UNDERSTANDING
TRADEMARK LAW
Second Edition

LexisNexis Law School Publishing Advisory Board

UNDERSTANDING TRADEMARK LAW

Second Edition

Mary LaFrance

William S. Boyd Professor of Law

William S. Boyd School of Law

University of Nevada, Las Vegas

 LexisNexis

ISBN: 978-1-4224-7232-3

Library of Congress Cataloging-in-Publication Data

LaFrance, Mary, 1958-
Understanding trademark law / Mary LaFrance. -- 2nd ed.
p. cm.
Includes index.
ISBN 978-1-4224-7232-3 (softbound)
1. Trademarks--Law and legislation--United States. I. Title.
KF3180.L34 2009
346.7304'88--dc22
2009024021

Editorial Offices
121 Chanlon Rd., New Providence, NJ 07974 (908) 464-6800
201 Mission St., San Francisco, CA 94105-1831 (415) 908-3200
www.lexisnexis.com

MATTHEW◆BENDER

Anna Egan LaFrance
1922–2008

When you are old and grey and full of sleep,
And nodding by the fire, take down this book
And slowly read, and dream of the soft look
Your eyes had once, and of their shadows deep.
—William Butler Yeats

PREFACE

This text offers a broad introduction to the fundamental principles of the law of trademarks and unfair competition. Although deeply rooted in the common law of torts, modern trademark law has branched in many directions, as evidenced by the development of dilution and cybersquatting laws, as well as state and federal registration systems. Practitioners and students of trademark law today must be familiar with all of these branches and their various sources — which include statutes as well as common law, and federal as well as state law.

Although trademark law has become increasingly federalized since the enactment of the Lanham Act in 1946, the federal law of trademarks and unfair competition has little preemptive effect on state law. As a result, many aspects of trademark and unfair competition law are governed by both state and federal law. The state and federal approaches often converge, and sometimes diverge, but despite the increasing scope of federal trademark and unfair competition law, federal law rarely preempts state law.

There is also the potential for conflict between, on the one hand, the state and federal regimes of trademark and unfair competition law and, on the other hand, the exclusively federal regimes of copyright and patent law. An understanding of trademark law, therefore, requires an understanding of its relationship with these other doctrines — in particular, which applications of trademark or unfair competition law would so interfere with the congressional schemes of patent and copyright protection that the latter must be given preemptive effect, as illustrated by the denial of trademark protection to functional aspects of trade dress.

The law of trademarks and unfair competition constantly evolves in response to changes in commercial markets. For example, the globalization of markets for goods and services has led to the internationalization of trademark and unfair competition law. Federal law, in particular, now considers certain foreign uses of trademarks in determining priority for federal registration and, conversely, recognizes that certain foreign activities may give rise to infringement claims under the Lanham Act. Federal law has also responded to the explosive growth of the Internet as a means for communication as well as a marketplace for goods and services. Although trademark law has traditionally protected the right of a trademark holder within the specific geographic markets where the mark is in use, such geographic boundaries are less relevant today, as brick-and-mortar locations are supplemented or displaced by Internet marketing. Internet activity can also blur the line between commercial activities subject to trademark regulation and expressive conduct that is protected by the First Amendment. In addition, activities such as keyword advertising raise fundamental questions about the meaning of trademark infringement.

For practitioners and students with no background in trademark and unfair competition law, this text may serve as a free-standing introduction. Those who already have some familiarity with these subjects will find the text to be a handy reference tool. Extensive footnoting and citation to authority is provided throughout, in order to assist those desiring to investigate a particular topic in greater depth.

The author would like to thank Gail Cline for her valuable assistance in the preparation of the second edition.

Table of Contents

Chapter 1   **NATURE AND PURPOSE OF TRADEMARK
                PROTECTION** 1

PART I: HISTORICAL OVERVIEW OF TRADEMARK LAW 6
§ 1.01   INTRODUCTION 1
§ 1.02   EARLY COMMON LAW: PASSING OFF 3
§ 1.03   EVOLUTION OF MODERN COMMON LAW AND STATE
         TRADEMARK STATUTES 3
§ 1.04   EARLY FEDERAL LAW: THE TRADEMARK CASES 6
§ 1.05   THE LANHAM ACT 6

PART II: TRADEMARK, COPYRIGHT, AND PATENT LAW
           COMPARED 11
§ 1.06   SUBJECT MATTER 9
§ 1.07   SCOPE OF RIGHTS 11
§ 1.08   DURATION OF PROTECTION 11
§ 1.09   GEOGRAPHIC SCOPE OF PROTECTION 13
§ 1.10   SOURCE OF CONGRESSIONAL AUTHORITY 13
§ 1.11   RELATIONSHIP BETWEEN STATE AND FEDERAL LAW 14

Chapter 2   **SUBJECT MATTER OF TRADEMARK
                PROTECTION** 15

.... 15
§ 2.01   INTRODUCTION 15

PART I: NATURE OF TRADEMARKS 15
§ 2.02   TRADEMARKS AS ORIGIN IDENTIFIERS 16
§ 2.03   THE REQUIREMENT OF NONFUNCTIONALITY 24

PART II: ESTABLISHING TRADEMARK RIGHTS 32
§ 2.04   USE IN TRADE 32
§ 2.05   DISTINCTIVENESS 46
§ 2.06   MAINTAINING TRADEMARK RIGHTS 48

PART III: TYPES OF TRADEMARKS 48
§ 2.07   PROTECTIBLE MARKS 64

PART IV: FEDERAL TRADEMARK REGISTRATION 111
§ 2.08   BENEFITS OF FEDERAL REGISTRATION 76
§ 2.09   MARKS ELIGIBLE FOR FEDERAL REGISTRATION 78
§ 2.10   REGISTRATION PROCESS 107
§ 2.11   JUDICIAL REVIEW 111

Table of Contents

§ 2.12　CANCELLATION 112

§ 2.13　INCONTESTABILITY 114

§ 2.14　THE SUPPLEMENTAL REGISTER 118

§ 2.15　DOMESTIC PRIORITY BASED ON FOREIGN TRADEMARK
　　　　REGISTRATIONS 123

PART V:　STATE TRADEMARK REGISTRATION 126

§ 2.16　STATE REGISTRATION STATUTES 127

PART VI:　UNREGISTERED MARKS 129

§ 2.17　PROTECTION OF UNREGISTERED MARKS 129

§ 2.18　ASSIGNMENTS AND LICENSES 129

Chapter 3　　　　**TRADEMARK INFRINGEMENT AND UNFAIR
　　　　　　　　　COMPETITION** **134**

.... 133

§ 3.01　INTRODUCTION 133

PART I:　TRADEMARK INFRINGEMENT 134

§ 3.02　ELEMENTS OF TRADEMARK INFRINGEMENT 134

PART II:　REVERSE PASSING OFF 192

§ 3.03　REVERSE PASSING OFF 192

PART III:　FEDERAL LAW OF FALSE ADVERTISING 197

§ 3.04　FALSE ADVERTISING 202

PART IV:　DILUTION 204

§ 3.05　THE CONCEPT OF TRADEMARK DILUTION 205

§ 3.06　STATE DILUTION LAWS 212

§ 3.07　THE FEDERAL TRADEMARK DILUTION ACT 221

PART V:　CYBERSQUATTING 237

§ 3.08　ANTICYBERSQUATTING CONSUMER PROTECTION ACT
　　　　(ACPA) 237

§ 3.09　ALTERNATIVE FORUMS FOR DOMAIN NAME DISPUTES 247

PART VI:　SECONDARY LIABILITY 249

§ 3.10　CONTRIBUTORY AND VICARIOUS LIABILITY 249

PART VII:　DEFENSES 260

§ 3.11　FIRST AMENDMENT CONSIDERATIONS 262

§ 3.12　AFFIRMATIVE DEFENSES 288

PART VIII:　REMEDIES 344

§ 3.13　NON-MONETARY REMEDIES 341

Table of Contents

§ 3.14   MONETARY AWARDS 348

§ 3.15   LIMITATIONS ON REMEDIES AGAINST CERTAIN
         DEFENDANTS 354

§ 3.16   CRIMINAL PENALTIES 360

PART IX: ADJUDICATION 360

§ 3.17   SUBJECT MATTER JURISDICTION 360

§ 3.18   STANDING 366

§ 3.19   DECLARATORY JUDGMENTS 367

Chapter 1

NATURE AND PURPOSE OF TRADEMARK PROTECTION

§ 1.01 INTRODUCTION

Trademark law has long been recognized as serving two purposes — protecting consumers from being confused or deceived about the source of goods or services in the marketplace, and encouraging merchants to stand behind their goods or services by protecting the goodwill they have developed in their trademarks. As the Supreme Court has noted:

> [T]rademark law, by preventing others from copying a source-identifying mark, "reduce [s] the customer's costs of shopping and making purchasing decisions," for it quickly and easily assures a potential customer that this item — the item with this mark — is made by the same producer as other similarly marked items that he or she liked (or disliked) in the past. At the same time, the law helps assure a producer that it (and not an imitating competitor) will reap the financial, reputation-related rewards associated with a desirable product.[1]

Trademark law is part of the broader law of unfair competition, which is rooted in English common law.[2] By the end of the twentieth century, United States trademark and unfair competition doctrines had expanded the scope of their protection to encompass a wider array of source indicators, had begun to protect the goodwill of especially famous trademarks even in the absence of confusion or competition, and had become extensively codified at both the state and federal level. In spite of these changes, however, even today these doctrines remain largely faithful to their common law roots.

Unlike other types of intellectual property, such as patents and copyrights, trademark rights are not property rights in gross. A fundamental principle of trademark law is that trademark rights arise only through the actual use of a mark to indicate the source of goods or services, and the public must actually recognize the mark as a source indicator in order for it to be protected. As noted in one of the Supreme Court's early trademark decisions: "There is no such thing as property in a trade-mark except as a right appurtenant to an established business or trade in connection with which the mark is employed."[3]

If a mark ceases to be used as a source indicator, or if the public ceases to recognize it as a source indicator, then it will cease to be protected as a trademark. Thus, it is crucial for a trademark owner to be vigilant in monitoring

---

[1] Qualitex Co. v. Jacobson Prods. Co. Inc., 514 U.S. 159, 163-64 (1995).

[2] Moseley v. V Secret Catalogue, Inc., 537 U.S. 418, 428 (2003).

[3] United Drug Co. v. Theodore Rectanus Co., 248 U.S. 90, 97 (1918).

the use of its mark as well as the public perception of its mark. However, regardless of a trademark owner's best efforts to police and protect its mark, the consumer remains the ultimate arbiter of whether that mark deserves continued protection. As the Second Circuit noted in holding that the public had begun to use the term "cellophane" generically:

> The rights of the complainant must be based upon a wrong which the defendant has done to it by misleading customers as to the origin of the goods sold and thus taking away its trade. Such rights are not founded on a bare title to a word or symbol but on a cause of action to prevent deception. It, therefore, makes no difference what efforts or money the DuPont Company expended in order to persuade the public that "cellophane" means an article of DuPont manufacture. So far as it did not succeed in actually converting the world to its gospel it can have no relief.[4]

PART I:
HISTORICAL OVERVIEW OF TRADEMARK LAW

§ 1.02   EARLY COMMON LAW: PASSING OFF

The law of trademarks and unfair competition has its roots in nineteenth-century tort law, specifically the common law tort of passing off (also known as "palming off"), which was concerned with protecting consumers from being deceived by merchants who falsely represented the source of their goods in order to divert sales from their competitors and capitalize on the good reputations of those competitors. In some cases, the deceit was carried out by falsely marking the goods with the competitor's trademark. In other cases, the deceit did not involve the use of a "technical trademark," but involved other means of suggesting a false origin for the goods — for example, imitating the competitor's packaging, or the appearance of its product itself. Imitation of another's technical trademark constituted trademark infringement. Use of other means, such as similar packaging or product appearance, to falsely suggest the origin of goods, constituted unfair competition. The distinction between trademark infringement and unfair competition was that trademark infringement involved the imitation of distinct product identifiers, whereas in the case of unfair competition the imitated features were descriptive aspects of the product that served as origin identifiers only because the public had come to associate them with a single source for the goods in question — in other words, the imitated features had acquired secondary meaning. Whether the infringement involved technical trademarks or unfair competition, the underlying concern was that the consumer was being deceived about the origin of the goods. Today, trademark infringement encompasses both the imitation of technical trademarks and the imitation of descriptive terms or features that have acquired secondary meaning.

---

[4] DuPont Cellophane Co. v. Waxed Prods. Co., 85 F.2d 75, 81 (2d Cir. 1936).

Because the law of passing off evolved as an offshoot of the law of fraud or deceit, throughout the nineteenth century fraudulent intent was an essential element of this cause of action. Although consumers might, of course, be equally confused by an inadvertent similarity between trademarks, in the absence of deceptive intent this confusion did not necessarily have a remedy. However, during the twentieth century the element of intent gradually decreased in importance, and the concern for avoiding consumer confusion became paramount.[5] Dispensing with the element of intent also made enforcement easier, because, as an evidentiary matter, the objective fact of consumer confusion was typically easier to prove than the defendant's subjective intent.

§ 1.03   EVOLUTION OF MODERN COMMON LAW AND STATE TRADEMARK STATUTES

Because the law of trademarks is a subset of the larger field of unfair competition,[6] both are governed by essentially the same principles.[7] However, unfair competition is based on principles of equity, and, unlike trademark infringement, it does not always involve the violation of one party's exclusive right to use a specific word, mark, symbol, or device as an indication of origin.[8]

In its narrowest formulation, unfair competition involves a defendant's fraudulent "passing off" (or "palming off") of his or her goods or services as originating from the plaintiff.[9] An unfair competition claim may be based on a defendant's unauthorized use of a distinctive mark that the plaintiff uses to identify its goods or services, or it may be based on the existence of other conduct or contextual factors that are likely to confuse consumers about the source of the defendant's goods or services. Thus, a plaintiff raising an unfair competition claim need not have a valid trademark at all. In some cases, for example, courts have refused to find trademark infringement where a plaintiff's mark has lost its trademark significance by becoming the generic term for a product, or where a plaintiff never had a valid trademark in the first place, but have upheld the plaintiff's unfair competition claim where the defendant affirmatively and falsely represented to consumers that the product it was selling was made by the plaintiff — a classic example of passing off.[10] In other cases, a mark might have become generic in the minds of most consumers, but perhaps not all; in such a case, the court may require competitors to take affirmative steps to inform consumers of the true source of the product being sold under the generic name.[11] Some courts have used the term "unfair competition" more broadly, however, to

---

[5] J. Thomas McCarthy, McCarthy on Trademarks and Unfair Competition § 5:2 (4th ed. 2009).

[6] Safeway Stores, Inc. v. Safeway Properties, Inc., 307 F.2d 495 (2d Cir. 1962).

[7] National Auto. Club v. National Auto Club, Inc., 365 F. Supp. 879 (S.D.N.Y. 1973).

[8] House of Westmore v. Denney, 151 F.2d 261 (3d Cir. 1945).

[9] Crowell Pub. Co. v. Italian Monthly Co., 28 F.2d 613 (2d Cir. 1928).

[10] See, e.g., Murphy Door Bed Co. v. Interior Sleep Sys., Inc., 874 F.2d 95 (2d Cir. 1989) (trademark had lost its significance); William R. Warner & Co. v. Eli Lilly & Co., 265 U.S. 526 (1924) (plaintiff did not have a protectable mark in the first place).

[11] See, e.g., DuPont Cellophane, 85 F.2d at 82.

describe any conduct that they perceive as exceeding the bounds of ethical competition.[12]

The modern common law of trademarks and unfair competition is reflected in the *Restatement (Third) of Unfair Competition*, which defines "passing off" in terms of the effect of the defendant's conduct on consumers' purchasing decisions rather than in terms of the subjective intent of the defendant:

> One is subject to liability to another . . . if, in connection with the marketing of goods or services, the actor makes a representation likely to deceive or mislead prospective purchasers by causing the mistaken belief that the actor's business is the business of the other, or that the actor is the agent, affiliate, or associate of the other, or that the goods or services that the actor markets are produced, sponsored, or approved by the other.[13]

The *Restatement* also reflects the fact that modern common law recognizes forms of unfair competition other than traditional passing off — including, among others, false advertising (defined by the *Restatement* as false statements about a merchant's own goods),[14] reverse passing off (that is, misrepresenting the source of another merchant's goods),[15] and the right of publicity (that is, the unauthorized appropriation of a person's name or likeness for commercial gain).[16]

Because these categories "do not fully exhaust the scope of statutory or common law liability for unfair methods of competition," the *Restatement* also recognizes "a residual category encompassing other business practices determined to be unfair,"[17] illustrated by the following examples:

> 5. *A* manufactures a computer designed for use by schoolchildren. *B*, a manufacturer of a competing product, sends letters to wholesalers and distributors stating that *A*'s computer infringes a patent owned by *B*. The letters contain a threat to institute an infringement action against anyone who markets *A*'s product. *B* knows that *A*'s product does not infringe the patent and has no intention of commencing the threatened litigation. *B* is subject to liability to *A*.

---

[12] *See, e.g.*, Addison-Wesley Pub. Co. v. Brown, 207 F. Supp. 678 (E.D.N.Y. 1962) (publishing answers to the problems presented in another publisher's physics textbook); Merchants' Syndicate Catalog Co. v. Retailers' Factory Catalog Co., 206 F. 545 (N.D. Ill. 1913) (misuse of confidential information).

[13] RESTATEMENT (THIRD) OF UNFAIR COMPETITION § 4 (1995).

[14] RESTATEMENT, *supra* note 13, at § 2). In contrast, the federal law of false advertising now applies to false statements about the defendant's own goods or services or those of another. *See* 15 U.S.C. § 43(a)(1)(B); *see also* § 3.04 *infra*.

[15] *Id.* § 5.

[16] *Id.* § 1. *See, e.g.*, Waits v. Frito-Lay, Inc., 978 F.2d 1093 (9th Cir. 1992) (holding that imitation of singer's voice was actionable), *cert. denied*, 506 U.S. 1080 (1993); White v. Samsung Elecs. America, Inc., 971 F.2d 1395 (9th Cir. 1992) (reversing summary judgment for defendant that used a robot to imitate celebrity's likeness), *cert. denied*, 508 U.S. 951 (1993).

[17] RESTATEMENT, *supra* note 13, at § 1 cmt. g.

6. *A* is the local distributor for a brand of wall paneling. *B*, a builder, makes a contract to install wall paneling in a school being constructed by *C*, a school district. *C* requests *B* to solicit bids for the wall paneling from suppliers. *B* then arranges to become the local distributor for a brand of paneling similar to that sold by *A*. Without informing *A* of this fact, *B* obtains a bid from *A* but alters *A*'s figures to increase the price before submitting *A*'s bid, together with its own lower bid, to *C*. *C* awards the supply contract to *B*. *B* is subject to liability to *A*.

7. *A* is involved in a dispute with *B*, a former licensee, concerning the use by *B* of a trade name similar to *A*'s. *A* files a change of address form under *B*'s name at the local post office, listing its own address as the new address of *B*'s business. As a result of the diversion of mail, *B* loses the opportunity to bid on several contracts. *A* is subject to liability to *B*.[18]

Although case law provides far fewer illustrations of such sui generis types of unfair competition than the more traditional forms such as passing off, two of the better-known cases include *Addison-Wesley Publishing Co. v. Brown*,[19] in which the distribution and sale of an answer key for problems contained in a physics textbook, which damaged the market for the textbook, was held to be actionable, and *International News Service v. Associated Press*, which held that one wire service could enjoin another from the virtually simultaneous and uncredited copying of its news items.[20]

Thus, while trademark law is a subset of the broader category of unfair competition law, it is by far the most significant component of this category, especially under its modern formulation, which recognizes that descriptive terms, product packaging, and even product configuration can serve as trademarks when they acquire secondary meaning. Distinctive product packaging and configuration have become known as "trade dress."

Trademarks, including trade dress, are protected under the common law of the states, regardless of whether they have been registered, provided that they are not a functional feature of a product, and provided that they distinguish, in the minds of consumers, the goods or services of one merchant from those of another. In addition to common law doctrines, many states have enacted trademark and unfair competition statutes that apply to unregistered trademarks and trade dress, and many have also enacted state registration systems that provide enhanced protection to registered marks. Many states also recognize the right of publicity as a matter of common law and/or statutory law.

---

[18] *Id.*

[19] 207 F. Supp. 678, 678-79 (E.D.N.Y. 1962).

[20] 248 U.S. 215 (1918). For additional examples, see McCarthy, *supra* note 5, at § 1:10.

§ 1.04 EARLY FEDERAL LAW: THE TRADEMARK CASES

Congress enacted the first federal trademark statute in 1870,[21] providing a system of federal registration for all trademarks used within the United States, regardless of whether they were used in interstate commerce. However, in 1879, the Supreme Court struck down this statute in *The Trademark Cases*[22] on the ground that it exceeded the scope of Congress's authority under either the Patent and Copyright Clause or the Commerce Clause of the Constitution. The statute exceeded Congress's power under the Patent and Copyright Clause, Article 1, Section 8, Clause 8, because it extended trademark protection without regard to the originality or creativity of the mark. It exceeded Congress's power under the Commerce Clause because it appeared to extend federal protection to trademarks without regard to whether they were used in "commerce" that fell within Congress's regulatory authority, which, under Article 1, Section 8, Clause 3, was limited to "commerce with foreign nations, and among the several states, and with the Indian tribes."[23] Congress corrected this constitutional defect in subsequent trademark statutes by expressly limiting the scope of federal law to activities that fall within the scope of Congress's power to regulate commerce.

However, Congress did not permit federal registration of marks used in interstate commerce until the Trademark Act of 1905.[24] The 1905 Act permitted registration only of "technical" trademarks — that is, marks that were inherently distinctive — thus excluding descriptive marks and most types of trade dress regardless of their degree of acquired distinctiveness. The 1905 Act had other inadequacies as well. Over the next 40 years, the federal trademark statutes were continuously revised, with coverage extended to descriptive marks with secondary meaning in the 1920 Act.[25] Finally, Congress undertook the most recent major overhaul of federal trademark law by enacting the Lanham Trademark Act of 1946.[26]

§ 1.05 THE LANHAM ACT

[A] Overview

The Lanham Act provides a federal registration scheme for trademarks and service marks that are used in any commerce that Congress has the authority to regulate, and provides an array of remedies against parties that infringe such registered marks. It also provides a federal scheme of protection against certain

---

[21] Act of July 8, 1870, 16 Stat. at L. 198.

[22] 100 U.S. 82 (1879).

[23] U.S. Const., art. I, § 8, cl. 3.

[24] Act of Feb. 20, 1905, 33 Stat. 724.

[25] Act of Mar. 19, 1920, 41 Stat. 533.

[26] Pub. L. No. 79-489, 60 Stat. 427 (1946). Section 45 of the Lanham Act provides that "[t]he intent of this chapter is to regulate commerce within the control of Congress," where " 'commerce' means all commerce which may lawfully be regulated by Congress." 15 U.S.C. § 1127.

acts of unfair competition that take place in federally regulated commerce, but that do not involve infringement of federally registered marks.

In enacting the Lanham Act, Congress recognized that commercial activities were increasingly taking place on a national scale, so that state-by-state remedial schemes were not necessarily adequate to protect consumers and merchants from injury due to unfair competition. This concern was noted in both the House and Senate Reports accompanying the Act:

> Trade is no longer local, but is national. Marks used in interstate commerce are properly the subject of Federal regulation. It would seem as if national legislation along national lines securing to the owners of trade-marks in interstate commerce definite rights should be enacted and should be enacted now.

> There can be no doubt under the recent decisions of the Supreme Court of the constitutionality of a national act giving substantive as distinguished from merely procedural rights in trade-marks in commerce over which Congress has plenary power, and when it is considered that the protection of trade-marks is merely protection to good will, to prevent diversion of trade through misrepresentation, and the protection of the public against deception, a sound public policy requires that trade-marks should receive nationally the greatest protection that can be given them.[27]

As originally enacted, the Lanham Act reflected the traditional common law view of trademark and unfair competition law as prohibiting only those uses that "convey a false impression to the public mind, and [are] of a character to mislead and deceive the ordinary purchaser in the exercise of ordinary care and caution in such matters."[28] The three most fundamental sections of the Act are sections 2, 32, and 43(a), although the significance of section 43(a) was less apparent in 1946 than it is today. Section 2 sets forth the standards for registering a trademark or service mark on the Principal Register of the Patent and Trademark Office (PTO). Section 32 protects federally registered trademarks and service marks against unauthorized uses that are likely to confuse or mislead consumers as to the origin of goods or services, and section 43(a) provides a federal unfair competition cause of action for a party that suffers a competitive injury as a result of false statements made by others in connection with the offering of goods or services, including infringement of an unregistered trademark.

In focusing almost exclusively on preventing consumer confusion and the injury to a trademark owner's goodwill that might result from such confusion, the Lanham Act in its original form reflected the traditional concerns underlying the common law tort of passing off:

> Trade-marks are merely a convenient way of distinguishing the goods of one trader from those of another. By furnishing a means of identifica-

---

[27] H.R. Rep. No. 219, 79th Cong. 1st Sess. 4 (1945); S. Rep. No. 1333, 79th Cong. 2d Sess. 5-6 (1946).

[28] McLean v. Fleming, 96 U.S. 245, 255 (1877).

tion, they perpetuate good will, and enable purchasers, by recognizing the marks, to buy again the goods which have pleased them before. . . . The public is thus assured of identity, and is given an opportunity to choose between competing articles. To protect trade-marks, i.e., marks which permit the goods of different makers to be distinguished from each other, is to promote competition and is sound public policy. The protection which is accorded is security against misrepresentation as to the origin of goods, by suppressing imitations which are calculated to mislead buyers into the belief that the goods of one maker are those of another.[29]

Sections 2 and 32 of the Lanham Act have undergone relatively minor modifications since 1946. Section 43(a), in contrast, has continuously expanded in importance. Although the language of section 43(a) was amended in the Trademark Law Revision Act (TLRA) of 1988, most of the expansion in the importance of section 43(a) has resulted from judicial interpretation of the pre-1988 language, and most of those judicial interpretations were endorsed by Congress in the 1988 amendments.

[B]   Recent Amendments

Over time, the Lanham Act has been amended to incorporate new types of trademark protection. Two of these changes — the addition of antidilution provisions in 1995 (followed by their 2006 amendments), and the addition of anticybersquatting provisions in 1999 — represent especially significant expansions of the scope of federal trademark law.

[1]   Dilution Doctrine

In 1995, Congress followed the lead of states that had enacted antidilution laws to protect trademark owners against certain unauthorized uses of their marks that could undermine the selling power, or tarnish the reputation, of their marks even in the absence of competition or likelihood of confusion. In the Federal Trademark Dilution Act (FTDA),[30] Congress added section 43(c) to the Lanham Act,[31] creating a cause of action for dilution of the selling power of "famous" marks. Thus, for the first time, federal trademark law afforded enhanced protection to certain trademarks purely for the purpose of protecting the trademark owners' investment in the goodwill of their marks, as opposed to the traditional common law purpose of preventing consumers from being deceived or confused, as exemplified in sections 32 and 43(a).[32] In 2006, Congress enacted the Trademark Dilution Revision Act (TDRA),[33] amending section 43(c) in response to ten years of judicial interpretations.

---

[29] H.R. Rep. No. 76-944, at 3 (1939) (internal citation omitted).

[30] PUB. L. No. 104-98, 109 STAT. 985-86.

[31] 15 U.S.C. § 1125(c).

[32] Federal dilution law is discussed in § 3.07, *infra.*

[33] PUB. L. No. 109-312, 120 STAT. 1730 (Oct. 6, 2006).

[2]   Anticybersquatting Provisions

With the proliferation of commercial transactions on the Internet, existing federal trademark protections under sections 32, 43(a), and 43(c) of the Lanham Act were not always adequate to protect trademark owners against parties that made unauthorized use of their trademarks in domain names in a way that could confuse or mislead consumers, or undermine the selling power of their marks. In particular, it was difficult in some cases to determine whether a party's domain name registration was being used in connection with the offering of goods or services in such a manner as to give rise to a valid infringement claim under section 32 or 43(a), or a valid dilution claim under section 43(c), or, alternatively, whether the unauthorized use should be protected, either as a noncommercial expression of ideas or as a valid method of competition by another merchant. In addition, trademark owners often had difficulty enforcing their rights against domain name registrants whose identity could not be determined, or whose physical location placed them outside the personal jurisdiction of the federal courts.

Congress sought to remedy these problems in 1999 with the Anticybersquatting Consumer Protection Act (ACPA),[34] which added section 43(d) to the Lanham Act.[35] In this provision, Congress sought to define with greater certainty the circumstances in which registration, use, or trafficking in a domain name that resembles a valid trademark violates the rights of a trademark owner, and to establish procedures for enforcing such rights even when the infringer is beyond the personal jurisdiction of the federal courts.[36]

PART II:
TRADEMARK, COPYRIGHT, AND PATENT LAW COMPARED

It is important to distinguish among the variety of state and federal doctrines that provide protection for different types of intellectual property rights. Some of these doctrines are mutually exclusive, while others allow for significant overlap.

§ 1.06   SUBJECT MATTER

Trademark and unfair competition law provide a means by which parties offering goods or services to the public can distinguish their goods or services from those offered by other parties. These doctrines allow parties to obtain exclusive rights to essentially any device that serves as an indication of the origin *exclusive* of their goods or services, provided that the device is not a functional feature of *right* the functional properties of those goods or services. The device may be a word, symbol, sound, fragrance, graphic design, or virtually any nonfunctional feature

---

[34] Pub. L. No. 106-113, 113 Stat. 1536 (1999).

[35] 15 U.S.C. § 1125(d).

[36] The anticybersquatting provisions are discussed in § 3.08, *infra*.

of the goods or services; it can even be an ornamental aspect of the design of the product or its packaging, in which case it is referred to as "trade dress." There is no requirement that the device be novel, nonobvious, or original.

The functionality limitation of trademark and unfair competition law is intended to prevent these doctrines from impermissibly overlapping with federal patent law, under which the inventor of a novel, nonobvious, and useful product may obtain exclusive rights to exploit that invention for a limited time, in exchange for disclosing the details of that invention to the public (as opposed to exploiting the useful invention while seeking to maintain its secrecy under the laws that protect the trade secrets of a business against improper appropriation). Novelty requires that the invention was generally unknown to the public before the applicant invented it, and nonobviousness requires that it embody more than a trivial change from the prior art. The standards for establishing that an invention is sufficiently novel and nonobvious to be worthy of patent protection are quite high, and the examination process is exacting. In contrast, a trademark may be protected without any showing of novelty, nonobviousness or originality. For this reason, the functionality bar to trademark protection is essential to preventing trademark and unfair competition law from serving as an "end run" around the rigorous requirements of federal patent law.

In some cases, the protections of trademark and unfair competition can permissibly overlap with those of federal patent law. The creator of an ornamental design may obtain the protection of a federal design patent if the design is sufficiently novel and nonobvious. Because design patents are available only for designs that are ornamental rather than functional, design patents and utility patents are mutually exclusive. Thus, a novel and nonobvious ornamental design that qualifies for a design patent will not qualify for a utility patent. For that same reason, however, an ornamental design that is eligible for design patent protection may also be eligible for trademark or trade dress protection if it is used to identify the origin of goods or services. Thus, these forms of protection are not mutually exclusive.

Copyright law protects "original works of authorship" when fixed in tangible form. Works of authorship include a wide variety of expressive works, including literary, artistic, and musical works, as well as sound recordings and audiovisual works. Many of these expressive works are also capable of serving as trademarks. Thus, for example, if a trademark consists of a graphic design that is sufficiently original to merit copyright protection, the same design may be protected by copyright as well as trademark law. As noted above, if the design is also novel and nonobvious, it may be eligible for design patent protection as well.[37] Thus, it is possible for a single ornamental design to be copyrighted, patented, and protected by trademark and unfair competition law at the same time.

---

[37] It is not unusual for trade dress to be protected both by a design patent and by trademark or unfair competition law. *See, e.g.*, In re World's Finest Chocolate, Inc., 474 F.2d 1012, 1015 (C.C.P.A. 1973) (collecting cases).

§ 1.07   SCOPE OF RIGHTS

Traditional trademark and unfair competition law recognizes a trademark owner's right to prevent competitors from using the same or confusingly similar marks in a way that will confuse or mislead consumers regarding the origin of goods or services. This right of priority belongs to the party that is the first to use the trademark in connection with the offering of goods or services, provided that party has not abandoned the mark before the date on which the junior user commences use. It does not protect against all unauthorized uses of the mark — only against uses in connection with the offering of goods or services. Thus, purely literary or artistic uses of the mark, or use in the context of news reporting or other protected speech, will typically not be actionable.

The scope of trademark protection is somewhat broader under state and federal dilution laws, which provide the trademark owner with a remedy against uses that are non-competing and non-confusing, if they threaten to undermine the selling power of the mark. Nonetheless, the offending use must be in connection with the offering of goods or services in order to be actionable.

In contrast, patent rights give the patent owner the exclusive right to make, use, or sell the patented invention (or, more precisely, the right to exclude others from engaging in these activities). Thus, the owner of a design patent may prevent others from making, using, or selling a design that is identical to, or an obvious variation on, the patented design, regardless of whether or not their use is in connection with the offering of goods or services. The design or utility patent owner may prevent others from making, using, or selling the patented invention regardless of whether those parties have copied the patented invention or developed it independently.

Copyright law provides a cause of action against one who copies the protected work of authorship, regardless of whether the copying is connected to the offering of goods or services. Copying occurs whenever the defendant's design is substantially similar to the copyrighted design, unless the defendant's design was independently created (that is, not copied from the plaintiff's design). In this context, "copying" is shorthand for copying, distributing, publicly performing, or publicly displaying the protected work, or adapting it into a new "derivative" work.

In contrast to copyright law, which protects against copying rather than parallel creation, trademark law protects against the use of confusingly similar or dilutive marks even if they were adopted in good faith, without knowledge of the trademark owner's prior use of the mark.

§ 1.08   DURATION OF PROTECTION

Under the common law of trademark and unfair competition, the rights of a trademark owner last as long as the owner continues to use the mark, provided it is not abandoned or forfeited, and provided the mark does not otherwise cease to function as an origin indicator. Thus, for example, if a mark ceases to function as a trademark because it has become the generic term for the goods or services with which it is associated, trademark protection for that mark will cease.

Similarly, trademark protection will not commence until the mark sought to be protected has begun to function as an origin identifier; thus, for example, a mark whose primary meaning is descriptive will not be protected as a trademark unless and until consumers begin to recognize it as an indication of source.

If a mark is federally registered, the additional rights obtained through federal registration commence on the effective date of that registration. In order to maintain those rights in force, the registration must be renewed. Failure to renew a mark's federal registration will terminate only the benefits of federal registration with respect to that mark; it will not affect the existence of common law rights in that mark.

In contrast to the indefinite, use-based, term of protection under trademark and unfair competition laws, federal patent and copyright laws provide protection for a fixed statutory term. Rights under utility patents and design patents commence on the date the patent is granted.[38] The term of a utility patent ends 20 years from the date on which the application was filed; the term of a design patent ends 14 years from the date on which the patent issues.[39] The term of copyright protection has changed over time, but for works created after December 31, 1977, the term is the life of the author plus 70 years, or, in the case of works made for hire, the shorter of 95 years from publication or 120 years from creation.[40] While the term of copyright protection is longer than that of patent protection, it can (in theory, at least) be shorter than the indefinite term of trademark protection. However, unlike trademark protection, which commences only upon use, and which ceases when the use is discontinued, copyright and patent protections endure even if the owner of the rights does not exploit the copyrighted or patented material, or ceases to exploit it.

The owner of an interest in a patent or copyright is said to own this property right "in gross," meaning that the federal right is treated much like other forms of property, and can be freely assigned and licensed subject only to minimal procedural restrictions. In contrast, a trademark is a more fragile right. It cannot be owned "in gross," because it is merely a symbol of goodwill. Without that goodwill, the trademark ceases to exist. The validity of a mark is tied to its continued ability to embody that goodwill — that is, its ability to function as a source identifier for the trademark owner's goods or services. Thus, if the trademark owner stops using the mark in connection with goods or services, or if the mark loses its ability to identify the source of those goods or services (for example, if it becomes generic), the trademark right ceases to exist. The same result follows if the trademark owner attempts to sell the mark unaccompanied by the goodwill of the business (an "assignment in gross") or licenses it without exercising sufficient quality controls over the licensee ("naked licensing").

---

[38]   35 U.S.C. §§ 154(a)(2), 173.

[39]   *Id.* Extensions of utility patent terms are permitted in very limited circumstances. *See* 35 U.S.C. § 156.

[40]   17 U.S.C. §§ 302-304.

§ 1.09   GEOGRAPHIC SCOPE OF PROTECTION

The exclusive rights of a federal patent or copyright owner are nationwide in scope. In contrast, the geographic scope of rights under trademark or unfair competition law depends on whether the mark derives its protection from common law, state statute, or federal registration.

Under common law, as well as section 43(a) of the Lanham Act, the exclusive rights of a trademark owner are generally limited to the geographic area in which the owner was the first to use the mark, and has used it continuously since that time. Thus, different parties may be entitled to use the same or very similar trademarks concurrently, for similar goods or services, if they are using them in distinct geographic areas.

Some state statutes may allow trademark owners to expand upon their common law rights, by obtaining statewide priority rights through the state trademark registration system. However, the statewide priority obtainable under a state registration scheme is still subject to the preexisting common law rights of a prior user.

The federal registration statutes allow trademark owners an even greater expansion of their common law rights by giving nationwide rights of priority to trademarks that are registered on the Principal Register. However, federal registration does not displace any preexisting common law rights. Because the federal registrant's nationwide priority is based on constructive rather than actual use, any party that had established common law priority rights through actual use of an identical or confusingly similar mark before the effective date of the federal registration, and who has not abandoned the mark, retains priority over the federal registrant in the geographic markets where that prior actual use has taken place.

§ 1.10   SOURCE OF CONGRESSIONAL AUTHORITY

Congress derives its power to grant patent and copyright protection from Article 1, Section 8, Clause 8 of the United States Constitution, which authorizes Congress "To Promote the Progress of Science and useful Arts, by securing for limited Times to Authors and Inventors the exclusive Right to their respective Writings and Discoveries." This clause has been variously referred to as the "Patent and Copyright Clause" or the "Intellectual Property Clause."

In contrast, congressional power to enact trademark and unfair competition laws derives from the Commerce Clause of the Constitution: Article 1, Section 8, Clause 3, which grants Congress the "Power to regulate commerce with foreign nations, and among the several States, and with the Indian tribes." Thus, in contrast to Congress's power to grant patents and copyrights, federal trademarks and unfair competition laws do not extend to purely intrastate activities — that is, activities that do not affect interstate commerce (although such purely intrastate activities are increasingly rare). However, because the Commerce Clause does not contain a "limited times" provision, Congress has the power to protect a trademark indefinitely.

§ 1.11   RELATIONSHIP BETWEEN STATE AND FEDERAL LAW

Patent law is exclusively federal. Copyright protection for tangible works of authorship is also exclusively federal, except in the case of sound recordings that were created prior to 1972. State laws that attempt to duplicate, or interfere with, federal patent or copyright law are generally held to be invalid or unenforceable under the doctrine of federal preemption. In some cases, state trademark or unfair competition laws have been held to conflict impermissibly with federal patent or copyright laws, and have been invalidated due to federal preemption.[41] This would be the case, for example, if a state provided trade dress protection for the functional features of a product, because this would interfere with Congress's exclusive authority to set the standards for patent protection.

In contrast, trademark and unfair competition laws exist concurrently at both the federal and state levels. As noted by the Court of Customs and Patent Appeals, a predecessor of the Federal Circuit: "Rights appurtenant to the ownership of a federal trademark registration . . . may be considered supplemental to those recognized at common law, stemming from ownership of a trademark."[42] Because there are significant variations in state trademark and unfair competition laws, some state doctrines are virtually identical to their federal counterparts, while others diverge. Only rarely have state laws been held to be unenforceable due to preemption by federal trademark or unfair competition laws.[43] Ordinarily, plaintiffs are free to include both their state and federal causes of action when filing a complaint alleging trademark infringement or unfair competition. As discussed in § 3.17 below, because federal courts do not have exclusive jurisdiction over trademark or unfair competition claims arising under the Lanham Act, a plaintiff alleging trademark infringement or unfair competition under both state and federal laws frequently has the choice of bringing both sets of claims either in federal court or state court.

---

[41] *See, e.g.*, Sears, Roebuck & Co. v. Stiffel Co. 376 U.S. 225 (1964) (state statute prohibiting copying of lamp design was preempted by federal patent law); Compco Corp. v. Day-Brite Lighting, Inc., 376 U.S. 234 (1964) (similar); Bonito Boats v. Thunder Craft Boats, 489 U.S. 141 (1989) (state statute prohibiting copying of boat hulls was preempted by federal patent law). *But see* Kohler v. Moen, 12 F.3d 632, 638-43 (7th Cir. 1993) (rejecting argument that trade dress protection for faucet design would impermissibly conflict with federal patent law).

[42] In re Beatrice Foods, 429 F.2d 466, 472-73 (C.C.P.A. 1970).

[43] One of those rare instances is illustrated by *Burger King of Florida, Inc. v. Hoots*, 403 F.2d 904 (7th Cir. 1968), discussed in § 2.16 [B] *infra*.

Chapter 2

SUBJECT MATTER OF TRADEMARK PROTECTION

§ 2.01 INTRODUCTION

This chapter explores the fundamental question: "What is a trademark?" As explained in the sections that follow, a trademark is a device that, when used on or in connection with goods or services, serves the exclusive function of identifying to consumers the source from which those particular goods or services have emanated. Although traditionally a trademark consisted of a word or symbol, trademarks today may take many forms, including a sound, a fragrance, or the overall appearance of a product or its packaging (known as trade dress). Although registration of trademarks is possible under both state and federal law, and federal registration can significantly enhance the legal protections available to the trademark owner, registration is not essential to trademark protection in the United States.

PART I:
NATURE OF TRADEMARKS

§ 2.02 TRADEMARKS AS ORIGIN IDENTIFIERS

The function of a trademark or service mark is to inform consumers about the source of the goods or services with which that mark is associated. Although consumers might not care specifically about the source, they typically care about the qualities and characteristics that they have come to associate with goods or services emanating from that source. The trademark is a shorthand form of communication from a merchant to its customers or potential customers, in which the merchant identifies which products or services it stands behind, and distinguishes them from competing products or services offered by other merchants. The shorthand is helpful because it is frequently not possible or practical for a consumer to test every product or service before purchasing it. Thus, a consumer who has found a brand of peanut butter that is particularly pleasing in its characteristics will be able to distinguish which jars of peanut butter on the supermarket shelf are most likely to possess those characteristics, simply by looking for one that bears the same identifying label.

Furthermore, trademarks enable consumers to hold merchants accountable for products or services that prove to be disappointing. A consumer can avoid brands that have been unsatisfactory in the past, and can also complain to a merchant whose brand has previously been satisfactory but that has declined in quality or has otherwise changed in ways that are displeasing to that consumer.

Sometimes the consumer's desire for a particular merchant's product is based not on actual experience with the product, but on expectations fueled by that merchant's marketing efforts. "A trademark is a merchandising shortcut which induces a purchaser to select what he wants, or what he has been led to believe he wants."[1] Here, too, the merchant's mark enables the consumer to identify which product promises to meet these expectations, and to hold the merchant accountable if the product does not live up to the merchant's promises.

The reputation that attaches to a trademark is often referred to as goodwill. It represents the cumulative experience of consumers who have used the product or service with which the mark is associated. As a predictor of future patronage, goodwill can represent a large portion of the value of a merchant's business.

Thus, while trademarks are origin identifiers, their primary importance to the public lies in the indirect assurances of quality and accountability that they provide. Their importance to merchants lies in their ability to capture the goodwill generated by the merchant's efforts to provide goods or services that are pleasing to consumers, and their ability to channel that goodwill toward the merchant that is responsible for creating it rather than toward the merchant's competitors, thus increasing the likelihood that the merchant will enjoy future patronage by satisfied customers. Thus, when a trademark is infringed, "[w]hat truly is infringed is the public's right to be secure from confusion and the corresponding right of each trademark's owner to control its own product's reputation."[2]

§ 2.03   THE REQUIREMENT OF NONFUNCTIONALITY

[A]   Public Policy

Under both state and federal law, the functionality bar denies trademark protection to any aspects of an article that contribute to the utility of the article. According to the Supreme Court's most comprehensive effort to define functionality, "a product feature is functional, and cannot serve as a trademark, if it is essential to the use or purpose of the article or if it affects the cost or quality of the article, that is, if exclusive use of the feature would put competitors at a significant non-reputation-related disadvantage."[3]

The proscription against trademark protection for the functional features of an article is a judicially created doctrine that predates the Lanham Act.[4] The functionality prohibition serves two related purposes: (1) it fosters competition by ensuring that all competitors are free to copy the useful features of a product, and (2) it prevents trademark law from conflicting with the scheme of federal patent protection by ensuring that trademark law does not provide

---

[1] Mishawaka Rubber & Woolen Mfg. Co. v. S.S. Kresge, 316 U.S. 203, 205 (1942).

[2] David Berg & Co. v. Gatto Int'l Trading Co., 884 F.2d 306, 310 (7th Cir. 1989).

[3] Qualitex Co. v. Jacobson Products Co., 514 U.S. 159, 165 (1995) (internal quotation marks omitted).

[4] Wilhelm Pudenz, GmbH v. Littelfuse, Inc. 177 F.3d 1204, 1207 (11th Cir. 1999).

patent-like protection of unlimited duration for the useful features of a product.[5] The Supreme Court articulated these policy concerns in *Qualitex Co. v. Jacobson Prods. Co.*:

> The functionality doctrine prevents trademark law, which seeks to promote competition by protecting a firm's reputation, from instead inhibiting legitimate competition by allowing a producer to control a useful product feature. It is the province of patent law, not trademark law, to encourage invention by granting inventors a monopoly over new product designs or functions for a limited time, after which competitors are free to use the innovation. If a product's functional features could be used as trademarks, however, a monopoly over such features could be obtained without regard to whether they qualify as patents and could be extended forever (because trademarks may be renewed in perpetuity).[6]

Thus, if a feature is functional, it may be the subject of a monopoly only if and to the extent that it qualifies for federal patent protection, and if it so qualifies, the monopoly should expire at the end of the federal patent term so that all other competitors will be free to incorporate the useful feature. The functionality bar applies to both state and federal law, even though the latter is not subject to supremacy clause preemption: "[W]hen the operation of the Lanham Act would upset the balance struck by the Patent Act, the Lanham Act must yield. The functionality doctrine serves this purpose by eliminating the possibility of a perpetual exclusive right to the utilitarian features of a product under trademark law, which would be impossible (as well as unconstitutional) under the Patent Act."[7]

For example, in *William R. Warner & Co. v. Eli Lilly & Co.*,[8] pharmacists had been substituting a cheaper quinine medication for the more expensive one requested by customers without disclosing the substitution. The deception was facilitated by the fact that the two medications were similar in appearance and flavor because both contained chocolate; indeed, there was some evidence that the defendant had deliberately set out to duplicate the plaintiff's formula as precisely as possible so that the medications would be indistinguishable. Although the Supreme Court agreed that the pharmacists had engaged in unfair competition in the nature of passing off, and that the manufacturer of the cheaper medication was liable for the activities of its sales representatives in encouraging the deception, the Court held that it would be improper to enjoin the defendant from continuing to use chocolate in its medication, because the chocolate was a functional ingredient that contributed to the taste and appearance of the medication, and also served as a suspension agent for the medicinal ingredients:

> Respondent has no exclusive right to the use of its formula. Chocolate is used as an ingredient not alone for the purpose of imparting a distinctive

---

[5] *Id.* at 1207-08; Qualitex Co. v. Jacobson Products Co., Inc., 514 U.S. 159, 164-65 (1995).

[6] 514 U.S. at 164-65.

[7] *Willhelm Pudenz*, 177 F.3d at 1208.

[8] 265 U.S. 526 (1924).

color, but for the purpose also of making the preparation peculiarly agreeable to the palate, to say nothing of its effect as a suspending medium. While it is not a medicinal element in the preparation, it serves a substantial and desirable use, which prevents it from being a mere matter of dress. It does not merely serve the incidental use of identifying the respondent's preparation, and it is doubtful whether it should be called a non-essential. The petitioner or anyone else is at liberty under the law to manufacture and market an exactly similar preparation containing chocolate and to notify the public that it is being done.[9]

While the defendant could not be enjoined from offering the same non-patented medication as the plaintiff, or from using chocolate to impart the same color and flavor, the Court did endorse an injunction requiring the defendant to take affirmative steps to prevent pharmacists from engaging in the fraudulent substitution of one medication for the other.

[B]   The Evolving Definition of Functionality

Although the concept of functionality was at the core of the Supreme Court's decision in *William R. Warner*, the Court did not use this term or attempt to define the concept at that time. In its 1982 decision in *Inwood Laboratories, Inc. v. Ives Laboratories, Inc.*, however, the Court held that "a product feature is functional if it is essential to the use or purpose of the article or if it affects the cost or quality of the article."[10] As discussed below, this remains the primary definition of functionality in trademark law, although the Supreme Court has articulated a secondary test as well.

Like *William R. Warner*, the *Inwood Laboratories* case involved an unfair competition claim that arose from the fraudulent activities of pharmacists who were able to pass off the defendant's cheaper medication as though it were the plaintiff's more expensive medication because the capsules were identical in color. The Supreme Court held that the plaintiff's claim was properly rejected by the district court for two reasons, either of which was sufficient by itself: (1) the color of the capsules lacked secondary meaning, and (2) the color of the capsules was functional. The Court found no error in the district court's explanation for its finding of functionality:

> In reaching its conclusion, the court found that the blue and blue-red colors were functional to patients as well as to doctors and hospitals: many elderly patients associate color with therapeutic effect; some patients commingle medications in a container and rely on color to differentiate one from another; colors are of some, if limited, help in identifying drugs in emergency situations; and use of the same color for brand name drugs and their generic equivalents helps avoid confusion on the part of those responsible for dispensing drugs.[11]

---

[9] *Id.* at 531.

[10] 456 U.S. 844, 850 n.10 (1982).

[11] *Id.* at 853.

In 1995, the Supreme Court again addressed the meaning of functionality in a new context — that of aesthetic functionality in *Qualitex Co. v. Jacobson Products Co.*,[12] which presented the question of whether color alone could be registered as a form of trade dress. In concluding that color was not, in this case, a functional feature of the registrant's product (a laundry press pad), the Court appeared to enlarge the definition of functionality. Noting that "sometimes color plays an important role in making a product more desirable," the Court found that color played no such role in this case. In concluding that color was not a functional feature of the registrant's press pad, the Court quoted the *Inwood Laboratories* standard, but added the language indicated in italics below:

> "[I]n general terms, a product feature is functional," and cannot serve as a trademark, "if it is essential to the use or purpose of the article or if it affects the cost or quality of the article," *that is, if exclusive use of the feature would put competitors at a significant non-reputation-related disadvantage*"[13]

Although the addition of the italicized language was not necessary to hold that the color of the press pad in this case was nonfunctional, it appeared to broaden the functionality definition in a way that would be crucial in situations in which color might in fact "play an important role in making a product more desirable." Implicit in this definition is the Court's recognition of the concept of "aesthetic functionality" — that is, the concept that certain aesthetic aspects of a product's design or packaging (that is, its trade dress) may contribute to its consumer appeal in ways that are unrelated to any origin-identifying function and that, therefore, should be denied trademark protection even if they have acquired secondary meaning.

More recently, the Court's 2001 opinion in *TrafFix Devices, Inc. v. Mktg. Displays, Inc.*,[14] appeared to articulate a hierarchy in this functionality analysis, making the original *Inwood Laboratories* test primary, and the *Qualitex* expansion relevant only where the primary test is not satisfied:

> Discussing trademarks, we have said " 'in general terms, a product feature is functional,' and cannot serve as a trademark, 'if it is essential to the use or purpose of the article or if it affects the cost or quality of the article.' " Expanding upon the meaning of this phrase, we have observed that a functional feature is one the "exclusive use of [which] would put competitors at a significant non-reputation-related disadvantage." The Court of Appeals in the instant case seemed to interpret this language to mean that a necessary test for functionality is "whether the particular product configuration is a competitive necessity." This was incorrect as a comprehensive definition. As explained in *Qualitex, supra,* and *Inwood, supra,* a feature is also functional when it is essential to the use or purpose of the device or when it affects the cost or quality of the device. The *Qualitex* decision did not purport to displace this traditional rule. Instead, it quoted the rule as *Inwood* had set it forth. It is proper

---

[12] 514 U.S. 159 (1995).

[13] *Id.* at 165 (emphasis added).

[14] 532 U.S. 23 (2001).

to inquire into a "significant non-reputation-related disadvantage" in cases of aesthetic functionality, the question involved in *Qualitex*. Where the design is functional under the *Inwood* formulation there is no need to proceed further to consider if there is a competitive necessity for the feature. In *Qualitex*, by contrast, aesthetic functionality was the central question, there having been no indication that the green-gold color of the laundry press pad had any bearing on the use or purpose of the product or its cost or quality.[15]

In *TrafFix*, the trade dress at issue was an aspect of the product's design that had been the subject of a since-expired utility patent, a dual-spring device that "provide[d] a unique and useful mechanism to resist the force of the wind."[16] The fact that the feature in question had been the subject of a utility patent was, in the Court's view, "strong evidence" that the feature was functional, and warranted imposing a "heavy burden" on the party seeking to refute this evidence of functionality — "for instance by showing that it is merely an ornamental, incidental, or arbitrary aspect of the device."[17] In this case, the utility of the device established that it was functional, and, in the Court's view, this made it unnecessary to inquire whether alternative design possibilities were available to competitors. The utilitarian function of the design in question was therefore distinguishable from the arbitrary selection of a color for the laundry press pad in *Qualitex*, where the exclusive use of one color by one party still left numerous alternative color choices for competitors:

> There is no need, furthermore, to engage, as did the Court of Appeals, in speculation about other design possibilities, such as using three or four springs which might serve the same purpose. Here, the functionality of the spring design means that competitors need not explore whether other spring juxtapositions might be used. The dual-spring design is not an arbitrary flourish in the configuration of MDI's product; it is the reason the device works. Other designs need not be attempted.

> Because the dual-spring design is functional, it is unnecessary for competitors to explore designs to hide the springs, say by using a box or framework to cover them, as suggested by the Court of Appeals. The dual-spring design assures the user the device will work. If buyers are assured the product serves its purpose by seeing the operative mechanism that in itself serves an important market need. It would be at cross-purposes to those objectives, and something of a paradox, were we to require the manufacturer to conceal the very item the user seeks.

---

[15] *Id.* at 32-33 (citations omitted).

[16] *Id.* at 33.

[17] *Id.* at 29-30. In a later decision interpreting *TrafFix*, a federal district court held that a particular design feature was not "essential to the use or purpose" of a patented adhesive spreader because the patent disclosure specifically stated that the feature was "not essential to the invention." However, because the patent disclosure also described several "desirable" functions of this design feature (adding strength, protecting the user's hand, and providing a surface on which information could be imprinted), the court held that a question of fact remained as to whether the feature affected "the cost or quality" of the device. Clark Tile Co. v. Red Devil, Inc., 2007 U.S. Dist. LEXIS 90107, *20-22 (Dec. 7, 2007).

In a case where a manufacturer seeks to protect arbitrary, incidental, or ornamental aspects of features of a product found in the patent claims, such as arbitrary curves in the legs or an ornamental pattern painted on the springs, a different result might obtain. There the manufacturer could perhaps prove that those aspects do not serve a purpose within the terms of the utility patent. The inquiry into whether such features, asserted to be trade dress, are functional by reason of their inclusion in the claims of an expired utility patent could be aided by going beyond the claims and examining the patent and its prosecution history to see if the feature in question is shown as a useful part of the invention. No such claim is made here, however. MDI in essence seeks protection for the dual-spring design alone. The asserted trade dress consists simply of the dual-spring design, four legs, a base, an upright, and a sign. MDI has pointed to nothing arbitrary about the components of its device or the way they are assembled. The Lanham Act does not exist to reward manufacturers for their innovation in creating a particular device; that is the purpose of the patent law and its period of exclusivity. The Lanham Act, furthermore, does not protect trade dress in a functional design simply because an investment has been made to encourage the public to associate a particular functional feature with a single manufacturer or seller. The Court of Appeals erred in viewing MDI as possessing the right to exclude competitors from using a design identical to MDI's and to require those competitors to adopt a different design simply to avoid copying it. MDI cannot gain the exclusive right to produce sign stands using the dual-spring design by asserting that consumers associate it with the look of the invention itself. Whether a utility patent has expired or there has been no utility patent at all, a product design which has a particular appearance may be functional because it is "essential to the use or purpose of the article" or "affects the cost or quality of the article."[18]

TrafFix appears to make *Inwood Laboratories* the primary test of functionality, so that the availability of alternative designs need not be considered where the *Inwood Laboratories* test is satisfied. Only if a product feature is deemed to be nonfunctional under the strictly utilitarian standard of *Inwood Laboratories* should a court inquire whether copying that feature was a competitive necessity, or whether competitors could instead have used alternative designs. The Fifth Circuit has already adopted this interpretation of *TrafFix*,[19] and the Second Circuit appears to have embraced it as well,[20] while the views of several other Circuits do not appear fully formed as yet.[21]

---

[18] *TrafFix*, 532 U.S. at 33-35.

[19] *See, e.g.*, Eppendorf-Netheler-Hinz GMBH v. Ritter GMBH, 289 F.3d 351 (5th Cir.), *cert. denied*, 537 U.S. 1071 (2002).

[20] Nora Beverages, Inc. v. Perrier Group of Am., Inc., 269 F.3d 114, 120 n. 4 (2d Cir. 2001) (mentioning the relevance of alternative design possibilities only in the context of aesthetic functionality).

[21] The Sixth Circuit stopped just short of endorsing the Fifth Circuit's interpretation in *Antioch Co. v. West Trimming Corp.*, 347 F.3d 150, 155-56 (6th Cir. 2003), where it held that courts are not *required* to consider evidence of alternative designs in applying the *Inwood Laboratories* test of

In contrast, the Federal Circuit's post-*TrafFix* opinion in *Valu Engineering v. Rexnord Corp.* held that the availability of alternative designs can still be considered as "a legitimate source of evidence to determine whether a feature is functional in the first place,"[22] without limiting the relevance of this inquiry to cases involving aesthetic functionality. The Federal Circuit continues to adhere to its pre-*TrafFix* distinction between product features that are "de facto" functional, and thus not precluded from trademark protection, and those that are "de jure" functional and therefore not a proper subject for trademark protection:

> Our decisions distinguish de facto functional features, which may be entitled to trademark protection, from de jure functional features, which are not. "In essence, de facto functional means that the design of a product has a function, i.e., a bottle of any design holds fluid." De facto functionality does not necessarily defeat registrability. De jure functionality means that the product has a particular shape "because it works better in this shape."[23]

Furthermore, in determining whether a feature is de jure functional, the Federal Circuit continues to apply the four-factor test articulated by its predecessor, the Court of Customs and Patent Appeals, in the 1982 case of *In re Morton-Norwich Products, Inc.*,[24] which considers: (1) the existence of a utility patent disclosing the utilitarian advantages of the design; (2) advertising materials in which the originator of the design touts the design's utilitarian advantages; (3) the availability to competitors of functionally equivalent designs; and (4) facts indicating that the design results in a comparatively simple or cheap method of manufacturing the product.[25] In the Federal Circuit's view, *TrafFix* did not alter the *Morton-Norwich* analysis.[26] The court's explanation, however, is hardly a model of clarity:

> We did not in the past under the third factor require that the opposing party establish that there was a "competitive necessity" for the product feature. Nothing in *TrafFix* suggests that consideration of alternative designs is not properly part of the overall mix, and we do not read the Court's observations in *TrafFix* as rendering the availability of alternative designs irrelevant. Rather, we conclude that the Court merely noted that once a product feature is found functional based on other considerations there is no need to consider the availability of alternative designs, because the feature cannot be given trade dress protection

---

functionality. The Third Circuit has interpreted *TrafFix* as making the *Inwood Laboratories* test primary, and the competitive necessity test secondary, although it has not opined on the relevance of alternative designs under either test. Shire US, Inc. v. Barr Labs., Inc., 329 F.3d 348, 353-54 (3d Cir. 2003).

[22] 278 F.3d 1268, 1276 (Fed. Cir. 2002).

[23] *Id.* at 1274 (citations omitted).

[24] 671 F.2d 1332, 1340-41 (C.C.P.A. 1982).

[25] *Valu Eng'g*, 278 F.3d at 1274.

[26] *Id.* at 1276. The Trademark Trial and Appeals Board, which is bound to follow Federal Circuit precedent, continues to apply the *Morton-Norwich* factors. *See, e.g.*, In re UDOR U.S.A., Inc., 2009 TTAB LEXIS 61 (Mar. 4, 2009); In re Vertex Group LLC, 2009 TTAB LEXIS 60, *32-39 (Feb. 13, 2009); Roller Derby Skate Corp. v. Bauer Nike Hockey, Inc., 2005 TTAB LEXIS 7, *6 (Jan. 7, 2005).

merely because there are alternative designs available. But that does not mean that the availability of alternative designs cannot be a legitimate source of evidence to determine whether a feature is functional in the first place.[27]

Notwithstanding the court's assertion to the contrary, it appears that, in response to *TrafFix*, the Federal Circuit has in fact modified the *Morton-Norwich* analysis so that, if a competitor establishes functionality under factors 1, 2, and 4, the court need not consider the availability of alternative designs (factor 3). If a competitor *cannot* make the functionality showing under factors 1, 2, and 4 alone, then consideration of factor 3 is appropriate. It is not entirely clear, however, whether the Federal Circuit meant to *foreclose* consideration of factor 3 when functionality was established under factors 1, 2, and 4, or whether it meant that consideration of factor 3 is simply not *required* in that situation. The former position would appear to be more consistent with *TrafFix*.

The Ninth Circuit, too, continues to treat the availability of alternative designs as an indicator of non-functionality, even after *TrafFix*:

> To determine whether a product feature is functional, this circuit typically considers four factors: (1) whether advertising touts the utilitarian advantages of the design, (2) whether the particular design results from a comparatively simple or inexpensive method of manufacture, (3) whether the design yields a utilitarian advantage and (4) whether alternative designs are available.

> In applying the[se] factors, we are mindful of the Supreme Court's recent pronouncement that once functionality is established, "there is no need . . . to engage . . . in speculation about other design possibilities. . . ." Therefore, the existence of alternative designs cannot negate a trademark's functionality. But the existence of alternative designs may indicate whether the trademark itself embodies functional or merely ornamental aspects of the product.[28]

Not surprisingly, a number of commentators have criticized the *TrafFix* decision for its lack of clarity, and for creating interpretive problems for the lower courts.[29] It appears likely that the Supreme Court will have to provide further clarification of the test(s) for functionality in the not-too-distant future.

---

[27] *Valu Eng'g*, 278 F.3d at 1276.

[28] Talking Rain Bev. Co. v. South Beach Bev. Co., 349 F.3d 601, 603 (9th Cir. 2003). Treatise author J. Thomas McCarthy agrees with this view. J. Thomas McCarthy, McCarthy on Trademarks and Unfair Competition § 7.75 (2009).

[29] *See, e.g.*, McCarthy on Trademarks, note 28 *supra* at § 7:75; Margreth Barrett, *Consolidating the Diffuse Paths to Trademark Functionality: Encountering* TrafFix *on the Way to* Sears, 61 Wash. & Lee L. Rev. 79, 129-35 (2004); Vincent N. Palladino, *Trade Dress Functionality after* TrafFix: *The Lower Courts Divide Again*, 93 TMR 1219 (2003); Mark Alan Thurmon, *The Rise and Fall of Trademark's Functionality Doctrine*, 56 Fla. L. Rev. 243 (2004).

[C]   Aesthetic Functionality

The concept of "aesthetic functionality," as opposed to the "utilitarian" type of functionality described in *Inwood Laboratories*, is somewhat controversial. As early as 1938, this concept was recognized in the *Restatement of Torts*, which noted that "[w]hen goods are bought largely for their aesthetic value, their features may be functional because they definitely contribute to that value and thus aid the performance of an object for which the goods are intended."[30] Even in the case of mundane products, such as toothpaste, mouthwash, food and beverages, lighting fixtures, and automobiles, there can be little doubt that aesthetic features — color, flavor, texture, aroma, or a pleasing appearance — can have a significant influence on purchasing decisions that may have nothing to do with any secondary meaning that might happen to attach to those features. For consumers who can taste the difference between Coke and Pepsi, their distinctive flavors function not only as source indicators but as the essential features that make consumers prefer one brand over another. In the case of products like colognes, soaps, and shampoos, aroma can serve a similar dual purpose.

The *Restatement (Third) of Unfair Competition* also recognizes aesthetic functionality:

> A design is functional because of its aesthetic value only if it confers a significant benefit that cannot practically be duplicated by the use of alternative designs.[31]

Many of the lower federal courts had recognized the concept of aesthetic functionality long before the Supreme Court addressed the concept in *Qualitex*.[32] Some of these courts found an aesthetic feature to be nonfunctional, and thus eligible for trademark protection, if it was "of such an arbitrary nature that depriving the public of the right to copy it is insignificant";[33] in contrast, if the aesthetic feature was dictated by functional considerations, it was ineligible for trademark protection.[34] Applying this standard in *Keene Corp. v. Paraflex Industries, Inc.*, for example, the Third Circuit denied trademark protection to the aesthetic features of an exterior wall-mounted lighting fixture:

> The luminaire itself is essentially a utilitarian product, used to light exterior area. However, because it is a wall-mounted luminaire, as distinguished from a free-standing street lamp, part of its function includes its architectural compatibility with the structure or building on which it is mounted. Thus its design configuration, rather than serving merely as an arbitrary expression of aesthetics, is intricately related to its function.[35]

---

[30] RESTATEMENT OF TORTS § 742, cmt. a (1938).

[31] RESTATEMENT (THIRD) OF UNFAIR COMPETITION, § 17, cmt. c (1993).

[32] *See* Keene Corp. v. Paraflex Indus., Inc., 653 F.2d 822, 825-26 (3d Cir. 1981) (collecting cases).

[33] *Id.* at 825 (quoting In re Mogen David Wine Corp., 328 F.2d 925, 933, 51 C.C.P.A. 1260 (C.C.P.A. 1964) (Rich, J., concurring)).

[34] *Id.*

[35] *Id.* at 826.

The Third Circuit noted that it was entirely possible for an aesthetic feature to be both functional and imbued with secondary meaning, and that in such cases trademark law should not prevent competitors from copying the functional feature:

> Keene also contends that the court failed to consider whether competition would be substantially hindered by restricting the copying of the Wall Cube, and that this consideration is the test of functionality. As we previously noted, the policy predicate for the entire functionality doctrine stems from the public interest in enhancing competition. Thus both the Restatement and courts considering this issue have referred to the question "whether prohibition of imitation by others will deprive the others of something which will substantially hinder them in competition." Restatement of Torts § 742, Comment a (1938).
>
> Judge Meanor gave ample consideration to this factor. He found that there is "a limited number of designs" possible for an outdoor wall-mounted luminaire. He noted that presently there are around twelve or fifteen wall-mounted luminaires from which to choose, and perceived a danger to competition in the luminaire market if manufacturers were given the exclusive right to a design. Although Keene would have us adopt a standard inquiring whether the specific design features of the product "were competitively essential," we believe that is an unnecessarily narrow view of functionality. This court has previously indicated that merely because there are other shapes and designs "which defendant could use and still produce a workable" product, the design used is not thereby non-functional. . . .
>
> . . .
>
> Because there are only a limited number of configurations or designs for a luminaire which are architecturally compatible with the type of structures on which they are placed, the selection of a luminaire design does not have the unlimited boundaries as does the selection of a wine bottle or ashtray design, and the court's finding that competition will be stifled is again not clearly erroneous.[36]

Shortly thereafter, in *Deere & Co. v. Farmhand, Inc.*, the Eighth Circuit affirmed a district court's use of the *Keene* analysis to deny trademark protection to the particular shade of green used by John Deere for its front-end loaders, tractors, and other farm equipment, in spite of strong evidence that the color had secondary meaning, because the court found that farmers preferred to buy their equipment in matching colors.[37]

Other courts adopted a slightly different test, treating an aesthetic element as functional if its presence was a "competitive necessity." For example, in *Brunswick Corp. v. British Seagull*,[38] the Federal Circuit upheld the PTO's

---

[36] *Id.* at 827.

[37] 560 F. Supp. 85, 98 (S.D. Iowa 1982) (following *Keene*), *aff'd*, 721 F.2d 253 (8th Cir. 1983) (per curiam).

[38] 35 F.3d 1527 (Fed. Cir. 1994).

refusal to register the color black for outboard motors, on the ground that, in this context, the color black was functional:

> [A]lthough the color black is not functional in the sense that it makes these engines work better, or that it makes them easier or less expensive to manufacture, black is more desirable from the perspective of prospective purchasers because it is color compatible with a wider variety of boat colors and because objects colored black appear smaller than they do when they are painted other lighter or brighter colors. The evidence shows that people who buy outboard motors for boats like the colors of the motors to be harmonious with the colors of their vessels, and that they also find it desirable under some circumstances to reduce the perception of the size of the motors in proportion to the boats.[39]

In upholding the PTO, the Federal Circuit noted that "[f]unctionality reflects a tension" between "a fundamental right to compete through imitation of a competitor's product" and "the individual's right to protect symbols which identify the source of particular goods."[40] Under the functionality doctrine, the right to protect source indicators as trademarks should, therefore, be limited by "the *need* to copy [articles that are not protected by patent or copyright], which is more properly termed the right to compete *effectively*."[41] The court distinguished between de facto functional features, which were eligible for trademark protection, and de jure functional features, which were not:

> In essence, de facto functional means that the design of a product has a function, i.e., a bottle of any design holds fluid. De jure functionality, on the other hand, means that the product is in its particular shape because it works better in this shape.[42]

The court rejected the argument that a feature is de jure functional only if it is "essential" to competitiveness. Rather, "[i]f the feature asserted to give a product distinctiveness is the best, or at least one, of a few superior designs for its *de facto* purpose, it follows that competition is hindered," and the functionality bar should therefore apply.[43] The court concluded that this "competitive necessity" test was met in the case of the black outboard motor.[44]

In an analysis reminiscent of *Inwood Laboratories*, the competitive necessity test was also applied in *Nor-Am Chemical v. O.M. Scott & Sons Co.* to deny trademark protection for the use of the color blue for fertilizer:

> First, the use of color assists commercial blenders of fertilizer in determining whether various components of a blend are sufficiently mixed. For example, by using color, visual inspection will reveal whether

---

[39] *Id.* at 1530-32 (quoting TTAB).

[40] *Id.* at 1530.

[41] *Id.* at 1531 (quoting In re Morton-Norwich Prods., Inc., 71 F.2d 1332, 1339 (C.C.P.A. 1982) (emphasis in original)).

[42] *Id.* (quoting In re R.M. Smith, Inc., 734 F.2d 1482, 1484 (Fed. Cir.1984)).

[43] *Id.* (quoting In re Bose Corp.,772 F.2d 866, 872 (Fed. Cir. 1985) (emphasis added)).

[44] *Id.* at 1531-32.

each component has been introduced into the blend. Also, color assists users in determining whether fertilizer has been applied to an area, and if so, whether it has been applied uniformly. Finally, the scientific community uses the color blue to designate nitrogen and the color blue commonly identifies nitrogen in fertilizers outside the specialty agricultural fertilizer market. These considerations suggest that the consuming public, including retail purchasers of blends containing nitrogen fertilizer, associate nitrogen with the color blue. For these reasons, I find that there is a competitive need for the color blue in all nitrogen fertilizer markets.[45]

A number of courts, however, declined to find trade dress aesthetically functional solely because it was aesthetically appealing. For example, in the *Keene* case mentioned earlier, the Third Circuit expressly rejected this interpretation of aesthetic functionality as overbroad, holding that "[i]nstead, the inquiry should focus on the extent to which the design feature is related to the utilitarian function of the product or feature."[46]

The Supreme Court has addressed aesthetic functionality in a series of cases — including *Inwood Laboratories*, *William R. Warner*, and *Qualitex*, as well as dictum in *TrafFix* — that have consistently indicated that aesthetic features such as color (as well as flavor, in *William R. Warner*) may be barred from trademark protection under the functionality doctrine.

The Supreme Court's discussion of aesthetic functionality in *Qualitex* provides the most comprehensive guidance to date on this somewhat unsettled area of the law. Although *Qualitex* was not itself an aesthetic functionality case, addressing instead the threshold question of whether color, by itself, is per se unregistrable (a question that the court answered in the negative), the question of functionality arose because the party opposing registration argued that granting trademark protection to colors would have an anticompetitive effect, because it would deplete the color choices available to competitors of the registrant. In rejecting that argument, the Court observed that "the trademark doctrine of 'functionality' normally would seem available to prevent the anticompetitive consequences" of color depletion,[47] and that a diminishing array of color choices would not hinder competition in cases in which color contributed nothing to the functionality of the product. The Court appeared to endorse the prevailing judicial interpretations of aesthetic functionality:

> The functionality doctrine, as we have said, forbids the use of a product's feature as a trademark where doing so will put a competitor at a significant disadvantage because the feature is "essential to the use or

---

[45] 4 U.S.P.Q.2d (BNA) 1316, 1320 (E.D. Pa. 1987); *cf.* Warner Lambert Co. v. McCrory's Corp., 718 F. Supp. 389, 396 (D.N.J. 1989) (holding that color is functional for mouthwash, because customers associate certain colors with certain flavors).

[46] Keene Corp. v. Paraflex Indus., Inc., 653 F.2d 822, 825 (3d Cir. 1981); *see also* American Greetings Corp. v. Dan-Dee Imports, Inc., 807 F.2d 1136, 1142 (3d Cir. 1986) (upholding district court's conclusion that "tummy graphics" on Care Bears were aesthetically functional not because they made the toys "more appealing to the eye," but because they "communicat[ed] the particular personality of each of the Care Bear characters").

[47] *Qualitex*, 514 U.S. at 169.

purpose of the article" or "affects [its] cost or quality." The functionality doctrine thus protects competitors against a disadvantage (unrelated to recognition or reputation) that trademark protection might otherwise impose, namely their inability reasonably to replicate important non-reputation-related product features. For example, this Court has written that competitors might be free to copy the color of a medical pill where that color serves to identify the kind of medication (e.g., a type of blood medicine) in addition to its source. And, the federal courts have demonstrated that they can apply this doctrine in a careful and reasoned manner, with sensitivity to the effect on competition. Although we need not comment on the merits of specific cases, we note that lower courts have permitted competitors to copy the green color of farm machinery (because customers wanted their farm equipment to match) and have barred the use of black as a trademark on outboard boat motors (because black has the special functional attributes of decreasing the apparent size of the motor and ensuring compatibility with many different boat colors). . . . The Restatement (Third) of Unfair Competition adds that, if a design's "aesthetic value" lies in its ability to "confer a significant benefit that cannot practically be duplicated by the use of alternative designs," then the design is "functional." The "ultimate test of aesthetic functionality," it explains, "is whether the recognition of trademark rights would significantly hinder competition."

The upshot is that, where a color serves a significant nontrademark function — whether to distinguish a heart pill from a digestive medicine or to satisfy the "noble instinct for giving the right touch of beauty to common and necessary things," G. Chesterton, *Simplicity and Tolstoy* 61 (1912) — courts will examine whether its use as a mark would permit one competitor (or a group) to interfere with legitimate (nontrademark-related) competition through actual or potential exclusive use of an important product ingredient. That examination should not discourage firms from creating esthetically pleasing mark designs, for it is open to their competitors to do the same. But, ordinarily, it should prevent the anticompetitive consequences of [the] hypothetical "color depletion" argument, when, and if, the circumstances of a particular case threaten "color depletion."[48]

As examples of "careful and reasoned" applications of the doctrine, the Court cited *Deere, Brunswick Corp.*, and *Nor-Am Chemical*.[49]

Six years after *Qualitex*, dictum in *TrafFix* confirmed that "[i]t is proper to inquire into a 'significant non-reputation-related disadvantage' in cases of aesthetic functionality."[50] The *TrafFix* opinion specifically refers to this as the "competitive necessity" test.[51]

---

[48] *Id.* at 169-70 (citing REST. (THIRD) OF UNFAIR COMPETITION § 17, cmt. c., pp. 175-76 (1993) (additional citations omitted)).

[49] *Id.*

[50] *TrafFix*, 532 U.S. at 33.

[51] *Id.*

Even after *Qualitex*, aesthetic functionality remains controversial. Leading commentator and treatise author J. Thomas McCarthy continues to reject the doctrine, arguing that purely ornamental features of trade dress should receive trademark protection only when they acquire secondary meaning, and consumer preferences as to ornamentation should not alter this analysis.[52] Aesthetic functionality was squarely rejected by the Fifth Circuit in 2008.[53]

In those courts that have expressly recognized aesthetic functionality, post-*Qualitex* decisions have revealed some confusion over how to apply the competitive necessity test to aesthetic features.

For example, in *Publications Int'l, Ltd. v. Landoll, Inc.*,[54] the Seventh Circuit applied *Qualitex* in holding that the use of gold-colored gilding on the edges of cookbook pages was aesthetically functional because "[g]old connotes opulence," and was a color commonly used both in food decoration and bookbinding.[55] Calling this "a prime example of aesthetic functionality,"[56] the court observed:

> It would be arbitrary as well as puritanical and even philistine to deny that one function of modern consumer packaging is to be beautiful, the motivation being sometimes a hope that the consumer will infer the quality of the product from the beauty of the package and sometimes a hope that the consumer will derive utility (and so be willing to pay more) from the packaging directly, as when a consumer displays a shapely bottle of champagne to his dinner guests. A producer cannot in the name of trade dress prevent his competitors from making their products as visually entrancing as his own. Ordinarily there is a sufficient variety of pleasing shapes, sizes, colors, and ornamentation to enable beauty without sacrificing differentiation. But if consumers derive a value from the fact that a product looks a certain way that is distinct from the value of knowing at a glance who made it, then it is a nonappropriable feature of the product.[57]

Several years later, in *Eco Mfg., LLC v. Honeywell Int'l, Inc.*,[58] the Seventh Circuit reiterated its agreement in principle with the concept of aesthetic functionality as elucidated in *Qualitex*, but declined to apply the doctrine where a thermostat maker claimed that a substantial number of consumers preferred the "look" of a round thermostat. Although the district court had found that the aesthetic appeal of the round shape was such that denying competitors the right to use the same shape would place them at a significant non-reputation-related disadvantage, the appellate court disagreed:

---

[52] McCarthy on Trademarks, note 28 *supra* at § 7:81.

[53] Board of Supervisors for Louisiana State Univ. v. Smack Apparel Co., 550 F.3d 465, 487-88 (5th Cir. 2008).

[54] 164 F.3d 337 (7th Cir. 1998).

[55] 164 F.3d at 342.

[56] *Id.* at 339.

[57] *Id.*

[58] 357 F.3d 649 (7th Cir. 2003) (*aff'g* 295 F. Supp. 2d 854, 872 (S.D. Ind. 2003)).

Aesthetic appeal *can* be functional; often we value products for their looks. Yet an understanding of "aesthetic functionality" as broad as Eco's would destroy protection of trade dress . . . It would always be possible to show that *some* consumers like the item's appearance; then the corner jewelry store could emulate the distinctive Tiffany blue box, which would lose its ability to identify origin. "Beauty lies in the eye of the beholder" therefore cannot by itself establish functionality of trade dress. Perhaps, however, a more complete record may show that consumers' desire for circular thermostats comes from more than familiarity with a shape that Honeywell made famous. After all, Honeywell did not invent the circle (or the wheel).[59]

A post-*Qualitex* decision in the Eleventh Circuit held that functionality barred trademark protection for the color, shape, and size of flash-frozen ice cream pellets. With respect to color, the plaintiff sought to prevent the defendant from using the exact same colors as the plaintiff to indicate the flavors of its flash-frozen ice cream pellets (brown for chocolate, white for vanilla, pink for strawberry, etc.). Notably, the court based its finding that ice cream color was functional on *both* the *Inwood Laboratories* test and the *Qualitex* "competitive necessity" test, finding that: (1) a significant non-reputation-related disadvantage would arise if trademark law gave one competitor the exclusive right to use certain colors to indicate the flavors of its ice cream,[60] and (2) the use of traditional colors for ice cream was "functional in this case it is essential to the purpose of the product and affects its quality," thus invoking the pure *Inwood Laboratories* standard rather than the competitive necessity test.[61] The court then applied the "competitive necessity" test to the color, shape, and size of the ice-cream pellets, treating all three as aesthetically functional aspects of the product's design:

> Likewise, the color, shape, and size of dippin' dots are "aesthetic functions" that easily satisfy the competitive necessity test because precluding competitors like FBD from copying any of these aspects of dippin' dots would eliminate all competitors in the flash-frozen ice cream market, which would be the ultimate non-reputation-related disadvantage. Therefore, DDI's argument that FBD could still compete in the ice cream market by producing, *e.g.*, soft-serve ice cream, which would not have many of the same functional elements as dippin' dots and thus would not infringe upon DDI's product trade dress, is unavailing. FBD does not want to compete in the ice cream business; it wants to compete in the flash-frozen ice cream business, which is in a different market from more traditional forms of ice cream . . .

Setting color aside, however, the shape of the ice cream pellets was actually an artifact of the flash-freezing process itself, and the size of the pellets was dictated by the need to minimize the formation of ice crystals in order to produce a

---

[59] *Id.* at 654 (emphasis in original).

[60] Dippin' Dots, Inc. v. Frosty Bites Dist., L.L.C., 369 F.3d 1197, 1203 (11th Cir. 2004), *cert. denied*, 160 L. Ed. 2d 777 (2005).

[61] *Id.* at 1206.

creamy flavor and texture.[62] Thus, whether this part of the court's analysis reflects aesthetic functionality or a more utilitarian concept of functionality is arguable.

A 2002 opinion from the Sixth Circuit expressly adopted the competitive necessity standard for aesthetic functionality, holding in *Abercrombie & Fitch Stores, Inc. v. American Eagle Outfitters, Inc.*,[63] that certain words and images that appeared on a company's clothing were aesthetically functional and therefore unprotected. It reached the same conclusion with respect to the company's in-store displays and its use of college students as sales associates, but found material issues of fact with regard to the functionality of the design of the clothing catalog.

Post-*Qualitex* decisions from courts in the Second Circuit, which had embraced aesthetic functionality even before *Qualitex*,[64] have reflected some confusion about the doctrine. In a muddled opinion issued immediately after *Qualitex*, the Court of Appeals held in *Knitwaves, Inc. v. Lollytogs, Ltd.*[65] that granting trade dress protection to a decorative design on a sweater would not hinder competition because alternative designs were available, but declined to grant such protection because "the designs were not primarily intended as source identification."[66] The court's requirement that trade dress be *intended* as source designation has no foundation in the law of trade dress, or in trademark law generally, because the status of a mark as an origin indicator is dictated by consumer perceptions rather than by a merchant's intent. A later Second Circuit opinion endorsed aesthetic functionality without mentioning intent, citing *Qualitex*'s "non-reputation-related disadvantage" formulation."[67] At the district court level, one opinion rejected the aesthetic functionality doctrine without mentioning *Qualitex*,[68] while a later opinion used the availability of alternative designs to rule that a jewelry design was not aesthetically functional.[69]

Confusion also reigns in the Ninth Circuit, where pre-*Qualitex* decisions had recognized aesthetic functionality but had vacillated in determining its scope.[70] A 2001 opinion (issued just a few months after *TrafFix*) flatly held that functional features are limited to those that have a utilitarian aspect, and thus should not include features that contribute only to a product's aesthetic appeal.[71] In

---

[62] *Id.* at 1206-07.

[63] 280 F.3d 619, 641-45 (6th Cir. 2002).

[64] *See, e.g.*, Wallace Int'l Silversmiths, Inc. v. Godinger Silver Art Co., 916 F.2d 76, 79-81 (2d Cir. 1990).

[65] 71 F.3d 996, 1006 (2d Cir. 1995).

[66] *Id.* at 1009. *Knitwaves'* intent requirement was immediately applied in Banff Ltd. v. Express, Inc., 921 F. Supp. 1065, 1071 (S.D.N.Y. 1995).

[67] Yurman Design, Inc. v. PAJ, Inc., 262 F.3d 101, 116 (2d Cir. 2001).

[68] Krueger Int'l v. Nightingale Inc., 915 F. Supp. 595, 606 (S.D.N.Y. 1996) (calling aesthetic functionality "unnecessary and illogical").

[69] Yurman Design, Inc. v. Golden Treasure Imps., Inc., 275 F. Supp. 2d 506, 512 (S.D.N.Y. 2003).

[70] MCCARTHY ON TRADEMARKS, *supra* note 28, at § 7:80.

[71] *See* Clicks Billiards, Inc. v. Sixshooters, Inc., 251 F.3d 1252, 1260 (9th Cir. 2001) (collecting cases). *But see* Vuitton et Fils S.A. v. J. Young Enters., Inc., 644 F.2d 769, 774 (9th Cir. 1981)

contrast, a 2006 opinion endorsed a broader view, applying the doctrine to "product features that serve an aesthetic purpose wholly independent of any source-identifying function."[72] Citing *TrafFix*, the court adopted the test of "whether protection of the feature as a trademark would impose a significant non-reputation-related competitive disadvantage."[73]

One aspect of aesthetic functionality is uncontroversial. Even where individual elements of a design are aesthetically functional, it is well-settled that the functionality test must be applied to the design as a whole. Thus, while individual design elements may be functional, the total combination of those elements may still be subject to trademark protection.[74]

PART II:
ESTABLISHING TRADEMARK RIGHTS

§ 2.04   USE IN TRADE

Under common law and state statutes, trademark rights may be established only through actual use of the mark in connection with the offering of goods or services to the public. Subject to very limited exceptions, this is true under the Lanham Act as well.[75] The Supreme Court has held that "there is no such thing as property in a trade-mark except as a right appurtenant to an established business or trade in connection with which the mark is employed. . . . The right to a particular mark grows out of its use, not its mere adoption."[76] Similarly, when a party discontinues use of a mark with no intent to resume such use, that mark will cease to function as a trademark, and will be deemed to be abandoned.

At common law, trademark rights are limited to the market or markets where the mark is actually being used. A major difference between common law and federal law, however, is that federal registration of a trademark or service mark gives rise to "constructive use" of that mark even in markets where the registrant has not actually used the mark. As between competing users in a particular market, the exclusive right to use the mark (referred to as "priority") belongs to the first user (referred to as the "senior user") of the mark in that

---

(suggesting that Ninth Circuit precedent would still prevent "the use of a trademark to monopolize a design feature which, in itself and apart from its identification of source, improves the usefulness or appeal of the object it adorns").

[72] Au-Tomotive Gold, Inc. v. Volkswagen of America, Inc., 457 F.3d 1062, 1073 (9th Cir. 2006).

[73] *Id.* at 1072 (citing both *Qualitex* and *TrafFix*). The opinion relies heavily on *TrafFix*, even though that case was not cited by either of the parties. *Id.* at 1070-72.

[74] *Dippin' Dots*, 369 F.3d at 1206-07; *Clicks Billiards*, 251 F.3d at 1259; *Landoll*, 164 F.3d at 342; Coach, Inc. v. We Care Trading Co., 67 Fed. Appx. 626 (2d Cir. 2002) (unpub.); Jeffrey Milstein, Inc. v. Greger, Lawlor, Roth, Inc., 58 F.3d 27, 32 (2d Cir. 1995); Fuddruckers, Inc. v. Doc's B.R. Others, Inc., 826 F.2d 837, 841 (9th Cir. 1987).

[75] The intent-to-use provisions of the Lanham Act provide a limited, and short-term, exception to this rule. *See* § 2.10 [B] *infra*. A second exception permits federal registration based on a foreign registration, provided use commences within six years. See § 2.15 [C] *infra*.

[76] United Drug Co. v. Theodore Rectanus Co., 248 U.S. 90, 97 (1918).

market, whether that use is actual or (in the case of federal registration) constructive.

As discussed below, under both common law and the Lanham Act, in order for the use of a mark to be sufficient to establish and maintain trademark rights, the use must be a bona fide use in connection with an actual offering of goods or services, rather than a "token" use designed merely to reserve rights in the mark.

Although many states have established registration systems, state law generally follows the common law rules regarding establishment of priority rights in both registered and unregistered marks.

[A] Establishing Priority of Use

At common law, trademark rights are established by the person who is the first to make bona fide use of the mark in connection with offering goods or services to the public.[77] Even before actual sales have occurred, bona fide use may be established through pre-sales publicity or sales solicitation using the mark, combined with intent to continue the use.[78]

The right to the exclusive use of a trademark or service mark is ordinarily founded on priority of use. Thus, "the first to use a mark on a product or service in a particular geographic market acquires rights in the mark in that market."[79] The problem of determining priority rights as between competing users of similar marks was succinctly stated by the Ninth Circuit in *Grupo Gigante S.A. de C.V. v. Dallo & Co.*:

> A fundamental principle of trademark law is first in time equals first in right. But things get more complicated when to time we add considerations of place, as when one user is first in time in one place while another is first in time in a different place.[80]

Resolution of priority issues with regard to common law marks (that is, marks that are not federally registered) is governed by common law principles based on actual use, business presence and reputation, and, in some cases, a "zone of expansion."[81] Where marks are confusingly similar, the principles that determine priority rights in the same or different geographical areas are derived from the Supreme Court's decisions in *Hanover Star Milling Co. v. Metcalf*[82] and *United Drug Co. v. Theodore Rectanus Co.*[83] Where similar marks are used in

---

[77] Societe de Developments et D'Innovations des Marches Agricoles et Alimentaires – SODIMA – Union des Cooperatives Agricoles v. International Yogurt Co., 662 F. Supp. 839, 853 (D. Or. 1987); Hydro-Dynamics, Inc. v. George Putnam & Co., Inc., 811 F.2d 1470, 1472 (Fed. Cir. 1987); Blue Bell, Inc. v. Farah Mfg. Co., 508 F.2d 1260 (5th Cir. 1975) (applying Texas law).

[78] *Societe de Developments et D'Innovations*, 662 F. Supp. at 853.

[79] Popular Bank of Fla. v. Banco Popular de Puerto Rico, 9 F. Supp. 2d 1347, 1353 (S.D. Fla. 1998).

[80] Grupo Gigante S.A. de C.V. v. Dallo & Co., 391 F.3d 1088, 1093 (9th Cir. 2004).

[81] *Popular Bank*, 9 F. Supp. 2d at 1354.

[82] 240 U.S. 403 (1916).

[83] 248 U.S. 90 (1918).

geographic areas that are remote from one another, each user will enjoy exclusive rights within its geographic area; however, where the geographic areas of use are the same or overlapping, exclusive rights belong to the "senior user" in that market.[84] The senior user in one market may find itself the junior user when it seeks entry in a different market, and may therefore be unable to extend its trademark to the new market.[85]

The geographic area in which the senior user of a mark has established priority of use is determined by considering the area in which the mark is actually used in offering goods or services, the area in which the user has established a reputation and business presence, and the user's natural "zone of expansion" or area of "market penetration," encompassing areas into which the use is likely to expand.[86] The geographic scope of the senior user's priority is a question of fact, and depends on the reputation, advertising, and sales in the area.[87]

Actual use: To establish priority through actual use, a party must prove a level of use in the ordinary course of business in that territory sufficient to acquire rights in the mark; insignificant or sporadic use is insufficient.[88] The extent of the party's sales in the territory is an important indicator of actual use. Thus, "[t]he number and dollar amounts of the sales in the area, the number of customers, the pattern of sales over time, and the potential growth of sales are all relevant factors that should be considered by the court in determining actual use."[89] Mere "token" sales or intracompany shipments generally will not satisfy the actual use requirement.[90]

Reputation and business presence: A business may acquire trademark priority in a territory where it has established a reputation for its mark, even though it does not offer its product or service in that area; accordingly, "the extent to which advertising has carried the reputation of the mark into a new territory is a factor to be considered in deciding whether the territory has been successfully appropriated by the mark's owner."[91] Similarly, if the trademark owner's customers transport their purchases to areas where the trademark owner does not conduct business, or if the business attracts customers from different locations, the trademark may become known in areas beyond the trademark owner's business territory. Thus, in determining the geographic scope of a mark, relevant factors include "the nature and extent of advertising

---

[84] *Hanover Star Milling*, 240 U.S. at 416.

[85] *United Drug Co.*, 248 U.S. at 100.

[86] *See, e.g.*, Tally-Ho, Inc. v. Coast Community College Dist., 889 F.2d 1018, 1025-27 (11th Cir. 1989); Spartan Food Sys., Inc. v. HFS Corp., 813 F.2d 1279, 1283 (4th Cir. 1987).

[87] Thrifty Rent-A-Car Sys., Inc. v. Thrift Cars, Inc., 639 F. Supp. 750, 753 (D. Mass. 1986), *aff'd*, 831 F.2d 1177 (1st Cir. 1987).

[88] RESTATEMENT (THIRD) OF UNFAIR COMPETITION, § 19 cmt. b (1995).

[89] *Popular Bank*, 9 F. Supp. 2d at 1354 (citing Sweetarts v. Sunline, Inc., 380 F.2d 923, 929 (8th Cir. 1967)).

[90] *See, e.g.*, Blue Bell Inc. v. Farah Mfg. Co., 508 F.2d 1260 (5th Cir. 1975) (applying Texas law).

[91] *Popular Bank*, 9 F. Supp. 2d at 1355 (citing *Thrifty Rent-A-Car Sys.*, 639 F. Supp. at 753).

and other promotional activities, the geographic distribution of catalogs and flyers, [and] the geographical origins of orders and customer inquiries."[92]

Zone of expansion: In some cases, courts have recognized common law priority rights in the trademark owner's natural zone of expansion. As one court has explained:

> Under this doctrine, a prior user who can prove neither use nor current association with the mark in the disputed area can still prevail over a subsequent good-faith user by establishing that the area is within the zone of the prior user's probable or natural expansion. Under the common law, the senior user could not monopolize markets that neither his use nor reputation could reach, but the "zone of natural expansion" doctrine provides the senior user with some limited "breathing space" in which to expand beyond its current use.[93]

Courts that recognize the zone of expansion doctrine have tended to define that zone narrowly; geographical proximity to areas where the trademark owner actually conducts business or advertises is a significant factor in defining the zone.[94] They typically consider the party's: (1) previous business activity; (2) previous expansion or lack thereof; (3) dominance of contiguous areas; (4) presently planned expansion; and, where applicable, (5) possible market penetration by means of products brought in from other areas.[95] In assessing "market penetration," courts typically look to: (1) the volume of sales of the trademarked product; (2) the growth trends in the area; (3) the number of people actually purchasing the product in relation to the potential number of customers; and (4) the amount of product advertising in the area.[96]

[B] Lanham Act

[1] Use in Commerce

As under common law, the ownership of trademark rights under the Lanham Act is conditioned on use.[97] Under the Lanham Act, however, the use must be not only a use in trade, but also a use in "commerce."

In general, the use in commerce that is required for federal trademark protection is similar to the use required to obtain common law rights in the mark.[98] The federal definition of a trademark requires that it be used "to

---

[92] *Id.* (citing RESTATEMENT (THIRD) OF UNFAIR COMPETITION, § 19 comment b (1995)); *see, e.g,.* Stork Restaurant v. Sahati, 166 F.2d 348 (9th Cir. 1948) (mark was entitled to nationwide protection based on its extensive advertising and national press coverage).

[93] *Popular Bank*, 9 F. Supp. 2d at 1355 (citing *Tally-Ho, Inc.*, 889 F.2d at 1027-28).

[94] *Id.* at 1355-56 (collecting authorities).

[95] *Spartan Food Sys.*, 813 F.2d at 1283.

[96] *Id.*

[97] General Healthcare, Ltd. v. Qashat, 364 F.3d 332, 335 (1st Cir. 2004); United Drug Co. v. Theodore Rectanus Co., 248 U.S. 90, 97 (1918) (establishing that "the right to a particular mark grows out of its use, not its mere adoption").

[98] *Societe de Developments et D'Innovations*, 662 F. Supp. at 853 (citing 1 J.T. MCCARTHY,

identify and distinguish [one person's] goods, including a unique product, from those manufactured or sold by others and to indicate the source of the goods," and the definition of a service mark requires that it be used "to identify and distinguish the services of one person, including a unique service, from the services of others and to indicate the source of the services."[99]

To qualify for federal registration, however, a trademark or service mark must not only be used to identify the source of goods or services, but also be "used in commerce,"[100] where "commerce" means "all commerce which may lawfully be regulated by Congress,"[101] thus encompassing "[c]ommerce with foreign Nations, and among the several States, and with the Indian Tribes."[102] Because Congress's authority extends to any activity that "substantially affects" interstate commerce,[103] a service mark used purely for intrastate restaurant services can be federally registered if the restaurant has an interstate clientele.[104]

The Lanham Act defines a "use in commerce" as "the bona fide use of a mark in the ordinary course of trade, and not made merely to reserve a right in a mark."[105] Thus, a mere token or *de minimis* use will not qualify.[106]

TRADEMARKS AND UNFAIR COMPETITION § 16:5, at 773, § 19:4, at 881 (2d ed. 1984)).

[99] 15 U.S.C. § 1127.

[100] *Id.* § 1051(a)(1).

[101] *Id.* § 1127.

[102] U.S. CONST., art. I, § 8, cl. 3.

[103] United States v. Lopez, 514 U.S. 549, 559 (1995). It has been said, however, that the concept of a "use in commerce" for registration purposes is slightly narrower than the "use in commerce" concept for purposes of establishing federal jurisdiction under sections 43(a) and 43(c) of the Lanham Act. *See, e.g,* Planned Parenthood Fed'n of America v. Bucci, 42 U.S.P.Q.2d (BNA) 1430 (S.D.N.Y. 1997), *aff'd,* 1998 U.S. App. LEXIS 22179 (2d Cir.), *cert. denied,* 525 U.S. 834 (1998); MCCARTHY ON TRADEMARKS, *supra* note 28, at § 25:57 ("It is difficult to conceive of an act of infringement which is not 'in commerce' in the sense of the modern decisions. . . . However, the Patent and Trademark Office still appears to adopt a higher standard of use in commerce for purposes of qualifying for federal registration in the first instance."); *see generally* § 3.02 [F] *infra* (discussing federal jurisdiction under section 43 of the Lanham Act).

[104] Larry Harmon Pictures Corp. v. Williams Rest. Corp., 929 F.2d 662, 666 (Fed. Cir.) *cert. denied,* 502 U.S. 823 (1991).

[105] 15 U.S.C. § 1127.

[106] *See, e.g,* Paramount Pictures Corp. v. White, 31 U.S.P.Q.2D (BNA) 1768, 1772-73 (T.T.A.B. 1994) (finding no bona fide use in ordinary course of trade where mark was affixed to a game consisting of three pieces of paper and distributed for the purpose of promoting musical group); Hydro-Dynamics, Inc. v. George Putnam & Co., Inc., 811 F.2d 1470 (Fed. Cir. 1987) (shipment of goods marked with trademark for sole purpose of obtaining distributor's opinion of them was not a use in commerce; Avakoff v. Southern Pacific Co., 765 F.2d 1097 (Fed. Cir. 1985) (shipment of software bearing trademark to trademark owner, and latter's mail solicitation sent to retailers concerning the software, did not establish a use in commerce); Gay Toys, Inc. v. McDonalds Corp., 585 F.2d 1067 (C.C.P.A. 1978) (placing trademark on mock-up of product at trade show was not a use in commerce); In re Chicago Rawhide Mfg. Co., 455 F.2d 563 (C.C.P.A. 1972) (putting mark for goods in invoice inserted in package containing goods was not use in commerce); Anvil Brand, Inc. v. Consolidated Foods Corp., 464 F. Supp. 474 (S.D.N.Y. 1978) (applying trademark label to promotional goods to exhaust existing inventory was not a trademark use designed to identify source of garment and goodwill of manufacturer, and thus did not preclude finding that mark was abandoned).

Furthermore, the use of a mark in advertising, without more, will not qualify as a use in commerce for purposes of federal registration.[107] In the case of services, for example, the advertised services must in fact be provided, or reservations accepted; announcement of future services is insufficient.[108]

Section 45 of the Lanham Act[109] distinguishes between the activities that constitute a use in commerce in the case of a trademark and those that constitute a use in commerce in the case of a service mark. In the case of goods, the mark must be placed on the goods, their containers, or associated displays, or on tags or labels affixed thereto, or, "if the nature of the goods makes such placement impracticable," on associated documents, and the goods must be "sold or transported in commerce."[110] In the case of goods, therefore, a use in commerce may be established either through sale *or* through transportation of the goods in commerce. A sale must be a bona fide business transaction; sham sales are disregarded.[111] However, because the actual *sale* of goods is not necessary to establish a use in commerce; transportation alone will qualify, provided that it takes place in commerce,[112] which means that the shipments cannot be purely intrastate. In addition, for the transportation of goods to qualify as a sufficient use in commerce, an element of public awareness is required.[113] The transportation must therefore be "sufficiently public to identify or distinguish the marked goods in an appropriate segment of the public mind as those of the adopter of the mark."[114] Accordingly, although the applicant's use of a mark need not have gained wide public recognition, secret, undisclosed shipments do not qualify.[115] In general, for a shipment to qualify as a "use in

---

[107] *See, e.g.,* Lands' End, Inc. v. Manback, 797 F. Supp. 511 (E.D. Va. 1992) (use of trademark in mail order catalog alongside picture of product and accompanying description constituted "display associated" with goods rather than mere advertising); Greyhound Corp. v. Armour Life Ins. Co., 214 U.S.P.Q. (BNA) 473, 474 (T.T.A.B. 1982) ("Advertising of a service, without performance of a service, will not support registration."); In re Universal Oil Products Co., 476 F.2d 653 (C.C.P.A. 1973) (use of mark as name of process, and mentioning name of process in brochure that advertises services is not a use in commerce); Koffler Stores, Ltd. v. Shoppers Drug Mart, Inc., 434 F. Supp. 697 (E.D. Mich. 1976) (advertising use alone is not sufficient to support a valid trademark), *aff'd without op.,* 559 F.2d 1219 (6th Cir. 1977).

[108] *Greyhound Corp.,* 214 U.S.P.Q. (BNA) at 474; Aycock Eng'g, Inc. v. Airflite, Inc., 560 F.3d 1350, 1359–61 (Fed. Cir. 2009).

[109] 115 U.S.C. § 1127 (definitions).

[110] *Id.; see, e.g.,* In re Marriott Corp., 459 F.2d 525 (C.C.P.A. 1972) (use on restaurant menu is use on "displays associated" with goods; physical contact with goods is not always necessary).

[111] Acme Valve & Fittings Co. v. Wayne, 386 F. Supp. 1162, 1169 (S.D. Tex. 1974).

[112] *See, e.g., General Healthcare,* 364 F.3d at 335; New England Duplicating Co. v. Mendes, 190 F.2d 415, 417 (1st Cir. 1951) ("The use of the disjunctive 'or' between 'sold' and 'transported' leaves no doubt that a transportation . . . is enough to constitute a 'use' even without a sale."); Ideal Toy Corp. v. Cameo Exclusive Prods., Inc., 170 U.S.P.Q. (BNA) 596 (T.T.A.B. 1971).

[113] *General Healthcare,* 364 F.3d at 335 (collecting cases).

[114] *Mendes,* 190 F.2d at 418; *accord, General Healthcare,* 364 F.3d at 336 (noting that the requirement that the use be public distinguishes the "use in commerce" requirement for purposes of federal registration from the "use in commerce" requirement for federal jurisdiction over section 43(a) claims).

[115] *General Healthcare,* 364 F.3d at 335 (citing Blue Bell, Inc. v. Farah Mfg. Co., 508 F.2d 1260 (5th Cir. 1975)).

commerce," it must not be a purely intra-company shipment.[116] Where the goods in question are new pharmaceuticals that cannot be sold to the public because they have not yet received FDA approval, shipments to investigators conducting clinical trials can satisfy the "use in commerce" requirement.[117]

In the case of services, a mark is "used in commerce" when:

> it is used or displayed in the sale or advertising of services and the services are rendered in commerce, or the services are rendered in more than one State or in the United States and a foreign country and the person rendering the services is engaged in commerce in connection with the services.[118]

A use in "commerce" need not be a profit-seeking use; accordingly, courts recognize the rights of nonprofit and civic organizations to protect the trademarks they use to identify themselves as the source of their noncommercial activities.[119]

In contrast, the TTAB and the Ninth Circuit have both held that the use of a term as part of a domain name does not, by itself, constitute use as an indicator of the source of goods or services.[120]

The TTAB and several courts of appeals have also held that, to establish a use in commerce for registration purposes, the applicant's use must be lawful — that is, the sale or transportation of the goods bearing the mark must comply with all applicable laws and regulations.[121]

Two other concepts relevant to priority of use are the *related companies* doctrine and the concept of *tacking*.

Related companies. The related companies doctrine, which is embodied in section 5 of the Lanham Act, provides that, for purposes of validity and registration, the use of a mark by a company related to the registrant/applicant inures to the benefit of the registrant/applicant, unless the mark has been used

---

[116] Sterling Drug, Inc. v. Knoll A.G. Chemische Fabriken, 159 U.S.P.Q. 628, 631 (T.T.A.B. 1968).

[117] *See* G.D. Searle & Co. v. Nutrapharm, Inc., 1999 U.S. Dist. LEXIS 16862 (S.D.N.Y. 1999) (citing 1988 legislative history); Alfacell Corp. v. Anticancer, Inc., 2002 TTAB LEXIS 617 (T.T.A.B. 2002) (nonprecedential) (similar).

[118] 15 U.S.C. § 1127.

[119] United We Stand Am., Inc. v. United We Stand, Am., N.Y., Inc., 128 F.3d 86, 92 (2d Cir. 1997), *cert. denied*, 523 U.S. 1076 (1998). *See, e.g., United We Stand*, 128 F.3d at 92-93; Kappa Sigma Fraternity v. Kappa Sigma Gamma Fraternity, 654 F. Supp. 1095, 1101 (D.N.H. 1987); American Diabetes Ass'n, Inc. v. Nat'l Diabetes Ass'n, 533 F. Supp. 16, 20 (E.D. Pa. 1981), *aff'd*, 681 F.2d 804 (3d Cir. 1982); United States Jaycees v. Philadelphia Jaycees, 490 F. Supp. 688, 691 (E.D. Pa. 1980), *rev'd on other grounds*, 639 F.2d 134 (3d Cir. 1981); United States Jaycees v. San Francisco Junior Chamber of Commerce, 354 F. Supp. 61, 64, 65 (N.D. Cal. 1972), *aff'd*, 513 F.2d 1226 (9th Cir. 1975).

[120] In re Roberts, 87 U.S.P.Q.2d (BNA) 1474 (T.T.A.B. 2008) (use of mark in domain name tells public where user's website can be found, but does not necessarily serve as origin indicator for user's services); Brookfield Comms., Inc. v. West Coast Entert. Corp., 174 F.3d 1036, 1051 (9th Cir. 1999) (mere registration of mark as domain name is insufficient, where public has never seen the mark).

[121] CreAgri, Inc. v. USANA Health Scis., Inc., 474 F.3d 626, 630 (9th Cir. 2007); United Phosphorus, Ltd. v. Midland Fumigant, Inc., 205 F.3d 1219, 1225 (10th Cir. 2000); In re Pepcom Indus., Inc., 192 U.S.P.Q. (BNA) 400, 401 (T.T.A.B. 1976).

in a deceptive manner.[122] A "substantial relationship" between the parties is required.[123] Courts have held that successors in interest and controlled corporations qualify as related companies.[124] The Lanham Act defines a "related company" as "any person whose use of a mark is controlled by the owner of the mark with respect to the nature and quality of the goods or services on or in connection with which the mark is used."[125] Where the mark is used by a licensee that is subject to quality controls, the licensee's use inures to the benefit of the registrant or applicant.[126]

Tacking. A trademark user that was not the first to use the exact mark at issue may still be able to establish priority based on its earlier use of a similar though technically distinct mark. However, the user may "tack" its rights in the later mark to its use of the earlier mark only if the marks are so similar that the relevant consumers consider them to be the same mark.[127] For a detailed discussion of tacking, see § 3.02[A] below.

[2]   Foreign Use

Section 45 defines "commerce" broadly, as "all commerce which may lawfully be regulated by Congress."[128] However, under the well-established "territoriality principle," the use of a mark exclusively outside the United States is not a "use in commerce," and thus will not establish ownership rights in the United States, either at common law or for purposes of the Lanham Act.[129]

In applying the territoriality principle, the question has arisen whether a use in commerce can be established where the goods and services associated with the mark are advertised or promoted in the United States, but are offered exclusively overseas. In response to this question, the Trademark Trial and Appeal Board (TTAB) has consistently held that where a mark is used exclusively for services offered outside the United States, a use in commerce

---

[122] 15 U.S.C. § 1055.

[123] Secular Orgs. for Sobriety, Inc. v. Ullrich, 213 F.3d 1125 (9th Cir. 2000).

[124] *See, e.g.*, Hylo Co. v. Jean Patou, Inc., 215 F.2d 282 (C.C.P.A. 1954) (successor in interest); Browne-Vintners Co. v. National Distillers & Chem. Corp., 151 F. Supp. 595 (S.D.N.Y. 1957) (controlled corporation); Hurricane Fence Co. v. A-1 Hurricane Fence Co., 468 F. Supp. 975 (S.D. Ala. 1979) (similar).

[125] 15 U.S.C. § 1127. Applying this definition, the D.C. Circuit held that the related companies doctrine can also be applied to nonprofit entities. Estate of Coll-Monge v. Inner Peace Movement, 524 F.3d 1341, 1347 (D.C. Cir. 2008).

[126] Turner v. H M H Pub. Co., 380 F.2d 224 (5th Cir. 1967), *cert. denied*, 389 U.S. 1006 (1967).

[127] Brookfield Comms., Inc. v. West Coast Entert. Corp., 174 F.3d 1036, 1047-48 (9th Cir. 1999).

[128] 15 U.S.C. § 1127.

[129] *See, e.g.*, Grupo Gigante S.A. de C.V. v. Dallo & Co., 391 F.3d 1088, 1097-98 (9th Cir. 2004); Person's Co. v. Christman, 900 F.2d 1565, 1568-69 (Fed. Cir. 1990); Fuji Photo Film Co., Inc. v. Shinohara Shoji Kabushiki Kaisha, 754 F.2d 591, 599 (5th Cir. 1985); Empresa Cubana Del Tabaco v. Culbro Corp., 70 U.S.P.Q.2d (BNA) 1650, 2004 U.S. Dist. LEXIS 4935, at *87-88 (S.D.N.Y. Mar. 26, 2004), *aff'd in part and rev'd in part,*, 2005 U.S. LEXIS 3242 (2d Cir. Feb. 24, 2005); Tactica Int'l, Inc. v. Atlantic Horizon, Int'l, Inc., 154 F. Supp. 2d 586, 599 (S.D.N.Y. 2001); *see also* MCCARTHY ON TRADEMARKS, note 28 *supra*, at § 29.2.

cannot be established solely through advertising to United States consumers.[130] The leading TTAB decision is *Mother's Restaurants, Inc. v. Mother's Other Kitchen, Inc.*,[131] in which the mark in question was used for a restaurant located in Canada. Although ads for the restaurant were broadcast only by Canadian radio stations, some of the signals crossed the border into the United States. Promotional materials and coupons for the restaurant were distributed in southern Ontario along major tourist routes from the United States. The TTAB ruled that these activities did not establish a right of priority in the United States based on use in commerce:

> [P]rior use and advertising of a mark in connection with goods or services marketed in a foreign country (whether said advertising occurs inside or outside the United States) creates no priority rights in said mark in the United States as against one who, in good faith, has adopted the same or similar mark for the same or similar goods or services in the United States prior to the foreigner's first use of the mark on goods or services sold and/or offered in the United States. . . .[132]

The Second Circuit adopted the rule of *Mother's Restaurant* in *Buti v. Impressa Perosa, S.R.L.*,[133] holding that no Lanham Act priority was established where the "Fashion Café" service mark was used for restaurant services offered exclusively in Italy, and where the restaurant was not the subject of a formal advertising campaign in the United States. Although during visits to the United States the operator of the restaurant had distributed "literally thousands of T-shirts, cards, and key chains with the Fashion Café name and logo to persons associated with the modeling and fashion industry which entitled them to free meals" at the restaurant,[134] under the rule of *Mother's Restaurant* the court found this activity insufficient to satisfy the "use in commerce" requirement.[135]

The Fourth Circuit, however, takes a broader view of what constitutes "use in commerce." In *International Bancorp, LLC v. Society des Bains de Mer et du*

---

[130] *See, e.g.*, Linville v. Rivard, 41 U.S.P.Q.2D (BNA) 1731, 1735-37 (T.T.A.B. 1997) (Canadian company's promotion of its hair salons by radio, television, and print media that occasionally reached the United States, and distribution of promotional handouts and coupons at a state fair in the United States, was not a use in commerce, because the services were rendered in Canada, even though most of the salons were located near the border and some of the customers came from the United States), *aff'd*, 133 F.3d 1446 (Fed. Cir. 1998); Intermed Communications, Inc. v. Chaney, 197 U.S.P.Q. (BNA) 501, 507-08 (T.T.A.B. 1977) (doctor who arguably had publicized a service mark in the U.S. was denied trademark registration due to a lack of evidence that the underlying services had been offered to anyone in the U.S. or in commerce); Oland's Breweries [1971] Ltd. v. Miller Brewing Co., 189 U.S.P.Q. (BNA) 481, 489 (T.T.A.B. 1976) (ads for Canadian beer in magazines circulated in United States, and on American radio stations, aimed at American tourists, "may not be sufficient to establish technical trademark use in the United States," even if it might cause confusion as to origin among U.S. consumers).

[131] 218 U.S.P.Q. (BNA) 1046 (T.T.A.B. 1983).

[132] *Id.* at 1048; *accord*, Techex, Ltd. v. Dvorkovitz, 220 U.S.P.Q. (BNA) 81, 83 (T.T.A.B. 1983).

[133] 139 F.3d 98 (2d Cir.), *cert. denied*, 525 U.S. 826 (1998).

[134] *Id.* at 100.

[135] *See also* Morningside Group, Ltd. v. Morningside Capital Group, L.L.C., 182 F.3d 133, 138 (2d Cir. 1999) (distinguishing *Buti*, on the ground that "material aspects of" Morningside's Hong Kong-based investment services were actually conducted in the U.S.).

Cercle des Etrangers a Monaco,[136] the court held that a mark was used "in commerce" where it identified the source of services that a foreign casino operator offered to United States citizens. In that case, the casino operator provided its services exclusively overseas, although it advertised in the United States through its New York office. The court's conclusion that the casino's services were provided "in commerce" was based on two findings: (1) "United States citizens went to and gambled at the casino," which was "a subject of a foreign nation,"[137] and (2) the casino used its mark in its United States advertising for the casino.[138] The casino's gambling services therefore constituted "foreign trade," falling within the scope of Congress's regulatory powers under the Commerce Clause:[139]

> Because SBM used its mark in the sale and advertising of its gambling services to United States citizens; because its rendering of gambling services to United States citizens constitutes foreign trade; because foreign trade is commerce Congress may lawfully regulate; and because commerce under the Lanham Act comprises all commerce that Congress may lawfully regulate, the services SBM renders under the "Casino de Monte Carlo" mark to citizens of the United States are services rendered in commerce, and the "use in commerce" requirement that the Lanham Act sets forth for the mark's protectibility is satisfied.[140]

Accordingly, the foreign casino would be entitled to priority in the "Casino de Monte Carlo" mark if it could establish that the mark was distinctive among United States consumers.[141]

The Fourth Circuit emphasized that both the services and the advertising must take place in qualifying commerce: "[A] mark owner must *both* engage in qualifying commerce *and* use or display its mark in the sale or advertising of these services to the consumers that engage in that qualifying commerce."[142] In other words, if the Casino de Monte Carlo had not provided services to visitors from the United States, *or* if it had not advertised its services to United States consumers, the court would have held that the mark was not used in commerce.

The Fourth Circuit distinguished cases from other circuits, which had held that marks associated with services rendered exclusively abroad were not used in commerce, on the ground that the marks used in those cases failed to meet the second prong of its two-part test — the requirement that the mark be used in United States advertising or sales of the services.[143] It also endorsed the TTAB's analysis in *Sterling Drug, Inc. v. Knoll A.G. Chemische Fabriken*,[144] which

---

[136] 329 F.3d 359 (4th Cir. 2003), *cert. denied*, 540 U.S. 1106 (2004).

[137] *Id.* at 365.

[138] *Id.*

[139] *Id.*

[140] *Id.* at 370.

[141] *Id.*

[142] *Id.* at 381.

[143] *Id.* at 374-75.

[144] 159 U.S.P.Q. (BNA) 628 (T.T.A.B. 1968).

denied Lanham Act protection to marks used on pharmaceuticals sold exclusively in Germany (where they were occasionally used by United States consumers), which were not marketed or advertised in the United States: "Again, the obvious element that is missing here is the use and display of the mark to advertise or sell the product to United States consumers engaging in qualifying foreign commerce."[145] The fact that German publications containing advertising for the product might occasionally be found in the United States did not change the analysis:

> Though German publications containing applicant's advertisements of "TALUSIN" or references to that mark were received in the United States, *there is no indication in the record that these publications obtained such circulation in the United States as to make the relevant public for applicant's goods, physicians and pharmacists, aware of applicant's use of "TALUSIN."* In other words, the advertising in a foreign publication which may occasionally be found in some library in the United States does not create protectible rights in the advertised mark in the United States.[146]

The Fourth's Circuit's interpretation of "use in commerce" has been criticized as overbroad on the ground that it could require a party seeking to use a trademark in the United States to cede priority to a party that has used the mark exclusively overseas.[147]

[3]   The Famous Marks Doctrine

Several state and federal courts have recognized a controversial exception to the territoriality principle, in what has become known as the "famous marks" doctrine (or alternatively, the "well-known marks" doctrine). Under this doctrine, use of a mark exclusively overseas may give the owner of that mark priority in the United States if the mark is sufficiently well-known to U.S. consumers, even if the goods and services are not offered in the United States.

The famous marks doctrine was first recognized by New York trial courts under the common law of unfair competition. In *Maison Prunier v. Prunier's Rest. & Cafe*,[148] the trial court granted preliminary relief to a Paris restauranteur against a New York restaurant that was using a confusingly similar name and slogan and promoting itself as "The Famous French Sea Food Restaurant." In the court's view, the defendant's bad faith justified creating an exception to the territoriality principle. In *Vaudable v. Montmartre, Inc.*,[149]

---

[145] 329 F.3d at 378.

[146] *Id.* (quoting, with added emphasis, *Sterling Drug*, 159 U.S.P.Q. (BNA) at 630).

[147] *See, e.g., Int'l Bancorp*, 329 F.3d at 388 (Motz, J., dissenting); Empresa Cubana Del Tabaco v. Culbro Corp., 70 U.S.P.Q.2d (BNA) 1650, 2004 U.S. Dist. LEXIS 4935, at *88 n.8 (S.D.N.Y. Mar. 26, 2004), *aff'd in part and rev'd in part*, 2005 U.S. LEXIS 3242 (2d Cir. Feb. 24, 2005); MCCARTHY ON TRADEMARKS, note 28 *supra*, at § 29:4. For a critique of the territoriality principle, see Graeme B. Dinwoodie, *Trademarks and Territory: Detaching Trademark Law from the Nation-State*, 41 HOUS. L. REV. 885 (2004).

[148] 159 Misc. 551, 557-58, 288 N.Y.S. 529, 535-36 (N.Y. Sup. Ct. 1936).

[149] 193 N.Y.S.2d 332, 334-36 (N.Y. Sup. Ct. 1959).

another New York court enjoined the use of the name "Maxim's" for a restaurant in New York, because the Paris restaurant of that name had long held a "unique and eminent position as a restaurant of international fame and prestige,"[150] even though its services were offered exclusively in Paris.[151]

Federal courts have reached conflicting decisions on whether the famous marks exception should apply to the Lanham Act. The TTAB has applied the doctrine in several opposition proceedings,[152] and it has also been invoked by several federal district courts.[153] Among the courts of appeal, however, only the Ninth Circuit has embraced the doctrine. In its 2004 decision in *Grupo Gigante S.A. de C.V. v. Dallo & Co.*,[154] the appellate court observed:

> While the territoriality principle is a long-standing and important doctrine within trademark law, it cannot be absolute. An absolute territoriality rule without a famous-mark exception would promote consumer confusion and fraud. Commerce crosses borders. In this nation of immigrants, so do people. Trademark is, at its core, about protecting against consumer confusion and "palming off." There can be no justification for using trademark law to fool immigrants into thinking that they are buying from the store they liked back home.

> It might not matter if someone visiting Fairbanks, Alaska, from Wellington, New Zealand, saw a cute hair-salon name — "Hair Today, Gone Tomorrow," "Mane Place," "Hair on Earth," "Mary's Hair'em," or "Shear Heaven" — and decided to use the name on her own salon back home in New Zealand. The ladies in New Zealand would not likely think they were going to a branch of a Fairbanks hair salon. But if someone

---

[150] *Id.* at 334.

[151] *See also* Maison Prunier v. Prunier's Restaurant & Cafe, Inc., 288 N.Y.S. 529, 537 (N.Y. Sup. Ct. 1936) (owner of three "Prunier" restaurants in Paris and London would be permitted to enjoin defendant's use of same name for a New York City restaurant if plaintiff could demonstrate that "its reputation extends far beyond the territorial limits of Paris and London and that it has a substantial following in New York City and in other parts of the world").

[152] London Regional Transport v. The William A. Berden & Edward C. Goetz, III Partnership, 2006 TTAB LEXIS 272 (T.T.A.B. 2006) (although opposer showed that large numbers of Americans had used the opposer's rail services in London, opposer failed to demonstrate that "London Underground" mark was familiar, much less famous, to a substantial percentage of Americans); The All England Lawn Tennis Club (Wimbledon) Ltd. v. Creations Aromatiques, Inc., 220 U.S.P.Q. (BNA) 1069, 1072 (T.T.A.B. 1983) (holder of "Wimbledon" mark for tennis tournament in England has right of priority in United States based on mark's "fame and notoriety"). The Board has also recognized the doctrine in dicta. *See* First Niagara Ins. Brokers, Inc. v. First Niagara Fin. Group, Inc., 77 U.S.P.Q.2d (BNA) 1334 (T.T.A.B. 2005), *rev'd on other grounds*, 476 F.3d 867 (Fed. Cir. 2007); Mother's Rest., Inc. v. Mother's Other Kitchen, Inc., 218 U.S.P.Q. (BNA) 1046 (T.T.A.B. 1983).

[153] Resorts Int'l, Inc. v. Greate Bay Hotel & Casino, Inc., 1991 U.S. Dist. LEXIS 21789 (D.N.J. 1991) (unpub.) (trade name "Paradise Island" used for Caribbean resort was entitled to protection from infringement in the United States, where 16% of Atlantic City casino-goers recognized it as name of Caribbean casino, and 64% had heard of it); Koffler Stores, Ltd. v. Shoppers Drug Mart, Inc., 434 F. Supp. 697, 704 (E.D. Mich. 1976) (use of trademark overseas established domestic priority because plaintiff had advertised and developed goodwill in United States; "where advertising and good will extend beyond the immediate selling market, this reputation will be protected"), *aff'd without op.*, 559 F.2d 1219 (6th Cir. 1977).

[154] 391 F.3d 1088 (9th Cir. 2004).

opened a high-end salon with a red door in Wellington and called it Elizabeth Arden's, women might very well go there because they thought they were going to an affiliate of the Elizabeth Arden chain, even if there had not been any other Elizabeth Ardens in New Zealand prior to the salon's opening. If it was not an affiliate, just a local store with no connection, customers would be fooled. The real Elizabeth Arden chain might lose business if word spread that the Wellington salon was nothing special.[155]

Accordingly, where a large Mexican grocery chain had used the "Gigante" mark exclusively in Mexico, but its reputation had spread to San Diego, the Ninth Circuit held that, under the Lanham Act, the Mexican trademark owner could have priority in San Diego if its mark had become sufficiently well-known to consumers in that market before the arrival of the junior user.

In contrast, in 2007 the Second Circuit expressly held that the famous marks exception does *not* apply to the Lanham Act in *ITC v. Punchgini, Inc.*[156] While acknowledging that "a persuasive policy argument can be advanced" in support of the doctrine, the court held that Congress had not yet incorporated the doctrine into the Lanham Act. However, the court left open the possibility that the famous marks exception might apply to an unfair competition claim brought under *common* law. When the Second Circuit certified this question to the New York Court of Appeals, the latter court held that, while the famous marks doctrine was not recognized as an independent theory of liability under New York's common law of unfair competition, nonetheless a plaintiff could make out a common law claim of unfair competition by showing that the defendant deliberately copied the plaintiff's mark or trade dress, and that the mark or trade dress had secondary meaning among the relevant New York consumers.[157]

Thus, the validity of the famous marks exception under the Lanham Act remains unsettled,[158] and its application under common law must be determined on a state-by-state basis.

Even where the famous marks exception has been recognized, there is little authority addressing the degree of fame necessary for a mark to qualify. Some courts have suggested that secondary meaning in the relevant United States market is sufficient.[159] In *Grupo Gigante*, however, the Ninth Circuit rejected this view, because setting the standard this low "would effectively cause the

---

[155] *Id.* at 1094–95.

[156] 482 F.3d 135 (2d Cir. 2007).

[157] ITC Ltd. v. Punchgini, Inc., 518 F.3d 159 (2d Cir. 2008) (citing ITC Ltd. v. Punchgini, Inc., 9 N.Y.3d 467, 850 N.Y.S.2d 366, 880 N.E.2d 852 (N.Y. 2007)).

[158] *See* Int'l Bancorp, LLC v. Societe des Bains de Mer et du Cercle des Etrangers a Monaco, 329 F.3d 359, 389 n.9 (4th Cir. 2003) (Motz, J., dissenting) ("Nor does the 'famous marks' doctrine provide [defendant] any refuge. That doctrine has been applied so seldom (never by a federal appellate court and only by a handful of district courts) that its viability is uncertain."). Professor McCarthy's view is that the famous marks doctrine applies to the Lanham Act. MCCARTHY ON TRADEMARKS, note 28 *supra*, at § 29:4.

[159] *See* ITC Ltd. v. Punchgini, 373 F.Supp.2d 275, 287–88 (S.D.N.Y. 2005) (collecting cases), *aff'd in part*, 482 F.3d 135 (2d Cir. 2007).

exception to eclipse the territoriality rule entirely."[160] Instead, the court adopted the following standard:

> [W]here the mark has not before been used in the American market, the court must be satisfied, by a preponderance of the evidence, that a *substantial* percentage of consumers in the relevant American market is familiar with the foreign mark. The relevant American market is the geographic area where the defendant uses the alleged infringing mark. In making this determination, the court should consider such factors as the intentional copying of the mark by the defendant, and whether customers of the American firm are likely to think they are patronizing the same firm that uses the mark in another country. While these factors are not necessarily determinative, they are particularly relevant because they bear heavily on the risks of consumer confusion and fraud, which are the reasons for having a famous-mark exception.[161]

In *ITC v Punchgini*, the Second Circuit certified to the New York Court of Appeals the question of what degree of fame is necessary to invoke the famous marks exception under New York common law. The state court responded that, at a minimum, United States consumers of the goods or services in question "must primarily associate the mark with the foreign plaintiff."[162] Factors relevant to this determination would include:

> (1) evidence that "the defendant intentionally associated goods with those of the foreign plaintiff in the minds of the public, such as public statements or advertising stating or implying a connection with the foreign plaintiff"; (2) "direct evidence, such as consumer surveys, indicating that consumers of defendant's goods or services believe them to be associated with the plaintiff"; and (3) "evidence of actual overlap between customers of the New York defendant and the foreign plaintiff."[163]

[4]   Intent to Use (ITU) Applications

Until 1989, applicants with similar marks sometimes found themselves in a "race" to be the first to use their mark in commerce in order to be the first to register the mark on the Principal Register. They sometimes resorted to "token" interstate uses of their trademarks, leading to costly litigation over whether these uses were sham transactions or bona fide uses in commerce as required by the Lanham Act's definition of a "use in commerce" as a "bona fide use of a mark in the ordinary course of trade, and not made merely to reserve a

---

[160] 391 F.3d at 1096.

[161] *Id.* at 1098 (emphasis in original). Professor McCarthy agrees with the Ninth Circuit's requirement that a "substantial percentage" of the relevant American consumers should be familiar with the foreign mark, and suggests a threshold of 50 percent. McCarthy on Trademarks, note 28 *supra*, at § 29:4.

[162] 518 F.3d at 161 (quoting ITC Ltd. v. Punchgini, Inc., 9 N.Y.3d 467, 479 (N.Y. 2007)).

[163] *Id.* at 161 (quoting *Punchgini*, 9 N.Y.3d at 479-80).

right in a mark."[164] Even in the absence of such contrivances, aspiring trademark applicants risked losing their investment in developing new trademarks if another applicant for the same or a confusingly similar mark edged them out in being the first to make a bona fide use of the mark.

In addition, domestic trademark applicants filing applications based on actual use in commerce sometimes found themselves edged out by applicants for foreign trademark registrations for the same or similar marks, because (as discussed in § 2.15 [C] below) in many cases the latter are entitled to federal registration priority based on their foreign application dates even if they have not yet used their marks anywhere in the world.

In response to these concerns, in the Trademark Law Revision Act of 1988 (TLRA), Congress amended section 1 of the Lanham Act to permit the filing of "intent to use" (ITU) applications for registration on the Principal Register. The ITU provisions, codified in section 1(b),[165] took effect in 1989. The ITU application allows a trademark applicant to file an application for registration on the Principal Register before the date on which the mark is first used in trade. If the ITU application eventually ripens into a valid trademark registration, the effective date of that registration will be the date on which the ITU application was filed. Accordingly, by using the ITU process, the successful applicant obtains a priority date for nationwide constructive use that corresponds to the applicant's ITU filing date, which is earlier than the date of the first actual use of the mark in trade.

The ITU application process is discussed in detail in § 2.10 [B] below.

[5]   Constructive Use

Although actual use in commerce is a prerequisite to registration of a mark on the Principal Register, registration of the mark constitutes constructive use of the mark throughout the United States, thus giving the registrant priority against later adopters of confusingly similar marks even in areas where the registrant has not actually used the mark.[166] Constructive use is discussed at § 2.08 below.

§ 2.05   DISTINCTIVENESS

A trademark or service mark must be capable of distinguishing the goods or services in connection with which it is used from goods or services offered by another source. Distinctiveness in the trademark context has been defined as the "tendency to identify the goods sold as emanating from a particular, though possibly anonymous, source."[167] If a word, symbol, or other device is incapable of distinguishing the source of goods or services, then it cannot qualify for

---

[164] 15 U.S.C. § 1127 (defining "use in commerce"); see, e.g., Blue Bell, Inc. v. Jaymar-Ruby, Inc., 497 F.2d 433, 437 (2d Cir. 1974).

[165] 15 U.S.C. § 1051(b).

[166] Id. § 1057(c) (constructive use).

[167] Paddington Corp. v. Attiki Imp. & Distrib., Inc., 996 F.2d 577, 585 (2d Cir. 1993).

trademark protection, either at common law or under the Lanham Act.

A mark can be distinctive in either of two ways. It can be inherently distinctive, or it can acquire distinctiveness through use. A mark is inherently distinctive if, starting from the moment its use commences, "[its] intrinsic nature serves to identify a particular source."[168] Inherently distinctive marks may be arbitrary ("Camel" cigarettes), fanciful ("Kodak" film), or suggestive ("Tide" detergent). Many marks, however, are not inherently distinctive, because when they are first used on a product or service they do not immediately convey to the consumer the message that they are source indicators. A descriptive mark, by definition, is not inherently distinctive, because it conveys information about the characteristics of the product or service in connection with which it is used. However, a descriptive mark may nonetheless possess acquired distinctiveness — also known as secondary meaning.[169] Secondary meaning arises when, "in the minds of the public, the primary significance of a [mark] is to identify the source of the product rather than the product itself."[170] Acquired distinctiveness, or secondary meaning, arises over time, after consumers have had repeated encounters with the mark.

There are important legal consequences to the determination of: (1) whether a mark is inherently distinctive, (2) whether a descriptive mark has acquired secondary meaning, and (3) whether a word, symbol, or other device is so lacking in distinctiveness that it cannot distinguish one merchant's goods or services from those of another (in which case it is characterized as either "generic" or "merely descriptive"). These consequences are discussed where relevant throughout the remainder of this text.

The "spectrum of distinctiveness" is discussed in § 2.07 [A] below.

§ 2.06 MAINTAINING TRADEMARK RIGHTS

Unlike patents and copyrights, which have statutorily limited terms of protection, trademark rights have potentially indefinite duration, both at common law and under the Lanham Act. However, once trademark rights have been established, they must also be maintained, or they will be lost. Because trademark rights are established through: (1) use and (2) distinctiveness, they can be lost through: (1) non-use or (2) loss of distinctiveness.

A loss of trademark rights through cessation of use is referred to as "abandonment." This topic is addressed in § 3.12 [A][1] below.

---

[168] Abercrombie & Fitch Co. v. Hunting World, Inc., 537 F.2d 4, 10-11 (2d Cir. 1976).

[169] "The phrase 'secondary meaning' originally arose in the context of word marks, where it served to distinguish the source-identifying meaning from the ordinary, or 'primary,' meaning of the word. 'Secondary meaning' has since come to refer to the acquired, source-identifying meaning of a non-word mark as well." Wal-Mart Stores, Inc. v. Samara Bros., Inc., 529 U.S. 205, 211 (2000).

[170] Inwood Laboratories, Inc. v. Ives Laboratories, Inc., 456 U.S. 844, 851, n. 11 (1982); see also Perini Corp. v. Perini Construction, Inc., 915 F.2d 121, 125 (4th Cir. 1990) ("Secondary meaning is the consuming public's understanding that the mark, when used in context, refers, not to what the descriptive mark ordinarily describes, but to the particular business that the mark is meant to identify.").

Trademark rights can also be lost if a mark loses its ability to distinguish the trademark owner's goods or services from those of another. This can occur if consumers begin to perceive the mark not as an origin indicator, but merely as a description of, or a synonym for, the goods or services in question. These topics are addressed below, in § 2.07 [A][3] (descriptive marks) and § 2.07 [A][4] (generic terms).

Although trademarks and service marks can be assigned or licensed, the ability to assign or license a mark is not unfettered. If the assignment or license causes the mark to become separated from its underlying goodwill, so that consumer expectations are frustrated, the mark may lose its protection. For this reason, an assignment of a mark must include the goodwill of the line of business in which the mark is used. An attempt to assign a mark without the accompanying goodwill constitutes an "assignment in gross," and leads to a loss of trademark protection. Likewise, if the licensor of a trademark fails to exercise quality control over its licensee, this constitutes a "naked license," and leads to a loss of trademark protection. These topics are addressed in § 3.12 [A][2][a] (naked licensing) and § 3.12 [A][2][b] (assignments in gross).

In the case of a federally registered mark, the registrant must also file periodic renewals and statements of use in order to maintain the federal registration and to continue to enjoy the legal benefits of that registration. This topic is addressed in § 2.10 [H] below.

PART III:
TYPES OF TRADEMARKS

§ 2.07   PROTECTIBLE MARKS

Section 45 of the Lanham Act defines a trademark as:

any word, name, symbol, or device, or any combination thereof —

(1) used by a person, or

(2) which a person has a bona fide intention to use in commerce and applies to register on the principal register established by this chapter,

to identify and distinguish his or her goods, including a unique product, from those manufactured or sold by others and to indicate the source of the goods, even if that source is unknown.[171]

The federal definition of a service mark is similar, substituting "services" where appropriate, and adding one additional sentence:

Titles, character names, and other distinctive features of radio or television programs may be registered as service marks notwithstand-

---

[171]   15 U.S.C. § 1127.

ing that they, or the programs, may advertise the goods of the sponsor.[172]

The concept of a trademark or service mark under common law dispenses with the requirement of use in interstate commerce, but otherwise parallels the Lanham Act definition. Thus, common law marks must be capable of distinguishing the origin of goods or services.

[A] Spectrum of Distinctiveness

Courts have developed a "spectrum of distinctiveness" to describe the ability of a particular mark to perform an origin-identifying function, as well the relative strength of one mark compared to other marks. Originating at common law, the spectrum of distinctiveness applies under the Lanham Act as well. In descending order of strength, the categories of protectible marks are categorized as (1) arbitrary or fanciful, (2) suggestive, and (3) descriptive. Marks falling into any of the first two categories are considered inherently distinctive, meaning they may be protected without a showing of secondary meaning, whereas descriptive marks are protectible only if they acquire distinctiveness through secondary meaning.[173] A fourth category consists of generic terms, which are so highly descriptive that they are incapable of acquiring distinctiveness even after prolonged use, and therefore, although such terms are often referred to as "generic marks," as a matter of both state and federal law, they are incapable of serving as either trademarks or service marks. The classification of a mark is a question of fact.[174]

Classification of a mark into one of these four categories is an important step in determining whether and under what circumstances it is eligible for protection under state or federal law, and can also be important in determining the relative strength of the mark, an important factor in determining the likelihood of confusion. Classification is easier in some cases than in others. As the Second Circuit noted in *Abercrombie & Fitch Co. v. Hunting World, Inc.,* one of the leading cases addressing issues of trademark classification:

> The lines of demarcation, however, are not always bright. Moreover, the difficulties are compounded because a term that is in one category for a particular product may be in quite a different one for another, because a term may shift from one category to another in light of differences in usage through time, because a term may have one meaning to one group of users and a different one to others, and because the same term may be put to different uses with respect to a single product.[175]

For example, "ivory" would be generic as applied to a product made from elephant tusks, but is probably arbitrary as applied to soap, the word "escalator" was originally fanciful or suggestive, but has since become generic, and "aspirin"

---

[172] *Id.*

[173] Secondary meaning is discussed in § 2.07 [A][3][b], *infra.*

[174] Bristol-Myers Squibb Co. v. McNeill-P.P.C., Inc., 973 F.2d 1033, 1039-40 (2d Cir. 1992).

[175] *Abercrombie & Fitch,* 537 F.2d at 9.

was fanciful before it became generic;[176] likewise, "apple" is arbitrary for computers, but would be descriptive for apple pies, and generic for apples themselves.

In some cases, a trademark proponent will adopt an alternate spelling for a descriptive or generic term. Where the two spellings are pronounced the same way, courts have treated these terms as their descriptive or generic equivalents.[177] Thus, "Lite" for beer was treated the same as "light," and was therefore held to be generic.[178] "Cush-N-Grip" was treated as equivalent to the generic "Cushion-Grip."[179] "Beanee" was the equivalent of "Beany," and was therefore descriptive for barbecued beans.[180]

In classifying marks into categories along the spectrum of distinctiveness, an element of subjectivity is sometimes unavoidable. As the Fifth Circuit has cautioned:

> These categories, like the tones in a spectrum, tend to blur at the edges and merge together. The labels are more advisory than definitional, more like guidelines than pigeonholes. Not surprisingly, they are somewhat difficult to articulate and to apply.[181]

In the case of a "composite mark" — that is, a mark which consists of several separable components, which may be words, designs, or any combination thereof — the distinctiveness of the mark must be determined by considering the mark as a whole, rather than by considering the distinctiveness of each individual component. This rule follows from the general principle that the distinctiveness of a mark depends on the overall commercial impression which the mark conveys to consumers. Thus, for example, it is possible for a composite mark to be inherently distinctive (e.g., arbitrary or suggestive) even if each of its individual components is merely descriptive of the product or service in question.[182] A few

---

[176] *Id.* at 9 nn. 6-8.

[177] *See, e.g.*, Soweco, Inc. v. Shell Oil Co., 617 F.2d 1178, 1186 n. 24 (5th Cir. 1980) (treating "larvacide" the same as its generic equivalent "larvicide"), *cert. denied*, 450 U.S. 981 (1981); Keller Prods., Inc. v. Rubber Linings Corp., 213 F.2d 382, 385-86 (7th Cir. 1954) (collecting cases).

[178] Miller Brewing Co. v. G. Heileman Brewing Co., 561 F.2d 75, 81 (7th Cir. 1977), *cert. denied*, 434 U.S. 1025 (1978).

[179] Nupla Corp. v. IXL Mfg. Co., 114 F.3d 191, 196 (Fed. Cir. 1997).

[180] Hesmer Foods, Inc. v. Campbell Soup Co., 346 F.2d 356, 358 (7th Cir. 1965), *cert. denied*, 382 U.S. 839 (1965).

[181] Zatarain's, Inc. v. Oak Grove Smokehouse, Inc., 698 F.2d 786, 790 (5th Cir. 1983).

[182] Union Carbide Corp. v. Ever-Ready, Inc., 531 F.2d 366, 379 (7th Cir. 1976); *see, e.g.*, California Cooler, Inc. v. Loretto Winery, Ltd., 774 F.2d 1451, 1455-56 (9th Cir. 1985) (rejecting argument that, because "California" and "cooler" are not distinctive, "California Cooler" is incapable of distinctiveness as a matter of law); Macia v. Microsoft Corp., 335 F. Supp. 2d 507, 513 (D. Vt. 2004) ("PocketMoney" may be suggestive even though "pocket" and "money" alone would be descriptive), *aff'd*, 164 Fed. Appx. 17 (2d. Cir. 2006); W.W.W. Pharm. Co. v. Gillette Co., 808 F. Supp. 1013, 1022 (S.D.N.Y. 1992)("SPORTSTICK" was suggestive even though "sport" and "stick" were generic or descriptive), *aff'd*, 984 F.2d 567 (2d Cir. 1993); *see generally* MCCARTHY ON TRADEMARKS, *supra* note 28, at § 11:26 (collecting cases).

courts, however, have held to the contrary.[183]

[1]   Arbitrary or Fanciful

The strongest marks are those that are either arbitrary or fanciful. Both are considered inherently distinctive, and thus are protectible without a showing of secondary meaning.[184]

Fanciful marks are coined terms that have no commonplace or dictionary meaning at all, having been "completely fabricated by their owners."[185] Frequently cited examples of fanciful marks include "Kodak" for photographic equipment and supplies,[186] "Xerox" for copying equipment and supplies,[187] "Aunt Jemima" for pancake syrup,[188] "Rolls Royce" for automobiles and airplane parts,[189] the "Toucan Sam" word mark and logo (a cartoonish image of a toucan) for cereal,[190] "Polaroid" for camera equipment,[191] "Exxon" for oil and gas products and services,[192] and "Clorox" for bleach.[193]

Arbitrary marks are words in common usage, with dictionary meanings, but that do not in any respect describe the goods or services to which they are attached.[194] Like fanciful marks, arbitrary marks are inherently distinctive. Unlike fanciful marks, however, "an arbitrary mark is distinctive only within its product market and entitled to little or no protection outside of that area,"[195] because the determination of arbitrariness depends on the nature of the goods or services to which the mark is applied. Because an arbitrary mark is not a coined word, it has a commonplace meaning that is unrelated to its origin-indicating function;[196] thus, the distinctiveness of an arbitrary mark arises from the fact that it is "mismatched" to a particular product or service, because its commonplace meaning has no relationship to that product or service.[197] Thus, "Apple" is arbitrary for computers, but would be generic for apples, and descriptive for apple-flavored candy, liquor, or pies.

---

[183] *See, e.g.*, National Conf. of Bar Examiners v. Multistate Legal Studies, Inc., 692 F.2d 478, 488 (7th Cir. 1982).

[184] Secondary meaning is discussed in § 2.07 [A][3][b].

[185] Kellogg Co. v. Toucan Golf, Inc., 337 F.3d 616, 624 (6th Cir. 2003).

[186] *Id.*

[187] *Id.*

[188] Arrow Distilleries, Inc. v. Globe Brewing Co., 117 F.2d 347, 349 (4th Cir. 1941).

[189] *Id.*

[190] Kellogg Co. v. Toucan Golf, Inc., 337 F.3d 616, 624 (6th Cir. 2003).

[191] Polaroid Corp. v. Polaroid, Inc., 319 F.2d 830 (7th Cir. 1963).

[192] Sara Lee Corp. v. Kayser-Roth Corp., 81 F.3d 455, 464 (4th Cir.), *cert. denied*, 519 U.S. 976 (1996).

[193] Clorox Chem. Co. Chlorit Mfg. Corp., 25 F. Supp. 702 (E.D.N.Y. 1938).

[194] *See* Moose Creek, Inc. v. Abercrombie & Fitch Co., 331 F. Supp. 2d 1214, 1222 (C.D. Cal.) (citing 2 J. Thomas McCarthy, McCarthy on Trademarks and Unfair Competition § 11:11 (4th ed. 2004)), *aff'd*, 114 Fed. Appx. (9th Cir. 2004).

[195] *Kellogg*, 337 F.3d at 626.

[196] *Abercrombie & Fitch*, 537 F.2d at 11.

[197] *Kellogg*, 337 F.3d at 626.

Other examples of arbitrary word marks include "Camel" for cigarettes,[198] "Toucan" for cereal,[199] "Black & White" for scotch whiskey,[200] "Domino" for sugar,[201] "Tea Rose" for flour,[202] and "Mustang" for motels.[203]

Non-word marks may be arbitrary or fanciful as well. For example, in determining whether a design is inherently distinctive, the Court of Customs and Patent Appeals has inquired "whether it was a 'common' basic shape or design, whether it was unique or unusual in a particular field, whether it was a mere refinement of a commonly adopted and well-known form of ornamentation for a particular class of goods viewed by the public as a dress or ornamentation for the goods, or whether it was capable of creating a commercial impression distinct from the accompanying words."[204]

[2] Suggestive

Like arbitrary and fanciful marks, suggestive marks are considered inherently distinctive, and thus are eligible for trademark protection without a showing of a secondary meaning.[205]

Suggestive marks are considered very strong marks, but less so than arbitrary and fanciful marks. This category of marks was not recognized at early common law, but was developed by courts in response to the common law rule that descriptive marks could not serve as trademarks,[206] a rule that (under section 5 of the 1905 Trademark Act[207]) also prevented descriptive marks from being federally registered until their owner could demonstrate ten years of exclusive use.[208] In order to avoid denying trademark protection to marks that

---

[198] Daddy's Junky Music Stores, Inc. v. Big Daddy's Family Music Center, 109 F.3d 275, 280-81 (6th Cir. 1997).

[199] *Kellogg*, 337 F.3d at 626.

[200] Fleischmann Distilling Corp. v. Maier Brewing Co., 314 F.2d 149 (9th Cir.), *cert. denied*, 374 U.S. 830 (1963).

[201] Amstar Corp. v. Domino's Pizza, Inc., 615 F.2d 252, 260 (11th Cir.) (noting, however, that the mark may originally have been descriptive with regard to sugar, because the plaintiff at one time sold sugar in domino-shaped pieces), *cert. denied*, 449 U.S. 899 (1980).

[202] *Sara Lee*, 81 F.3d at 464 (4th Cir.), *cert. denied*, 519 U.S. 976 (1996).

[203] Mustang Motels, Inc. v. Patel, 226 U.S.P.Q. 526 (C.D. Cal. 1985).

[204] Seabrook Foods, Inc. v. Bar-Well Foods, Ltd., 568 F.2d 1342, 1344 (C.C.P.A. 1977).

[205] Blinded Veterans Ass'n v. Blinded American Veterans Found., 872 F.2d 1035, 1040 (D.C. Cir. 1989). Secondary meaning is discussed in § 2.07 [A][3][b] *infra*.

[206] *See, e.g.*, William R. Warner & Co. v. Eli Lilly & Co., 265 U.S. 526, 529 (1924); In re Anti-Cori-Zine Chem. Co., 34 App. D.C. 191 (App. D.C. 1909). However, even under early common law, many courts protected descriptive marks under the doctrine of unfair competition, provided the mark had acquired secondary meaning; this did not afford the senior user exclusive rights in the mark, but protected the senior user against a junior user's efforts to palm off the junior user's goods or services as those of the senior user. *See, e.g.*, Cridlebaugh v. Rudolph, 131 F.2d 795, 801 (3d Cir. 1942), *cert. denied*, 318 U.S. 779 (1943); Folmer Graflex Corp. v. Graphic Photo Serv., 44 F. Supp. 429, 431-33 (D. Mass. 1942); Coalgate Abstract Co. v. Coal County Abstract Co., 180 Okla. 8 (Okla. 1937) (collecting cases).

[207] 33 Stat. 724, 726.

[208] *See Abercrombie & Fitch*, 537 F.2d at 11; Pinaud, Inc. v. Huebschman, 27 F.2d 531, 535

were only somewhat descriptive, courts categorized these marks as suggestive rather than descriptive.[209] As one contemporaneous court observed:

> It is pretty clear that the two terms are not mutually exclusive. There must be some description in almost any suggestion or the suggesting process will not take place. So what we have in any trade-mark case is a matter of judgment as to what side of the line the question mark falls upon. It is desirable to protect the trader who has built up public association with a product under his trade-mark from having his business taken by somebody else. It is also desirable to keep the channels of expression open by not giving protection to people who go out and take ordinary, descriptive words and then claim something like a property right in them.[210]

Having created the "suggestive" category, however, courts found it difficult to define.[211] Suggestive marks have a descriptive aspect, but differ from descriptive marks in that they merely suggest, rather than describe, certain qualities of the goods or services to which they are attached. A suggestive mark only indirectly conveys an impression of the goods or services to which it is attached,[212] and thus "requires the observer or listener to use imagination and perception to determine the nature of the goods."[213] Most courts have adopted some variation of this "imagination" test to identify suggestive marks. In a much-quoted comparison between descriptive and suggestive marks, one court observed:

> A term is suggestive if it requires imagination, thought and perception to reach a conclusion as to the nature of goods. A term is descriptive if it forthwith conveys an immediate idea of the ingredients, qualities or characteristics of the goods.[214]

Examples of marks that courts have determined to be suggestive include "Citibank" for banking services (connoting "an urban or modern bank"),[215] "Goliath" for wood pencils (connoting "a large size"),[216] "Safari" for ice chests, axes, tents, and smoking tobacco (connoting wilderness expeditions),[217] "Roach

---

(E.D.N.Y.), aff'd, 27 F.2d 538 (2d Cir.), cert. denied, 278 U.S. 644 (1928).

[209] Abercrombie & Fitch, 537 F.2d at 10.

[210] Q-Tips, Inc. v. Johnson & Johnson, 206 F.2d 144, 146 (3d Cir.), cert. denied, 346 U.S. 867 (1953).

[211] Abercrombie & Fitch, 537 F.2d at 10.

[212] Blinded Veterans Ass'n, 872 F.2d at 1040.

[213] Induct-O-Matic Corp. v. Inductotherm Corp., 747 F.2d 358 (6th Cir. 1984).

[214] Blinded Veterans Ass'n, 872 F.2d at 1040 (quoting Stix Prods., Inc. v. United Merchants & Mfrs., Inc., 295 F. Supp. 479, 488 (S.D.N.Y. 1068); see also General Shoe Corp. v. Rosen, 111 F.2d 95, 98 (4th Cir. 1940) (per curiam) (suggestive terms "shed some light upon the characteristics of the good" only "through an effort of the imagination on the part of the observer"); Union Carbide Corp. v. Ever-Ready, Inc., 531 F.2d 366, 378-80 (7th Cir. 1976) (adopting similar test).

[215] DeGidio v. West Group Corp., 355 F.3d 506, 510-511 (6th Cir.), cert. denied, 542 U.S. 904 (2004).

[216] Id.

[217] Abercrombie & Fitch, 537 F.2d at 14.

Motel" for insect traps (connoting housing for roaches),[218] "Q-Tips" for cotton swabs (connoting cuteness and, therefore, babies),[219] "L'eggs" (connoting attractiveness and legginess),[220] "Penguin" (for refrigerators),[221] "The Real Yellow Pages,"[222] and "Wite-Out,"[223] as well as "Coppertone," "Orange Crush," and "Playboy."[224]

The line between suggestive and descriptive marks can be difficult to draw. To assist in this task, some courts have employed a six-factor test developed by leading trademark scholar Thomas McCarthy:

(1) How much imagination on the buyer's part is required in trying to cull a direct message from the mark about the quality, ingredients or characteristics of the product or service?

(2) Does the mark directly convey a real and unequivocal idea of some characteristic, function, quality or ingredient of the product or service to a reasonably informed potential buyer? Is some reflection or multi-stage reasoning process necessary to cull some direct information about the product from the term used as a mark?

(3) Does the mark so closely tell something about the product or service that other sellers of like products would be likely to want to use the term in connection with their goods? Perhaps a more realistic way to pose this question is to ask whether, without any prior knowledge of this mark, others would be likely to want to use it to describe their products?

(4) Are, in fact, other sellers now using this term to describe their products?

(5) Even though the mark may tell something about the goods or services, is it just as likely to conjure up some other, purely arbitrary connotation? E.g., "Sugar & Spice" baked goods, or "Poly Pitcher" plastic pitchers.

(6) How does the mark fit into the basic concept that descriptive marks cannot pinpoint one source by identifying and distinguishing only one seller? That is, are buyers likely to regard the mark really as a symbol of origin, or merely as another form of self-laudatory advertising?[225]

---

[218] American Home Prods. Corp. v. Johnson Chem. Co., 589 F.2d 103, 106 (2d Cir. 1978). The court noted that this mark might even be arbitrary due to its high degree of incongruity: "While roaches may live in some motels against the will of the owners, motels are surely not built for roaches to live in." *Id.*

[219] Q-Tips, Inc. v. Johnson & Johnson, 206 F.2d 144 (3d Cir.), *cert. denied*, 346 U.S. 867 (1953).

[220] Sara Lee Corp. v. Kayser-Roth Corp., 81 F.3d 455, 465 (4th Cir.), *cert. denied*, 519 U.S. 976 (1996).

[221] Union Nat'l Bank of Texas v. Union Nat'l Bank of Texas, 909 F.2d 839, 845 (5th Cir. 1990).

[222] BellSouth Adv'g & Pub'g Corp. v. The Real Color Pages, 792 F. Supp. 775, 781 (M.D. Fla. 1991).

[223] BIC Corp. v. Far Eastern Source Corp., 2000 U.S. Dist. LEXIS 18226 (S.D.N.Y. Dec. 19, 2000).

[224] *Sara Lee*, 81 F.3d at 464.

[225] *See* MCCARTHY ON TRADEMARKS, *supra* note 28, at § 11:71 (expanding on each of these factors);

Another commentator suggests: "Imagine that a potential consumer is told the mark without being told what product the mark is associated with." If the consumer would be unlikely to guess the correct product, but sees the connection once the product is revealed, then the mark is probably suggestive.[226]

Because suggestive marks are considered inherently distinctive, under common law as well as the Lanham Act they may be protected without a showing of secondary meaning. Because suggestive terms are not as informative as descriptive marks, there is less reason to be concerned that withdrawing a suggestive mark from general circulation will impair the ability of competitors to describe their own goods or services.[227]

[3]　Descriptive

A descriptive mark specifically describes a quality, function, characteristic, or ingredient of a product or service.[228] In contrast to suggestive marks, it takes no imagination to understand what characteristics of a product or service are being conveyed by a descriptive mark. Examples of descriptive marks include "Rich 'N Chips" for chocolate chip cookies,[229] "Rocktober" for an October rock music broadcast,[230] "After Tan" for post-tanning lotion,[231] "5 Minute Glue" for fast-drying glue,[232] "Yellow Pages" for a phone directory with yellow-colored pages,[233] "King Size" for men's clothing,[234] as well as such general laudatory terms as "Best," "Superior," and "Preferred."[235] One court has described "Coca-Cola" as "the paradigm of a descriptive mark that has acquired a secondary meaning."[236]

[a]　Common Law Proscription

Traditionally, under the common law of trademarks, descriptive marks were considered incapable of serving as trademarks.[237] It was thought that withdrawing a descriptive term from general circulation for the exclusive use of

---

DeGidio, 355 F.3d at 510-511 (6th Cir.) (applying the McCarthy factors); A La Carte v. Culinary Enters., 1997 Dist. LEXIS 12755, *13-14 (N.D. Ill. 1997) (similar).

[226] GILSON, 1-2 TRADEMARK PROTECTION AND PRACTICE § 2.04[1] (2008).

[227] *Abercrombie & Fitch*, 537 F.2d at 11.

[228] *Induct-O-Matic Corp.*, 747 F.2d at 362; Blinded Veterans Ass'n v. Blinded Am. Veterans Found., 872 F.2d 1035, 1039-40 (D.C. Cir. 1989).

[229] Application of Keebler Co., 479 F.2d 1405 (C.C.P.A. 1973).

[230] Metromedia, Inc. v. American Broadcasting Co's., Inc., 210 U.S.P.Q. 21 (S.D.N.Y. 1980).

[231] *Sara Lee*, 81 F.3d at 464.

[232] *Id.*

[233] *Id.*

[234] *Id.*

[235] Champions Golf Club, Inc. v. The Champions Golf Club, Inc., 78 F.3d 1111, 1117 (6th Cir. 1996).

[236] *Sara Lee*, 81 F.3d at 464. Coca-Cola was named after two of its original ingredients — coca leaves and kola nuts. Secondary meaning is discussed in § 2.07 [A][3][b] *infra.*

[237] *See, e.g.*, Armstrong Paint & Varnish Works v. Nu-Enamel Corp., 305 U.S. 315, 334 (1938); William R. Warner & Co. v. Eli Lilly & Co., 265 U.S. 526, 529 (1924); Delaware & Hudson Canal Co.

one competitor would impair the ability of other competitors to describe their own goods or services. However, it is now well settled that descriptive marks can be protected as trademarks under state and federal trademark and unfair competition laws once they have achieved distinctiveness in the minds of consumers — that is, once they acquire secondary meaning.[238]

[b]   Secondary Meaning

A descriptive mark, while not inherently distinctive, may nonetheless acquire distinctiveness through use, if the public comes to recognize the mark as an indication of source, thus giving it "secondary meaning." The question of whether a mark has acquired secondary meaning is a question of fact.[239]

The role of secondary meaning has been described as follows:

> It contemplates that a word or phrase originally, and in that sense primarily, incapable of exclusive appropriation with reference to an article on the market, because geographically or otherwise descriptive, might nevertheless have been used so long and so exclusively by one producer with reference to his article that, in that trade and to that branch of the purchasing public, the word or phrase had come to mean that the article was his product; in other words, had come to be, to them, his trade-mark. So it was said that the word had come to have a secondary meaning, although this phrase, 'secondary meaning,' seems not happily chosen, because, in the limited field, this new meaning is primary rather than secondary; that is to say, it is, in that field, the natural meaning.[240]

For a descriptive mark to have sufficient secondary meaning to serve as a source indicator, it is not necessary that the public be able to identify the source by name; "[i]t is sufficient if the public is aware that the product comes from a single, though anonymous, source."[241] However, it is essential that "the primary significance of the term in the minds of the consuming public is not the product but the producer."[242]

---

v. Clark, 80 U.S. (13 Wall.) 311, 323 (1872); In re Anti-Cori-Zine Chem. Co., 34 App. D.C. 191 (App. D.C. 1909); *see generally Blinded Veterans Ass'n*, 872 F.2d at 1041 n.11 (noting the historical use of the terms "trade name" or "nontechnical trademark" to refer to marks that were not considered to be trademarks at common law, and were protectible, if at all, only under the law of unfair competition).

[238] *See, e.g.*, Colston Inv. Co. v. Home Supply Co., 74 S.W.3d 759, 764-65 (Ky. Ct. App. 2001); Yocono's Restaurant v. Yocono, 100 Ohio App. 3d 11, 17-18 (Ohio Ct. App. 1994); Zapata Corp. v. Zapata Trading Int'l, Inc., 841 S.W.2d 45, 47-48 (Tex. Ct. App. 1992).

[239] Japan Telecom, Inc. v. Japan Telecom Am., Inc., 287 F.3d 866, 873 (9th Cir. 2002).

[240] G & C Merriam Co. v. Saalfield, 198 F. 369, 373 (6th Cir. 1912), *cert. denied*, 243 U.S.C. 651 (1917).

[241] Union Carbide Corp. v. Ever-Ready, Inc., 531 F.2d 366, 380 (7th Cir. 1976) (citing Spangler Candy Co. v. Crystal Pure Candy Co., 353 F.2d 641, 647 (7th Cir. 1965)), *cert. denied*, 429 U.S. 830 (1976).

[242] Kellogg Co. v. Nat'l Biscuit Co., 305 U.S. 111 (1938).

Under both state and federal law, the existence of secondary meaning is determined by considering a number of factors. Although the precise formulation varies by jurisdiction, the factors tend to be similar. For example, the Ninth Circuit considers: survey evidence; direct consumer testimony; exclusivity, manner and length of use of the mark; amount and manner of advertising; amount of sales and number of customers; established place in the market; and proof of intentional copying by the defendant.[243] The Fourth Circuit considers, without limitation: advertising expenditures; consumer studies linking the mark to a source; sales success; unsolicited media coverage of the product; attempts to plagiarize the mark; and the length and exclusivity of the mark's use.[244] However, the Fourth Circuit has also held that proof that a defendant directly and intentionally copied the plaintiff's mark gives rise to a rebuttable presumption that the plaintiff's mark has secondary meaning.[245] Although the importance of each secondary meaning factor may vary from case to case, survey evidence often provides the strongest indication of consumer recognition and association.[246]

Where several parties have used the same descriptive mark in the same geographic area, priority will depend not on which party was the first to use the mark in that market, but which party's mark was the first to acquire distinctiveness (that is, secondary meaning) in that market.[247]

Just as a descriptive term may acquire distinctiveness over time, it may also lose that distinctiveness over time. If the secondary meaning of a descriptive mark weakens, so that the public no longer perceives it as an origin indicator, the mark may lose its trademark status, unless it is a federally registered mark that has become incontestable. (Incontestability is discussed in § 2.13 below.)

Descriptive marks may describe any aspect of a good or service. As discussed in § 2.07 [B] below, personal names are typically treated as descriptive marks. So, too, are geographic indicators.[248]

[4] Generic Terms

A generic term is one that is commonly used as the name or description of a kind of goods.[249] A generic term may be synonymous with the good or service itself (e.g., "apple" is generic for apples), or may describe a broader category to

---

[243] Filipino Yellow Pages, Inc. v. Asian Journal Publ'n, Inc., 198 F.3d 1143, 1151 (9th Cir. 1999).

[244] Perini Corp. v. Perini Construction, Inc., 915 F.2d 121, 125 (4th Cir. 1990).

[245] Larsen v. Terk Technologies, 151 F.3d 140, 148-49 (4th Cir. 1998).

[246] Levi Strauss & Co. v. Blue Bell, Inc., 778 F.2d 1352, 1358 (9th Cir. 1985).

[247] Investacorp, Inc. v. Arabian Inv. Banking Corp., 931 F.2d 1519, 1524 (11th Cir.), *cert. denied*, 502 U.S. 1005 (1991); Grupo Gigante S.A. de C.V. v. Dallo & Do., 119 F. Supp. 2d 1083, 1092, *aff'd*, 391 F.3d 1088 (9th Cir. 2004).

[248] *See, e.g.*, Madison Reprographics v. Cook's Reprographics, 203 Wis. 2d 226 (Wis. Ct. App. 1996) ("Madison Repro" is descriptive for a copy shop in Madison, Wisconsin).

[249] Induct-O-Matic Corp. v. Inductotherm Corp., 747 F.2d 358, 362 (6th Cir. 1984); *accord*, G. Heileman Brewing Co. v. Anheuser-Busch, Inc., 873 F.2d 985, 997 (7th Cir. 1989) (generic mark "denominate[s] a type, kind, genus or subcategory of goods"); Dayton Progress Corp. v. Lane Punch Corp., 917 F.2d 836, 839 (4th Cir. 1990) (generic mark "identifies the general nature of an article").

which the particular good or service belongs (e.g., "fruit" is also generic for apples). It is sometimes said that a generic term describes the *genus* of which a particular merchant's product is a *species*. For example, "cola" describes a genus of sweet caramel-colored carbonated beverages, of which "Coca-Cola" and "Pepsi-Cola" are species, and "laundry detergent" describes a genus of cleaning products, of which "Tide" and "Arm & Hammer" are species. A term may sometimes be generic if it names a distinctive *characteristic* of the genus of which the product in question is a species; for example, "Matchbox" was held to be generic for toy vehicles because they were sold in matchbox-sized boxes.[250]

Generic terms are per se ineligible for trademark protection under either state or federal law. Unlike descriptive terms, which can serve as trademarks if and when they acquire secondary meaning — that is, if and when the public comes to perceive them as indicators of source — generic terms are, as a matter of law, incapable of serving as indicators of source. As one court has noted, "no matter how much money and effort the user of a generic term has poured into promoting the sale of its merchandise and what success it has achieved in securing public identification, it cannot deprive competing manufacturers of the product of the right to call an article by its name."[251]

Examples of generic terms include "cereal" for breakfast cereal,[252] "Bermuda" for shorts,[253] "Convenient Store" for a retail store,[254] "Dry Ice" for solid carbon dioxide,[255] "Light Beer" for low-calorie beer,[256] "Crab House" for a restaurant that serves crab,[257] and "Multistate Bar Examination" for an attorney competency exam used by many states.[258]

A term may be generic with respect to more than one category of product or service. One court held, for example, that "safari" is generic not only for an expedition into the African wilderness, but also for a certain type of clothing that was originally associated with such activities but later became popular with a broader group of consumers.[259]

Conversely, a term may be generic even if there are other synonyms for the product or service; "the test for genericness is whether the public perceives the

---

Although generic terms are sometimes referred to as "common descriptive" terms, they must be distinguished from the category of descriptive terms, discussed above, which are also called "merely descriptive" terms. *Blinded Veterans Ass'n*, 872 F.2d at 1039 n. 4.

[250] *Sara Lee*, 81 F.3d at 464 n.10.

[251] *Abercrombie & Fitch*, 537 F.2d at 9.

[252] Kellogg Co. v. Toucan Golf, Inc., 337 F.3d 616, 624 (6th Cir. 2003).

[253] *Abercrombie & Fitch*, 537 F.2d at 13.

[254] *Sara Lee*, 81 F.3d at 464.

[255] *Id.*

[256] *Id.*

[257] Hunt Masters, Inc. v. Landry's Seafood Rest., Inc., 240 F.3d 251 (4th Cir. 2001).

[258] National Conference of Bar Examiners v. Multistate Legal Studies, Inc., 692 F.2d 478, 488 (7th Cir. 1982), *cert. denied*, 464 U.S. 814 (1983).

[259] *Abercrombie & Fitch*, 537 F.2d at 11-12.

term primarily as the designation of the article."[260]

A term may be generic for one class of goods, but not for another. Thus, while "apple" would be generic for apples, it is arbitrary for computers. In cases presenting closer questions, the Seventh Circuit held that "hog" was generic for motorcycles but descriptive for motorcycle clubs,[261] and the Second Circuit held that "self-actualization" was generic for a yoga organization but descriptive for yoga books and classes.[262]

Although many generic terms are nouns, other types of words, such as verbs[263] or adjectives,[264] can be generic as well. And while case law addressing genericism most frequently involves word marks, designs can also be generic. The Ninth Circuit, for example, held that while a grape leaf design was at one time a suggestive (and thus inherently distinctive) trademark for wine, over time the use of such an image by numerous winemakers had caused it to become generic.[265]

Under both state and federal law, a protected trademark will lose its protected status if it becomes generic. Thus, a term that initially enjoys state or federal trademark protection because of inherent or acquired distinctiveness will lose that protection if the public begins to use the mark as a synonym for the product itself rather than as an indication of the product's source. Whether the owner of a mark has made diligent efforts to "police" its mark — that is, to maintain the trademark status of the mark by discouraging the public from using the term generically and by taking prompt action against infringers — does not determine whether the mark has become generic. What matters is how the public perceives the mark. In some cases, even diligent policing of a mark is insufficient to prevent the public from adopting the mark as a generic term for the product or service.[266]

Although both descriptive marks and generic marks are "descriptive" in a sense, there is a significant difference. Whereas a descriptive mark describes a "quality, function, or characteristic" of a product or service,[267] a generic mark connotes the "basic nature" of the product or service,[268] or the broader genus of

---

[260] *Blinded Veterans Ass'n*, 872 F.2d at 1041.

[261] H-D Michigan, Inc. v. Top Quality Serv., Inc., 496 F.3d 755, 761-62 (7th Cir. 2007).

[262] Self-Realization Fellowship Church v. Ananda Church of Self-Realization, 59 F.3d 902, 909-10 (2d Cir. 1995).

[263] Although no court has held "Xerox" to be generic, at one time the widespread use of this term as a verb meaning "to photocopy" posed a risk of genericide. *See* Union Nat'l Bank v. Union Nat'l Bank, 909 F.2d 839, 845 n.15 (5th Cir. 1990). "Google" faces a similar risk today. "Park 'n Fly" presents a close question as well, although the infringement defendant that raised this argument failed to marshal the evidence to support it. *See* Park 'N Fly, Inc. v. Dollar Park and Fly, Inc., 718 F.2d 327, 330-31 (9th Cir. 1984), *rev'd on other grounds*, 465 U.S. 1078 (1984).

[264] *See, e.g.*, Rudolph Int'l, Inc. v. Realys, Inc., 482 F.3d 1195, 1198-99 (9th Cir. 2007) (finding "disinfectable" generic for nail files).

[265] Kendall-Jackson Winery, Ltd. v. E. & J. Gallo Winery, 150 F.3d 1042, 1048-49 (9th Cir. 1998).

[266] *See, e.g.*, King-Seeley Thermos Co. v. Aladdin Indus., Inc., 321 F.2d 577 (2d Cir. 1963).

[267] *Blinded Veterans Ass'n*, 872 F.2d at 1039-40.

[268] Zatarain's, Inc. v. Oak Grove Smokehouse, Inc., 698 F.2d 786, 790 (5th Cir. 1983). Some

which the particular product or service is a species.[269]

Marks associated with unique or patented products or services, and marks that have been featured in particularly strong advertising campaigns, run a particular risk of becoming generic. If a product or service is significantly different from others available to the public, or if the advertising has been especially effective in creating market dominance, consumers may begin to use the mark as a synonym for the product or service.[270] The term "aspirin," for example, was originally a trademark until, through popular usage, it become the generic term for the pain medication to which it was attached; the public preferred the term "aspirin" over the cumbersome alternative "acetylsalicylic acid."[271] Other former trademarks that became generic include "yo-yo,"[272] "Murphy bed,"[273] "Singer" (for sewing machines, although by now that usage is obsolete),[274] "trampoline,"[275] "brassiere,"[276] "cellophane,"[277] "escalator,"[278] "shredded wheat,"[279] and "dry ice."[280] A similar fate befell "thermos," a term that consumers preferred over the clumsy phrase "vacuum bottle," although "Thermos" (with a capital "T") remains protected.[281]

In some cases, trademarks have been saved from the brink of genericism when their owners began promoting the use of convenient alternative generic terms for their branded products. For example, "Xerox" avoided becoming generic when its owner began promoting its products as "Xerox" brand "copiers," and "Sanka" avoided genericism when its owner began promoting "Sanka" brand "decaf."[282] The former owner of the "Yo-Yo" trademark was less successful, however, in its effort to persuade the public to refer to its "Yo-Yo" brand toy as a "return top."[283] The owners of the "Tabasco" and "Jell-O" marks have tried to avoid genericism by expanding the variety of products on which their marks appear (for example, Jell-O brand pudding). Other well-known

---

authorities refer to generic terms as "common descriptive" terms, and descriptive terms as "merely descriptive" terms. *Blinded Veterans Ass'n*, 872 F.2d at 1039 n. 4.

[269] Ty, Inc. v. Softbelly's, Inc., 353 F.3d 528, 532 (7th Cir. 2003) (noting that owner of "Beanies" mark "may be fighting a losing war" to keep its mark from becoming generic, unless it can persuade public to use the cumbersome "plush beanbag animals" as a generic alternative).

[270] *See, e.g.*, Dresser Indus., Inc. v. Heraeus Engelhard Vacuum, Inc., 395 F.2d 457 (3d Cir.), *cert. denied*, 393 U.S. 934 (1968); King-Seeley Thermos Co. v. Aladdin Indus., Inc., 321 F.2d 577 (2d Cir. 1963).

[271] Bayer Co. v. United Drug Co., 272 F. 505 (S.D.N.Y. 1921).

[272] Donald F. Duncan, Inc. v. Royal Tops Mfg. Co., 343 F.2d 655, 668 (7th Cir. 1965).

[273] Murphy Door Bed Co. v. Interior Sleep Sys., Inc., 874 F.2d 95, 101 (2d Cir. 1989).

[274] Singer Mfg. Co. v. June Mfg. Co., 163 U.S. 169 (1896).

[275] Nissen Trampoline Co. v. American Trampoline Co., 193 F. Supp. 745 (S.D. Iowa 1961).

[276] Charles R. DeBevoise Co. v. H. & W. Co., 60 N.J. Eq. 114, 60 A. 407 (1905).

[277] DuPont Cellophane Co. v. Waxed Prods. Co., 85 F.2d 75 (2d Cir. 1936).

[278] Haughton Elev. Co. v. Seeberger, 85 U.S.P.Q. (BNA) 80 (Comm'r Pat. & Trademarks 1950).

[279] Kellogg Co. v. National Biscuit Co., 305 U.S. 111 (1938).

[280] Ty, Inc. v. Softbelly's, Inc., 353 F.3d 528, 532 (7th Cir. 2003).

[281] King-Seeley Thermos Co. v. Aladdin Indus., Inc., 321 F.2d 577 (2d Cir. 1963).

[282] *Ty, Inc.*, 353 F.3d at 532.

[283] *Donald F. Duncan*, 343 F.2d at 668.

marks that are at risk of genericism, if they have not already succumbed, include "Band-Aid," "Q-tip," "Kleenex," and "PowerPoint."

The question of whether a mark is, or has become, generic is a question of fact.[284] A mark may become generic in one market but retain its distinctiveness in others. In such cases, courts have held that the mark retains its trademark status only in those markets where it is still distinctive of the trademark owner's goods or services.[285]

As discussed in §§ 2.09 [B][5][a] and 2.12 [A] below, a generic mark cannot be federally registered, and if a mark becomes generic after it has been registered, its registration can be cancelled.

[B] Personal Names

An individual's name can serve as a trademark. However, because a personal name is not considered to be inherently distinctive, a mark consisting of a personal name is generally treated as a descriptive mark that can be protected only upon a showing of secondary meaning.[286] Nonetheless, personal names frequently serve as trademarks, and can be very strong ones at that. The "McDonald's" mark for fast food restaurants exemplifies a personal name mark with extremely strong secondary meaning. Other examples are "Gallo" for wine, "Avery Dennison" for office products, "Howard Johnson" for restaurants and hotels, "Bacardi" for rum, "Liz Claiborne" and "Levi Strauss" for clothing, and "Sardi's" and "Wolfgang Puck" for restaurants.

For a personal name to serve as a mark, it must be associated with the offering of goods or services to the public (and not perceived simply as the identity of an individual), and it must have secondary meaning. For a personal name to have secondary meaning, it is not enough that the public perceives the product or service as emanating from a person that has that particular name; the public must have the impression that this product or service comes from the same source whenever it is offered under that name.[287] Thus, for example, even though the name "McDonald's" is a very common surname, the public perceives the name "McDonald's" on a fast-food restaurant as an indicator that this restaurant is affiliated with all of the other McDonald's fast-food restaurants, and not as an indicator that one of the many people having the surname McDonald happens to own this particular restaurant. This particular mark is so strong that the public barely perceives it as a personal name at all; thus, its

---

[284] Bath & Body Works, Inc. v. Luzier Personalized Cosmetics, Inc., 76 F.3d 743, 748 (6th Cir. 1996).

[285] *Abercrombie & Fitch*, 537 F.2d at 10.

[286] *See, e.g.*, E. & J. Gallo Winery v. Gallo Cattle Co., 967 F.2d 1280, 1288 (9th Cir. 1992); Marker Int'l v. DeBruler, 844 F.2d 763 (10th Cir. 1988); Buscemi's, Inc. v. Anthony Buscemi Delicatessen, 96 Mich. App. 2d 714, 717-18 (Mich. Ct. App. 1980). *But see* Peaceable Planet, Inc. v. Ty, Inc., 362 F.3d 986, 988-90 (7th Cir. 2004) (rejecting characterization of personal names as descriptive marks).

[287] *See, e.g.*, Lewis v. Marriott Int'l, Inc., 527 F. Supp. 2d 422, 426-27 (E.D. Pa. 2007) (noting that "a personal name acquires secondary meaning as a mark when the name and the business become synonymous in the public mind") (quoting Tillery v. Leonard & Sciolla, LLP, 437 F. Supp. 2d 312, 321 (E.D. Pa. 2006) (internal quotations omitted).

source-indication function has overtaken its personal identification function, which is the essence of secondary meaning.

Individual entertainers and musical groups who establish secondary meaning for their names (including real names, nicknames, and stage names) are entitled to register them as service marks (and also as trademarks, if they engage in merchandising).[288] Thus, for example, the public's ability to recognize such names as Madonna, Britney Spears, Lindsay Lohan, and the Rolling Stones as sources of entertainment services qualifies those names for registration on the Principal Register. For a musician or musical group to register a name as a mark in the category of sound recordings, the PTO requires the applicant to show that the name has been used on more than one recording, so that it signifies to the public that the entertainer is the source of any recordings that bear his or her name.[289] A similar rule requires authors to use their names on multiple works of authorship in order to qualify for registration.[290] Professional athletes may also be able to show sufficient secondary meaning to obtain registration, although their registrations are most often for merchandise. For example, both Tiger Woods and Michael Jordan have registrations covering a variety of merchandise. Drawing a rather formalistic distinction, the PTO has sometimes rejected applications to register the names of well-known athletes as service marks on the rationale that the name merely identifies the athlete rather than indicating the source of the athlete's services.[291] Other athletes, however, have succeeded in obtaining service mark registrations; for example, TIGER WOODS is a registered service mark for "entertainment in the nature of competitions in the field of golf" and for "entertainment services, namely, personal appearances by a sports celebrity."[292]

In some cases, a mark may have two meanings, only one of which is a personal name.[293] For federal registration purposes, the "primary" significance of the mark will be determinative,[294] and there is authority, albeit limited, for applying the same test under the common law.[295]

At one time courts recognized a virtually absolute right to use one's own name as a trademark.[296] Today, however, most courts hold that the ordinary

---

[288] See, e.g., In re Carson, 197 U.S.P.Q. (BNA) 554 (T.T.A.B. 1977).

[289] Trademark Manual of Examining Procedure (TMEP) § 1202.09(a).

[290] Id. § 1301.02(b).

[291] See, e.g., In re Mancino, 219 U.S.P.Q. (BNA) 1047 (T.T.A.B. 1983); In re Lee Trevino Enters., 182 U.S.P.Q. (BNA) 253 (T.T.A.B. 1974).

[292] Reg. No. 2,442,618.

[293] Peaceable Planet, Inc., 362 F.3d at 992 (noting that "Niles" for a stuffed camel toy could be perceived as a personal name or as a reference to the Nile River); Lane Capital Mgt., Inc. v. Lane Capital Mgt., Inc., 192 F.3d 337, 346 (2d Cir. 1999) (noting dual meanings of "King" and "Cotton"); In re Nelson Souto Major Piquet, 5 U.S.P.Q.2D (BNA) 1367, 1368 (T.T.A.B. 1987) (dictionary reference to "obscure card game" did not rebut prima facie showing that "N. Piquet" was primarily merely a surname; affirming refusal to register).

[294] In re Hutchinson Tech., Inc., 852 F.2d 552, 554 (Fed. Cir. 1988).

[295] See, e.g., Brody's, Inc. v. Brody Bros., Inc., 308 Pa. Super. 417, 424 (1982) ("names primarily understood to be personal names are inherently distinctive").

[296] Basile, S.p.A. v. Basile, 899 F.2d 35, 39 (D.C. Cir. 1990) (reviewing this history).

rules of trademark priority apply to personal names; thus, there is no absolute right to use one's own name as a trademark, if such use would conflict with another's prior use of that name as a mark in such a way as to cause consumer confusion.[297] Thus, for example, a New York court held that one Findlay brother could be enjoined from using his last name on an art gallery located on the same street as his brother's well-established gallery, without regard for whether his intentions were predatory or bona fide. Noting that the established gallery had developed a particularly strong reputation under the Findlay name, and that the likelihood of confusion was high if both brothers were allowed to operate galleries under the Findlay name, the court determined that the proposed injunction was not overly broad:

> The defendant has the right to use his name. The plaintiff has the right to have the defendant use it in such a way as will not injure his business or mislead the public. Where there is such a conflict of rights, it is the duty of the court so to regulate the use of his name by the defendant that, due protection to the plaintiff being afforded, there will be as little injury to him as possible.[298]

Some courts, however, remain reluctant to enjoin the use of a proprietor's own name to identify the source of his or her goods or services, unless the name was adopted as a mark for the purpose of confusing the public.[299] Thus, where intent to confuse or mislead is absent, an injunction will be "carefully tailored to balance the interest in using one's own name against the interest in avoiding public confusion."[300] Such an injunction may require, for example, that the junior user's name be used in combination with a modifier or disclaimer so that the two marks are distinguishable.[301] In cases involving predatory intent or other equitable considerations, however, more sweeping injunctions are warranted.[302]

For the rules governing federal registration of surnames, see § 2.09 [B][5][e] below. For rules governing the unauthorized use of celebrity names or likenesses, see § 2.07[F] below.

---

[297] *See, e.g.,* John R. Thompson Co. v. Holloway, 366 F.2d 108 (5th Cir. 1966); Little Tavern Shops v. Davis, 116 F.2d 903 (4th Cir. 1941); David B. Findlay, Inc. v. Findlay, 18 N.Y.2d 12, 271 N.Y.S.2d 652 (App. Div. 1966), *cert. denied,* 385 U.S. 930 (1966).

[298] *David B. Findlay,* 18 N.Y.2d at 21.

[299] *See, e.g.,* E. & J. Gallo Winery v. Gallo Cattle Co., 967 F.2d 1280, 1288 (9th Cir. 1992); Brody's, Inc. v. Brody Bros., Inc., 308 Pa. Super. 417, 423-24 (1982); Poloskey v. Pantano, 25 Pa. D. & C.2d 307, 311-12 (1961); Haltom v. Haltom's Jewelers, Inc., 691 S.W.2d 823, 826-27 (Tex. Ct. App. 1985).

[300] *E. & J. Gallo Winery,* 967 F.2d at 1288.

[301] *See, e.g.,* Sardi's Rest. Corp. v. Sardie, 755 F.2d 719, 725 (9th Cir. 1985) (collecting cases). *But see* A.W. Cox Dep't Store Co. v. Cox's, Inc., 159 W. Va. 306, 315-16 (1976) (questioning effectiveness of such "halfway limitations").

[302] *See, e.g.,* Taylor Wine Co. v. Bully Hill Vineyards, Inc., 569 F.2d 731, 735 (2d Cir. 1978) (collecting cases).

[C]   Trade Dress

The term *trade dress* refers to the distinctive features of a product's packaging or the distinctive features of the product configuration itself; it is "the total image of a product and may include features such as size, shape, color or color combinations, texture, graphics, or even particular sales techniques."[303] Services as well as goods may be associated with a distinctive trade dress; for example, the color brown is widely recognized as trade dress used by United Parcel Service (UPS) by virtue of its use on the UPS delivery trucks and uniforms. Although few cases have addressed the question, it appears that the overall appearance of a website may be eligible for trade dress protection as well.[304]

Like other types of trademarks, trade dress is protectible only if it is capable of distinguishing, in the minds of the public, the goods or services of one person from those of another. As the Seventh Circuit has noted:

> [T]he term 'trade dress' refers to the appearance of a product when that appearance is used to identify the producer. To function as an identifier, the appearance must be distinctive by reason of the shape or color or texture or other visible or otherwise palpable feature of the product or its packaging. If it isn't distinctive, it won't be associated in the mind of the consumer with a specific producer.[305]

The appearance of a line of products or its packaging need not be identical in order to receive trade dress protection; it is enough that the design conveys a recognizable and consistent overall look.[306] If the design is not sufficiently consistent, consumers will fail to recognize that the products come from the same source — in other words, the design will be unprotectible due to lack of distinctiveness.

Under federal law, in order for trade dress to qualify for trademark protection, it must be both nonfunctional and distinctive.[307] Thus, a plaintiff seeking trade dress protection under section 43(a) must prove that: (1) the trade dress of the two products is confusingly similar; (2) the features of the trade dress are primarily nonfunctional; and (3) the trade dress is inherently distinctive or has acquired secondary meaning.[308]

Trade dress that is both nonfunctional and distinctive may be registered on the Principal Register if it otherwise satisfies the requirements of section 2 of the

---

[303] Two Pesos, Inc. v. Taco Cabana, Inc. 505 U.S. 763, 765 n. 1 (1992) (quoting John H. Harland Co. v. Clarke Checks, Inc., 711 F.2d 966, 980 (11th Cir. 1983)).

[304] *See, e.g.*, Blue Nile, Inc. v. Ice.com, Inc., 478 F. Supp. 2d 1240, 1246 (W.D. Wash. 2007).

[305] Publications Int'l, Ltd. v. Landoll, Inc., 164 F.3d 337 (7th Cir. 1998), *cert. denied*, 526 U.S. 1088 (1999).

[306] Rose Art Indus., Inc. v. Swanson, 235 F.3d 165, 173 (3d Cir. 2000).

[307] *See, e.g.*, Nora Bevs., Inc. v. Perrier Group of Am., Inc., 164 F.3d 736, 743 (2d Cir. 1998).

[308] Dippin' Dots, Inc. v. Frosty Bites Dist., LLC, 369 F.3d 1197 (11th Cir. 2004), *cert. denied*, 125 S. Ct. 911 (2005).

Lanham Act.[309] Examples of registered trade dress include bottle shapes,[310] the shape of a household cleaner spray pump,[311] various aspects of a maple syrup jug,[312] the pink color of fiberglass insulation,[313] the triangular shape of a chemical cake,[314] the design of a candy bar wrapper,[315] a jewelry design,[316] and the design of a faucet and faucet handles.[317]

Unregistered trade dress may also be protected under section 43(a). However, in this case the party asserting trade dress protection has the additional burden of establishing that the trade dress is nonfunctional.[318] In this respect, federal protection of trade dress differs from federal protection of other types of trademarks.

Federal law treats trade dress differently from other types of trademarks in one other respect. Other trademarks may be protected regardless of whether they are inherently distinctive (arbitrary, fanciful, and suggestive marks) or are descriptive but have acquired distinctiveness through secondary meaning. As discussed below, however, when trade dress takes the form of product configuration (as opposed to product packaging), the Supreme Court has added an additional layer to the distinctiveness requirement.

In *Two Pesos, Inc. v. Taco Cabana, Inc.*,[319] the Supreme Court held that, like other trademarks, inherently distinctive trade dress may be protected under section 43(a) without regard to whether it has acquired secondary meaning; the

---

[309] Wal-Mart Stores, Inc. v. Samara Bros., 529 U.S. 205, 209 (2000) (expressly agreeing with lower courts that have treated trade dress as both registrable under section 2 and protectible under section 43(a)); *see, e.g.*, In re Owens-Corning Fiberglas Corp., 774 F.2d 1116 (Fed. Cir. 1985) (reversing PTO's refusal to register pink color for fiberglass insulation); *see also id.* at 1120 (collecting cases). In the case of trade dress, of course, the functionality bar to registration, as well as the corresponding grounds for cancellation and defense to incontestability, will frequently be implicated. 15 U.S.C. §§ 1052(e)(5), 1064(3), 1115(b)(8); *see, e.g.*, Eco Mfg., LLC v. Honeywell Int'l, Inc., 357 F.3d 649 (7th Cir. 2003) (suggesting that plaintiff's otherwise incontestable registration for round shape of thermostat may be invalid on functionality grounds); Wilhelm Pudenz, GmbH v. Littlefuse, Inc., 177 F.3d 1204 (11th Cir. 1999) (holding that otherwise-incontestable registration for shape of auto fuse may be challenged on functionality grounds); Brunswick Corp. v. British Seagull, 35 F.3d 1527 (Fed. Cir. 1994) (holding that functionality barred registration of the color black for outboard motors). The eligibility rules for federal trademark registration are discussed in § 2.09 *infra*.

[310] Ex parte Haig & Haig, Ltd., 118 U.S.P.Q. (BNA) 229 (Comm'r Pat. 1958) (whiskey bottle); In re Mogen David Wine Corp., 328 F.2d 925 (C.C.P.A. 1964) (wine bottle); In re Days-Ease Home Products Corp., 197 U.S.P.Q. (BNA) 566 (T.T.A.B. 1977) (drain cleaner bottle).

[311] In re Morton-Norwich Products, Inc., 671 F.2d 1332 (C.C.P.A. 1982).

[312] Maple Grove Farms v. Euro-Can Prods., 974 F. Supp. 85 (D. Mass. 1997).

[313] In re Owens-Corning Fiberglas Corp., 774 F.2d 1116 (Fed. Cir. 1985).

[314] In re Minnesota Mining and Mfg. Co., 335 F.2d 836 (C.C.P.A. 1964) (on the Supplemental Register).

[315] In re World's Finest Chocolate, Inc., 474 F.2d 1012 (C.C.P.A. 1973).

[316] In re Penthouse Int'l Ltd., 565 F.2d 679 (C.C.P.A. 1977).

[317] Kohler Co. v. Moen, Inc., 12 F.3d 632 (7th Cir. 1993).

[318] 15 U.S.C. § 43(a)(3). *See Dippin' Dots*, 369 F.3d at 1202 (under section 43(a), plaintiff must establish that product design features are "primarily non-functional").

[319] 505 U.S. 763 (1992). *Two Pesos* involved trade dress protection for the décor of a Mexican-themed restaurant.

Court found nothing in section 43(a) to warrant treating trade dress differently from traditional trademarks in this regard.[320] Just three years later, however, in *Wal-Mart Stores, Inc. v. Samara Brothers., Inc.*,[321] the Court refined its position, drawing a distinction between product *packaging* and product *configuration*, and holding that, as a matter of law, trade dress protection for product configuration may not be obtained on the basis of inherent distinctiveness:

> It seems to us that design, like color, is not inherently distinctive. The attribution of inherent distinctiveness to certain categories of word marks and product packaging derives from the fact that the very purpose of attaching a particular word to a product, or encasing it in a distinctive packaging, is most often to identify the source of the product. Although the words and packaging can serve subsidiary functions — a suggestive word mark (such as "Tide" for laundry detergent), for instance, may invoke positive connotations in the consumer's mind, and a garish form of packaging (such as Tide's squat, brightly decorated plastic bottles for its liquid laundry detergent) may attract an otherwise indifferent consumer's attention on a crowded store shelf — their predominant function remains source identification. Consumers are therefore predisposed to regard those symbols as indication of the producer. . . . In the case of product design, as in the case of color, we think consumer predisposition to equate the feature with the source does not exist. Consumers are aware of the reality that, almost invariably, even the most unusual of product designs — such as a cocktail shaker shaped like a penguin — is intended not to identify the source, but to render the product itself more useful or more appealing.
>
> The fact that product design almost invariably serves purposes other than source identification not only renders inherent distinctiveness problematic; it also renders application of an inherent-distinctiveness principle more harmful to other consumer interests. Consumers should not be deprived of the benefits of competition with regard to the utilitarian and esthetic purposes that product design ordinarily serves by a rule of law that facilitates plausible threats of suit against new entrants based upon alleged inherent distinctiveness. How easy it is to mount a plausible suit depends, of course, upon the clarity of the test for inherent distinctiveness, and where product design is concerned we have little confidence that a reasonably clear test can be devised . . .[322]

Accordingly, as a result of the *Wal-Mart* decision, the party asserting trade dress protection under federal law for an element of its product *design* must establish that the design element has secondary meaning. In contrast, a party may obtain trade dress protection for an element of its product *packaging* on the basis of either inherent or acquired distinctiveness. Thus, as a result of

---

[320] *Id.* at 773-74.

[321] 529 U.S. 205 (2000).

[322] *Id.* at 212-14. The Court added that, assuming the theoretical possibility that some product designs might be inherently source-identifying, protection for such designs would be available through copyright or design patent protection without proof of secondary meaning. *Id.* at 214.

Wal-Mart, the rule of *Two Pesos* now applies only to product packaging, and not to product design. The Court's decision in *Wal-Mart* did not overrule its prior trade dress decisions in either *Two Pesos* or *Qualitex Co. v. Jackson Products, Inc.*; *Two Pesos* did not involve product design,[323] and *Qualitex*, which involved product design, held that color, like a descriptive mark, could be registered as a trademark only upon a showing of secondary meaning.[324]

Because the *Wal-Mart* decision applies specifically to protection of product configuration trade dress under section 43(a), the question arises whether the same rule should apply to federal registration under section 2 — that is, can product configuration trade dress be registered on the basis of inherent distinctiveness, or can it be registered only upon proof of acquired distinctiveness under section 2(f)? The answer, according to the Federal Circuit, is that a showing of acquired distinctiveness is necessary in order to register a product configuration on the Principal Register.[325] The Court's public policy concerns in *Wal-Mart* are equally applicable to registered and unregistered marks. Furthermore, the *Wal-Mart* Court drew support for its analysis from its previous decision in *Qualitex*,[326] where it held that, for purposes of section 43(a) as well as section 32, color can never be inherently distinctive.

In contrast, because the Supreme Court recognized in *Two Pesos* that product packaging (as opposed to product configuration) can be inherently distinctive, an applicant can register product packaging on the Principal Register without a showing of secondary meaning if the packaging is arbitrary, fanciful, or suggestive. However, if the packaging is not inherently distinctive, the applicant will need to establish secondary meaning as required by section 2(f).

Even if the individual elements of a party's trade dress are not themselves inherently distinctive, it is possible that inherent distinctiveness may exist in the particular combination of those elements:

> Trade dresses often utilize commonly used lettering styles, geometric shapes, or colors, or incorporate descriptive elements, such as an illustration of the sun on a bottle of suntan lotion. While each of these elements individually would not be inherently distinctive, it is the combination of elements and the total impression that the dress gives to the observer that should be the focus of a court's analysis of distinctiveness. If the overall dress is arbitrary, fanciful, or suggestive, it is inherently distinctive despite its incorporation of generic or descriptive elements. One could no more deny protection to a trade dress for using commonly used elements than one could deny protection to a trademark because it consisted of a combination of commonly used letters of the alphabet.[327]

---

[323] The *Wal-Mart* opinion distinguishes the restaurant décor in *Two Pesos* as "either product packaging . . . or else some *tertium quid* that is akin to product packaging." 529 U.S. at 215.

[324] 514 U.S. 159, 162-63 (1995). For further discussions of Qualitex, see § 2.03 *supra* (addressing functionality), and §2.07 [D] *infra* (addressing color as trademark).

[325] *In re Slokevage*, 441 F.3d 957, 961 (Fed. Cir. 2006).

[326] 514 U.S. at 162-63.

[327] Paddington Corp. v. Attiki Imp. & Distrib., Inc., 996 F.2d 577, 584 (2d Cir. 1993).

[D]   Color, Sound, Scent

Under federal law, the types of devices capable of serving as trademarks may include color alone (for example, the color of the product's packaging, or even the color of the product itself), sound (a melody or even a single sound), scent, and virtually anything else that is nonfunctional and capable of indicating the source of goods or services.

Prior to 1995, the federal courts had split on the question of whether color alone could serve as a trademark.[328] The Supreme Court resolved the split in *Qualitex Co. v. Jacobson Prods. Co.*,[329] in which it held that no per se rule precluded the federal registration of a trademark consisting of color. *Qualitex* rejected arguments that allowing registration of a trademark in color alone would deplete the number of colors available to competitors, that it would lead to confusion where competitors used slightly different shades, and that color trademarks already had sufficient federal protection under section 43(a).[330] The Court held that, while color alone cannot be inherently distinctive, it can serve as a trademark if it is nonfunctional and acquires secondary meaning.[331]

Sound and scent, like color, are not likely to be inherently distinctive, because typically they are not immediately recognizable as source identifiers, but they are capable of serving as trademarks if they are non-functional and acquire secondary meaning.[332] Thus, for example, fragrance cannot serve as a trademark for food, soap or perfume, because in those contexts it would be functional, but it can serve as a trademark for thread.[333] And fans of the television series *Law and Order: SVU* have come to recognize the "doink-doink" sound as a trademark for that series; the mark's secondary meaning was further strengthened through a series of commercials featuring this sound.

For trade dress to be protectible, it must also be consistent — that is, the trade dress as used on one item offered by the merchant must be similar to the trade dress as used on other items offered by that merchant.[334] Trade dress protection does not apply to a "generalized type of appearance."[335] Too much

---

[328] *Compare* NutraSweet Co. v. Stadt Corp., 917 F.2d 1024, 1028 (8th Cir. 1990) (absolute prohibition against protection of color alone), *cert. denied*, 499 U.S. 983 (1991), *with* In re Owens-Corning Fiberglas Corp., 774 F.2d 1116, 1128 (Fed. Cir. 1985) (allowing registration of color pink for fiberglass insulation), *and* Master Distributors, Inc. v. Pako Corp., 986 F.2d 219, 224 (8th Cir. 1993) (declining to establish per se prohibition against protecting color alone as a trademark).

[329] 514 U.S. 159 (1995).

[330] *Id.* at 166-72.

[331] *Id.* at 163-65.

[332] *See. e.g.*, In re Vertex Group LLC, 89 U.S.P.Q.2d (BNA) 1694 (T.T.A.B. 2009).

[333] In re Clarke, 17 U.S.P.Q.2d 1238 (T.T.A.B. 1990).

[334] *See, e.g.*, Maharishi Hardy Blechman Ltd. v. Abercrombie & Fitch Co., 292 F. Supp. 2d 535, 549-550 & n.12 (S.D.N.Y. 2003) (eliminating variations in the styling of merchant's pants left only the unprotectible elements of "roll-up pants with elasticized cinch devices"); Walt Disney Co. v. Goodtimes Home Video Corp., 830 F. Supp. 762, 766-68 (S.D.N.Y. 1993) (denying trade dress protection where overall look of video packaging was inconsistent).

[335] Jeffrey Milstein, Inc. v. Gregor, Lawlor, Roth, Inc., 58 F.3d 27, 32 (2d Cir. 1995).

variation in the putative trade dress undermines the argument that the public recognizes it as a distinctive origin identifier.

When considering whether trade dress is distinctive and nonfunctional, and thus protectible as a trademark, courts emphasize that the trade dress must be considered as a whole; thus, while individual elements may be functional or nondistinctive, the overall trade dress may still be protectible if the particular combination of those elements is nonfunctional and distinctive.[336]

[E] Artistic, Musical, and Other Expressive Works

Works of artistic[337] or musical[338] expression may qualify for common law and federal trademark protection if they acquire distinctiveness. Both artistic designs and musical "jingles" are common types of trademarks. Slogans and catch-phrases, which are also types of expressive works, are widely recognized as trademarks under common law and the Lanham Act. Even the design of a building can qualify as a trademark, if the specific images (drawings, photographs, or other renderings) that are used to indicate the source of goods or services are sufficiently consistent to create a "consistent and distinct commercial impression."[339]

However, the application of trademark concepts to expressive works becomes problematic when the expressive work functions as both the product and the source indicator.

To begin with, classifying such an expressive work along the spectrum of distinctiveness can be difficult. For example, in *Foxworthy v. Custom Tees, Inc.*,[340] a federal district court held that section 43(a) protected the phrase "You might be a redneck . . . ," where comedian Jeff Foxworthy had become well-known for using this phrase in his jokes about rural southerners. Rather than treating this mark as descriptive, and therefore protectible only upon a showing of secondary meaning, the court characterized Foxworthy's catchphrase as a suggestive mark. A strong argument can be made, however, that the phrase is descriptive, because it is a substantial ingredient of Foxworthy's redneck jokes; it is impossible to tell one of those jokes without using the phrase, or some close variation of it.

Second, the expressive work can function as a trademark only with respect to goods or services other than the expressive work itself. For example, where an advertising agency invented a slogan for a client, the agency had no trademark rights in the slogan; only the client that actually used the slogan in connection with goods or services could assert trademark rights.[341]

---

[336] *See, e.g., id.*

[337] *E.g.*, In re Swift & Co., 223 F.2d 950 (C.C.P.A. 1955).

[338] *E.g.*, Oliveira v. Frito-Lay, Inc., 251 F.3d 56 (2d Cir. 2001).

[339] Rock & Roll Hall of Fame & Museum, Inc. v. Gentile Prods., 134 F.3d 749, 755 (6th Cir. 1988).

[340] 879 F. Supp. 1200 (N.D. Ga. 1995).

[341] American Express Co. v. Goetz, 515 F.3d 156, 159-60 (2d Cir. 2008).

An even greater problem, however, is the potential for conflict between trademark protection and other forms of intellectual property protection for expressive works. Although copyright and trademark protection (as well as design patent protection) are not mutually exclusive, special problems may arise when a claim for trademark protection appears to conflict with the overall scheme of federal copyright law.

For example, in *Hartford House, Ltd. v. Hallmark Cards, Inc.*,[342] the Tenth Circuit upheld a preliminary injunction that barred the defendant from producing a line of greeting cards similar in style and subject matter to the plaintiff's cards, on the ground that the overall appearance of the plaintiff's cards was nonfunctional, distinctive, and thus protectible as trade dress under section 43(a), and that the defendant's close imitation of plaintiff's cards was likely to cause confusion. In *Romm Art Creations, Ltd. v. Simcha Int'l, Inc.*,[343] the plaintiff brought trade dress claims under New York law and section 43(a) of the Lanham Act, alleging that the defendant's art posters unlawfully imitated the distinctive style and subject matter of the plaintiff's art posters. Relying in part on *Hartford House*, the district court found that the artistic style of the plaintiff's posters was nonfunctional and inherently distinctive ("arbitrary or fanciful"), and granted a preliminary injunction upon finding a likelihood of confusion.

In contrast, *Leigh v. Warner Bros., Inc.*[344] rejected a section 43(a) claim by a photographer who alleged that the defendant had closely imitated the subject matter and style of a photograph he had produced for the cover of a successful book. Treating this as a trade dress claim, the court held that the style and subject matter of the photograph did not function as a trademark for the plaintiff's goods or services:

> In applying these rules to pictures or artwork, one must be careful to avoid confusing use of the work to identify the artist with use of the work to identify the source of goods or services. "In determining the existence of trademark rights in a picture, the focus is on whether that picture serves to identify the source of goods and services in connection with which the picture is used. The identity of the designer or artist who created the image is irrelevant unless that person is identified as the source of the product or service sold under the trademark image." Thus, it follows that if a picture or work of art merely identifies the artist rather than any products or services, it cannot be protected as a trademark. This rule applies even if the work is an example of an artist's unique artistic style. Style is a matter more properly protected by copyright law.[345]

---

[342] 846 F.2d 1268, 1274 (10th Cir.), *cert. denied*, 488 U.S. 908 (1988).

[343] 786 F. Supp. 1126 (E.D.N.Y. 1992).

[344] 10 F. Supp. 2d 1371 (S.D. Ga. 1998), *aff'd in relevant part*, 212 F.3d 1210, 1218 (11th Cir. 2000).

[345] *Id.* at 1381 (citations omitted) (*quoting* MCCARTHY ON TRADEMARKS at § 3:4 (4th ed. 1998)).

The court rejected the *Romm Art* analysis as "contrary to the basic tenets of trademark law."[346] The Eleventh Circuit affirmed, noting that the plaintiff's photograph "strikes us not as a separate and distinct mark *on the good*, but, rather, as the good itself."[347] Other courts have applied a similar analysis in rejecting trademark claims that are based on copying or imitation of works of art.[348]

Romm Art's analysis is indeed questionable, as it provides an alternative form of copyright protection for the uncopyrightable elements (style and general subject matter) of an expressive work. First, the state law claims arguably should have been treated as preempted by federal copyright law. Second, the Lanham Act claims would be unlikely to succeed today, in light of the Supreme Court's holding in *Dastar Corp. v. Twentieth Century Fox Film Corp.*[349] that, for purposes of section 43(a), the "origin" of goods and services does not refer to their artistic or intellectual origin, but only to their physical origin. Finally, the doctrine of aesthetic functionality might be applied to the facts of *Hartford House*, *Romm Art*, and *Leigh*, to bar trade dress protection for the artistic features of an artistic product, regardless of the distinctiveness of those features.

Another potential conflict with copyright law arises when a party seeks trademark protection for an expressive work after the copyright in that work has expired. An expressive work passes into the public domain when its copyright expires. Recognizing trademark rights in such a work would arguably limit the ability of the public to copy that work freely. This conflict can be resolved, however, by allowing the expressive work to function as a trademark only for goods or services other than the expressive work itself. This would place the public domain expressive work in the same position as any public domain symbol, work, or device that is available for adoption as a trademark. In *Fredrick Warne & Co. v. Book Sales, Inc.*,[350] a publisher asserted trademark rights under sections 32 and 43(a) of the Lanham Act in several of the illustrations that had appeared in Beatrix Potter's "Peter Rabbit" series, which had originally been published by the plaintiff but were no longer protected by copyright. The defendant had reproduced those illustrations in a new volume containing the public domain stories. The court held that the plaintiff would have to prove that the illustrations had secondary meaning that caused the public to associate them with the publisher: "[I]t would not be enough that the illustrations in question have come to signify Beatrix Potter as author of the books; plaintiff must show that they have come to represent its goodwill and reputation as Publisher of

---

[346] *Id.*

[347] 212 F.3d 1210, 1218 (11th Cir. 2000) (quoting Rock & Roll Hall of Fame & Museum, Inc. v. Gentile Prods., 134 F.3d 749, 754 (6th Cir. 1998)).

[348] *See, e.g.*, Hughes v. Design Look Inc., 693 F. Supp. 1500, 1505 (S.D.N.Y. 1988) (holding estate of Andy Warhol had no trademark rights in Warhol paintings that were copied and included in defendant's calendar as they were never used by artist to identify source of goods or services); Galerie Furstenberg v. Coffaro, 697 F. Supp. 1282, 1290 (S.D.N.Y. 1988) (holding unique artistic style of Salvador Dali is not protected by trademark law; rather any protection available is through copyright law).

[349] 539 U.S. 23 (2003).

[350] 481 F. Supp. 1191 (S.D.N.Y. 1979).

those books."[351] The court rejected the defendant's argument that the expiration of the copyright prevented the publisher from claiming a trademark right in the illustrations: "[T]he proper factual inquiry in this case is not whether the cover illustrations were once copyrightable and have fallen into the public domain, but whether they have acquired secondary meaning, identifying Warne as the publisher or sponsor of goods bearing those illustrations, and if so, whether defendant's use of these illustrations in 'packaging' or 'dressing' its editions is likely to cause confusion."[352]

[F]   Celebrity Likenesses and Fictional Characters

Most courts hold that the name or likeness of a celebrity can function as a trademark only if it is used to identify the source of particular goods or services (and, in the case of a likeness, only if the same image is consistently used as the source indicator, so as to create a continuing and distinct commercial impression[353]).[354] However, courts have also used a "false endorsement theory under section 43(a) to extend federal protection to a celebrity's name, nickname, physical likeness, voice, and other identifying characteristics.[355] Such cases often combine section 43(a) claims or state law unfair competition claims with claims arising under a state law "right of publicity" doctrine, which provides an individual with a cause of action against unauthorized commercial uses of his or her name or likeness. Although the right of publicity doctrine varies considerably among the different states where it is recognized, right of publicity claims typically differ from state or federal trademark and unfair competition claims in that they do not require the plaintiff to establish that the defendant's use creates a likelihood of confusion. In addition, some states limit or prohibit the post-mortem assertion of a right of publicity, whereas a section 43(a) false endorsement claim or common law unfair competition claim may be asserted by any party that owns the goodwill associated with the deceased celebrity's identity.

Courts have also extended section 43(a) and state unfair competition laws to the names, images, or characteristics of fictional characters,[356] although not to the copyrighted materials embodying them. For example, in *Comedy III Prods.,*

---

[351] *Id.* at 1195.

[352] *Id.* at 1198.

[353] *See, e.g.,* Pirone v. MacMillan, Inc., 894 F.2d 579, 583 (2d Cir. 1990); Estate of Presley v. Russen, 513 F. Supp. 1339, 1363-64 (D.N.J. 1981).

[354] *See* ETW Corp. v. Jireh Pub., Inc., 332 F.3d 915, 922-23 (6th Cir. 2003) (collecting cases).

[355] *See, e.g.,* Wendt v. Host Int'l, Inc., 125 F.3d 806 (9th Cir. 1997) (celebrities' distinctive characteristics embodied by animatronic robots); White v. Samsung Elecs. America, Inc., 971 F.2d 1395 (9th Cir. 1992) (celebrity's likeness embodied by a robot); Waits v. Frito-Lay, Inc., 978 F.2d 1093 (9th Cir. 1992) (imitation of celebrity's distinctive voice); Allen v. National Video, Inc., 610 F. Supp. 612 (S.D.N.Y. 1985) (celebrity impersonator resembling plaintiff used in advertisement for video rental store).

[356] *See, e.g.,* Edgar Rice Burroughs, Inc. v. Manns Theatres, 195 U.S.P.Q. (BNA) 159 (C.D. Cal. 1976) (finding likelihood of confusion and dilution arising from defendant's unauthorized use of name of plaintiff's "Tarzan" character in title of X-rated film).

Inc. v. New Line Cinema,[357] the Ninth Circuit rejected a section 43(a) claim arising from the defendant's incorporation of a public domain "Three Stooges" film clip into another film. The defendant asserted a trademark right in the name, characters, likenesses, and overall "act" of the Three Stooges. However, the court found that the film clip was incapable of serving as a trademark, regardless of secondary meaning. Allowing trademark protection of the clip would allow the plaintiff to avoid the limitations of copyright law: "If material covered by copyright law has passed into the public domain, it cannot then be protected by the Lanham Act without rendering the Copyright Act a nullity."[358] The court distinguished cases extending section 43(a) to celebrity likenesses, noting that those cases recognized trademark rights in the likenesses, rather than in the copyrightable materials embodying those likenesses. The court added: "Had New Line used the likeness of The Three Stooges on t-shirts which it was selling, Comedy III might have an arguable claim for trademark violation."[359]

The names and likenesses of real people or fictional characters can also become federally registered trademarks if the requirements for federal registration are otherwise satisfied. (The eligibility rules for federal trademark registration are discussed in § 2.09 below.)

[G] Titles of Expressive Works

The titles of literary or artistic works present a special problem in descriptive trademarks. It is clear that the title of a *series* of such works (such as the name of a newspaper, periodical, or a series of books or films) can enjoy trademark protection, including federal registration, if it acquires secondary meaning — that is, if the public perceives the name of the series as an indication that each work in the series comes from the same source as the others."[360]

However, with respect to the titles of individual works, the standards for federal registration diverge from the standards for providing protection under the common law and section 43(a) of the Lanham Act. Federal registration is not permitted for the title of a single work.[361] Such a title is considered merely descriptive: "Each literary title is regarded as a designation used to describe the literary work itself, rather than a trademark used to identify and distinguish the literary work of one source from that of another."[362] In contrast, courts have held that the titles of individual works can be protected as common law marks under section 43(a) of the Lanham Act if they acquire secondary meaning.[363]

---

[357] 200 F.3d 593, 595 (9th Cir. 2000).

[358] *Id.* (citing Smith v. Chanel, Inc., 402 F.2d 562, 565 (9th Cir. 1968)).

[359] *Id.* at 596.

[360] In re Cooper, 254 F.2d 611, 615 (C.C.P.A. 1958); *accord,* In re Scholastic, 23 U.S.P.Q.2d (BNA) 1774, 1779 (T.T.A.B. 1992).

[361] Herbko Int'l, Inc. v. Kappa Books, Inc., 308 F.3d 1156, 1162-63 (Fed. Cir. 2002); TMEP § 1202.08 (applying this prohibition to both the Principal and Supplemental Registers).

[362] *Scholastic,* 23 U.S.P.Q.2d (BNA) at 1779.

[363] *Herbko Int'l, Inc.,* 308 F.3d at 1162 n.2; *see, e.g.,* Estate of Jenkins v. Paramount Pictures Corp., 90 F. Supp. 2d 706, 709-11 (E.D. Va. 2000), *aff'd sub nom.,* Evans v. Paramount Pictures Corp.,

[H]   Numbers and Alphanumeric Combinations

Numbers and alphanumeric combinations can serve as trademarks under common law as well as federal law, if they have inherent or acquired distinctiveness. The "501" mark for Levi's jeans, for example, is a federally registered mark.[364] In some cases, numeric or alphanumeric marks are arbitrary, in which case no secondary meaning is required.[365] In other cases, however, the mark may have originated as a model number or part number, in which case trademark protection is available only if and when the mark acquires secondary meaning.[366]

[I]   Foreign Words

When the mark for which protection is sought consists of a word or phrase in a language other than English, in some cases the English translation will determine whether the word or phrase qualifies for trademark protection. Under the "doctrine of foreign equivalents," if the foreign word in question is from a relatively common language, its English translation will be used to determine genericness, descriptiveness, as well as similarity of connotation in order to assess whether it is confusingly similar to English-language word marks already in use.[367] However, if it is unlikely that "the average American purchaser" will translate the foreign mark, then the doctrine will be withheld.[368]

---

248 F.3d 1134, *reported in full at* 7 Fed. Appx. 270 (4th Cir. 2001); Simon & Schuster v. Dove Audio, 936 F. Supp. 156, 163 (S.D.N.Y. 1996); Tri-Star Pictures, Inc. v. Leisure Time Prods., B.V., 749 F. Supp. 1243 (S.D.N.Y. 1990); Orion Pictures Co. v. Dell Pub. Co., 471 F. Supp. 392, 395 (S.D.N.Y. 1979).

[364] Reg. No. 1,552,985.

[365] Eastman Kodak Co. v. Bell & Howell Document Mgt. Prods. Co., 994 F.2d 1569, 1576 (Fed. Cir. 1993) (holding that alphanumeric designation can be inherently distinctive).

[366] Ideal Indus., Inc. v. Gardner Bender, Inc., 612 F.2d 1018 (7th Cir. 1980) (recognizing that alphanumeric model numbers such as "71B," which originally designated sizes of plaintiff's electrical connectors, had acquired secondary meaning, and therefore warranted trademark protection), *cert. denied*, 447 U.S. 924 (1980); Arrow Fastener Co. v. Stanley Works, 59 F.3d 384, 392-93 (2d Cir. 1995) (finding that model number "T-50" was descriptive but had acquired secondary meaning).

[367] Palm Bay Imps., Inc. v. Veuve Clicquot Ponsardin Maison Fondee En 1772, 396 F.3d 1369, 1377 (Fed. Cir. 2005); *see, e.g.*, Otokoyama Co. v. Wine of Japan Import, Inc., 175 F.3d 266 (2d Cir. 1999) (district court erred in upholding registration of "otokoyama" mark without considering evidence that it was generic for a type of sake); In re Sarkli, Ltd., 721 F.2d 353 (Fed. Cir. 1983) (finding no likelihood of confusion between REPECHAGE and SECOND CHANCE marks, because the latter is not the English equivalent); Blue & White Food Prods. Corp. v. Shamir Food Indus., Ltd., 350 F. Supp. 2d 514 (S.D.N.Y. 2004) (registration of "Shamir" was not invalid due to genericness even though mark translates as "dill," because it was applied to food products not containing dill); *Popular Bank*, 9 F. Supp. 2d at 1359 (applying both Florida law and the Lanham Act, and finding likelihood of confusion between "Banco Popular" and "Popular Bank" due to the large Spanish-speaking population in the area where the banks conducted business); In re Am. Safety Razor Co., 2 U.S.P.Q.2d (BNA) 1459, 1460, 1987 TTAB LEXIS 95 (T.T.A.B. 1987) (finding BUENOS DIAS for soap confusingly similar to GOOD MORNING for shaving cream).

[368] *Palm Bay Imps.*, 396 F.3d at 1377 (finding it unlikely that average American will translate "Veuve" mark as "Widow"); *see also* In re Tia Maria, Inc., 188 U.S.P.Q. (BNA) 524 (T.T.A.B. 1975) (finding no likelihood of confusion between "Tia Maria" mark for restaurant and "Aunt Mary" mark for canned vegetables, because it was unlikely that average American would translate "Tia Maria" as "Aunt Mary").

The translation need not be literal; idiomatic uses are sufficient.[369] Courts treat the doctrine of foreign equivalents not as an absolute rule, but merely as a guideline, based on assessing the likelihood that the "average American" would translate the mark.[370]

The doctrine of foreign equivalents is based on the assumption that "there are (or someday will be) customers in the U.S. who speak that foreign language;" accordingly, the doctrine is generally withheld when the foreign language is an obscure, obsolete, or "dead" language.[371] A second policy justification is international comity; the United States opposes foreign trademark protection of generic English words, and therefore refuses to protect generic foreign words.[372]

In practice, the doctrine of foreign equivalents has been applied somewhat differently in the context of federal registration than it has in the context of protecting unregistered marks. Registration has been refused solely on the basis that a foreign word mark and an English-language word mark have the same meaning, even if the two marks are not similar in sight or sound.[373] In contrast, in determining whether an unregistered mark warrants protection under state law or section 43(a), most courts have treated similarity of meaning as just one part of a three-part test, which considers sight, sound, and meaning. Thus, although the English translation of the mark is considered relevant to determining similarity of meaning, most courts will consider the foreign word itself (untranslated) in determining similarity of sight and sound.[374] In contrast, courts will consider the meaning alone when assessing whether the foreign mark is generic or descriptive.[375] Although the translated meaning is certainly sufficient to determine genericness or descriptiveness, it is a more difficult question whether meaning alone should be sufficient to determine confusing

---

[369] Enrique Bernat F., S.A. v. Guadalajara, 210 F.3d 439, 443-45 (5th Cir. 2000) (collecting cases).

[370] *Palm Bay Imps.*, 396 F.3d at 1377.

[371] *Enrique Bernat*, 210 F.3d at 443 (quoting Otokoyama Co. Ltd. v. Wine of Japan Import, Inc., 175 F.3d 266, 270 (2d Cir. 1999)).

[372] *Id.* at 445.

[373] *See, e.g.*, Weiss Noodle Co. v. Golden Cracknel & Specialty Co., 290 F.2d 845 (C.C.P.A. 1961) (cancelling HA-LUSH-KA mark for noodles because it was phonetic equivalent in English of Hungarian name for noodles); In re La Peregrina Ltd., 86 U.S.P.Q.2d (BNA) 1645 (T.T.A.B. 2008) (finding LA PEREGRINA confusingly similar to PILGRIM based on similarity of meaning, despite differences in appearance and pronunciation); In re Am. Safety Razor Co., 2 U.S.P.Q.2d (BNA) 1459, 1460, 1987 TTAB LEXIS 95 (T.T.A.B. 1987) (finding BUENOS DIAS for soap confusingly similar to GOOD MORNING for shaving cream); Ex parte Odol-Werke Wien Gesellschaft M.B.H., 111 U.S.P.Q.(BNA) 286 (Com'r Patents & Trademarks 1956) (finding confusing similarity between CHAT NOIR and BLACK CAT based on meaning alone); *see also* In re Sarkli, Ltd., 721 F.2d 353, 355 (Fed. Cir. 1983) (noting that "the PTO may reject an application ex parte solely because of similarity in meaning of the mark sought to be registered with a previously registered mark").

[374] *See, e.g.*, Horn's, Inc. v. Sanofi Beaute, Inc., 963 F. Supp. 318, 323 (S.D.N.Y. 1997) (although DECI DELA mark was identical in meaning to HERE AND THERE mark, differences in sight and sound outweighed similarity of meaning); *Popular Bank*, 9 F. Supp. 2d at 1359 (applying similar analysis under Florida law and Lanham Act).

[375] *See, e.g., Enrique Bernat*, 210 F.3d at 445 ("chupa" trademark for lollipops was generic and its registration was therefore invalid).

similarity, either in the context of common law protection or in the context of federal registration.

[J]   Abbreviations of Generic or Descriptive Terms

Courts have not reached a consensus on whether and under what circumstances trademark protection can extend to abbreviations of words or phrases that are themselves either generic or merely descriptive. In the context of federal registration, the CCPA and the TTAB have taken a liberal view, permitting such abbreviations to be registered "unless they have become so generally understood as representing descriptive words as to be accepted as substantially synonymous therewith."[376] In contrast, the Seventh Circuit imposes a "heavy burden" on the trademark proponent to establish that the abbreviation has a meaning distinct from the underlying unprotectable expression.[377] Several courts have suggested that *all* abbreviations of descriptive phrases are inherently descriptive.[378] Others have held that such abbreviations can acquire secondary meaning,[379] and still others have held that they can be suggestive,[380] arbitrary, or fanciful.[381]

PART IV:
FEDERAL TRADEMARK REGISTRATION

§ 2.08   BENEFITS OF FEDERAL REGISTRATION

Although federal registration is not a prerequisite to protecting a trademark under section 43 of the Lanham Act or under state law, registration does confer significant benefits.

First, under sections 7(b) and 33(a), registration on the Principal Register is prima facie evidence that the mark in question is valid and owned by the registrant, and that the latter has the exclusive right to use the mark in commerce on or in connection with the goods or services for which it is registered, subject to any conditions or limitations stated in the registration.[382] Thus, in an action for infringement, the registered mark will be presumed valid for the goods or services for which it is registered, and the registrant need not affirmatively prove validity in order to make out a prima facie case of infringe-

---

[376] Modern Optics v. Univis Lens Co., 234 F.2d 504, 506 (C.C.P.A. 1956); *accord*, Racine Indus., Inc. v. Bane-Clene Corp., 35 U.S.P.Q.2d (BNA) 1832 (T.T.A.B. 1995).

[377] G. Heileman Brewing Co. v. Anheuser-Busch, Inc., 873 F.2d 985, 994 (7th Cir. 1989).

[378] CPP Ins. Agency, Inc. v. General Motors Corp., 212 U.S.P.Q. (BNA) 257 (C.D. Cal. 1980), *aff'd without op.*, 676 F.2d 709 (9th Cir. 1982); U.S. Conference of Catholic Bishops v. Media Research Center, 432 F. Supp. 2d 616, 624 (E.D. Va. 2006).

[379] Welding Services, Inc. v. Forman, 509 F.3d 1351, 1359 (11th Cir. 2007).

[380] Anheuser-Busch, Inc. v. Stroh Brewery Co., 750 F.2d 631, 635-36 (8th Cir. 1984).

[381] Grove Labs. v. Brewer & Co., 103 F.2d 175 (1st Cir. 1939) (arbitrary or fanciful).

[382] 15 U.S.C. §§ 1057(b), 1115(a); The Coca-Cola Co. v. Overland, Inc., 692 F.2d 1250, 1254 (9th Cir. 1982).

ment. Instead, the defendant bears the burden of showing that the mark should not have been registered in the first place, or that it was valid when registered but subsequently lost its validity.

Second, section 7(c) provides that, subject to several exceptions, if the application to register a mark on the Principal Register is ultimately successful, then the filing of the application will constitute constructive use of the mark, conferring nationwide priority with respect to the goods or services for which the mark is registered, as of the date on which the application was filed.[383] The exceptions to this rule apply when another party has taken any one of the following actions *prior to* the applicant's filing date: (1) used the mark, (2) filed an application to register the mark, which either is pending or has resulted in registration of the mark, or (3) has filed a foreign application to register the mark on the basis of which that party has acquired a right of priority, and timely files a registration application under 15 U.S.C. § 1126(d), which either is pending or has resulted in registration of the mark. For any of the exceptions to apply, however, the party taking one of these three actions must not have subsequently abandoned the mark.[384]

Third, under section 22, registration on the Principal Register constitutes constructive notice of the registrant's ownership of the mark, thus giving the registrant priority over junior users even in markets where the registrant has not yet used the mark.[385] It also precludes a subsequent user from arguing that it adopted the mark in good faith and without knowledge of the registration.[386] Prior to enactment of the Lanham Act in 1946, there was no constructive notice provision; thus, a party that was the first to use a mark in a particular region could obtain rights in the mark within that region if it adopted the mark without actual notice of an existing registration.[387] However, for post-1989 applications, the constructive notice provision has reduced importance in light of the more powerful use provision in section 7(c).

Fourth, once a mark has been registered on the Principal Register for five years, it can become incontestable,[388] as discussed in § 2.13 below.

Fifth, under section 42, federal registration significantly improves the trademark owner's ability to block the importation of infringing goods.[389]

Finally, in an infringement action, the owner of a mark that is registered on the Principal Register has access to a broader array of remedies under sections

---

[383] 15 U.S.C. § 1057(c).

[384] *Id.* Priority based on foreign applications is discussed at § 2.15 *infra.*

[385] 15 U.S.C. § 1072; Value House v. Phillips Mercantile Co., 523 F.2d 424, 429 (10th Cir. 1975); Old Dutch Foods, Inc. v. Dan Dee Pretzel & Potato Chip Co., 477 F.2d 150 (6th Cir. 1973); John R. Thompson Co. v. Holloway, 366 F.2d 108, 115 (5th Cir. 1966); Dawn Donut Co. v. Hart's Food Stores, Inc., 267 F.2d 358, 362 (2d Cir. 1959).

[386] *Value House*, 523 F.2d at 429.

[387] *Dawn Donut*, 267 F.2d at 362.

[388] 15 U.S.C. § 1065.

[389] 15 U.S.C. § 1124. In addition, only registered marks can be recorded with the U.S. Customs Service, and once the mark is recorded, Customs agents can seize infringing goods under 19 U.S.C. § 1526.

34(d), 35(b), and 35(c) than does the owner of an unregistered mark.[390]

Where a trademark owner brings an infringement action for use of its registered mark on goods or services other than those for which the mark is registered, the advantages of federal registration do not apply, and the mark will be treated as an unregistered mark. The trademark owner's rights and remedies, therefore, will be limited to those available under the applicable state law and section 43(a) of the Lanham Act.[391]

The benefits of federal registration provide trademark owners with an incentive to seek registration rather than rely on protection under state law or section 43(a). Federal registration offers benefits to the public as well as to the registrant:

> [R]egistration of a trademark, in addition to serving the interests of the registrant by providing constructive notice, serves the interests of other participants in the market place. Entrepreneurs, for example, who plan to promote and to sell a new product under a fanciful mark, should be able to rely on a search of the trademark registry and their own knowledge of whether the mark has been used so that what may be substantial expenditures of money promoting the mark will not be wasted. Consumers are also benefited by the registration of national trademarks, because such registration helps to prevent confusion about the source of products sold under a trademark and to instill in consumers the confidence that inferior goods are not being passed off by use of a familiar trademark. In short, therefore, the benefits of prior registration under the Lanham Act are justified in light of the order such registration brings to the market place.[392]

Indeed, one of the major policies underlying the enactment of the Lanham Act "was to encourage the presence on the register of trademarks of as many as possible of the marks in actual use so that they are available for search purposes."[393]

§ 2.09 MARKS ELIGIBLE FOR FEDERAL REGISTRATION

[A]   General Standard

Section 2 of the Lanham Act sets forth the general substantive standards for registering a mark on the Principal Register of the PTO. It is structured, however, as a series of rules specifying which marks will be refused registration. The general standard that precedes the specific bars to registration simply states that "[n]o trademark by which the goods of the applicant may be

---

[390] 15 U.S.C. §§ 1116(d), 1117(b), (c). For more on remedies, see Part VIII *infra.*

[391] Natural Footwear Ltd. v. Hart, Schaffner & Marx, 760 F.2d 1383, 1396-97 (3d Cir. 1985); Universal Nutrition Corp. v. Carbolite Foods, Inc., 325 F. Supp. 2d 526, 532 (D.N.J. 2004).

[392] Natural Footwear Ltd. v. Hart, Schaffner & Marx, 760 F.2d 1383, 1395 (3d Cir. 1984).

[393] Bongrain Int'l Corp. v. Delice de France, Inc., 811 F.2d 1479, 1485 (Fed. Cir. 1987).

distinguished from the goods of others shall be refused registration on the principal register on account of its nature" unless it falls within one of the statutory bars listed in sections 2(a) through (e).[394] Section 3 makes clear that the registration rules of section 2 apply equally to service marks.[395]

To fall within this broad permissive language, however, the applicant's mark must meet the federal definition of a trademark or a service mark. Section 45 defines a "trademark" to include:

any word, name, symbol, or device, or any combination thereof —

(1) used by a person, or

(2) which a person has a bona fide intention to use in commerce and applies to register on the principal register established by this Act

to identify and distinguish his or her goods, including a unique product, from those manufactured or sold by others and to indicate the source of the goods, even if that source is unknown.[396]

A "service mark" is defined as:

any word, name, symbol, or device, or any combination thereof —

(1) used by a person, or

(2) which a person has a bona fide intention to use in commerce and applies to register on the principal register established by this Act,

to identify and distinguish the services of one person, including a unique service, from the services of others and to indicate the source of the services, even if that source is unknown. Titles, character names, and other distinctive features of radio or television programs may be registered as service marks notwithstanding that they, or the programs, may advertise the goods of the sponsor.

A trademark or service mark, therefore, must be used to identify and distinguish goods or services, and to indicate their source. If the applicant's mark does not serve this function, it cannot be registered.[397]

Although this standard appears to be the same as the general standard used to determine whether a mark qualifies for protection under the common law or section 43(a),[398] the PTO in some circumstances interprets this standard more narrowly in the registration context. For example, titles of individual books or movies may not be registered, but have been protected under section 43(a).[399] These differences arise because, to be registered, a mark must be capable of distinguishing specific goods or services that originate from the owner of the

---

[394] 15 U.S.C. § 1052.

[395] *Id.* § 1053.

[396] *Id.* § 1127.

[397] *Id.*

[398] *See* § 2.07 *supra*.

[399] *See* § 2.07 [G] *supra*.

mark. The mark must therefore be used to indicate the origin of specific goods or services rather than merely to identify an individual person, character, or literary/dramatic work.

If an applicant's mark satisfies the federal definition of a trademark or service mark, it must still run the gauntlet of the bars to registration under sections 2(a) through (e). The bars to registration reflect a variety of concerns related to public policy or international law.

Failure of a mark to qualify for registration on the Principal Register does not preclude protection for such marks under section 43(a) of the Lanham Act, or under state common law or statutory law. In addition, some marks that fail to qualify for the Principal Register may obtain a lesser degree of protection by being registered on the Supplemental Register.[400]

[B]   Marks Ineligible for Registration on the Principal Register

If a mark is capable of distinguishing the applicant's goods or services from those of another, the mark may be registered on the Principal Register unless it falls within one of the five categories described in sections 2(a) through (e). With respect to the first four of these categories, sections 2(a) through (d), registration of a mark falling into that category is completely prohibited. With respect to marks that are barred from registration under section 2(e), however, section 2(f) distinguishes between marks that are completely unregistrable and those that may overcome the presumption of unregistrability if they have acquired secondary meaning.

"Composite marks" are marks which consist of several separable components, which may be words, designs, or combinations thereof. When an applicant seeks to register a composite mark that includes some components that are unregistrable, pursuant to section 6 of the Lanham Act the applicant may disclaim, or may be required by the Director of the PTO to disclaim, the portions of the mark that are unregistrable.[401] With respect to the disclaimed portions of the mark, the applicant surrenders any entitlement to exclusivity that would otherwise arise from the fact of registration.[402] The disclaimer, however, does not prejudice the applicant's ability to seek registration of the

---

[400] *See* § 2.14 *infra.*

[401] 15 U.S.C. § 1056 (a); *see, e.g.,* In re Best Software, Inc., 63 U.S.P.Q.2d (BNA) 1109 (T.T.A.B. 2002) (requiring disclaimer of BEST, and acknowledging applicant's voluntary disclaimer of HRMS, in application to register BEST! IMPERATIV HRMS). Sometimes, the registrable and unregistrable components of a composite mark are so interdependent (either graphically or semantically) that the mark is considered "unitary," in which case a disclaimer will not be required. For example, the term BLACK MAGIC would be considered unitary, because the meaning of the two words combined has nothing to do with the color black; thus, although BLACK is a descriptive term it would not have to be disclaimed even if the BLACK MAGIC mark were applied to goods that were black in color. Trademark Manual of Examining Procedure (TMEP) § 1213.05 (5th ed.) (giving additional examples).

[402] United States Steel Corp. v. Vasco Metals Corp., 394 F.2d 1009, 1012 (C.C.P.A. 1968).

disclaimed matter at another time[403] — for example, where the disclaimed matter is descriptive but later acquires secondary meaning. However, a disclaimer may not be used to avoid a rejection based on deceptiveness under section 2(a),[404] or based on a determination that a mark is primarily geographically deceptively misdescriptive under section 2(e)(3).[405] The rationale for these exceptions is that the public that encounters the trademark will be unaware that any portion of it has been disclaimed; thus, permitting registration of a mark that contains a deceptive component would lead to consumer confusion notwithstanding the disclaimer.[406]

There are conflicting authorities on the question of whether an applicant may disclaim each individual component of a composite mark, but still obtain registration for the mark as a whole. For example, registration of the mark MINITMIX was permitted, subject to disclaimers of both MINIT and MIX,[407] but a registration for PILATES STUDIO was cancelled, notwithstanding disclaimers of both PILATES and STUDIO, because "a composite mark cannot be amended to disclaim all portions of the mark individually and remain valid."[408]

Only one mark can be registered in a single application.[409] In *In re International Flavors & Fragrances, Inc.*,[410] the Federal Circuit invoked this rule to bar "phantom" registrations, in which an applicant seeks to register an incomplete mark so that the registered mark can be used in combination with various other terms in order to obtain protection for an open-ended "family" of related marks in a single registration. In that case, the applicant applied for three registrations — for LIVING XXXX FLAVOR, LIVING XXXX FLAVORS, and LIVING XXXX. In each case, XXXX was merely a placeholder for the name of "a specific herb, fruit, plant or vegetable" or "a botanical or extract thereof" that the applicant would later insert for each product marketed under the mark — for example, LIVING GREEN BELL PEPPER FLAVORS,

---

[403] 15 U.S.C. § 1056(b).

[404] American Speech-Language-Hearing Ass'n v. National Hearing Aid Soc'y, 224 U.S.P.Q. (BNA) 798 (T.T.A.B. 1984).

[405] In re Wada, 48 U.S.P.Q.2d (BNA) 1689 (T.T.A.B. 1998) (noting that the NEW YORK WAYS GALLERY mark for goods not originating in New York will have the same effect on consumers regardless of whether NEW YORK is disclaimed in the registration). This aspect of *In re Wada* appears to remain good law despite the Federal Circuit's subsequent reinterpretation of "primarily geographically deceptively misdescriptive marks" in section 2(e)(3) to include only deceptive marks in *In re California Innovations, Inc.*, 329 F.3d 1334 (Fed. Cir. 2003). *See* § 2.09 [B][5][d] *infra.*

[406] *Wada*, 48 U.S.P.Q. 2d (BNA) at 1692 (describing PTO policy as stated in the Official Gazette and § 1210.06 of the Trademark Manual of Examining Procedure (1997)).

[407] Ex Parte Pillsbury Flour Mills Co., 23 U.S.P.Q. (BNA) 168 (Comm'r 1934) (applying pre-Lanham Act PTO policy); *see also United States Steel*, 394 F.2d at 1012 (citing *Pillsbury* with approval, and noting that "it is entirely possible to disclaim all the components of [a design mark] and still have a registrable whole").

[408] Pilates, Inc. v. Georgetown Bodyworks Deep Muscle Massage Ctrs., Inc., 157 F. Supp. 2d 75, 82 (D.D.C. 2001); *see also* In re Midy Labs, 104 F.2d 617, 618 (C.C.P.A. 1939) (applying pre-Lanham Act PTO policy).

[409] In re International Flavors & Fragrances, Inc., 183 F.3d 1361, 1366 (Fed. Cir. 1999).

[410] 183 F.3d 1361 (Fed. Cir. 1999).

LIVING CILANTRO FLAVOR, LIVING FLOWERS, and LIVING MINT. Thus, with only three registrations, the applicant sought to obtain protection for an indefinite array of marks conforming to the patterns specified in the registrations. The Federal Circuit held that these applications were unregistrable, because allowing registrations in this incomplete and indefinite form would make trademark searches too difficult, and would thus fail to provide the public with constructive notice of what was registered.[411]

[1]   Immoral, Deceptive, Scandalous, or Disparaging Matter; False Geographic Indications for Wines and Spirits

Section 2(a) bars registration of a mark that comprises any of the following: (1) immoral, deceptive, or scandalous matter; (2) matter that may disparage, or falsely suggest a connection, with persons (either living or dead), institutions, beliefs, or national symbols, or bring them into "contempt, or disrepute"; or (3) with respect to marks used on or in connection with wines or spirits, a geographical indication that is not the place where the goods originated, but only if such use of the mark by the applicant commenced on or after January 1, 1995 (the effective date of the WTO Agreement in the U.S.).[412]

A mark is immoral or scandalous if "the mark would be offensive to the conscience or moral feelings of a substantial composite of the general public."[413] Whether a particular mark is so immoral or scandalous as to be unregistrable is a somewhat subjective judgment, and changing social and cultural norms may lead to different decisions over time. According to the Federal Circuit,

> In meeting its burden, the PTO must consider the mark in the context of the marketplace as applied to the goods described in the application for registration. In addition, whether the mark consists of or comprises scandalous matter must be determined from the standpoint of a substantial composite of the general public (although not necessarily a majority), and in the context of contemporary attitudes, keeping in mind changes in social mores and sensitivities.[414]

The Federal Circuit has held that a finding that a mark is vulgar is sufficient to establish that it is immoral or scandalous.[415] Although the personal opinion of the examining attorney cannot be the basis for a determination that a mark is scandalous, where the evidence shows that a mark has only one pertinent meaning, the dictionary meaning alone can satisfy the PTO's burden of proof for a section 2(a) refusal, because "dictionary definitions represent an effort to distill

---

[411] *International Flavors*, 183 F.3d at 1368. The court gave this example: "[S]uppose IFF begins using LIVING SPICE FLAVOR. However, since IFF seeks only to register LIVING XXXX FLAVOR, it is very possible that a potential trademark holder wanting to use LIVELY SPICE would not locate IFF's registration while doing a trademark search and therefore would not be on notice that LIVELY SPICE might infringe IFF's mark." *Id.* at 1368 n.6.

[412] 15 U.S.C. § 1052(a).

[413] In re Wilcher Corp., 40 U.S.P.Q.2d (BNA) 1929 (T.T.A.B. 1996).

[414] In re Boulevard Entertainment, Inc., 334 F.3d 1336, 1340 (Fed. Cir. 2003).

[415] *Id.*

the collective understanding of the community with respect to language and thus clearly constitute more than a reflection of the individual views of either the examining attorney or the dictionary editors."[416]

Registration has been denied for the term "BUBBY TRAP" for brassieres,[417] for an image of a man and woman kissing that displayed full frontal nudity,[418] for an image of a defecating dog,[419] and for the terms "BULLSHIT"[420] and "JACK-OFF."[421] Registrations of "MADONNA"[422] and "MESSIAS"[423] for wine were refused, on the ground that the juxtaposition would be offensive or scandalous. However, the term "BLACK TAIL"[424] and the image of a condom with stars and stripes resembling an American flag[425] were both held to be registrable.

Whether a particular mark is immoral, scandalous, or disparaging can be a close question. For example, at one stage of a 15-year cancellation proceeding, the Trademark Trial and Appeal Board ruled that the term "REDSKINS" for a football team was disparaging and therefore unregistrable, only to be reversed by the federal district court for lack of substantial evidence. According to the district court, the TTAB erred, *inter alia*, by concluding that the mark was disparaging based on the perceptions of the general public; rather, the Board should have considered whether the mark was perceived as disparaging by the relevant group — in this case, Native Americans.[426]

The test of whether a mark is "deceptive" is somewhat more objective. To be deceptive, (1) the mark must falsely describe the goods or services, (2) the misdescription must be one that the prospective purchaser is likely to believe is true, and (3) that mistaken belief must be likely to materially affect the consumer's purchasing decision.[427] For example, the "LOVEE LAMB" trademark for car seat covers made of fuzzy synthetic material was held to be unregistrable as deceptive, because purchasers were likely to believe the material was lambskin, and this belief was likely to have a material affect on their purchasing decision.[428]

---

[416] *Id.*

[417] In re Runsdorf, 171 U.S.P.Q. (BNA) 443 (T.T.A.B. 1971).

[418] In re McGinley, 660 F.2d 481 (C.C.P.A. 1981).

[419] Greyhound Corp. v. Both Worlds, Inc., 6 U.S.P.Q.2d (BNA) 1635 (T.T.A.B. 1988).

[420] In re Tinseltown, Inc., 212 U.S.P.Q. (BNA) 863 (T.T.A.B. 1981).

[421] In re Boulevard Ent., Inc., 334 F.3d 1336 (Fed. Cir. 2003).

[422] In re Riverbank Canning Co., 95 F.2d 327 (C.C.P.A. 1938); In re P.J. Valckenbeg, GmbH, 122 U.S.P.Q. (BNA) 334 (T.T.A.B. 1959).

[423] In re Sociedade Agricola v. Commercial Dos Vinhos Messias, S.A.R.L., 159 U.S.P.Q. (BNA) 275 (T.T.A.B. 1968).

[424] Boswell v. Mavety Media Group, Ltd., 52 U.S.P.Q.2d (BNA) 1600 (T.T.A.B. 1999).

[425] In re Old Glory Condom Corp., 26 U.S.P.Q.2d (BNA) 1216 (T.T.A.B. 1993).

[426] Pro-Football, Inc. v. Harjo, 284 F. Supp. 2d 96 (D.D.C. 2003).

[427] In re Budge Mfg. Co., 857 F.2d 773 (Fed. Cir. 1988).

[428] *Id.* at 775-77.

The test used by the TTAB to determine whether a mark falsely suggests a connection with persons, institutions, beliefs, or national symbols is also objective. In order to establish a false connection, the TTAB must find that: (1) the applicant's mark is the same as, or closely approximates, another's previously used name or identity; (2) the mark would be recognized as such; (3) the other party (person, institution, etc.) is not connected with the activities performed by the applicant under the mark; and (4) the name or identity of the other party is of sufficient fame or reputation that when the applicant's mark is used on goods or services, a connection with the other party would be presumed.[429]

[2]   National, State, or Municipal Insignia

Section 2(b) bars registration of a mark that comprises or simulates the flag, coat of arms, or insignia of the United States, any state or municipality, or any foreign nation.[430] Thus, for example, section 2(b) barred registration of the official seals of England[431] and the United States Department of Justice,[432] and the seal and coat of arms of the state of Maryland,[433] but did not bar registration of an image of the Statue of Liberty, which was found to be, at most, a "national symbol" subject to evaluation under section 2(a).[434]

[3]   Name, Portrait, or Signature

Section 2(c) bars registration of any mark that comprises (1) a name, portrait, or signature identifying a particular living individual, except with that person's written consent, or (2) the name, signature, or portrait of a deceased U.S. President during the life of his or her surviving spouse, except with the spouse's written consent.[435] The purpose of this bar is to protect individuals' rights of privacy and publicity.[436]

[4]   Marks Likely to Cause Confusion with Existing Marks

Section 2(d) incorporates the common law "likelihood of confusion" test, barring registration of any trademark that comprises a mark which so resembles a mark already registered at the PTO, or already used in the United States by another and not abandoned, as to be likely, when used on or in connection with the applicant's goods or services, to cause confusion or mistake,

---

[429] Buffett v. Chi-Chi's, Inc., 228 U.S.P.Q. (BNA) 428, 429 (T.T.A.B. 1985).

[430] 15 U.S.C. § 1052(b).

[431] In re Gorham Mfg. Co., 41 App. D.C. 263 (1913) (noting that the lion is "[t]he official emblem of the British Assay Office").

[432] In re William Connors Paint Mfg. Co., 27 App. D.C. 389 (1906).

[433] In re Cahn, Belt, & Co., 27 App. D.C. 173 (1906).

[434] Liberty Mutual Ins. Co. v. Liberty Ins. Co., 185 F. Supp. 895 (E.D. Ark. 1960).

[435] 15 U.S.C. § 1052(c).

[436] University of Notre Dame du Lac v. J.C. Gourmet Food Imports Co., Inc., 703 F.2d 1372, 1376 (Fed. Cir. 1983); Canovas v. Venezia, 220 U.S.P.Q. (BNA) 660, 661 (T.T.A.B. 1983).

or to deceive.[437] To enjoy a right of priority under section 2(d), a party must show that it was the first to establish proprietary rights in the mark. Proprietary rights "may arise from a prior registration, prior trademark or service mark use, prior use as a trade name, prior use analogous to trademark or service mark use, or any other use sufficient to establish proprietary rights."[438]

[a]   Priority of Use

When two or more parties seek to register confusingly similar marks for similar goods or services, based on either intended or actual use in commerce, the question of which party has the right of priority will depend on which party used the mark first. Although use *in commerce* is essential to obtaining trademark registration, an applicant who is the first to use a mark in commerce may be denied registration under section 2(d) if another party has used a confusingly similar mark on similar goods or services *anywhere* in the United States, even if that use was not "in commerce" because it was purely intrastate.[439] Thus, priority under section 2(d) depends on which party was the first to use the mark in connection with the goods or services in question, whether or not that use involved interstate commerce. In the case of an intent-to-use application, the applicant's priority date will be either the filing date of the intent-to-use application, or the date on which that applicant commenced use of the mark in connection with goods and services (whether or not that use was interstate), whichever is earlier.[440]

[b]   Priority through Analogous Use

Although technical trademark use is a prerequisite to registration, prior use of a mark in interstate or intrastate commerce can defeat another user's registration (or attempted registration) of a similar mark if the prior use is analogous to trademark use.[441] Under the doctrine of "analogous use," a use that would not by itself be a technical trademark use may nonetheless be sufficient, under section 2(d), to establish which party is the senior user of the mark — that is, which party has priority in the mark.[442] For example, using a mark merely to advertise goods, without actually affixing the mark to the goods and shipping them to consumers or retailers, is not a technical trademark use, and thus is not a sufficient use in commerce to permit registration of the mark. However, if the use "was of such nature and extent as to create an association by

---

[437] 15 U.S.C. § 1052(d).

[438] Herbko Int'l, Inc. v. Kappa Books, Inc., 308 F.3d 1156, 1162 (Fed. Cir. 2002).

[439] First Niagara Ins. Brokers, Inc. v. First Niagara Financial Group, Inc., 476 F.3d 867, 870-71 (Fed. Cir. 2007).

[440] Aktieselskabet AF 21.November 2001 v. Fame Jeans, Inc., 525 F.3d 8, 18-20 (D.C. Cir. 2008); Fair Indigo LLC v. Style Conscience, 85 U.S.P.Q.2d (BNA) 1536, 1539 (T.T.A.B. 2007); Corporate Document Services, Inc. v. I.C.E.D. Mgt., Inc., 48 U.S.P.Q.2d (BNA) 1477, 1479 (T.T.A.B. 1998).

[441] Jimlar Corp. v. Army & Air Force Exchange Serv., 24 U.S.P.Q.2d (BNA) 1216, 1221 (T.T.A.B. 1992).

[442] *Aktieselskabet*, 525 F.3d at 20.

the purchasing public of the goods with the user,"[443] then it is an analogous use.[444] The analogous use need not be in the context of advertising, and it need not even be a use by the party claiming the right of priority; for example, a third-party use of the mark by the news media or by the public (such as the popular slang "Tar-Jay" for "Target," "Mickey Dee's" for "McDonald's," or "Jacques Pennay" for "JC Penney") can inure to the benefit of the party claiming a right of priority by virtue of analogous use, even if that party has not itself used the term.[445] It does not matter whether the analogous use is purely intrastate.[446]

In an opposition or interference proceeding, an analogous use by the party seeking to register a mark may establish the applicant's priority date, regardless of whether the application is based on actual use or intent to use.[447] Likewise, an analogous use by an opposer may establish the opposer's right of priority for purposes of preventing another's registration of a confusingly similar mark for similar goods or services.[448] Using analogous use to antedate actual use (or constructive use, in the case of an intent-to-use application) is a species of "tacking." (Tacking is discussed in § 3.02[A] below.)

Analogous use may be tacked to actual use (or constructive use based on the filing date of an intent-to-use application) even if there is a delay between the analogous use and the actual or constructive use, provided that the delay is commercially reasonable.[449] The user "need not necessarily have a capacity to

---

[443] IT&T Corp. v. General Instr. Corp., 152 U.S.P.Q.(BNA) 821 (T.T.A.B. 1967).

[444] See Jim Dandy Co. v. Martha White Foods, 458 F.2d 1397, 1398 (C.C.P.A. 1972) (advertising sufficient to establish analogous use "must have been of such a nature and extent that the term or slogan has become popularized in the public mind as identifying the product of the user thereof"); Dyneer Corp. v. Automotive Prods. PLC, 37 U.S.P.Q.2d 1251 (T.T.A.B. 1995) (analogous use "must be of 'such a nature and extent as to create an association of said [term] with a single source . . . sufficient to create a proprietary right in the user deserving of protection'") (quoting Era Corp. v. Electronic Realty Associates, Inc., 211 U.S.P.Q. (BNA) 734, 745 (T.T.A.B. 1981)); Liqwacon Corp. v. Browning-Ferris Industries, Inc., 203 U.S.P.Q. (BNA) 305, 308 (T.T.A.B. 1979) (use must be "calculated to attract the attention of potential customers or customers in the applicable field of trade" so as to create an association of the term with a single source, even if anonymous). Some courts use different terminology to express the same idea. See, e.g., Goetz v. American Express, 515 F.3d 156, 161-62 (2d Cir. 2008) (analogous use must be "open and notorious," so that relevant consuming public identifies the marked goods or services with the mark's adopter); T.A.B. Sys. v. Pactel Teletrac, 77 F.3d 1372, 1376 (Fed. Cir. 1996) (noting that an "open and notorious public use" is the same as a use that causes a mark to become "popularized in the public mind," and that under any formulation of the test, "it is actual public perception that is required.")

[445] National Cable Television Ass'n, Inc. v. American Cinema Editors, Inc., 937 F.2d 1572, 1577-78 (Fed. Cir. 1991); American Stock Exch., Inc. v. American Express Co., 207 U.S.P.Q. (BNA) 356, 364 (T.T.A.B. 1980).

[446] L. & J.G. Stickley, Inc. v. Cosser, 81 U.S.P.Q.2d (BNA) 1956, 1965 (T.T.A.B. 2007); Corporate Document Services Inc. v. I.C.E.D. Management Inc., 48 U.S.P.Q.2d (BNA) 1477, 1479 (T.T.A.B. 1998).

[447] Fair Indigo LLC v. Style Conscience, 85 U.S.P.Q.2d (BNA) 1536 (T.T.A.B. 2007).

[448] IT&T Corp. v. General Instr. Corp., 152 U.S.P.Q. (BNA) 821 (T.T.A.B. 1967).

[449] Dyneer Corp. v. Automotive Prods. PLC, 37 U.S.P.Q.2d (BNA) 1251 (T.T.A.B. 1995); see also Evans Chemetics, Inc. v. Chemetics International Ltd., 207 U.S.P.Q. (BNA) 695, 700 (T.T.A.B. 1980) (question is whether services "were actually rendered or available for performance soon enough after the initial advertising . . . to preclude a finding that the advertising was merely an attempt to

produce goods for sale under the involved mark at the time of the analogous use."[450] However, in the event of delay, the TTAB will inquire whether the user "had a continuing intent to cultivate an association of the mark with itself and its goods and whether members of the relevant purchasing public in fact made such an association."[451] This inquiry is analogous to the analysis of abandonment.[452]

[c]   Factors Indicating Likelihood of Confusion

In determining whether a likelihood of confusion exists under section 2(d), the PTO focuses on how the marks will be perceived by consumers in the marketplace, and specifically considers the following list of factors (known as the *DuPont* factors), to the extent that relevant evidence is present in the record:

(1) The similarity or dissimilarity of the marks in their entireties as to appearance, sound, connotation, and commercial impression.

(2) The similarity or dissimilarity and nature of the goods or services as described in an application or registration or in connection with which a prior mark is in use.

(3) The similarity or dissimilarity of established, likely-to-continue trade channels.

(4) The conditions under which and buyers to whom sales are made, i.e. "impulse" versus careful, sophisticated purchasing.

(5) The fame of the prior mark (sales, advertising, length of use).

(6) The number and nature of similar marks in use on similar goods.

(7) The nature and extent of any actual confusion.

(8) The length of time during and conditions under which there has been concurrent use without evidence of actual confusion.

(9) The variety of goods on which a mark is or is not used (house mark, "family" mark, product mark).

(10) The market interface between applicant and the owner of a prior mark, including:

    (a) a mere "consent" to register or use.

    (b) agreement provisions designed to preclude confusion, i.e., limitations on continued use of the marks by each party.

---

preempt a mark for use at an indefinite future date"); Computer Food Stores Inc. v. Corner Store Franchises, Inc., 176 U.S.P.Q. (BNA) 535, 538 (T.T.A.B. 1973) (use analogous to trademark use must be "in a manner sufficient to . . . inform or apprise prospective purchasers of the present or future availability" of the goods or services).

[450] *Dyneer Corp*, 37 U.S.P.Q.2d (BNA) at 1255 (citing PacTel Teletrac v. T.A.B. Systems, 32 U.S.P.Q.2d (BNA) 1668 (T.T.A.B. 1994)).

[451] *Id.*

[452] *Id.* For a discussion of abandonment, see § 3.12 [A] below.

    (c)   assignment of mark, application, registration and goodwill of the related business.

    (d)   laches and estoppel attributable to owner of prior mark and indicative of lack of confusion.

(11)   The extent to which applicant has a right to exclude others from use of its mark on its goods.

(12)   The extent of potential confusion, i.e., whether *de minimis* or substantial.

(13)   Any other established fact probative of the effect of use.[453]

The weight accorded to each factor will vary, depending on the particular circumstances of the case.[454] Typically, however, the similarity of the marks and the similarity of the goods or services are especially important.[455]

[d]   Concurrent Use

If the Director of the PTO determines that the confusion, mistake, or deception can be avoided by imposing certain conditions on the parties' use of the same or similar marks, concurrent registrations can be issued. The Director may also issue concurrent registrations when a court of competent jurisdiction determines that more than one person is entitled to use the same or similar marks in commerce. In either case, for concurrent registrations to issue, the Director must impose conditions and limitations (1) as to either the mode or the place of use of each mark,[456] or (2) as to the goods in connection with which each mark is registered.[457]

Concurrent registrations will issue only to applicants that became entitled to use the marks as a result of their concurrent lawful use in commerce prior to the earliest of (1) the filing dates of the pending applications, or (2) any registration actually issued for the mark. This timing requirement is waived if the owner of such registration or pending application consents to the granting of a concurrent registration to the applicant.

In the leading case on concurrent registrations, *Application of Beatrice Foods*,[458] the Court of Customs and Patent Appeals noted that the Lanham Act's concurrent use provision reflects "a recognition, by the framers of that statute, that occasions do and will arise where two or more persons will

---

[453] In re E.I. DuPont de Nemours & Co., 476 F.2d 1357, 1361 (C.C.P.A. 1973).

[454] *Id.* at 1361-62.

[455] In re Azteca Rest. Enters., Inc., 50 U.S.P.Q.2d (BNA) 1209 (T.T.A.B. 1999); *see, e.g.,* In re Dixie Rests., 105 F.3d 1405 (Fed. Cir. 1997) (affirming rejection of THE DELTA CAFÉ mark for restaurant services in light of existing registration of DELTA for hotel, motel, and restaurant services).

[456] Old Dutch Foods, Inc. v. Dan Dee Pretzel & Potato Chip Co., 477 F.2d 150 (6th Cir. 1973).

[457] *E.g.,* Alfred Dunhill of London, Inc. v. Dunhill Tailored Clothes, Inc., 293 F.2d 685 (C.C.P.A. 1961), *cert. denied,* 369 U.S. 864 (1962); Avon Shoe Co. v. David Crystal, Inc., 279 F.2d 607 (2d Cir.), *cert. denied,* 364 U.S. 909 (1960).

[458] 429 F.2d 466 (C.C.P.A. 1970).

independently adopt the same or a similar trademark and use it under the same or similar circumstances, and indicates their concern that a mechanism be provided for an equitable resolution of the problems which such concurrent use creates."[459]

Beatrice Foods involved co-pending applications by two parties who had been using the same mark concurrently for dairy products since 1953 and 1956, respectively. When one of the parties applied to register the mark, the other party filed an opposition. The parties then entered an agreement dividing the entire United States into two geographic territories, and each applicant requested a registration that was limited to its agreed-upon region. The TTAB rejected this arrangement on the ground that the designated regions included states where neither party was using the mark, and that each party's registration should be limited to the states in which it was actually using the mark.[460] Both parties objected to the TTAB's resolution. The prior user argued that it was presumptively entitled to priority everywhere except those areas where another party was actually using the mark, a position that was consistent with the rights that it would have been entitled to had it been the sole applicant. The junior user argued that its registration should reflect its planned expansion from its areas of actual use into several of the neighboring states, a plan to which the senior user had consented.

The Court of Customs and Patent Appeals agreed with both parties that the TTAB had erred in restricting them to their regions of actual use, rather than allocating the entire United States between them. Leaving territories unallocated, it held, would simply increase the potential for consumer confusion.[461]

The Court of Customs and Patent Appeals outlined the principles that should determine whether to grant concurrent use applications:

1. The parties must already be entitled to use their respective marks concurrently, meaning that each party must already have made more than a token use of its mark in commerce.

2. Continued concurrent use must not create a likelihood of confusion, mistake, or deception as to the source of the parties' goods.

3. The respective territories must then be restricted as necessary to avoid a likelihood of confusion.[462]

In concurrent use proceedings in which neither party owns a registration for the mark, the court held, the following rules should govern the allocation of the parties' territories:

1. The prior user is prima facie entitled to nationwide registration.

2. If the prior user applies for registration before registration is granted to

---

[459] *Id.* at 472.

[460] *Id.* at 470-71.

[461] *Id.* at 473.

[462] *Id.* at 473-74.

another party, then the prior user should be granted nationwide registration, *except* to the extent that another user

(a)   has established common law priority in a particular territory through actual use before the registrant's application date, *and*

(b)   establishes that granting the registrant exclusive rights in the other user's territory would create a likelihood of confusion, mistake, or deception.[463]

However, if the prior user does *not* apply for registration before registration is granted to another, the court noted that "there may be valid grounds, based on a policy of rewarding those who first seek federal registration, and a consideration of the rights created by the existing registration, for limiting [the prior user's] registration to the area of actual use and permitting the prior registrant to retain the nationwide protection of the act restricted only by the territory of the prior user."[464]

In determining how to restrict the parties' respective territories so as to avoid confusion, mistake, or deception, *Beatrice Foods* notes that the PTO may consider, although it is not required to adopt, any restrictions that have been agreed upon by the parties themselves. Where such agreements are undertaken in good faith, the court noted, "there can be no better assurance of the absence of any likelihood of confusion, mistake, or deception than the parties' promises to avoid any activity which might lead to such likelihood."[465] The concurrent registrations should, together, encompass all parts of the United States except those areas where another user has established common law rights through actual use; leaving any regions unallocated would frustrate the goal of avoiding likelihood of confusion.[466]

Beatrice Foods also considered "what circumstances, if any, short of actual use of the trademark, may create rights in a territory sufficient to warrant inclusion of that territory in a geographically restricted registration, and up to what time prior to registration may proof regarding the territorial extent of trademark rights be submitted."[467] Evidence of a likelihood of expansion, the court concluded, is an important consideration in light of the goal of preventing confusion, mistake, or deception:

Where a party has submitted evidence sufficient to prove a strong probability of future expansion of his trade into an area, that area would then become an area of likelihood of confusion if a registration covering it was granted to the other party. For example, many forms of evidence which would ordinarily be proffered to show a likelihood of expansion would be the same kind submitted to argue a likelihood of confusion if another party began use of the mark in that area. Thus, based on the

---

[463] *Id.* at 474.

[464] *Id.* at 474 & n.13.

[465] *Id.* at 474.

[466] *Id.*

[467] *Id.* at 475.

premise that territorially restricted registrations must issue and, further, that said registrations combined will encompass the entire United States, if a likelihood of confusion is to be avoided, the territories of the parties must be limited in such a way as to exclude from each the area of probable expansion of the other party.[468]

The court also held that, in determining the conditions and limitations of each party's registration, the public interest would be best served if the PTO also considered any expansion of a party's exclusive use that took place *after* the filing of the registration application.[469] Although use in commerce prior to registration is essential to establishing the *right* to register the mark, in allocating territories between parties that have already satisfied this requirement the PTO should take account of any changes in their areas of use that take place during the examination process, so that the concurrent registrations will accurately reflect the areas of each party's actual use at the time the registrations are granted.[470]

[5]   Descriptive, Misdescriptive, or Functional Marks

The section 2(e) bar[471] applies to a variety of marks that are descriptive, misdescriptive, or functional, and to any mark that is primarily merely a surname. In some cases, such marks are completely unregistrable. As discussed in § 2.09 [B][6] below, however, under section 2(f) some marks that are presumptively barred under section 2(e) can be registered on the Principal Register once they have acquired sufficient secondary meaning.

[a]   Merely Descriptive

Subsection (e)(1) bars registration of a mark that is "merely descriptive" of the applicant's goods.[472] The determination of descriptiveness is based specifically on the goods or services for which registration of the mark is sought. Any mark that is denied registration on section (e)(1) grounds is still eligible for registration if and when it acquires sufficient distinctiveness (that is, secondary meaning) to satisfy section 2(f).[473] In fact, many descriptive marks have been successfully registered upon a showing of secondary meaning.[474] However, if the mark is so descriptive as to be generic, no amount of secondary meaning will

---

[468] *Id.; accord, Old Dutch Foods*, 477 F.2d 150.

[469] *Beatrice Foods*, 429 F.2d at 475.

[470] *Id.*

[471] 15 U.S.C. § 1052(e).

[472] For a discussion of the standards for determining whether a mark is descriptive, see §§ 2.07 [A][2] and [3] *supra*. An example of a mark deemed unregistrable because of descriptiveness is "Continuous Progress" for educational materials. Educational Dev't Corp. v. Economy Co., 562 F.2d 26 (10th Cir. 1977) (also finding that the term lacked secondary meaning).

[473] Roux Labs., Inc. v. Clairol, Inc., 427 F.2d 823, 829 (C.C.P.A. 1970).

[474] *See, e.g.*, Union Carbide Corp. v. Ever-Ready, Inc., 531 F.2d 366 (7th Cir. 1976) (finding that EVEREADY for batteries and light bulbs had acquired secondary meaning, and thus its registration was valid regardless of whether the mark was deemed to be descriptive or suggestive), *cert. denied*, 429 U.S. 830 (1976).

make it registrable.[475] Thus, "COCOA PUFFS" is a registered trademark for breakfast cereal,[476] while "CORN FLAKES" (except as part of the "KELLOGG'S CORN FLAKES" mark[477]) is not.

[b]   Deceptively Misdescriptive

Subsection (e)(1) also bars registration of a mark that is "deceptively misdescriptive" of the applicant's goods. A mark is deceptively misdescriptive if it misdescribes the goods or services to which it is affixed, and if the public is likely to believe the misdescription to be true. The difference between a mark that is deceptively misdescriptive under section 2(e)(1) and one that is deceptive under section 2(a) is that, in the latter case, the consumer's mistaken belief also has a material affect on the decision to purchase. Thus, for example, the "GLASS WAX" mark for a glass cleaner that contained no wax was held to be deceptively misdescriptive under (e)(1), but not deceptive under (a), because there was no evidence that consumers would be influenced to purchase the product based on the belief that it contained wax.[478]

A mark may be misdescriptive without being deceptively so. For example, the trademark "SOLID GOLD" for a chocolate bar would be misdescriptive, but consumers would be unlikely to believe that the chocolate bar is really made of gold. Similarly, the mark "APPLE" for computers is misdescriptive but not deceptively so, because no one would believe that the computers were made of apples, or that they were apple-flavored. A mark that is misdescriptive but not deceptively so is, in fact, a type of arbitrary mark.

A mark that is merely deceptively misdescriptive, such as "GLASS WAX," can be registered on the Principal Register if it acquires sufficient secondary meaning to satisfy section 2(f). In contrast, a mark that is deceptive under section 2(a) cannot be registered at all.

[c]   Primarily Geographically Descriptive

Subsection (e)(2) bars registration of a mark that is "primarily geographically descriptive" of the applicant's goods. As in the case of other descriptive marks, allowing one competitor to monopolize a mark that describes the geographic origin of goods or services would make it difficult for competitors to accurately describe their goods or services that have a similar origin. The prohibition applies only when the term is "primarily" geographically descriptive with respect to the goods or services in question; it does not apply when the geographic meaning of the mark is obscure or remote, or when the mark has a popular significance apart from its geographic meaning.[479] The bar is also

---

[475] *Roux Labs.*, 427 F.2d at 829.

[476] Reg. No. 902,727.

[477] Reg. No. 1,411,563.

[478] Gold Seal Co. v. Weeks, 129 F. Supp. 928 (D.D.C. 1955), *aff'd sub nom.* S.C. Johnson & Son, Inc. v. Gold Seal Co., 230 F.2d 832 (D.C. Cir.), *cert. denied*, 352 U.S. 829 (1956).

[479] In re Int'l Taste, Inc., 53 U.S.P.Q.2d (BNA) 1604 (T.T.A.B. 2000) (popular significance of the term "Hollywood" prevents it from being primarily geographically descriptive).

inapplicable to certification marks.[480]

[d]   Primarily Geographically Deceptively Misdescriptive

Subsection (e)(3) bars registration of a mark that is "primarily geographically deceptively misdescriptive" of the applicant's goods. Although at one time such marks could be registered after they acquired secondary meaning, in 1993 the North American Free Trade Agreement (NAFTA) amendments to section 2 changed subsection (e)(3) to an absolute registration bar, comparable to that of section 2(a). Accordingly, marks in this category may not be registered even if they have become distinctive, subject to a narrow exception in the nature of a grandfather clause, spelled out in subsection (f), for marks that became distinctive of the applicant's goods before NAFTA's enactment date (December 8, 1993).

Prior to 2003, the courts and the PTO used a two-part test for determining whether a mark was "primarily geographically deceptively misdescriptive," requiring that the mark "(1) have as its primary significance a generally known geographic place, and (2) identify products that purchasers are likely to believe mistakenly are connected with that location."[481] A TTAB decision explained the rationale for this test:

> If the evidence shows that the geographical area named in the mark is an area sufficiently renowned to lead purchasers to make a goods-place association but the record does not show that goods like applicant's or goods related to applicant's are a principal product of that geographical area, then the deception will most likely be found not to be material and the mark, therefore, not deceptive. On the other hand, if there is evidence that goods like applicant's or goods related to applicant's are a principal product of the geographical area named by the mark, then the deception will most likely be found material and the mark, therefore, deceptive.[482]

In 2003, however, the Federal Circuit held in *In re California Innovations*[483] that this test ceased to be appropriate when the NAFTA amendments converted the defeasible registration bar for primarily geographically deceptively misdescriptive marks into a complete bar analogous to that of section 2(a). Instead, under the new test imposed by the Federal Circuit, for a misdescriptive geographic mark to fall within section 2(e)(3), not only must the mark satisfy the two-part test set forth above, the misrepresentation of geographic origin must also be "a material factor in the consumer's decision" to purchase the applicant's goods or services.[484] Thus, the new test for "geographically deceptively misde-

---

[480]   15 U.S.C. § 1052(e)(2) (referencing 15 U.S.C. § 1054).

[481]   In re Wada, 194 F.3d 1297, 1300 (Fed. Cir. 1999).

[482]   In re House of Windsor, Inc., 221 U.S.P.Q. (BNA) 53, 57 (T.T.A.B. 1983).

[483]   In re California Innovations, Inc., 329 F.3d 1334 (Fed. Cir. 2003).

[484]   *Id.* at 1338; *accord* In re Les Halles de Paris, J.V., 334 F.3d 1371 (Fed. Cir. 2003) (applying same test to service marks).

scriptive" marks is now identical to the test for deceptive marks under section 2(a). If the Federal Circuit stands by its ruling, it will have rendered section 2(e)(3) largely superfluous. Furthermore, if the section 2(e)(3) bar now applies only to deceptive marks, then the grandfather clause of section 2(f) (for marks that became distinctive before NAFTA's enactment) may be completely inoperative. Indeed, in applying the *California Innovations* standard, the TTAB has held that a geographically deceptively misdescriptive mark cannot be registered, even if it became distinctive prior to December 8, 1993.[485]

In the case of services, the test for primarily geographically deceptively misdescriptive marks, both before and after *California Innovations*, differs slightly from the test that applies to goods. With respect to goods, the second prong of the test — which asks whether purchasers are likely to believe the goods came from the location implied by the mark — often requires little more than a showing that the place is a known source for the product.[486] In the case of services, however, this part of the test is modified:

> In the case of a services-place association, however, a mere showing that the geographic location in the mark is known for performing the service is not sufficient. Rather the second prong of the test requires some additional reason for the consumer to associate the services with the geographic location invoked by the mark. Thus, a services-place association in a case dealing with restaurant services . . . requires a showing that the patrons of the restaurant are likely to believe the restaurant services have their origin in the location indicated by the mark. In other words, to refuse registration under section 2(e)(3), the PTO must show that patrons will likely be misled to make some meaningful connection between the restaurant (the service) and the relevant place.

> For example, the PTO might find a services-place association if the record shows that patrons, though sitting in New York, would believe the food served by the restaurant was imported from Paris, or that the chefs in New York received specialized training in the region in Paris, or that the New York menu is identical to a known Parisian menu, or some other heightened association between the services and the relevant place . . .[487]

The new third prong of the (e)(3) test — the materiality requirement — applies equally to both goods and services,[488] but again its application to services differs slightly from its application to goods. In the case of goods, the materiality test is likely to be satisfied where the geographic area in question "is famous as a source of the goods at issue."[489] The Federal Circuit offered this example of a situation in which the geographic origin of services might be material to a purchasing decision:

---

[485] In re Beaverton Foods, Inc., 84 U.S.P.Q.2d (BNA) 1253 (T.T.A.B. 2007).

[486] In re Les Halles de Paris J.V., 334 F.3d 1371, 1374 (Fed. Cir. 2003).

[487] *Id.*

[488] *Id.*

[489] *Id.*

For restaurant services, the materiality prong might be satisfied by a particularly convincing showing that identifies the relevant place as famous for providing the specialized culinary training exhibited by the chef, and that this fact is advertised as a reason to choose this restaurant. In other words, an inference of materiality arises in the event of a very strong services-place association. Without a particularly strong services-place association, an inference would not arise, leaving the PTO to seek direct evidence of materiality.[490]

In 2009, the Federal Circuit clarified that the materiality test of (e)(3) requires that "a substantial portion of the relevant consumers" are likely to be deceived.[491]

[e]   Primarily Merely a Surname

Subsection (e)(4) bars registration of a mark that is "primarily merely a surname." Such marks may still be registered, however, if they acquire sufficient secondary meaning to satisfy section 2(f). The rationale for the (e)(4) bar is that the primary significance of a surname is to identify an individual's family name. Only when the public begins to recognize the surname as an indication of the origin of specific goods or services is the surname capable of serving a trademark function. The "McDonald's" mark for fast food restaurants is an example of a surname that has acquired strong secondary meaning.

Some marks may have several meanings, only one of which is a surname. In such cases, the test under subsection (e)(4) is whether the purchasing public perceives the mark as "primarily" a surname when it is used in association with goods or services, or whether the other meanings of the word are more significant.[492] In fact, the surname significance of some words may not be recognized by consumers at all; in such cases, the mark clearly would not fall under subsection (e)(4).[493]

The TTAB considers five factors in determining whether a mark is primarily merely a surname: (1) the degree of the surname's rareness; (2) whether anyone connected with the applicant uses the term as a surname; (3) whether the mark has any recognized meaning other than as a surname; (4) whether the mark has the "look and sound" (or the "structure and pronunciation") of a surname; and (5) whether the manner in which the mark is displayed may negate any surname

---

[490] *Id.* at 1374-75.

[491] In re Spirits Int'l, N.V., 563 F.3d 1347, 1353 (Fed. Cir. 2009).

[492] *See, e.g.*, Savin Corp. v. Savin Group, 391 F.3d 439, 451 (2d Cir. 2004) (noting that while "Savin" is a surname, it also has a dictionary meaning); Williamson-Dickie Mfg. Co. v. Davis Mfg. Co., 149 F. Supp. 852 (E.D. Pa. 1957), *aff'd*, 251 F.2d 924 (3d Cir. 1957) (although Dickie was the surname of one of the parties related to the litigation, it was not primarily merely a surname, because in ordinary usage it was perceived primarily as a nickname or diminutive of "Richard").

[493] *See, e.g.*, IMAF, S.P.A. v. J.C. Penney Co., 806 F. Supp. 449, 455 (S.D.N.Y. 1992) ("The name (or word) Adiansi is not likely to be immediately identified with a person by an average buyer of a sweater at J.C. Penney. Thus, the fact that Adiansi is a surname is not dispositive on the issue of inherent distinctiveness.").

significance.[494] The Examining Attorney has the initial burden to make a prima facie showing of surname significance.[495]

[f]   Functional Marks

Subsection (e)(5) bars registration of a mark if it "comprises any matter that, as a whole, is functional." This reflects the familiar rule, under common law and section 43(a) of the Lanham Act, that one party cannot be given exclusive rights in a functional mark, because such protection would impede competition by affording a patent-like monopoly to functional designs without regard to whether the requirements of patent law had been satisfied.[496] This rule recognizes that a manufacturer "does not have rights under trade dress law to compel its competitors to resort to alternative designs which have a different set of advantages and disadvantages."[497] Although the functionality bar was not codified until 1998,[498] the legislative history of the 1998 amendment indicates Congress's intent to endorse the historical practice of the PTO in refusing registration of functional marks.[499]

Functionality issues arise most often in the case of trade dress, either product packaging or product configuration. However, in the case of product configurations, the Federal Circuit and the TTAB distinguish between designs that are "de jure" functional and those that are "de facto" functional. Only de jure functionality will trigger the subsection (e)(5) bar.[500]

A product configuration is de jure functional if it is "a superior design essential for competition"; in contrast, if the configuration "merely performs some function or utility," but is not significantly better than other possible configurations, it is only de facto functional, and will not be subject to the functionality bar to registration.[501] Thus, for example, the shape of a bottle may be de facto functional, because it enables the bottle to hold a liquid,[502] but it may not be de jure functional, because the particular bottle design chosen by the manufacturer may serve a purpose other than enhancing the bottle's ability to hold a liquid, in which case the bottle shape could be registered if it serves as an

---

[494] In re Benthin Mgt. GmbH, 37 U.S.P.Q.2d (BNA) 1332 (T.T.A.B. 1995).

[495] In re Yeley, 85 U.S.P.Q.2d (BNA) 1150 (T.T.A.B. 2007).

[496] *See* Talking Rain Bev. Co. v. South Beach Bev. Co., 349 F.3d 601, 604 (9th Cir. 2003); § 2.03 *supra*.

[497] Tie Tech, Inc. v. Kinedyne Corp., 296 F.3d 778, 786 (9th Cir. 2002) (evidence that design of cutting device was functional was sufficient to overcome presumption of validity that attached to registration) (quoting Leatherman Tool Group, Inc. v. Cooper Indus., Inc., 199 F.3d 1009, 1012 (9th Cir. 1999)).

[498] Technical Corrections to Trademark Act of 1946, Pub. L. No. 105-330, § 201(b), 112 Stat. 3064 (1998).

[499] Valu Eng'g, Inc. v. Rexnord Corp., 278 F.3d 1268, 1274 (Fed. Cir. 2002).

[500] In re Morton-Norwich Prods., Inc., 671 F.2d 1332, 1337-41 (C.C.P.A. 1982).

[501] In re Ennco Display Sys., Inc., 56 U.S.P.Q.2d (BNA) 1279 (T.T.A.B. 2000); *Valu Eng'g, Inc.*, 278 F.3d at 274.

[502] In re R.M. Smith, Inc., 734 F.2d 1482, 1484 (Fed. Cir. 1984).

origin indicator.[503] In contrast, the design of a drinking bottle was held to be de jure functional, and its registration therefore invalid, where several elements of the design made the bottle especially easy for a bicycle rider to use while cycling.[504] Where a design is de jure functional, the Supreme Court's decision in *TrafFix Devices, Inc. v. Marketing Displays, Inc.* indicates that the existence of alternative designs that would perform the same function is irrelevant.[505]

Because section 2(f) does not apply to marks determined to be de jure functional, the subsection (e)(5) bar is insurmountable even if acquired distinctiveness can be shown. In contrast, if a mark is only de facto functional, the insurmountable (e)(5) bar will not apply. However, in practice, registration of de facto functional marks will frequently be denied on the ground that the mark lacks inherent distinctiveness, a rejection that can be overcome upon a showing of acquired distinctiveness under section 2(f).

For a more detailed discussion of functionality, see § 2.03, *supra*.

[6]   Overcoming Bars to Registration Under Section 2(f)

With respect to most of the section 2 registration bars, the prohibition against registration applies regardless of whether the mark has acquired secondary meaning. The bars that are absolute in this respect are subsections (a), (b), (c), (d), (e)(3) and (e)(5).

In contrast, the bars under (e)(1), (e)(2), and (e)(4) are all subject to the exception set forth in section 2(f), which allows an otherwise unregistrable mark to be registered if it has in fact become distinctive of the applicant's goods. This acquired distinctiveness corresponds to secondary meaning under the common law.

In order to demonstrate acquired distinctiveness under subsection (f), an applicant may submit evidence demonstrating that the mark has acquired secondary meaning. Relevant evidence includes the amount and manner of advertising, the volume of sales, the length and manner of the applicant's use of the mark, direct consumer testimony, and consumer surveys.[506] The applicant must establish acquired distinctiveness by a preponderance of evidence.[507]

An applicant need not, however, submit exhaustive evidence of secondary meaning. As an alternative, subsection (f) provides that the Director of the PTO may accept, as prima facie evidence that a mark has become distinctive of the applicant's goods, proof of *substantially exclusive and continuous use* thereof as a mark by the applicant in commerce for the five years immediately preceding the date on which the claim of distinctiveness is asserted. However,

---

[503] *Valu Eng'g*, 278 F.3d at 1274.

[504] *Talking Rain*, 349 F.3d at 603-05.

[505] 532 U.S. 23, 33-34 (2001), *cited in Talking Rain*, 349 F.3d at 604.

[506] Union Carbide Corp. v. Ever-Ready, Inc., 531 F.2d 366 (7th Cir. 1976), *cert. denied*, 429 U.S. 830 (1976).

[507] In re Rogers, 53 U.S.P.Q.2d (BNA) 1741 (T.T.A.B. 1999).

the Director is not *required* to accept this as proof of distinctiveness.[508]

In light of the savings clause of section 2(f), it is crucial to distinguish between, on the one hand, the subsection (a) prohibition against registering "deceptive" marks and, on the other hand, the subsection (e)(1) prohibition against registering "deceptively misdescriptive" marks. Whereas the latter can be overcome by a showing of secondary meaning under subsection (f), the former cannot. Thus, if a mark is deceptively misdescriptive, but not in fact *deceptive*, it can be registered once it acquires secondary meaning. In contrast, a mark that is *both* deceptively misdescriptive *and* deceptive appears to pose a much greater risk of misleading consumers, and cannot be registered even after it acquires secondary meaning.

In the case of the subsection (e)(3) bar against registering a mark that is "primarily geographically deceptively misdescriptive," the prohibition is absolute *only* if the mark in question became distinctive of the applicant's goods in commerce on or after December 8, 1993 (the effective date of the North American Free Trade Agreement (NAFTA)). Marks that became distinctive before that date, therefore, can be registered if they satisfy the secondary meaning requirement of section 2(f).

To summarize, the registration bars that can be overcome by a showing of secondary meaning include: the (e)(1) bar against "merely descriptive" and "deceptively misdescriptive" marks; the (e)(2) bar against "primarily geographically descriptive" marks; the (e)(4) bar against registering a mark that is "primarily merely a surname"; and, only with respect to marks that became distinctive before December 8, 1993, the (e)(3) bar against marks that are "primarily geographically deceptively misdescriptive."

In contrast, marks that are misdescriptive, but not deceptively so, are not subject to any registration bars at all. Under common law, these would fall into the "arbitrary" category, consisting of marks that have a dictionary meaning that bears no relationship to the nature of the goods in question.

Marks that have been denied registration under subsection (e)(1), (e)(2), or (e)(4), as well as pre-NAFTA marks denied registration under subsection (e)(3), can be registered on the Supplemental Register[509] until they meet the section 2(f) requirements. In contrast, marks that have been denied registration under any other provision of section 2 are eligible for neither the Principal nor the Supplemental Register.

[7] Dilutive Marks

Section 2 also permits the PTO to refuse registration of a mark which would be likely to cause dilution by blurring or dilution by tarnishment under section 43(c).[510] However, such refusal may occur only pursuant to an opposition

---

[508] In re Deister Concentrator Co., 289 F.2d 496 (C.C.P.A. 1961); In re Garcia, 175 U.S.P.Q. (BNA) 732 (T.T.A.B. 1972).

[509] *See* § 2.14 *infra.*

[510] The dilution language appears at the end of section 2, immediately following subsection 2(f).

proceeding brought under section 13.[511] Thus, in contrast to the other grounds for refusing to register a mark under section 2, the PTO may not, in an ex parte examination proceeding, refuse to register a mark on dilution grounds.

For an opposition to succeed on dilution grounds against an intent-to-use application, the TTAB has held that the opposer's mark must have become famous before the filing date of the application.[512] Where the application is based on actual use, however, the TTAB takes the position that the opposer's mark must have become famous prior to the applicant's first use of its mark.[513]

In determining whether the opposer's mark will be diluted by the mark for which registration is sought, the TTAB has considered "the similarity of the marks, the renown of the party claiming fame and whether purchasers are likely to associate two different products and/or services with the mark even if they are not confused as to the different origins of the products and/or services."[514] It has required the opposer to prove that the marks "are identical or very or substantially similar."[515] However, these TTAB decisions were issued prior to the 2006 amendments to section 43(c). Because those amendments now specify six non-exclusive factors for courts to consider in determining the likelihood of dilution by blurring,[516] it is likely that future TTAB decisions under section 2 will consider those six factors when the opposer contends that there is a likelihood of dilution by blurring.

This provision was first enacted in the Trademark Amendments Act of 1999, Pub. L. 106-43, sec. 2(a), 106th Cong., 1st Sess. (1999), then amended by the Trademark Dilution Revision Act of 2006 (TDRA), Pub. L. 109-312, 109th Cong., 2d Sess. (2006). The 1999 amendment applied to registration applications filed on or after January 16, 1996, and overruled Babson Bros. Co. v. Surge Power Corp., 39 U.S.P.Q.2d (BNA) 1953 (T.T.A.B. 1996), in which the TTAB had held that the Federal Trademark Dilution Act of 1995 (FTDA) did not provide grounds for opposition or cancellation proceedings. See Enterprise Rent-A-Car Co. v. Advantage Rent-A Car, Inc., 330 F.3d 1333, 1344 (Fed. Cir.) (discussing legislative history), cert. denied, 540 U.S. 1089 (2003). Although the 1999 version of this registration bar applied to any mark "which when used would cause dilution," the 2006 version (applicable on and after October 6, 2006) reflects the TDRA's adoption of the less demanding "likelihood of dilution" standard. Dilution under section 43(c) is discussed in § 3.07 infra.

[511] 15 U.S.C. § 1063. Similarly, a registration may be cancelled on these same grounds only pursuant to cancellation proceedings brought under 15 U.S.C. § 1064 (generally limited to the first five years after registration), or 15 U.S.C. § 1092 (applicable to marks registered on the Supplemental Register). The possibility that the mark would cause dilution under state law, in contrast, is not grounds for refusing or cancelling federal registration, unless it would also lead to a likelihood of confusion under section 2(d). Enterprise Rent-A-Car, 330 F.3d at 1344-45. In addition, the 1995 version of section 43(c) provided that registration on the Principal Register was a complete defense to a claim of dilution under state law; as a result of ambiguous drafting in the 2006 TDRA amendments to section 43(c), it is unclear whether registration is also a complete defense to a federal dilution claim. See § 3.07 [K] infra.

[512] Toro Co. v. ToroHead Inc., 61 U.S.P.Q.2d (BNA) 1164, 1174-75 (T.T.A.B. 2001); Nike, Inc. v. Nikepal Int'l, Inc., 2005 TTAB LEXIS 176, *16 (April 21, 2005).

[513] Toro, 61 U.S.P.Q.2d (BNA) at 1174 n. 9.

[514] Nike, 2005 TTAB LEXIS at *17.

[515] Id. at *17-18 (finding insufficient similarity, and thus no dilution, between NIKE and NIKEPAL).

[516] The blurring factors are discussed in § 3.07 [G][2] infra.

The Federal Circuit has held that an applicant's prior use of a mark, even in a limited geographic area, bars a registrant's claim of dilution as a basis for opposing the prior user's application to register its mark. In *Enterprise Rent-A-Car Co. v. Advantage Rent-A-Car, Inc.*,[517] the court held that the applicant's use of its mark in a limited geographic area prior to the date on which the opposer's mark became famous was a complete bar to a dilution-based opposition. Between 1992 and 1995 the applicant, Advantage, had used the slogan "We'll Even Pick You Up" in television commercials that aired only in San Antonio, Texas, although in later years the ads were aired in Texas as well as three adjoining states. In 1994, Enterprise began using the slogans "Pick the Company that Picks You Up," and "Pick Enterprise, We'll Pick You Up," in national advertising, and during 1996 and 1997, Enterprise obtained registration for these two phrases as well as the phrase "We'll Pick You Up." When Advantage applied to register its slogan in 1999, Enterprise filed an opposition based on dilution of its three registered marks. However, the TTAB rejected the opposition because it found that Enterprise's slogans had not become famous prior to Advantage's first use of its slogan in San Antonio. The Board also refused to limit Advantage's registration to the geographic areas of its prior use as might have been appropriate in the case of concurrent registrations under section 2(d), on the ground that this practice was limited to cases involving confusing similarity under section 2(d).[518] The Federal Circuit agreed, reasoning that the language of section 43(c) evinced congressional intent to provide relief only where a plaintiff's mark had achieved fame before the defendant made *any* use in commerce of its allegedly dilutive mark.[519] The authoritativeness of these decisions appears to be unaffected by the 2006 amendments to section 43(c).

[C]   Certification Marks

A mark may be registered as a certification mark, rather than as a trademark or service mark, pursuant to section 4 of the Lanham Act.[520] Section 45 defines a certification mark as:

any word, name, symbol, or device, or any combination thereof —

(1)   used by a person other than its owner, or

(2)   which its owner has a bona fide intention to permit a person other than the owner to use in commerce and files an application to register on the principal register established by this Act, to certify regional or other origin, material, mode of manufacture, quality, accuracy, or other characteristics of such person's goods or services or that the work or labor on the goods or services was performed by members of a union or other organization.[521]

---

[517] 330 F.3d 1333 (Fed. Cir.), *cert. denied*, 540 U.S. 1089 (2003).

[518] *Id.* at 1337 (citing 37 C.F.R. § 2.133(c)).

[519] *Id.* at 1341-43

[520] 15 U.S.C. § 1054.

[521] *Id.* § 1127.

Examples of certification marks include the "Underwriters Laboratory" or "UL" mark, which signifies that a product complies with certain safety standards,[522] and the "Roquefort" mark, which signifies that cheese has been manufactured according to a particular process and within a particular region of France.[523]

The prohibition against registering primarily geographically descriptive marks contains an exception for certification marks, which can be registered even if they describe the geographic origin of goods or services and lack secondary meaning.[524] However, a nongeographic mark that is generic or primarily descriptive cannot be registered as a certification mark, because consumers would not recognize such a mark as a certification of quality.[525]

A certification mark is neither a trademark nor a service mark, and will become invalid if it is used as such. Thus, the owner of a certification mark is prohibited from producing or marketing the goods or services to which that mark is applied; such activities are grounds for refusal or cancellation of a certification mark's registration.[526] However, a certification mark registrant is not prohibited from using its certification mark in advertising or promoting its certification program or the goods or services meeting its certification standards, provided that the registrant does not itself produce, manufacture, or sell any of the certified goods or services to which its certification mark is applied.[527]

Under section 14(5) of the Lanham Act,[528] registration of a certification mark may also be cancelled if the registrant (1) does not control, or is not able legitimately to exercise control over, the use of such mark;[529] (2) permits the use of the certification mark for purposes other than to certify; or (3) discriminately refuses to certify or to continue to certify the goods or services of any person who maintains the standards or conditions that such mark certifies. A certification mark must be made available, without discrimination, to any product or service that meets the certification standards.[530]

[D]   Collective Marks

Section 4 of the Lanham Act permits registration of collective marks, which are trademarks or service marks indicating that the user is a member of the particular association or collective group that owns that mark. Thus, the origin-signifying function of a collective mark is not to signify that the goods or

---

[522] Midwest Plastic Fabricators, Inc. v. Underwriters Laboratories, Inc., 906 F.2d 1568 (Fed. Cir. 1990).

[523] Community of Roquefort v. William Faehndrich, Inc., 303 F.2d 494 (2d Cir. 1962).

[524] Id.

[525] In re Prof'l Photographers of Ohio, Inc., 149 U.S.P.Q. (BNA) 857 (T.T.A.B. 1966).

[526] In re Florida Citrus Comm'n, 160 U.S.P.Q. (BNA) 495 (T.T.A.B. 1968).

[527] 15 U.S.C. § 1064(5).

[528] Id.

[529] See Midwest Plastic Fabricators, 906 F.2d at 1573 (rejecting claims that UL failed to exercise sufficient control over use of its certification mark).

[530] 15 U.S.C. § 1064; Roquefort, 303 F.2d at 497.

services come from a particular source, but to indicate that their source is affiliated with a particular group. Unlike certification marks, collective marks do not signify that the product or service bearing the mark has particular qualities or characteristics.

Section 45 defines a collective mark as:

a trademark or service mark —

(1)   used by the members of a cooperative, an association, or other collective group or organization, or

(2)   which such cooperative, association, or other collective group or organization has a bona fide intention to use in commerce and applies to register on the principal register established by this Act, and includes marks indicating membership in a union, an association, or other organization.[531]

A collective mark's registration may be canceled if the association (as distinguished from individual members) begins to use the mark on goods or services, or transfers ownership of the mark to a particular member of the group.[532] However, the association is free to license its mark to nonmembers subject to the generally applicable rule requiring trademark licensors to exercise proper control over licensees' use of the mark.[533] Like trademarks and service marks, a collective mark must be distinctive in order to be registered on the Principal Register.[534]

Examples of collective marks include "REALTOR" and "REALTORS," registered by the National Association of Realtors,[535] and "LIONS INTERNA-TIONAL," registered by the International Association of Lions Clubs.[536]

[E]   Service Marks

Service marks, as defined in section 45 of the Lanham Act,[537] may be registered, subject to all of the same rules and protections that apply to trademarks for goods.[538] If the same mark is used for both goods and services, two separate registrations may be obtained.[539]

For a mark to be registered as a service mark, the owner must use the mark in connection with offering bona fide services, as opposed to activities that

---

[531]   15 U.S.C. § 1127.

[532]   F.R. Lepage Bakery, Inc. v. Roush Bakery Prods. Co., 851 F.2d 351 (Fed. Cir.), *modified and remanded*, 863 F.2d 43 (Fed. Cir. 1988).

[533]   Professional Golfers Ass'n of America v. Bankers Life & Cas. Co., 514 F.2d 665, 668 (5th Cir. 1975).

[534]   Racine Industries Inc. v. Bane-Clene Corp., 35 U.S.P.Q.2d (BNA) 1832, 1837 (T.T.A.B. 1994).

[535]   Zimmerman v. National Ass'n of Realtors, 70 U.S.P.Q.2d (BNA) 1425 (T.T.A.B. 2004).

[536]   Int'l Ass'n of Lions Clubs v. Mars, Inc., 221 U.S.P.Q. (BNA) 187 (T.T.A.B. 1984).

[537]   *See* § 2.09 [A] *supra*.

[538]   15 U.S.C. § 1053.

[539]   In re Burger King of Florida, Inc., 136 U.S.P.Q. (BNA) 396 (T.T.A.B. 1963).

constitute merely the advertising, promotion, or aftermarket support of the merchant's goods.[540] In some cases, this distinction can be difficult to draw — for example, where the mark is used in connection with a contest or a sporting event that provides entertainment services to the public while simultaneously promoting the merchant's goods.[541]

On occasion, advertising agencies have attempted to register marks for their advertising services even though the marks are in fact licensed to their clients for use in promoting the clients' own goods or services. For example, one agency attempted to register "THE ROAD AUTHORITY" for the advertising services that it provided in promoting the goods and services of auto parts stores. The agency licensed this slogan to various auto parts stores on a territorially exclusive basis. Because the slogan did not serve to identify the origin of the agency's advertising services — if anything, it identified the origin of the goods and services offered by the auto parts stores — the agency was not entitled to register the mark.[542] In contrast, an advertising agency may obtain a service mark registration for a slogan that it uses to promote its advertising services, even if it *also* uses (or allows clients to use) the same slogan to promote the goods or services of the clients.[543]

§ 2.10   REGISTRATION PROCESS

Under section 1 of the Lanham Act, there are two types of applications for registration on the Principal Register of the PTO — one based on use, and the other based on intent to use. In the alternative, an application may be based on the existence of a foreign or international trademark registration, or application therefor; these applications are filed under section 44 or section 66 of the Act, rather than section 1. Applications under section 1 are discussed in subsections [A] and [B] below. Applications under section 44 are discussed in § 2.15[C], and applications under section 66 (applying the Madrid Protocol) are discussed in § 2.15[D].

[A]   Use

An application based on use must contain all the information required by section 1(a) of the Lanham Act, including, *inter alia*, the date of the applicant's first use of the mark,[544] the goods or services with which the mark is used, a

---

[540] *See, e.g.*, In re Orion Research, Inc., 669 F.2d 689 (C.C.P.A. 1980) (guarantee to repair or replace merchant's own merchandise is not a "service").

[541] *See, e.g.*, In re Dr. Pepper Co., 836 F.2d 508 (Fed. Cir. 1987); In re Heavenly Creations, Inc., 168 U.S.P.Q. (BNA) 317 (T.T.A.B. 1971).

[542] In re Application of Admark, Inc., 214 U.S.P.Q. (BNA) 302 (T.T.A.B. 1982); *accord*, In re Local Trademarks, Inc., 220 U.S.P.Q. (BNA) 728 (T.T.A.B. 1983) (refusing to register "WHEN IT'S TIME TO ACT" as mark for advertising agency's services, because slogan was in fact used by agency's clients to promote their insurance services).

[543] In re Advertising & Marketing Dev., Inc. 821 F.2d 614, 620-21 (Fed. Cir. 1987) (reversing refusal to register "THE NOW GENERATION" as mark for advertising services where slogan was used both for agency's promotional services and for clients' banking services).

[544] The application must indicate the date of the applicant's first use of the mark *anywhere* (even

drawing of the mark,[545] and a specimen.[546] In the case of sound, scent, or other nonvisual marks, a detailed description is required in place of a drawing.[547] If the applicant intends to rely on section 2(f) to establish acquired distinctiveness, the application may also include evidence of such distinctiveness.[548] An application for concurrent use must also provide the information necessary for the PTO to determine the appropriate restrictions on that registration.[549] Similarly, applications for registration of collective marks or certification marks must provide the information necessary to determine whether the marks qualify for the type of registration requested.[550]

If the PTO examiner determines that the mark is entitled to registration, the mark is published in the Official Gazette of the PTO.[551] If no opposition is filed within the statutory period (30 days, subject to extensions for good cause), the certificate of registration will issue.[552] If the examiner determines that the mark is not entitled to registration, the applicant may appeal that decision to the Trademark Trial and Appeals Board (TTAB).[553]

[B]   Intent to Use

An application based on intent to use a mark in commerce is governed by section 1(b) of the Lanham Act. In general, the requirements are similar to those for an application based on actual use. However, rather than assert the date of first use in commerce, the intent-to-use (ITU) applicant must state a bona fide intent to use the mark in commerce. In addition, no specimen is required at the time of filing.[554] A complete ITU application must specify the goods or services for which the mark will be used, and must include a drawing of the mark, the filing fee, a statement of the applicant's bona fide intention to use the mark, and a statement that the applicant knows of no other party that is entitled to use the same or a confusingly similar mark in commerce.[555]

---

intrastate) in connection with the specified goods or services, as well as the date of its first use in commerce. 37 C.F.R. § 2.34.

[545] The requirements for the drawing vary depending on whether the mark is a simple word mark or requires such elements as color, motion, three dimensions, or a specific font. *Id.* § 2.52. Where a drawing cannot adequately capture the significant features of the mark, a verbal description may also be required. *Id.* § 2.52(b)(5).

[546] *Id.* § 2.56(a).

[547] *Id.* § 2.52(e).

[548] *Id.* §§ 2.41, 2.43.

[549] *Id.* § 2.42.

[550] *Id.* §§ 2.44-2.45.

[551] 15 U.S.C. § 1062.

[552] *Id.* § 1063.

[553] *Id.* § 1070; 37 C.F.R. § 2.141.

[554] 37 C.F.R. §§ 2.33(b)(2), 2.56(a).

[555] 15 U.S.C. § 1051(b)(1)-(3). Although subsection (b)(2) refers only to "goods," section 3 of the Lanham Act makes clear that the ITU provisions, like other provisions of the Lanham Act, are equally applicable to services. *Id.* § 1053.

Once the ITU application is filed, the PTO conducts an initial examination of the mark and, if the trademark examiner determines that the applicant will be entitled to register the mark on the Principal Register upon commencing use of the mark in commerce, the mark will be published in the PTO's Official Gazette.[556] (An intent-to-use application may also be amended to allege actual use at any time before the examiner approves the mark for publication; this converts the ITU application in a regular use-based application.[557]) If no opposition is filed within the post-publication statutory period (30 days, subject to extensions for good cause), or if any opposition filed is unsuccessful, then a Notice of Allowance (rather than a certificate of registration) will issue.[558]

Within six months of the date on which the Notice of Allowance is issued, the applicant must file a verified statement that the mark is being used in commerce, indicating the first date on which such use occurred, and describing the goods or services on which the mark is being used (which must correspond to goods or services that were specified in the Notice of Allowance).[559] The applicant must also submit such specimens or facsimiles of the mark used in commerce as the Director of the PTO may require.[560]

An applicant who is unable to file the verified statement of use within the prescribed six-month period may obtain a six-month extension upon filing a written request before the expiration of the original six-month term.[561] Further six-month extensions totaling no more than 24 months are available, but only for good cause.[562] The requirements for establishing good cause are not onerous:

> The showing of good cause must include a statement of the applicant's ongoing efforts to make use of the mark in commerce on or in connection with each of the relevant goods or services. Those efforts may include product or service research or development, market research, manufacturing activities, promotional activities, steps to acquire distributors, steps to obtain governmental approval, or other similar activities. In the alternative, the applicant must submit a satisfactory explanation for the failure to make efforts to use the mark in commerce.[563]

Every request for an extension of the time to file a verified statement of use, including the initial extension for which good cause need not be shown, must be made in writing, must be filed before the expiration of the preceding extension, and must include the prescribed fee as well as a verified statement indicating the goods or services specified in the Notice of Allowance as to which the applicant

---

[556] *Id.* § 1062(a).

[557] 15 U.S.C. § 1051(c); 37 C.F.R. § 2.76.

[558] 15 U.S.C. § 1063(b). In contrast, at this point in the application process for an application based on use, the mark would be registered on the Principal Register. *Id.*

[559] *Id.* § 1051(d)(1); 37 C.F.R. § 2.88.

[560] 15 U.S.C. § 1051(d)(1).

[561] *Id.* § 1051(d)(2).

[562] *Id.*; 37 C.F. R. § 2.89(c). Thus, if the applicant uses all of the available extensions, the maximum period of time that may pass between the filing of the ITU application and the filing of the verified statement of use is 36 months.

[563] 37 C.F.R. § 2.89(d).

has a continued bona fide intention to use the mark in commerce.[564] Any goods or services listed in the Notice of Allowance that are not listed in the verified statement of intent to use that accompanies the extension request will be excluded from the extension, and thus will not be included in any trademark registration that ultimately issues from the ITU application.[565] Failure to timely file a statement of use or an extension request will cause the ITU application to be abandoned, unless the applicant demonstrates that the failure was unintentional.[566]

If the actual use and specimen requirements are satisfied within the statutory period (including any extensions), then the PTO will then conduct an examination to determine whether the marks, as used, qualify for registration pursuant to section 2 of the Lanham Act.[567] If the marks so qualify, then a certificate of registration will issue, but only with respect to the goods or services that were specified in the applicant's statement of use.[568] This notice of registration will be published in the PTO's Official Gazette.[569] The effective date of this registration will be the filing date of the ITU. Thus, a successful ITU application permits the applicant to establish nationwide constructive use, and thus nationwide priority, prior to the date on which the mark was actually used in commerce.[570]

An adverse decision on an intent-to-use application may be appealed to the TTAB.[571]

[C]   Who May Register a Mark

Only the *owner* of a mark is entitled to register the mark;[572] in the case of an intent-to-use application, the applicant must be "the person who is entitled to use the mark in commerce."[573] A licensee — even an exclusive licensee — is not entitled to register the licensed mark.[574] An application from an applicant who is not the owner of the mark (or the person entitled to use it) at the time of filing is void, and cannot be amended, because the application right is not assignable; however, an error in the manner of setting forth the applicant's name is correctable.[575] Joint owners of a mark may file a joint application.[576]

---

[564] 15 U.S.C. § 1051(d)(2).

[565] 87 C.F.R. § 2.89 (f).

[566] 15 U.S.C. § 1051(d)(4). A petition to revive the application on the ground that the failure was unintentional must meet timeliness and other requirements specified in 37 C.F.R. § 2.66.

[567] 15 U.S.C. §§ 1051(d)(1), 1052.

[568] *Id.* Thus, if the statement of use indicates that the mark is being used on or in connection with fewer than all of the goods or services that were specified in Notice of Allowance, the registration will be granted only for this smaller subset of goods or services.

[569] *Id.* § 1051(d)(1).

[570] *Id.* § 1057(c).

[571] *Id.* § 1070; 37 C.F.R. § 2.141.

[572] 15 U.S.C. § 1051(a)(1); Huang v. Tzu Wei Chen Food Co., 849 F.2d 1458 (Fed. Cir. 1988).

[573] TMEP § 803.01.

[574] In re Phillips Beverage Co., Nos. 75/313,751 & 75/313,753, 2000 TTAB LEXIS 656 (T.T.A.B. Sept. 13, 2000); Marcon Ltd. v. Avon Prods., Inc., 4 U.S.P.Q.2d (BNA) 1474 (T.T.A.B. 1987).

[575] TMEP § 803.01; 37 C.F.R. § 2.71(d).

[D] Opposition

In the case of both use and intent-to-use applications, the opposition period begins on the date the mark is published in the Official Gazette, and is limited to 30 days unless extensions are granted. After notice to all parties, opposition proceedings, which are *inter partes*, take place before the TTAB, which determines whether the opposed mark should be registered, and what, if any, restrictions to impose on the registration.[577]

An opposition may be filed by any person who anticipates being damaged (for example, due to likelihood of confusion with, or dilution of, another mark) by the registration of the applicant's mark on the Principal Register.[578] To have standing to bring an opposition, an opposer must have a "real interest" in the proceeding.[579] The nature of that interest will depend on the grounds for the opposition. For example, where the opposer claims priority in a confusingly similar mark under section 2(d), the opposer must have "a real commercial interest in its own mark or trade name, plus a reasonable basis for its belief that it would be damaged by the registration in question."[580] In an opposition based on section 2(d) or the false suggestion of an affiliation under section 2(a), the opposer must have a proprietary right in the mark at issue.[581] Where the opposer alleges that the applicant's mark is merely descriptive (or generic), the opposer must be a competitor of the applicant with respect to the goods or services in question.[582] Standing to oppose a mark that is merely a surname, or that is geographically merely descriptive, can be asserted by a competitor with the same surname, or whose goods come from the same geographic area, respectively.[583]

An opposition under section 2(d) may be brought by either the owner or the exclusive licensee of a mark that is confusingly similar to the mark sought to be registered.[584] Whether a non-exclusive licensee has standing to oppose remains unsettled.[585]

---

[576] TMEP § 803.03(d).

[577] 15 U.S.C. § 1067.

[578] 15 U.S.C. § 1063(a).

[579] Lipton Industries, Inc. v. Ralston Purina Co., 670 F.2d 1024, 1028 (CCPA 1982); Compuclean Mktg. & Design v. Berkshire Prods., Inc., 1 U.S.P.Q.2d (BNA) 1323 (T.T.A.B. 1986).

[580] National Ass'n of Certified Home Inspectors, Inc. v. American Soc'y of Home Inspectors, Inc., Opposition No. 91166484 (T.T.A.B. Aug. 28, 2008).

[581] Jewelers Vigilance Comm., Inc. v. Ullenberg Corp., 229 U.S.P.Q. (BNA) 860 (T.T.A.B. 1987).

[582] No Nonsense Fashions, Inc. v. Consolidated Foods Corp., 226 U.S.P.Q.2d (BNA) 502, 504 (T.T.A.B. 1985); Fioravanti v. Fioravanti Corrado S.R.L., 230 U.S.P.Q. (BNA) 36 (T.T.A.B. 1986).

[583] Fioravanti v. Fioravanti Corrado S.R.L., 230 U.S.P.Q. (BNA) 36 (T.T.A.B. 1986).

[584] J.L. Prescott Co. v. Blue Cross Laboratories (Inc.), 216 U.S.P.Q. (BNA) 1127, 1128 (T.T.A.B. 1982).

[585] National Ass'n of Certified Home Inspectors, Inc. v. American Soc'y of Home Inspectors, Inc., Opposition No. 91166484 (T.T.A.B. Aug. 28, 2008) (suggesting, without deciding, that non-exclusive licensees have standing); *see* Ramex Records, Inc. v. Guerrero, 2002 TTAB LEXIS 407 (T.T.A.B. June 26, 2002) (holding that "licensee or distributor" has standing); William & Scott Co. v. Earl's Restaurants Ltd., 30 U.S.P.Q.2d (BNA) 1870, 1872 n.2 (T.T.A.B. 1994) (similar).

[E]   Interferences

The Director may declare an interference between two applications for registration, or between such an application and a not-yet-incontestable registration, if the marks in question so resemble one another as to give rise to a likelihood of confusion when applied to the respective applicants' goods or services, but only upon a showing of extraordinary circumstances that would unduly prejudice a party in the absence of an interference. Ordinarily, however, the availability of an opposition or cancellation proceeding will eliminate such prejudice.[586] Typically, an interference is declared only where a party would otherwise have to engage in multiple opposition or cancellation proceedings in which the issues are substantially the same.[587] An interference can be declared only upon petition to the Director.[588] Once the examiner determines that each of the marks in question is registrable, the marks will be published in the Official Gazette for opposition, and, upon notice to the parties, the TTAB will conduct the interference, which is an *inter partes* proceeding at which the respective priorities of the parties, and their rights to registration, will be determined.[589]

[F]   Concurrent Use Proceedings

Under section 2(d), concurrent use proceedings may be instituted where an applicant seeks to register a mark that resembles another mark already registered or in use, but the Director determines that confusion, mistake, or deception will not arise from concurrent registrations if appropriate conditions and limitations are imposed on the use of each mark. However, concurrent registrations are permitted only if (a) both users became entitled to use their respective marks through concurrent lawful use prior to the earliest filing date to which either is entitled, or (b) the user with the earlier filing date consents to concurrent registration by the other user. In addition, the Director may issue concurrent registrations when a court of competent jurisdiction has determined that more than one party is entitled to use the same or similar marks in commerce. In either case, the Director may limit the mode or place of use of each mark, or the range of goods or services encompassed by each registration.[590] The substantive standards for granting concurrent use registrations are discussed in § 2.09 [B][4][d] above.

Like other trademark applications, concurrent use applications are published in the Official Gazette for opposition. If there are no successful oppositions, concurrent use proceedings will be initiated upon notice to all concurrent users and registrants, unless such proceedings are unnecessary because a court of competent jurisdiction has already resolved the respective rights of the

---

[586] 37 C.F.R. § 2.91.

[587] TMEP § 1507; In re Family Inns of America, Inc., 180 U.S.P.Q. (BNA) 332 (Comm'r of Patents 1974).

[588] TMEP § 1507; 37 C.F.R. § 2.91(a).

[589] 15 U.S.C. § 1067; 37 C.F.R. §§ 2.92-.93.

[590] 15 U.S.C. § 1052(d).

concurrent users, and the concurrent use application complies fully and exactly with the court's decree.[591]

Intent-to-use applications are subject to concurrent use proceedings only after the statement of actual use has been filed as required by section 1(d).[592]

[G] Dividing Applications

Pending trademark applications (whether based on use or intent to use) may be divided into two or more separate applications. In the case of intent-to-use applications, division is mandatory if the applicant files an amendment to allege use under section 1(c) before making use of the mark on all of the goods or services listed in the application, or files a statement of use under section 1(d) before using the mark on all of the goods specified in the notice of allowance.[593]

[H] Maintaining and Renewing Registrations

To maintain a federal trademark registration, the owner of the registration must periodically file: (1) an affidavit of use and (2) a renewal application. Because the time frames for these filings coincide, registrants may choose to combine them into a single document, provided that it meets the statutory requirements for both filings.[594]

[1] Affidavit of Use

Under section 8 of the Lanham Act,[595] the owner must file an affidavit of use (and pay the applicable fee) between the fifth and sixth years after initial registration, another between nine and ten years after initial registration, and another in the year preceding every tenth year thereafter.[596] The affidavit must indicate either: (1) the goods or services recited in the registration on or in connection with which the mark is being used in commerce, in which case it must be accompanied by specimens or facsimiles demonstrating use, or (2) the goods or services recited in the registration on or in connection with which the mark is *not* being used in commerce, in which case the affidavit must demonstrate that the nonuse is excused by special circumstances and is not due to any intention to abandon the mark.[597] If the registrant pays the applicable surcharge, a six-month grace period applies to each affidavit deadline, and deficient affidavits may be corrected.[598] Otherwise, failure to timely file the

---

[591] 37 C.F.R. § 2.99.

[592] *Id.* § 2.99(g).

[593] TMEP §§ 1104.03(a), 1109.03, 1110; 37 C.F.R. §§ 2.76(c), 2.87(a), 2.88(c).

[594] TMEP § 1606.15.

[595] 15 U.S.C. § 1058.

[596] The six- and ten-year affidavits of use are also required for marks that were registered under the Trademark Acts of 1881 or 1905 and that were subsequently republished under 15 U.S.C. § 1062(c) in order to claim the benefits of the Lanham Act. *Id.* § 1058(b). In this case, the initial six-year period is measured from the republication date. *Id.*

[597] 15 U.S.C. § 1058(b).

[598] *Id.* § 1058(c).

affidavit will lead to cancellation of the mark.[599]

Under section 71 of the Lanham Act,[600] affidavits of use are also required to maintain registrations arising from extensions of protection under the Madrid Protocol. In general, the statutory periods for filing are the same. However, for the ten-year filings, the affidavit must be filed within the last six months of each ten-year period (rather than within the last year). Although there is a six-month grace period for late filings of the ten-year affidavits, there is no grace period for the six-year affidavit, and there is no provision for correcting deficiencies.[601]

[2]   Renewal

Under section 9 of the Lanham Act,[602] a federal trademark registration may be renewed for a ten-year period beginning ten years after the initial registration, and continuing at successive ten-year intervals thereafter.[603] The renewal application may be filed during the final year of each ten-year registration period, or, upon payment of a fee, within six months after the end of that registration period.[604] Failure to timely file the renewal application will cause the registration to be cancelled.[605] If a renewal application is rejected, the Director must notify the registrant of the reasons for the rejection.[606] The registrant has the option to renew the registration for fewer than all of the classes of goods or services covered by the initial registration or prior renewals thereof.[607]

Although the person filing the renewal application need not be the owner of the registered mark, the application must be signed by the registrant or the registrant's representative,[608] and the renewal registration will be issued in the name of the registration's owner of record. If the mark has been assigned since its initial registration (or any subsequent renewal thereof), the assignee can become the owner of record only by recording the assignment or other document of title with the PTO's Assignment Services Branch, and notifying the Post Registration examiner, at the time the renewal application is filed, that such documentation has been recorded.[609]

Section 9 applies to all registrations except for extensions of protection under the Madrid Protocol; these must be renewed by application to WIPO's International Bureau.[610]

---

[599]   *Id.* § 1058(a).

[600]   *Id.* § 1141k.

[601]   TMEP § 1613.

[602]   15 U.S.C. § 1059.

[603]   *Id.* § 1059(a).

[604]   *Id.*; 37 C.F.R. § 2.182.

[605]   TMEP § 1606.03 (collecting cases).

[606]   15 U.S.C. § 1059(b).

[607]   TMEP § 1606.02; 37 C.F.R. § 2.183.

[608]   TMEP § 1606.06; 37 C.F.R. § 2.183(a).

[609]   TMEP § 1606.06.

[610]   TMEP § 1606.01(b).

§ 2.11 JUDICIAL REVIEW

Under section 21 of the Lanham Act,[611] two alternative routes of appeal from adverse decisions of the TTAB or the Director of the PTO are available to an applicant for trademark registration or renewal, a party to an interference or cancellation proceeding, a party to a concurrent use application, or a registrant who has filed a continuing use affidavit under section 8.[612] The dissatisfied party may appeal the decision to the United States Court of Appeals for the Federal Circuit, in which case the court will limit its review to the record before the PTO,[613] or the party may commence a civil action in federal district court.[614] These procedures apply to registrations on either the Principal or the Supplemental Register.

In an appeal to the Federal Circuit, decisions on questions of law are reviewed de novo. Prior to 1999, questions of fact were reviewed under the "clearly erroneous" standard of review. However, in 1999 the Supreme Court held in *Dickinson v. Zurko*[615] that PTO findings of fact must be reviewed according to the standards established in section 706 of the Administrative Procedure Act.[616] The Federal Circuit subsequently determined that section 706 requires it to apply the "substantial evidence" standard of review to the PTO's findings of fact.[617] This standard requires the court to uphold the PTO's findings if "a reasonable person might find that the evidentiary record supports the agency's conclusion," and "involves examination of the record as a whole, taking into account evidence that both justifies and detracts from an agency's decision."[618]

For example, when the PTO finds that a mark is unregistrable under section 2(d) because its similarity to another mark would create a likelihood of confusion, the Federal Circuit treats this as a question of law subject to de novo review, but it reviews the factual findings on which the PTO bases its legal conclusion — the *DuPont* factors[619] — under the more deferential "substantial evidence" standard.[620] Abandonment, too, is a question of fact, subject to substantial evidence review.[621]

If a party elects to commence a civil action in federal district court rather than to seek a review in the Federal Circuit, the standard of review for questions of law is de novo, but the standard of review for findings of fact is somewhat

---

[611] 15 U.S.C. § 1071.

[612] *Id.* § 1058.

[613] *Id.* § 1071(a)(4).

[614] *Id.* § 1071(b).

[615] 527 U.S. 150 (1999).

[616] 5 U.S.C. § 706.

[617] In re Gartside, 203 F.3d 1305, 1315 (Fed. Cir. 2000); Recot, Inc. v. M.C. Becton, 214 F.3d 1322 (Fed. Cir. 2000).

[618] On-Line Careline, Inc. v. America Online, Inc., 229 F.3d 1080, 1085-86 (Fed. Cir. 2000).

[619] In re E.I. DuPont DeNemours & Co., 476 F.2d 1357, 1361 (C.C.P.A. 1973). *See* § 2.09 [B][4] *supra.*

[620] *On-Line Careline*, 229 F.3d at 1084.

[621] *Id.* at 1087.

unsettled; the weight of authority, however, holds that the district court must review the factual findings of the TTAB under the substantial evidence standard of review, but because the parties may also submit new evidence in a district court proceeding, the court may make new findings of fact based on the newly submitted evidence.[622] In addition, several circuits have held that a party bringing a section 21(b) action in a district court may also introduce new issues not brought before the TTAB.[623]

For purposes of appellate review, the Federal Circuit has treated PTO determinations under sections 2(a) and 2(d) as questions of law based on underlying factual findings.[624] However, at least one district court has rejected this approach, treating section 2(a) and 2(d) determinations as question of fact, and basing this decision on authorities that have treated "likelihood of confusion" determinations under sections 32 and 43(a) as questions of fact.[625]

§ 2.12 CANCELLATION

[A]   Grounds for Cancellation

Once a trademark has been registered on the Principal Register, it is entitled to a presumption of validity under section 7(b) of the Lanham Act.[626] Nonetheless, the registration is subject to cancellation under the conditions set forth in section 14.[627] Some grounds of cancellation apply regardless of the length of time the mark has been registered, while others apply only during the first five years of registration.

Under sections 14(3) and 14(5), a mark may be cancelled *at any time* on one of the following grounds, even after it has become incontestable:[628] if the mark becomes generic, if it is functional, if it has been abandoned, if its registration was obtained fraudulently, if its registration was obtained contrary to section 4 of the Lanham Act (dealing with collective and certification marks) or the registration prohibitions of sections 2(a), (b), or (c), or if it is being used by, or with the permission of, the registrant to misrepresent the source of the goods or services with respect to which it is used. If a mark becomes generic with respect to some, but not all, of the goods or services for which it is registered, then it is subject to cancellation only with respect to those goods or services as to which it has become generic.[629]

---

[622] Pro-Football, Inc. v. Harjo, 284 F. Supp. 2d 96, 102, 115-16 (D.D.C. 2003).

[623] Aktieselskabet AF 21. November 2001 v. Fame Jeans, Inc., 525 F.3d 8, 12 (D.C. Cir. 2008); CAE, Inc. v. Clean Air Eng'g, Inc., 267 F.3d 660, 674 (7th Cir. 2001); PHC, Inc. v. Pioneer Healthcare, Inc., 75 F.3d 75, 80 (1st Cir. 1996).

[624] *See, e.g.*, In re Mavety Media Group Ltd., 33 F.3d 1367, 1371 (Fed. Cir. 1994); Weiss Assocs., Inc. v. HRL Assocs. Inc., 902 F.2d 1546, 1547-48, 14 U.S.P.Q.2d (BNA) 1840, 1841 (Fed. Cir. 1990).

[625] *Pro-Football, Inc.*, 284 F. Supp. 2d 96, 116-17 (collecting cases).

[626] 15 U.S.C. § 1057(b).

[627] *Id.* § 1064.

[628] *Id.* § 1065.

[629] *See, e.g., Abercrombie & Fitch Co. v. Hunting World, Inc.*, 537 F.2d 4, 13 (2d Cir. 1976)

A certification mark may also be cancelled at any time if the registrant (1) does not control, or is unable legitimately to exercise control, over the use of the mark, (2) engages in the production or marketing of any goods to which the certification mark is applied, (3) permits the use of the mark for purposes other than to certify, or (4) discriminately refuses to certify or continue to certify goods that meet the standards or conditions that the mark certifies.[630]

In addition to the grounds on which a mark may be cancelled at any time, a mark that has been registered on the Principal Register for less than five years may be cancelled if it becomes subject to any of the bars to registration under section 2 — for example, if it is found to be merely descriptive under section 2(e)(1), or if it is found, under section 2(d), to bear a confusing resemblance to a mark already in use in the United States.[631]

Sections 2, 14, and 24[632] of the Lanham Act permit cancellation of a registered mark that would be likely to cause dilution by blurring or dilution by tarnishment under section 43(c).[633] A dilution-based cancellation petition may be filed against any registration that was filed on or after January 16, 1996.[634] In order to prevail, however, the petitioning party must establish that its mark became famous prior to the registrant's first use of the allegedly dilutive mark.[635]

[B]   Procedure

A petition for cancellation may be filed by any person who believes he or she has been, or will be, damaged by the registration of a mark on the Principal Register, including as a result of dilution under section 43(c).[636] The TTAB conducts an *inter partes* proceeding to rule on the petition, and its decision is subject to judicial review by the Federal Circuit.[637]

In a court action involving a registered mark, a court may order full or partial cancellation of a registration if it determines that the registration is wholly or partly invalid.[638]

(finding partial cancellation appropriate where "Safari" mark was generic as to some goods but not others).

[630] 15 U.S.C. § 1064(5); *see, e.g., Midwest Plastic Fabricators Inc. v. Underwriters Labs., Inc.*, 906 F.2d 1568 (Fed. Cir. 1990) (rejecting cancellation petition alleging that UL failed to exercise adequate control over use of its certification mark).

[631] These grounds for cancellation cease to be available once the mark has been registered in the Principal Register for five years, regardless of whether the registrant has also filed for incontestable status under section 15. 15 U.S.C. § 1065. *See, e.g.*, Gracie v. Gracie, 2003 TTAB LEXIS 514 (T.T.A.B. 2003) (holding that registration of GRACIE may not be cancelled after five years on ground that it is primarily merely a surname, even though registrant has not sought incontestable status).

[632] 15 U.S.C. § 1092.

[633] Pub. L. 106-43, sec. 2(a), 106th Cong., 1st Sess. (1999).

[634] Toro Co. v. ToroHead, Inc., 61 U.S.P.Q.2d (BNA) 1164, 1172 (T.T.A.B. 2001).

[635] *Id.* at 1174 n. 9.

[636] 15 U.S.C. § 1064.

[637] *Id.* §§ 1067(a), 1071.

[638] *Id.* § 1119; Abercrombie & Fitch Co. v. Hunting World, Inc., 537 F.2d 4 (2d Cir. 1976).

Because a registration is entitled to a presumption of validity, the Federal Circuit requires the petitioner in a cancellation proceeding to establish grounds for cancellation by a preponderance of the evidence.[639] Although several other courts agree,[640] some circuits require "clear and convincing" evidence, at least where the ground for cancellation is fraud or abandonment.[641] Even where the preponderance of the evidence standard applies, the longer a party waits to commence a cancellation proceeding, the more persuasive that party's evidence will need to be, because the registration is entitled to a presumption of validity under section 7(b), and typically the trademark owner will have built up goodwill in the registered mark in the time since registration.[642]

§ 2.13   INCONTESTABILITY

[A]   Effect of Incontestable Status

In a significant departure from the common law principles on which the Lanham Act is based, section 15 of the Act[643] permits certain registered marks to become *incontestable*.[644] Incontestable status conclusively establishes the validity of a registered mark, as well as the registrant's ownership of, and exclusive right to use, the mark in commerce, with respect to the goods or services for which it has become incontestable.[645]

There are several important exceptions to the conclusive presumptions of validity, ownership, and exclusivity. The conclusive presumptions do not apply to the extent that grounds exist for cancelling the mark under paragraphs (3) or (5) of section 14.[646] They also do not apply to the extent, if any, that the use of the registered mark infringes any common law right established by another's continuous use of a mark from a date prior to the registration date.[647]

---

[639] West Fla. Seafood v. Jet Rests., 31 F.3d 1122, 1128 (Fed. Cir. 1994); Cerveceria Centroamericana, S.A. v. Cerveceria India, Inc., 892 F.2d 1021, 1023 (Fed. Cir. 1989).

[640] Creative Gifts, Inc. v. UFO, 235 F.3d 540, 545 (10th Cir. 2000); *Pro-Football, Inc.*, 284 F. Supp. 2d at 122.

[641] *Pro-Football*, 284 F. Supp. 2d at 122; Woodstock's Enters., Inc. v. Woodstock's Enters., Inc., 43 U.S.P.Q.2d (BNA) 1440 (T.T.A.B. 1997) (requiring "clear and convincing" evidence of fraud); *compare* Eurostar, Inc. v. "Euro-Star" Reitmoden GMBH & Co., 34 U.S.P.Q.2d (BNA) 1266 (T.T.A.B. 1995) (requiring "clear and convincing" evidence of abandonment), *with* Cerveceria Centroamericana, 892 F.2d at 1024 (applying "preponderance of the evidence" to abandonment), *and* Auburn Farms, Inc. v. McKee Foods Corp., 51 U.S.P.Q.2d (BNA) 1439 (T.T.A.B. 1999) (similar).

[642] *See Cerveceria Centroamericana*, 892 F.2d at 1023-24; *Pro-Football*, 284 F. Supp. 2d at 123 (collecting authorities).

[643] 15 U.S.C. § 1065.

[644] Other significant departures from common law are section 22's provision for constructive notice of registration, *id.* § 1072, and modification of the common law rule that allowed acquisition of concurrent rights by users in distinct geographic areas if the later adopter began using the mark without knowledge of the prior use. Park N' Fly v. Dollar Park and Fly, Inc., 469 U.S. 189, 200 (1985).

[645] 15 U.S.C. § 1115(b).

[646] *Id.* § 1064(3), (5).

[647] *Id.* § 1065.

When a mark becomes incontestable, the grounds on which its registration can be cancelled are more limited than in the case of other registered marks. Under section 14 of the Lanham Act, an incontestable mark can be cancelled only on the following grounds: (1) with respect to any goods or services as to which it becomes generic; (2) if it is functional; (3) if it is abandoned; (4) if its registration was obtained fraudulently or in violation of section 2(a), (b), or (c)[648]; (5) in the case of collective or certification marks, if the registration was obtained contrary to the requirements of section 4; or (6) if the mark is used by, or with the permission of, the registrant in a manner that misrepresents the source of goods or services.[649]

Notably, an incontestable mark cannot be cancelled on the ground that it was granted in violation of section 2(d). Thus, even if the mark should not have been registered because it was confusingly similar to a mark already in use or already registered, once the mark becomes incontestable this confusing similarity cannot be grounds for cancellation.

Incontestability also offers a significant benefit to descriptive marks that have been registered on the basis of acquired distinctiveness under section 2(f). Until they achieve incontestable status, such marks are vulnerable to invalidation, and thus cancellation, on the grounds that they are insufficiently distinctive to maintain their registration. Once such a mark becomes incontestable, however, mere descriptiveness (short of genericness) is insufficient grounds for cancellation. In effect, incontestability serves to quiet title to the mark.

In addition to limiting the grounds on which a mark's registration may be cancelled, incontestability also limits the defenses that are available to an alleged infringer. Under section 33(b), defenses to infringement of incontestable marks are limited to the following:

(1)   that the registration, or incontestable status, was obtained fraudulently,[650]

(2)   that the registrant has abandoned the mark,[651]

(3)   that the registrant (or a party acting with the consent of, or in privity with, the registrant) is using the mark to misrepresent the source of goods or services,

(4)   that the defendant's use of the mark is a *fair use*,[652]

(5)   that the mark used by the defendant was adopted without knowledge of

---

[648]   *Id.* § 1052(a), (b), (c).

[649]   *Id.* § 1064(3).

[650]   Fraud on the PTO occurs when an applicant makes material representations of fact which it knows or should know are false or misleading. Torres v. Cantine Torresella S.r.l., 808 F.2d 46, 48 (Fed. Cir. 1986); Medinol Ltd. v. Neuro Vasx, Inc., 67 U.S.P.Q.2d (BNA) 1205 (T.T.A.B. 2003). In May 2009, the Federal Circuit heard oral arguments in a case that challenges the "knew or should have known" standard. In re Bose, No. 08–1448 (Fed. Cir. May 6, 2009).

[651]   Abandonment is discussed at § 3.12 [A] *infra.*

[652]   The fair use defense is discussed at §§ 3.12 [F] and [G] *infra.*

the registrant's prior use, and has been used continuously by the adopter, or those in privity with the adopter, since a date prior to the effective date of registration of the mark alleged to be infringed,[653]

(6)   that the mark used by the defendant was registered and used before the registration of the mark alleged to be infringed, and was not abandoned,

(7)   that the mark has been or is being used to violate federal antitrust laws,

(8)   that the mark is functional,[654] or

(9)   that equitable principles (including laches, estoppel, and acquiescence) are applicable.

The prior use defenses under subsections (5) and (6) — which differ in that subsection (6) requires both prior use and prior registration — apply only to the areas in which the defendant's prior use is established.[655]

The Supreme Court's decision in *Park N' Fly v. Dollar Park and Fly*[656] established that descriptiveness is not a defense to infringement of an incontestable mark.[657] In contrast, genericness is grounds for cancellation of an incontestable mark as well as a defense to infringement of an incontestable mark. Even though genericness is not specifically mentioned as a defense in section 33(b), courts have inferred its availability as a defense from the language of section 15(4), which provides that "no incontestable right shall be acquired in a mark which is the generic name of the goods or services or a portion thereof, for which it is registered,"[658] and from section 14(3), which permits cancellation of an incontestable mark that becomes generic.[659]

For purposes of the likelihood-of-confusion test for infringement,[660] the fact that a mark is incontestable does not necessarily establish that it is a strong mark.[661]

---

[653] Whether the effective date is the application date, the date on which the registration was granted, or another date, depends on whether the registration was applied for before or after the effective date of the Trademark Law Revision Act of 1988. 15 U.S.C. § 1115(b)(5)(A)-(C).

[654] *See, e.g.*, Baughman Tile Co. v. Plastic Tubing, Inc., 211 F. Supp. 2d 720 (E.D.N.C. 2002).

[655] 15 U.S.C. §§ 1115(b)(5), (6); *see, e.g.*, Burger King of Fla., Inc. v. Hoots, 403 F.2d 904 (7th Cir. 1968) (applying "limited area" defense under § 33(b)(5) to limit the common law rights of prior user to geographic area of use prior to effective date of plaintiff's registration); Lucky Brand Dungarees, Inc. v. Ally Apparel Resources LLC, 2008 U.S. Dist. LEXIS 8210 (S.D.N.Y. Feb. 5, 2008) (unpub.) (concluding that the geographic scope of rights under § 33(b)(6) is the same as under § 33(b)(5)).

[656] 469 U.S. 189, 201 (1985).

[657] *See, e.g.*, Salton, Inc. v. Cornwall Corp., 477 F. Supp. 975 (D.N.J. 1979) (rejecting descriptiveness as defense to infringement of HOTRAY mark for electric food warmers).

[658] 15 U.S.C. § 1065(4).

[659] 15 U.S.C. § 1064(3); *see, e.g.*, Te-Ta-Ma Truth Found. — Family of U.R.I., Inc. v. World Church of the Creator, 297 F.3d 662, 665 (7th Cir. 2002), *cert. denied*, 537 U.S. 1111 (2003).

[660] The likelihood-of-confusion test is discussed in § 3.02 [B] *infra*.

[661] *Compare* Oreck Corp. v. U.S. Floor Sys., Inc., 803 F.2d 166 (5th Cir. 1986), *cert. denied*, 481 U.S. 1069 (1987), *and* American Soc'y of Plumbing Eng'rs v. TMB Publ'g., Inc., 109 Fed. Appx. 781

Although incontestability conclusively establishes a registrant's exclusive right to use the mark in question with respect to the goods or services for which it has been registered, it does not guarantee the registrant's right to register that mark for additional goods or services.[662]

[B]   Establishing Incontestability

Section 15 of the Lanham Act sets forth the conditions under which a mark can become incontestable. To become incontestable with respect to goods and services for which it is registered, it must have been in continuous use in commerce with respect to those goods or services for at least five consecutive years from the date of registration on the Principal Register.[663] In addition, there must not have been any final decision adverse to the registrant's right to claim of ownership in the mark or right to obtain or maintain the mark's registration, and there must be no pending proceeding in the courts or the PTO with respect to those rights.[664] To obtain incontestable designation for a qualifying mark, the registrant must file an affidavit with the Director within one year after the end of any such five-year period, asserting that the mark has been in continuous use for this period, and is still in use, and specifying the goods or services for which the mark is registered and has been in continuous use.[665] A mark cannot become incontestable with respect to any goods or services as to which it has become generic.[666]

§ 2.14   THE SUPPLEMENTAL REGISTER

Registration on the Supplemental Register offers benefits for certain marks that lack the distinctiveness to be registered on the Principal Register, but that nonetheless have the capacity to acquire distinctiveness through use.[667] A major purpose for the creation of the Supplemental Register was to provide a type of domestic trademark registration for marks that had not yet acquired secondary meaning, because United States copyright owners often needed a domestic registration in order to qualify for a foreign registration. Although this function has since diminished in importance as foreign countries have abandoned the domestic registration prerequisite, the Supplemental Register also serves other useful purposes, providing a searchable public record of marks that have been adopted for use in commerce, and preventing the registration of confusingly similar marks.

(7th Cir. 2004) (unpub.), *with* Dieter v. B&H Indus. of Southwest Fla., Inc., 880 F.2d 322 (11th Cir. 1989), *cert. denied*, 498 U.S. 950 (1990).

[662] *See, e.g.*, In re Best Software, Inc., 63 U.S.P.Q.2d (BNA) 1109 (T.T.A.B. 2002).

[663] 15 U.S.C. § 1065.

[664] *Id.* § 1065(1), (2).

[665] *Id.* § 1065(3).

[666] *Id.* § 1065(4).

[667] In re Simmons Co., 278 F.2d 517 (C.C.P.A. 1960).

[A]   Eligible Marks

Under section 23 of the Lanham Act,[668] marks registrable on the Supplemental Register include "any trademark, symbol, label, package, configuration of goods, name, word, slogan, phrase, surname, geographical name, numeral, device, any matter that as a whole is not functional, or any combination of any of the foregoing, but such mark must be capable of distinguishing the applicant's goods or services."[669] Thus, marks that are ineligible for registration on the Principal Register may be registered on the Supplemental Register, unless they are functional or barred by sections 2(a), (b), (c), (d), or (e)(3).[670] The Supplemental Register primarily benefits marks that lack sufficient secondary meaning to satisfy section 2(f). For example, a mark that is merely descriptive, or primarily merely a surname, may be registered on the Supplemental Register prior to acquiring distinctiveness through secondary meaning, provided the PTO considers it to be capable of becoming distinctive. Once such a mark acquires distinctiveness, the owner of the mark may pursue its registration on the Principal Register under section 2(f). In contrast, a mark that is deceptive under section 2(a) cannot be registered on either the Principal or the Supplemental Register. The same is true of generic marks, which are considered incapable of distinguishing the applicant's goods or services under any circumstances.[671]

To be eligible for supplemental registration, a mark must be in lawful use in commerce in connection with the goods or services for which it is registered.[672] Where a mark is the subject of an intent-to-use application for the Principal Register under section 1(b), the mark is eligible for supplemental registration only after an amendment to allege use or a statement of use has been filed.[673]

Although applications for the Supplemental Register may be filed under section 44 (foreign registrations),[674] they may not be filed under section 66(a)[675] (the Madrid Protocol).[676]

---

[668] 15 U.S.C. § 1091.

[669] *Id.* § 1091(c).

[670] *Id.* § 1091(a), (c). The section 2(e)(3) bar is inapplicable, however, to marks that were in lawful use in commerce in connection with goods or services prior to December 8, 1993 (the effective date of NAFTA). *Id.* § 1091(a).

[671] *See, e.g.*, In re Helena Rubenstein, Inc., 410 F.2d 438 (CCPA 1969); Clairol, Inc. v. Roux Distr. Co., Inc., 280 F.2d 863 (CCPA 1960); In re Sealol, Inc., 168 U.S.P.Q. (BNA) 320 (T.T.A.B. 1970).

[672] 15 U.S.C. § 1091(a); 27 C.F.R. § 2.47(a).

[673] 15 U.S.C. § 1094; 37 C.F.R. § 2.47(d).

[674] 15 U.S.C. § 1126; *see* § 2.15 [C] below.

[675] 15 U.S.C. § 1141f; *see* § 2.15 [D] below.

[676] 37 C.F.R. §§ 2.47(b)-(c).

[B] Registration Procedure

A mark may be registered on the Supplemental Register after it is examined for eligibility, and upon compliance with sections 1(a) and 1(e) of the Lanham Act, to the extent applicable.[677] Such marks are not subject to opposition, and are not published in the PTO's Official Gazette until after registration.[678] They are, however, subject to cancellation.[679]

If a mark is refused registration on the Supplemental Register, the applicant may appeal that decision using the same procedures that apply to refusal of registration on the Principal Register.[680]

[C] Effect of Supplemental Registration

Under section 26,[681] a mark registered on the Supplemental Register is denied many of the benefits conferred by registration on the Principal Register. The certificate of supplemental registration does not constitute prima facie evidence of the validity, ownership, or exclusive right to use the mark. The constructive notice and constructive use provisions do not apply, and the mark may not become incontestable. Under section 28,[682] the owner of a supplemental registration may not invoke the provisions of section 42[683] barring importation of counterfeit goods.

Except as provided in section 26, if a mark is registered on the Supplemental Register, it constitutes a "registered" mark for purposes of Title 15. Thus, it can be the basis for refusing registration on the Principal Register to a confusingly similar[684] or dilutive mark (although refusing registration on dilution grounds requires an opposition proceeding).[685] A mark registered on the Supplemental Register can also be the basis for a refusal to register a confusingly similar mark on the Supplemental Register.

Although supplemental registration does not provide constructive notice of ownership under section 22, it does provide a searchable database that enables potential adopters of a mark to determine whether a similar mark is already in use.

---

[677] 15 U.S.C. § 1091(a), (b).

[678] *Id.* § 1092.

[679] 15 U.S.C. § 1092; *see, e.g.*, Professional Economics Inc. v. Professional Economic Servs., Inc., 205 U.S.P.Q. (BNA) 368 (T.T.A.B. 1979).

[680] 15 U.S.C. §§ 1091(b), 1062(b), 1071. For the appeal procedures, see §§ 2.10 [A] and 2.11 *infra.*

[681] 15 U.S.C. § 1094.

[682] *Id.* § 1096.

[683] *Id.* § 1124.

[684] *Id.* § 1052(d).

[685] *Id.* § 1052 (language following subsec. (f)).

[D]   Cancellation

A mark registered on the Supplemental Register is not published for opposition, and may not be the subject of an opposition proceeding, but will be published in the Official Gazette upon registration. Any person who believes that he or she is or will be damaged by registration of that mark on the Supplemental Register may then file a petition to cancel the registration under section 24. However, if cancellation is sought on the ground that the registered mark is likely to dilute a famous mark by blurring or tarnishment under section 43(c), then cancellation is allowed only if the petitioner's mark became famous *before* the effective filing date of the registration on the Supplemental Register.[686]

After a cancellation petition has been filed, and upon notice to the registrant, the TTAB will conduct a hearing, and if the mark is ineligible for registration, or if it has been abandoned, then the Director will cancel the registration.[687]

§ 2.15   DOMESTIC PRIORITY BASED ON FOREIGN TRADEMARK REGISTRATIONS

[A]   International Agreements

The United States is a signatory to a number of international agreements pertaining to trademarks and unfair competition, including multilateral agreements as well as agreements with individual nations. The multilateral agreements include, among others, the International Convention for the Protection of Industrial Property (the "Paris Convention"), the General Inter-American Convention for Trade Mark and Commercial Protection, and the Madrid Protocol.

For example, under the 1883 Paris Convention, which pertains to trademarks as well as other forms of industrial property, the United States and the other 167 member nations must provide "national treatment" to one another's nationals (including corporations), meaning that foreign nationals must be afforded trademark rights at least equal to those provided to the member's own nationals.[688] In addition, a national of any signatory country who applies to register a trademark in one member nation may use that filing to establish an effective filing date in any other member nation where that applicant applies for registration within six months of the first filing.[689] However, the Paris Convention (unlike the Madrid Agreement and the Madrid Protocol, discussed in § 2.15 [D] below) does not provide a mechanism for filing a multinational application.

---

[686] *Id.* § 1092.

[687] *Id.* § 1094.

[688] Paris Convention, Art. 2(1).

[689] Paris Convention, Art. 4(A)(1)(C); 15 U.S.C. § 1441g.

The requirements of these international agreements have been incorporated throughout the Lanham Act, most notably in section 44.[690]

[B]   National Treatment

The requirement of national treatment is implemented in section 44(b), which provides that nationals of a country that is (1) a party to a trademark treaty or convention to which the United States is a party, or that (2) extends reciprocity to United States nationals, are entitled to "the rights to which any owner of a mark is otherwise entitled" under the Lanham Act. They also enjoy certain additional rights specifically provided to such foreign persons by section 44. Section 44(g) provides that trade names or commercial names of such parties are protected even without registration, and even if they do not constitute trademarks, section 44(h) entitles them to "effective protection against unfair competition," including the remedies afforded by the Lanham Act.[691]

[C]   Domestic Priority Based on Foreign Registration

Under section 44(d), nationals of trademark treaty partners or countries providing reciprocity (as prescribed by section 44(b)) may take advantage of an exception (in addition to the section 1(b) intent-to-use exception that is available to all applicants) to the general rule that a mark can be federally registered only after its use in commerce has commenced.[692] Section 44(d) implements Article 4 of the Paris Convention by giving foreign nationals a right of priority for six months after filing a foreign application, even if the applicant has not yet used the mark anywhere in the world. To take advantage of section 44(d), both the applicant and the country where the foreign application is filed must qualify under section 44(b),[693] and the United States application must include a statement of bona fide intent to use the mark in commerce.[694] Where these conditions are satisfied, a domestic application that is filed within six months after the foreign application is filed will be treated as having the same filing date as the previously filed foreign application. The filing date of the foreign application becomes the effective date of the applicant's constructive use in the United States.[695] Thus, where a qualifying applicant files a United States application before the expiration of this six-month period, an intervening use of a similar mark in the United States that commences during the priority period will not invalidate the foreign applicant's right to register the mark.[696] Therefore, a competing user can establish common law priority rights, or

---

[690]   15 U.S.C. § 1126.

[691]   Havana Club Holding, S.A. v. Galleon, S.A., 203 F.3d 116 (2d Cir.), *cert. denied*, 531 U.S. 918 (2000) (rights under § 44(h) are coextensive with treaty rights under § 44(b), including treaty rights relating to repression of unfair competition).

[692]   Crocker Nat'l Bank v. Canadian Imperial Bank of Commerce, 223 U.S.P.Q. (BNA) 909 (T.T.A.B. 1984).

[693]   15 U.S.C. § 1126(d).

[694]   *Id.* § 1126(d)(2).

[695]   *Id.* § 1126(d).

[696]   *Id.* § 1126(d); *see, e.g.*, SCM Corp. v. Langis Foods, Ltd., 539 F.2d 196 (D.C. Cir. 1976).

federal registration priority, only where the competing use of the mark (or domestic application to register the mark) predates the filing of the foreign application that caused the six-month grace period to commence.[697] However, the foreign applicant may not file an infringement action based on any acts committed prior to the date on which the mark becomes registered, unless the registration is based on use in commerce.[698]

Notwithstanding the priority rights conferred by section 44(d), section 44(c) provides that a federal registration will not issue until either (1) the mark has been registered in the applicant's country of origin, or (2) the applicant alleges use of the mark in commerce.[699] The applicant's "country of origin" is defined as "the country in which he has a bona fide and effective industrial or commercial establishment, or if he has not such an establishment the country in which he is domiciled, or if he has not a domicile in any of the countries described in subsection (b) of this section, the country of which he is a national."[700]

Section 44(e) confers a second significant privilege on foreign applicants. Once the applicant has obtained a trademark registration in the country of origin, the mark may be registered on the Principal Register (if eligible) or on the Supplemental Register. Although the foreign applicant must state a bona fide intent to use the mark in commerce, the registration may issue even if the use in commerce has not commenced.

The section 44(e) registration privilege is significantly more generous than the intent-to-use provisions of section 1(b) in that a registration pursuant to an intent-to-use application will not issue until after the use in commerce has commenced. A section 44(e) registration requires only that the mark be the subject of a valid registration in the country of origin (as defined in section 44(c)) at the time the federal registration issues. Because many foreign countries do not require use of a mark prior to registration, it is therefore possible for a foreign applicant to obtain a federal registration for a mark without ever having used that mark in the United States or anywhere else in the world.

A foreign applicant that obtains a federal registration under section 44(e) may maintain that registration for up to six years without actually using the mark in commerce.[701] Upon proof of use in commerce before the end of that six-year period, the registration will be subject to the same rules as a use-based registration.[702]

---

[697] 15 U.S.C. § 1126(d)(3).

[698] *Id.* § 1126(d)(4).

[699] *Id.* § 1126(c); *see also* In re Societe d'Exploitation de da Marque le Fouquet's, 67 U.S.P.Q.2d (BNA) 1784 (T.T.A.B. 2003). (underlying foreign registration must be valid at time U.S. registration issues).

[700] 15 U.S.C. § 1126(c).

[701] *Id.* § 1058(a).

[702] *Id.* § 1058(a)-(b).

[D]   The Madrid Agreement and the Madrid Protocol

The United States is not a signatory to the Madrid Agreement Concerning the International Registration of Marks (1891) (the "Madrid Agreement"), which is administered by the World Intellectual Property Organization (WIPO), and which had 56 signatories as of November 2008. Nationals (including corporations) of signatory countries that have registered a mark in their home country may file a single international trademark registration in their home country's trademark office in which they request registration in some or all of the member nations.[703] Any country wishing to refuse to register the mark must do so within 12 months, or protection will be automatically granted.[704] International registrations under the Madrid Agreement last for 20 years,[705] and may be renewed.[706] However, if the applicant's home country registration is invalidated within the first five years, the international registration will be invalidated as well.[707]

The United States has not joined the Madrid Agreement, based on concerns that United States nationals would be disadvantaged compared with the nationals of other countries. In the United States, trademark registration is generally more difficult and takes longer to obtain, and can be more difficult to defend against challenges, than in most countries that are signatories to the Agreement. This would lead to several problems: (1) it would be more difficult for a United States national to obtain the predicate home country registration than it would be for nationals of other Madrid signatories to do so, (2) the United States PTO might have difficulty completing its examination of a Madrid registration application before the end of the 12-month period for refusing a foreign application, and (3) a home country registration in the United States would be more vulnerable to invalidation during its first five years than a home country registration elsewhere. Another obstacle was that the Madrid Agreement requires applications to be filed in French.[708]

Effective November 2, 2003, however, the United States joined the Protocol Relating to the Madrid Agreement Concerning the International Registration of Marks (1989), also known as the Madrid Protocol, which had 78 signatories as of November 2008.[709] Under the Protocol, a United States national[710] that applies for, or has already obtained, a United States trademark registration may also

---

[703] Madrid Agreement, Arts. 1(2), 3(1), 3ter(1).

[704] Id. Arts. 5(2), 5(5).

[705] Id. Arts. 3ter(2), 6(1).

[706] Id. Art. 7(1).

[707] Id. Art. 6(3).

[708] Common Regulations Under the Madrid Agreement Concerning the International Registration of Marks and the Protocol Relating to that Agreement, Rule 6(1)(a).

[709] Nations may join the Madrid Agreement, the Madrid Protocol, or both. There is significant overlap in their membership.

[710] Under section 61 of the Lanham Act, a United States trademark registration or application may serve as the basis for an international registration under the Madrid Protocol only if the registrant or applicant is a United States national or domiciliary, or a party that maintains "a real and effective industrial or commercial establishment" in the United States. 15 U.S.C. § 1141a(b).

file a single international application covering any countries that are Protocol signatories.[711] The registration date for a properly filed international application that is promptly forwarded to WIPO's International Bureau by the United States PTO will be the date on which that application was filed at the PTO.[712] Member countries may elect a period of either 18 months or 12 months as their time limit for refusing registration to an international applicant.[713] Due to the length of the examination process under the Lanham Act, the United States has elected 18 months.[714]

Conversely, a party that obtains an international trademark registration from a Protocol country *other than* the United States may request an extension of that protection to the United States.[715] Under section 66 of the Lanham Act, such a request must be accompanied by a declaration of bona fide intent to use the mark in commerce.[716] A request for extension of protection is subject to examination to determine whether the mark meets the requirements for registration on the Principal Register under section 2 of the Lanham Act. If the trademark examiner determines that the mark fails to meet these requirements, then the extension of protection will be refused.[717] However, registration may *not* be refused on the ground that the mark has not been used in commerce.[718] If the examiner determines that the mark meets the requirements of section 2

---

[711] Madrid Protocol, Art. 2(1); 15 U.S.C. § 1141a(a). Note that Art. 2(1) of the Madrid Protocol allows the international registration to be filed on the basis of a trademark *application* in the applicant's home country, whereas Art. 1(2) of the Madrid Agreement requires that the international applicant have already obtained a home country *registration*. Because the registration process in the United States is lengthier than that of many other countries, joining the Protocol rather than the Agreement allows United States nationals to obtain their international registrations that much sooner, and eliminates the advantage that nationals of countries with faster registration systems would enjoy under the Agreement.

[712] Madrid Protocol, Art. 3(4). If the international application does not reach WIPO's International Bureau within two months of its filing at the PTO, the international registration's effective date will be the date on which the application was actually received by the International Bureau. *Id.*

[713] *Id.* Art. 5(2).

[714] 15 U.S.C. §§ 1141h(c)(1), (4). In determining whether to grant or refuse an international application that is submitted to the PTO by WIPO's International Bureau pursuant to the Madrid Protocol procedure, while the PTO must refuse to register a mark that does not meet the requirements for registration on the Principal Register, *id.* § 1141h(a)(4), it may not refuse to register a mark on the ground that the applicant's mark has not been used in commerce, *id.* § 1141h(a)(3). However, the international application must declare a bona fide intent to use the mark in commerce. *Id.* § 1141f(a). Unless registration is refused, the PTO must issue a "certificate of extension of protection" for the mark, which, as of the date such certificate issues, has the same effect as a registration on the Principal Register. *Id.* § 1141i. In addition, the foreign applicant's submission of the international registration application to WIPO constitutes constructive use in the United States under section 7(c) of the Lanham Act, *id.* § 1057(c), as of the earliest of the following dates: (1) the Paris Convention priority date (if applicable), (2) the date on which the international registration application was filed (if it designated the United States as one of the Protocol nations where protection was sought), or (3) the date on which the applicant requested trademark protection in the United States (if that request was not included in the original international application). *Id.* § 1141f(b).

[715] *Id.* § 1141e.

[716] *Id.* § 1141f (a).

[717] *Id.* § 1141h(a)(4).

[718] *Id.* § 1141h(a)(3).

(other than use in commerce), then the mark will be published in the Official Gazette, and will be subject to opposition. Within 18 months of receiving the request for extension of protection, the Director must transmit to WIPO's International Bureau any of the following that are relevant: (1) a notification of refusal based on examination of the request; (2) a notification of refusal based on the filing of an opposition; or (3) a notification that an opposition may be filed after the end of the 18-month period. In the latter case, if the opposition results in a refusal, the Director must send notice of this refusal within a statutory time period. If the Director does not send a notice of refusal within the designated time frames, then the extension of protection must be granted,[719] and the PTO must issue a "certificate of extension of protection" for the mark, which, as of the date such certificate issues, has the same effect as a registration on the Principal Register.[720]

Unless the request for extension of protection is refused, the filing of the request for extension of protection constitutes constructive use of the mark under section 7(c) of the Lanham Act,[721] as of the earliest of (1) the international registration date (if the request for extension of protection to the United States was filed in the international application), (2) the date of recordal of the request for extension of protection to the United States, if the request was made after the international registration date, or (3) any earlier priority date claimed pursuant to Article 4 of the Paris Convention.[722]

All international registrations under the Protocol last for ten years,[723] and may be renewed in a single application.[724] However, during the first five years of an international registration under the Protocol, the registration will be cancelled if the home country application is rejected, withdrawn, or lapses, or if the home country registration is cancelled or otherwise terminates.[725] If the home country's rejection, withdrawal, cancellation, or termination applies to some but not all categories of goods or services for which the registration was sought or obtained, then the international cancellation will apply only to those categories.[726] The same results follow if the home country application is rejected, or the home country registration cancelled, after the end of the five-year period, if this outcome results from a legal action that commenced during the five-year period.[727] However, when a mark loses its international registration as a result of adverse action in the home country, the applicant has a three-month grace period in which to file country-by-country applications in the Protocol nations without losing the priority date that was based on the

---

[719] *Id.* § 1141h.

[720] *Id.* § 1141i.

[721] *Id.* § 1057(c).

[722] *Id.* §§ 1141f(b), (g).

[723] Madrid Protocol, Art. 6(1).

[724] *Id.* Art. 7.

[725] *Id.* Art. 6(3).

[726] *Id.*

[727] *Id.*

international registration.[728] This option — known as "transformation" — is not available under the Madrid Agreement.

As permitted by the Madrid Protocol (in contrast to the Madrid Agreement),[729] the United States PTO requires international applications to be filed in English.[730]

By taking advantage of the international filing mechanism of the Madrid Protocol, United States nationals seeking foreign trademark registrations can avoid having to file separate applications in each signatory country where protection is desired, and can thereafter renew all of these registrations in a single renewal application. In addition, the Paris Convention's six-month grace period allows for additional foreign applications by United States nationals — which must be filed country-by-country in any of nearly 100 countries that are Paris signatories but not Protocol signatories — to obtain a priority date based on the filing date of the United States application.

International trademark registrations under either the Madrid Agreement or the Madrid Protocol are searchable on WIPO's Madrid Express database.[731]

PART V:

STATE TRADEMARK REGISTRATION

§ 2.16   STATE REGISTRATION STATUTES

[A]   General

Many states have supplemented common law protection of trademarks by enacting their own registration systems. Many of the state registration requirements are modeled after, and closely resemble, the federal scheme,[732] including preclusions similar to those in section 2 of the Lanham Act,[733] and in such cases their terms are typically interpreted *in pari materia*. State trademark registration can benefit parties that cannot use the federal registration system because they do not use their marks in interstate commerce. State registration schemes typically do not displace common law rights.[734]

---

[728] *Id.* Art. 9 *quinquies.* This option is not available, however, where the home country registration was voluntarily cancelled by the trademark owner. *Id.*

[729] *Common Regulations Under the Madrid Agreement Concerning the International Registration of Marks and the Protocol Relating to that Agreement*, Rule 6(1)(b).

[730] 37 C.F.R. § 7.3.

[731] http://www.wipo.int/madrid/en/madrid_express.htm. For further information on the Madrid Agreement and the Madrid Protocol, see *Madrid System for the International Registration of Marks*, at http://www.wipo.int/madrid/en/index.html.

[732] *See, e.g.*, CAL. BUS. & PROF. CODE § 14220 (2005); § 765 I.L.C.S. 1036/10 (2005); N.Y. GEN. BUS. L. § 360-a (2005).

[733] 15 U.S.C. § 1052.

[734] *See, e.g.*, CAL. BUS. & PROF. CODE § 14210 (2005); § 765 1036/80 (2005); N.Y. GEN. BUS. L. § 360-o (2005).

[B]   Federal Preemption

In general, state common law and state legislation with regard to trademarks and unfair competition are not preempted by the Lanham Act, regardless of whether they parallel the Lanham Act or depart from it, except to the extent that they interfere with rights conferred under the Lanham Act. Thus, for example, common law trademarks are typically protected by both state law and section 43(a) of the Lanham Act. A trademark owner may obtain federal registration for the mark, or state registration, or both; the standards in some states are similar to those of section 2, while in others they may differ. Likewise, the same activities by a junior user of a mark may serve as the basis for infringement claims under both state and federal law, although the standards for establishing infringement may differ under the two regimes, and a particular plaintiff may prevail on state law claims but not federal claims, or vice versa.

If, however, in a particular situation, the enforcement of state trademark law would interfere with rights conferred under the Lanham Act, federal law will preempt the state law provisions. For example, trademark registration systems in some states may give state registrants a right of priority throughout the state, even in parts of the state where the registrant does not actually use the mark, and thus has not established common law priority.[735] These statewide priority rights would not automatically be preempted by the Lanham Act. However, if another party were to obtain federal registration for the same (or a confusingly similar) mark, the nationwide priority rights of the federal registrant would supersede the statewide priority rights of the state registrant in any area where the state registrant had not established common law priority through actual use. Thus, in a battle for priority based on constructive use, federal registration "trumps" state registration, even if the federal registration took place *after* the effective date of the state registration.[736] If a mark qualifies for federal registration, therefore, it is generally unwise to obtain a state registration without also obtaining a federal registration.

For example, in *Burger King of Florida, Inc. v. Hoots*,[737] the defendants had used their mark in one part of the state, and had also obtained a state registration for the mark, before the effective date of the plaintiffs' federal registration for the same mark.[738] The defendants argued that the state registration gave them a right of priority in the mark throughout the state, not merely in the area of actual use. The court held that even if this interpretation of the state registration statutes was accurate, the defendants' claim of statewide priority through registration could no longer be given effect once the

---

[735] *See, e.g.*, First Nat'l Bank v. First Wyo. S&L Ass'n, 192 P.2d 697, 704-05 (Wyo. 1979) (noting that Wyoming statutes do not have this effect, but that statutes in other states may).

[736] Burger King of Fla., Inc. v. Hoots, 403 F.2d 904 (7th Cir. 1968); *accord* Spartan Food Sys., Inc. v. HFS Corp., 813 F.2d 1279 (4th Cir. 1987).

[737] 403 F.2d 904 (7th Cir. 1968).

[738] At the time *Burger King* was decided, the limited area exception of section 33(b)(5) grandfathered any common law rights established before a federal registration was issued; in the Trademark Law Revision Act of 1988, the exception was narrowed to encompass only those common law rights established prior to the effective date of the registration, which is the application date. 15 U.S.C. § 1115(b)(5).

plaintiffs had obtained nationwide priority rights through their federal registration. Thus, the defendants' priority was limited to the area in which they had actually used the mark prior to the effective date of the plaintiffs' federal registration — that is, the area where they had established priority rights under common law. Their claim of statewide priority was superseded by the plaintiff's nationwide priority, even though the federal registration took place after the state registration.

Although the Lanham Act makes clear that a federal registrant has nationwide priority, some courts will not enjoin (or award damages for) the use of the mark by a junior user unless and until the registrant shows a likelihood of entry into the junior user's trading territory.[739] The leading case articulating this position is *Dawn Donut Co. v. Hart's Food Stores, Inc.*[740] In that case, the owner of the federal registration for a mark had not exploited the mark at the retail level in a particular geographic area for some 30 years. Even though the Second Circuit held that the plaintiff's mark was not abandoned (because abandonment due to cessation of use occurs only when the registrant no longer uses the mark anywhere in the United States),[741] the court refused to issue an injunction under the Lanham Act to prevent a junior user from adopting the same mark at the retail level in that territory, unless and until the plaintiff resumed its retail use of the registered mark in that territory. The court also refused to award damages. The court reasoned that:

> [B]ecause no likelihood of public confusion arises from the concurrent use of the mark in connection with retail sales of doughnuts and other baked goods in separate trading areas, and because there is no present likelihood that plaintiff will expand its retail use of the mark into defendant's market area, plaintiff is not now entitled to any relief under the Lanham Act.[742]

The junior user's right to exploit the mark in the limited trading area would cease, however, if and when the federal registrant expanded its retail activities to that area.[743]

Although the approach of *Dawn Donut* has been endorsed by the majority of circuits,[744] the Sixth Circuit has rejected it, holding instead that injunctive relief is warranted whenever infringement is established under the circuit's multi-

---

[739] KeyCorp. v. Key Bank & Trust, 99 F. Supp. 2d 814, 822 n. 5 (N.D. Ohio 2000).

[740] 267 F.2d 358 (2d Cir. 1959)

[741] *Id.* at 363.

[742] *Id.* at 360.

[743] *Id.*

[744] *See, e.g.,* Comidas Exquisitos, Inc. v. O'Malley & McGee's, Inc., 775 F.2d 260, 262 (8th Cir. 1985); Pizzeria Uno Corp. v. Temple, 747 F.2d 1522, 1536 (4th Cir. 1984); Foxtrap, Inc. v. Foxtrap, Inc., 671 F.2d 636, 640 (D.C. Cir. 1982) (per curiam); Value House, Inc. v. Phillips Mercantile Co., 523 F.2d 424, 429 (10th Cir. 1975); Holiday Inns of America, Inc. v. B & B Corp., 409 F.2d 614, 618-19 (3d Cir. 1969); Mister Donut of America, Inc. v. Mr. Donut, Inc., 418 F.2d 838, 844 (9th Cir. 1969); American Foods, Inc. v. Golden Flake, Inc., 312 F.2d 619, 625-26 (5th Cir. 1963); *cf.* Citibank, N.A. v. Citibanc Group, Inc., 724 F.2d 1540, 1546 (11th Cir. 1984) (implicitly endorsing *Dawn Donut*). *Compare* Members First Fed. Credit Union v. Members 1st Fed. Credit Union, 54 F. Supp. 2d 393, 402 (M.D. Pa. 1999) (questioning *Dawn Donut's* continuing applicability in the Third Circuit) *with*

factor likelihood-of-confusion analysis (which considers, *inter alia*, the likelihood that the plaintiff will enter the defendant's trading area in the future).[745]

PART VI:
UNREGISTERED MARKS

§ 2.17 PROTECTION OF UNREGISTERED MARKS

[A]   State Law

Even in states that have established trademark registration systems, unregistered marks that are capable of distinguishing a merchant's goods or services are still protected under the common law, under principles similar to those embodied in section 43(a) of the Lanham Act.[746]

[B]   Federal Law

Sections 43(a), 43(c), and 43(d) of the Lanham Act[747] protect unregistered marks against, respectively, unfair competition, dilution, and bad faith appropriation through domain name registrations. These provisions are discussed in §§ 3.02 – 3.09 below.

§ 2.18 ASSIGNMENTS AND LICENSES

[A]   Assignments

Under both common law and the Lanham Act, any assignment of a mark (that is, any transfer of ownership) must include a transfer of the accompanying goodwill of the line of business in which the mark is used.[748] An attempt to transfer rights in the mark without the accompanying goodwill constitutes an "assignment in gross" (sometimes called a "naked assignment"), and results in abandonment of the mark, as discussed more fully in § 3.12 [A][2][b] below. However, where some of the goodwill of a business is not associated with the mark that is being assigned — for example, where the mark is used in one line of business but not another, or where some of the goodwill of the business is

---

Commerce Bancorp, Inc. v. BankAtlantic, 285 F. Supp. 2d 475, 501 n.12 (D.N.J. 2003) (applying *Dawn Donut*).

[745] Circuit City Stores, Inc. v. CarMax, Inc., 165 F.3d 1047, 1056 (6th Cir. 1999).

[746] *See, e.g.*, HQM, Ltd. v. Hatfield, 71 F. Supp. 2d 500, 504 n.17 (D. Md. 1999) (noting that Maryland common law of unfair competition tracks § 43(a)); Great S. Bank v. First S. Bank, 625 So. 2d 463, 466-67 (1993) (using § 43(a) precedents to analyze unfair competition claim under Florida law).

[747] 15 U.S.C. §§ 1125(a), (c), (d).

[748] Oklahoma Beverage Co. v. Dr. Pepper Love Bottling Co. (of Muskogee), 565 F.2d 629 (10th Cir. 1977) (no particular words are necessary for assignment of trademark accompanied by transfer of seller's business and goodwill, where transferee continues operation under same trademark).

associated with other marks — only the goodwill associated with the particular mark being assigned must be included in the transfer.[749]

Because of the prohibition against assignments in gross, an intent-to-use application under section 1(b)[750] cannot be assigned until the verified statement of use has been filed under section 1(d)[751] or the application has been amended to allege use pursuant to section 1(c);[752] the only exception is when the application is assigned to a successor to the business of the applicant to which the mark pertains, if the business is ongoing.[753]

Assignments of registered marks, or of marks that are the subject of pending applications, must be in writing and duly executed.[754] Recording of the assignment in the PTO's Assignments Services Branch is prima facie evidence of execution.[755] An assignment is void against any subsequent purchaser for valuable consideration without notice, unless the assignment is properly recorded in the PTO within three months after the assignment or prior to the subsequent purchase.[756] In contrast, no writing requirement applies to assignments of common law marks.

If a mark is assigned while federal registration is still pending, the assignee should record the assignment in the PTO so that the registration will ultimately issue in the assignee's name.[757] The assignee becomes entitled to conduct the prosecution of the registration application.[758] If a mark is assigned after registration, the assignee should record the assignment in the PTO to ensure that future renewals will issue in the assignee's name.

If the ownership of a trademark registration changes with respect to some, but not all, of the goods and services listed in the registration, then the owners may, upon recording these assignment(s), request that the registration be divided into two or more separate registrations.[759] Thus, for example, the sole owner of a registration may assign to another party the right to use the mark with respect to some of the goods or services covered in the registration, and may retain the right to use the mark with respect to the remaining goods or services, or may transfer that right to a third party.[760] Likewise, one joint owner of a registration may transfer his or her share of the ownership to

---

[749] 15 U.S.C. §§ 1060(a)(1)-(2).

[750] *Id.* § 1051(b).

[751] *Id.* § 1051(d).

[752] *Id.* § 1051(c); Clorox Co. v. Chemical Bank, 40 U.S.P.Q.2d (BNA) 1098 (T.T.A.B. 1996).

[753] 15 U.S.C. § 1060(a)(1).

[754] *Id.* § 1060(a)(3).

[755] *Id.*

[756] *Id.* § 1060(a)(4).

[757] *Id.* § 1057(d); TMEP § 501.01(a).

[758] 37 C.F.R. § 3.71.

[759] TMEP §§ 1615-1615.02.

[760] Visa, USA, Inc. v. Birmingham Trust Nat'l Bank, 696 F.2d 1371 (Fed. Cir. 1982); TMEP § 501.06.

another party.[761] The requirement for a transfer of accompanying goodwill applies in each of these situations.

In contrast to other trademark registrations, an extension of protection under the Madrid Protocol (discussed in § 2.15 [D] above) may be assigned only to another person who is entitled to the benefits of the Protocol.[762]

[B]   Licensing

Prior to the Lanham Act, many courts held that a trademark was abandoned when it was licensed to another party outside of the business in which it was previously used, on the grounds that its use by another party was misleading.[763] In the Lanham Act, however, Congress adopted the more liberal view endorsed by other courts — that a trademark can be validly licensed provided that the licensor maintains adequate control over the licensee's use of the mark.[764]

As in the case of assignments, neither common law nor the Lanham Act imposes specific formalities on the licensing of trademarks or service marks. However, in order to avoid abandonment, it is essential that the licensor exercise adequate quality control over the licensee's use of the mark. Failure to exercise quality control constitutes "naked licensing," which will lead to a finding of abandonment. Naked licensing is discussed in § 3.12 [A][2][a] below.

---

[761] TMEP § 501.06.

[762] 15 U.S.C. § 1141l; TMEP § 501.01(b).

[763] *Dawn Donut*, 267 F.2d at 366 (collecting cases).

[764] *Id.* (citing 15 U.S.C. §§ 1055, 1127 (definition of "related company")).

Chapter 3

TRADEMARK INFRINGEMENT AND UNFAIR COMPETITION

---

§ 3.01 INTRODUCTION

A cause of action for infringement of trademarks and service marks may arise under common law, state statutes, or the Lanham Act. Under all three sources of law, traditional trademark infringement claims require the senior user of a mark to establish that the junior user's mark creates a likelihood of confusion with regard to the origin of the latter's goods or services, and that this confusion is likely to cause a competitive injury to the senior user.

However, modern trademark and unfair competition laws are even broader in scope. Under the broadly interpreted unfair competition provisions of the Lanham Act, and comparable provisions of state statutes and common law, false or misleading representations about the source, sponsorship, or affiliation of goods, services, or commercial activities are actionable even where no trademark misuse occurs, provided that the representations are likely to cause confusion. Furthermore, under the antidilution provisions of the Lanham Act, as well as statutes that have been adopted by a majority of states, an actionable injury to the rights of a trademark owner may arise in the absence of a likelihood of confusion, if the plaintiff can establish that the defendant's activities diluted the selling power of the plaintiff's mark or tarnished the reputation of that mark; under many dilution statutes, however, this extraordinary protection is limited to marks that are especially strong and/or "famous."[1] In addition, the Lanham Act contains a false advertising provision that provides a cause of action for false or misleading statements made about products or services in the context of commercial advertising or promotion.[2] Finally, under the Lanham Act's "anti-cybersquatting" provisions, certain unauthorized uses of another person's mark in a domain name are actionable as well.[3]

---

[1] For the elements of a dilution claim, see § 3.05 *infra*.

[2] For the elements of a federal false advertising claim, see § 3.04 *infra*.

[3] For the elements of a cybersquatting claim, see § 3.08 *infra*.

PART I:
TRADEMARK INFRINGEMENT

§ 3.02   ELEMENTS OF TRADEMARK INFRINGEMENT

In the case of federally registered marks (on the Principal or the Supplemental Register), a federal cause of action for infringement arises under section 32 of the Lanham Act.[4] State statutes similar to section 32 govern infringement of marks registered under state law.

Where the mark in question is not registered, but nonetheless qualifies as a mark at common law, the owner of the mark can bring an unfair competition claim under section 43(a) of the Lanham Act or under the state law of unfair competition.[5] The elements of an unfair competition claim under state law are similar to those of section 43(a), regardless of whether the state law claim arises under the common law or under an unfair competition statute.[6] In fact, courts typically use the principles of section 43(a) as a "measuring stick" for analyzing state law unfair competition claims, and will frequently dispense with analyzing the plaintiff's state law claims once they have reached a decision on the Lanham Act claims.[7]

Although the provisions of sections 32 and 43(a) are not identical, the rules governing infringement of registered and common law marks under federal law are similar in their purpose — permitting the owner of a trademark to obtain relief against any person whose unauthorized imitation of that mark is likely to confuse consumers with regard to the origin of the goods or services in connection with which the unauthorized use occurs.

Section 32(1)(a) gives the owner of a federal trademark registration a cause of action against:

Any person who shall, without the consent of the registrant —

(a)   use in commerce any reproduction, counterfeit, copy, or colorable imitation of a registered mark in connection with the sale, offering for sale, distribution, or advertising of any goods or services on or in connection with which such use is likely to cause confusion, or to cause mistake, or to deceive . . .[8]

Similarly, section 43(a)(1)(A) authorizes the owner of a common law mark to bring an infringement claim against

---

[4] 15 U.S.C. § 1114. In the case of registered marks, certain federal causes of action may also arise under section 43(a) — for example, claims of false advertising. See 15 U.S.C. § 1125(a)(1)(B).

[5] 15 U.S.C. § 1125(a). In the case of both registered and common law marks, claims of dilution or cybersquatting, which differ from traditional trademark infringement, arise under sections 43(c) and 43(d), respectively, 15 U.S.C. § 1125(c), (d). See § 3.05 infra (dilution), § 3.08 infra (cybersquatting).

[6] See, e.g., Ohio Rev. Code Ann. § 4165.02 (2005) (codifying unfair competition principles).

[7] See, e.g., Planetary Motion, Inc. v. Techsplosion, Inc., 261 F.3d 1188, 1193 n. 4 (11th Cir. 2001).

[8] 15 U.S.C. § 1114(1)(a).

Any person who, on or in connection with any goods or services, or any container for goods, uses in commerce any word, term, name, symbol, or device, or any combination thereof, or any false designation of origin, false or misleading description of fact, or false or misleading representation of fact, which —

(A)   is likely to cause confusion, or to cause mistake, or to deceive as to the affiliation, connection, or association of such person with another person, or as to the origin, sponsorship, or approval of his or her goods, services, or commercial activities by another person . . .[9]

Section 43(a) is, however, more than a trademark infringement statute. It also provides a remedy for false or misleading representations that do not involve unauthorized use of a trademark.[10] The misrepresentations may pertain to the origin of goods or services, the affiliation of one business with another,[11] or, under the false advertising provisions of section 43(a)(1)(B), the qualities or characteristics, or even the geographic origin, of any merchant's goods or services.[12] Section 43(a) is broadly construed.[13]

Under both federal law and state law, claims of trademark infringement (other than dilution claims) generally involve a two-step analysis: First, the plaintiff must establish that its mark is valid and enforceable, and that the plaintiff is the owner of that mark, with a right of priority over the defendant with respect to that mark.[14] Second, the plaintiff must establish that the defendant has used the mark in connection with goods or services in a way that is likely to cause consumer confusion as to the origin of those goods or services.[15] The analysis under the first step — validity and priority — depends on whether the claim is brought under state or federal law, and on whether the mark has been registered on the Principal Register. These differences are noted in the discussion that follows. However, the analysis of the likelihood of confusion remains essentially the same regardless of whether the mark is registered,[16] and

---

[9] 15 U.S.C. § 1125(a)(1)(A). Section 43(a)(1)(B), which addresses false advertising, is discussed in § 3.04, *infra*.

[10] Zyla v. Wadsworth, 360 F.3d 243, 251 (1st Cir. 2004); Dastar Corp. v. Twentieth Century Fox Film Corp., 539 U.S. 23, 25-28 (2003).

[11] Schlotzky's Ltd. v. Sterling, 520 F.3d 393, 399 (5th Cir. 2008) (§ 43(a) applicable where defendant falsely claimed to be plaintiff's exclusive purchasing agent).

[12] Empresa Cubana Del Tabaco v. Culbro Corp., 399 F.3d 462, 478 (2d Cir. 2005); Gnesys, Inc. v. Greene, 437 F.3d 482, 488-89 (6th Cir. 2005). The false advertising provisions of section 43(a) are discussed in § 3.04 *infra*.

[13] *Schlotzky's Ltd.*, 520 F.3d at 399.

[14] If ownership rights are not established, a court will not evaluate the likelihood of confusion. Custom Mfg. & Eng'g, Inc. v. Midway Servs., 508 F.3d 641, 648 & n.8 (11th Cir. 2007).

[15] *See, e.g.*, Lamparello v. Falwell, 420 F.3d 309, 313 (4th Cir. 2005); SunAmerica Corp. v. Sun Life Assurance Co. of Canada, 77 F.3d 1325, 1334 (11th Cir.), *cert. denied*, 519 U.S. 822 (1996).

[16] *See, e.g.*, Louis Vuitton Malletier v. Dooney & Bourke, Inc., 454 F.3d 108, 114 (2d Cir. 2006); Matrix Motor Co. v. Toyota Jidosha Kabushiki Kaisha, 290 F. Supp. 2d 1083, 1090 (C.D. Cal. 2003), *aff'd*, 120 Fed. Appx. 30 (9th Cir. 2005) (mem.) (unpub.); Rolls-Royce Motors, Ltd. v. A & A Fiberglass, Inc., 428 F. Supp. 689 (N.D. Ga. 1977).

regardless of whether the claim is brought under state statute, common law, or the Lanham Act.[17]

In addition to establishing ownership of a valid mark, and a likelihood of confusion arising from the defendant's activities, a plaintiff bringing a trademark infringement claim under either section 32 or section 43(a) of the Lanham Act must also establish that the defendant's infringing activities took place "in commerce." Likewise, an unfair competition claim under section 43(a) must also involve activities taking place in commerce. In contrast, a claim of trademark infringement or unfair competition that is brought under state law may arise from activities that are purely intrastate, and thus do not meet the "in commerce" jurisdictional requirement of federal law.

Each of these requirements is discussed below.

[A]   Ownership of a Valid Mark

If a mark is registered on the Principal Register, section 7(b) of the Lanham Act provides that the certificate of registration is prima facie evidence of the validity of the mark and its registration, of the registrant's ownership of the mark, and of the registrant's exclusive right to use the registered mark in commerce.[18] However, this applies only to the goods or services specified on the registration certificate. Thus, if the trademark owner uses the registered mark on other goods or services, it will not be entitled to the presumption of validity. When the presumption applies to a registered mark, it shifts the burden of production to the infringement defendant, who must present evidence that the mark is invalid — for example, because the mark is descriptive and lacks secondary meaning.[19] The presumption of validity does not apply to marks that are registered only on the Supplemental Register.[20]

If a mark registered on the Principal Register has become incontestable, the registration is *conclusive* evidence of the validity of the mark and its registration, of the registrant's ownership of the mark, and of the registrant's exclusive right to use the mark in commerce, subject only to a narrow list of exceptions.[21]

However, in the case of a common law mark, or a mark that is registered on the Supplemental Register, the plaintiff bears the burden of establishing ownership of a valid mark. Thus, the plaintiff must establish that it has used the mark in connection with the offering of goods or services to the public, and that its mark either (1) is inherently distinctive (that is, arbitrary, fanciful, or suggestive) or (2) has acquired secondary meaning. The date on which the

---

[17] As discussed in § 3.02 [B] *infra*, each federal court of appeals and each state uses a multi-factor analysis to determine whether the activities of the junior user give rise to a likelihood of consumer confusion. While the specific list of factors varies according to the jurisdiction, the substance of the analysis is similar. *See, e.g., Matrix Motor*, 290 F. Supp. 2d at 1090 n. 7.

[18] 15 U.S.C. § 1057(b).

[19] Custom Vehicles, Inc. v. Forest River, Inc., 476 F.3d 481, 486 (7th Cir. 2007).

[20] 15 U.S.C. § 1094; E.T. Browne Drug Co. v. Cococare Prods., 538 F.3d 185, 190 (3d Cir. 2008).

[21] 15 U.S.C. § 1115(b).

plaintiff began using its mark, and the market in which it uses the mark, will determine whether it is in fact the senior user, with priority over the accused infringer.

Sometimes, a trademark owner will make minor changes to its mark over time. In the context of an infringement action, the trademark owner may argue that its priority rights should be based on the earlier versions of the mark, rather than the most recent version. Under the practice known as "tacking," a trademark owner may claim priority in a mark based on the date on which it commenced use of a similar but not identical mark. However, tacking is permitted only when "the previously used mark is 'the legal equivalent of the mark in question or indistinguishable therefrom' such that consumers 'consider both as the same mark.' "[22] Where consumers regard the new and old marks as essentially the same, tacking furthers the goals of trademark law by protecting consumers from confusion while allowing some flexibility to trademark owners: "Without tacking, a trademark owner's priority in his mark would be reduced each time he made the slightest alteration to the mark, which would discourage him from altering the mark in response to changing consumer preferences, evolving aesthetic developments, or new advertising and marketing styles."[23]

The standard for tacking, however, has been described as "exceedingly strict."[24] The degree of similarity required is greater than the similarity required under the "likelihood of confusion" test.[25] The earlier and later versions of the mark "must create the same, continuing commercial impression, and the later mark should not materially differ from or alter the character of the mark attempted to be tacked."[26] Consistent with the strictness of this standard, tacking is rarely allowed.[27] Courts are especially reluctant to tack an earlier mark with a "narrow commercial impression" to a later mark with a "broader

---

[22] Brookfield Comms., Inc. v. West Coast Entertainment Corp., 174 F.3d 1036, 1047-48 (9th Cir. 1999) (quoting Data Concepts, Inc. v. Digital Consulting, Inc., 150 F.3d 620, 623 (6th Cir. 1998)); accord, Van Dyne-Crotty, Inc. v. Wear-Guard Corp., 926 F.2d 1156, 1159 (Fed. Cir. 1991)).

[23] Brookfield, 174 F.3d at 1048.

[24] Id.

[25] Id.

[26] Id. (quoting Van Dyne-Crotty, 926 F.2d at 1159) (adding emphasis); accord Data Concepts, 150 F.3d at 623.

[27] Sufficient similarity to support tacking was found in: Hess's of Allentown, Inc. v. National Bellas Hess, Inc., 169 U.S.P.Q. (BNA) 673, 674-75 (T.T.A.B. 1971) ("Hess Brothers" and "Hess" tacked onto "Hess's"); and Laura Scudder's v. Pacific Gamble Robinson Co., 136 U.S.P.Q. (BNA) 418, 419-20 (T.T.A.B. 1962) ("BLUE BIRD" tacked onto "BLUE ROBIN"). In contrast, sufficient similarity to support tacking was absent in: Brookfield, 174 F.3d at 1049 ("moviebuff.com" and "The Movie Buff's Movie Store" could not be tacked); Data Concepts, 150 F.3d at 623-24 ("DCI" and "dci" could not be tacked); Van Dyne-Crotty, 926 F.2d at 1160 ("CLOTHES THAT WORK. FOR THE WORK YOU DO" could not be tacked to "CLOTHES THAT WORK."); Pro-Cuts v. Schilz-Price Enters., 27 U.S.P.Q.2d (BNA) 1224, 1227 (T.T.A.B. 1993) ("PRO-CUTS" and "PRO-KUT" could not be tacked); and American Paging, Inc. v. American Mobilphone, Inc., 13 U.S.P.Q.2d (BNA) 2036 (T.T.A.B. 1989) (tacking not allowed for "American Mobilphone" with a star-and-stripe design and "American Mobilphone Paging" with identical design), aff'd, 17 U.S.P.Q.2d (BNA) 1726 (Fed. Cir. 1990).

commercial impression."[28] However, courts disagree on whether tacking is a question of law or fact.[29]

In a section 43(a) action for infringement of unregistered trade dress, establishing ownership of a valid mark requires one additional element: the plaintiff must establish, as part of its prima facie case, that the trade dress it seeks to protect is not functional.[30] In contrast, under state law, while functionality will bar an infringement claim, it is up to the individual states to determine whether nonfunctionality is part of the plaintiff's prima facie case or whether the plaintiff need address it only to rebut a functionality defense.

[B]   Likelihood of Confusion

[1]   Overview

In a cause of action for infringement of a registered or common law trademark, or for a false designation of origin claim under unfair competition doctrine, the key inquiry is whether the defendant's false or misleading representation as to the origin of goods or services is likely to confuse the consuming public. More specifically, the likelihood-of-confusion test inquires whether "an appreciable number of ordinarily prudent consumers" are likely to be misled or confused into believing that the junior user's product or service either originated with the senior user, or had some connection (such as sponsorship, endorsement, or affiliation) to the senior user.[31]

Under this test, the likelihood of confusion is evaluated from the point of view of the "ordinarily prudent consumer."[32] The ordinarily prudent consumer is not necessarily assumed to be highly intelligent, or to exercise a high degree of care in purchasing decisions, but is instead assumed to possess those characteristics that are typical of buyers for the particular goods or services at issue.[33] The

---

[28] In *Van Dyne-Crotty*, 926 F.2d at 1160, the Federal Circuit noted the following examples: *Polo Fashions, Inc. v. Extra Special Products, Inc.*, 451 F. Supp. 555 (S.D.N.Y. 1978) (earlier use of "Marco Polo" mark could not be tacked to later use of "Polo" mark); *Corporate Fitness Programs v. Weider Health and Fitness*, 2 U.S.P.Q.2d (BNA) 1682 (T.T.A.B. 1987) (refusing to tack applicant's earlier use of "SHAPE UP" mark to later use of "SHAPE" mark); and *Viviane Woodard Corp. v. Roberts*, 181 U.S.P.Q. (BNA) 840 (T.T.A.B. 1974) (refusing to tack prior use of "ALTER EGO" mark to later use of "EGO" mark).

[29] *See* Quiksilver, Inc. v. Kymsta Corp., 466 F.3d 749, 759 (9th Cir. 2006) (collecting cases).

[30] 15 U.S.C. § 1125(a)(3). For a discussion of functionality, *see* § 2.03 *supra.*

[31] *See, e.g.*, Mushroom Makers, Inc. v. R.G. Barry Corp., 580 F.2d 44, 47 (2d Cir.1978), *cert. denied*, 439 U.S. 1116 (1979); HMH Pub. Co. v. Lambert, 482 F.2d 595 (9th Cir. 1973); J.R. Wood & Sons, Inc. v. Reese Jewelry Corp., 278 F.2d 157 (2d Cir. 1960); CBS, Inc. v. Liederman, 866 F. Supp. 763 (S.D.N.Y. 1994), *aff'd*, 44 F.3d 174 (2d Cir. 1995) (per curiam); Toys "R" Us, Inc. v. Canarsie Kiddie Shop, Inc., 559 F. Supp. 1189, 1195 (E.D.N.Y. 1983).

[32] *See, e.g.*, S.S. Kresge Co. v. Winget Kickernick Co., 96 F.2d 978 (8th Cir. 1938); Walgreen Drug Stores v. Obear-Nester Glass Co., 113 F.2d 956 (8th Cir. 1940), *cert. denied*, 311 U.S. 708 (1940).

[33] *See, e.g.*, Volkswagenwerk Aktiengesellschaft v. Tatum, 344 F. Supp. 235, 237 (S.D. Fla. 1972) (standard for determining confusion is "not that of a careful and discriminating purchaser, but that of an ordinary and casual buyer, or perhaps even an ignorant, inexperienced and gullible purchaser"); *see also* Stork Rest. v. Sahati, 166 F.2d 348 (9th Cir. 1948); Coca-Cola Co. v. Snow Crest Beverages, Inc., 162 F.2d 280 (1st Cir. 1947), *cert. denied*, 332 U.S. 809 (1947); Drexel Enters., Inc. v. Hermitage

question of what characteristics typify this consumer is an important one, however, and as discussed below,[34] is incorporated into the portions of the likelihood-of-confusion analysis that consider the sophistication of the targeted consumer group as well as the circumstances surrounding the typical purchasing decision. However, courts express varying views on the extent to which careless consumers should be considered in determining the likelihood of confusion; some decisions have held that a probability of confusion on the part of careless consumers argues in favor of likelihood of confusion,[35] while others suggest that careless consumers should be disregarded.[36] In some cases, the nature of a product as an "impulse purchase" has led courts to assume that even the ordinarily prudent consumer would be somewhat careless.[37]

There is no fixed standard as to what constitutes an "appreciable number" of confused consumers.[38] Most courts do not require that a majority of consumers be confused.[39] Surveys showing relatively low percentages of actual confusion (15 to 20%, and sometimes even lower) are typically deemed persuasive evidence of actual confusion, which, in turn, is strongly probative of the likelihood of confusion.[40]

Confusion must be probable, not merely possible.[41] In describing the relationship between the probability of confusion and the level of prudence expected of consumers, the Second Circuit has noted: "The test . . . is not whether confusion is possible; nor is it whether confusion is probable among customers who are not knowledgeable. Rather, the test . . . is whether confusion is probable among numerous customers who are ordinarily prudent."[42]

It is not necessary for a plaintiff to prove that consumers would erroneously believe that the plaintiff actually produced the goods or services in question; it is

---

Cabinet Shop, Inc., 266 F. Supp. 532 (N.D. Ga. 1967); Ralston Purina Co. v. Saniwax Paper Co., 26 F.2d 941 (W.D. Mich. 1928).

[34] See § 3.02 [B][2][d] *infra*.

[35] *See, e.g.*, Fleischmann Distilling Corp. v. Maier Brewing Co., 314 F.2d 149, 156 (9th Cir. 1963); Harold F. Ritchie, Inc. v. Chesebrough-Pond's, Inc., 281 F.2d 755 (2d Cir. 1960); American Chicle Co. v. Topps Chewing Gum, Inc., 208 F.2d 560 (2d Cir. 1953); Stork Restaurant v. Sahati, 166 F.2d 348, 359 (9th Cir. 1948) (trademark law should protect "the vast multitude which includes the ignorant, the unthinking and the credulous who . . . do not stop to analyze, but are governed by appearance and general impressions").

[36] *See, e.g.*, Indianapolis Colts, Inc. v. Metropolitan Baltimore Football Club L.P., 34 F.3d 410, 414-415 (7th Cir. 1994); Dawn Donut Co. v. Day, 450 F.2d 332 (10th Cir. 1971); Oriental Foods, Inc. v. Chun King Sales, Inc. 244 F.2d 909 (9th Cir. 1957); Life Savers Corp. v. Curtiss Candy Co., 182 F.2d 4 (7th Cir. 1950).

[37] Beer Nuts, Inc. v. Clover Club Foods Co., 805 F.2d 920 (10th Cir. 1986); Playboy Enters., Inc. v. Chuckleberry Pub., Inc., 687 F.2d 563 (2d Cir. 1982); Beech-Nut, Inc. v. Warner-Lambert Co., 480 F.2d 801 (2d Cir. 1973).

[38] Alderman v. Iditarod Props., 32 P.3d 373, 390 (Alaska 2001).

[39] *Id.*

[40] *Id.*; *see* § 3.02 [B][2][e] *infra* (discussing survey evidence of actual confusion).

[41] A&H Sportswear Co. v. Victoria's Secret Stores, Inc., 166 F.3d 197, 205-06 (3d Cir. 1999); Elvis Presley Enters. v. Capece, 141 F.3d 188, 193 (5th Cir. 1998); *Alderman*, 32 P.3d at 390.

[42] Estee Lauder v. Gap, Inc., 108 F.3d 1503, 1511 (2d Cir. 1997).

enough that consumers would believe that the plaintiff endorsed or was affiliated with those goods or services.[43] Although the most common type of confusion is that which occurs at the time of purchasing — sometimes called "point of sale" confusion — infringement claims may also be based on initial interest confusion (that is, pre-sale confusion that dissipates before the purchase is made) or post-sale (or "aftermarket") confusion.[44] Initial interest confusion and post-sale confusion are discussed in § 3.02 [D] below.

[2]   Factors

The federal courts of appeals, and the courts of each state, have developed their own versions of a multi-factor balancing test that functions as a flexible guide for evaluating the likelihood of confusion under federal or state law, respectively. Although the tests used in different jurisdictions differ as to the precise factors, the overall scope of the analysis is largely the same. Furthermore, jurisdictions generally agree that (1) no single factor is decisive, (2) evidence of actual confusion is helpful but not essential, (3) the list of factors adopted in any particular jurisdiction is non-exhaustive, and (4) on any given set of facts, some of the factors may be more significant than others. Ultimately, the likelihood of confusion depends on the circumstances of the particular case, and must be "proved by inference drawn from the totality of relevant facts."[45]

In the Second Circuit, the following factors (known as the *Polaroid* factors) are considered in assessing the likelihood of confusion: (1) the strength of the senior mark; (2) the degree of similarity between the two marks; (3) the proximity of the products or services; (4) the likelihood that the prior owner will "bridge the gap"; (5) evidence of actual confusion; (6) the defendant's good faith (or bad faith) in adopting the mark in question; (7) the quality of defendant's product or service; and (8) the sophistication of the buyers.[46] Depending on the complexity of the issues, "the court may have to take still other variables into account."[47]

Outside of the Second Circuit, each federal court of appeals, and each state, has adopted some variation on the *Polaroid* test. Several of the *Polaroid* factors are universally recognized — i.e., the strength of the senior mark, the similarity of the marks, the similarity of the parties' goods or services, evidence of actual confusion, and the junior user's intent. One factor — the quality of the junior user's goods or services — has received little attention outside the Second Circuit. Beyond these factors, there are slight variations among the different jurisdictions, but these generally amount to different categorizations rather

---

[43] *See, e.g.,* Conagra, Inc. v. Singleton, 743 F.2d 1508, 1512 n.2 (11th Cir. 1984).

[44] *See, e.g.,* Louis Vuitton Malletier v. Dooney & Bourke, Inc., 340 F. Supp. 2d 415, 431 (S.D.N.Y. 2004), aff'd in part, vacated and remanded in part, 454 F.3d 108 (2d Cir. 2006).

[45] A&H Sportswear Co. v. Victoria's Secret Stores, Inc., 166 F.3d 197, 206-07 (3d Cir. 1999) (quoting Richard L. Kirkpatrick, Likelihood of Confusion in Trademark Law, § 1.8 (PLI, 1997); Dieter v. B&H Indus., Inc., 880 F.2d 322, 326 (11th Cir. 1989)).

[46] Polaroid Corp. v. Polarad Elecs. Corp., 287 F.2d 492, 495 (2d Cir.), *cert. denied,* 368 U.S. 820 (1961).

[47] *Id.*

than differences in substance.[48] For example:

The Ninth Circuit uses the *Sleekcraft* factors: (1) the similarity of the marks; (2) the relatedness or proximity of the two parties' products or services; (3) the strength of the senior user's mark; (4) the marketing channels used; (5) the degree of care likely to be exercised by the purchaser in selecting the goods or services; (6) the accused infringer's intent in selecting its mark; (7) evidence of actual confusion; and (8) the likelihood of expansion in product lines (that is, "bridging the gap").[49]

In the Seventh Circuit, courts consider the following factors: (1) the similarity of the marks; (2) the similarity of the products or services; (3) the area and manner of concurrent use; (4) the degree of care likely to be used by consumers; (5) the strength of the plaintiff's mark; (6) whether any actual confusion exists; and (7) the defendant's intent to palm off its goods or services as those of the plaintiff.[50]

Because these lists are nonexhaustive, and infringement cases are highly fact-specific, virtually any facts and circumstances relevant to the potential for consumer confusion can be taken into consideration. For example, where a court found that purchasers or users of a product were unlikely to see the disputed trademark because it appeared on a particular subcomponent that was not visible without dismantling the product, the court held that an examination of the specific likelihood-of-confusion factors was unnecessary.[51]

Although district courts are expected to analyze each factor in the likelihood-of-confusion analysis with care,[52] and must justify the conclusion that a particular factor is inapplicable in a given case,[53] courts have repeatedly cautioned against rigid application of any particular test.[54]

---

[48] For tests used in other federal circuits, *see* AMF Inc. v. Sleekcraft Boats, 599 F.2d 341 (9th Cir. 1979) (8-factor test); Scott Fetzer Co. v. House of Vacuums, Inc., 381 F.3d 477 (5th Cir. 2004) (7-factor test); Sullivan v. CBS Corp., 385 F.3d 772, 776-77 (7th Cir. 2004) (7-factor test); Palm Bay Imports, Inc. v. Veuve Clicquot Ponsardin Maison Fondee en 1772, 396 F.3d 1369 (Fed. Cir. 2005) (13-factor test, developed by Federal Circuit's processor in In re E.I. DuPont de Nemours & Co., 476 F.2d 1357, 1361 (C.C.P.A. 1973)); Frisch's Restaurants v. Elby's Big Boy, 670 F.2d 642, 648 (6th Cir. 1982) (8-factor test); SquirtCo v. Seven-Up Co., 628 F.2d 1086, 1091 (8th Cir. 1980) (6-factor test); and Jellibeans, Inc. v. Skating Clubs of Georgia, Inc., 716 F.2d 833 (11th Cir. 1983) (7-factor test).

[49] *Sleekcraft*, 599 F.2d at 346.

[50] Sullivan v. CBS Corp., 385 F.3d 772, 776-77 (7th Cir. 2004).

[51] Custom Mfg. & Eng'g, Inc. v. Midway Servs., 508 F.3d 641, 649-52 (11th Cir. 2007).

[52] *See, e.g.*, New Kayak Pool v. R & P Pools, Inc., 246 F.3d 183, 185 (2d Cir. 2001); Sunbeam Prods., Inc. v. West Bend Co., 123 F.3d 246, 257 (5th Cir. 1997), *cert. denied*, 523 U.S. 1118 (1998).

[53] *See, e.g.*, *New Kayak Pool*, 246 F.3d at 185.

[54] *See, e.g.*, Indianapolis Colts, Inc. v. Metropolitan Balt. Football Club P'Ship, 34 F.3d 410, 414 (7th Cir. 1994) (noting that "[t]he legal standard [for confusion] under the Act has been formulated variously, but the various formulations come down to whether it is likely that the challenged mark if permitted to be used by the defendant would cause the plaintiff to lose a substantial number of consumers"); Bristol-Myers Squibb. Co. v. McNeil-P.P.C., Inc., 973 F.2d 1033, 1044 (2d Cir. 1992) (noting that the Polaroid factors are "merely tools designed to help grapple with the vexing problem of resolving the likelihood of confusion issue, and the ultimate conclusion as to whether a likelihood of confusion exists is not to be determined in accordance with some rigid formula.") (internal quotation marks omitted).

In addition, if the junior use occurs in the context of parody, some courts treat the parodic context as an additional likelihood-of-confusion factor.[55] Parodies are discussed in § 3.11 below.

In reviewing trial court decisions regarding the likelihood of confusion, appellate courts treat determinations under each individual factor as questions of fact, reviewable only for clear error.[56] However, appellate courts disagree on the standard of review that applies to the ultimate conclusion of whether a likelihood of confusion exists.[57] Although a majority of courts treat this as a question of fact,[58] others treat it as a question of law subject to de novo review.[59] Even where the ultimate conclusion is treated as a question of fact, de novo review is proper if this conclusion was premised on an incorrect legal standard.[60]

[a]   Similarity of Marks

Although likelihood of confusion, and infringement, may be found even though the junior and senior users' marks are not identical, the similarity of the junior and senior users' marks receives considerable weight in the likelihood-of-confusion analysis.[61]

A few courts have expressed the view that, in the case of directly competing goods, a strong showing of similarity or dissimilarity of the marks can obviate the need to undertake the rest of the likelihood-of-confusion analysis,[62] but it seems unlikely that such a foreshortened analysis will be common.[63] Extreme dissimilarity of marks will almost always dictate a finding of non-infringement even under the full likelihood-of-confusion analysis, but determining what degree of dissimilarity is sufficient to make further analysis unnecessary would be a somewhat subjective determination. In the case of extremely *similar* marks used on directly competing goods, it would be highly unlikely that federal

---

[55] *See, e.g., Elvis Presley Enters.*, 141 F.3d at 194.

[56] *See, e.g.*, Tumblebus, Inc. v. Cranmer, 399 F.3d 754, 764 (6th Cir. 2005).

[57] *See* ConAgra, Inc. v. George A. Hormel & Co., 990 F.2d 368 (8th Cir. 1993) (collecting cases).

[58] *See* 3 Gilson, Trademark Protection and Practice § 8.14 (Matthew Bender 2005); *see, e.g.*, Facenda v. N.F.L. Films, Inc., 542 F.3d 1007, 1024 (3d Cir. 2008); General Motors Corp. v. Urban Gorilla, LLC, 500 F.3d 1222, 1227 (10th Cir. 2007); Everest Capital, Ltd. v. Everest Funds Mgt., L.L.C., 393 F.3d 755 (8th Cir. 2005); Thane Int'l v. Trek Bicycle Corp., 305 F.3d 894, 901 (9th Cir. 2002); Elvis Presley Enters. v. Capece, 141 F.3d 188, 196 (5th Cir. 1998); Scandia Down Corp. v. Euroquilt, Inc., 772 F.2d 1423, 1428 (7th Cir. 1985); *Jellibeans, Inc.*, 716 F.2d at 840 n.16 (rejecting earlier precedents to the contrary).

[59] Leelanau Wine Cellars v. Black & Red, 502 F.3d 504, 515 (6th Cir. 2007); China Healthways Inst., Inc., v. Wang, 491 F.3d 1337, 1339 (Fed. Cir. 2007), *cert. denied*, __ U.S. __, 128 S. Ct. 661 (2007).

[60] *Elvis Presley Enters.*, 141 F.3d at 196.

[61] Daddy's Junky Music Stores, Inc. v. Big Daddy's Family Music Center, 109 F.3d 275, 283 (6th Cir. 1997)

[62] A & H Sportswear, Inc. v. Victoria's Secret Stores, Inc., 237 F.3d 198, 214 (3d Cir. 2000); Brookfield Communs., Inc. v. West Coast Ent. Corp., 174 F.3d 1036, 1054, 1056 (9th Cir. 1999).

[63] *See, e.g.*, Dippin' Dots, Inc. v. Frosty Bites Dist., L.L.C., 369 F.3d 1197, 1208 n.13 (11th Cir. 2004), *cert. denied*, 125 S. Ct. 911 (2005).

registrations could be validly obtained for both marks under section 2(d)[64] of the Lanham Act. Where similar marks are *un*registered, the full likelihood-of-confusion analysis is not foreclosed, because even identical unregistered marks on directly competing goods may be non-infringing under appropriate circumstances, such as where the marks are relatively weak and are used in remote geographic locations.

In assessing the similarity of trademarks, or trade dress, courts have stressed that each mark must be considered as a whole.[65] In the case of a composite mark (that is, a mark consisting of a combination of words and/or images),[66] the "anti-dissection" rule requires courts to "view marks in their entirety and focus on their overall impressions, not individual features."[67] Only by viewing the marks in their entirety can a court understand the overall impression that each would make on a consumer in the marketplace.

Similarly, where one of the marks at issue is a subordinate mark — that is, a mark that is always used in conjunction with another mark — this may undercut the similarity between the senior and junior users' marks. For example, where the defendant always used its "Alpha" mark for cameras in conjunction with its "Polaroid" mark, this reduced the likelihood that its cameras would be confused with the plaintiff's cameras, which were sold under the "Alpha" mark.[68]

The anti-dissection rule applies even in the case of a registered composite mark in which part of the mark has been disclaimed. In comparing the registered mark with the allegedly infringing marks, courts consider the

---

[64] 15 U.S.C. § 1052(d).

[65] Clicks Billiards, Inc. v. Sixshooters, Inc., 251 F.3d 1252, 1259 (9th Cir. 2001); *see also* The Forschner Group, Inc. v. Arrow Trading Co., Inc., 124 F.3d 402, 409 (2d Cir. 1997) ("[W]e are not so much concerned with dissecting the competing trade dress and enumerating discrete points of similarity, but rather we focus on the overall image created."); Union Carbide Corp. v. Ever-Ready, Inc., 531 F.2d 366, 379 (7th Cir.) ("[D]issecting marks often leads to error. Words which would not individually become a trademark may become one when taken together."), *cert. denied*, 429 U.S. 830 (1976).

[66] TMEP § 1213.02 (defining "composite mark").

[67] *Daddy's Junky Music Stores, Inc.*, 109 F.3d at 283-84; *see, e.g.*, AutoZone, Inc. v. Tandy Corp., 373 F.3d 786, 795-96 (6th Cir. 2004); AM General Corp. v. DaimlerChrysler Corp., 311 F.3d 796, 825 (7th Cir. 2002) ("[l]imiting the focus to the grille and ignoring all that surrounds the grille seems to blink the general rule that courts evaluate similarity in light of what happens in the marketplace"); Packman v. Chicago Tribune Co., 267 F.3d 628, 644 (7th Cir. 2001) (although marks contained exact same words in their marks, "the words' appearances do not resemble each other and are not likely to cause confusion"); Little Caesar Enters., Inc. v. Pizza Caesar, Inc. 834 F.2d 568, 571 (6th Cir. 1987) (emphasis on the "prominent" feature of a mark and not on its totality violates the rule against comparing component parts of "dissected" marks); Henri's Food Prods. Co., Inc. v. Kraft, Inc., 717 F.2d 352, 355 (7th Cir. 1983) (adding that it is important to examine similarity of the marks' "sound, sight, and meaning"); Sweetwater Brewing Co. LLC v. Great American Restaurants, Inc., 266 F. Supp. 2d 457, 462 (E.D. Va. 2003) (focusing on dominant portion of marks but noting that anti-dissection rule applies as well); MB Financial Bank, N.A. v. MB Real Estate Services, L.L.C., 2003 U.S. Dist. LEXIS 21051 (N.D. Ill. 2003) (collecting cases).

[68] Pignons S.A. de Mecanique de Precision v. Polaroid Corp., 657 F.2d 482, 487 (1st Cir. 1981); *see also* Fisher Stoves, Inc. v. All Nighter Stove Works, Inc., 626 F.2d 193, 194-95 (1st Cir. 1980); Keebler Co. v. Rovira Biscuit Corp., 624 F.2d 366, 378-79 (1st Cir. 1980); Alpha Indus., Inc. v. Alpha Steel Tube & Shapes, Inc., 616 F.2d 440, 444 (9th Cir. 1980); Bose Corp. v. Linear Design Labs, Inc., 467 F.2d 304, 310 (2d Cir. 1972); R.G. Barry Corp. v. A. Sandler Co., 406 F.2d 114, 116 (1st Cir. 1969).

plaintiff's mark as a whole, including the disclaimed portion, because this is how consumers experience the plaintiff's mark.[69]

In *Daddy's Junky Music Stores, Inc. v. Daddy's Junky Music Center*, the Sixth Circuit outlined several important principles that guide the assessment of similarity:

> When analyzing similarity, courts should examine the pronunciation, appearance, and verbal translation of conflicting marks. The appearance of the litigated marks side by side in the courtroom does not accurately portray market conditions. Rather, courts must determine whether a given mark would confuse the public when viewed alone, in order to account for the possibility that sufficiently similar marks "may confuse consumers who do not have both marks before them but who may have a 'general, vague, or even hazy, impression or recollection' of the other party's mark. Moreover, courts must view marks in their entirety and focus on their overall impressions, not individual features."[70]

In addition, the court held, in order to assess the similarity of the marks as the consumer would actually experience them, the comparison must be made "in light of what happens in the marketplace and not merely by looking at the two marks side-by-side."[71] Thus, where consumers do not normally encounter the marks together, minor stylistic differences between the marks should be disregarded.[72]

In the case of composite marks, notwithstanding the anti-dissection rule, "[i]f one word or feature of a composite trademark is the salient portion of the mark, it may be given greater weight than the surrounding elements."[73] This is particularly true where the surrounding elements are very weak. For example, in *International Kennel Club, Inc. v. Mighty Star, Inc.*, the Seventh Circuit found that the only significant difference between the plaintiff's "International Kennel Club of Chicago" mark and the defendant's "International Kennel Club" mark was "the common geographic term 'of Chicago,'" and concluded, therefore, that the "similarity" factor weighed in the plaintiff's favor because the defendant had appropriated "the dominant portion" of the plaintiff's mark.[74] Similarly,

---

[69] *See, e.g.*, Sleeper Lounge Co. v. Bell Mfg. Co., 253 F.2d 720 (9th Cir. 1958).

[70] *Daddy's Junky Music Stores*, 109 F.3d at 283 (citations and internal quotes omitted).

[71] Sullivan v. CBS Corp., 385 F.3d 772, 777 (7th Cir. 2004).

[72] *Sullivan*, 385 F.3d at 777; International Kennel Club, Inc. v. Mighty Star, Inc., 846 F.2d 1079, 1088 (7th Cir. 1988).

[73] *Sullivan*, 385 F.3d at 777.

[74] 846 F.2d 1079, 1088 (7th Cir. 1988); *see also* Meridian Mut. Ins. Co. v. Meridian Ins. Group, Inc., 128 F.3d 1111, 1116 (7th Cir. 1997) (focusing on "Meridian" portion of marks, and concluding they were "essentially the same"); Induct-O-Matic Corp. v. Inductotherm Corp., 747 F.2d 358, 361 (6th Cir. 1984) (addition of weak and nondistinctive terms does little to reduce likelihood of confusion); MB Financial Bank, N.A. v. MB Real Estate Services, L.L.C., 2003 U.S. Dist. LEXIS 21051 (N.D. Ill. 2003) (focusing on "MB" portion of marks, but cautioning that the rest of the mark should be considered as well); Sweetwater Brewing Co. LLC v. Great American Restaurants, Inc., 266 F. Supp. 2d 457, 462 (E.D. Va. 2003) (focusing on "Sweetwater" part of composite mark); Lycee Francais de New York v. Reynaud, 143 U.S.P.Q. (BNA) 311, 311 (N.Y. Sup. 1964) ("[t]he fact that plaintiff uses the words 'de New York' after the words 'Lycee Francais' to describe its institution, while defendant

courts routinely disregard top-level domain names (that is, ".com," ".org," etc.) in assessing similarity between domain names and trademarks.[75] Where a portion of a mark has been disclaimed, the non-disclaimed portion is generally considered to be dominant.[76]

In some cases, a trademark owner may establish rights in an entire family of marks sharing a common and distinctive characteristic, which is called the "formative." The owner of rights in a family of marks may obtain trademark protection against a party whose mark uses the same formative in a manner that is likely to lead consumers to believe that its goods or services emanate from the same "family."[77] The existence of a family of marks is a question of fact based on "the distinctiveness of the common formative component and other factors, including the extent of the family's use, advertising, promotion, and its inclusion in a number of registered and unregistered marks owned by a single party."[78] Furthermore, courts have held that the existence of third-party uses or registrations of marks using the same formative does not preclude recognition of a party's rights to a family of marks using that formative.[79]

For example, in *J&J Snack Foods Corp. v. McDonald's Corp.*, the Federal Circuit held that the McDonald's restaurant chain had established a family of marks that consisted of a variety of generic food names preceded by the "Mc" prefix, even if it had not used or registered the "Mc" prefix by itself. The court explained the elements necessary to establish ownership of a family of marks:

---

uses the word 'Kennedy' thereafter, is of little significance. Both would ordinarily be called . . . 'Lycee Francais.' ").

[75] *See, e.g.*, Brookfield Communications, Inc. v. West Coast Entertainment Corp., 174 F.3d 1036, 1055 (9th Cir. 1999) (disregarding.com portion of defendant's domain name, which was otherwise identical to plaintiff's "MovieBuff" trademark); Public Serv. Co. v. Nexus Energy Software, Inc., 36 F. Supp. 2d 436 (D. Mass. 1999) (finding "energyplace.com" and "Energy Place" to be virtually identical); Minnesota Mining & Mfg. Co. v. Taylor, 21 F. Supp. 2d 1003, 1005 (D. Minn. 1998) (finding "post-it.com" and "Post-It" to be the same); Interstellar Starship Servs. Ltd. v. Epix, Inc., 983 F. Supp. 1331, 1335 (D. Or. 1997) ("In the context of Internet use, ['epix.com'] is the same mark as ['EPIX']."); Planned Parenthood Federation of America, Inc. v. Bucci, 1997 U.S. Dist. LEXIS 3338 (S.D.N.Y. Mar. 24, 1997) (concluding that "plannedparenthood.com" and "Planned Parenthood" were essentially identical), *aff'd*, 152 F.3d 920 (2d Cir. 1998), *cert. denied*, 525 U.S. 834 (1998).

[76] Citigroup Inc. v. City Holding Co., 2003 U.S. Dist. LEXIS 1845, *63 (S.D.N.Y. Feb. 10, 2003); *see, e.g.*, Quantum Fitness Corp. v. Quantum Lifestyle Ctrs., L.L.C., 83 F. Supp. 2d 810, 824 (S.D. Tex. 1999) (finding that disclaimer of FITNESS from QUANTUM FITNESS mark required focus on QUANTUM word for the purpose of analyzing the likelihood of confusion and ruling as a result that prospective purchasers are likely to believe that the two uses are associated); Am. Throwing Co. v. Famous Bathrobe Co., 250 F.2d 377, 381-82 (C.C.P.A. 1957) (finding disclaimer of WIPER and KNIT from WIPER-KINS and KNIT-KINS marks respectively required relegation of disclaimed words to "minor importance" for confusion analysis).

[77] *See* McDonald's Corp. v. McBagel's, Inc., 649 F. Supp. 1268, 1271-72 (S.D.N.Y. 1986); Medical Modalities Association, Inc. v. ARA Corporation, 203 U.S.P.Q. (BNA) 295 (T.T.A.B. 1979). The fact that a party has not registered the formative by itself does not preclude recognition that it owns a family of marks using that formative. Toys "R" Us v. Abir, 1997 U.S. Dist. LEXIS 22431, *7-*8 (S.D.N.Y. 1997) (fact that Toys "R" Us does not own registration for "R Us" does not prevent recognition of "R Us" as common component of family of marks).

[78] *McBagel's*, 649 F. Supp. at 1272.

[79] *J&J Snack Foods*, 932 F.2d at 1463 (third-party registrations of various "Mc" names did not defeat McDonald's specific family of marks using prefix "Mc" with generic food names to create fanciful words); *accord* McDonald's Corp. v. McKinley, 13 U.S.P.Q.2d (BNA) 1895 (T.T.A.B. 1989).

A family of marks is a group of marks having a recognizable common characteristic, wherein the marks are composed and used in such a way that the public associates not only the individual marks, but the common characteristic of the family, with the trademark owner. Simply using a series of similar marks does not of itself establish the existence of a family. There must be a recognition among the purchasing public that the common characteristic is indicative of a common origin of the goods. . . .

Recognition of the family is achieved when the pattern of usage of the common element is sufficient to be indicative of the origin of the family. It is thus necessary to consider the use, advertisement, and distinctiveness of the marks, including assessment of the contribution of the common feature to the recognition of the marks as of common origin. McDonald's showed extensive usage and promotion of various marks using the "Mc" formative, in association with the McDONALD'S mark, in advertising and at McDonald's restaurants. McDonald's showed that in 1987 it operated 7,600 outlets in the United States with sales of over $14 billion; that it engaged in extensive nationwide advertising, spending $405 million in 1987; that its current menu is diverse; and that two of its restaurants have sold pretzels.

J & J does not challenge the renown of the individual marks, but argues that a trademark owner must own trademark rights to the formative itself, in order to establish rights to a family based on that formative. J & J points out that the "Mc" mark, standing alone, is registered by McCormick & Company for use with spices. However, it is not correct that the formative itself must be a trademark in order to sustain a family of marks . . .[80]

In like manner, courts have recognized that Toys "R" Us owns a family of marks, enabling it to prevent others from using such marks as "Adults R Us" and "Kids R Us."[81]

In contrast, a district court found no likelihood of confusion between Citigroup's family of marks based on the "CITI" prefix (CITIBANK, CITICORP,

---

[80] 932 F.2d 1460, 1463 (Fed. Cir. 1991); *accord* McDonald's Corp. v. Dorothy Jill McKinley dba McKinley & Co., 13 U.S.P.Q.2d (BNA) 1895 (T.T.A.B. 1989) (recognizing McDonald's strong family of marks using "Mc" and "Mac" formatives, and sustaining its opposition to registration of "McTeddy"); *see also* Phat Fashions, L.L.C. v. Phat Game Ath. Apparel, Inc., 2002 U.S. Dist. LEXIS 15734, *25-27 (E.D. Cal. 2002) (holding that plaintiff had established family of marks in which word "PHAT" was always followed by a one-syllable four-letter word, so that defendant's "PHAT GAME" mark was similar enough to cause confusion); AMF, Inc. v. American Leisure Prods., Inc., 474 F.2d 1403, 1406 (C.C.P.A. 1973) (holding that opposer had established family of marks of "fish" names for sailboats); Motorola, Inc. v. Griffiths Elecs., Inc., 317 F.2d 397, 399 (C.C.P.A. 1963) (holding that opposer had established family of "golden" marks); International Diagnostics Technology, Inc. v. Miles Labs., Inc., 746 F.2d 798, 800 (Fed. Cir. 1984) (holding that opposer had established family of "STIX" marks).

[81] Toys "R" Us, Inc. v. Akkaoui, 40 U.S.P.Q.2d (BNA) 1836, 1996 U.S. Dist. LEXIS 17090 (N.D. Cal. 1996) (with respect to "Adults R Us"); Geoffrey, Inc. v. Stratton, 16 U.S.P.Q.2D (BNA) 1691, 1694 (C.D. Cal. 1990) (with respect to "Phones R Us"); Toys "R" Us, Inc. v. Canarsie Kiddie Shop, Inc., 559 F. Supp. 1189 (E.D.N.Y. 1983) (with respect to "Kids R Us").

CITICARD, etc.) and a defendant's various "CITY" marks (CITY NATIONAL BANK, CITY FINANCIAL GROUP, etc.). While the "CITI" portion of the plaintiff's marks was very strong, both in terms of inherent and acquired distinctiveness,[82] the plaintiff failed to establish a likelihood of confusion because, inter alia, "the aural identity" of the marks was "overcome by the written differentiation,"[83] and the "CITY" portion of the defendant's composite marks had been used by the defendant as well as third parties for substantial periods without causing confusion with the "CITI" family of marks.[84] In a later proceeding, however, the court held that the defendant did not have a "CITY" family of marks at all, but merely a small number of marks utilizing the word "CITY." The court distinguished between a family of marks and a series of composite marks that merely shared a common component:

> It is now held that City Holding does not have a family such as would provide protection under trademark law under the family of marks doctrine because of the lack of distinctiveness of the CITY "surname" and the lack of any association between the common CITY surname and City Holding. According to the leading commentator:
>
>> To be effective, the "family of marks" argument must rest in the ultimate analysis on proof . . . that the designation constituting the "surname" of the family is in fact recognized by the public as a trademark in and of itself. Usually this requires some proof that the "family surname" has been so extensively advertised that buyers would be likely to think that [the infringer's] product originates with [the owner of the family being infringed]. This is a matter of fact, not supposition. The mere fact of registration of many marks with a common syllable does not in itself prove that a family of marks exists in fact.
>
> 3 J. Thomas McCarthy, McCarthy on Trademarks and Unfair Competition, § 23:61, p. 23-170 . . . There is no question that City Holdings has registered, or attempted to register, nine marks with a common surname of "CITY." There is no evidence, however, that consumers recognize CITY as a trademark in and of itself that belongs to City Holding. . . .
>
> In the absence of any indication that consumers recognize that the nine marks are somehow related, . . . City Holdings is not entitled to the added protections afforded by the family of marks doctrine.
>
> By contrast, Citigroup owns a family of CITI marks. This is because, to use the examples discussed at oral argument, Citigroup's CITI surname is a rare spelling of a common surname, such as Smyth is a rare spelling of the common surname Smith. Further, the largesse of advertising has associated that distinctive spelling of CITI with Citigroup. City Holding, on the other hand, relies on the common spelling of "city," and is one

---

[82] Citigroup, Inc. v. City Holding Co., 171 F. Supp. 2d 333, 345-47 (S.D.N.Y. 2001).

[83] *Id.* at 349.

[84] *Id.* at 350-51.

Smith among many in the absence of any sort of effort to associate the plain spelling of CITY only with City Holding and its subsidiaries.[85]

[b]   Competitive Proximity

Competitive proximity refers to the likelihood that consumers will assume that the junior user's product or service is associated with the senior user.[86] In determining the proximity of the goods or services associated with the junior and senior users' marks, courts consider the "content, geographic distribution, market position, and audience appeal," of those goods or services.[87] For example, in *CBS v. Liederman*, the district court found little proximity between a California television production facility and a television-themed restaurant in New York:

> CBS produces televisions shows at Television City in California. The mark is to protect the name in that context. The intended use of defendants' proposed restaurant will primarily be serving food. There simply is little or no overlap between the services provided by each of the parties. Additionally, the production site and the proposed restaurant are on opposite coasts. While it is true that an avid fan of television may be attracted to both places, it does not mean that they would visit one at the expense of the other. The individual would have two entirely different experiences. CBS invites the public into CBS Television City to make up the audiences for its game shows and other television programs produced on site. While there, CBS provides a tour of the facility. However, there was testimony that the public is excluded from CBS Television City for all purposes other than for seeing a show produced. . . . There is little overlap of markets between plaintiff's and defendants' services.[88]

When goods are in direct competition, the degree of similarity between the marks that is necessary to establish a likelihood of confusion is lower than in the case of dissimilar products.[89] In contrast, where the parties' goods or services do not directly compete, a higher degree of similarity between the marks will normally be necessary.[90] The Sixth Circuit has expanded this observation into a

---

[85] *Citigroup Inc.*, 2003 U.S. Dist. LEXIS 1845, at *53-56 & n. 10.

[86] CBS v. Liederman, 866 F. Supp. 763, 767 (S.D.N.Y. 1994), *aff'd*, 44 F.3d 174 (2d Cir. 1995).

[87] *Id.*

[88] *Id.*

[89] Sara Lee Corp. v. Kayser-Roth Corp., 81 F.3d 455, 465-66 (4th Cir. 1996).

[90] Kellogg Co. v. Toucan Golf, Inc., 337 F.3d 616, 625 (6th Cir. 2003); *see, e.g.*, Recot, Inc. v. Becton, 214 F.3d 1322, 1328 (Fed. Cir. 2000) (finding likelihood of confusion between "Frito Lay" and "Fido Lay" even though one is used for snack chips and one is used for dog food); Hunt Foods & Indus., Inc. v. Gerson Stewart Corp., 367 F.2d 431, 435, 54 C.C.P.A. 751 (C.C.P.A. 1966) (holding "Hunt's" for canned goods and "Hunt" for cleaning products confusingly similar); American Sugar Refining Co. v. Andreassen, 296 F.2d 783, 784, 49 C.C.P.A. 782 (C.C.P.A. 1961) (finding "Domino" for sugar and "Domino" for pet food confusingly similar); Yale Elec. Corp. v. Robertson, 26 F.2d 972, 974 (2d Cir. 1928) (finding "Yale" for flashlights and locks confusingly similar); Quality Inns Int'l, Inc. v. McDonald's Corp., 695 F. Supp. 198, 221-22 (D. Md. 1988) (finding similarity between "McSleep Inn" and McDonald's' trademarks); John Walker & Sons, Ltd. v. Bethea, 305 F. Supp. 1302, 1307-08

sliding scale analysis:

> First, if the parties compete directly by offering their goods or services, confusion is likely if the marks are sufficiently similar; second, if the goods or services are somewhat related but not competitive, the likelihood of confusion will turn on other factors; third, if the goods or services are totally unrelated, confusion is unlikely.[91]

Although ordinarily the similarity between marks must be weighed against the other likelihood-of-confusion factors, some courts have gone so far as to state that, where the parties' goods or services are directly competing, a court rarely needs to look beyond the similarity of the marks.[92]

Even where goods or services do not directly compete, if they serve the same purpose, are closely related, or are likely to be used together, this can contribute to a likelihood of confusion.[93] For example, in *E. & J. Gallo Winery v. Gallo Cattle Co.*, wine, cheese, and salami were found to be complementary goods because they are often served together, a fact that increased the likelihood of confusion where similar marks were used on these goods.[94]

There is wide variation in what courts consider to be similar or related goods or services; especially in older cases, where the user's mark is particularly strong, courts have found non-competing goods to be related even where the relationship is quite tenuous.[95] Such cases today would more likely be litigated under antidilution laws, which protect especially strong marks against non-competing uses even in the absence of a likelihood of confusion.[96]

This aspect of the likelihood-of-confusion analysis also takes account of the marketing channels through which the senior and junior users advertise and sell their goods or services. In some jurisdictions, such as the Second Circuit, this factor is subsumed in the analysis of the proximity of the parties' goods or

---

(D.S.C. 1969) (finding "Johnnie Walker" whiskey and "Johnny Walker" hotels confusingly similar).

[91] *Daddy's Junky Music Stores*, 109 F.2d at 282.

[92] *See, e.g.,* A & H Sportswear Co. v. Victoria's Secret Stores, Inc., 166 F.3d 197, 202 (3d Cir. 1999); Interpace Corp. v. Lapp, Inc., 721 F.2d 460, 462 (3d Cir. 1983); Members First Federal Credit Union v. Members 1st Federal Credit Union, 54 F. Supp. 2d 393, 402 n.15 (M.D. Pa. 1999).

[93] Restatement (Third) of Unfair Competition § 21, cmt. j (Tent. Draft No. 2, 1990); *see, e.g.,* Lange v. Retirement Living Pub. Co., 949 F.2d 576, 582 (2d Cir. 1991) (finding that defendant's magazine and plaintiff's books and tapes were not used together); *Yale Electric Corp.*, 26 F.2d at 974 (finding likely confusion between Yale locks and Yale flashlights); Aunt Jemima Mills Co. v. Rigney & Co., 247 F. 407, 409-10 (2d Cir. 1917) (finding likely confusion between Aunt Jemima pancake syrup and Aunt Jemima pancake flour); Schieffelin & Co. v. Jack Co., 850 F. Supp. 232, 244-45 (S.D.N.Y. 1994) (finding insufficient evidence that champagne and popcorn are consumed together). *Compare* Time, Inc. v. Life Television Corp., 123 F. Supp. 470, 475 (D. Minn. 1954) (finding likely confusion between Life magazine and Life television sets because Life magazine endorsed various products), *with* Time, Inc. v. T.I.M.E., Inc., 123 F. Supp. 446, 456-57 (S.D. Cal. 1954) (finding no likely confusion between Time magazine and T.I.M.E. trucking service).

[94] 967 F.2d 1280, 1291 (9th Cir. 1992).

[95] *See* Fleischmann Distilling Corp. v. Maier Brewing Co., 314 F.2d 149, 153 n.2A (9th Cir. 1963) (collecting cases).

[96] *See* § 3.05 *infra*.

services,[97] while in others the similarity of the parties' marketing channels is treated as a separate factor.[98] Where there is no overlap between the marketing channels for the parties' goods, confusion is less likely. Thus, for example, where one party sold its food products directly to consumers, while another sold exclusively to commercial food brokers, the Second Circuit held that there was no consumer who would encounter both marks, and thus no consumer to be confused.[99] On the other hand, the fact that the parties' goods are sold in the same types of stores does not necessarily receive great weight, because "modern marketing methods tend to unify widely different types of products in the same retail outlets or distribution networks"[100] — for example, selling groceries, DVDs, fishing gear, computers, and home improvement supplies in a single "big box" store or on Amazon.com.

[c]   Strength of Plaintiff's Mark

The "strength" of a trademark refers to its distinctiveness or, more precisely, its tendency to identify the goods or services sold under the mark as emanating from a particular, although possibly anonymous, source.[101] As a general rule, the stronger the plaintiff's mark, the greater the likelihood of confusion: "The more deeply a plaintiff's mark is embedded in the consumer's mind, the more likely it is that the defendant's mark will conjure up the image of the plaintiff's product instead of that of the junior user."[102]

A mark's strength is measured by two factors: (1) the degree to which it is inherently distinctive (that is, arbitrary, fanciful, or suggestive); and (2) the degree to which it is distinctive in the marketplace.[103] Thus, while the spectrum of distinctiveness provides a useful guide to the strength of a plaintiff's mark for purposes of the likelihood of confusion test, the extent of the mark's recognition in the marketplace is also important.[104] Some courts refer to a mark's position

---

[97] *See, e.g.*, Patsy's Brand, Inc. v. I.O.B. Realty, Inc., 317 F.3d 209, 218 (2d Cir. 2003) (balancing the fact that one merchant's sauces were sold only at its restaurants, while the other merchant's sauces were sold only at retail stores, against the geographic proximity of those sales locations, the fact that the two sauces appealed to similar consumers, and the fact that patrons of the restaurant locations were also likely to be patrons of the nearby retail stores).

[98] *See, e.g., Dippin' Dots*, 369 F.3d 1197, *cert. denied*, 125 S. Ct. 911 (2005).

[99] Dawn Donut Co. v. Hart's Food Stores, Inc., 267 F.2d 358 (2d Cir. 1959).

[100] Vitarroz Corp. v. Borden, Inc., 644 F.2d 960, 967 (2d Cir. 1981) (quoting Continental Connector Corp. v. Continental Specialties Corp., 492 F. Supp. 1088, 1096 (D. Conn. 1979)) (noting also that the products were typically shelved in different sections of the store).

[101] McGregor-Doniger, Inc. v. Drizzle, Inc., 599 F.2d 1126, 1131 (2d Cir. 1979) (citing E.I. DuPont de Nemours & Co. v. Yoshida Int'l, Inc., 393 F. Supp. 502, 512 ((E.D.N.Y. 1975).

[102] Hormel Foods Corp. v. Jim Henson Prods., 73 F.3d 497, 503 (2d Cir. 1996); *accord*, McGregor-Doniger Inc. v. Drizzle Inc., 599 F.2d 1126, 1132 (2d Cir. 1979). In *Hormel*, however, the court noted that parody can be an exception to this rule. 73 F.3d at 503. *See* § 3.11 *infra*.

[103] Virgin Enters., Ltd. v. Nawab, 335 F.3d 141, 147-48 (2d Cir. 2003); W.W.W. Pharm. Co. v. Gillette, 984 F.2d 567, 572 (2d Cir. 1993); Kraft Gen. Foods, Inc. v. Allied Old English, Inc., 831 F. Supp. 123, 128 (S.D.N.Y. 1993).

[104] "The more likely a mark is to be remembered and associated in the public mind with the mark's owner, the greater protection the mark is accorded by trademark law." GoTo.com v. Walt Disney Co., 202 F.3d 1199, 1207 (9th Cir. 2000); *accord*, Miss World (UK), Ltd. v. Mrs. America

on the spectrum of distinctiveness as its "conceptual strength," and its degree of recognition by consumers as its "commercial strength."[105] (The concept of commercial strength is virtually synonymous with secondary meaning.) A mark may be conceptually strong, yet commercially weak, or vice versa.[106] For example, a mark may be fanciful, and thus inherently distinctive, but may not be known to a large number of consumers, or may be considered relatively weak for other reasons. The image of a moose used in conjunction with the "Moose Creek" word mark for apparel was held to be arbitrary but still "conceptually weak" under the "crowded field" doctrine, because moose images are commonly used in connection with the marketing of apparel, even though they are not necessarily used as trademarks.[107] Likewise, a descriptive mark with strong secondary meaning may qualify as a very strong mark for purposes of the likelihood-of-confusion analysis because, while it lacks conceptual strength, it has a high degree of commercial strength.

The Second Circuit has explained the relevance of conceptual strength to the likelihood of consumer confusion as follows:

> If a mark is arbitrary or fanciful, and makes no reference to the nature of the goods it designates, consumers who see the mark on different objects offered in the marketplace will be likely to assume, because of the arbitrariness of the choice of mark, that they all come from the same source. For example, if consumers become familiar with a toothpaste sold under an unusual, arbitrary brand name, such as ZzaaqQ, and later see that same inherently distinctive brand name appearing on a different product, they are likely to assume, notwithstanding the product difference, that the second product comes from the same producer as the first. The more unusual, arbitrary, and fanciful a trade name, the more unlikely it is that two independent entities would have chosen it. In contrast, every seller of foods has an interest in calling its product "delicious." Consumers who see the word delicious used on two or more different food products are less likely to draw the inference that they must all come from the same producer.[108]

In the case of federally registered marks, section 7(b) of the Lanham Act provides that registration on the Principal Register creates a rebuttable presumption of validity.[109] Accordingly, registration on the Principal Register creates a rebuttable presumption that the mark either is inherently distinctive or has acquired secondary meaning. Incontestability makes this presumption conclusive, subject to the defenses of section 33(b).[110] In addition, several circuits

---

Pageants, Inc., 856 F.2d 1445, 1449 (9th Cir. 1988).

[105] *See, e.g.*, Moose Creek, Inc. v. Abercrombie & Fitch Co., 331 F. Supp. 2d 1214, 1224 (C.D. Cal.), *aff'd*, 114 Fed. Appx. 921 (2004).

[106] *See, e.g.*, Oxford Indus., Inc. v. JBJ Fabrics, Inc., 6 U.S.P.Q.2d (BNA) 1756 (S.D.N.Y. 1988); McGregor-Doniger, Inc. v. Drizzle, Inc., 599 F.2d 1126, 1131-32 (2d Cir. 1979).

[107] *Moose Creek*, 331 F. Supp. 2d at 1225 (C.D. Cal.), *aff'd*, 114 Fed. Appx. 921 (9th Cir. 2004).

[108] *Virgin Enters.*, 335 F.3d at 148.

[109] 15 U.S.C. § 1057(b); Zyla v. Wadsworth, 360 F.3d 243 (1st Cir. 2004).

[110] Retail Servs. v. Freebies Pub'g, 364 F.3d 535, 548 (4th Cir. 2004).

have held that the PTO's decision to register a mark on the Principal Register without requiring proof of secondary meaning gives rise to a rebuttable presumption that the mark is inherently distinctive (that is, arbitrary, fanciful, or suggestive) rather than descriptive.[111]

Regardless of whether a mark derives its strength from inherent characteristics of the mark or from its history of use in the marketplace, "the strength of a mark ultimately depends on distinctiveness, or its 'origin-indicating' quality, in the eyes of the purchasing public."[112] The relevant public, for this purpose, is not necessarily the general public, but the consumer market for the particular good or service.[113]

The fact that a registered mark has become incontestable may be relevant to an assessment of its strength, but it is far from conclusive. As the Sixth Circuit has noted:

> Even where a trademark is incontestable and "worthy of full protection," the significance of its presumed strength will depend upon its recognition among members of the public. Treating a valid, incontestable trademark as an exceptionally strong mark for the purpose of determining whether confusion is likely to occur, without examining whether the mark is distinctive and well-known in the general population, would shift the focus away from the key question of "whether relevant consumers are likely to believe that the products or services offered by the parties are affiliated in some way."[114]

In the case of a composite mark, validity and distinctiveness must be tested by considering the mark as a whole, rather than by dissecting it into its component parts.[115] When considered as a whole, a composite mark may be stronger than its individual components.[116] Thus, for example, a combination of two descriptive terms may result in a suggestive mark.[117]

Evidence of a mark's strength can take many forms. Evidence of long and continuous use, extensive advertising, sales, and recognition in the commercial

---

[111] *See, e.g.*, Abercrombie & Fitch Co. v. Hunting World, Inc., 537 F.2d 4, 11 (2d Cir. 1976); GTE Corp. v. Williams, 904 F.2d 536, 538-39 (10th Cir. 1990); Pizzeria Uno Corp. v. Temple, 747 F.2d 1522, 1528-29 (4th Cir. 1984); Money Store v. Harriscorp Fin., Inc., 689 F.2d 666, 673 (7th Cir. 1982).

[112] *McGregor-Doniger*, 599 F.2d at 1131-32.

[113] Macia v. Microsoft, 335 F. Supp. 2d 507, 514-15 (D. Vt. 2004).

[114] Therma-Scan, Inc. v. Thermoscan, 295 F.3d 623, 632-33 (6th Cir. 2002) (*quoting* Homeowner's Group, Inc. v. Home Marketing Specialists, 931 F.2d 1100, 1107 (6th Cir. 1991)).

[115] GoTo.com, Inc. v. Walt Disney Co., 202 F.3d 1199, 1207 (9th Cir. 2000); Courtenay Comms. Corp. v. Hall, 334 F.3d 210, 215 (2d Cir. 2003).

[116] Union Carbide Corp. v. Ever-Ready, Inc., 531 F.2d 366, 379 (7th Cir. 1976).

[117] *See, e.g.*, W.W.W. Pharm. Co. v. Gillette Co., 808 F. Supp. 1013, 1022 (S.D.N.Y. 1992) (consolidation of two descriptive or generic terms, "sport" and "stick," was a suggestive mark), *aff'd*, 984 F.2d 567 (2d Cir. 1993); Banff, Ltd. v. Federated Dept. Stores, Inc., 841 F.2d 486, 489 (2d Cir. 1988) (combination of arbitrary and generic terms in mark "Bee Wear" resulted in suggestive or arbitrary mark); Macia v. Microsoft, 335 F. Supp. 2d 507, 514-15 (D. Vt. 2004) (finding that while "Pocket" and "Money" were each arguably descriptive of financial management software, "Pocket-Money" was suggestive).

field of use, and use on a broad variety of products can all help to establish the extent of its secondary meaning.[118]

Even if a mark is otherwise strong, its strength may be undermined where other parties have used the same or similar marks at the same time as the plaintiff. Thus, extensive use of a mark by third parties will reduce the likelihood of confusion when another new entrant begins to use the mark.[119] For example, the mark "Domino" for sugar, while a strong mark in its field, was held to be a weak mark due to the widespread third-party use of "Domino" for other types of products; this led a court to conclude that the public was unlikely to associate "Domino" sugar with "Domino's Pizza."[120]

A subordinate mark — that is, a mark that is always used in conjunction with another mark — also tends to be weaker than a mark that stands alone. For example, where the subordinate mark "Drizzler" for raincoats was used only in conjunction with the plaintiff's "McGregor" mark, it was held to be a relatively weak mark that was unlikely to be confused with the defendant's "Drizzle" mark for women's raincoats.[121]

[d]   Consumer Sophistication

In general, more sophisticated consumers are presumed to be less easily confused than consumers who are less sophisticated, because the former are presumed to have greater powers of discrimination, and thus to exercise a higher degree of care in making their purchasing decisions.[122] Thus, in evaluating the likelihood of confusion, courts consider the sophistication of the typical consumer who would encounter the junior user's product or service.

The nature of the junior user's goods or services is often relevant to the question of consumer sophistication.[123] Certain products or services (high-end

---

[118] *See, e.g.*, Scarves by Vera, Inc. v. Todo Imports, Ltd., 544 F.2d 1167 (2d Cir. 1976); Levi Strauss & Co. v. Blue Bell, Inc., 632 F.2d 817 (9th Cir. 1980); Minnesota Mining & Mfg. Co. v. 3M Electrical Corp., 184 U.S.P.Q. (BNA) 470 (S.D. Fla. 1974).

[119] *See, e.g.*, Sun Banks of Florida, Inc. v. Sun Federal Sav. & Loan Ass'n., 651 F.2d 311 (5th Cir. 1981) (widespread use of "Sun" in names of financial institutions weakens "Sun Banks' " mark so that public is unlikely to confuse it with "Sun Federal").

[120] Amstar Corp. v Domino's Pizza, Inc., 615 F.2d 252 (5th Cir.), *cert. denied*, 449 U.S. 899 (1980).

[121] McGregor-Doniger, Inc. v Drizzle, Inc., 599 F.2d 1126 (2d Cir. 1979).

[122] *See, e.g.*, Virgin Enters. v. Nawab, 335 F.3d 141, 151 (2d Cir. 2003) (professional buyers would exercise a higher degree of care than retail customers); TCPIP Holding Co. v. Haar Communications, Inc., 244 F.3d 88, 102 (2d Cir. 2001) (sophisticated consumers less likely to be misled); Ashe v. Pepsico, Inc., 205 U.S.P.Q. (BNA) 451 (S.D.N.Y. 1979) (tennis players encountering expensive tennis rackets under ADVANTAGE mark and sunglasses under ADVANTAGE ASHE mark are sophisticated and not likely to be confused as to sources of these products); Reddy Comms., Inc., v. Environmental Action Foundation, 477 F. Supp. 936 (D.D.C. 1979) (subscribers to publication that criticizes power companies are sophisticated and not likely to be confused by use of parodic version of "Reddi Kilowatt" character in those publications); TCPIP Holding Co. v. Haar Communications, Inc., 244 F.3d 88, 102 (2d Cir. 2001)

[123] *See, e.g*, Merriam-Webster, Inc. v. Random House, Inc., 35 F.3d 65, 72 (2d Cir. 1994) (considering "the general impression of the ordinary purchaser, buying under normally prevalent conditions of the market and giving the attention such purchasers usually give in buying that class of goods.") (quoting McGregor-Doniger, Inc. v. Drizzle, Inc., 599 F.2d 1126, 1137 (2d Cir. 1979)).

designer clothing or certain financial services, for example) may be of interest largely to sophisticated consumers, while others (such as laundry detergent, standard grocery items, or plumbing repair services) are of interest to a broader demographic, and still others may be marketed to relatively unsophisticated persons, such as children. Where a product is relatively expensive, the process of purchasing it typically involves a higher level of purchaser engagement (sometimes referred to as the "degree of care"), that will tend to mitigate the likelihood of confusion.[124] In contrast, confusion is more likely in the case of impulse purchases.[125] The average educational level of the relevant consumers can also be an important indicator of sophistication.[126]

[e]   Actual Confusion

Where evidence of actual confusion exists, it will often be the best evidence of likelihood of confusion,[127] and as a result it receives substantial weight in the likelihood-of-confusion analysis.[128] However, evidence of actual confusion is not required to establish likelihood of confusion, both because such evidence can be difficult to obtain,[129] and because requiring such evidence would compel plaintiffs to postpone legal action until both they and the consumer have suffered harm from the defendant's infringing activities. Indeed, in many cases, actual confusion will be difficult or impossible to demonstrate, because the senior user brings the infringement claim before the junior user has commenced its use of the mark in question, or shortly after the use has commenced but before there has been an opportunity for significant confusion to arise.[130] Because the policy of trademark law is to encourage trademark owners to take legal action before they suffer actual injury from the infringing use, the absence of evidence of actual confusion in such a case will have little or no impact on the likelihood-of-confusion analysis.[131] However, the absence of evidence of actual confusion can weaken a plaintiff's case where the competing marks have been in concurrent use for an extended period; if long-term concurrent use has not yet yielded actual confusion, this suggests that such confusion is unlikely to occur in the future, even if the defendant's use continues.[132]

---

[124] *See, e.g.*, Deere & Co. v. MTD Holdings, Inc., 70 U.S.P.Q.2d (BNA) 1009, 1023-24 (S.D.N.Y. 2004).

[125] *See, e.g., id.*; Citigroup, Inc. v. City Holding Co., 171 F. Supp. 2d 333, 349 (S.D.N.Y. 2001) ("There would appear to be a difference between a one shot purchase of an item to wear or consume and initiating a continuing financial relationship.").

[126] *See, e.g.*, Information Clearing House, Inc. v. Find Magazine, 492 F. Supp. 147, 163 (S.D.N.Y. 1980).

[127] Amstar Corp. v. Domino's Pizza, Inc., 615 F.2d 252, 263 (5th Cir.), *cert. denied*, 449 U.S. 899 (1980).

[128] International Kennel Club v. Mighty Star, Inc., 846 F.2d 1079, 1089-90 (7th Cir. 1988).

[129] *See, e.g.*, Brookfield Comms., Inc. v. West Coast Entert. Corp., 174 F.3d 1036, 1050 (9th Cir. 1999); Eclipse Assocs. Ltd. v. Data Gen. Corp., 894 F.2d 1114, 1118-19 (9th Cir. 1990); *Sleekcraft*, 599 F.2d at 353.

[130] *See, e.g.*, Lobo Enters., Inc. v. Tunnel, Inc., 822 F.2d 331, 333 (2d Cir. 1987).

[131] CBS v. Liederman, 866 F. Supp. 763, 768 (S.D.N.Y. 1994), *aff'd*, 44 F.3d 174 (2d Cir. 1995) (per curiam).

[132] *See, e.g.*, Libman Co. v. Vining Indus., Inc., 69 F.3d 1360, 1361 (7th Cir. 1995) ("Vining sold

The strength of the actual confusion evidence will influence the weight it receives in the overall likelihood-of-confusion analysis. Isolated instances of confusion, or evidence of confusion that is unclear or insubstantial, will be given little weight.[133]

In addition, the weight given to evidence of actual confusion will vary according to the identity of those confused, the value of the services involved, and the context in which the confusion occurs.[134] Also, courts have given little weight to the absence of actual confusion evidence where the goods in question were inexpensive impulse purchases, because consumers are less likely to report their confusion in these cases.[135]

Evidence of actual confusion may take the form of anecdotal accounts by actual consumers, or survey evidence.[136] If a survey is well-constructed, survey evidence can be especially persuasive evidence of actual confusion.[137] When survey evidence is used, the question arises as to what percentage of survey respondents must have been confused in order for the evidence to be persuasive; in general, percentages of 15 to 20 percent or higher have been deemed persuasive,[138] although in some instances lower percentages have been deemed persuasive as well.[139] Questions may also arise, however, regarding the

---

several hundred thousand of the allegedly infringing brooms, yet there is no evidence that any consumer ever made such an error; if confusion were likely, one would expect at least one person out of this vast multitude to be confused . . .").

[133] *See, e.g.*, Alpha Industries, Inc. v. Alpha Steel Tube & Shapes, Inc., 616 F.2d 440, 445 (9th Cir. 1980); *Sleekcraft*, 599 F.2d at 352; De Costa v. Columbia Broadcasting System, Inc., 520 F.2d 499, 514-15 (1st Cir. 1975), *cert. denied*, 423 U.S. 1073 (1976); McFly, Inc. v. Universal City Studios, 228 U.S.P.Q. (BNA) 153 (C.D. Cal. 1985); Schwartz v. Slenderella Systems of California, Inc., 43 Cal.2d 107, 271 P.2d 857 (1954).

[134] Imperial Service Systems, Inc. v. ISS Int'l Service System, Inc., 701 F. Supp. 655, 659 (N.D. Ill. 1988); *see, e.g.*, A La Carte, Inc. v. Culinary Enters., Inc., 1997 U.S. Dist. LEXIS 12755, *20 n. 1 (N.D. Ill. 1997) ("Although the plaintiff has introduced evidence of several instances of confusion, only one of these incidents involved a consumer, and this incident did not occur in the context of a purchasing decision.").

[135] *See, e.g.*, AmBrit, Inc. v. Kraft, Inc., 805 F.2d 974, 987-88 (11th Cir. 1986), *cert. denied*, 481 U.S. 1041 (1987); Foxworthy v. Custom Tees, 879 F. Supp. 1200, 1216-17 (N.D. Ga. 1995).

[136] *See, e.g.*, Resource Developers Inc. v. Statue of Liberty-Ellis Island Foundation, Inc., 926 F.2d 134, 140 (2d Cir. 1991); Schieffelin & Co. v. Jack Co., 850 F. Supp. 232, 245 (E.D.N.Y. 1994).

[137] *See, e.g.*, Blockbuster Ent. Grp. v. Laylco, Inc., 869 F. Supp. 505 (E.D. Mich. 1994)

[138] *See, e.g.*, *Blockbuster*, 869 F. Supp. at 513; Novartis Consumer Health, Inc. v. Johnson & Johnson-Merck Consumer Pharms. Co., 290 F.3d 578, 594 (3d Cir. 2002); Sara Lee Corp. v. Kayser-Roth Corp., 81 F.3d 455, 466-67 & n. 15 (4th Cir. 1996); Exxon Corp. v. Texas Motor Exch., Inc., 628 F.2d 500, 507 (5th Cir. 1980); RJR Foods, Inc. v. White Rock Corp., 603 F.2d 1058 (2d Cir. 1979); James Burrough, Ltd. v. Sign of Beefeater, Inc., 540 F.2d 266 (7th Cir. 1976); Schieffelin & Co. v. Jack Company of Boca, 850 F. Supp. 232, 247 (S.D.N.Y. 1994).

[139] *See, e.g.*, Mutual of Omaha Ins. Co. v. Novak, 836 F.2d 397, 400 (8th Cir. 1987) (10% was sufficient); Coca-Cola Co. v. Tropicana Prods., Inc., 690 F.2d 312 (2d Cir. 1982) (reversing district court's conclusion that 7.5% confusion was insufficient); Goya Foods, Inc. v. Condal Distribs., Inc., 732 F. Supp. 453, 457 n. 7 (S.D.N.Y. 1990) (9-10% confusion was sufficient); Nat'l Football League Props., Inc. v. New Jersey Giants, Inc., 637 F. Supp. 507, 517 (D.N.J. 1986) (citing decisions relying on surveys showing 8.5% to 15% confusion); Grotrian, Helfferich, Schulz, Th. Steinweg Nachf. v. Steinway & Sons, 365 F. Supp. 707, 716 (S.D.N.Y. 1973) (survey showing 8.5% confusion was "strong evidence" of a likelihood of confusion).

manner in which the survey was constructed or administered, and expert testimony on these questions may be important in determining how much, if any, weight to assign to the survey evidence;[140] flawed survey methodologies may undermine or negate the evidentiary value of the survey.[141] One court has suggested that the following principles should govern the relevance and weight of survey evidence:

> The trustworthiness of surveys depends upon foundation evidence that (1) the "universe" was properly defined, (2) a representative sample of that universe was selected, (3) the questions to be asked of interviewees were framed in a clear, concise and nonleading manner, (4) sound interview procedures were followed by competent interviewers who had no knowledge of the litigation or the purpose for which the survey was conducted, (5) the data gathered was accurately reported, (6) the data was analyzed in accordance with accepted statistical principles and (7) objectivity of the entire process was assured.[142]

[f]   Bridging the Gap

This factor considers whether the senior user is likely to expand into the junior user's market.[143] If the two fields are closely related, this factor will tend to favor the senior user. In *Scarves by Vera, Inc. v. Todo Imports, Ltd.*, for example, the Second Circuit held that the fact that other women's fashion designers had crossed over into cosmetics, perfume, and toiletries, together with evidence that the plaintiff (a women's fashion designer) was exploring that market, helped to establish that perfumes were sufficiently related to women's fashion products that the parties' use of VERA in both fields was likely to cause confusion.[144] In contrast, if the parties' fields are unrelated, the senior user is unlikely to prevail on this factor.[145] Thus, the court in *CBS v. Liederman* held

---

[140] *See, e.g., Blockbuster*, 869 F. Supp. at 514.

[141] Indianapolis Colts, Inc. v. Metropolitan Baltimore Football Club L.P., 34 F.3d 410, 414-15 (7th Cir. 1994); Anheuser-Busch, Inc. v. Balducci Pubs., 28 F.3d 769, 775 n. 4 (8th Cir. 1994); Lois Sportswear, U.S.A., Inc. v. Levi Strauss & Co., 799 F.2d 867, 875 (2d Cir. 1986); ConAgra, Inc. v. Geo. A. Hormel & Co., 784 F. Supp. 700, 734 (D. Neb. 1992), *aff'd*, 990 F.2d 368 (8th Cir. 1993); Conopco, Inc. v. Cosmair, Inc., 49 F. Supp. 2d 242, 252-55 (S.D.N.Y. 1999); Novo Nordisk of N. Am. v. Eli Lilly & Co., 1996 U.S. Dist. LEXIS 12807 (S.D.N.Y. 1996).

[142] Toys "R" Us, Inc. v. Canarsie Kiddie Shop, Inc., 559 F. Supp. 1189, 1205 (E.D.N.Y. 1983); *see also* Simon Prop. Group L.P. v. mySimon, Inc., 104 F. Supp. 2d 1033, 1038-39 (S.D. Ind. 2000) (collecting cases); Schieffelin & Co. v. Jack Co., 850 F. Supp. 232, 245 (S.D.N.Y. 1994); Hutchinson v. Essence Communications, Inc., 769 F. Supp. 541, 557 (S.D.N.Y. 1991); Weight Watchers Intern. v. Stouffer Corp., 744 F. Supp. 1259, 1272 (S.D.N.Y. 1990).

[143] CBS, Inc. v. Liederman, 866 F. Supp. 763, 767 (S.D.N.Y. 1994), *aff'd*, 44 F.3d 174 (2d Cir. 1995).

[144] 544 F.2d 1167 (2d Cir. 1976).

[145] Westward Coach Mfg. Co. v. Ford Motor Co., 388 F.2d 627 (7th Cir.) (where plaintiff's "Mustang" campers and trailers did not compete with defendant's "Mustang" sport automobiles, and it was unlikely that plaintiff would expand into automobile field, confusion was unlikely, especially because "Mustang" was a weak mark), *cert. denied*, 392 U.S. 927 (1968); McGregor-Doniger, Inc. v. Drizzle, Inc., 599 F.2d 1126 (2d Cir. 1979) (lack of competition between women's fashionable rainwear and men's lightweight rain jackets, combined with improbability that plaintiff would expand from the latter market into the former market, makes it unlikely that customers will be confused between DRIZZLER mark for men's jackets and DRIZZLE mark for women's raincoats).

that the senior user's field of television production was so unrelated to the junior user's field of restaurant services that even the senior user's stated intent to enter the restaurant business was irrelevant to the likelihood-of-confusion analysis.[146] In *Procter & Gamble Co. v. Johnson & Johnson, Inc.*, the district court found it unlikely that the plaintiff would expand the use of its SURE mark for deodorant into the market for tampons, because the plaintiff was already marketing tampons under the RELY mark; thus, the court concluded, the junior user's adoption of ASSURE for tampons and SURE & NATURAL for maxipads was unlikely to cause confusion.[147]

Bridging the gap applies to geographic markets as well as product markets. Thus, if the parties are not currently operating in the same territories, courts may consider the likelihood that the senior user will enter the junior user's territory in the future.[148]

[g]   Defendant's Good Faith

This factor considers whether the junior user adopted its mark "with the intention of capitalizing on plaintiff's reputation and goodwill and any confusion between [the junior user's] and the senior user's" goods or services.[149] Although a finding of bad faith is not necessary to finding a likelihood of confusion,[150] if the junior user adopted its mark with the intent of capitalizing on consumer confusion, this will weigh in favor of the senior user.

There will typically be no direct evidence of the junior user's intent in adopting the mark. However, courts have held that a rebuttable presumption of bad faith may be warranted when the junior user's mark is identical to another mark that was already well-known and had acquired a secondary meaning at the time the junior user adopted it:[151]

> On the assumption that a businessman will ordinarily act to his commercial advantage, and that the attraction of an established business' good will to the newcomer's product is such an advantage, the inference to be drawn from imitation is the imitator's own expectation of confusion as to the source of origin of his product. Where . . . there is little to distinguish the marks themselves and the prior mark is a

---

[146] *Liederman*, 866 F. Supp. at 767.

[147] 485 F. Supp. 1185 (S.D.N.Y.), *aff'd without op.*, 636 F.2d 1203 (2d Cir. 1979).

[148] Cork 'N Cleaver of Colorado, Inc. v. Keg 'N Cleaver of Utica, Inc., 192 U.S.P.Q. (BNA) 148 (N.D.N.Y. 1975) (likelihood that plaintiff's Colorado-based restaurant chain would expand into New York State supported finding of infringement against junior user in New York state); Sun Banks of Florida, Inc. v. Sun Federal Sav. & Loan Ass'n, 200 U.S.P.Q. (BNA) 758 (N.D. Fla. 1978) (holding that defendant's use of dominant SUN portion of plaintiff's mark for banking services was likely to cause confusion where plaintiff was likely to expand its own banking services into defendant's territories).

[149] W.W.W. Pharmaceutical Co. v. Gillette Co., 984 F.2d 567, 575 (2d Cir. 1993); *accord*, Lang v. Retirement Living Pub. Co., 949 F.2d 576, 583 (2d Cir. 1991); Macia v. Microsoft, 335 F. Supp. 2d 507 (D. Vt. 2004); Edison Bros. Stores, Inc. v. Cosmair, Inc., 651 F. Supp. 1547, 1560 (S.D.N.Y. 1987).

[150] Tisch Hotels, Inc. v. Americana Inn, Inc., 350 F.2d 609, 613 (7th Cir. 1965).

[151] Stern's Miracle-Gro Prods., Inc. v. Shark Prods., Inc., 823 F. Supp. 1077, 1087 (S.D.N.Y 1993).

long-established one of which the newcomer was aware, doubts about intent are resolved against the newcomer, and a reasonable explanation of its choice is essential to establish lack of intent to deceive.[152]

Bad faith may also be inferred from a junior user's continued use of a mark after being notified of the senior user's objections.[153]

Mere knowledge that another party is already using a similar mark, however, does not necessarily establish a junior user's bad faith. Thus, for example, courts have held that bad faith was not established where the junior user relied on legal advice that confusion with the senior user's mark was unlikely under the circumstances.[154] It has also been held that failure to conduct a trademark search before adopting a mark does not, by itself, establish bad faith.[155] Conversely, where a junior user seeks advice of counsel and undertakes a trademark investigation before determining that adoption of a mark will not lead to confusion, this has been treated as evidence of good faith.[156]

Bad faith in the context of trademark infringement or unfair competition under state law or under sections 32 or 43(a) of the Lanham Act should not be confused with "bad faith intent to profit" under the "cybersquatting" provisions of section 43(d) of the Lanham Act. The latter is discussed in § 3.08 below.

[h]   Relative Quality of Defendant's Goods or Services

Although the quality of the defendant's goods or services is one of the *Polaroid* factors used by the Second Circuit, its role in the analysis is somewhat ambiguous, and it seems to have little relevance in other jurisdictions.[157]

The ambiguity of this factor arises from the fact that a marked difference in quality between the senior and junior users' goods cuts both ways. It can reduce the likelihood of confusion, but where the junior user's goods are significantly lower in quality, any confusion that does occur will not only divert sales from the

---

[152] Toys "R" Us, Inc. v. Canarsie Kiddie Shop, Inc., 559 F. Supp. 1189, 1199 (E.D.N.Y. 1983).

[153] *Stern's Miracle-Gro*, 823 F. Supp. at 1088; *see also* Mobil Oil Corp. v. Pegasus Petroleum Corp., 818 F.2d 254, 258-59 (2d Cir. 1987); Eastman Kodak Co. v. Rakow, 739 F. Supp. 116, 119 (W.D.N.Y. 1989).

[154] *See, e.g.*, W.W.W. Pharmaceutical Co. v. Gillette Co., 984 F.2d 567 (2d Cir. 1993); Procter & Gamble Co. v. Johnson & Johnson, Inc., 485 F. Supp. 1185, 1202 (S.D.N.Y. 1979).

[155] Paco Sport, Ltd. v. Paco Rabanne Parfums, 86 F. Supp. 2d 305 (S.D.N.Y.), *aff'd*, 2000 U.S. App. LEXIS 29570 (2d Cir. 2000).

[156] *See, e.g.*, Information Clearing House, Inc. v. Find Magazine, 492 F. Supp. 147 (S.D.N.Y. 1980) (defendant showed good faith by studying market and seeking advice of counsel before adopting mark); Lever Bros. Co. v. American Bakeries Co., 537 F. Supp. 248 (E.D.N.Y.), *aff'd*, 693 F.2d 251 (2d Cir. 1982) (finding good faith where defendant adopted AUTUMN GRAIN mark for bread after conducting trademark investigation and obtaining advice of counsel regarding plaintiff's AUTUMN mark for margarine).

[157] AMF, Inc. v. Sleekcraft Boats, 599 F.2d 341, 353-54 (9th Cir. 1979) (noting that current high quality of defendant's goods is no guarantee of their continued quality, and that equivalence of quality may contribute to consumer confusion); *see also* Drexel Enterprises, Inc. v. Hermitage Cabinet Shop, Inc., 266 F. Supp. 532 (N.D. Ga. 1967) (holding that it makes no difference whether noncompetitive user's goods or services are of higher, equal, or inferior quality).

senior user, but will also tend to injure the senior user's reputation.[158] As the Second Circuit has noted:

> The next factor, quality of the junior user's product, is the subject of some confusion. Essentially, there are two issues with regard to quality, but only one has relevance to determining the likelihood of confusion. If the quality of the junior user's product is low relative to the senior user's, then this increases the chance of actual injury where there is confusion, i.e., through dilution of the senior user's brand. A marked difference in quality, however, actually tends to reduce the likelihood of confusion in the first instance, because buyers will be less likely to assume that the senior user whose product is high-quality will have produced the lesser-quality products of the junior user. Conversely, where the junior user's products are of approximately the same quality as the senior user's, there is a greater likelihood of confusion, but less possibility of dilution.[159]

Yet, when courts consider quality in the traditional likelihood-of-confusion analysis, they do not always acknowledge the ambiguous role of this factor. In some cases, courts have squarely held that there is less likelihood of confusion when the defendant's goods are at least equal in quality to the plaintiff's, because in such a case any consumer confusion about the origin of the defendant's goods is less likely to injure the plaintiff's reputation.[160] Other courts have squarely held that there is less likelihood of confusion where the defendant's goods are inferior to the plaintiff's, because "dissimilarity between the goods as well as between the groups of consumers that each party targets substantially lessens the likelihood of consumers' misapprehending the source of either type of products."[161] On other occasions, courts have acknowledged that this factor is more relevant to assessing the extent of the senior user's injury, and fashioning

---

[158] Hormel Foods Corp. v. Jim Henson Prods., Inc., 73 F.3d 497, 505 (2d Cir. 1996) (*citing* Nikon, Inc. v. Ikon Corp., 987 F.2d 91, 95 (2d Cir. 1993)); New Colt Holding Corp. v. RJG Holdings of Fla., Inc., 312 F. Supp. 2d 195, 227 (D. Conn. 2004).

[159] Savin Corp. v. Savin Group, 391 F.3d 439, 460-61 (2d Cir. 2004) (citations and internal quotation marks omitted); *accord* Empresa Cubana Del Tabaco v. Culbro Corp., 70 U.S.P.Q.2d (BNA) 1650, 2004 U.S. Dist LEXIS 4935, *137-38 (S.D.N.Y. 2004).

[160] *See, e.g.*, Gruner + Jahr USA Pub'g v. Meredith Corp., 991 F.2d 1072, 1079 (2d Cir. 1993) (rejecting the argument that similarity of quality favors the plaintiff "because it means the products closely compete," and treating this factor as neutral, because "[g]enerally, quality is weighed as a factor when there is an allegation that a low quality product is taking unfair advantage of the public good will earned by a well-established high quality product"); W.W.W. Pharm. Co. v. Gillette Co., 984 F.2d 567, 575 (2d Cir. 1993) (holding that plaintiff's failure to allege that defendant's goods are inferior weakens plaintiff's case, because "[i]f an infringing product is of inferior quality, the senior user is entitled to protect 'the good reputation associated with his mark from the possibility of being tarnished by inferior merchandise of the junior user") (internal quotation marks omitted); Lever Bros. Co. v. American Bakeries Co., 693 F.2d 251 (2d Cir. 1982) (high quality of both products reduces likelihood of confusion); M&G Elecs. Sales Corp. v. Sony Kabushiki Kaisha, 250 F. Supp. 2d 91 (E.D.N.Y. 2003) (where plaintiff did not dispute high quality of defendants' products, quality-of-products factor favored defendants); *accord* Scarves by Vera, Inc. v. Todo Imports, Ltd., 544 F.2d 1167, 1172 (2d Cir. 1976); Essence Communications, Inc. v. Singh Indus., 703 F. Supp. 261, 270 (S.D.N.Y. 1988).

[161] Plus Prods. v. Plus Discount Foods, Inc., 722 F.2d 999, 1007 (2d Cir. 1983) (inferior quality of defendant's goods lessens likelihood of confusion).

an appropriate remedy, than to determining the existence of likelihood of confusion, because the plaintiff's reputation might have been tarnished if the defendant's goods were of low quality.[162]

Where inferior quality is reflected in the price of the defendant's goods, however, courts generally hold that a significant price differential reduces the likelihood of confusion.[163] The same applies if the defendant's goods are higher in price.[164]

Similarity in quality may be especially significant in the post-sale context, where it will tend to increase the likelihood of confusion by nonpurchasers, because, unlike the purchasers, they do not benefit from knowing the price differential.[165]

[3]   Jurisdictional Variations on the *Polaroid* Test

Outside of the Second Circuit, the list of factors considered by some jurisdictions includes factors that, while not expressly listed in the *Polaroid* test, are nonetheless subsumed under the broad sweep of such factors as the proximity of the goods and the sophistication of the consumers.[166]

For example, several jurisdictions explicitly consider the "degree of care" exercised by consumers in selecting goods or services of the type in question,[167] an important element that, in the *Polaroid* analysis, is usually considered under the "sophistication of the consumers" factor,[168] although the "degree of care"

---

[162] Virgin Enters., Ltd. v. Nawab, 335 F.3d 141, 152 (2d Cir. 2003).

[163] *See, e.g.*, Field Enters. Educ. Corp. v. Grosset & Dunlap, Inc., 256 F. Supp. 382 (S.D.N.Y. 1966) (no likelihood of confusion where plaintiff's books sold for $129 and defendant's books sold for $1 each); Field Enters. Educ. Corp. v. Cove Industries, Inc., 297 F. Supp. 989 (E.D.N.Y. 1969) (no likelihood of confusion where plaintiff's encyclopedia sold for about $200 and defendant's encyclopedia for about $40); McGregor-Doniger, Inc. v. Drizzle, Inc., 446 F. Supp. 160 (S.D.N.Y.), *aff'd*, 599 F.2d 1126 (2d Cir. 1978) (no likelihood of confusion between low-priced men's rain jackets and more expensive and stylish women's rainwear).

[164] *See, e.g.*, W.F. & John Barnes Co. v. Vandyck-Churchill Co., 207 F. 855 (S.D.N.Y.), *aff'd*, 213 F. 637 (2d Cir. 1913); Gort Girls Frocks, Inc. v. Princess Pat Lingerie, Inc., 73 F. Supp. 364 (S.D.N.Y. 1947) (plaintiff's reputation would not be endangered if consumers misattributed defendant's higher priced dresses).

[165] For example, in *Lois Sportswear, U.S.A., Inc. v. Levi Strauss & Co.*, 799 F.2d 867, 875 (2d Cir. 1986), the court noted that the high quality of the defendant's knock-off jeans arguably reduced the risk of injury to the plaintiff's reputation as a result of consumer confusion, but added:

> It must be noted, however, that under the circumstances of this case the good quality of appellants' product actually may increase the likelihood of confusion as to source. Particularly in the post-sale context, consumers easily could assume that quality jeans bearing what is perceived as appellee's trademark stitching pattern to be a Levi's product. The fact that appellants have produced a quality copy suggests that the possibility of their profiting from appellee's goodwill is still likely.

[166] For authorities listing some of the multi-factor tests used outside the Second Circuit, see note 48 *supra*.

[167] *See, e.g.*, AMF Inc. v. Sleekcraft Boats, 599 F.2d 341 (9th Cir. 1979); Sullivan v. CBS Corp., 385 F.3d 772, 776-77 (7th Cir. 2004); Frisch's Restaurants v. Elby's Big Boy, 670 F.2d 642, 648 (6th Cir. 1982).

[168] *See, e.g.*, Deere & Co. v. MTD Holdings, Inc., 70 U.S.P.Q.2d 1009 (S.D.N.Y. 2004); Tommy Hilfiger Licensing, Inc. v. Nature Labs, LLC, 221 F. Supp. 2d 410, 420 (S.D.N.Y. 2002).

focuses specifically on the state of mind that the consumer brings to the particular purchasing decision. When a high degree of care is exercised at the time of purchase, this generally reduces the likelihood of confusion.[169] Thus, for example, consumers are thought to exercise a higher degree of care in selecting banking or financial services,[170] educational services,[171] or other expensive items,[172] than they do in making inexpensive impulse purchases.[173] It can be argued that the "degree of care" approach is more useful than the "sophistication" approach, because the latter implies that consumers bring the same level of sophistication to *every* purchasing decision, while the former recognizes that even sophisticated consumers exercise more care in some transactions than in others.

Several jurisdictions also list an additional likelihood of confusion factor, which they describe as either the "marketing channels used" by the junior and senior user in promoting their goods,[174] or the "area and manner of concurrent use" of the parties' marks.[175] In the Second Circuit's *Polaroid* test, this consideration is subsumed under the broader "proximity of the goods" factor.

[C]   Reverse Confusion

Trademark infringement under sections 32 or 43(a) of the Lanham Act may be based on either "forward" or "reverse" confusion.[176] Forward (or "ordinary") confusion is the more common type of confusion, in which the junior user adopts a mark that so closely resembles the senior user's mark that consumers are likely to be misled into believing that the senior user is the source of the junior user's goods or services. In reverse confusion, the similarity between the marks has the opposite effect: consumers are likely to be misled into believing that the senior user's goods originate with the junior user.[177] In other words,

---

[169] Sally Beauty Co. v. Beautyco., Inc., 304 F.3d 964, 975 (10th Cir. 2002); Heartsprings, Inc. v. Heartspring, Inc., 143 F.3d 550, 557 (10th Cir. 1998).

[170] *See, e.g.*, First National Bank, in Sioux Falls v. First National Bank, South Dakota, 153 F.3d 885, 889-90 (8th Cir. 1998) ("Consumers tend to exercise a relatively high degree of care in selecting banking services. As a result, customers are more likely to notice what, in other contexts, may be relatively minor differences in names."); First Franklin Fin. Corp. v. Franklin First Fin., LTD, 356 F. Supp. 2d 1048 (N.D. Cal. 2005) (mortgage consumers exercise high degree of care).

[171] *Heartsprings*, 143 F.3d at 557.

[172] *Sally Beauty Co.*, 304 F.3d at 975; *Tommy Hilfiger*, 221 F. Supp. 2d at 420.

[173] *Sally Beauty Co.*, 304 F.3d at 975; Beer Nuts, Inc. v. Clover Club Foods Col, 805 F.2d 920, 926 (10th Cir. 1986).

[174] *See, e.g., Sleekcraft*, 599 F.2d 341.

[175] *See, e.g., Sullivan*, 385 F.3d at 776-77.

[176] Trouble v. Wet Seal, 179 F. Supp. 2d 291, 295-96 (S.D.N.Y. 1991).

[177] Lange v. Retirement Living Pub. Co., 949 F.2d 576, 583 (2d Cir. 1991); Restatement (Third) of Unfair Competition § 20(1)(c) & cmt. f; Banff, Ltd. v. Federated Dept. Stores, Inc., 841 F.2d 486, 490 (2d Cir. 1988); Sterling Drug, Inc. v. Bayer AG, 14 F.3d 733, 741 (2d Cir. 1994) (collecting cases); Trouble v. Wet Seal, 179 F. Supp. 2d 291, 295-96 (S.D.N.Y. 1991); Trustees of Columbia University v. Columbia/HCA Healthcare Corp., 964 F. Supp. 733, 743 (S.D.N.Y. 1997); Sunenblick v. Harrell, 895 F. Supp. 616, 625-26 (S.D.N.Y. 1995) (collecting cases); Dreamwerks Prod. Grp. v. SKG Studio, 142 F.3d 1127, 1130 (9th Cir. 1998) (issue in reverse confusion is "whether consumers doing business with the senior user might mistakenly believe that they are dealing with the junior user"); Fuji Photo Film

"consumers encountering Plaintiff's products will assume that they are made by Defendant."[178] Most commonly, this results from the success of the junior user's marketing success, which causes the junior user to become better known than the senior user:

> [T]he junior user saturates the market with a similar trademark and overwhelms the senior user. The public comes to assume the senior user's products are really the junior user's or that the former has become somehow connected to the latter. The result is that the senior user loses the value of the trademark — its product identity, corporate identity, control over its goodwill and reputation, and ability to move into new markets.[179]

Where reverse confusion occurs, the junior user's goodwill may so overwhelm that of the senior user that consumers may mistakenly believe that the senior user and the junior user are the same or related entities,[180] or even that the senior user is infringing the junior user's mark.[181]

Courts have applied the Lanham Act to encompass claims of reverse confusion because providing such protection to trademark owners "comports with the dual purposes of the Act — namely, to protect the public from confusion as to the source of goods, and at the same time to protect the trademark holder from misappropriation of its mark."[182] The earliest federal court opinion recognizing a reverse confusion claim noted that the consequence of refusing to recognize such claims

> would be the immunization from unfair competition liability of a company with a well-established trade name and with the economic power to advertise extensively for a product name taken from a competitor. If the law is to limit recovery to passing off, anyone with adequate size and resources can adopt any trademark and develop a new meaning for that trademark as identification of the second user's products.[183]

Co. v. Shinohara Shoji Kabushiki Kaisha, 754 F.2d 591, 596 (5th Cir. 1985) (collecting cases).

[178] Becoming, Inc. v. Avon Products, Inc., No. 01 Civ. 5863, 2001 U.S. Dist. LEXIS 11929, *28 (S.D.N.Y. Aug. 15, 2001).

[179] Ameritech, Inc. v. American Information Technologies Corp., 811 F.2d 960, 964 (6th Cir. 1987); see also Sunenblick, 895 F. Supp. at 625 (describing reverse confusion as "the phenomenon in which the junior user's advertising so greatly overshadows that of the senior user that consumers come to the mistaken conclusion that the junior user is in fact the source of the senior user's goods.").

[180] Home Box Office, Inc. v. Showtime/The Movie Channel, Inc., 832 F.2d 1311, 1314 (2d Cir. 1987).

[181] See, e.g., W.W.W. Pharm. Co. v. Gillette Co., 984 F.2d 567, 571 (2d Cir. 1993); Banff, Ltd. v. Federated Dept. Stores, Inc., 841 F.2d 486, 490 (2d Cir. 1988); Sunenblick, 895 F. Supp. at 625-26.

[182] Sterling Drug, 14 F.3d at 741.

[183] Big O Tire Dealers, Inc. v. Goodyear Tire & Rubber Co., 561 F.2d 1365, 1372 (10th Cir. 1977) (quoting Big O Tire Dealers, Inc. v. Goodyear Tire & Rubber Co., 408 F. Supp. 1219, 1236 (D. Colo. 1976)).

For example, in *Plus Products v. Plus Discount Foods, Inc.*,[184] the senior user had established a reputation for high-quality, premium-priced products offered under its PLUS trademark. The junior user later adopted the PLUS trademark for goods sold through its chain of bargain-basement, self-service, cash-only discount stores. The senior user based its trademark infringement claim on a theory of reverse confusion, arguing that consumers would believe that the senior user's premium products were in fact produced by the junior user, and that, as a result of this mistaken belief, the senior user's reputation for high-quality merchandise would "become tarnished because of [the junior user's] bargain-basement, no-frills image."[185]

In contrast to forward confusion, the injury to the senior user arising from reverse confusion may not involve an immediate diversion of sales. Instead, it typically involves an erosion of the senior user's goodwill or a loss of control over the senior user's reputation.[186] For example, consumers may come to believe that the senior user is an infringer trying to ride the coattails of the junior user.[187] Alternatively, if the junior user engages in conduct that gives rise to negative public opinion, this could tarnish the reputation of the senior user by eroding the goodwill associated with the mark.[188] Courts occasionally mention, as another source of potential injury to the senior user, that consumers who experience problems with the quality of the junior user's goods or services may erroneously attribute their negative experience to the senior user;[189] however, these courts appear to be in error, because this type of harm really arises from forward confusion.[190] Where evidence exists to support both forward and reverse confusion, a senior user may utilize both theories in its infringement claim.[191]

---

[184] 722 F.2d 999 (2d Cir. 1983).

[185] *Id.* at 1003-04.

[186] *See, e.g.*, Lange v. Retirement Living Pub. Co., 949 F.2d 576, 583 (2d Cir. 1991) ("because this case involves reverse confusion, the commercial injury [the senior user] has suffered is an erosion of goodwill and a loss of control over her reputation, and as such is a more subtle injury than the customary diversion of trade engendered by direct confusion"); Sands, Taylor & Wood Co. v. Quaker Oats Co., 978 F.2d 947, 957 (7th Cir. 1992) ("The result is that the senior user loses the value of the trademark — its product identity, Corporate identity, control over its goodwill and reputation, and ability to move in to new markets.") (quoting Ameritech, Inc. v. American Information Technologies Corp., 811 F.2d 960, 964 (6th Cir. 1987)).

[187] Banff, Ltd. v. Federated Dep't Stores, Inc., 841 F.2d 486, 490 (2d Cir. 1988); W.W.W. Pharm. Co. v. Gillette Co., 984 F.2d 567, 571 (2d Cir. 1993); Sunenblick v. Harrell, 895 F. Supp. 616, 625 (S.D.N.Y. 1995), *aff'd without op.*, 101 F.3d 684 (2d Cir. 1996).

[188] Dreamwerks Prod. Grp. v. SKG Studio, 142 F.3d 1127, 1129 (9th Cir. 1998). It has also been suggested that the senior user could also be harmed if the junior user's dominance impedes the senior user from expanding into the junior user's line of business. *Id.*

[189] *See, e.g.*, Becoming, Inc. v. Avon Products, Inc., No. 01 Civ. 5863, 2001 U.S. Dist. LEXIS 11929, *28 (S.D.N.Y. Aug. 15, 2001) (stating that reverse confusion doctrine "recognizes the danger that a junior user's products may tarnish the image of the senior user's products"); Brockmeyer v. Hearst Corp., 2002 U.S. Dist. LEXIS 11725 (S.D.N.Y. June 27, 2002).

[190] For example, in Lange v. Retirement Living Publishing Co., Inc., 949 F.2d 576 (2d Cir. 1991), the plaintiff's evidence of actual confusion included evidence that consumers had erroneously contacted the plaintiff regarding the defendant's product. The court held that this evidence did not support the reverse confusion claim:

The misdirected phone calls are not relevant because, even if we infer in [plaintiff] Lang's

In determining the likelihood of reverse confusion, courts generally consider the same likelihood of confusion factors that they apply to claims of "ordinary" confusion,[192] with occasional modification.[193] However, with respect to one of these factors — the strength of the mark — courts disagree on whether the reverse confusion analysis should focus on the strength of the senior user's mark or that of the junior user's mark.[194] Of the courts that focus on the strength of the senior user's mark, several have suggested that the threshold for establishing secondary meaning should be somewhat lower than it would be in a case

---

favor that they reflect consumer confusion, those consumers erroneously believed that the senior user (Lang) was the source of the junior user's (Retirement Living) magazine. Evidence of actual reverse confusion that might support Lang's claim would involve purchasers or prospective purchasers of Lang's products who believed that they were produced by or affiliated with Retirement Living's magazine.

Id. at 583.

[191] For example, in Banff, Ltd. v. Federated Dept. Stores, Inc., 841 F.2d 486 (2d Cir. 1988), the court recognized that some consumers might perceive the senior user (Banff) as the source of the junior user's (Bloomingdales') goods, while others might make the opposite mistake:

The principal marks in question, "Bee Wear" and various typestyles of "B Wear," may create both types of confusion. Consumers who know of Banff's "Bee Wear" may believe that Bloomingdale's standard typestyle "B Wear," ribbon-style "B Wear," or stylized lower-case "b Wear" goods originate with Banff. The Lanham Act protects against this kind of confusion in order to prevent Bloomingdale's from appropriating Banff's reputation, limiting Banff's expansion, or causing Banff a loss of patronage. Other consumers initially aware of Bloomingdale's apparel may believe that Banff's "Bee Wear" mark they later encounter originates with Bloomingdale's. These consumers may consider Banff an unauthorized infringer, and Bloomingdale's use of the mark may in that way injure Banff's reputation and impair its good will. Thus, reverse confusion also inhibits fair competition and deprives Banff of its reputation and good will.

Id. at 490 (citations omitted). *See also* Trustees of Columbia University v. Columbia/HCA Healthcare Corp., 964 F. Supp. 733, 743 (S.D.N.Y. 1997) (considering plaintiff's allegations under both theories); Trouble v. Wet Seal, 179 F. Supp. 2d 291, 295-96 (S.D.N.Y. 1991) ("allegations of forward confusion and reverse confusion do not form distinct claims — they are alternative theories that can be used separately or together in a trademark infringement claim under the Lanham Act").

[192] *See, e.g.*, Dreamwerks Prod. Grp., 142 F.3d at 1129; Sands, Taylor & Wood Co. v. Quaker Oats Co., 978 F.2d 947, 959 (7th Cir. 1992); Banff, Ltd. v. Federated Dept. Stores, Inc., 841 F.2d 486, 491 (2d Cir. 1988); M & G Elecs. Sales Corp. v. Sony Kabushiki Kaisha, 250 F. Supp. 2d 91, 100 (E.D.N.Y. 2003). In the Ninth Circuit, three of the likelihood-of-confusion factors are considered especially important in determining the likelihood of reverse confusion: (1) the strength of the marks, (2) the relatedness of the goods, and (3) the similarity of the marks. Matrix Motor Co., Inc. v. Toyota Jidosha Kabushiki Kaisha, 290 F. Supp. 2d 1083, 1090 (C.D. Cal. 2003), *aff'd*, 120 Fed. Appx. 30 (2005). However, consideration of the other likelihood-of-confusion factors is not foreclosed. *Matrix Motor*, 290 F. Supp. 2d at 1090; *Dreamwerks*, 142 F.3d at 1130.

[193] *See, e.g.*, Commerce Nat'l Ins. Servs. v. Commerce Ins. Agency, 214 F.3d 432, 444 (3d Cir. 2000) (giving less weight to the weakness of the senior user's mark, and revising the "intent" factor "to focus on whether the defendant was aware of the senior user's use of the mark in question, or whether the defendant conducted an adequate name search for other companies marketing similar goods or services under that mark.").

[194] *Compare Commerce Nat'l Ins.*, 214 F.3d at 444 (senior user's mark); *Trustees of Columbia University*, 964 F. Supp. at 744-45 (similar); *and* Ernst Hardware Co. v. Ernst Home Ctr., 134 Or. App. 560, 563-64 (Or. Ct. App. 1995) (similar), *with Dreamwerks*, 142 F.3d at 1130 n. 5 (junior user's mark); *Sands, Taylor & Wood*, 978 F.2d at 959 (similar); *Sunenblick*, 895 F. Supp. at 626 (similar); and Sunmark Inc. v. Ocean Spray Cranberries, Inc., 1994 U.S. Dist. LEXIS 15186, (N.D. Ill. 1994) *58 (similar).

involving forward confusion: Otherwise, "a larger company could with impunity infringe the senior mark of a smaller one."[195]

Although reverse confusion is now well-recognized under the Lanham Act, the doctrine is of relatively recent vintage, and only a few decisions have discussed its viability under state law.[196]

Claims of reverse confusion should not be confused with claims of reverse passing-off. Reverse confusion, like forward confusion, arises when two parties each sell their own goods under similar marks, while reverse passing off involves a defendant that is selling the plaintiff's goods under the defendant's mark, thus falsely representing itself as the maker of those goods.[197]

[D]   Confusion Before or After the Purchasing Decision

Consumer confusion occurring at the time a transaction takes place (sometimes called "point of sale" confusion) is not the only type of consumer confusion recognized under the Lanham Act. As discussed below, a number of courts have recognized "initial interest confusion" and "post-sale confusion." This expansive view of confusion has been traced to the 1962 amendments to section 2 of the Lanham Act, which removed references to "purchasers."[198] Many courts have interpreted this broadening of the statute as a recognition that the Lanham Act protects *trademark owners* in addition to consumers.

[1]   Initial Interest Confusion

Initial interest confusion occurs when one party has used another's mark "in a manner calculated 'to capture initial consumer attention, even though no actual sale is finally completed as a result of the confusion.' "[199] Here, the similarity between a junior user's mark and a senior user's mark is what draws

---

[195] *Commerce Nat'l Ins.*, 214 F.3d at 444 (quoting *Banff*, 841 F.2d at 491).

[196] The majority of these cases have concluded that the state laws in question encompassed reverse confusion. *See, e.g.*, Big O Tire Dealers, Inc. v. Goodyear Tire & Rubber Co., 561 F.2d 1365, 1371 (10th Cir. 1977), *cert. dismissed*, 434 U.S. 1052 (1978) (concluding that Colorado's common law of trademark infringement encompassed claims of reverse confusion); Ameritech, Inc. v. American Info. Tech. Corp., 811 F.2d 960 (6th Cir. 1987) (recognizing claim for reverse confusion under Ohio law); Capital Films Corp. v. Charles Fries Productions, 628 F.2d 387 (5th Cir. 1980) (recognizing reverse confusion under Texas law); *cf.* Ernst Hardware Co. v. Ernst Home Ctr., 134 Or. App. 560, 563-64 (Or. Ct. App. 1995) (implicitly recognizing reverse confusion as a valid claim under Oregon law, but concluding that the plaintiff's mark lacked secondary meaning). However, the earliest reported case addressing reverse confusion, Westward Coach Mfg. Co. v. Ford Motor Co., 388 F.2d 627, 633-34 (7th Cir.), *cert. denied*, 392 U.S. 927 (1968), held that such claims were not actionable under Indiana law.

[197] For a discussion of reverse passing-off, see § 3.03 *infra*.

[198] *See* Checkpoint Sys. v. Check Point Software Techs., Inc., 269 F.3d 270, 295 (3d Cir. 2001). The Federal Circuit disagrees, however, noting that the legislative history indicates that the term "purchasers" was deleted from section 2 in order to make clear that the Lanham Act's protection also extends to *potential* purchasers. Electronic Design & Sales, Inc. v. Electronic Data Sys. Corp., 954 F.2d 713, 716 (Fed. Cir. 1992) (citing S. Rep. No. 2107, 87th Cong., 2d Sess. 4 (1962), *reprinted in* 1962 U.S.C.C.A.N. 2844, 2847).

[199] Brookfield Comms., Inc. v. West Coast Ent. Corp., 174 F.3d 1036, 1062 (6th Cir. 1999) (quoting Dr. Seuss Enters. v. Penguin Books, 109 F.3d 1394, 1405 (9th Cir. 1997).

the consumer's initial attention to the goods or services of the junior user, but the consumer is no longer confused by the time the purchasing decision is made.[200] To employ the Ninth Circuit's now-famous analogy:

> Suppose [Blockbuster Video] puts up a billboard on a highway reading — "West Coast Video: 2 miles ahead at Exit 7" — where West Coast is really located at Exit 8 but Blockbuster is located at Exit 7. Customers looking for West Coast's store will pull off at Exit 7 and drive around looking for it. Unable to locate West Coast, but seeing the Blockbuster store right by the highway entrance, they may simply rent there. Even consumers who prefer West Coast may find it not worth the trouble to continue searching for West Coast since there is a Blockbuster right there. Customers are not confused in the narrow sense: they are fully aware that they are purchasing from Blockbuster and they have no reason to believe that Blockbuster is related to, or in any way sponsored by, West Coast. Nevertheless, the fact that there is only initial consumer confusion does not alter the fact that Blockbuster would be misappropriating West Coast's acquired goodwill.[201]

For example, in *Elvis Presley Enterprises, Inc. v. Capece*, the Fifth Circuit found that initial interest confusion was likely to arise from the defendant's use of the name "The Velvet Elvis" for its restaurant:

> The witnesses all testified that, upon entering and looking around the [defendants'] bar, they had no doubt that [plaintiff was] not affiliated with it in any way. Despite the confusion being dissipated, this initial-interest confusion is beneficial to the Defendants because it brings patrons in the door; indeed, it brought at least one of the [plaintiff's] witnesses into the bar. Once in the door, the confusion has succeeded because some of the patrons may stay, despite realizing that the bar has no relationship with [plaintiff]. This initial-interest confusion is even more significant because the Defendants' bar sometimes charges a cover charge for entry, which allows the Defendants to benefit from initial-interest confusion before it can be dissipated by entry into the bar.[202]

Similarly, in *Grotrian, Helfferich, Schulz, Th. Steinweg Nachf. v. Steinway & Sons*,[203] the Second Circuit found that, despite the high degree of care exercised

---

[200] *See* Playboy Enters. v. Netscape Communs. Corp., 354 F.3d 1020, 1025 (9th Cir. 2004) ("Although dispelled before an actual sale occurs, initial interest confusion impermissibly capitalizes on the goodwill associated with a mark and is therefore actionable trademark infringement.").

[201] *Brookfield*, 174 F.3d at 1064. The Second Circuit explains the concept as follows:

> A likelihood of confusion arises "not in the fact that a third party would do business with Pegasus Petroleum believing it related to Mobil [and its winged horse trademark], but rather in the likelihood that Pegasus Petroleum would gain crucial credibility during the initial phases of a deal. For example, an oil trader might listen to a cold phone call from Pegasus Petroleum — an admittedly oft used procedure in the oil business — when otherwise he might not, because of the possibility that Pegasus Petroleum is related to Mobil."

Mobil Oil Corp. v. Pegasus Petroleum Corp., 818 F.2d 254, 259 (2d Cir. 1987).

[202] 141 F.3d 188, 204 (5th Cir. 1998).

[203] 523 F.2d 1331, 1341-42 (2d Cir. 1975).

by consumers in purchasing pianos, the resemblance between the Steinway mark and the Grotrian-Steinweg mark could initially confuse consumers into considering the latter brand. While closer examination of the latter product would eliminate their initial confusion, some of them might decide to purchase it based on cost and quality. In the court's view, this impermissibly allowed the maker of the Grotrian-Steinweg piano to benefit from confusion with the Steinway mark.

At least seven circuits now recognize initial interest confusion as a valid basis for an infringement claim.[204]

Because the likelihood of initial interest confusion depends on the familiar likelihood-of-confusion factors, the analysis in any given case will be highly fact-specific. For example, the likelihood of initial interest confusion presented a close question where a grocery store's house brand adopted trade dress that was similar to that of a name brand competitor.[205] Although consumers may be highly sophisticated about house brands, and the store may present the competing goods in a way that draws attention to the fact that they are different brands and invites customers to make comparisons, this does not always outweigh the similarities between the marks.[206]

Initial interest confusion has played a significant role in infringement claims arising from the unauthorized use of trademarks in Internet domain names and metatags (a term that refers to computer code embedded in a website that is readable by search engines but that does not appear as actual text on the web page). A consumer looking for a senior user's website will search for a domain name incorporating the familiar trademark, either by entering the most likely domain name directly into a browser, or by using a search engine to find websites incorporating a key word or words contained in the trademark. A junior user may divert that consumer to its own website by incorporating the senior user's exact trademark, or a common misspelling, into the domain name, or by incorporating the trademark in the text of the web page or as a metatag, so that the search engine perceives the website as relevant to the user's search request.[207] The more frequently the trademark appears in the text or in metatags, the higher the rank a search engine will assign to the web page in the

---

[204] *See* Mobil Oil Corp. v. Pegasus Petroleum Corp., 818 F.2d 254 (2d Cir. 1987); SecuraComm. Consulting, Inc. v. SecuraCom Inc., 984 F. Supp. 286 (D.N.J. 1997), *rev'd on other grounds*, 166 F.3d 182 (3d Cir. 1999), *appeal after remand*, 224 F.3d 273 (3d Cir. 2000); Elvis Presley Enters., Inc. v. Capece, 141 F.3d 188, 204 (5th Cir. 1998); Forum Corp. of N. Am. v. Forum, Ltd., 903 F.2d 434, 442, n. 2 (7th Cir. 1990); Brookfield Comm'ns., Inc. v. West Coast Ent. Corp., 174 F.3d 1036 (9th Cir. 1999); Australian Gold v. Hatfield, 436 F.3d 1228, 1238-39 (10th Cir. 2006); HRL Assocs., Inc. v. Weiss Assocs., Inc., 12 U.S.P.Q.2d 1819 (TTAB 1989), *aff'd on other grounds*, 902 F.2d 1546 (Fed. Cir. 1990). The Sixth Circuit has implicitly recognized it as well. *See* Gibson Guitar Corp. v. Paul Reed Smith Guitars, LP, 423 F.3d 539, 549-50 (6th Cir. 2005); PACCAR, Inc. v. TeleScan Techs., L.L.C., 319 F.3d 243, 253 (6th Cir. 2003).

[205] McNeil Nutritionals, LLC v. Heartland Sweeteners, LLC, 511 F.3d 350 (3d Cir. 2007), *aff'g in part and rev'g in part*, 512 F. Supp. 2d 217 (E.D. Pa. 2007).

[206] *Id.* at 367-69.

[207] For a good introduction to the mechanics of initial interest confusion on the Internet, see Brookfield Communications, Inc. v. West Coast Entertainment Corp., 174 F.3d 1036, 1044-45 (9th Cir. 1999).

list of search results it provides to the user[208] (although as search engines become more sophisticated they can better discriminate). Even where a consumer (or a search engine utilized by the consumer) is confused only briefly by a junior user's use of metatags or similar devices, the consumer may remain on the junior user's website long enough to learn about its products or services, or those that it is advertising, and may even decide to make a purchase; thus, the temporary nature of the confusion does not preclude a finding that the junior user has misappropriated the senior user's goodwill, and thereby infringed.[209] Courts sometimes describe this as a type of "bait and switch" advertising.[210]

The Ninth Circuit treats three of the likelihood-of-confusion factors used in that circuit (the *Sleekcraft* factors,[211] which differ slightly from the Second Circuit's *Polaroid* factors[212]) as especially relevant to initial interest confusion on the Internet. This "Internet trinity" consists of: (1) the similarity of the marks, (2) the relatedness of the goods or services, and (3) the parties' simultaneous use of the Internet as a marketing channel.[213] If these three factors suggest confusion, then the remaining *Sleekcraft* factors would have to weigh strongly against a likelihood of confusion in order to avoid a finding of infringement.[214] In contrast, the Ninth Circuit considers the strength of the senior user's mark to be a relatively unimportant factor in the Internet context.[215]

A leading case involving initial interest confusion on the Internet is *Brookfield Communications, Inc. v. West Coast Entertainment Corp.*,[216] in which a video rental company planned to use "moviebuff.com" as the domain name for its Web site, and to use a similar term as a metatag on its site, which could be read by search engines. The Ninth Circuit held that the defendant's actions infringed the plaintiff's rights in its registered "MovieBuff" trademark, which it used in connection with software and databases related to the entertainment industry:

> Given the virtual identity of "moviebuff.com" and "MovieBuff," the relatedness of the products and services accompanied by those marks, and the companies' simultaneous use of the Web as a marketing and advertising tool, many forms of consumer confusion are likely to result.

---

[208] *Id.* at 1045.

[209] Promatek Indus., Ltd. v. Equitrac Corp., 300 F.3d 808, 812-13 (7th Cir. 2002).

[210] *See, e.g.,* Dorr-Oliver, Inc. v. Fluid-Quip, Inc., 94 F.3d 376, 382 (7th Cir. 1996).

[211] AMF Inc. v. Sleekcraft Boats, 599 F.2d 341 (9th Cir. 1979). The *Sleekcraft* factors are listed in § 3.02 [B][2] *supra.*

[212] Polaroid Corp. v. Polarad Elecs. Corp., 287 F.2d 492, 495 (2d Cir.), *cert. denied,* 368 U.S. 820 (1961).

[213] *See, e.g.,* SMC Promotions, Inc. v. SMC Promotions, 355 F. Supp. 2d 1127 (C.D. Cal. 2005); Interstellar Starship Servs. v. Epix, Inc., 304 F.3d 936, 942 (9th Cir. 2002); GoTo.com, Inc. v. Walt Disney Co., 202 F.3d 1199, 1207 (9th Cir. 2000). The Sixth Circuit has endorsed this approach as well, *see* Paccar v. Telescan Techs., 319 F.3d 243, 254-55 (6th Cir. 2003), although it later denied that this approach to domain name confusion was specific to initial interest confusion, *see* Gibson Guitar Corp. v. Paul Reed Smith Guitars, LP, 423 F.3d 539, 550-51 (6th Cir. 2005) (questioning the validity of initial interest confusion in non-Internet contexts).

[214] *Interstellar Starship Servs.,* 304 F.3d at 942; *SMC Promotions,* 355 F. Supp. 2d at 1135.

[215] *GoTo.com,* 202 F.3d at 1208; *SMC Promotions,* 355 F. Supp. 2d at 1134.

[216] 174 F.3d 1036, 1057-58 (9th Cir. 1999).

People surfing the Web for information on "MovieBuff" may confuse "MovieBuff" with the searchable entertainment database at "moviebuff-.com" and simply assume that they have reached Brookfield's web site. In the Internet context, in particular, entering a web site takes little effort — usually one click from a linked site or a search engine's list; thus, Web surfers are more likely to be confused as to the ownership of a web site than traditional patrons of a brick-and-mortar store would be of a store's ownership. Alternatively, they may incorrectly believe that West Coast licensed "MovieBuff" from Brookfield, or that Brookfield otherwise sponsored West Coast's database. Other consumers may simply believe that West Coast bought out Brookfield or that they are related companies.

Yet other forms of confusion are likely to ensue. Consumers may wrongly assume that the "MovieBuff" database they were searching for is no longer offered, having been replaced by West Coast's entertainment database, and thus simply use the services at West Coast's web site. And even where people realize, immediately upon accessing "moviebuff.com," that they have reached a site operated by West Coast and wholly unrelated to Brookfield, West Coast will still have gained a customer by appropriating the goodwill that Brookfield has developed in its "MovieBuff" mark. A consumer who was originally looking for Brookfield's products or services may be perfectly content with West Coast's database (especially as it is offered free of charge); but he reached West Coast's site because of its use of Brookfield's mark as its second-level domain name, which is a misappropriation of Brookfield's goodwill by West Coast.[217]

The Ninth Circuit extended its *Brookfield* analysis to banner ads in *Playboy Enters. v. Netscape Communs. Corp.*,[218] in which the court held that the provider of an Internet search engine could be liable (whether directly or contributorily, it did not decide) for allowing banner ads to be triggered when consumers entered certain search terms. The practice at issue involved "keying" banner ads to related search terms — for example, causing banner ads for seed companies to be displayed whenever a user enters gardening-related search terms into the search engine.[219] The court agreed with the plaintiff that the keying of banner ads could lead to initial interest confusion:

> In this case, PEI claims that defendants, in conjunction with advertisers, have misappropriated the goodwill of PEI's marks by leading Internet users to competitors' websites just as West Coast video misappropriated the goodwill of Brookfield's mark. Some consumers, initially seeking PEI's sites, may initially believe that unlabeled banner advertisements are links to PEI's sites or to sites affiliated with PEI. Once they follow the instructions to "click here," and they access the site, they may well realize that they are not at a PEI-sponsored site. However, they may be

---

[217] *Id.*

[218] 354 F.3d 1020 (9th Cir. 2004).

[219] *Id.* at 1022-23.

perfectly happy to remain on the competitor's site, just as the *Brookfield* court surmised that some searchers initially seeking Brookfield's site would happily remain on West Coast's site. The Internet user will have reached the site because of defendants' use of PEI's mark. Such use is actionable.[220]

The court noted, however, that initial interest confusion would not arise if a keyword-trigger banner ad conveyed sufficient information to alleviate confusion *before* the user clicked on the link contained in the banner ad and was taken to the advertiser's website — for example, where the banner ad clearly identified its source or overtly compared its own goods or services with those offered by the owner of the trademarked keyword.[221]

Brookfield's conclusion that initial interest confusion can arise from the use of a mark solely in a metatag has met with mixed reviews. Although many courts have agreed with *Brookfield*,[222] some authorities have criticized the decision.[223] It has also been suggested that the use of a mark in a metatag may be justified where the competitor's website includes explicit comparative advertising pointing out similarities or differences between the trademark owner's goods or services and those of the competitor.[224] The likelihood that confusion will result from unauthorized use of a mark in a metatag has probably decreased in recent years, however, because most search engines such as Google have changed their methodologies so that metatags no longer significantly influence their search results.[225]

In the Internet context, the similarity of the parties' goods or services plays an important role in determining the likelihood of initial interest confusion. For example, in *Nissan Motor Co. v. Nissan Computer Corp.*, the Ninth Circuit held that initial interest confusion arose when the junior user, whose surname happened to be Nissan, used the "nissan.com" domain name to advertise automobile-related goods and services, but not when it used the same domain name to sell other computer-related goods and services:

> Nissan Computer's use of nissan.com to sell non-automobile-related goods does not infringe because Nissan is a last name, a month in the Hebrew and Arabic calendars, a name used by many companies, and

---

[220] *Id.* at 1025-26.

[221] *Id.* at 1025 n. 16, 1030 n. 44.

[222] *E.g.*, North Am. Med. Corp. v. Axiom Worldwide, Inc., 522 F.3d 1211, 1222 (11th Cir. 2008) (dicta); Australian Gold, Inc. v. Hatfield, 436 F.3d 1228, 1240 (10th Cir. 2007); Promatek Indus., LTD v. Equitrac Corp., 300 F.3d 808 (7th Cir. 2002); Eli Lilly & Co. v. Natural Answers, Inc., 86 F. Supp. 2d 834, 844 (S.D. Ind. 2000), *aff'd on other grounds*, 233 F.3d 456 (7th Cir. 2000); Tdata Inc. v. Aircraft Technical Publishers, 411 F. Supp. 2d 901, 907 (S.D. Ohio 2006).

[223] J.G. Wentworth, S.S.C. Ltd. P'ship v. Settlement Funding LLC, 85 U.S.P.Q.2d (BNA) 1780, 1786 (E.D. Pa. 2007); Playboy Enters., Inc. v. Netscape Comm'ns Corp., 354 F.3d 1020, 1035-36 (9th Cir. 2004) (Berzon, J., concurring) (arguing that use of marks as keywords triggering competitors' pop-up ads merely brings competing alternatives to a consumer's attention); *see also* J. Thomas McCarthy, McCarthy on Trademarks and Unfair Competition § 25:69 n. 17 (4th ed. 2009).

[224] North Am. Med. Corp. v. Axiom Worldwide, Inc., 522 F.3d 1211, 1224 n. 10 (11th Cir. 2008).

[225] E. Goldman, *Deregulating Relevancy in Internet Trademark Law*, 54 Emory L. J. 507, 567 (2005); McCarthy, *supra* note 223 at § 25:69.

"the goods offered by these two companies differ significantly." However, Nissan Computer traded on the goodwill of Nissan Motor by offering links to automobile-related websites. Although Nissan Computer was not directly selling automobiles, it was offering information about automobiles and this capitalized on consumers' initial interest. An internet user interested in purchasing, or gaining information about Nissan automobiles would be likely to enter nissan.com. When the item on that website was computers, the auto-seeking consumer "would realize in one hot second that she was in the wrong place and either guess again or resort to a search engine to locate" Nissan Motor's site. A consumer might initially be incorrect about the website, but Nissan Computer would not capitalize on the misdirected consumer. However, once nissan.com offered links to auto-related websites, then the auto-seeking consumer might logically be expected to follow those links to obtain information about automobiles. Nissan Computer financially benefited because it received money for every click. Although nissan-.com itself did not provide the information about automobiles, it provided direct links to such information. Due to the ease of clicking on a link, the required extra click does not rebut the conclusion that Nissan Computer traded on the goodwill of Nissan Motor's mark.[226]

Applying similar reasoning, the First Circuit held in *Hasbro Inc. v. Clue Computing, Inc.*[227] that the defendant's use of the domain name www.clue.com for a website promoting its computer services did not infringe the senior user's trademark for a board game, because the products were sufficiently disparate and there was no evidence of actual confusion.

Clearly, then, not every use of another's trademark as a domain name will give rise to liability for initial interest confusion. In *Interstellar Starship Services v. Epix, Inc.*, the Ninth Circuit distinguished between the use of a famous mark as a domain name and the use of a mark with less renown:

If an apple grower adopts a famous trademark, like www.DRSEUSS-.com, as a domain name, initial interest confusion probably results, even if that business's goods differ significantly from those of Dr. Seuss. Marks of renown, like DR. SEUSS, describe the source of only one company's products, and the apple grower's adoption of the www-.DRSEUSS.com domain name inevitably trades on the favorable cachet associated with that company, its works, and its reputation. Actionable initial interest confusion probably results even if every consumer realizes that DRSEUSS.com is owned by an apple grower, and no consumer ever consummates a Winesap, Delicious, or Granny Smith purchase thinking that Dr. Seuss grows apples or endorses, sponsors, or licenses his name to the apple grower.[228]

---

[226] 378 F.3d 1002, 1019 (9th Cir. 2004) (citations omitted), *cert. denied*, 2005 U.S. LEXIS 3332 (2005).

[227] 232 F.3d 1, 2 (1st Cir. 2000).

[228] *Interstellar Starship*, 304 F.3d at 943-44.

In contrast, if the apple grower adopted the domain name "www.apple.com," the Ninth Circuit's view is that initial interest confusion would not necessarily result:

> Although APPLE is a famous registered trademark of Apple Computer, Inc., many other companies also use the term APPLE to describe a variety of products. Indeed, the apple distributor probably does not infringe Apple Computer's mark because APPLE is also a common noun, used by many companies, and the goods offered by these two companies differ significantly.

> If, however, the apple grower adopted the www.apple.com domain name, and then competed directly with Apple Computer by selling computers, initial interest confusion probably would result. In that circumstance, the apple grower would have acted in a way which traded on the goodwill of Apple Computer's trademark while preventing Apple Computer from using the APPLE trademark itself. This conduct would be actionable because confusion would inevitably result from the apple grower's actions. For example, a consumer might read about the apple grower's computers on www.apple.com, where she expected to find computers sold by Apple Computer, and decide to buy one, thereby permitting the apple grower to capitalize on the goodwill of Apple Computer's APPLE trademark — even if the consumer is never confused about the apple grower's lack of connection with Apple Computer.[229]

The Ninth Circuit justified its distinction between the "Dr. Seuss" and "Apple" scenarios by noting that "[c]onsumers expect that owners of famous, fanciful trademarks will own the corresponding domain name, like www.X-EROX.com or www.KODAK.com, for no other companies identify themselves or their products using these marks," whereas "consumers would not be shocked to find an apple grower at www.apple.com."[230]

Because initial interest confusion involves a misappropriation of the senior user's goodwill, it is actionable even if the confusion completely disappears before the purchasing decision takes place. For this reason, disclaimers on a website are generally ineffective to negate the possibility of initial interest confusion.[231]

Although a significant body of case law has applied initial interest confusion to domain names, the Sixth Circuit has held that the use of another's trademark in the post-domain URL path of a website does not constitute infringement, because it is not likely to be perceived by consumers as an indication of source.[232]

---

[229] *Id.* at 944 (citations and footnotes omitted).

[230] *Id.*

[231] *See, e.g.*, SMC Promotions, Inc. v. SMC Promotions, 355 F. Supp. 2d 1127 (C.D. Cal. 2005); OBH, Inc. v. Spotlight Magazine, Inc., 86 F. Supp. 2d 176, 190 (W.D.N.Y. 2000); Toys "R" Us v. Abir, 1997 U.S. Dist. LEXIS 22431, *12 (S.D.N.Y. 1997); Planned Parenthood v. Bucci, 1997 U.S. Dist. LEXIS 3338, *12 (S.D.N.Y. 1997).

[232] Interactive Prods. Corp. v. A2Z Mobile Office Solutions, Inc., 326 F.3d 687, 696-98 (6th Cir. 2003).

The doctrine of initial interest confusion is not universally recognized, nor is the scope of its application entirely clear. In *Lamparello v. Falwell*,[233] for example, the Fourth Circuit raised a fundamental question about the validity of the doctrine, but also suggested, in the alternative, that if the doctrine had validity at all, it should be limited to situations where defendants were motivated by financial gain. The court therefore refused to apply the doctrine to a domain name consisting of a common misspelling of a public figure's name, where the website was devoted to criticism of the public figure. In *Gibson Guitar Corp. v. Paul Reed Smith Guitars*,[234] the Sixth Circuit questioned whether initial interest confusion should apply at all outside of the Internet context and, more specifically, whether it should apply to trade dress.

In evaluating infringement claims involving unauthorized use of trademarks or service marks in metatags or in keyword advertising, some courts do not reach the question of initial interest confusion at all, because they conclude, as a threshold matter, that such activities do not involve "trademark use" within the meaning of section 32 or section 43(a). This issue is addressed in § 3.02 [E] below.

[2] Post-sale Confusion

Consumer confusion about the origin of goods or services may occur even after the purchasing decision has been made.[235] Typically, the consumer experiencing such post-sale (or "aftermarket") confusion is not the same consumer who made the purchasing decision. One court has described the injury as arising from the likelihood that "the senior user's potential purchasers or ongoing customers might mistakenly associate the inferior quality work of the junior user with the senior user and, therefore, refuse to deal with senior user in the future."[236] Many courts have recognized the likelihood of post-sale confusion as a valid basis for an infringement claim under the Lanham Act.[237]

The likelihood-of-confusion analysis will often lead to different results with respect to purchasers and nonpurchasers; for example, the fact that the senior user and junior user sell their products in completely different packaging, with different labels, at different prices, or in different stores will often make point-of-sale confusion unlikely, while consumers who encounter the products after

---

[233] 420 F.3d 309, 316 (4th Cir. 2005).

[234] 423 F.3d 539, 551 n. 15 (6th Cir. 2005).

[235] Section 43(a) refers to false designations of origin or other false or misleading representations that are likely to cause confusion as to, inter alia, "affiliation, connection, or association," or "origin, sponsorship, or approval." 15 U.S.C. § 1125(a)(1)(A). Section 32 of the Lanham Act refers to any use of a registered mark that "is likely to cause confusion, or to cause mistake, or to deceive." 15 U.S.C. § 1114(1)(a). Prior to its amendment in 1962, section 32 specifically required confusion "of purchasers as to the source of origin of such goods or services." Pub. L. No. 87-772, 76 Stat. 769, 773 (1962). The 1962 amendment made clear that section 32 extends to confusion by nonpurchasers. Payless Shoesource, Inc. v. Reebok Int'l, Ltd., 998 F.2d 985, 989 (Fed. Cir. 1993) (collecting cases); Lois Sportswear, U.S.A., Inc. v. Levi Strauss & Co., 799 F.2d 867, 872-73 (2d Cir. 1986).

[236] Acxiom Corp. v. Axiom, Inc., 27 F. Supp. 2d 478, 497 (D. Del. 1998).

[237] *E.g.*, General Motors Corp. v. Urban Gorilla, LLC, 500 F.3d 1222, 1227 (10th Cir. 2007); Chrysler Corp. v. Silva, 118 F.3d 56, 59 (1st Cir. 1997); Esercizio v. Roberts, 944 F.2d 1235, 1244-45 (6th Cir. 1991); Polo Fashions v. Craftex, Inc., 816 F.2d 145, 148 (4th Cir. 1987); *Lois Sportswear*, 799 F.2d at 871.

they have been purchased will not have the benefit of these signals as to origin. Thus, the consumer who purchases a knock-off Gucci bag from a street vendor is less likely to be confused than the person who receives that bag as a gift and finds that the stitching has unraveled after a few weeks of use.

For example, in *Payless Shoesource v. Reebok Int'l*, shoe manufacturer Reebok alleged that retailer Payless sold shoes that infringed Reebok's trademarks and trade dress in violation of sections 32 and 43(a) of the Lanham Act. Applying the traditional likelihood-of-confusion factors, the district court concluded that confusion at the point of sale was "inconceivable."[238] The appellate court agreed that point-of-sale confusion was unlikely, but found that the district court had given inadequate consideration to the possibility of post-sale confusion:

> In reaching its determination concerning trademark infringement, the district court focused on the likelihood of confusion between Reebok's and Payless' shoes in the marketplace. Particularly persuasive to the district court were what it considered "vast" differences in the manner of marketing and the channels of trade employed by the two companies. For example, the court found that Payless and Reebok shoes were never sold in the same stores, that Payless shoes were only available in Payless stores, that Payless shoes generally sell for much less than Reebok shoes, and that the self-service nature of Payless stores requires customers to become highly knowledgeable concerning the selection of Payless shoes. Additionally, the court found that the degree of care consumers exercise in purchasing athletic footwear further lessens the likelihood of confusion.

> However, by exclusively focusing on confusion at the point of sale, the district court effectively disregarded Reebok's argument relating to "post-sale confusion." Reebok contended that such confusion occurs, for example, when a consumer observes someone wearing a pair of Payless accused shoes and believes that the shoes are Reebok's. As a consequence, the consumer may attribute any perceived inferior quality of Payless shoes to Reebok, thus damaging Reebok's reputation and image.[239]

Because post-sale confusion occurs after the purchasing decision has been made, the nature of the injury to the trademark owner is different from the injury experienced by confusion that actually affects the purchasing decision. The purchaser was not confused, and therefore the senior user cannot complain that the junior user diverted that particular sale. However, if a consumer who encounters the goods or services after the point of sale is confused about their origin, any perceived defects in those goods or services, or in the vendor's aftermarket support for those goods or services, will be attributed to the wrong merchant, thereby injuring that merchant's goodwill and possibly diverting future sales. The Eleventh Circuit has emphasized that failure to protect

---

[238] Payless Shoesource, Inc. v. Reebok, Int'l, Ltd., 804 F. Supp. 206, 212 (D. Kan. 1992), *vacated and remanded on other grounds*, 998 F.2d 985 (Fed. Cir. 1993).

[239] 998 F.2d 985, 989 (Fed. Cir. 1993).

consumers against post-sale confusion can undermine the incentives of trademark owners to produce goods of high quality:

> It . . . is important to recognize that the enforcement of trademark laws benefits consumers even in cases where there is no possibility that consumers will be defrauded. For, to the extent that trademarks provide a means for the public to distinguish between manufacturers, they also provide incentives for manufacturers to provide quality goods. Traffickers of these counterfeit goods, however, attract some customers who would otherwise purchase the authentic goods. Trademark holders' returns to their investments in quality are thereby reduced. This reduction in profits may cause trademark holders to decrease their investments in quality below what they would spend were there no counterfeit goods. This in turn harms those consumers who wish to purchase higher quality goods.[240]

In *Karl Storz – Endoscopy America, Inc. v. Surgical Technologies, Inc.*,[241] post-sale confusion arose where hospitals sent used endoscopes to the defendant for repair and refurbishment. Even after extensive refurbishment, the endoscopes still displayed the original manufacturer's trademark, and were not marked as having been refurbished. The Ninth Circuit held that the refurbishment was extensive enough that, in effect, the hospitals were purchasing refurbished endoscopes. Although the hospitals that engaged the defendant to perform the repairs clearly knew that the repaired endoscopes were not identical to new ones, so that there was no confusion at the point of sale, the doctors to whom the endoscopes were ultimately furnished by the hospital believed that they were using the manufacturer's original product, and attributed defects in the equipment to the manufacturer. This constituted post-sale confusion that had the potential to injure the manufacturer's reputation.[242]

Not all instances of post-sale confusion will support an infringement action; the confusion must be "commercially relevant." Confusion is commercially relevant if the defendant's use of the mark "could inflict commercial injury in the form of . . . a diversion of sales, damage to goodwill, or loss of control over reputation."[243] The trademark owner alleging aftermarket confusion need not prove an actual loss of sales in order to establish the requisite injury; damage to goodwill or reputation will suffice.[244] This view is in accord with the *Restatement*

---

[240] United States v. Torkington, 812 F.2d 1347, 1353 n. 6 (11th Cir. 1987) (citation omitted).

[241] 285 F.3d 848 (9th Cir. 2002).

[242] *Id.* at 854-55.

[243] Beacon Mut. Ins. Co. v. OneBeacon Ins. Group, 376 F.3d 8, 15 (1st Cir. 2004) (quoting The Sports Authority, Inc. v. Prime Hospitality Corp., 89 F.3d 955, 963 (2d Cir. 1996) (internal quotation marks omitted)).

[244] *See, e.g.*, Balance Dynamics Corp. v. Schmitt Indus., Inc., 204 F.3d 683, 693 (6th Cir. 2000) (damages may be awarded under § 43(a) for actual confusion that causes harm to goodwill even in the absence of lost sales); Landscape Forms, Inc. v. Columbia Cascade Co., 113 F.3d 373, 382-83 (2d Cir. 1997) (nonpurchaser confusion is relevant if "related to the goodwill of the aggrieved manufacturer"); Meridian Mutual Ins. Co. v. Meridian Ins. Group, Inc., 128 F.3d 1111, 1118 (7th Cir. 1997); Insty*Bit, Inc. v. Poly-Tech Indus., 95 F.3d 663, 672 (8th Cir. 1996) (confusion under § 43(a) "includes confusion of nonpurchasers as well as direct purchasers"); Champions Golf Club, Inc. v. The Champions Golf

(Third) of Unfair Competition, which treats confusion as relevant when it creates "a significant risk to the sales or good will of the trademark owner," and notes that actionable confusion "must threaten the commercial interests of the owner of the mark, but it is not limited to the confusion of persons doing business directly with the actor."[245]

Because the potentially confused parties in a post-sale scenario are not actual purchasers, it is not always clear whose confusion should "count." Certainly, any party that has the potential to be a future customer of the senior user should count. Also, as illustrated by *Karl Storz-Endoscopy America,* when an infringing product is purchased for use by a third party whose satisfaction or dissatisfaction with the product may influence the purchaser's future decisions, any confusion experienced by the third-party user has the potential to harm the trademark owner. Thus, courts have held that the post-sale confusion inquiry extends to foreseeable users.[246] However, some parties who encounter the mark in a post-sale context may be so unlikely to purchase, or to influence purchasers of, the product or service in question that their potential confusion should be disregarded.[247]

Some courts have implied that commercially relevant post-sale confusion, and thus actionable injury, may arise even if the junior use's merchandise is not inferior to that of the senior user, because the junior user has made it possible for the purchaser to enjoy the prestige associated with appearing to own the senior user's merchandise:

> Trademark laws exist to protect the public from confusion. The creation of confusion in the post-sale context can be harmful in that if there are too many knockoffs in the market, sales of the originals may decline because the public is fearful that what they are purchasing may not be an original. Furthermore, the public may be deceived in the resale market if it requires expertise to distinguish between an original and a knockoff. Finally, the purchaser of an original is harmed by the

---

Club, Inc., 78 F.3d 1111, 1119-20 (6th Cir. 1996) (confusion includes confusion among suppliers); Perini Corp. v. Perini Constr., Inc., 915 F.2d 121, 128 (4th Cir. 1990) (non-purchaser confusion is relevant if it "adversely affects the plaintiff's ability to control his reputation among its laborers, lendors, investors, or other group with whom the plaintiff interacts"); International Kennel Club of Chicago, Inc. v. Mighty Star, Inc., 846 F.2d 1079, 1091 (7th Cir. 1988) ("the owner of a mark is damaged by a later use of a similar mark which places the owner's reputation beyond its control, though no loss in business is shown" (internal quotation marks omitted)); In re Artic Electronics Co., 220 U.S.P.Q. (BNA) 836, 838 (T.T.A.B. 1983) ("The notion that likelihood of confusion is limited to purchaser confusion is simply not correct.")

[245] Restatement (Third) of Unfair Competition § 20 cmt. b (1995); *accord* CMM Cable Rep., Inc. v. Ocean Coast Props., 888 F. Supp. 192, 200 (D. Me. 1995), *aff'd,* 97 F.3d 1504 (1st Cir. 1996). One court has speculated that commercially relevant nonpurchaser confusion "may well extend beyond the confusion of those persons positioned to influence directly the decisions of purchasers." *Beacon Mut. Ins. Co.,* 376 F.3d at 16-17.

[246] Custom Mfg. & Eng'g, Inc. v. Midway Servs., 508 F.3d 641, 651 & n. 9 (11th Cir. 2007).

[247] *Id.* at 651 n. 9 (where infringing mark appeared on a single and not-readily-visible component of a water meter system, potential confusion of repair technicians and fire marshals should be disregarded because they were not "foreseeable users").

widespread existence of knockoffs because the high value of originals, which derives in part from their scarcity, is lessened.[248]

For example, in *Foxworthy v. Custom Tees*, the defendant's T-shirts were printed with the plaintiff's "redneck" jokes, including a slight variation on his signature phrase "You might be a redneck if. . . ." The district court noted that confusion was likely not only at the point of sale, but also post-sale. Without addressing any quality differences between the plaintiff's authorized T-shirts and the defendant's knock-offs, the court deemed it "significant . . . that the placement of the defendants' T-shirts on the market, and in the public after sale, would cause the public viewing the T-shirts to associate the shirts with plaintiff, regardless of whether the purchaser himself or herself was confused."[249]

[E]   Trademark Use

In order for an infringement (or dilution) claim to arise, a defendant must use another's registered or unregistered trademark to identify the source or affiliation of goods or services that are offered to the public. In most cases, the question of whether the defendant is using the mark to identify the source of goods or services is fairly clear-cut. For example, this requirement is generally not satisfied where a defendant uses another's trademark on a website that is devoted purely to commentary about that party's goods or services.[250] In contrast, if the website also offers goods or services to the public, or if it contains commercial advertising, courts typically treat this as satisfying the threshold requirement.

Other cases, however, present a closer question — for example, where one party uses another's trademark in an expressive work that is offered for sale to the public,[251] where a trademark is used in the domain name of a noncommercial website that contains links to commercial websites[252] or solicits contributions for

---

[248] Hermes, Int'l v. Lederer de Paris Fifth Ave., Inc., 219 F.3d 104, 108 (2d Cir. 2000); *accord*, Mastercrafters Clock & Radio Co. v. Vacheron & Constantin-Le Coutre Watches, Inc., 221 F.2d 464, 466 (2d Cir. 1955) ("At least some customers would buy [the copier's] cheaper clock for the purpose of acquiring the prestige gained by displaying what many visitors at the customers' homes would regard as a prestigious article. [The] wrong thus consisted of the fact that such a visitor would be likely to assume that the clock was an Atmos clock."); Lois Sportswear, U.S.A., Inc. v. Levi Strauss & Co., 799 F.2d 867, 875 (2d Cir. 1986) ("The fact that appellants have produced a quality copy suggests that the possibility of their profiting from appellee's goodwill is still likely.").

[249] 879 F. Supp. 1200, 1216 (N.D. Ga. 1995).

[250] *See, e.g.*, Utah Light Ministry v. Found. for Apologetic Info & Resch., 527 F.3d 1045 (10th Cir. 2008). Bosley Med. Inst., Inc. v. Kenner, 403 F.3d 672 (9th Cir. 2005); Savannah College of Art & Design, Inc. v. Houeix, 369 F. Supp. 2d 929 (S.D. Ohio 2004).

[251] *See, e.g.*, Felix the Cat Prods., Inc. v. New Line Cinema Corp., 54 U.S.P.Q. 2d (BNA) 1856, 1857 (C.D. Cal. 2000).

[252] *Compare Bosley Med. Inst.*, 403 F.3d at 677–80; *and Savannah College*, 369 F. Supp. 2d at 944–48; *with* Nissan Motor Co. v. Nissan Computer Corp., 378 F.3d 1002 (9th Cir. 2004); Taubman Co. v. Webfeats, 319 F.3d 770, 775 (6th Cir. 2003); PETA v. Doughney, 263 F.3d 359 (4th Cir. 2001); OBH, Inc. v. Spotlight Magazine, Inc. 86 F. Supp. 2d 176 (N.D.N.Y. 2000); *and* Jews for Jesus v. Brodsky, 993 F. Supp. 282 (D.N.J.), *aff'd*, 159 F.3d 1351 (3d Cir. 1998).

a cause antithetical to that of the trademark owner,[253] or where an Internet search engine triggers pop-up advertising for a merchant's goods or services whenever a user enters a competitor's trademark as a search term.[254] Some courts have held that the unauthorized use of a merchant's trademark in a domain name may be a use in connection with goods or services if it tends to impede or frustrate consumers trying to find the merchant's official website.[255]

In analyzing these claims, an important threshold question is whether the unauthorized use of the trademark is a "use in connection with . . . goods or services" so as to be actionable under section 32, 43(a), or 43(c).[256] Some courts phrase the question differently, asking whether the defendant's activity involves a "use in commerce" as that term is defined in section 45 of the Lanham Act.[257] In this context, however, the focus of the analysis is not whether the defendant's use of the mark involves commerce that Congress has the authority to regulate, but whether it involves "commerce" in the dictionary sense — offering goods or services to the public.[258] As a result, the issue of trademark "use" arises even where the trademark, unfair competition, or dilution claims arise under state rather than federal law.[259]

The requirement that a mark be used "in commerce" does not limit the protections of the Lanham Act to profit-seeking activities; thus, the Lanham Act also applies to nonprofit activities that involve the offering of goods or services.[260] However, using a registered or unregistered mark in a context that does not involve the sale, distribution, or advertising of goods or services does not constitute infringement under section 32 or 43(a) of the Lanham Act because it does not involve the use of a mark in commerce.[261] For example, the use of a well-known cartoon character to "set the mood" of a film, rather than to indicate

---

[253] *See, e.g.*, Planned Parenthood Federation of America, Inc. v. Bucci, 42 U.S.P.Q. (BNA) 1430, 1435 (S.D.N.Y. 1997).

[254] *See, e.g.*, 1-800 Contacts, Inc. v. WhenU.com, Inc., 414 F.3d 400, 408 (2d Cir. 2005); Google, Inc. v. American Blind & Wallpaper Factory, Inc., 74 U.S.P.Q. (BNA) 1385 (N.D. Cal. 2005); U-Haul Int'l, Inc. v. WhenU.com, Inc., 279 F. Supp. 2d 723, 731 (E.D. Va. 2003); Wells Fargo & Co. v. WhenU.com, Inc., 293 F. Supp. 2d 734, 760 (E.D. Mich. 2003); GEICO v. Google, Inc., 330 F. Supp. 2d 700, 703 (E.D. Va. 2004).

[255] *See, e.g.*, PETA v. Doughney, 263 F.3d 359, 365 (4th Cir. 2001); *but see Bosley Med. Inst.*, 403 F.3d at 679–80 (rejecting this argument); Ford Motor Co. v. 2600 Enters., 177 F. Supp. 2d 661, 664 (E.D. Mich. 2001) (similar).

[256] Occasionally, however, courts have found initial interest confusion without explicitly addressing the question of use. *See, e.g.*, Australian Gold, Inc. v. Hatfield, 436 F.3d 1228, 1239 (10th Cir. 2006).

[257] *E.g.*, Boston Duck Tours, LP v. Super Duck Tours, LLC, 527 F. Supp. 2d 205 (D. Mass. 2007); Merck & Co. v. Mediplan Health Consulting, 425 F. Supp. 2d 402, 415 (S.D.N.Y. 2006).

[258] Bosley Medical Inst., Inc. v. Kremer, 403 F.3d 672, 677 (9th Cir. 2005).

[259] *See, e.g.*, FragranceNet.com, Inc. v. FragranceX.com, Inc., 493 F. Supp. 2d 545, 547 n. 4 (E.D.N.Y. 2007).

[260] United We Stand America, Inc. v. United We Stand, America New York, Inc., 128 F.3d 86, 92-93 (2d Cir. 1997), *cert. denied*, 523 U.S. 1076 (1998).

[261] *See, e.g.*, Marvel Enters., Inc. v. NCSoft Corp., CV 04-9253-RGK (PLAx) (C.D. Cal. Mar. 9, 2005) (because game players' use of registered trademarks as names for game characters was a non-infringing "recreational" use, maker of game was not contributorily liable for providing "character creation engine" that made this possible); Lucasfilm, Ltd. v. High Frontier, 622 F. Supp. 931, 934 (D.D.C. 1985) (use that did not involve affixation of mark to any good or service offered for

its source, was held not to be a use in commerce.[262] However, if such a mark is used to suggest a false or misleading source or affiliation for a work of entertainment, such a use is considered to be "in commerce" and can constitute an infringement.[263]

The discussion that follows focuses on four areas of ostensible trademark use: keyword advertising, metatags, domain names, and expressive works.

[1]   Keyword-Triggered Advertising

Internet search engines such as Google and Yahoo sometimes sell advertisers "keyword" rights in the trademarks or service marks of others. Under these arrangements, when a user enters that keyword as a search term, this triggers the appearance of links to the advertiser's website (referred to as "sponsored links"). In other situations, software (sometimes called "adware") is used to detect trademarks or service marks that are being used in Internet searches and to trigger banner or pop-up advertisements for competing or related goods and services. When, as is typically the case, the advertisements or sponsored links are not authorized by the actual owner of the trademark or service mark, this can give rise to an infringement claim based on likelihood of consumer confusion, most often in the nature of "initial interest confusion," as discussed in § 3.02 [D][1] above. Dilution claims may arise as well (see § 3.05 below).[264]

Despite extensive litigation, courts remain divided about whether "trademark use" occurs in these contexts. Federal district courts in the First,[265] Third,[266] Eighth[267] and Ninth[268] circuits have held, and a district court in the Seventh Circuit[269] has expressly assumed, that keyword-triggered advertising (in the form of sponsored links or banner ads) constitutes trademark use. The opposite conclusion has been reached by district courts in the Second[270] and Sixth[271]

---

sale was non-infringing); Felix the Cat Prods., Inc. v. New Line Cinema Corp., 54 U.S.P.Q.2d (BNA) 1856, 1857 (C.D. Cal. 2000) (use of trademarked cartoon character in movie was non-infringing because it did not make use of the goodwill associated with the character, and thus was not a use in connection with advertising or sale of goods or services in commerce).

[262] *Felix the Cat Prods.*, 54 U.S.P.Q.2d (BNA) at 1858.

[263] *Id.*

[264] *E.g.*, Rescuecom Corp. v. Google, Inc., 456 F. Supp. 2d 393, 404 (N.D.N.Y. 2006); Playboy Enters. v. Netscape Comm. Corp., 354 F.3d 1020, 1023 (9th Cir. 2004).

[265] Boston Duck Tours, LP v. Super Duck Tours, LLC, 527 F. Supp. 2d 205 (D. Mass. 2007).

[266] J.G. Wentworth, S.S.C. Ltd. P'ship v. Settlement Funding LLC, 2007 U.S. Dist. LEXIS 288, at *16-17 (E.D. Pa. Jan. 4, 2007); Buying for the Home, LLC v. Humble Abode, LLC, 459 F. Supp. 2d 310, 323 (D.N.J. 2006); 800-JR Cigar, Inc., v. GoTo.com, Inc., 437 F. Supp. 2d 273 (D.N.J. 2006).

[267] Edina Realty, Inc. v. TheMLSonline.com, 2006 U.S. Dist. LEXIS 13775, *9-10 (D. Minn. Mar. 20, 2006).

[268] Google Inc. v. American Blind and Wallpaper Factory Inc., 2007 U.S. Dist. LEXIS 32450, *21 (N.D. Cal. Apr. 18, 2007).

[269] International Profit Assocs., Inc. v. Paisola, 461 F. Supp. 2d 672, 677 n. 3 (N.D. Ill. 2006).

[270] S&L Vitamins, Inc. v. Australian Gold, Inc., 521 F. Supp. 2d 188, 199-202 (E.D.N.Y. 2007); Site Pro-1, Inc. v. Better Metal, LLC, 506 F. Supp. 2d 123 (E.D.N.Y. 2007); FragranceNet.com, Inc. v. FragranceX.com, Inc., 493 F. Supp. 2d 545, 550 (E.D.N.Y. 2007); Merck & Co., Inc. v. Mediplan Health Consulting, Inc., 425 F. Supp. 2d 402, 415 (S.D.N.Y. 2006), *on reconsid.*, 431 F. Supp. 2d 425,

circuits, on the ground that when the mark is used merely as a keyword it is not being displayed to consumers, and thus is not being used to indicate the source of any goods or services. As discussed below, however, the most recent of the district court decisions in the Second Circuit has been reversed on appeal, casting doubt on the validity of the others. In the Fourth Circuit, two district courts have held that sponsored linking involves trademark use,[272] while another has held that no trademark use occurs when user-installed software employs a directory of trademarks to generate relevant pop-up ads based on the user's searches or visits to websites.[273]

There is less authority at the appellate level, although the trend of authority recognizes at least some keyword advertising as a trademark use. In *Playboy Enters., Inc. v. Netscape Communications Corp.*, where the Ninth Circuit held that keyword-triggered banner ads on a search results page could support a trademark infringement claim, the court noted that there was "no dispute" on the question of trademark use.[274] In *Australian Gold v. Hatfield*, the Tenth Circuit tacitly assumed that keyword-triggered sponsored links involved trademark use.[275]

The most thorough consideration of keyword advertising has come from the Second Circuit. In the often-cited case of *1-800 Contacts v. WhenU.com, Inc.*[276] the Second Circuit addressed the question whether trademark use occurred when the defendant's adware triggered pop-up ads of the plaintiff's competitors whenever a user visited the plaintiff's website. The adware functioned by maintaining a directory of website addresses, including the plaintiff's. Because the plaintiff's website address incorporated its trademark, the plaintiff argued that the adware's use of its website address to trigger pop-up ads constituted trademark use. Following the reasoning of district court decisions from the Fourth and Sixth Circuits, the Second Circuit held that no trademark use occurred, because the adware did not "place" the plaintiff's mark on any goods or services to indicate their origin, and indeed did not display the mark to the user.[277] In addition, however, the court noted that what triggered the pop-up ads was not the plaintiff's mark but the plaintiff's web address, which was slightly different from its mark. Accordingly, the court expressly declined to decide whether the inclusion of the actual trademark in the adware directory would constitute trademark use.[278] The court also noted that the ads for the

---

427 (S.D.N.Y. 2006); Rescue.com Corp. v. Google, Inc., 456 F. Supp. 2d 393, 404 (N.D.N.Y. 2006), *vacated and remanded*, 562 F.3d 123 (2d Cir. 2009).

[271] Wells Fargo & Co. v. WhenU.Com, Inc., 293 F. Supp. 2d 734, 762 (E.D. Mich. 2003).

[272] Market America v. Optihealth Prods., 2008 U.S. Dist. LEXIS 95337, *17-19 (M.D.N.C. 2008) (in context of determining personal jurisdiction rather than infringement analysis); Gov't Employees Ins. Co. v. Google, Inc., 330 F. Supp. 2d 700, 704 (E.D. Va. 2004).

[273] U-Haul Intern. Inc. v. WhenU.com, Inc., 279 F. Supp. 2d 723, 728 (E.D. Va. 2003) (drawing analogy to comparative advertising).

[274] 354 F.3d 1020, 1024 (9th Cir. 2004).

[275] 436 F.3d 1228, 1239 (10th Cir. 2006).

[276] 414 F.3d 400 (2d Cir. 2005).

[277] *Id.* at 408-09.

[278] *Id.* at 409 & n.11.

plaintiff's competitors would also be triggered when a user entered a search for purely generic terms relevant to those products or services — e.g., "contacts" or "eye care."[279] Because the adware did not alter or interfere with the plaintiff's website, did not divert or misdirect consumers away from that website, did not alter the results of a search using the plaintiff's mark or web address, and did not involve the sale of trademarks as keywords triggering pop-up ads, the court held that there was no basis for finding trademark use.[280]

In 2009, however, the Second Circuit issued its opinion in *Rescuecom Corp. v. Google, Inc.*,[281] distinguishing *1-800 Contacts* and holding that Google's keyword advertising system involved trademark use. Google's system had two components — AdWords and Keyword Suggestion Tool. AdWords allowed an advertiser to purchase keywords — including a competitor's trademark — which, when entered as search terms in Google's search engine, would cause the advertiser's ad and link to be displayed in the user's search results, generally accompanied by the label "sponsored link." The Keyword Suggestion Tool actively suggested to each advertiser certain keywords which that advertiser might be interested in purchasing; these suggestions sometimes included the trademarks of the advertiser's competitors. The district court had dismissed the plaintiff's infringement claim on the ground that, under *1-800 Contacts*, Google's activities did not involve a "trademark use." On appeal, however, the Second Circuit reversed. The court distinguished *1-800 Contacts* on two grounds: (1) the advertisers' pop-up ads in that case were triggered when users entered a competitor's website address, not its trademark (although the court acknowledged that the two were often very similar); and (2) instead of being triggered by specific keywords, the pop-up ads in *1-800 Contacts* were triggered by the general category of goods or services that corresponded to the search term or website address entered by a user. In contrast, Google's keyword system recommended, displayed, and "sold" the plaintiff's mark to advertisers; thus, in the court's view, Google's use of the plaintiff's mark fit literally within the language of § 1127's definition of a "use in commerce," because Google used the plaintiff's mark "in the sale of [Google's advertising] services . . . rendered in commerce."[282] The court declined to rule on the narrower question whether the inclusion of a trademark in Google's internal search algorithm, without more, could constitute trademark use. It also rejected the argument that Google's scheme was analogous to a retail store's side-by-side display of brand name and generic products in order to induce customers to consider the cheaper generic product. However, the court's rationale for rejecting this analogy — that Google's practice involved consumer deception — strayed well beyond the threshold question of "trademark use" and into the realm of likelihood of confusion, an issue that was not yet before the court.

It is important to remember that even when a court decides that trademark use has occurred within the meaning of the Lanham Act, this does not

---

[279] *Id.* at 410.

[280] *Id.* at 411-12.

[281] 562 F.3d 123 (2d Cir. 2009).

[282] *Id.* at 128-29.

necessarily mean that the use is also infringing or dilutive; these are separate determinations. Conversely, at least one court has held that even if sponsored linking does not, by itself, involve trademark use, if the plaintiff's mark is also displayed in the advertiser's sponsored link when it appears in the list of search results, this display can constitute trademark use.[283]

[2]   Metatags

Courts are somewhat less divided on the question whether incorporating trademarks into a website's metatags constitutes trademark use. Metatags are computer codes, invisible to the average user, that give search engines information about the content of a website. A search engine may use this information in determining how high to rank the website when displaying search results. Thus, if a website contains a metatag that incorporates a trademark, that website could appear high on the list of search results displayed to a user who is searching for products bearing that trademark; as discussed in § 3.02 [D][1], this has led to claims of initial interest confusion.

The Ninth[284] and Eleventh[285] Circuits have held that metatags involve trademark use, as have district courts in the First[286] and Third[287] Circuits. The First,[288] Seventh[289] and Tenth[290] Circuits, and a district court in the Fourth Circuit,[291] have tacitly assumed trademark use. In the Second Circuit, while early district court decisions either held[292] or tacitly assumed[293] that metatags involve trademark use, later decisions reached the opposite conclusion, relying on the Second Circuit's analysis of keyword advertising in *1–800–Contacts*.[294]

---

[283] Hamzik v. Zale Corp./Delaware, 2007 U.S. Dist. LEXIS 28981, at *3 (N.D.N.Y. Apr. 19, 2007); *see also* Tiffany, Inc. v. eBay, Inc., 576 F. Supp. 2d 463 (S.D.N.Y. 2008) (implying agreement with *Hamzik*).

[284] Brookfield Communs., Inc. v. West Coast Entertainment Corp., 174 F.3d 1036, 1064-66 (9th Cir. 1999).

[285] North American Medical Corp. v. Axiom Worldwide Inc., 522 F.3d 1211 (11th Cir. 2008).

[286] Niton Corp. v. Radiation Monitoring Devices, Inc., 27 F. Supp. 2d 102 (D. Mass. 1998).

[287] J.G. Wentworth S.S.C. LP v. Settlement Funding LLC, 2007 U.S. Dist. LEXIS 288, *16-17 (E.D. Pa. 2007) (but finding no actionable confusion). The Fourth Circuit has also held that metatags involve trademark use, but this ruling was made in the context of determining personal jurisdiction. Market America v. Optihealth Prods., 2008 U.S. Dist. LEXIS 95337, *17-19 (M.D.N.C. 2008)

[288] Venture Tape Corp. v. McGills Glass Warehouse, 540 F.3d 56, 60 & n. 5 (1st Cir. 2008), *cert. denied*, 129 S. Ct. 1622 (2009).

[289] Promatek Indus., LTD v. Equitrac Corp., 300 F.3d 808, 812-13 (7th Cir. 2002); Eli Lilly & Co. v. Natural Answers, Inc., 233 F.3d 456 (7th Cir. 2000).

[290] Australian Gold v. Hatfield, 436 F.3d 1228, 1239 (10th Cir. 2006).

[291] Playboy Enters., Inc. v. Asiafocus Int'l, Inc., 1998 U.S. Dist. LEXIS 10359, *8 (E.D. Va. Apr. 10, 1998). In a more recent decision, a defendant conceded trademark use. Deltek, Inv. v. Iuvo Sys., 2009 U.S. Dist. LEXIS 33555, *18 (E.D. Va. Apr. 20, 2009).

[292] Bihari v. Gross, 119 F. Supp. 2d 309, 318 (S.D.N.Y. 2000).

[293] New York State Soc'y of CPA's, 79 F. Supp. 2d 331, 341-42 (S.D.N.Y. 1999).

[294] FragranceNet.com, Inc. v. FragranceX.com, Inc., 493 F. Supp. 2d 545, 550 (E.D.N.Y. 2007); S&L Vitamins, Inc. v. Australian Gold, Inc., 521 F. Supp. 2d 188 (E.D.N.Y. 2007); Site Pro-1, Inc. v. Better Metal, LLC, 506 F. Supp. 2d 123 (E.D.N.Y. 2007). These cases adopted the reasoning of the Second Circuit in 1-800 Contacts, Inc. v. WhenU.com, 414 F.3d 400 (2d Cir. 2005), *cert. denied*, 546

Courts that treat metatags as trademark use do not necessarily find such uses to be infringing. Courts have held that the unauthorized use of another's mark in a metatag can be a fair use,[295] if the mark fairly and in good faith describes the contents of the website.[296]

The use of trademarks in metatags is unlikely to be extensively litigated in the future; due to changes in searching methodology, search engines today make little or no use of metatags.[297]

[3] Domain Names

Courts have also failed to reach consensus on whether the use of a trademark in a domain name, without more, constitutes trademark use. The question is whether the mere presence of a trademark in a domain name involves using the mark to indicate the origin of goods or services. If the website itself is considered a good or service, then trademark use would be established. However, if the website itself is not considered a good or service, then the trademark use question would turn on whether consumers encountering the website would perceive the trademark in question as indicating the origin of the goods or services offered or promoted on the website, or offered at other websites that are linked to that site. Unless trademark use is established, claims of likelihood of confusion or dilution cannot be based solely on the presence of the mark in the domain name.

Some courts have held that incorporating a trademark into a domain name involves trademark use because consumers searching for the trademark owner's official website will mistakenly encounter the unauthorized website, frustrating their efforts to reach the official website, thus interfering with the trademark owner's offering of goods or services (although in most of these cases the defendant's website also included links to commercial websites).[298] Other courts have rejected this analysis.[299] Courts are especially reluctant to adopt this theory of trademark use where the website whose domain name incorporates the trademark is devoted to criticizing or parodying the trademark owner or its goods or services.[300] In contrast, courts have held that registering a domain

---

U.S. 1033 (2005), even though that case involved adware rather than metatags.

[295] Fair use is discussed in § 3.12 [F]-[G] *infra*.

[296] *See, e.g.*, Playboy Enters., Inc. v. Welles, 279 F.3d 796 (9th Cir. 2002); Bijur Lubricating Corp. v. Devco Corp., 332 F. Supp. 722 (D.N.J. 2004); Trans Union L.L.C. v. Credit Research, Inc., 142 F. Supp. 2d 1029 (N.D. Ill. 2001); Bihari v. Gross, 119 F. Supp. 2d 309, 321-23 (S.D.N.Y. 2000); *accord, Promatek*, 300 F.3d at 814 & n.3 (noting that "legitimate use" of another's trademark in a metatag would be permissible); *Brookfield Communs.*, 174 F.3d at 1065-66 (similar, dicta).

[297] Standard Process, Inc. v. Banks, 554 F. Supp. 2d 866, 871 (E.D. Wis. 2008).

[298] *E.g.*, PETA v. Doughney, 263 F.3d 359, 366 (4th Cir. 2001); OBH, Inc. v. Spotlight Magazine, Inc., 86 F. Supp. 2d 176, 185-86 (W.D.N.Y. 2000); Jews for Jesus v. Brodsky, 993 F. Supp. 282, 309 (D.N.J. 1998); Planned Parenthood Fed'n v. Bucci, 1997 U.S. Dist. LEXIS 3338, *14 (S.D.N.Y. 1997), *aff'd*, 152 F.3d 90 (2d Cir. 1998).

[299] *E.g.*, Utah Lighthouse Ministry v. Found. for Apologetic Info & Resch., 527 F.3d 1045, 1053–54 (10th Cir. 2008); Bosley Medical Inst., Inc. v. Kremer, 403 F.3d 672, 679 (9th Cir. 2005).

[300] *E.g., Utah Lighthouse Ministry*, 527 F.3d at 1053; *Bosley Medical Inst.*, 403 F.3d at 679; Taubman Co. v. Webfeats, 319 F.3d 770, 777-778 (6th Cir. 2003); Savannah College of Art & Design,

name incorporating another's trademark in order to compel the trademark owner to purchase the domain name is trademark use, regardless of whether any goods or services are offered or advertised on the website.[301]

The problem of determining whether a domain name constitutes unauthorized trademark use has been somewhat alleviated by the Anticybersquatting Consumer Protection Act ("ACPA"),[302] which creates a specific cause of action for use of a trademark in a domain name with a "bad faith intent to profit" from the mark, without requiring the plaintiff to establish that the defendant was using the mark to indicate the origin of goods or services. Many claims that formerly would have required a threshold determination of trademark use in order to establish a likelihood of confusion or dilution can now be brought under the ACPA instead. The ACPA is discussed in § 3.08 below.

[4]   Expressive Works

Although the unauthorized use of trademarks in expressive works also implicates important First Amendment issues (see § 3.11 below), a few courts have held, as a threshold matter, that no trademark use is involved, because the mark is being used in connection with ideas rather than goods or services.[303] In other cases, however, courts have proceeded directly to the infringement or dilution analysis and the First Amendment considerations.[304]

[F]   Use in Commerce as Jurisdictional Predicate

In an infringement action under section 32 or section 43(a) of the Lanham Act, or in a dilution action under section 43(c), the defendant's infringing conduct must take place "in commerce." This phrase refers to the offering of goods or services *only* in those markets that Congress has the authority to regulate. The reason for this requirement is that Congress's authority to regulate trademarks derives from its powers under the Commerce Clause of the Constitution.[305] Thus, under section 32 the defendant must have used the plaintiff's registered mark in commerce, under section 43(a) the defendant must have made a false or misleading misrepresentation in commerce, and under

---

Inc. v. Houeix, 369 F. Supp. 2d 929, 947-48 (W.D. Ohio 2004); Ford Motor Co. v. 2600 Enters., 177 F. Supp. 2d 661, 664-65 (E.D. Mich. 2001); Northland Ins. Cos. v. Blaylock, 115 F. Supp. 2d 1108, 1122-23 (D. Minn. 2000).

[301] *E.g.*, Panavision International, L.P. v. Toeppen, 141 F.3d 1316, 1325 (9th Cir. 1998); Intermatic Inc. v. Toeppen, 947 F. Supp. 1227, 1239 (N.D. Ill. 1996).

[302] 15 U.S.C. § 1125(d).

[303] *E.g.*, Felix the Cat Prods. v. New Line Cinema, 54 U.S.P.Q.2d (BNA) 1856 (C.D. Cal. 2000); Lucasfilm, Ltd. v. High Frontier, 622 F. Supp. 931, 934 (D.D.C. 1985); L.L. Bean Inc. v. Drake Publishers, Inc., 811 F.2d 26 (1st Cir.), *cert. denied*, 483 U.S. 1013 (1987).

[304] *E.g.*, Mattel, Inc. v. MCA Records, 296 F.3d 894, 900-01 (9th Cir. 2002); Dr. Seuss Enters. L.P. v. Penguin Books USA, Inc., 109 F.3d 1394, 1403-04 (9th Cir. 1997); Hormel Foods Corp. v. Jim Henson Prods., Inc., 73 F.3d 497 (2d Cir. 1996); Dallas Cowboys Cheerleaders, Inc. v. Pussycat Cinema, Ltd., 604 F.2d 200 (2d Cir. 1979).

[305] *See* § 1.04 *supra*.

section 43(c) the defendant must have made a dilutive use of another's mark or trade name in commerce.

Under the Commerce Clause, Congress may regulate commerce among the states, with foreign nations, or with Indian tribes. Congress may not regulate purely *intrastate* commerce. However, as discussed below, it is increasingly rare to find transactions that are purely intrastate. Intrastate activities are considered to be "in commerce" if they have a substantial effect on commerce. In contrast, claims arising under state laws governing trademark infringement, unfair competition, or dilution may arise from activities that are purely intrastate and do not have a substantial effect on commerce, provided that they involve the offering of goods or services.

The "in commerce" requirement for establishing subject matter jurisdiction for an infringement or dilution action under the Lanham Act is different from the "use in commerce" requirement for establishing ownership of a trademark for purposes of federal registration.[306] The latter, embodied in the section 45 definition of a "use in commerce," inquires whether the applicant for registration has made a qualifying use of the mark in commerce that Congress has the authority to regulate. In contrast, the "in commerce" requirement for infringing or dilutive activities focuses on whether a defendant's allegedly infringing activities have taken place in commerce that Congress has the authority to regulate. As discussed below, the jurisdictional scope of this "in commerce" requirement is broader than the definition of a "use in commerce" for registration purposes.[307]

Because purely intrastate disputes do not fall within the commerce clause, they cannot serve as the basis for infringement or dilution claims under the Lanham Act.[308] However, the jurisdictional scope of the Lanham Act has been construed to be "at least as broad as the definition of commerce employed in any other federal statute."[309] Courts have held that the "use in commerce" jurisdictional requirement is satisfied when either (1) the defendant's activity takes place in commerce, or (2) the defendant's conduct involves purely intrastate activities that nonetheless have a substantial effect on interstate commerce. In light of the broad sweep of the commerce clause, it is difficult to find an infringing activity that does not have a significant effect on commerce.

Courts have found sufficient interstate activity to satisfy the jurisdictional requirement where goods bearing the infringing mark were sold in interstate

---

[306] *See* § 2.04 [B][1] *supra* (discussing registration requirements). Recent dicta from the Second Circuit urges Congress to amend the Lanham Act to clarify this distinction. Rescuecom Corp. v. Google, Inc., 562 F.3d 123, 140–41 (2d Cir. 2009).

[307] Planned Parenthood Fed. of America v. Bucci, 42 U.S.P.Q.2d (BNA) 1430, 1437 n. 7 (S.D.N.Y. 1997).

[308] Jellibeans, Inc. v. Skating Clubs of Georgia, Inc., 716 F.2d 833, 838 (11th Cir. 1983); Iding v. Anaston, 266 F. Supp. 1015, 1019 (N.D. Ill. 1967)).

[309] *Jellibeans*, 716 F.2d at 838; *accord*, Shatel Corp. v. Mao Ta Lumber & Yacht Corp., 697 F.2d 1352, 1356 n. 3 (11th Cir. 1983); Bulova Watch Co. v. Steele, 194 F.2d 567, 570 n. 11 (5th Cir. 1952), *aff'd*, 344 U.S. 280 (1952).

commerce,[310] where the infringing mark was used in advertisements in more than one state,[311] where infringing goods moved in interstate commerce from manufacturer to reseller,[312] and where infringing goods were shipped from one state to another in an effort to qualify for federal trademark registration.[313]

Where the defendant's infringing activity is intrastate, courts generally agree that a substantial effect on interstate commerce is demonstrated where the infringing conduct damages goodwill that the plaintiff built up through the use of its mark in interstate commerce:[314]

> Congress's power to protect a plaintiff's mark used in interstate commence necessarily implies the power to regulate a defendant's unauthorized use of the mark within a state's borders. "If a registrant's right to employ its trademark were subject within every state's borders to preemption or concurrent use by local business, the protection afforded a registrant by the Lanham Act would be virtually meaning-less."[315]

Other effects on interstate commerce have also been held to be sufficient. For example, in *University of Florida v. KPB, Inc.*,[316] the defendant's sale of study guides specific to the courses at a single university was found to have a sufficient effect on interstate commerce because (1) 15 percent of the student body was from out of state, and (2) one of the university's employees had a contract to produce a competing product for an out-of-state publisher.

Activities utilizing the Internet are generally considered to be "in commerce" because they reach a national audience. For example, an Internet domain name was held to be used "in commerce" where the website provided news and information to Chinese-speaking people within the United States, even though it did not offer to sell them any goods or services.[317] In *Planned Parenthood Federation of America v. Bucci*, a federal district court held that the defendant's maintenance of a website that used the plaintiff's mark in its domain name

---

[310] *See, e.g.*, Department of Justice v. Calspan Corp., 578 F.2d 295 (C.C.P.A. 1978).

[311] *See, e.g.*, American Hosp. Ass'n v. Bankers Commercial Life Ins. Co., 275 F. Supp. 563 (D. Tex. 1967), *aff'd*, 403 F.2d 718 (5th Cir. 1968), *cert. denied*, 394 U.S. 1018 (1969).

[312] *See, e.g.*, Admiral Corp. v. Penco, Inc., 203 F.2d 517 (2d Cir. 1953), *overruled on other grounds*, Monsanto Chem. Co. v. Perfect Fit Prods. Mfg. Co., 349 F.2d 389 (2d Cir. 1965), *cert. denied*, 383 U.S. 942 (1966), *disapproved on other grounds*, Fleischmann Distilling Corp. v. Maier Brewing Co., 386 U.S. 714 (1967).

[313] *See, e.g.*, Drop Dead Co. v. S.C. Johnson & Son, Inc., 326 F.2d 87 (9th Cir. 1963), *cert. denied*, 377 U.S. 907 (1964).

[314] *See, e.g.*, Franchised Stores of New York, Inc. v. Winter, 394 F.2d 664 (2d Cir. 1968); Pure Foods, Inc. v. Minute Maid Corp., 214 F.2d 792 (5th Cir. 1954), *cert. denied*, 348 U.S. 888 (1954); Tiffany & Co. v. Boston Club, Inc., 231 F. Supp. 836 (D. Mass. 1964).

[315] United We Stand America, Inc. v. United We Stand, America New York, Inc., 128 F.3d 86, 93 (2d Cir. 1997), *cert. denied*, 523 U.S. 1076 (1998) (quoting Dawn Donut Co. v. Hart's Food Stores, Inc., 267 F.2d 358, 365 (2d Cir. 1959)).

[316] 89 F.3d 773, 775 n. 3 (11th Cir. 1996).

[317] Cable News Network L.P. v. CNNews.com, 177 F. Supp. 2d 506, 516-18 (E.D. Va. 2001), *aff'd in relevant part*, 56 Fed. Appx. 599, 66 U.S.P.Q.2d (BNA) 1057 (4th Cir. 2003).

satisfied the jurisdictional predicate for an infringement action under the Lanham Act because the website (1) affected the plaintiff's interstate activities, and (2) reached an interstate audience:

> It is well settled that the scope of "in commerce" as a jurisdictional predicate of the Lanham Act is broad and has a sweeping reach. The activity involved in this action meets the "in commerce" standard for two reasons. First, defendant's actions affect plaintiff's ability to offer plaintiff's services, which, as health and information services offered in forty-eight states and over the Internet, are surely "in commerce." Thus, even assuming, arguendo, that defendant's activities are not in interstate commerce for Lanham Act purposes, the effect of those activities on plaintiff's interstate commerce activities would place defendant within the reach of the Lanham Act. Second, Internet users constitute a national, even international, audience, who must use interstate telephone lines to access defendant's web site on the Internet. The nature of the Internet indicates that establishing a typical home page on the Internet, for access to all users, would satisfy the Lanham Act's "in commerce" requirement. Therefore, I conclude that defendant's actions are "in commerce" within the meaning of that term for jurisdictional purposes.[318]

[G]   Territorial Limitations

The issue of whether, and when, a federal court may adjudicate a Lanham Act claim arising from activities taking place outside of the United States is a question of subject matter jurisdiction. Today, it is well settled that federal courts may enjoin extraterritorial conduct under the Lanham Act when necessary to prevent harm to commerce in the United States. Although infringement of registered or unregistered marks is actionable under sections 32 or 43(a) of the Lanham Act (and dilution is actionable under section 43(c)) only when the defendant's activities involve a "use in commerce" of the plaintiff's mark, section 45 of the Act defines "commerce" broadly to include "all commerce which may lawfully be regulated by Congress,"[319] and expressly states that the intent of the Lanham Act is:

> to regulate commerce within the control of Congress by making actionable the deceptive and misleading use of marks in such commerce; to protect registered marks used in such commerce from interference by State, or territorial legislation; to protect persons engaged in such commerce against unfair competition; to prevent fraud and deception in such commerce by the use of reproductions, copies, counterfeits, or colorable imitations of registered marks; and to provide rights and

---

[318] 42 U.S.P.Q.2d (BNA) 1430 (S.D.N.Y. 1997) (citations omitted), aff'd, 1998 U.S. App. LEXIS 22179 (2d Cir. Feb. 9, 1998), cert. denied, 525 U.S. 834 (1998); see also Intermatic, Inc. v. Toeppen, 947 F. Supp. 1227, 1239 (N.D. Ill. 1996) (quoting 1 Gilson, Trademark Protection and Practice, § 5.11[2], p.5-234: "there is little question that the 'in commerce' requirement would be met in a typical Internet message").

[319] 15 U.S.C. § 1127.

remedies stipulated by treaties and conventions respecting trade-marks, trade names, and unfair competition entered into between the United States and foreign nations.[320]

The leading case on the extraterritorial reach of the Lanham Act is the Supreme Court's decision in *Steele v. Bulova Watch Co.*[321] In that case, the United States corporation that owned the "Bulova" trademark for watches alleged that the unauthorized use of its registered trademark by the defendant, a citizen and resident of the United States, was actionable under the Lanham Act even though the defendant's use of the mark took place exclusively in Mexico, where he obtained a Mexican registration for the mark, and began assembling and selling watches bearing the mark using components obtained from the United States and elsewhere. The plaintiff learned of these activities when it began to receive reports from retail jewelers in the Mexican border areas that customers were bringing in the defective watches for repair, believing them to be genuine Bulovas. Noting the general principle that "[t]he legislation of Congress will not extend beyond the boundaries of the United States unless a contrary legislative intent appears,"[322] the Court found that such intent was clearly expressed in section 45, and therefore concluded that "Congress has the power to prevent unfair trade practices in foreign commerce by citizens of the United States, although some of the acts are done outside the territorial limits of the United States."[323] Accordingly, the Court held that the defendant's activities in Mexico were actionable under the Lanham Act because:

> His operations and their effects were not confined within the territorial limits of a foreign nation. He bought component parts of his wares in the United States, and spurious "Bulovas" filtered through the Mexican border into this country; his competing goods could well reflect adversely on Bulova Watch Company's trade reputation in markets cultivated by advertising here as well as abroad.[324]

Moreover, the issuance of an injunction against the defendant's infringing activities in Mexico would not create a conflict with Mexican law because the Mexican government had already canceled his trademark registration: "Where, as here, there can be no interference with the sovereignty of another nation, the District Court in exercising its equity powers may command persons properly before it to cease or perform acts outside its territorial jurisdiction."[325]

Several of the circuit courts of appeal have distilled the *Bulova* analysis into a three-factor test that considers: (1) whether the defendant is a United States citizen; (2) whether the foreign activity has a substantial effect on United States commerce; and (3) whether exercising jurisdiction would interfere with the

---

[320] *Id.*

[321] 344 U.S. 280 (1952).

[322] *Id.* at 285.

[323] *Id.* at 286 (quoting Branch v. Federal Trade Commission, 141 F.2d 31, 35 (1944)).

[324] *Id.* at 286.

[325] *Id.* at 289.

sovereignty of another nation.[326] Under this standard of extraterritoriality, the infringing conduct must have a "substantial" effect on United States commerce.[327] For example, the Eleventh Circuit found a substantial effect on commerce where foreign-made counterfeit jeans were found at the defendants' premises in the United States and were shipped through the United States, documents connected to the transactions falsely stated that the jeans were made in the United States, and many of the defendants' illegal activities, including locating and negotiating with prospective buyers and arranging shipments, took place in the United States.[328] The same court found a substantial effect where sales of cordless telephones took place abroad, but the telephones were shipped through a United States free-trade zone, negotiations had occurred in the United States, and sales had been orchestrated from a Florida office.[329] In the Second Circuit, a substantial effect was established where a defendant advertised its product in the United States, and sold it by mail to United States customers,[330] where a defendant's foreign activities created confusion among United States customers as to the source of products sold in the United States,[331] where $6 million of an American plaintiff's foreign sales were diverted,[332] and where the defendant's actions created a danger of irreparable injury to a plaintiff's good will and reputation.[333]

Applying the same standard, the Second Circuit has held that a substantial effect is not established by non-infringing domestic activities that are designed to support the infringing foreign activities; the court noted that the Supreme Court's finding of a substantial effect in *Bulova* was not solely based on the fact that the defendant bought some of its watch components in the United States, but also on the fact that the counterfeit watches were coming into the United States and damaging Bulova's domestic goodwill.[334] In the Second Circuit's view:

> Where (i) an alleged infringer's foreign use of a mark does not mislead American consumers in their purchases or cause them to look less favorably upon the mark; (ii) the alleged infringer does not physically use the stream of American commerce to compete with the trademark owner by, for example, manufacturing, processing, or transporting the competing product in United States commerce; and (iii) none of the alleged infringer's American activities materially support the foreign

---

[326] *See* Int'l Café v. Hard Rock Café Int'l, 252 F.3d 1274, 1278 (11th Cir. 2001); Scanvec Amiable, Ltd. v. Chang, 80 Fed. Appx. 171, 181 (3d Cir. 2003) (unpub.); Atl. Richfield Co. v. ARCO Globus Int'l Co., 150 F.3d 189, 192 (2d Cir. 1998); Nintendo of Am., Inc. v. Aeropower Co., 34 F.3d 246, 250-51 (4th Cir. 1994).

[327] *Atl. Richfield Co.*, 150 F.3d at 192.

[328] Levi Strauss & Co. v. Sunrise Int'l Trading Inc., 51 F.3d 982, 985 (11th Cir. 1995).

[329] Babbit Elecs., Inc. v. Dynascan Corp., 38 F.3d 1161, 1179 (11th Cir. 1994).

[330] Vanity Fair Mills, Inc. v. T. Eaton Co., 234 F.2d 633, 643 (2d Cir. 1956).

[331] Sterling Drug v. Bayer AG, 14 F.3d 733, 747 (2d Cir. 1994).

[332] Warnaco, Inc. v. VF Corp., 844 F. Supp. 940, 951 (S.D.N.Y. 1994).

[333] *Warnaco*, 844 F. Supp. at 945, 951; Calvin Klein Indus., Inc. v. BFK Hong Kong, Ltd., 714 F. Supp. 78, 80 (S.D.N.Y. 1989).

[334] *Atl. Richfield*, 150 F.3d at 192-93.

use of the mark, the mere presence of the alleged infringer in the United States will not support extraterritorial application of the Lanham Act.[335]

In determining whether application of the Lanham Act would create a conflict with foreign law, courts applying the *Bulova* analysis have found such a conflict where the defendant is operating under a presumptively valid trademark in its home country.[336] In some cases, a pending application for the foreign registration may suffice to create this conflict,[337] although the opposite result was reached where it appeared that the defendant's foreign application would be rejected based on the plaintiff's priority rights.[338]

In contrast, the Ninth Circuit has adopted a different test, known as the *Timberlane* factors, derived from precedent addressing the extraterritorial reach of antitrust law: (1) there must be some effect on American foreign commerce; (2) the effect must be sufficiently great to present a cognizable injury to plaintiffs under the federal statute; and (3) the interests of and links to American foreign commerce must be sufficiently strong in relation to those of other nations to justify an assertion of extraterritorial authority.[339] In explaining its rejection of the approach adopted by other circuits, the Ninth Circuit noted that, while the effect on United States commerce, the citizenship of defendants, and the existence of a conflict with foreign law were all "relevant to the resolution of the jurisdictional issue," nonetheless "the absence of one of the factors is not necessarily determinative of the issue." Instead, the court treated each of these factors as "just one consideration to be balanced in the 'jurisdictional rule of reason' of comity and fairness adopted by us in *Timberlane*."

In applying the *Timberlane* "rule of reason," the Ninth Circuit considers the following seven factors to determine whether "the contacts and interests of the United States are sufficient to support the exercise of extraterritorial jurisdiction:"[340]

> The degree of conflict with foreign law or policy, the nationality or allegiance of the parties and the locations or principal places of business of corporations, the extent to which enforcement by either state can be expected to achieve compliance, the relative significance of effects on the United States as compared with those elsewhere, the extent to which there is explicit purpose to harm or affect American commerce, the foreseeability of such effect, and the relative importance to the violations charged of conduct within the United States as compared with conduct abroad.[341]

---

[335] *Id.* at 193.

[336] *Vanity Fair Mills*, 234 F.2d at 643; Aerogroup Int'l v. Marlboro Footworks, 955 F. Supp. 220, 229 (S.D.N.Y. 1997).

[337] American White Cross Labs., Inc. v. H.M. Cote, Inc., 556 F. Supp. 753 (S.D.N.Y. 1983).

[338] Les Ballets Trockadero De Monte Carlo, Inc. v. Trevino, 945 F. Supp. 563, 567-68 (S.D.N.Y. 1996).

[339] Wells Fargo & Co. v. Wells Fargo Express Co., 556 F.2d 406 (9th Cir. 1977) (citing Timberlane Lumber Co. v. Bank of America, 549 F.2d 597 (9th Cir. 1976).

[340] *Wells Fargo*, 556 F.2d at 428-29 (quoting *Timberlane*, 549 F.2d at 614-15 (footnotes omitted)).

[341] Reebok Int'l, Ltd. v. Marnatech Enters., Inc., 970 F.2d 552, 555 (9th Cir. 1992).

Under the Ninth Circuit's approach, it is not necessary that the defendant be a United States citizen; the "nationality or allegiance of the parties and the locations or principal places of business of corporations" is but one factor in the overall comity analysis. Moreover, even where a conflict might exist between plaintiff's and the defendant's registration in a country, jurisdiction to enjoin the defendant's activities is not necessarily foreclosed.[342]

The Fifth Circuit has adopted a slight variation on the *Timberlane* factors:

[C]ertain factors are relevant in determining whether the contacts and interests of the United States are sufficient to support the exercise of extraterritorial jurisdiction. These include the citizenship of the defendant, the effect on United States commerce, and the existence of a conflict with foreign law. The absence of any one of these is not dispositive. Nor should a court limit its inquiry exclusively to these considerations. Rather, these factors will necessarily be the primary elements in any balancing analysis.[343]

Notably, both the Ninth and Fifth Circuits have rejected the requirement that the defendant's foreign activities must have a substantial effect on United States commerce; in these circuits, it is sufficient if those activities have "some" effect.[344] In adopting this less demanding standard, the Ninth Circuit explained: "[S]ince the origins of the "substantiality" test apparently lie in the effort to distinguish between intrastate commerce, which Congress may not regulate as such, and interstate commerce, which it can control, it may be unwise blindly to apply the factor in the area of foreign commerce over which Congress has exclusive authority."[345]

For example, the Ninth Circuit found that the foreign manufacturing of counterfeit REEBOK shoes had a sufficient effect on United States commerce, and caused an actionable injury to Reebok warranting application of the Lanham Act, where (1) the defendant organized and directed the manufacture of counterfeit REEBOK shoes from the United States, (2) the defendant knew that the counterfeit shoes entered the United States with regular frequency, and (3) the defendant's sales of the shoes "decreased the sale of genuine REEBOK shoes in Mexico and the United States and directly decreased the value of Reebok's consolidated holdings."[346]

The Fifth Circuit found a sufficient effect on commerce where the defendant's sale of rice under an infringing trademark took place abroad, but where "essential steps" leading to those sales (including processing, packaging, transportation, and distribution) took place in the United States.[347]

---

[342] *Wells Fargo,* 556 F.2d at 429.

[343] American Rice, Inc. v. Ark. Rice Growers Co-op. Ass'n, 701 F.2d 408, 414 (5th Cir. 1983) (citing *Vanity Fair Mills,* 234 F.2d at 642 (2d Cir.), *cert. denied,* 352 U.S. 871 (1956)).

[344] *Wells Fargo,* 556 F.2d at 428 (citing *Timberlane,* 549 F.2d at 612); *American Rice,* 701 F.2d at 414 n. 8.

[345] *Id.* (citing *Timberlane,* 549 F.2d at 612); *accord, American Rice,* 701 F.2d at 414.

[346] *Reebok,* 970 F.2d at 554-55.

[347] *American Rice,* 701 F.2d at 414-15.

Recently, the First Circuit articulated its own test for extraterritorial application of the Lanham Act where the defendants are not United States citizens, holding in *McBee v. Delica Co.* that the Lanham Act can be applied to extraterritorial conduct by foreign defendants only where their conduct "has a substantial effect on United States commerce.[348] Where such an effect is established, the court may take considerations of comity into account as a prudential matter, but such considerations do not preclude the court's exercise of Lanham Act jurisdiction.[349] Like the Ninth Circuit in *Timberlane*, the First Circuit derived its analysis from Supreme Court precedents involving antitrust law.[350]

PART II:
REVERSE PASSING OFF

§ 3.03   REVERSE PASSING OFF

Section 43(a) has been held to apply also to actions for "reverse passing off" (or "reverse palming off"). Reverse passing off occurs when a defendant offers the public goods or services produced by another person, but represents them as the defendant's own goods or services.[351] The *Restatement (Third) of Unfair Competition* recognizes this cause of action at common law, noting that an actor may be liable to another "if, in marketing goods or services manufactured, produced or supplied by the other, the actor makes a representation likely to deceive or mislead prospective purchasers by causing the mistaken belief that the actor or a third person is the manufacturer, producer, or supplier of the goods or services if the representation is to the likely commercial detriment of the other. . . ."[352]

The injury to the plaintiff in a case of reverse passing off is different from, and arguably less significant than, the injury caused by traditional passing off. The Ninth Circuit has described the harm caused by reverse passing off as follows:

> [S]uch conduct, like traditional palming off, is wrongful because it involves an attempt to misappropriate or profit from another's talents and workmanship. Moreover, in reverse palming off cases, the originator of the misidentified product is involuntarily deprived of the advertising value of [his] name and the goodwill that otherwise would stem from public knowledge of the true source of the satisfactory product. The

---

[348]   417 F.3d 107, 120 (1st Cir. 2005).

[349]   *Id.* at 121.

[350]   *Id.* at 119-21.

[351]   *See, e.g.,* Lipscher v. LRP Pubs., Inc., 266 F.3d 1305, 1312 (11th Cir. 2001); *See, e.g.,* Lamothe v. Atlantic Recording Co., 847 F.2d 1403, 1405 (9th Cir. 1988); Truck Equipment Service Co. v. Fruehauf Co., 536 F.2d 1210, 1216 (8th Cir. 1976); Kasco Corp. v. General Services, Inc., 905 F. Supp. 29, 33-35 (D. Mass. 1995); Smith v. Montoro, 648 F. 2d 602, 607 (9th Cir. 1981); Cleary v. News Corp., 30 F.3d 1255 (9th Cir. 1994).

[352]   Restatement (Third) of Unfair Competition, § 5 (1995).

ultimate purchaser (or viewer) is also deprived of knowing the true source of the product and may even be deceived into believing that it comes from a different source.[353]

Reverse passing off may be "express" — where the defendant places its own origin indicator on goods produced by someone else — or "implied" — where the defendant omits the plaintiff's origin indicator but does not substitute its own.[354] However, courts disagree on whether and under what circumstances the mere *removal* of origin-identifying information from a product would violate section 43(a).[355]

Although reverse passing off may occur when a defendant passes off the plaintiff's unaltered goods as its own, it may also occur when a defendant modifies the plaintiff's goods before relabeling them as its own.[356] In the latter group of cases, courts have distinguished between minor modifications, which support a finding of liability,[357] and more substantial modifications, which create a "new product" and do not amount to reverse passing off.[358]

Courts often use the term "reverse passing off" to describe situations in which a seller merely uses the goods of another as samples or illustrations of its own goods in order to solicit customers.[359] In *Bangor Punta Operations, Inc., v.*

---

[353] *Montoro*, 648 F.2d at 607; *see also* Rest. (Third) of Unfair Competition, § 5, cmt. a (1995) ("Reverse passing off . . . may sometimes misrepresent the relative capabilities or accomplishments of the parties, thus creating the likelihood of a future diversion of trade to the actor. This Section subjects the actor to liability only if the actual producer can establish both the fact of a misrepresentation and a likelihood of harm to its commercial relations.").

[354] *See, e.g.*, Summit Mach. Tool Mfg. Corp. v. Victor CNC Sys., Inc., 7 F.3d 1434, 1437 (9th Cir. 1993); Roho, Inc. v. Marquis, 902 F.2d 356, 359 (5th Cir. 1990); *Montoro*, 684 F.2d 604.

[355] *Compare* CCS Communications Control, Inc. v. Law Enforcement Assoc., Inc., 628 F. Supp. 1457, 1460 (S.D.N.Y. 1986) (stating that "removal of [product's] identifying letters and its resale is not a violation of [section 43(a)] because it 'makes actionable the application of a 'false designation of origin,' not the removal of a true designation' ") (internal citation omitted), *and* PIC Design Corp. v. Sterling Precision Corp., 231 F. Supp. 106 (S.D.N.Y. 1964) (holding that mere removal of plaintiff's mark was not actionable under section 43(a) absent substitution of defendant's own mark), *with* Lamothe, 847 F.2d at 1407 n. 2 (suggesting disagreement with CCS Communs.), *and* Montoro, 648 F.2d at 605 (" 'Implied' reverse passing off occurs when the wrongdoer simply removes or otherwise obliterates the name of the manufacturer or source and sells the product in an unbranded state."). In *Commodore Import Co. v. Hiraoka*, 422 F. Supp. 628 (S.D.N.Y. 1976), the district court found no section 43(a) violation where the defendant obtained goods that had been abandoned by plaintiff and replaced plaintiff's labels with its own.

[356] *See* General Univ. Sys. v. Lee, 379 F.3d 131, 148 n. 41 (5th Cir. 2004).

[357] *See* Arrow United Indus., Inc. v. Hugh Richards, Inc., 678 F.2d 410, 412, 415 (2d Cir. 1982) (preliminary injunction issued prohibiting defendant from modifying Arrow-Foil dampers in size and other minor respects and relabeling them); Matsushita Elec. Corp. of Am. v. Solar Sound Sys., Inc., 381 F. Supp. 64, 66-67, 70 (S.D.N.Y. 1974) (defendant enjoined from using one of plaintiff's radios, which had been slightly modified and then relabeled, to advertise the sale of defendant's radio).

[358] *Roho, Inc.*, 902 F.2d at 360-61 (5th Cir. 1990).

[359] *See, e.g.*, Alpo Petfoods, Inc. v. Ralston Purina Co., 913 F.2d 958, 963-964, n. 6 (D.C. Cir. 1990); Arrow United Indus., Inc. v. Hugh Richards, Inc., 678 F.2d 410, 415 (2d Cir. 1982); Alum-A-Fold Shutter Corporation v. Folding Shutter Corporation, 441 F.2d 556 (5th Cir. 1971); American Precast Corp. v. Maurice Concrete Products, 360 F. Supp. 859 (D. Mass. 1973), *aff'd*, 502 F.2d 1159 (1st Cir. 1974); Crossbow, Inc. v. Dan-Dee Imports Inc., 266 F. Supp. 335, 339-40 & n. 1 (S.D.N.Y. 1967) (collecting cases).

Universal Marine Co.,[360] for example, the defendant used a picture of plaintiff's trawler in its advertising materials, representing it to be a picture of its own trawler. Although several authorities have described this as "implied reverse passing off,"[361] in fact this is not true reverse passing off, because the defendant does not in fact sell the plaintiff's goods; rather, it is a form of false advertising, in which the defendant falsely claims that the sample or illustration depicts its own goods.[362] True reverse passing off occurs only when a defendant actually sells a plaintiff's goods to consumers under the pretense that they are the defendant's own goods. In fact, cases holding defendants liable for true reverse passing off are rare.[363] However, few courts have recognized this distinction,[364] and for that reason both usages must be recognized in practice.[365]

In order to state a claim for true reverse passing off under section 43(a), a plaintiff must establish that: (1) the defendant misbranded plaintiff's goods; (2) such misbranding was "material"; (3) the defendant caused the plaintiff's goods to enter interstate commerce; and (4) the defendant's misbranding caused a likelihood of confusion.[366]

Until 2003, perhaps the most significant use of true reverse passing off claims under section 43(a) was in cases alleging failure to properly attribute authorship of ideas or creative expression. In fact, these claims comprised the majority of section 43(a) cases in which courts held that the plaintiffs had at least a colorable claim of true reverse passing off. For example, plaintiffs won favorable rulings in the following situations: where an actor's name was removed from film credits and advertising materials and replaced with another actor's name,[367] where a publisher's name was removed from the songs printed in a hymnal and replaced

---

[360] Bangor Punta Operations, Inc. v. Universal Marine Co., 543 F.2d 1107, 1109 (5th Cir. 1976).

[361] *Lamothe,* 847 F.2d at 1406; *Montoro,* 648 F.2d at 604 (citing 1 R. Callman, Unfair Competition, Trademarks and Monopolies, § 18.2(b)(1), at 294 (1980 Supp. to 3d ed.)).

[362] Rest. (Third) of Unfair Competition § 5 (1995), cmt. a.

[363] Pioneer Hi-Bred Int'l v. Holden Found. *Seeds,* 35 F.3d 1226, 1242 (8th Cir. 1994); Web Printing Controls Co. v. Oxy-Dry Corp., 906 F.2d 1202, 1203-04 (7th Cir. 1990); Williams v. Curtiss-Wright Corp., 691 F.2d 168, 1172-73 (3d Cir. 1982); Federal Elec. Co. v. Flexlume Corp., 33 F.2d 412, 414-15 (7th Cir. 1929).

[364] This distinction was recognized in Bretford Mfg. v. Smith Sys. Mfg. Co., 286 F. Supp. 2d 969, 971-72 (N.D. Ill. 2003), which rejected a reverse passing off claim arising from the defendant's use of the plaintiff's product as a component of the sample merchandise defendant displayed to potential customers, on the ground that the sample merchandise was not the actual good offered for sale. Customers who placed orders in fact received merchandise made by the defendant.

[365] For example, both usages can be found in *Montoro,* 648 F.2d at 604-05. In Dastar Corp. v. Twentieth Century Fox Film Corp., 539 U.S. 23 (2003), the Supreme Court used the term "reverse passing off" to refer to a group of precedents that includes both true reverse passing off cases and cases involving false advertising. One reason for the failure of courts to distinguish between the two types of claims is that these cases, like most cases applying section 43(a) to reverse passing off, arose under the pre-1988 version of section 43(a), which did not contain a separate false advertising provision. Today, it can be argued, courts should pay closer attention to the precise wording of sections 43(a)(1)(A) and 43(a)(1)(B) in order to determine which prong of section 43(a) applies to a particular set of facts.

[366] Web Printing Controls Co. v. Oxy-Dry Corp., 906 F.2d 1202, 1204 (7th Cir. 1990).

[367] *Montoro,* 648 F. 2d at 607.

by the name of the parish,[368] where the names of two co-authors were omitted from a record album cover and sheet music featuring their compositions,[369] where a defendant published a biography without giving attribution to its authors,[370] where one publisher copied another publisher's books,[371] where a defendant copied the plaintiff's cookbooks without attribution,[372] and where a defendant incorporated the plaintiff's copyrighted software into its CD-ROMs without attribution.[373] In fact, the federal courts had reached a strong consensus that false or omitted authorship attributions were actionable under section 43(a). The only major point of disagreement among the circuits was the degree of copying necessary to find a likelihood of confusion, with some courts requiring only "substantial similarity,"[374] while others imposed the higher "bodily appropriation" standard.[375]

However, the Supreme Court rejected the application of section 43(a) to misattribution of creative or expressive works in its 2003 decision in *Dastar Corp. v. Twentieth Century Fox Film Corp.*,[376] thus implicitly overruling all of these precedents. In *Dastar*, the defendant re-edited a television series that had originally been produced by the plaintiff, but that had lost its copyright and entered the public domain. The defendant then released the re-edited series on videocassette, identifying itself as the producer and omitting any reference to the plaintiff. The plaintiff brought a claim of reverse passing off under section 43(a), alleging "bodily appropriation" of its film series. The Supreme Court rejected the plaintiff's claim of reverse passing off under section 43(a), holding that the term "origin" in section 43(a) refers to "the producer of the tangible goods that are offered for sale, and not to the author of any idea, concept, or communication embodied in those goods."[377] Although the Court acknowledged that, in general, section 43(a) encompasses claims of reverse passing off,[378] it held that such a claim is limited to false designations of the physical producer of goods, and thus may not be based on failure to identify the origins of ideas or expression embodied in those goods. Although the Court acknowledged, in dicta, that reverse passing off would "undoubtedly" have been established if the defendant had repackaged videocassettes that had been physically produced by the plaintiff,[379] the same conclusion did not follow when the defendant copied only

---

[368] F.E.L. Publications, Ltd. v. Catholic Bishop of Chicago, 214 U.S.P.Q. (BNA) 409, 416-17 (7th Cir. 1982).

[369] Lamothe v. Atlantic Recording Co., 847 F.2d 1403, 1405 (9th Cir. 1998).

[370] Dodd v. Fort Smith Special School Dist., 666 F. Supp. 1278, 1284-85 (W.D. Ark. 1987).

[371] Waldman Pub. Corp. v. Landoll, Inc., 43 F.3d 775, 780 (2d Cir. 1994).

[372] Marling v. Ellison, 218 U.S.P.Q. (BNA) 702 (S.D. Fla. 1982).

[373] Montgomery v. Noga, 168 F.3d 1282, 1299 n. 27 (11th Cir. 1999).

[374] *See, e.g.*, Waldman Pub. Corp. v. Landoll, Inc., 43 F.3d 775, 780 (2d Cir. 1994)

[375] *See, e.g.*, Cleary v. News Corp., 30 F.3d 1255, 1261 (9th Cir. 1994); Shaw v. Lindheim, 919 F.2d 1353, 1364 (9th Cir. 1990).

[376] 539 U.S. 23 (2003).

[377] *Id.* at 37.

[378] In reaching this conclusion, the Court bowed to what it described as "the unanimous court-of-appeals jurisprudence on that subject." *Id.* at 30.

[379] 539 U.S. at 28. The Court added that a similar cause of action would arise if Coca-Cola were

the plaintiff's intangible intellectual property:

> The dictionary definition of "origin" is "the fact or process of coming into being from a source," and "that from which anything primarily proceeds; source." And the dictionary definition of "goods" (as relevant here) is "[w]ares; merchandise." We think the most natural understanding of the "origin" of "goods" — the source of wares — is the producer of the tangible product sold in the marketplace, in this case the physical Campaigns videotape sold by Dastar. The concept might be stretched (as it was under the original version of § 43(a)) to include not only the actual producer, but also the trademark owner who commissioned or assumed responsibility for ("stood behind") production of the physical product. But as used in the Lanham Act, the phrase "origin of goods" is in our view incapable of connoting the person or entity that originated the ideas or communications that "goods" embody or contain. Such an extension would not only stretch the text, but it would be out of accord with the history and purpose of the Lanham Act and inconsistent with precedent.[380]

In the Court's view, consumers do not normally care about the creative origins of the goods they purchase; thus, full disclosure of creative — as opposed to physical — origins is not required by the Lanham Act.[381] The Court acknowledged that this generalization might not apply to communicative works, whose creative origins might in fact be a matter of concern to consumers.[382] Nonetheless, the Court concluded that giving different treatment to communicative works would create a conflict between the Lanham Act and federal copyright law: "The right to copy, and to copy without attribution, once a copyright has expired, like the right to make [an article whose patent has expired] — including the right to make it in precisely the shape it carried when patented — passes to the public."[383]

Dastar leaves many questions unanswered. For example, although the case involved an expired copyright, much of the Court's reasoning appears equally applicable to subsisting copyrights, and courts have consistently so held.[384]

---

to pass off Pepsi-Cola as a Coca-Cola product. *Id.* at 32. This analogy obfuscates more than it clarifies, however, since each of these beverages has unique and distinct characteristics, which are more important to brand-loyal purchasers than the identity of the actual manufacturer. To the sensitive palate, Pepsi could no more substitute for Coke than it could for orange juice.

[380] *Id.* at 28-29 (emphasis added) (citations omitted) (quoting Webster's New International Dictionary 1079, 1720-1721 (2d ed. 1949)).

[381] *Id.* at 32.

[382] *Id.* at 33.

[383] *Id.* at 33 (internal quotation marks omitted).

[384] *E.g.*, Zyla v. Wadsworth, 360 F.3d 243, 251-52 (1st Cir. 2004) (textbook); Richard Feiner & Co. v. New York Times Co., 2008 U.S. Dist. LEXIS 58454, *9-11 (S.D.N.Y. Aug. 1, 2008) (still images from motion pictures); Thomas Pub'g Co., LLC v. Technology Evaluation Ctrs., Inc., 2007 U.S. Dist. LEXIS 55086 (S.D.N.Y. July 27, 2007) (directory); Antidote Int'l Films, Inc. v. Bloomsbury Pub'g, PLC, 467 F. Supp. 2d 394 (S.D.N.Y. 2007) (novel); Beckwith Builders, Inc. v. Depietri, 81 U.S.P.Q.2d (BNA) 1302 (D.N.H. 2006) (architectural plans); Auscape Int'l v. National Geographic Soc'y, 409 F. Supp. 2d 235, 250 (S.D.N.Y. 2004) (photographs in a collective work); Smith v. New Line Cinema, 2004 U.S. Dist. LEXIS 18382 (Sept. 13, 2004) (motion picture screenplay); Williams v. UMG

Under this interpretation, *Dastar* forecloses any application of section 43(a) to reverse passing off of the ideas or content of expressive works, whether or not they are protected by copyright.

The holding in *Dastar* also casts doubt on the application of section 43(a) to traditional (that is, non-reverse) passing off claims involving expressive works. For example, in *Gilliam v. American Broadcasting Cos., Inc.*,[385] the Monty Python comedy troupe brought a successful claim under section 43(a) against a television network that edited their television programs without their consent. The Second Circuit held in that case that the network had falsely designated the origin of the altered programs by attributing them to the Monty Python troupe. Similarly, in *King v. Innovation Books*,[386] the Second Circuit held that section 43(a) was violated when the film credits for "Lawnmower Man" implicitly exaggerated Stephen King's creative contribution to the film. In each of these cases, the false designation of origin pertained to the creative source of the work, rather than its physical source. After *Dastar*, it is not clear whether these precedents can still be considered good law.[387]

In addition, *Dastar* noted the possibility that some false attribution claims pertaining to expressive works might still be brought under section 43(a)(1)(B), the false advertising provision of the Lanham Act.[388] As discussed in the next section, however, attempts to bring such claims have not succeeded.

PART III:
FEDERAL LAW OF FALSE ADVERTISING

§ 3.04 FALSE ADVERTISING

Section 43(a)(1)(B) of the Lanham Act permits a plaintiff to bring a federal claim for false advertising. Such a claim arises when a defendant uses, in connection with any goods or services in commerce, "any false designation of origin, false or misleading description of fact, or false or misleading representation of fact . . . which, in commercial advertising or promotion, misrepresents the nature, characteristics, qualities, or geographic origin of his or her or another person's goods, services, or commercial activities."[389] A false or misleading representation may be actionable under section 43(a)(1)(B) whether it pertains to the plaintiff's or the defendant's goods, services, or commercial activities.

To prevail on a false advertising claim, a plaintiff must prove by a preponderance of the evidence (1) that the defendant has made false or misleading statements as to his own product (or another's); (2) that there is actual deception

---

Recordings, 281 F. Supp. 2d 1177 (C.D. Cal. 2003) (contributions to motion picture).

[385] 538 F.2d 14 (2d Cir. 1976).

[386] 976 F.2d 824 (2d Cir. 1992).

[387] One court has suggested, in brief dicta, that *Gilliam* remains good law. Auscape Int'l v. National Geographic Soc'y, 409 F. Supp. 2d 235, 251 n. 85 (S.D.N.Y. 2004).

[388] *Dastar*, 539 U.S. at 37. For more on false advertising, see § 3.04 *infra*.

[389] 15 U.S.C. § 1125(a)(1)(B).

of, or at least a tendency to deceive, a substantial portion of the intended audience; (3) that the deception is material in that it is likely to influence purchasing decisions; (4) that the advertised goods traveled in interstate commerce; and (5) that there is a likelihood of injury to the plaintiff (e.g., declining sales or loss of good will).[390]

To prove that a defendant's statements were false or misleading, the plaintiff must establish either that (1) the advertisement is literally false, or (2) although the advertisement is literally true or ambiguous, it is likely to deceive or confuse consumers.[391] Where the advertised claim is literally false, the court may enjoin the continued assertion of the false claim "without reference to the advertisement's impact on the buying public,"[392] — that is, without proof of consumer deception.[393] However, in the absence of such literal falsity, the plaintiff must show that the public was actually misled.[394] Such proof may take the form of consumer testimony, marketing surveys, proof of lost sales, or other evidence of consumer deception.[395] Thus, a false advertising plaintiff must prove either literal falsity or consumer confusion, but not both.[396]

In contrast, claims that fall into the category of mere "puffery" are not actionable. Puffery consists of "exaggerated advertising, blustering, and boasting upon which no reasonable buyer would rely,"[397] and includes representations of product superiority that are vague or highly subjective.[398] In contrast, false statements regarding specific or absolute characteristics of a product, and specific, measurable claims of product superiority that are based on product testing are not puffery and are actionable.[399]

In determining whether claims are literally false, a court will first identify the unambiguous claims made by the advertisement or by the product's name, and then determine whether those claims are false.[400] A literally false claim need not

---

[390] *See, e.g.,* AT&T v. Winback & Conserve Program, 42 F.3d 1421, 1428 n. 9 (3d Cir. 1994).

[391] Lipton v. Nature Co., 71 F.3d 464, 474 (2d Cir. 1995).

[392] McNeil-P.C.C., Inc. v. Bristol-Myers Squibb Co., 938 F.2d 1544, 1549 (2d Cir. 1991) (quoting Coca-Cola v. Tropicana Prods., Inc., 690 F.2d 312, 317 (2d Cir. 1982).

[393] Vidal Sassoon, Inc. v. Bristol-Myers Co., 661 F.2d 272, 277 (2d Cir. 1981).

[394] Clorox Co. v Procter & Gamble Commer. Co., 228 F.3d 24 (1st Cir. 2000); United Indus. Corp. v. Clorox Co., 140 F.3d 1175, 1182 (8th Cir. 1998).

[395] *See, e.g.,* Warner-Lambert Co. v. BreathAsure, Inc., 204 F.3d 87, 96 (3d Cir. 2000); McNeilab, Inc. v. American Home Prods. Corp., 501 F. Supp. 517, 525 (S.D.N.Y. 1980).

[396] Castrol Inc. v. Pennzoil Co., 987 F.2d 939, 943 (3d Cir. 1993). The Eighth Circuit, however, has taken the position that proof that the defendant acted willfully and in bad faith can substitute for proof of consumer confusion. United Indus. Corp. v. Clorox Co., 140 F.3d 1175, 1183 (8th Cir. 1998).

[397] *United Indus. Corp.,* 140 F.3d at 1180 (quoting Southland Sod Farms v. Stover Seed Co., 108 F.3d 1134, 1145 (9th Cir. 1997)); *see also* Castrol Inc. v. Pennzoil Co., 987 F.2d 939, 945 (3d Cir. 1993).

[398] United Indus. Corp., 140 F.3d at 1180 (citing Southland, 108 F.3d at 1145); *see also* Cook, Perkiss & Liehe, Inc. v. Northern California Collection Serv., Inc., 911 F.2d 242, 246 (9th Cir. 1990) (advertising that merely states in general terms that one product is superior is not actionable).

[399] United Indus. Corp., 140 F.3d at 1180; *see also Southland,* 108 F.3d at 1145; *Castrol,* 987 F.2d at 945.

[400] *Clorox,* 228 F.3d at 34; Novartis Consumer Health, Inc. v. Johnson & Johnson-Merck Consumer Pharms. Co., 290 F.3d 578, 586 (3d Cir. 2002).

be explicit; it may be "conveyed by necessary implication when, considering the advertisement in its entirety, the audience would recognize the claim as readily as if it had been explicitly stated."[401] However, the claim must still be unambiguous in order to be literally false: "The greater the degree to which a message relies upon the viewer or consumer to integrate its components and draw the apparent conclusion, . . . the less likely it is that a finding of literal falsity will be supported."[402]

In determining whether a false claim is necessarily implied by a product's name or advertisement, so that the plaintiff will not be required to submit evidence of consumer confusion, courts inquire whether, "based on a facial analysis of the product name or advertising, the consumer will unavoidably receive a false message from the product's name or advertising."[403] Thus, for example, literal falsity by necessary implication was found where a defendant claimed that its "BreathAsure" capsules were superior to gums, mints, and mouthwash at fighting bad breath because the capsules were to be swallowed, and would "fight the product at its source," falsely implying that the stomach was the source of bad breath; accordingly, both the product's name and advertising necessarily and falsely implied that the product would "assure" fresh breath.[404] Similarly, literal falsity was found where the maker of a professional model food processor ran an advertisement stating: "Robot-Coupe: 21, Cuisinart: 0. WHEN ALL 21 OF THE THREE-STAR RESTAURANTS IN FRANCE'S MICH-ELIN GUIDE CHOOSE THE SAME PROFESSIONAL MODEL FOOD PROCESSOR, SOMEBODY KNOWS THE SCORE-SHOULDN'T YOU?"[405] This statement necessarily implied (1) that Cuisinart made a professional model food processor, and that (2) the restaurants in question had chosen the Robot-Coupe model over the Cuisinart model. Because both of these implied claims were false on their face, the court issued a preliminary injunction.[406] And where a shampoo commercial depicted a female fashion model stating that the product had been tested on "over nine hundred women like me," when in fact the number of adult women tested was far smaller than that, the Second Circuit concluded that this statement was facially false and thus subject to an injunction without the necessity of proving consumer deception.[407]

In *Novartis Consumer Health, Inc. v. Johnson & Johnson-Merck Pharms. Co.*,[408] the Third Circuit considered whether the name and/or advertising of the defendant's "Mylanta Night Time Strength" heartburn remedy were "literally false by necessary implication," because they implied two claims: (1) that the product was "specially formulated" for nighttime relief, and (2) that the product

---

[401] *Clorox*, 228 F.3d at 35.

[402] *Novartis*, 290 F.3d at 587.

[403] *Id.*

[404] Warner-Lambert Co. v. BreathAsure, Inc., 204 F.3d 87, 96-97 (3d Cir. 2000).

[405] Cuisinart, Inc. v. Robot-Coupe Int'l Corp., 1982 U.S. Dist. LEXIS 13594 (S.D.N.Y. June 9, 1982).

[406] *Id.* at *6.

[407] Vidal Sassoon, Inc. v. Bristol-Myers Co., 661 F.3d 272, 277 (2d Cir. 1981).

[408] 290 F.3d 578 (3d Cir. 2002).

was superior to competing products at providing nighttime relief.[409] The court concluded that the first claim indeed followed by necessary implication from the product's name:

> [T]he MNTS name is literally false by necessary implication because it conveys the unambiguous message that the product is specially formulated to relieve nighttime heartburn. The Court found that "the product name Mylanta 'Night Time Strength' necessarily implies a false message . . . that it possesses a quality that is particularly efficacious for those suffering from heartburn at night." . . . We agree with the District Court that the term "nighttime" conveys a different meaning than the terms "regular," "extra," and "maximum." The latter terms describe different degrees of strength. . . . By contrast, the "nighttime" designation describes not a degree of strength, but rather a time when the product will be effective. The phrase "nighttime strength" therefore necessarily conveys a message that the MNTS product is specially made to work at night.[410]

However, the court held that the second claim — that the defendant's product was superior at providing nighttime relief — did not follow by necessary implication from either the name of the product or its advertising: "[C]onsumers will only receive a message of superior relief from the MNTS name and advertising if they assume that a product that provides 'Night Time' relief is more effective than a [competing] product that provides 'Extra Strength' or 'Maximum' relief. The MNTS name and advertising alone do not require that this inference will be made."[411] Because the message of superior performance was not literally conveyed (explicitly or implicitly) by the defendant's statements, the plaintiff was therefore required "to prove through a consumer survey that the name and advertising actually misled or had a tendency to mislead consumers into believing that the product provided nighttime heartburn relief superior to any other product on the market."[412]

The plaintiff's burden in establishing literal falsehood depends on the nature of the false claim. For example, a defendant's advertising may falsely claim that its product has a certain superior characteristic, or, instead, it may falsely claim that "tests prove" that the product has the claimed characteristic. Where the defendant's advertising asserts only the characteristic, and not the existence of probative tests, the plaintiff must adduce evidence affirmatively proving that the advertised assertion is false.[413] In contrast, where the defendant's advertising

---

[409] *Id.* at 587.

[410] *Id.* at 589.

[411] *Id.* at 588.

[412] *Id.*

[413] Castrol, Inc. v. Quaker State Corp., 977 F.2d 57, 63 (2d Cir. 1992); Procter & Gamble Co. v. Chesebrough-Pond's, Inc., 747 F.2d 114, 119 (2d Cir. 1984); BASF Corp. v. Old World Trading Co., 41 F.3d 1081, 1090-91 (7th Cir. 1994); United Indus. Corp. v. Clorox, 140 F.3d 1175, 1182 (8th Cir. 1998). Notably, however, the Third Circuit has taken a different position, holding that a plaintiff may establish literal falsity simply by proving that the defendant's claim is unsubstantiated. Novartis Consumer Health, Inc. v. Johnson & Johnson-Merck Pharms. Co., 290 F.3d 578, 589 (3d Cir. 2002) ("although the plaintiff normally has the burden to demonstrate that the defendant's advertising

asserts that "tests prove" that its product has the superior characteristic, the plaintiff need only establish that the tests on which the defendant rests its claim "were not sufficiently reliable to permit one to conclude with reasonable certainty that they established the proposition for which they were cited."[414] Thus, in the latter case, the plaintiff need not prove that the defendant's product in fact lacks the claimed superior characteristic; the plaintiff need only prove that the tests in question fail to support that claim. Once the plaintiff has voiced a challenge to the defendant's tests, the defendant bears the burden of identifying the tests on which it relied.[415] The plaintiff may then satisfy its burden of proof by showing either (1) that the tests are insufficiently reliable to prove the defendant's claim, or (2) that, even if reliable, the test results do not support the defendant's claim.[416]

If an advertisement is not literally false, then the plaintiff may still prevail by demonstrating that the statement has a tendency to confuse or deceive consumers. To prevail on this basis, the plaintiff must establish that (1) the defendant has made false or misleading statements of fact concerning his own product or another's; (2) the statement actually or tends to deceive a substantial portion of the intended audience; (3) the statement is material; (4) the advertisements were introduced into interstate commerce; and (5) there is some causal link between the challenged statements and injury to the plaintiff (or likelihood thereof).[417] A false or misleading statement is material if it is likely to influence a consumer's purchasing decision.[418]

Misrepresentations are actionable under section 43(a)(1)(B) only if they take place in "commercial advertising or promotion." In determining whether a particular activity constitutes commercial advertising or promotion, some courts have adopted the following approach:

> In order for representations to constitute "commercial advertising or promotion" under Section 43(a)(1)(B), they must be: (1) commercial speech; (2) by a defendant who is in commercial competition with plaintiff; (3) for the purpose of influencing consumers to buy defendant's goods or services. While the representations need not be made in a "classic advertising campaign," but may consist instead of more informal types of "promotion," the representations (4) must be disseminated sufficiently to the relevant purchasing public to constitute "advertising" or "promotion" within that industry.[419]

---

claim is false, a court may find that a completely unsubstantiated advertising claim by the defendant is per se false without additional evidence from the plaintiff to that effect").

[414] *Castrol*, 977 F.2d at 63; *accord, Chesebrough-Pond's*, 747 F.2d at 119; *BASF*, 41 F.3d at 1090-91; *United Indus. Corp.*, 140 F.3d at 1182.

[415] *Castrol*, 977 F.2d at 63.

[416] *Id.*

[417] American Council of Certified Podiatric Physicians & Surgeons v. American Bd. of Podiatric Surgery, Inc., 185 F.3d 606 (6th Cir. 1999); *accord* Pizza Hut, Inc. v. Papa John's Int'l, Inc., 227 F.3d 489 (5th Cir. 2000); *Novartis*, 290 F.3d at 590.

[418] Cashmere & Camel Hair Mfrs. Inst. v. Saks Fifth Ave., 284 F.3d 302 (1st Cir. 2002).

[419] Procter & Gamble Co. v. Haugen, 222 F.3d 1262, 1273-74 (10th Cir. 2000); *accord,* Coastal Abstract Serv., Inc. v. First Am. Tit. Ins. Co., 173 F.3d 725, 734 (9th Cir. 1999); Seven-Up Co. v.

Other courts have adopted only three prongs of this test, dispensing with the requirement that the parties be competitors.[420] For purposes of this test, courts generally follow the Supreme Court's definition of commercial speech as "speech which does no more than propose a commercial transaction."[421]

Nontraditional activities that may qualify as commercial advertising or promotion have been held to include disparaging comments made about competitors in a variety of contexts — e.g., in the course of phone conversations with customers,[422] in a trade publication,[423] and in an anonymous memorandum.[424]

However, courts have cautioned against interpreting commercial advertising or promotion so broadly as to encompass protected speech. Thus, for example, where an article in a trade publication contained comments by the owners of one art gallery challenging the authenticity of works offered by a competing gallery, the Second Circuit held that these statements were not commercial advertising or promotion even if they were widely disseminated and were intended to influence purchasers to choose the defendants' gallery over the competing gallery:

> We have little hesitation in deciding that as a matter of law the ARTnews article, and the Khidekels' statements quoted in that article, are not commercial speech. The article itself addresses a matter of public concern — fraud in the art market — and is certainly protected. The Khidekels' statements contained in the article are inextricably intertwined with the reporters' coverage of their topic. The statements by the Khidekels in ARTnews contribute to reporters' discussion of an issue of public importance and occur in a forum that has traditionally been granted full protection under the First Amendment. As always with the public expression of opinion, "we have been careful not to permit overextension of the Lanham Act to intrude on First Amendment values."[425]

Statements may be actionable under section 43(a)(1)(B) even if the speaker has not yet begun to compete in the same market as the party whose commercial activities it is disparaging.[426] Otherwise, a business entity could "destroy an

---

Coca-Cola Co., 86 F.3d 1379, 1384 (5th Cir. 1996); Gordon & Breach Sci. Pubs., S.A. v. American Inst. of Physics, 859 F. Supp. 1521, 1535-36 (S.D.N.Y. 1994).

[420] See, e.g., Galerie Gmurzynska v. Hutton, 355 F.3d 206, 210 (2d Cir. 2004).

[421] Id. (quoting City of Cincinnati v. Discovery Network, Inc., 507 U.S. 410, 422 (1993) (internal quotation marks omitted)).

[422] National Artists Mgt. Co. v. Weaving, 769 F. Supp. 1224 (S.D.N.Y. 1991).

[423] Semco, Inc. v. Amcast, Inc., 52 F.3d 108, 113-14 (6th Cir. 1995); Fuente Cigar, Ltd. v. Opus One, 985 F. Supp. 1448, 1456 (M.D. Fla. 1997). But see Gordon & Breach, 859 F. Supp. at 1541-42 (where journal of non-profit entity made disparaging comments about journal of for-profit entity, this was not "commercial advertising or promotion").

[424] H&R Indus. v. Kirshner, 899 F. Supp. 995, 1006 (E.D.N.Y. 1995).

[425] Boule v. Hutton, 328 F.3d 84, 91-92 (2d Cir. 2003) (quoting Groden v. Random House, Inc., 61 F.3d 1045, 1052 (2d Cir. 1995); see also Galerie Gmurzynska v. Hutton, 355 F.3d 206 (2d Cir. 2004) (per curiam) (neither art experts' opinions nor criticisms published in museum catalog are commercial advertising or promotion).

[426] See, e.g., Fuente Cigar, Ltd. v. Opus One, 985 F. Supp. 1448, 1456 (M.D. Fla. 1997) (party that

anticipated competitor through false representations made during the period before the commencement of the new business, and then pick up the pieces of the ruined business."[427]

Actionable misrepresentations under section 43(a)(1)(B) may pertain to goods, services, or "commercial activities." Courts have interpreted the latter phrase as encompassing a variety of commercial activities other than those that involve the offering of goods or services to the public.[428] Typically, actionable false statements pertaining to "commercial activities" are those that have the effect of tarnishing the plaintiff's general business reputation. For example, actionable misrepresentations involving a party's commercial activities have been held to include allegations that a competing manufacturer donated a share of its profits to Satan, because, "[g]iven the common association of Satan and immorality, a direct affiliation with the church of Satan could certainly undermine a corporation's reputation and goodwill by suggesting the corporation conducts its commercial activities in an unethical or immoral manner."[429] Other examples of actionable false statements regarding commercial activities other than the offering of goods or services include false allegations of improper and unethical practices,[430] of failure to pay bills,[431] and of improper solicitation of customers.[432]

Another variety of false advertising takes place when a party presents its potential customers with a picture or sample of a competitor's product, implying that this is a picture or sample of its own product, in order to solicit their patronage.[433] This type of false advertising has sometimes been treated as a false designation of origin.[434]

As noted in § 3.03 above, the Supreme Court in *Dastar Corp. v. Twentieth Century Fox Film Corp.*[435] held that a false attribution of the authorship of an *expressive* work is not actionable as a false designation of origin under section

---

made disparaging remarks in trade publication was planning to compete with the plaintiff in the market for premium cigars); National Artists Mgt. Co. v. Weaving, 769 F. Supp. 1224, 1233 (S.D.N.Y. 1991) (speaker who disparaged former employer in phone calls to customers was planning to set up competing business).

[427] *Fuente Cigar*, 985 F. Supp. at 1456 (quoting *National Artists*, 769 F. Supp. at 1234).

[428] Procter & Gamble Co. v. Haugen, 222 F.3d 1262 (10th Cir. 2000); *see also* Fuente Cigar, Ltd. v. Opus One, 985 F. Supp. 1448, 1454 (M.D. Fla. 1997) (where senior user accused junior user of deliberately imitating its trademark in order to trade on senior user's reputation, this statement concerned the commercial activities of the junior user for purposes of § 43(a)(1)(B)).

[429] *Haugen*, 222 F.3d at 1272-73.

[430] *National Artists*, 769 F. Supp. at 1229-36.

[431] Coastal Abstract Serv., Inc. v. First Am. Tit. Ins. Co., 173 F.3d 725, 732 (9th Cir. 1999).

[432] H & R. Indus., Inc. v. Kirshner, 899 F. Supp. 995, 1005-06 (E.D.N.Y. 1995).

[433] *See, e.g.*, Innovative Design Enters. v. Circulair, Inc. 1997 U.S. Dist. LEXIS 12799, *39-40 (N.D. Ill. 1997); Accurate Leather & Novelty Co. Inc. v. LTD Commodities Inc., 18 U.S.P.Q. (BNA) 2d 1327, 1329 (N.D. Ill. 1990).

[434] *See, e.g.*, Truck Equipment Service Co. v. Fruehauf Corp., 536 F.2d 1210, 1216 (8th Cir.) (misrepresenting pictures of plaintiff's product as pictures of defendant's product in sales literature is a false designation of origin actionable under § 43(a)), *cert. denied*, 429 U.S. 861 (1976); *Innovative Design*, 1997 U.S. Dist. LEXIS 12799 at *39-40 (describing this as "implied passing off"). Courts have sometimes characterized these claims as "implied reverse passing off." *See* § 3.03 *supra*.

[435] 539 U.S. 23 (2003).

43(a)(1)(A), because the term "origin" in the Lanham Act refers to the origin of tangible goods, not their intangible ideas or expressive content, and because permitting a Lanham Act claim in such circumstances would impermissibly create a "mutant" form of copyright. Although the Court also noted that some of these claims might be actionable as false advertising under section 43(a)(1)(B), the Court did not explain how a false advertising claim for misattribution of authorship would avoid the conflict with federal copyright law, nor did it explain what might constitute "commercial advertising or promotion" in the case of expressive works.[436]

Post-*Dastar*, attempts to bring false advertising claims for false attribution of authorship have been unsuccessful. The Ninth Circuit has held that *Dastar* precludes a section 43(a)(1)(B) claim arising from a defendant's actions in falsely labeling its karaoke recordings as fully licensed by the copyright owner, even though the plaintiff was not the copyright owner or exclusive licensee, but merely a competitor in the karaoke industry, and thus would have no standing to bring a copyright infringement claim.[437] Other courts have applied *Dastar* to preclude section 43(a)(1)(B) claims alleging false assertions of inventorship,[438] authorship of copyrightable works,[439] and authorship of research data,[440] on the ground that the false advertising claims were nothing more than restated claims of reverse passing-off.

PART IV:
DILUTION

§ 3.05   THE CONCEPT OF TRADEMARK DILUTION

The concept of trademark dilution gained acceptance in the mid- to late twentieth century, as trademark protection began to expand beyond its traditional goal of preventing consumer confusion and deception, and began to protect particularly strong trademarks as a form of property in themselves, whose value should be protected against unauthorized appropriation by others.

---

[436] *See, e.g.*, Zyla v. Wadsworth, 360 F.3d 243, 251-52 & n. 8 (1st Cir. 2004) (applying *Dastar* to foreclose reverse passing off claim based in failure to attribute authorship, and finding insufficient facts to conclude that the acknowledgements section of a book qualified as "commercial advertising or promotion").

[437] Sybersound Records, Inc. v. UAV Corp., 517 F.3d 1137, 1143-44 (9th Cir. 2008).

[438] Baden Sports, Inc. v. Kabushiki Kaisha Molten, 2007 U.S. Dist. LEXIS 51252 (W.D. Wash. July 16, 2007); Monsanto Co. v. Syngenta Seeds, Inc., 443 F. Supp. 2d 648, 652-53 (D. Del. 2006), *aff'd*, 503 F.3d 1352, *cert. dismissed*, __ U.S. __, 129 S. Ct. 394 (2008).

[439] Wilchcombe v. Teevee Toons, Inc., 515 F. Supp. 2d 1297, 1305-06 (N.D. Ga. 2007) (holding that false advertising claim was precluded to extent it restated reverse passing off claim, but also rejecting claim on the merits); Antidote Int'l Films, Inc. v. Bloomsbury Pub'g, PLC, 467 F. Supp. 2d 394 (S.D.N.Y. 2007) (claim based on false assertions as to novel's authorship and its semi-autobiographical nature); Thomas Pub'g Co., LLC v. Technology Evaluation Ctrs., Inc., 2007 U.S. Dist. LEXIS 55086 (July 27, 2007) (claim based on false assertion of authorship).

[440] Radolf v. University of Connecticut, 364 F. Supp. 2d 204, 222 (D. Conn. 2005).

Dilution doctrine recognizes that trademark law should protect "strong, well-recognized marks even in the absence of a likelihood of confusion, if defendant's use is such as to tarnish, degrade or dilute the distinctive quality of the mark."[441] Whereas traditional trademark infringement law has focused primarily on protecting consumers against confusion or deception about the origin of goods or services, dilution laws (also called "antidilution" laws) protect the trademark owner's investment in the goodwill that is embodied in a mark.[442]

The Ninth Circuit has offered this simple example of dilution:

> [F]or example, if a cocoa maker began using the "Rolls Royce" mark to identify its hot chocolate, no consumer confusion would be likely to result. Few would assume that the car company had expanded into the cocoa making business. However, the cocoa maker would be capitalizing on the investment the car company had made in its mark. Consumers readily associate the mark with highly priced automobiles of a certain quality. By identifying the cocoa with the Rolls Royce mark, the producer would be capitalizing on consumers' association of the mark with high quality items. Moreover, by labeling a different product "Rolls Royce," the cocoa company would be reducing the ability of the mark to identify the mark holder's product. If someone said, "I'm going to get a Rolls Royce," others could no longer be sure the person was planning on buying an expensive automobile. The person might just be planning on buying a cup of cocoa. Thus, the use of the mark to identify the hot chocolate, although not causing consumer confusion, would cause harm by diluting the mark.[443]

In contrast to the more immediate harm arising from trademark infringements that give rise to a likelihood of consumer confusion (for example, by diverting sales), some commentators describe dilution as a phenomenon that *gradually* undermines the unique selling power of a mark:

> The gravamen of a dilution complaint is that the continuing use of a mark similar to the plaintiff's mark will inexorably have an adverse effect upon the value of the plaintiff's mark, and that, if he is powerless to prevent such use, in some cases the plaintiff's mark will eventually be deprived of all distinctiveness. . . . Dilution . . . is a cancer which, if allowed to spread, will *slowly* destroy the advertising value of the mark.[444]

Because it disassociates trademark protection from consumer protection, dilution doctrine has been criticized as anticompetitive and as an unwarranted

---

[441] 2 J. Thomas McCarthy, Trademarks & Unfair Competition § 24.13, at 155 (1973).

[442] Comparing dilution with traditional infringement, the First Circuit has noted that, in dilution doctrine, "an entirely different issue is at stake — not interference with the source signaling function but rather protection from an appropriation of or free riding on the investment [the trademark holder] has made in its [trademark]." I.P. Lund Trading ApS v. Kohler Co. 163 F.3d 27, 50 (1st Cir. 1998); *accord,* Playboy Enters., Inc. v. Welles, 279 F.3d 796, 805 (9th Cir. 2002).

[443] *Playboy,* 279 F.3d at 805-06.

[444] 3 Callman, The Law of Unfair Competition, Trademarks and Monopolies § 22:13 (4th ed. 2008).

extension of trademark law. Courts have applied the doctrine warily, "lest it swallow up all competition in the claim of protection against trade name infringement."[445] Although no likelihood of confusion is necessary, the senior and junior users' use of the marks must trigger some sort of mental association in the mind of the consumer;[446] thus, dilution will ordinarily be found only if "there is at least some subliminal connection in a buyer's mind between the two parties' uses of their marks."[447]

Unlike traditional trademark and unfair competition law, the dilution doctrine is not based on common law. Rather, it is a creature of statute that owes its origin largely to an influential 1927 law review article by Frank Schechter, recommending the expansion of unfair competition doctrine beyond the common law tradition of protecting against consumer deception or confusion. Schechter argued that unfair competition law should serve the broader goal of preserving the "uniqueness of a trademark" by protecting the trademark owner against "the gradual whittling away or dispersion of the identity and hold upon the public mind of the mark or name by its use upon non-competing goods."[448]

Dilution statutes typically encompass two distinct types of injury to the trademark owner, known as "blurring" and "tarnishment."[449] Blurring has been defined as "the whittling away of an established trademark's selling power through its unauthorized use by others upon dissimilar products."[450] Hypothetical examples include "Dupont" shoes, "Buick" aspirin tablets, "Schlitz" varnish, "Kodak" pianos, and "Bulova" gowns.[451] Affording trademark owners a remedy against blurring provides them with protection in situations in which the public knows that the defendant is not affiliated with the plaintiff, so that there is no likelihood of confusion as to source, but where "the ability of the plaintiff's mark to serve as a unique identifier of the plaintiff's goods or services is weakened because the relevant public now also associates that designation with a new and different source."[452]

Tarnishment, in contrast, typically occurs when a plaintiff's mark is "linked to products of shoddy quality, or is portrayed in an unwholesome or unsavory context, with the end result that the public will associate the lack of quality or lack of prestige in the defendant's goods with the plaintiff's unrelated goods."[453]

---

[445] Coffee Dan's, Inc. v. Coffee Don's Charcoal Broiler, 305 F. Supp. 1210, 1217 n. 13 (N.D. Cal. 1969).

[446] Mead Data Cent., Inc. v. Toyota Motor Sales, U.S.A., Inc., 875 F.2d 1026, 1031 (2d Cir. 1989).

[447] Fruit of the Loom, Inc. v. Girouard, 994 F.2d 1359, 1363 (9th Cir. 1993).

[448] Schecter, *The Rational Basis of Trademark Protection*, 40 Harv. L. Rev. 813, 825 (1927).

[449] *See* New York Stock Exch., Inc., v. New York, New York Hotel, LLC, 293 F.3d 550, 557 (2d Cir. 2002).

[450] Mead Data Central, Inc. v. Toyota Motor Sales, U.S.A., Inc., 875 F.2d 1026, 1031 (2d Cir. 1989).

[451] *Id.* (quoting the legislative history of New York's antidilution statute).

[452] Mastercard Int'l, Inc. v. Nader 2000 Primary Comm., Inc., 70 U.S.P.Q.2d (BNA) 1046, 1052 (S.D.N.Y. 2004) (citing Federal Express Corp. v. Federal Espresso, Inc., 201 F.3d 168, 174 (2d Cir. 2000); Sports Auth. v. Prime Hospitality Corp., 89 F.3d 955, 965-66 (2d Cir. 1996)).

[453] *New York Stock Exch.*, 293 F.3d at 558 (internal quotation marks omitted); *See, e.g.,* Dallas

These negative associations result in injury to the goodwill associated with the plaintiff's mark.[454] For example, tarnishment is routinely found where the defendant uses the plaintiff's mark in connection with pornographic material.[455]

However, courts have also held that "tarnishment is not limited to seamy conduct."[456] For example, the Second Circuit allowed the New York Stock Exchange (NYSE) to proceed with its dilution claim against a New York-themed casino for using modified versions of the NYSE's marks in various aspects of its gaming activities. In that case, the court found no blurring of the capacity of the NYSE's marks to serve as a unique identifier of its products and services, and it also found that the context in which the casino used the marks was humorous; nonetheless, the court found that tarnishment was possible:

> NYSE would also like to preserve a reputation for integrity and transparency in the trading conducted on its floor. A reasonable trier of fact might therefore find that the Casino's humorous analogy to its activities — deemed by many to involve odds stacked heavily in favor of the house — would injure NYSE's reputation.[457]

Circuit Judge Posner has identified three possible rationales for granting trademark owners protection against unauthorized uses that are both non-competing and non-confusing:

> First, there is concern that consumer search costs will rise if a trademark becomes associated with a variety of unrelated products. Suppose an upscale restaurant calls itself "Tiffany." There is little danger that the consuming public will think it's dealing with a branch of the Tiffany jewelry store if it patronizes this restaurant. But when consumers next see the name "Tiffany" they may think about both the restaurant and the jewelry store, and if so the efficacy of the name as an identifier of the store will be diminished. Consumers will have to think harder — incur as it were a higher imagination cost — to recognize the name as the name of the store. So "blurring" is one form of dilution.

Cowboys Cheerleaders, Inc. v. Pussycat Cinema, Ltd., 604 F.2d 200, 205 & n. 8 (2d Cir. 1979) (finding injury to business reputation where defendant's adult film featured cheerleader uniforms similar to plaintiff's); Eastman Kodak Co. v. Rakow, 739 F. Supp. 116 (W.D.N.Y. 1989) (issuing preliminary injunction against use of stage name "Kodak" by entertainer who performed "raunchy" comedy act); Coca-Cola Co. v. Gemini Rising, Inc., 346 F. Supp. 1183, 1191-92 (E.D.N.Y. 1972) (granting preliminary injunction where defendant's poster displayed "Enjoy Cocaine" in lettering and colors similar to senior user's "Enjoy Coca-Cola" mark).

[454] *New York Stock Exch.*, 293 F.3d at 558; Hormel Foods Corp. v. Jim Henson Productions, Inc., 73 F.3d 497, 507 (2d Cir. 1996).

[455] *See, e.g.*, Lucent Techs., Inc. v. Johnson, 56 U.S.P.Q.2d (BNA) 1637 (C.D. Cal 2000) (allegation that defendant used plaintiff's mark as domain name for pornographic web site stated a claim for dilution); Mattel, Inc. v. Internet Dimensions, Inc., 2000 U.S. Dist. LEXIS 9747 (S.D.N.Y. July 13, 2000) (finding defendant's registration of barbiesplaypen.com to divert users to a site displaying pornographic content tarnished the goodwill of plaintiff's BARBIE mark); Hasbro Inc. v. Internet Entertainment Group, Ltd., 40 U.S.P.Q.2D (BNA) 1479, 1480, 1996 U.S. Dist. LEXIS 11626 (W.D. Wash. 1996) (finding defendants had diluted plaintiff's mark for its board game "Candy Land," by registering the domain name candyland.com and displaying pornography there).

[456] *N.Y. Stock Exch.*, 293 F.3d at 558 (quoting *Hormel Foods*, 73 F.3d at 507).

[457] *Id.*

Now suppose that the "restaurant" that adopts the name "Tiffany" is actually a striptease joint. Again, and indeed even more certainly than in the previous case, consumers will not think the striptease joint under common ownership with the jewelry store. But because of the inveterate tendency of the human mind to proceed by association, every time they think of the word "Tiffany" their image of the fancy jewelry store will be tarnished by the association of the word with the strip joint. So "tarnishment" is a second form of dilution. Analytically it is a subset of blurring, since it reduces the distinctness of the trademark as a signifier of the trademarked product or service.

Third, and most far-reaching in its implications for the scope of the concept of dilution, there is a possible concern with situations in which, though there is neither blurring nor tarnishment, someone is still taking a free ride on the investment of the trademark owner in the trademark. Suppose the "Tiffany" restaurant in our first hypothetical example is located in Kuala Lumpur and though the people who patronize it (it is upscale) have heard of the Tiffany jewelry store, none of them is ever going to buy anything there, so that the efficacy of the trademark as an identifier will not be impaired. If appropriation of Tiffany's aura is nevertheless forbidden by an expansive concept of dilution, the benefits of the jewelry store's investment in creating a famous name will be, as economists say, "internalized" — that is, Tiffany will realize the full benefits of the investment rather than sharing those benefits with others — and as a result the amount of investing in creating a prestigious name will rise.[458]

The question whether trademarks, even famous ones, should be protected against dilution remains controversial. Many respected commentators view the alleged harm from dilution as highly speculative.[459]

§ 3.06 STATE DILUTION LAWS

Dilution laws are of much more recent vintage than traditional trademark and unfair competition laws. The first dilution statute in the United States was enacted by Massachusetts in 1947.[460] Today, however, nearly three-quarters of the states have enacted dilution legislation.[461] With rare exceptions, state dilution laws are exclusively statutory.

Like traditional trademark laws, state dilution laws protect only those trademarks that are distinctive — that is, marks that are arbitrary, fanciful, or

---

[458] Ty, Inc. v. Perryman, 306 F.3d 509, 511-12 (7th Cir. 2002) (citations omitted) (expressing doubt regarding the merits of the third rationale).

[459] See, e.g., McCarthy on Trademarks, supra note 223, at § 24:67 & n. 16.

[460] Mass. Gen. Laws Ann. Ch. 110B, § 12 (2005).

[461] These include Alabama, Alaska, Arizona, Arkansas, California, Connecticut, Delaware, Florida, Georgia, Hawaii, Idaho, Illinois, Iowa, Kansas, Louisiana, Maine, Massachusetts, Minnesota, Mississippi, Missouri, Montana, Nebraska, Nevada, New Hampshire, New Jersey, New Mexico, New York, Oregon, Pennsylvania, Rhode Island, South Carolina, Tennessee, Texas, Utah, Washington, West Virginia, and Wyoming.

suggestive, or those that, while descriptive, have achieved distinctiveness through the acquisition of secondary meaning in the marketplace.[462] In some states, any distinctive mark is eligible for dilution protection.[463] In other states, however, it is not enough for the mark merely to be distinctive enough to serve as a trademark; it must be "highly distinctive," "strong," or "famous." In some states, this requirement is expressly imposed by the dilution statute,[464] while in others it results from judicial interpretations of the statute.[465] However, the trend is increasingly toward incorporating a "fame" requirement into the statute itself, reflecting the tendency of the states after 1995 to conform their dilution laws to the federal statute. Where there have already been some third-party uses of a mark, it may be especially difficult for the senior user to establish that the mark is strong enough to warrant protection against dilution; a court may find that the mark has already been so diluted that it lacks the degree of distinctiveness necessary to merit protection against further dilution.[466]

The requirement that a mark be more than merely distinctive in order to be protected from dilution is endorsed by the *Restatement (Third) of Unfair Competition*, which notes:

> The cause of action for dilution protects the selling power of a mark. Not all marks that identify the source or sponsorship of goods or services warrant such protection. To possess the selling power protected by the anti-dilution statutes, the mark must have a degree of distinctiveness beyond that needed for the designation to function as a valid trademark. The required standard of distinctiveness, however, cannot be defined by bright-line rules. A trademark is sufficiently distinctive to be diluted by a nonconfusing use if the mark retains its source significance when encountered outside the context of the goods or services with which it is used by the trademark owner. For example, the trademark KODAK evokes an association with the cameras sold under that mark whether the word is displayed with the cameras or used in the abstract. On the other hand, the designation ALPHA may become sufficiently distinctive to identify a source of cameras when it is affixed to the cameras, but its use alone and out of its market context may continue to evoke many different associations, including nothing more than the first letter of the

---

[462] *See, e.g.*, O.C.G.A. § 10-1-451(b) (2004); Dolphin Homes Corp. v. Tocome Dev. Corp., 223 Ga. 455 (1967).

[463] *See, e.g.*, Or. Rev. Stat. § 647.107 (2003).

[464] *See, e.g.*, Rev. Code Wash. § 19.77.010(6), .160 (2008).

[465] *See, e.g.*, Advantage Rent-A-Car, Inc. v. Enter. Rent-A-Car Co., 238 F.3d 378, 381 (5th Cir. 2001) (using factors similar to federal "fame" factors to assess whether mark is distinctive enough for protection under Texas statute); Scholastic, Inc. v. Time Warner Ent. Co., L.P., 221 F. Supp. 2d 425, 437-38 (S.D.N.Y. 2002) (requiring mark to be "extremely strong" under New York statute), *aff'd*, Scholastic, Inc. v. Stouffer, 81 Fed. Appx. 396, 2003 U.S. App. LEXIS 24243 (2d Cir. 2003); ESPN, Inc. v. Quiksilver, Inc., 2008 U.S. Dist. LEXIS 95690, *21 (S.D.N.Y. 2008) (mark must be "extremely strong" under New York statute, but need not be "famous"); *but see* Wedgwood Homes, Inc. v. Lund, 58 Or. App. 240, 245-51 (1982) (refusing to impose such a gloss on Oregon statute), *aff'd*, 294 Or. 493 (1983).

[466] *See, e.g.*, Astra Pharmaceutical Prods., Inc. v. Beckman Instruments, Inc., 718 F.2d 1201, 1210 (1st Cir. 1983) (applying Massachusetts law).

Greek alphabet. A mark that evokes an association with a specific source only when used with the particular goods or services that it identifies is not sufficiently distinctive to be protected under the antidilution statutes.[467]

The *Restatement* applies the following test to determine whether a mark is highly distinctive:

A number of factors are relevant to whether a mark has acquired sufficient distinctiveness to be protected from dilution, including the inherent distinctiveness and uniqueness of the mark, the duration and extent of its use, the duration and extent of advertising that emphasizes the mark, and the degree of recognition by prospective purchasers. Third party uses of the mark either as a trade symbol or in other contexts also is an important factor in assessing distinctiveness. Concurrent use by other firms makes it unlikely that consumers will form a single mental association with the mark.

There is nothing in the requirement that the mark be highly distinctive that necessarily limits dilution protection to coined or fanciful marks. It is possible that an arbitrary mark, or even a mark that was originally descriptive but that has acquired secondary meaning, may by extensive advertising and long and exclusive use acquire a sufficiently high degree of distinctiveness to justify protection against dilution. However, this will rarely be the case because competitors and others remain entitled to use such words in their primary, lexicographic sense, and this permissible alternative use makes it unlikely that consumers will associate the designation exclusively with the trademark owner.[468]

While dilution is broadly defined as "the gradual 'whittling away' of a trademark's value,"[469] state dilution laws generally recognize two types of dilution: blurring and tarnishment. Blurring occurs when another's use of a mark creates "the possibility that the mark will lose its ability to serve as a unique identifier of the plaintiff's product," while tarnishment occurs "when a famous mark is improperly associated with an inferior or offensive product or service."[470]

Apocryphal but oft-cited examples of dilution in the absence of competition include "DuPont" shoes, "Buick" aspirin, "Kodak" pianos, "Schlitz" varnish, and "Bulova" gowns;[471] case law has protected the "Tiffany" mark for jewelry stores

---

[467] Rest. (Third) of Unfair Competition § 25, comment e (Tent. Draft No. 2, 1990).

[468] *Id.*; *see, e.g.*, Great Southern Bank v. First Southern Bank, 625 So.2d 463, 470-71 (1993) (applying Restatement analysis to Florida statute).

[469] Academy of Motion Picture Arts & Sciences v. Creative House Promotions, Inc., 944 F.2d 1446, 1457 (9th Cir. 1991) (citing J. McCarthy, Trademarks and Unfair Competition, § 24:13 (2d ed. 1984)).

[470] Playboy Enters., Inc. v. Welles, 279 F.3d 796, 805 (9th Cir. 2002); Panavision Int'l, L.P. v. Toeppen, 141 F.3d 1316, 1326 n. 7 (9th Cir. 1998).

[471] *See, e.g.*, Mead Data Cent., Inc. v. Toyota Motor Sales, U.S.A., Inc., 875 F.2d 1026, 1031 (2d Cir. 1989); 141 Cong. Rec. H14317 (daily ed. Dec. 12, 1995) (statement of Rep. Moorehead), *quoted in* Viacom, Inc. v. Ingram Enters., Inc., 141 F.3d 886, 888 (8th Cir. 1998).

against appropriation by a movie company[472] as well as a restaurant,[473] and has granted relief to the maker of "Rolls Royce" automobiles against "Rolls Royce" radio tubes.[474]

Courts generally do not require marks to be identical in order to find dilution. Examples of marks found to be sufficiently similar to be dilutive include "Polaroid" and "Polaraid,"[475] "The Greatest Show on Earth" and "The Greatest Used Car Show on Earth"[476] "Saks Fifth Avenue" and "Sacks Thrift Avenue"[477] and "Godiva" and "Dogiva" (as well as "Cativa").[478] However, the Second Circuit held that "LEXIS" and "LEXUS" were not sufficiently similar to support a dilution claim; reversing the finding of the District Court, the Court of Appeals insisted that, even when the words were heard rather than seen, there was "no substantial similarity" between the marks.[479]

Many state dilution laws provide relief to plaintiffs that establish a *likelihood* of dilution. In those states, a plaintiff need not offer evidence that dilution has already occurred;[480] it is enough to establish that the defendant's activities create a likelihood of dilution either through blurring or tarnishment (referred to in many states as "injury to business reputation").[481] Typically, the court's assessment of the likelihood of dilution is based upon a number of factors that bear a slight resemblance to the "likelihood of confusion" factors, with the notable exception that they do not consider the existence of actual confusion. For example, federal courts interpreting New York's dilution statute[482] often (though not always) consider the following list of factors to determine a likelihood of blurring: "(i) the similarity of the marks; (ii) the similarity of the products covered; (iii) the sophistication of the consumers; (iv) the existence of predatory intent; (v) the renown of the senior mark; and (vi) the renown of the junior mark."[483]

---

[472] Tiffany & Co. v. Tiffany Prods., Inc., 264 N.Y.S. 459 (N.Y. Sup. Ct. 1932), *aff'd*, 260 N.Y.S. 821 (N.Y. App. Div. 1932), *aff'd*, 262 N.Y. 482 (1933).

[473] Tiffany & Co. v. Boston Club, Inc., 231 F. Supp. 836, 844 (D. Mass. 1964).

[474] Wall v. Rolls-Royce of America, Inc., 4 F.2d 333 (3d Cir. 1925).

[475] Polaroid Corp. v. Polaraid, Inc., 319 F.2d 830 (7th Cir. 1963).

[476] Ringling Bros.-Barnum & Bailey Combined Shows, Inc. v. Celozzi-Ettelson Chevrolet, Inc., 855 F.2d 480 (7th Cir. 1988).

[477] Saks & Co. v. Hill, 843 F. Supp. 620, 625 (S.D. Cal. 1993) (describing marks as "similar in sight and sound"), *appeal dismissed*, 65 F.3d 175 (9th Cir. 1995).

[478] Grey v. Campbell Soup Co., 650 F. Supp. 1166 (C.D. Cal. 1986), *aff'd*, 830 F.2d 197 (9th Cir. 1987).

[479] Mead Data Cent., Inc. v. Toyota Motor Sales, U.S.A., Inc., 875 F.2d 1026, 1030 (2d Cir. 1989).

[480] *See, e.g.*, Pfizer, Inc. v. Y2K Shipping & Trading, Inc., 2004 U.S. Dist. LEXIS 10426, at *28, n. 8 (2004) (applying New York statute).

[481] Glen Raven Mills, Inc. v. Ramada Int'l, Inc., 852 F. Supp. 1544, 1556-57 (M.D. Fla. 1994) (applying Florida statute); E. & J. Gallo Winery v. Consorzio Del Gallo Nero, 782 F. Supp. 457, 469 (N.D. Cal. 1991) (applying California statute).

[482] N.Y. Gen. Bus. L. § 360-l (McKinney Supp. 2004).

[483] *See, e.g.*, N.Y. Stock Exch., Inc. v. New York, New York Hotel, L.L.C., 293 F.3d 550, 558 (2d Cir. 2002).

In contrast, the language of some state dilution statutes provides relief against activities that "cause dilution" of a plaintiff's mark. As illustrated by the Supreme Court's interpretation of similar language in the original (1995) version of the federal dilution statute in *Moseley v. V Secret Catalog*,[484] this can be interpreted to require proof of *actual* dilution, rather than a mere likelihood of dilution. This is particularly problematic for state dilution statutes that track the language of the original federal statute, and that have not been revised since the 2003 *Moseley* decision or the legislative overruling of that decision in 2006.[485] As discussed in § 3.07 [G] below, actual dilution is significantly harder to prove than mere likelihood of dilution.

In jurisdictions that require a mark to be highly distinctive, strong, or famous in order to be protected against dilution, the question arises as to what segment of the consuming public must be examined to make this determination. For example, in *Mead Data Central, Inc. v. Toyota Motor Sales, U.S.A., Inc.*, the Second Circuit held that, for purposes of New York's dilution statute, the plaintiff's mark could be protected against dilution only if it had "a distinctive quality for a significant percentage of the defendant's market."[486] Because the plaintiff's mark was well-known only to a small segment of the general public, it did not have sufficient fame to be protected:

> [I]f a mark circulates only in a limited market, it is unlikely to be associated generally with the mark for a dissimilar product circulating elsewhere. . . . [S]uch distinctiveness as LEXIS possesses is limited to the narrow market of attorneys and accountants. Moreover, the process which LEXIS represents is widely disparate from the product represented by LEXUS. For the general public, LEXIS has no distinctive quality that LEXUS will dilute.[487]

Under certain circumstances, federal law provides a complete defense to a state law dilution claim. Despite the variations in state dilution laws, section 43(c) of the Lanham Act provides that if the allegedly dilutive mark is the subject of a valid registration on the Principal Register,[488] the owner of the federal registration has a complete defense to any state law claim asserting blurring, tarnishment, or other harm to the distinctiveness or reputation of a mark.[489]

Unlike the federal dilution statute, many state dilution laws do not contain express exceptions for news reporting or other noncommercial speech.[490] Nonetheless, it is clear that state dilution laws should not be enforced where they

---

[484] 537 U.S. 418 (2003). See § 3.07 [G][1]*infra*.

[485] *See, e.g.*, Nev. Rev. Stat. § 600.435(1) (2005).

[486] 875 F.2d 1026, 1031 (2d Cir. 1989).

[487] *Id.*

[488] The defense also applies if the allegedly dilutive mark was registered under the Act of March 3, 1881, or February 20, 1905. 15 U.S.C. § 1125(c)(3).

[489] 15 U.S.C. § 1125(c)(6).

[490] *E.g.*, N.Y. Gen. Bus. § 360-l (2008); Ann. Laws Mass. ch. 110H, § 13 (2008); 10 Me. Rev. Stat. § 1530 (2008). However, there are exceptions. *E.g.*, Pa. C.S. § 1124 (containing exceptions paralleling those in the 1995 version of section 43(c).

would interfere with speech protected by the First Amendment.[491]

§ 3.07   THE FEDERAL TRADEMARK DILUTION ACT

[A]   History

In 1995, the Federal Trademark Dilution Act (FTDA)[492] added section 43(c) to the Lanham Act, affording the trademark owner a federal remedy "against another person's commercial use in commerce of a mark or trade name, if such use begins after the mark has become famous and causes dilution of the distinctive quality of the mark,"[493] regardless of the absence of competition or confusion.[494] The legislative history of the Act indicates that its purpose was "to protect famous trademarks from subsequent uses that blur the distinctiveness of the mark or tarnish or disparage it, even in the absence of a likelihood of confusion."[495] By providing a federal remedy for dilution, Congress sought to discourage forum-shopping and provide plaintiffs with the opportunity for nationwide injunctive relief.[496] The protection of section 43(c) is available to both registered and unregistered marks.

In 2006, Congress enacted the Trademark Dilution Revision Act (TDRA)[497] in order to clarify several aspects of section 43(c). In the discussion below, major differences between the 1995 and 2006 versions of the federal dilution statute are noted where relevant.

[B]   Elements of a Federal Dilution Claim

To qualify for relief under the 2006 amendments to section 43(c), the plaintiff must establish that:

(1)   the plaintiff owns a mark that is both famous and distinctive; and

(2)   after the plaintiff's mark became famous, the defendant commenced use of a mark or trade name in commerce that is likely to cause dilution of the famous mark either by blurring or by tarnishment.[498]

---

[491]   *See, e.g.*, L.L. Bean, Inc. v. Drake Pub., Inc., 811 F.2d 26 (1st Cir. 1987); American Family Life Ins. Co. v. Hagan, 266 F. Supp. 2d 682, 693 (N.D. Ohio 2002); Mattel, Inc. v. MCA Records, Inc., 28 F. Supp. 2d 1120, 1154 n. 53 (C.D. Cal. 1998), *aff'd*, 296 F.3d 894 (9th Cir. 2002), *cert. denied*, 537 U.S. 1171 (2003); New Kids on the Block v. News America Publishing, Inc., 745 F. Supp. 1540, 1542 n. 1 (C.D. Cal. 1990), *aff'd*, 971 F.2d 302 (9th Cir. 1992). For further discussion of conflicts between trademark and unfair competition laws and the First Amendment, see § 3.11 *infra*.

[492]   P.L. 104-98, § 3(a), 109 Stat. 985 (1995).

[493]   15 U.S.C. § 1125(c)(1).

[494]   TCPIP Holding Co. v. Haar Communications, Inc., 244 F.3d 88, 95 (2d Cir. 2001).

[495]   H.R. Rep. No. 374, 104th Cong., 1st Sess. 3 (1995); 1995 U.S. Code Cong. & Admin. News 1029, 1030.

[496]   Ringling Bros.-Barnum & Bailey Combined Shows, Inc. v. B.E. Windows Corp., 937 F. Supp. 204, 208 (S.D.N.Y. 1996).

[497]   P.L. 109-312, 120 Stat. 1730 (Oct. 6, 2006).

[498]   15 U.S.C. § 1125(c)(1); PepsiCo, Inc. v. #1 Wholesale, LLC, 84 U.S.P.Q.2d (BNA) 1040 (N.D. Ga. July 20, 2007).

Liability for dilution by blurring or tarnishment may arise even where there is no actual or likely confusion, no competition, and no actual economic injury.

The amended statute's reference to dilution by blurring and dilution by tarnishment is more specific than the original version of section 43(c), which defined dilution simply as "the lessening of the capacity of a famous mark to identify and distinguish goods or services." Although the lower federal courts had interpreted this definition to encompass both blurring and tarnishment,[499] in 2003 the Supreme Court cast doubt on this conclusion in *Moseley v. V Secret Catalog*.[500] Comparing the language of section 43(c) with the language of state antidilution laws that expressly referred to injury to business reputation as well as dilution of the distinctive quality of a mark, the Court suggested that this contrast "arguably supports a narrower reading of" section 43(c).[501] In response, Congress amended this language in the 2006 TDRA to make clear that section 43(c) encompasses both blurring and tarnishment claims. To accomplish this, the TDRA eliminated the general definition of dilution, and replaced it with specific definitions of dilution by blurring and dilution by tarnishment. Section 43(c) now defines "dilution by blurring" as an "association arising from the similarity between a mark or trade name and a famous mark that impairs the distinctiveness of the famous mark,"[502] and defines "dilution by tarnishment" as an "association arising from the similarity between a mark or trade name and a famous mark that harms the reputation of the famous mark."[503]

Under the 1995 version of section 43(c)(1), a dilution claim could be brought only where the defendant's use of the famous mark constituted a "commercial use in commerce." As discussed in § 3.07 [H][2] below, this limitation to "commercial" uses created some confusion, because section 43(c)(4) expressly exempted "any noncommercial use" of a mark. The TDRA reduced this confusion by broadening the language of section 43(c)(1) to refer simply to the

---

[499] Deborah Heart & Lung Ctr. v. Children of the World Found., Ltd., 99 F. Supp. 2d 481 (D.N.J. 2000). *See, e.g.*, Kraft Foods Holdings, Inc. v. Helm, 205 F. Supp. 2d 942 (N.D. Ill. 2002) (finding likely tarnishment of "Velveeta" mark where defendant used "VelVeeda" on website depicting graphic sexuality and illustrations of drug use and paraphernalia); Hasbro, Inc. v. Internet Ent. Group., Ltd., 1996 U.S. Dist. LEXIS 11626, *2 (W.D. Wash. 1996) (finding likely dilution of "Candy Land" mark where defendant used "candyland.com" as the domain name of a sexually explicit website).

[500] 537 U.S. 418 (2003).

[501] *Id.* at 432.

[502] 15 U.S.C. § 1125(c)(2)(B).

[503] *Id.* § 1125(c)(2)(C). The Fourth Circuit incorporated these definitions into its statement of the elements of a TDRA dilution claim in *Louis Vuitton Malletier S.A. v. Haute Diggity Dog, LLC*, 507 F.3d 252, 264-65 (4th Cir. 2007):

[T]o state a dilution claim under the TDRA, a plaintiff must show:

(1) that the plaintiff owns a famous mark that is distinctive;

(2) that the defendant has commenced using a mark in commerce that allegedly is diluting the famous mark;

(3) that a similarity between the defendant's mark and the famous mark gives rise to an association between the marks; and

(4) that the association is likely to impair the distinctiveness of the famous mark or likely to harm the reputation of the famous mark.

"use of a mark or trade name in commerce." Although this language has not yet been interpreted by the court, under the Lanham Act a "use in commerce" is considered to be a use "in the ordinary course of trade" on goods that are sold or transported in commerce, or on services that are rendered in commerce, where "commerce" refers to all trade that Congress has the authority to regulate.[504]

Section 43(c) requires the dilution plaintiff to be the "owner" of the famous mark.[505] This requirement was in the original FTDA, and was not altered by the 2006 amendments. This standing requirement roughly parallels the standing rule for infringement of registered marks under section 32(1),[506] and differs from the more liberal rules for unfair competition and false advertising claims under section 43(a).[507]

[C]   Trademark Use

Occasionally, courts have considered the question whether a defendant's use of another's famous mark must be a "trademark use" in order to be dilutive.[508] While the statutory language makes clear that the defendant must be using the famous mark "in commerce" — meaning in connection with offering goods or services to the public in trade that Congress has the authority to regulate,[509] it is not clear whether that use must be as an *origin indicator*. On this point, the language of both the 1995 and 2006 versions of the statute is ambiguous: The FTDA applied to a "commercial use in commerce of a mark or trade name, if such use . . . causes dilution" of the famous mark, and the TDRA applies to a "use of a mark or trade name in commerce that is likely to cause dilution . . . of the famous mark."

Courts interpreting the original FTDA reached conflicting conclusions on this question.[510] However, the TDRA is somewhat less ambiguous than the FTDA on this point, and appears to permit dilution liability to be premised on use of a

---

[504] 15 U.S.C. § 1127; *see also* § 3.02 [F] *supra*.

[505] *See* Hyundai Constr. Equip. U.S.A., Inc. v. Chris Johnson Equip., Inc., 2008 U.S. Dist. LEXIS 84687, *9-10 (N.D. Ill. Sept. 10, 2008) (dilution plaintiff must have property interest in famous mark at time of offending conduct); *see also* § 3.18 [C] *infra*.

[506] 15 U.S.C. § 1114(1); *see* § 3.18 [B] *infra*.

[507] 15 U.S.C. § 1125(a); *see* § 3.18 [D] *infra*.

[508] Nabisco, Inc. v. PF Brands, Inc., 191 F.3d 208, 223 (2d Cir. 1999) (finding it unnecessary to resolve this "complicated" question).

[509] For a broader discussion of the "trademark use" requirement, see § 3.02 [E] *supra*.

[510] *Compare* Avery Dennison Corp. v. Sumpton, 189 F.3d 868, 880 (9th Cir. 1999) (defendants did not make commercial use of plaintiffs' marks because they "[did] not use trademarks qua trademarks," but instead "used words that happen to be trademarks for their non-trademark value") *and* Bird v. Parsons, 289 F.3d 865, 880 (6th Cir. 2002) (offering domain name for sale is not commercial use) *with* Panavision Int'l, L.P. v. Toeppen, 141 F.3d 1316, 1325 (9th Cir. 1998) (registering trademarks as domain names containing famous marks and selling them back to their trademark owners was commercial use); Horphag Research, Ltd. v. Garcia, 475 F.3d 1029, 1033-37 (9th Cir. 2007) (finding dilution where defendant used plaintiff's mark as metatag and as generic term for product); *and* Kinetic Concepts, Inc. v. Bluesky Med. Group, 2005 U.S. Dist. LEXIS 32353, *14 (W.D. Tex. Nov. 1, 2005) (even where defendant is not using marks to indicate origin of own products, its "associational, non-trademark use" supports dilution claim).

mark other than as an indication of origin for the defendant's goods or services. As discussed in § 3.07 [H] below, the TDRA's exemptions from dilution liability include "any fair use, including a nominative or descriptive fair use" of the famous mark "other than as a designation of source" for the defendant's own goods or services. Congress's decision to restrict this exemption to "fair use" situations implies that it did not intend to create a general exception for all uses "other than as a designation of source." So far, the one court that has addressed this question under the TDRA has held that liability for dilution is not restricted to use of the famous mark as an origin indicator for the defendant's goods, so long as consumers perceive the mark as *someone's* trademark.[511]

Most state dilution statutes are ambiguous on this point as well,[512] although the state law question has rarely, if ever, been litigated.

[D]   Distinctive and Famous Marks

Unlike state dilution laws that require merely that the senior user's mark have sufficient distinctiveness to warrant trademark protection, section 43(c) protects only those marks that are both *distinctive* and *famous*. Under the 1995 statute, the requirement of distinctiveness was implicit; however, the 2006 amendments made this requirement explicit and also clarified its meaning. And while the 1995 statute explicitly stated that protection was limited to famous marks, the 2006 amendments clarified and narrowed the meaning of fame.

[1]   Distinctiveness

Under the 1995 statute, there were conflicting interpretations of the requirement that the mark be distinctive. Most circuits interpreted this as a requirement that the mark be *either* (1) inherently distinctive, or (2) descriptive with secondary meaning.[513] In some cases, courts seemed to assume that a famous mark was *per se* distinctive; once the court determined that the mark was famous, it treated the mark as eligible for protection under section 43(c) without undertaking an explicit analysis of the mark's distinctiveness.[514] A leading commentator suggested that the latter approach was consistent with the intent of Congress, and that treating distinctiveness as a requirement separate

---

[511] Adidas Am., Inc. v. Payless Shoesource, Inc., 2008 U.S. Dist. LEXIS 69260, *20-22 (D. Or. Sept. 12, 2008).

[512] *See, e.g.,* N.Y. Gen. Bus. § 360-l (2008).

[513] *See, e.g.,* Thane, Int'l v. Trek Bicycle Corp., 305 F.3d 894, 912 (9th Cir. 2002); *Times Mirror Magazines*, 212 F.3d at 166 ("The Sporting News" is descriptive mark with high degree of acquired distinctiveness, and is also famous for purposes of section 43(c)); NBBJ East L.P. v. NBBJ Training Acad., Inc., 201 F. Supp. 2d 800, 806 (S.D. Ohio 2001). *Cf.* Avery Dennison Corp. v. Sumpton, 189 F.3d 868, 876-77 (9th Cir. 1999) (plaintiff's marks were surnames with sufficient acquired distinctiveness to satisfy section 43(c), but they lacked sufficient renown to be famous).

[514] *See, e.g.,* Ty, Inc. v. Perryman, 306 F.3d 509, 511, 513-14 (7th Cir. 2002) (recognizing that "Beanie Babies" mark is descriptive, but also famous for purposes of section 43(c)); Ringling Bros.-Barnum & Bailey Combined Shows v. Utah Div. of Travel Dev't, 955 F. Supp. 605, 613 & n. 4 (E.D. Va. 1997) (concluding, based on survey evidence indicating high degree of consumer recognition, that "The Greatest Show on Earth" is a famous mark), *aff'd,* 170 F.3d 449 (4th Cir. 1999).

from fame was simply redundant.[515]

The Second Circuit adopted a more restrictive view. Even though the first item listed in the 1995 "fame and distinctiveness" factors was "the degree of inherent *or* acquired distinctiveness of the mark," the Second Circuit required the plaintiff's mark to have *both* inherent and acquired distinctiveness, and therefore refused to extend the protection of section 43(c) to descriptive marks regardless of their degree of secondary meaning.[516] Under this approach, federal dilution law protected only arbitrary, fanciful, or suggestive marks.[517]

The TDRA clearly rejects the Second Circuit's approach. Now, section 43(c)(1) explicitly extends dilution protection to famous marks that are "distinctive, inherently or through acquired distinctiveness." Thus, under the 2006 amendments, a descriptive mark with secondary meaning is entitled to the same federal dilution protection as a mark that is arbitrary, fanciful, or suggestive — in each case, the dilution statute applies once the mark has become famous.

[2]   Fame

Although the 1995 statute included a list of factors that a court could (but was not required to) consider in assessing whether a mark was famous and distinctive,[518] determining whether a particular mark was famous proved to be a difficult interpretive problem. In general, courts applied a rigorous standard, reflecting the perspective that "[d]ilution is a cause of action invented and reserved for a select class of marks — those marks with such powerful

---

[515] McCarthy on Trademarks, *supra* note 223, at § 24:91.

[516] *See, e.g., Savin Corp.*, 391 F.3d at 449; *TCPIP Holding Co.*, 244 F.3d at 97-98.

[517] Even under the 1995 statute, this interpretation was unsupported by the statutory language; in addition to the clearly disjunctive test for distinctiveness that was outlined in the first "fame" factor, section 43(c)(1) stated that the owner of a famous mark was entitled to injunctive relief whenever a defendant's use diluted "the distinctive quality" of that mark. Because section 43(c) did not provide a specialized definition of distinctiveness, the meaning of that term elsewhere in the Lanham Act should have controlled. Section 2(f) of the Lanham Act specifically contemplates that a descriptive mark may become distinctive through use, 15 U.S.C. § 1052(f), as is true of unregistered marks protected by section 43(a), *id.* § 1125(a).

[518] To guide a court's assessment as to whether a particular mark was both "distinctive and famous," the 1995 version of section 43(c)(1) provided the following non-exhaustive list of factors that might be considered:

(A) the degree of inherent or acquired distinctiveness of the mark;

(B) the duration and extent of use of the mark in connection with the goods or services with which the mark is used;

(C) the duration and extent of advertising and publicity of the mark;

(D) the geographical extent of the trading area in which the mark is used;

(E) the channels of trade for the goods or services with which the mark is used;

(F) the degree of recognition of the mark in the trading areas and channels of trade used by the mark's owner and the person against whom the injunction is sought;

(G) the nature and extent of use of the same or similar marks by third parties; and

(H) whether the mark was registered under the Act of March 3, 1881, or the Act of February 20, 1905, or on the principal register.

15 U.S.C. § 1125(c)(1) (prior to 2006 amendments).

consumer associations that even non-competing uses can impinge their value."[519] The First Circuit, for example, held that a mark was famous only if it was "truly prominent and renowned,"[520] and the Second Circuit reserved this status for marks that were "household words."[521] Professor McCarthy argued that "a mark should not be recognized as 'famous' unless it is known to more than 50 percent of the defendant's potential customers."[522] As indicators of fame, courts typically considered how long the mark had been in use, the amount of sales, revenues, and advertising expenditures associated with the mark, and whether the mark was nationally advertised.[523] Marks that courts determined to be famous under the 1995 statute included "Victoria's Secret,"[524] "Beanie Babies" (and "Beanies"),[525] "Wawa,"[526] "Coca-Cola,"[527] "The Greatest Show on Earth,"[528] as well as "7-Eleven," "Nike," and "Pinehurst."[529] The legislative history of the FTDA gives the additional examples of "Buick," "DuPont," and "Kodak."[530]

However, in determining whether a mark was sufficiently well-known in the marketplace to qualify as famous under the 1995 statute, courts disagreed on

---

[519] Everest Capital Ltd. v. Everest Funds Mgt., L.L.C., 393 F.3d 755, 762 (8th Cir. 2005); *see also* I.P. Lund Trading ApS v. Kohler Co., 163 F.3d 27, 46 (1st Cir. 1998) (Congress intended courts to be "discriminating and selective in categorizing a mark as famous"); Avery Dennison Corp. v. Sumpton, 189 F.3d 866, 876-79 (9th Cir. 1999) (noting that fame requires more than distinctiveness, and applying statutory "fame" factors to reverse district court's conclusion that "Avery" and "Dennison" are famous marks); *cf.* Palm Bay Imports, Inc. v. Veuve Clicquot Ponsardin Maison Fondee En 1772, 396 F.3d 1369, 1374-75 (Fed. Cir. 2005) (fame for likelihood of confusion purposes, and for dilution purposes, are different concepts; former varies along a spectrum, while latter is "an either/or proposition").

[520] I.P. Lund Trading ApS v. Kohler Co., 163 F.3d 27, 46 (1st Cir. 1998) (quoting 3 J. Thomas McCarthy, McCarthy on Trademarks and Unfair Competition, § 24.91).

[521] TCPIP Holding Co., Inc. v. Haar Communs., Inc., 244 F.3d 88, 99 (2d Cir. 2001).

[522] Grupo Gigante S.A. de C.V. v. Dallo & Co., Inc., 391 F.3d 1088, 1108 (9th Cir. 2004) (Graber, J., concurring) (quoting McCarthy on Trademarks at § 24:112 (4th ed. 2002)).

[523] *See, e.g.,* Savin Corp. v. Savin Group, 391 F.3d 439, 450 (2d Cir. 2004); Nabisco, Inc. v. PF Brands, Inc., 50 F. Supp. 2d 188, 202 (S.D.N.Y. 1999), *aff'd,* 191 F.3d 208 (2d Cir. 1999); Best Cellars, Inc. v. Wine Made Simple, Inc., 2003 U.S. Dist. LEXIS 3958, 2003 WL 1212815 at *18 (S.D.N.Y. March 14, 2003) (dismissing dilution claim due to absence of national advertising campaign or any other evidence that mark was well-known to broad spectrum of public). *But see* I.P. Lund Trading ApS v. Kohler Co., 163 F.3d 27, 47 (1st Cir. 1998) (holding that plaintiff's faucet design was not famous even though it was strong, had secondary meaning, had been featured and advertised in national magazines and displayed in museums, and had been used for 20 years).

[524] *Moseley,* 537 U.S. at 432.

[525] Ty, Inc. v. Perryman, 306 F.3d 509, 511 (7th Cir. 2002).

[526] Wawa, Inc. v. Haaf, 40 U.S.P.Q. 2d (BNA) 1629 (E.D. Pa. 1996), *aff'd without op.,* 116 F.3d 471 (3d Cir. 1997).

[527] *I.P. Lund Trading,* 163 F.3d at 47 (citing Coca-Cola as an example of a mark so famous that judicial notice may be appropriate).

[528] Ringling Bros.-Barnum & Bailey Combined Shows, Inc. v. Utah Div. of Travel Dev't, 170 F.3d 449, 453 (4th Cir. 1999).

[529] Savin Corp. v. Savin Group, 391 F.3d 439, 452 (2d Cir. 2004).

[530] H.R. Rep. No. 104-374, 104th Cong., 1st Sess. 3 (1995).

the scope of the marketplace that should be considered.[531] While some courts concluded that the mark must be famous in the general marketplace,[532] others held that it was sufficient for the mark to be famous in a "niche" market.[533] Some authorities suggested that fame in a niche market was sufficient only where the senior and junior users were both using the mark within the same niche market.[534] Others suggested that the narrowness of the marketplace in which the senior user's mark had achieved fame was simply one factor to consider in determining whether the mark was famous.[535]

In the 2006 amendments, Congress attempted to clarify the meaning of fame. Section 43(c)(2)(A) now provides that "a mark is famous if it is widely recognized by the general consuming public of the United States as a designation of source of the goods or services of the mark's owner." This language repudiates the concept of "niche" fame.[536]

The 2006 amendments also provide a non-exhaustive list of factors that a court "may" consider in determining whether a mark "possesses the requisite degree of recognition" to be considered famous:

(i)   The duration, extent, and geographic reach of advertising and publicity of the mark, whether advertised or publicized by the owner or third parties.

---

[531] *See, e.g.*, Everest Capital Ltd. v. Everest Funds Mgt., L.L.C., 393 F.3d 755 (8th Cir. 2005) (collecting cases, and upholding jury verdict that plaintiff's mark was not "famous in the relevant consumer market"); Syndicate Sales, Inc. v. Hampshire Paper Corp., 192 F.3d 633, 640 (7th Cir. 1999) (collecting cases).

[532] *E.g., Savin Corp.*, 391 F.3d at 450 & n. 6; TCPIP Holding Co. v. Haar Comms., Inc., 244 F.3d 88, 98-99 (2d Cir. 2001); Sporty's Farm L.L.C. v. Sportsman's Market, Inc., 202 F.3d 489, 497 n. 10 (2d Cir. 2000); Thane Intern., Inc. v. Trek Bicycle Corp., 305 F.3d 894 (9th Cir. 2002); Ott v. Target Corp., 153 F. Supp. 2d 1055 (D. Minn. 2001).

[533] *E.g.*, Times Mirror Magazines, Inc. v. Las Vegas Sports News, L.L.C., 212 F.3d 157, 174 (3d Cir. 2000), *cert. denied*, 531 U.S. 1071 (2001); Syndicate Sales, Inc. v. Hampshire Paper Corp., 192 F3d 633, 640-41 (7th Cir. 1999).

[534] The Restatement (Third) of Unfair Competition notes:

A mark that is highly distinctive only to a select class or group of purchasers may be protected from diluting uses directed at that particular class or group. For example, a mark may be highly distinctive among purchasers of a specific type of product. In such circumstances, protection against a dilution of the mark's distinctiveness is ordinarily appropriate only against uses specifically directed at that particular class of purchasers; uses of the mark in broader markets, although they may produce an incidental diluting effect in the protected market, are not normally actionable.

Restatement (Third) of Unfair Competition § 25 cmt. e (1995); *see also* Syndicate Sales, 192 F.3d at 640-41(citing McCarthy on Trademarks § 24:112, at 24-204 to 24-205); Avery Dennison Corp. v. Sumpton, 189 F.3d 868, 878 (9th Cir. 1999).

[535] *See, e.g., Syndicate Sales*, 192 F.3d at 640-41; *I.P. Lund*, 163 F.3d at 47. This view was consistent with factor (F) on the list of statutory factors to be considered in assessing fame under the 1995 version of section 43(c)(1): "the degree of recognition of the mark in the trading areas and channels of trade used by the mark's owner and the person against whom the injunction is sought." 15 U.S.C. § 1125(c)(1)(F).

[536] "[T]he legislation expands the threshold of "fame" and thereby denies protection for marks that are famous only in 'niche' markets." H.R. Rep. No. 109-23, 109th Cong., 1st Sess. (Mar. 17, 2005); Top Tobacco, LP v. North Atlantic Operating Co., 509 F.3d 380, 384 (7th Cir. 2007).

(ii)   The amount, volume, and geographic extent of sales of goods or services offered under the mark.

(iii)   The extent of actual recognition of the mark.

(iv)   Whether the mark was registered under the Act of March 3, 1881, or the Act of February 20, 1905, or on the principal register.[537]

In addition, a court may consider any other relevant factors.[538] The new list of "fame" factors replaces the factors listed in the 1995 statute for determining both fame and distinctiveness.

Marks held to be famous and distinctive under the 2006 amendments have included "Pepsi," "Diet Pepsi," "Mountain Dew," "Sierra Mist," "Aquafina," "Cheetos," "Doritos," "Fritos,"[539] "eBay,"[540] "Visa,"[541] "Audi,"[542] "Nissan,"[543] "Hershey,"[544] "Nike,"[545] "Tiffany,"[546] "Victoria's Secret,"[547] "Louis Vuitton,"[548] and the three-stripe mark used by Adidas.[549] Marks held not to meet this standard include "Milbank,"[550] "Top,"[551] "Charlotte,"[552] "Mensa,"[553] "Jarritos,"[554] and "ComponentOne."[555]

---

[537] 15 U.S.C. § 1125(c)(2)(A).

[538] *Id.*

[539] PepsiCo, Inc. v. #1 Wholesale, LLC, 2007 U.S. Dist. LEXIS 53768, *12 (N.D. Ga. July 20, 2007) (basing this conclusion on long period of use and extensive sales).

[540] Perfumebay.com, Inc. v. eBay, Inc., 506 F.3d 1165, 1180 & nn.7-8 (9th Cir. 2007) (applying federal standards to state law dilution claim).

[541] Visa Int'l Serv. Ass'n v. JSL Corp., 2008 U.S. Dist. LEXIS 101399, *18-19 (D. Nev. Dec. 16, 2008).

[542] Audi AG v. Shokan Coachworks, Inc., 2008 U.S. Dist. LEXIS 92021, *78-79 (N.D.N.Y. Nov. 13, 2008).

[543] Nissan Motor Co. v. Nissan Computer Corp., 2007 U.S. Dist LEXIS 90487, *31-36 (C.D. Cal. Sept. 21, 2007).

[544] Hershey Co. v. Art Van Furn., Inc., 2008 U.S. Dist. LEXIS 87509, *36 (E.D. Mich. Oct. 24, 2008).

[545] Nike, Inc. v. Nikepal Int'l, Inc., 84 U.S.P.Q.2d (BNA) 1521 (E.D. Cal. Sept. 10, 2007).

[546] Tiffany, Inc. v. eBay, Inc., 576 F. Supp. 2d 463, 523 (S.D.N.Y. July 14, 2008).

[547] V Secret Catalogue, Inc. v. Moseley, 558 F. Supp. 2d 734, 743-44 (W.D. Ky. 2008).

[548] Louis Vuitton Malletier S.A. v. Haute Diggity Dog, 507 F.3d 252, 265 (4th Cir. 2007).

[549] Adidas Am., Inc. v. Payless Shoesource, Inc., 546 F. Supp. 2d 1029, 1063 (D. Or. 2008).

[550] Milbank Tweed Hadley & McCloy LLP v. Milbank Holding Corp., 82 U.S.P.Q.2d (BNA) 1583 (C.D. Cal. 2007).

[551] Top Tobacco, LP v. North Atlantic Operating Co., 509 F.3d 380, 383-84 (7th Cir. 2007).

[552] GMA Accessories, Inc. v. Croscill, Inc., 2008 U.S. Dist. LEXIS 16052, *34-35 (S.D.N.Y. Mar. 3, 2008).

[553] American Mensa, Ltd. v. Inpharmatica, Ltd., 2008 U.S. Dist. LEXIS 99394, *42 (D. Md. Nov. 6, 2008).

[554] Jarritos, Inc. v. Los Jarritos, 2007 U.S. Dist. LEXIS 32245, *54-55 (N.D. Cal. May 2, 2007).

[555] Componentone, L.L.C. v. Componentart, Inc., 2007 U.S. Dist. LEXIS 89772, *7 (W.D. Pa. Dec. 6, 2007).

[E] Trade Dress and other Nontraditional Marks

Although trade dress and other nontraditional marks were not mentioned specifically in the FTDA, courts have held that they can qualify as famous and therefore eligible for dilution protection, and this continues to be the rule under the TDRA. For example, the Second Circuit applied section 43(c) to protect Pepperidge Farm's Goldfish cracker, described by the court as a "goldfish-shaped orange, cheddar-cheese-flavored, bite-sized cracker,"[556] and the Tenth Circuit considered a federal dilution claim alleging that after-market car kits infringed General Motors' trade dress in the appearance of its "Hummer" vehicles.[557] Protection has also been granted to the titles of expressive works, as well as the names and images of fictional characters, whether or not registered; thus, for example, section 43(c) was applied to the title and characters of Dr. Seuss' "The Cat in the Hat."[558] Although both of these cases were decided under the original FTDA, neither involved "niche" fame; thus, the marks in question would qualify as famous even under the heightened standard of the TDRA.

In the case of dilution claims involving unregistered trade dress, the TDRA added a new subsection (c)(4), which expressly requires the dilution plaintiff to prove not only that its trade dress is famous, but also that it is not functional.[559] Requiring the owner to prove nonfunctionality parallels the similar requirement that applies to trade dress infringement claims under section 43(a)(3).[560] If the unregistered trade dress includes any registered marks, then the owner must prove that the unregistered component of the trade dress, taken as a whole, is famous "separate and apart from" the fame of the registered marks.

[F] Similarity

Although section 43(c) permits a finding of dilution even if the junior user's mark is not identical to the senior's mark, it does not specify the necessary degree of similarity. Courts agree, however, that the degree of similarity necessary to support a dilution claim is greater than that required to establish a likelihood of confusion;[561] the reason for imposing the more stringent standard, as the Sixth Circuit has noted, is that the similarity between the marks must be "great enough that even a noncompeting, nonconfusing use is harmful to the senior user."[562] Most courts have required the marks to be identical, or nearly so,[563] while other courts have adopted a variety of phrasings, all connoting a

---

[556] Nabisco, Inc. v. PF Brands, Inc., 191 F.3d 208, 217 (2d Cir. 1999).

[557] General Motors v. Urban Gorilla, 500 F.3d 1222 (10th Cir. 2007).

[558] Dr. Seuss Enters., L.P. v. Penguin Book USA, Inc., 924 F. Supp. 1559, 1570, 1573 (S.D. Cal. 1996), aff'd, 109 F.3d 1394 (9th Cir. 1997).

[559] 15 U.S.C. § 1125(c)(4).

[560] See § 3.02 [A] supra.

[561] See, e.g., Thane Int'l v. Trek Bicycle Corp., 305 F.3d 894, 906 (9th Cir. 2002).

[562] Jet, Inc. v. Sewage Aeration Sys., 165 F.3d 419, 424-425 (6th Cir. 1999).

[563] See, e.g., Nissan Motor Co. v. Nissan Computer Corp., 378 F.3d 1002, 1011 (9th Cir. 2004); Thane Int'l v. Trek Bicycle Corp., 305 F.3d 894, 905 (9th Cir. 2002); Playboy Enters., Inc. v. Welles, 279 F.3d 796, 806 (9th Cir. 2002); HI Limited Partnership v. Winghouse of Florida, Inc., 347 F. Supp.

high degree of similarity.[564] Several circuits have held that the marks must be similar enough that a significant segment of the relevant consumers would perceive them as "essentially the same."[565] However, it is difficult to determine whether these differences in phrasing by the courts are substantive or largely semantic.

The 2006 amendments to section 43(c) do not appear to alter the standard of similarity,[566] although the new multi-factor test for the likelihood of dilution by blurring mentions the similarity of the marks as just one of six factors to be considered. This arguably implies that a strong showing under some of the other factors might outweigh certain dissimilarities,[567] but thus far courts applying the multi-factor test have continued to require that the marks be nearly identical.[568]

[G]   Actual Dilution versus Likelihood of Dilution

[1]   The FTDA and the *Moseley* Decision

Under the 1995 dilution statute, a circuit split emerged as to whether section 43(c) required a plaintiff to prove that the defendant's unauthorized use had in fact caused dilution of the plaintiff's famous mark, or merely that such dilution was likely to occur.[569] Courts that adopted the "likelihood of dilution" standard generally evaluated that likelihood by applying a multi-factor analysis analogous to the traditional likelihood-of-confusion analysis, but geared toward determining whether the selling power of the plaintiff's mark had been undermined without regard to the likelihood of consumer confusion.[570] However, the tests adopted by some courts were criticized for bearing too close

---

2d 1256 (M.D. Fla. 2004) (in dilution claim based on trade dress, junior user's trade dress must be identical or nearly so). *See also* AutoZone, Inc. v. Tandy Corp., 373 F.3d 786, 806 (6th Cir. 2004) ("Every federal court to decide the issue has ruled that a high degree of similarity, ranging from 'nearly identical' to 'very similar,' is required for a dilution claim to succeed.").

[564] *See, e.g., Autozone*, 373 F.3d at 806 (requiring "a higher degree of similarity than is necessary in infringement claims"); Eli Lilly & Co. v. Natural Answers, Inc., 233 F.3d 456, 469 (7th Cir. 2000) (holding that dilution claim was likely to succeed because PROZAC and HERBROZAC were "highly similar"); Ringling Bros., 170 F.3d at 458 (requiring "a sufficient similarity between the junior and senior marks to evoke an instinctive mental association of the two"); *Nabisco*, 191 F.3d at 218 (stating that "the marks must be of sufficient similarity so that, in the mind of the consumer, the junior mark will conjure an association with the senior," but not requiring that marks be completely identical).

[565] *E.g., Thane Int'l*, 305 F.3d at 905; Playboy Enters. v. Welles, 279 F.3d 796, 806 n.41 (9th Cir. 2002); Luigino's, Inc. v. Stouffer Corp., 170 F.3d 827, 832 (8th Cir. 1999); I.P. Lund Trading ApS v. Kohler Co., 163 F.3d 27, 50 (1st Cir. 1998).

[566] *See* Century 21Real Estate LLC v. Century Ins. Group, 2007 U.S. Dist. LEXIS 9720 (D. Ariz. 2007) (TDRA does not alter requirement that marks be identical, nearly identical, or substantially similar).

[567] *See id.* at *48-49.

[568] *See* § 3.07[G][3][a] *infra*.

[569] *Compare Ringling Bros.*, 170 F.3d at 464 (requiring proof of actual dilution), *with* Nabisco, Inc. v. PF Brands, Inc., 191 F.3d 208 (2d Cir. 1999) (applying a non-exhaustive 10-factor analysis, derived from the likelihood-of-confusion factors, to determine likelihood of dilution).

[570] *See, e.g., Times Mirror*, 212 F.3d at 168; *Nabisco*, 191 F.3d at 217-22.

a resemblance to the likelihood-of-confusion analysis.[571] For example, some likelihood-of-dilution tests actually took account of actual confusion and/or the likelihood of confusion.[572] Others considered the sophistication of the consumers who encounter the defendant's mark;[573] however, sophistication seems more relevant to determining whether a person would be easily confused than whether a particular use of a mark might affect that person's subliminal response to that mark.

In 2003, the Supreme Court resolved this circuit split, holding in *Moseley v. V Secret Catalogue, Inc.*,[574] that the 1995 version of section 43(c) required the trademark owner to establish actual dilution rather than merely a likelihood of dilution.[575] The mere fact that consumers made a mental association between the plaintiff's mark and the defendant's mark would not, by itself, establish actionable dilution.[576] In the Court's view, proof of actual dilution required objective proof of actual injury to the economic value of the mark.[577] However, the Court noted that "direct evidence of dilution such as consumer surveys will not be necessary if actual dilution can reliably be proved through circumstantial evidence — the obvious case [being] one where the junior and senior marks are identical."[578] Although, initially, courts interpreting this language disagreed on whether the Court meant to establish that identity between the senior and junior marks established a presumption of actual dilution, or whether the Court was merely suggesting that circumstantial evidence of actual dilution could be sufficient to establish dilution in situations where the parties' marks were identical,[579] many courts came to agree that identity between the senior and junior users' marks supported a presumption of actual dilution.[580] Courts noted, however, that the standard of identity was more exacting in the dilution context than in the likelihood-of-confusion context; while close similarity between marks might be sufficient to support a finding of likelihood of confusion, close similarity was *not* sufficient to support a presumption of dilution.[581] In the dilution

---

[571] *Times Mirror*, 212 F.3d at 168 (*citing* McCarthy on Trademarks at § 24:94.1); *I.P. Lund Trading*, 163 F.3d at 49-50.

[572] *See, e.g., Nabisco*, 191 F.3d at 228 (considering actual confusion and likelihood of confusion); *Times Mirror*, 212 F.3d at 168-69 (adopting *Nabisco* factors).

[573] *See, e.g., Times Mirror*, 212 F.3d at 168.

[574] 537 U.S. 418 (2003).

[575] *Id.* at 433.

[576] *Id.*

[577] *Id.* at 422. In subsequent case law, objective evidence of actual dilution has rarely been submitted. Ironically, in one of those cases, the "dilution" evidence submitted was evidence of actual consumer confusion. Horphag Research Ltd. v. Garcia, 475 F.3d 1029, 1036 (9th Cir. 2007). In another case, consumer surveys also indicated a likelihood of consumer confusion; they showed that a minority of consumers (7-28%) believed that the defendant's product was either made by the plaintiff or made with the plaintiff's permission. Jada Toys, Inc. v. Mattel, Inc., 496 F.3d 974, 982 (9th Cir. 2007).

[578] *Moseley*, 537 U.S. at 434.

[579] *See, e.g.*, Savin Corp. v. Savin Group, 391 F.3d 439, 451-52 (2d Cir. 2004) (collecting cases).

[580] *Horphag Research*, 475 F.3d at 1036; *Jada Toys, Inc.*, 496 F.3d at 982; Carefirst of Md., Inc. v. First Care, P.C., 434 F.3d 263, 274 (4th Cir. 2006); *Savin Corp.*, 391 F.3d at 452-53.

[581] General Motors v. Urban Gorilla, 500 F.3d 1222, 1229 (10th Cir. 2007) (claim for dilution of

context, determining whether two marks were identical could itself be context-and/or media-dependent, as well as highly fact-specific — as, for example, where the marks were spelled identically but appeared in different fonts, sizes, or colors, or had different pronunciations, or where they were identical in some contexts (such as website addresses) but not in others.[582]

[2] Likelihood of Dilution under the TDRA

In the 2006 TDRA, however, Congress legislatively overruled *Moseley*'s holding that section 43(c) requires a showing of actual dilution, calling it "an undue burden for trademark holders."[583] The amended language in section 43(c)(1) now explicitly permits the owner of a famous mark to obtain injunctive relief against an unauthorized use "that is likely to cause dilution by blurring or dilution by tarnishment."

Whereas the 1995 version of section 43(c) offered no guidance to courts in assessing the likelihood of dilution, the 2006 amendments suggest six factors that courts may consider in determining whether dilution by blurring is likely. In contrast, it does not suggest any factors to consider in determining the likelihood of dilution by tarnishment.

In assessing the likelihood of dilution by blurring, section 43(c) now indicates that a court may consider "all relevant factors," and specifically notes that courts may consider the following:

(i)   The degree of similarity between the mark or trade name and the famous mark.

(ii) The degree of inherent or acquired distinctiveness of the famous mark.

(iii) The extent to which the owner of the famous mark is engaging in substantially exclusive use of the mark.

(iv) The degree of recognition of the famous mark.

(v)   Whether the user of the mark or trade name intended to create an association with the famous mark.

(vi) Any actual association between the mark or trade name and the famous mark.[584]

---

trade dress unlikely to succeed where products not identical and plaintiff offered no direct evidence of actual economic harm); *Savin Corp.*, 391 F.3d at 453; *Jada Toys, Inc.*, 496 F.3d at 982 (insufficient that marks are "nearly identical"); Omega S.A. v. Omega Eng'g, Inc., 2005 U.S. Dist. LEXIS 33480, *8-9 (D. Conn. 2005); Mashantucket Pequot Tribe v. Redican, 403 F. Supp. 2d 184, 194 (D. Conn. 2005).

[582] *Savin Corp.*, 391 F.3d at 453-54; *Horphag Research*, 475 F.3d at 1036.

[583] H.R. Rep. No. 109-23, 109th Cong., 1st Sess. (March 17, 2005). The House Report expressly endorsed the view of the International Trademark Association that, under the *Moseley* standard, "[b]y the time measurable, provable damage to the mark has occurred much time has passed, the damage has been done, and the remedy, which is injunctive relief, is far less effective." H.R. Rep. No. 109-23, 109th Cong., 1st Sess. (March 17, 2005).

[584] 15 U.S.C. § 1125(c)(2)(B).

In using the permissive "may," the statute does not expressly *require* courts to consider any or all of these factors. In practice, however, courts are likely to address all of them. In *Louis Vuitton Malletier S.A. v. Haute Diggity Dog LLC*, the Fourth Circuit stated that "the TDRA directs the court to consider all factors relevant to the issue, including [the] six factors that are enumerated in the statute,"[585] thus implying that courts are required to consider all six factors. In some cases, of course, certain factors may be more relevant than others.[586] In a situation where some factors suggest that dilution is likely and other factors weigh against such likelihood, the statute offers no guidance as to how a court should weigh each respective factor. Nonetheless, the Fourth Circuit held that "a trial court must offer a sufficient indication of which factors it has found persuasive and explain why they are persuasive so that the court's decision can be reviewed."[587]

In adopting the likelihood-of-dilution standard, the TDRA now enables the owners of famous marks to prevent irreparable harm to their goodwill *before* it occurs. However, this change may also lead courts to grant injunctive relief in doubtful cases.

The TDRA also made conforming amendments to sections 2(f), 13(a), 14, and 24 of the Lanham Act, reflecting the adoption of the likelihood of dilution standard and the clarification that dilution includes both blurring and tarnishment.

[3]   Judicial Interpretations

[a]   Likelihood of Dilution by Blurring

The first case to apply the new multifactor test for the likelihood of dilution by blurring, *Louis Vuitton Malletier S.A. v. Haute Diggity Dog LLC*,[588] did so in the context of a parody. The plaintiff alleged that its famous "Louis Vuitton" mark was likely to be diluted by the defendant's use of the "Chewy Vuiton" mark on dog toys. Because the defendant was using the mark as a source indicator for its own goods, it was not eligible for the "fair use" exception under the 2006 version of section 43(c)(4)(A). Nonetheless, the Fourth Circuit held that the parodic context was relevant to its analysis of the six statutory blurring factors.[589] Drawing from existing case law on parodies and dilution,[590] the court noted that "[w]hile a parody intentionally creates an association with the famous mark in order to be a parody, it also intentionally communicates, if it is successful, that it is *not* the famous mark, but rather a satire of the famous

---

[585] 507 F.3d 252, 266 (4th Cir. 2007).

[586] *Id.*

[587] *Id.*

[588] 507 F.3d 252 (4th Cir. 2007).

[589] *Id.* at 267.

[590] For a discussion of these cases, see § 3.11 *infra*.

mark."[591] In addition, "by making the famous mark an object of the parody, a successful parody might actually enhance the famous mark's distinctiveness by making it an icon. The brunt of the joke becomes yet more famous."[592] Applying these principles, the court concluded that the "Chewy Vuiton" mark was a successful parody that was unlikely to dilute the plaintiff's mark:

> Even as Haute Diggity Dog's parody mimics the famous mark, it communicates simultaneously that it is not the famous mark, but is only satirizing it. And because the famous mark is particularly strong and distinctive, it becomes more likely that a parody will not impair the distinctiveness of the mark. In short, as Haute Diggity Dog's "Chewy Vuiton" marks are a successful parody, we conclude that they will not blur the distinctiveness of the famous mark as a unique identifier of its source.[593]

The court noted, however, that the outcome might be different where the mark used in the parody "is so similar to the famous mark that it likely could be construed as actual use of the famous mark itself," because the unauthorized use of the famous marks *themselves* "might diminish the capacity of these trademarks to distinctively identify a single source."[594] In this case, however, the defendant's imitation of the plaintiff's marks "did not come so close to them as to destroy the success of its parody and, more importantly, to diminish the LVM marks' capacity to identify a single source."[595]

The parodic aspect of the "Chewy Vuiton" mark was also relevant to the analysis of factors (v) and (vi) — whether the defendant intended to create an association with the famous mark, and whether there was any actual association between the marks — because the defendant intentionally associated its mark with the plaintiff's mark, but did so "imperfectly," in order to convey the simultaneous messages essential to a successful parody: "[A]s a parody, it separated itself from the LVM marks in order to make fun of them."[596]

Other than the *Louis Vuitton* decision, there is as yet little case law applying the new blurring factors. However, as discussed below, a handful of district court decisions have provided some useful perspectives on three of those factors — the degree of similarity between the marks, the junior user's intent to create an association between the marks, and any actual association between the marks. Because the decisions are so recent, it remains to be seen whether these interpretations will be upheld by the appellate courts.

---

[591] 507 F.3d at 267 (citing People for Ethical Treatment of Animals (PETA) v. Doughney, 263 F.3d 359, 366 (4th Cir. 2001)).

[592] *Id.* (citing Hormel Foods Corp. v. Jim Henson Prods., Inc., 73 F.3d 497, 506 (2d Cir. 1996) (observing that a successful parody "tends to increase public identification" of the famous mark with its source); Yankee Publ'g Inc. v. News Am. Publ'g Inc., 809 F. Supp. 267, 272-82 (S.D.N.Y. 1992) (suggesting that a sufficiently obvious parody is unlikely to blur the targeted famous mark)).

[593] *Id.* (citing *PETA*, 263 F.3d at 366).

[594] *Id.* at 268.

[595] *Id.*

[596] *Id.*

Degree of similarity: Although, as a threshold matter, courts have required marks to be "nearly identical" in order to support a dilution claim under section 43(c), the first blurring factor still calls for an analysis of the *degree* of similarity. Where there are small differences between the junior and senior marks, courts have considered the context in which those marks appear. For example, when a defendant used the "evisa" mark in the domain name "evisa.com," the district court observed that, while the difference between "Visa" and "evisa" might be significant in some other settings, in the domain name context the two marks were very similar, because consumers would tend to disregard the "e" prefix as a commonplace prefix denoting the online aspect of a business.[597] In contrast, another court opined that the marks "Starbucks" and "Mr. Charbucks" were dissimilar enough to completely defeat a dilution claim, and that, at a minimum, analysis of the similarity factor favored the defendant.[598] "Victoria's Secret" and "Victor's Little Secret" were sufficiently similar that this factor weighed in the plaintiff's favor; the court noted that the word "Little" in the junior user's mark was "substantially smaller" than the rest of the mark.[599]

Running counter to the general trend toward strict application of the "nearly identical" standard, one district court held that "Nike" and "Nikepal" were "nearly identical" because (1) the dominant feature of each mark was "Nike," and (2) survey evidence showed that consumers associated the two marks.[600] The correctness of this finding is questionable. It appears that the court improperly merged its analysis of two separate blurring factors — the degree of similarity and the extent of actual association.

Although the Fourth Circuit rejected a likelihood-of-dilution-by-blurring claim in the *Louis Vuitton* case because the defendant's mark was a parody, as a threshold matter the court may have given inadequate consideration to the differences between the marks. While "Louis Vuitton" and "Chewy Vuiton" are similar, they are arguably no more similar than "Starbucks" and "Charbucks," and a different court might have found the differences between the marks to be dispositive. Indeed, most successful parodies are likely to involve dissimilar marks, because the dissimilarity is typically necessary to convey the parodic message.

Intent to create association: One court has held that, even if the junior user did *not* intend to create an association with the famous mark, the more important question is the degree to which consumers *actually* associate the two marks, because "trademark dilution is an objective inquiry into whether an alleged diluter's mark is likely to contribute to the gradual whittling away of a senior mark's value."[601]

Conversely, even where a junior user intends to create an association with a famous mark, it has been held that this factor does not necessarily favor the

---

[597] Visa Int'l Serv. Ass'n v. JSL Corp., 2008 U.S. Dist. LEXIS 101399, *23-24 (D. Nev. Dec. 16, 2008).

[598] Starbucks Corp. v. Wolfe's Borough Coffee, Inc., 559 F. Supp. 2d 472, 477 (S.D.N.Y. 2008).

[599] V Secret Catalogue, Inc. v. Moseley, 558 F. Supp. 2d 734, 745 (W.D. Ky. 2008).

[600] Nike, Inc. v. Nikepal Int'l, Inc., 84 U.S.P.Q.2d (BNA) 1521 (E.D. Cal. 2007).

[601] *Visa Int'l*, 2008 U.S. Dist. LEXIS 101399, at *31.

plaintiff. In *Starbucks Corp. v. Wolfe's Borough Coffee, Inc.*,[602] the district court found that the defendant adopted the "Mr. Charbucks" mark for the purpose of "alluding to the dark roasted characteristic of the Starbucks product," in order "to signal to purchasers that 'Mr. Charbucks' is a very dark roast and unlike Defendant's other coffee products." Because the two marks were far from identical, the court held that the association conjured up by the junior user's "playful dissimilar" mark was analogous to the association conjured up by a successful parody, as in *Louis Vuitton*.[603]

Actual association: In determining the extent of any actual association between the famous mark and the allegedly dilutive marks, courts have given significant weight to consumer survey evidence.[604] In one case, the testimony of a single customer was found to be indicative of actual association, yet the fact that the customer was fully aware that the junior and senior user were unaffiliated, and, indeed, was "offended" by the junior user's imitation of the famous mark, led the court to conclude that the association supported a claim of tarnishment rather than blurring.[605]

[b]   Likelihood of Dilution by Tarnishment

Faced with little statutory guidance on how to assess the likelihood of dilution by tarnishment, the few courts that have considered post-TDRA tarnishment claims have not departed significantly from their pre-TDRA approaches. They focus almost entirely on the nature of the junior user's goods, and are most inclined to find tarnishment where they perceive those goods to be unwholesome, offensive, or poor in quality.

In the first decision to address a tarnishment claim under the TDRA, the Fourth Circuit in the *Louis Vuitton* case found no likelihood of dilution by tarnishment, rejecting as "flimsy" the plaintiff's assertion that the defendant's "Chewy Vuiton" dog toys posed a choking hazard.[606] Although the court acknowledged that a $10 dog toy was inferior in quality to an expensive Louis Vuitton handbag, the court gave no weight to this difference in quality, and offered no explanation for disregarding it. In all likelihood, the appellate court's analysis of tarnishment, like its analysis of blurring, was influenced by its determination that the "Chewy Vuiton" mark was a parody.[607]

In the *Starbucks* decision, the district court considered survey evidence showing that some respondents associated a hypothetical "Charbucks" brand with burnt, bitter coffee. However, the court found no indication that this affected their perceptions of the plaintiff's famous "Starbucks" coffee. In

---

[602] 559 F. Supp. 2d 472 (S.D.N.Y. 2008).

[603] *Id.* at 478.

[604] *E.g., Visa Int'l*, 2008 U.S. Dist. LEXIS 101399, at 827 (73% of respondents indicated that "evisa" reminded them of "Visa"); Nike, Inc. v. Nikepal Int'l, Inc., 84 U.S.P.Q.2d (BNA) 1521 (E.D. Cal. 2007) (87% of respondents associated "Nikepal" with "Nike").

[605] V Secret Catalogue, Inc. v. Moseley, 558 F. Supp. 2d 734, 748-49 (W.D. Ky. 2008).

[606] *Louis Vuitton*, 507 F.3d at 268-69.

[607] *Id.* at 269. The court's analysis of blurring is discussed in § 3.07 [G][3][a], *supra*.

addition, the court found it significant that the actual Charbucks product produced by the defendant was of high quality. Accordingly, the court found no likelihood of tarnishment.[608]

Upon remand of the *Moseley* case, the district court offered only a brief explanation for its conclusion that that a store called "Victor's Little Secret" which sold "adult" novelties was likely to tarnish the reputation of the "Victoria's Secret" mark for lingerie.[609] Although the only evidence of consumer perception considered by the court was the testimony of a single customer who was offended by defendant's imitation of the famous mark, the court found this evidence to be persuasive.[610] The court was clearly influenced by the sexually explicit nature of the junior user's merchandise.

[H]   Exceptions

Unlike many state dilution statutes, the federal dilution statute sets forth specific circumstances in which the unauthorized use of a famous mark will not give rise to liability for dilution. Three such exceptions were included in the 1995 statute. The 2006 amendments retained these exceptions, but with several modifications that affect their scope.

The original FTDA included the following exceptions:

(A)   "Fair use of a famous mark by another person in comparative commercial advertising or promotion to identify the competing goods or services of the owner of the famous mark," (section 43(c)(4)(A);

(B)   "Noncommercial use of a mark" (section 43(c)(4)(B)); and

(C)   "All forms of news reporting and news commentary" (section 43(c)(4)(C)).

In 2006, however, the TDRA significantly revised section 43(c)'s "fair use" exception to dilution liability, while leaving the noncommercial use and news reporting exceptions intact. As amended (and renumbered), section 43(c)(3) now exempts:

(A)   Any fair use, including a nominative or descriptive fair use, or facilitation of such fair use, of a famous mark by another person other than as a designation of source for the person's own goods or services, including use in connection with —

    (i)   advertising or promotion that permits consumers to compare goods or services; or

    (ii) identifying and parodying, criticizing, or commenting upon the famous mark owner or the goods or services of the famous mark owner.

(B)   All forms of news reporting and news commentary.

---

[608] *Starbucks*, 599 F. Supp. 2d at 480.

[609] 558 F. Supp. 2d at 750.

[610] *Id.*

(C)   Any noncommercial use of a mark.

Each of these exceptions is discussed below.

[1]   Fair Use

The Ninth Circuit described the reasoning behind the 1995 version of the fair use exception as follows: "Uses that do not create an improper association between a mark and a new product but merely identify the trademark holder's products should be excepted from the reach of the anti-dilution statute. Such uses cause no harm."[611]

Under this exception, the Ninth Circuit held that nominative fair uses are non-dilutive as a matter of law.[612] A "nominative" fair use occurs when (1) a defendant uses a plaintiff's trademark to describe or identify the plaintiff's goods or services, even though the defendant's ultimate goal is to describe the defendant's own goods or services,[613] or (2) where the plaintiff's mark is the only practical way to refer to a particular subject matter.[614] For example, in *Playboy Enterprises v. Welles*,[615] the defendant, who was the "Playboy Playmate of the Year 1981" maintained a website in which she described herself by that title and made other uses of Playboy's trademarked terms, including uses in metatags and banner advertising for her site. In holding that most of these uses were nominative, and therefore non-dilutive under section 43(c)(4)(A), the Ninth Circuit explained:

> When Welles refers to her title, she is in effect referring to a product of [plaintiff] PEI's. She does not dilute the title by truthfully identifying herself as its one-time recipient any more than Michael Jordan would dilute the name "Chicago Bulls" by referring to himself as a former member of that team, or the two-time winner of an Academy Award would dilute the award by referring to him or herself as a "two-time Academy Award winner." Awards are not diminished or diluted by the fact that they have been awarded in the past.[616]

In contrast, the defendant's repeated use of the abbreviation "PMOY" (for "Playmate of the Year") in the wallpaper (i.e., background) of her website was held not to be a nominative use, and thus was not covered by the (c)(4)(A) exemption.[617]

---

[611]   Playboy Enters., Inc. v. Welles, 279 F.3d 796, 806 (9th Cir. 2002).

[612]   *Id.* at 806 (concluding that some, but not all, uses by former "Playmate of the Year" of Playboy's trademarks on her website were nominative and thus immune from liability under federal dilution law). For a detailed discussion of comparative advertising and nominative uses, see §§ 3.12 [G] and [H] *infra.*

[613]   *Ee.g.,* Cairns v. Franklin Mint Co., 292 F.3d 1139, 1151 (9th Cir. 2002).

[614]   *E.g.,* New Kids on the Block v. News Am. Publ'g, Inc., 971 F.2d 302, 308 (9th Cir. 1992) (noting that nominative fair use may occur where plaintiff's trademark is the "only word reasonably available to describe a particular thing").

[615]   279 F.3d 796 (9th Cir. 2002).

[616]   *Id.* at 806.

[617]   *Id.*

In other cases applying this exemption, courts have rejected federal dilution claims against defendants that used a plaintiff/competitor's trademark to describe their own products as identical or comparable to, or as replacements for, the competitor's trademarked goods.[618]

The 2006 amendments make clear that the fair use exception applies not only to traditional comparative advertising, but also to nominative fair use as well as parodies or criticisms of famous marks.[619] However, as the Fourth Circuit noted in *Louis Vuitton Malletier S.A. v. Haute Diggity Dog LLC*,[620] the exception expressly does not apply if the person accused of dilution used the mark as a source designation for that person's own goods or services. Accordingly, the fair use exception did not apply to a defendant's use of "Chewy Vuiton" as a mark for dog toys;[621] however, as discussed in § 3.07 [G][3] above, the Fourth Circuit held that the parodic context was nonetheless relevant to the determination whether dilution was likely to occur.[622]

[2]   Noncommercial Use

The FTDA's second (now third) exception, section 43(c)(4)(B) (redesignated as subsection (c)(3)(C) by the 2006 amendments), refers simply to the "[n]oncommercial use of a mark." The scope of this exception is somewhat unsettled. Under the 1995 FTDA, it was unclear why Congress thought it necessary to include a noncommercial use exception at all, because a dilution claim under section 43(c)(1) applied only where the dilutive activity involved a "commercial use in commerce."[623] (In contrast, the 2006 amendments deleted the phrase "commercial use," requiring only that the defendant make a dilutive use of the mark "in commerce.") The answer, according to the Second Circuit, was that "noncommercial use" in this context referred to "a use that consists entirely of noncommercial, or fully constitutionally protected, speech."[624] According to this interpretation, the noncommercial use exception functioned as a catch-all for speech that was protected by the First Amendment but that fell outside of the FTDA's exceptions for comparative advertising and news reporting.[625] The noncommercial use exception therefore encompassed any

---

[618] *See, e.g.*, Bijur Lubricating Corp. v. Devco Corp., 332 F. Supp. 2d 722, 733-34 (D.N.J. 2004); Avery Dennison Corp. v. Acco Brands, Inc., 1999 U.S. Dist. LEXIS 21464, *28-29 (C.D. Cal. 1999); Cumberland Packing Corp. v. Monsanto Co., 32 F. Supp. 2d 561, 581 (E.D.N.Y. 1999).

[619] Nominative fair use is discussed in § 3.12 [G]*infra.*

[620] 507 F.3d 252 (4th Cir. 2007).

[621] *Id.* at 266.

[622] *Id.* at 266-67.

[623] Mattel, Inc. v. MCA Records, Inc., 296 F.3d 894, 904 (9th Cir. 2002), *cert. denied*, 537 U.S. 1171 (2003).

[624] *Id.* at 905; *accord*, American Family Life Ins. Co. v. Hagan, 266 F. Supp. 2d 682, 695-98 (N.D. Ohio 2002).

[625] Support for this interpretation can be found in the legislative history, which contains references to "noncommercial expression," "consumer product reviews," "artistic and expressive speech," and "parody, satire, editorial and other forms of expression that are not a part of a commercial transaction." Mattel, 296 F.3d at 905-906 (collecting sources); *see, e.g.*, 141 Cong. Rec. S19310 (daily ed. Dec. 29, 1995) (statement of Sen. Hatch) (noting that section 43(c)(4)(B)

speech that was not purely commercial — that is, any speech that "d[id] more than propose a commercial transaction."[626] Courts interpreted this to include comedy, parody, satire, consumer criticism, editorial commentaries, and other forms of expression, even when they were sold for profit.[627] This interpretation appears to be correct under the 2006 amendments as well.

Using this analysis, courts interpreting the 1995 statute applied the noncommercial use exception to uses that were partly commercial but that nonetheless enjoyed a high degree of First Amendment protection, such as the use of Mattel's "Barbie" trademark in a pop song,[628] and a literary parody of O.J. Simpson's murder trial, which incorporated famous characters from books by "Dr. Seuss."[629] They also applied the exemption to political speech, including a presidential candidate's television commercial that closely imitated a credit card company's series of television ads,[630] and a political candidate's Internet commercials that included a quacking cartoon duck that was "highly reminiscent" of the duck character featured in an insurance company's television ads.[631]

Under the FTDA, the noncommercial use exception was frequently applied to websites that incorporated famous marks in their domain names and were dedicated to criticism or commentary aimed at the owners of those marks. For example, the exception was applied to a dilution claim by the Ford Motor Co. against an "artist and social critic" who established a website under the domain name "fuckgeneralmotors.com," which contained programming code incorporating Ford's trademarks so as to create an automatic hyperlink that transported visitors to Ford's official website. Treating this as an exempt noncommercial use, the court noted that "[i]f the FTDA's 'commercial use' requirement is to have any meaning, it cannot be interpreted so broadly as to include any use that might disparage or otherwise commercially harm the mark owner."[632] The noncommercial use exception was also applied (although without

---

encompassed "parody, satire, editorial and other forms of expression that are not part of a commercial transaction).

[626] *Id.* at 906.

[627] Ford Motor Co. v. 2600 Enters., 177 F. Supp. 2d 661, 664-65 (E.D. Mich. 2001); Charles Atlas, Ltd. v. D.C. Comics, Inc., 112 F. Supp. 2d 330, 336 (S.D.N.Y. 2000); Northland Ins. Cos. v. Blaylock, 115 F. Supp. 2d 1108, 1122-23 (D. Minn. 2000); World Championship Wrestling v. Titan Sports, Inc., 46 F. Supp. 2d 118, 122-23 (D. Conn. 1999); Mattel, Inc. v. MCA Records, 1998 U.S. Dist. LEXIS 7310, *14-15 (C.D. Cal. Feb. 18, 1998); Bally Total Fitness Holding Corp. v. Faber, 29 F. Supp. 2d 1161, 1166-67 (C.D. Cal. 1998); Dr. Seuss Enterprises v. Penguin Books USA, Inc., 924 F. Supp. 1559, 1574 (S.D. Cal. 1996); Panavision Int'l, L.P. v. Toeppen, 945 F. Supp. 1296, 1303 (C.D. Cal. 1996).

[628] *Mattel*, 296 F.3d at 906-07.

[629] *Dr. Seuss Enterprises*, 924 F. Supp. at 1573-74 (S.D. Cal. 1996), *aff'd*, 109 F.3d 1394 (9th Cir. 1997).

[630] Mastercard Int'l Inc. v. Nader 2000 Primary Comm., Inc., 70 U.S.P.Q.2d (BNA) 1046, 2004 U.S. Dist. LEXIS 3644 (S.D.N.Y. 2004).

[631] *American Family Life Ins.*, 266 F. Supp. 2d at 686, 698-701; *accord*, Griffith v. Fenrick, 486 F. Supp. 2d 848, 853 (W.D. Wis. 2007) (use of famous actor's name by political candidate was noncommercial use).

[632] *Ford Motor Co.*, 177 F. Supp. 2d at 665. In contrast, commercial use has been found where a defendant used a plaintiff's trademark in a domain name in order to redirect consumers to another

a specific reference to section 43(c)(4)) to bar a dilution claim against a website called "ballysucks.com," which reported consumer complaints about Bally Total Fitness health clubs,[633] and to a website containing critical commentary about a college and incorporating a well-known abbreviation for the college in its domain name.[634]

The 2006 amendments retained the language of the original "noncommercial use" exception, and Congress appears to have tacitly approved the case law interpreting that exception.[635]

[3] News Reporting and News Commentary

The exception for news reporting and news commentary was contained in the original FTDA, and was preserved without change by the 2006 amendments. The exception makes explicit what is already required by the First Amendment. Although the underlying purpose of the exception is clear, issues may arise regarding its scope, particularly where a defendant's "news" reporting has commercial aspects. For example, where a defendant operated a website that reported on real estate transactions in various neighborhoods, and identified by name a law firm whose attorneys were involved in several of those transactions, also providing links to the law firm's website, the parties disagreed on whether these references to the law firm constituted exempt news reporting or a dilutive use.[636] In another case, a court applied the news reporting exception to a blog; while noting that not every blog will qualify as news reporting, the court based its decision on the content of the blog and the intent of its author.[637]

[I] Remedies

The remedies available to plaintiffs under section 43(c) of the Lanham Act are more limited than those available for claims under sections 32 or 43(a).[638] Unless the defendant's dilutive activity is willful, the plaintiff is entitled only to injunctive relief under section 34.[639] The plaintiff may also bar importation of diluting goods.[640]

---

website in order to solicit contributions or sell merchandise. *See, e.g.*, Jews for Jesus v. Brodsky, 993 F. Supp. 282 (D.N.J.), *aff'd*, 159 F.3d 1351 (3d Cir. 1998); Planned Parenthood Federation of America, Inc. v. Bucci, 1997 U.S. Dist. LEXIS 3338, No. 97 Civ. 0629 (KMW) (March 24, 1997).

[633] Bally Total Fitness Holding Corp. v. Faber, 29 F. Supp. 2d 1161, 1166-67 (C.D. Cal. 1998).

[634] Savannah College of Art & Design, Inc. v. Houeix, 369 F. Supp. 2d 929, 957-58 (S.D. Ohio 2004)

[635] The 2006 amendments did revise section 43(c)(1) so that a dilution claim may now be brought against any "use in commerce" rather than any "commercial use in commerce." However, this change does not appear to be substantive; rather, it makes the noncommercial use exception no longer redundant.

[636] Jones Day v. Blockshopper, LLC, 2008 U.S. Dist. LEXIS 94442, *8-11 (N.D. Ill. Nov. 13, 2008).

[637] BidZirk, LLC v. Smith, 2007 U.S. Dist. LEXIS 78481, *16-19 (D.S.C. Oct. 22, 2007).

[638] For a detailed discussion of Lanham Act remedies, *see* §§ 3.13–3.15 *infra*.

[639] 15 U.S.C. §§ 1116, 1125(c)(1), (c)(5).

[640] *Id.* § 1125(b).

The dilution statute's provisions on monetary awards were revised by the TDRA in order to clarify the meaning of willfulness. Under section 43(c)(5), the owner of a famous mark may recover damages and/or profits, costs and attorney fees under section 35(a),[641] and may obtain an order for destruction of infringing articles under section 36,[642] only if, in the case of a blurring claim, the defendant "willfully intended to trade on the recognition of the famous mark,"[643] or, in the case of a tarnishment claim, the defendant "willfully intended to harm the reputation of the famous mark."[644] Furthermore, as discussed below, the availability of these additional remedies depends on whether the defendant first used the dilutive mark in commerce before or after October 6, 2006.[645]

[J]   Effective Date of TDRA

In several instances, courts have considered which version of section 43(c) — the 1995 FTDA or the 2006 TDRA — should apply to dilution claims in which the allegedly dilutive activity commenced before the effective date of the TDRA (October 6, 2006). Courts have consistently reached the conclusion that the TDRA applies to such activities with respect to claims for injunctive relief.[646] With respect to damages claims, however, courts have held that the original FTDA (and, thus, the more stringent actual dilution standard) applies to conduct predating the TDRA.[647] This conclusion reflects the language of section 43(c)(5)(A), which provides that monetary relief is available only where the defendant's first use in commerce of the mark that is likely to cause dilution takes place after October 6, 2006.

Accordingly, where a trademark owner has sought injunctive relief against dilutive conduct that commenced on or before October 6, 2006, the trademark owner has been required to show only a likelihood of dilution, rather than actual dilution. However, in order to obtain damages for willful dilution arising from that same conduct, the trademark owner in this situation would have to establish actual dilution, under the pre-TDRA standards as interpreted by the Supreme Court in *Moseley* and by the lower federal courts.[648] To recover damages for willful dilutive activity commencing *after* October 6, 2006, however, the applicable standard is likelihood of dilution.

---

[641] *Id.* § 1117(a).

[642] *Id.* § 1118.

[643] *Id.* § 1125(c)(5)(B)(i).

[644] *Id.* § 1125(c)(5)(B)(ii).

[645] *Id.* § 1125(c)(5)(A). Prior to the 2006 amendments, remedies under sections 35 and 36 were available for actual dilution, subject to the principles of equity and the discretion of the court, if the plaintiff established that the defendant "willfully intended to trade on the owner's reputation or to cause dilution of the famous mark." *Id.* § 1125(c)(2) (prior to 2006 amendments).

[646] Jada Toys, Inc. v. Mattel, Inc., 518 F.3d 628, 634 n.2 (9th Cir. 2007); Starbucks Corp. v. Wolfe's Borough Coffee, Inc., 477 F.3d 765, 766 (2d Cir. 2007).

[647] *Starbucks*, 477 F.3d at 766; University of Kansas v. Sinks, 565 F. Supp. 2d 1216, 1258 (D. Kan. 2008); *accord, Jada Toys*, 518 F.3d at 634 n.2 (holding that TDRA applies to pre-TDRA activities where plaintiff seeks injunctive relief, but not explicitly addressing which statute applies to damages claims).

[648] *See* § 3.07 [G][1] *supra.*

[K]   Federal Registration as a Dilution Defense

Under the original FTDA, ownership of a valid registration on the Principal Register (or under the 1881 or 1905 Trademark Acts) was a complete bar to any state law claim, with respect to that mark, brought against the owner of the registration and seeking "to prevent dilution of the distinctiveness of a mark, label, or form of advertisement."[649] The registration defense did not preclude *federal* dilution claims.

However, the TDRA revised the wording of the registration defense, which is now contained in section 43(c)(6). The amended language reads:

(6) Ownership of valid registration a complete bar to action.

The ownership by a person of a valid registration under the Act of March 3, 1881, or the Act of February 20, 1905, or on the principal register under this Act shall be a complete bar to an action against that person, with respect to that mark, that —

(A)

   (i)   is brought by another person under the common law or a statute of a State; and

   (ii)   seeks to prevent dilution by blurring or dilution by tarnishment; or

(B)   asserts any claim of actual or likely damage or harm to the distinctiveness or reputation of a mark, label, or form of advertisement.[650]

The reference in clause (B) to "any claim of actual or likely damage or harm to the distinctiveness or reputation" of a mark appears to preclude *federal* as well as state claims, which would be a significant change from the original FTDA provision.

Barring federal dilution claims against registered marks appears to conflict with the language of sections 2(f), 14, and 24 of the Lanham Act,[651] all of which provide that the registration for a mark that is likely to cause dilution may be canceled. One might reconcile these provisions by concluding that Congress intended to make cancellation the exclusive remedy for dilutive uses of a registered mark. Any continued use of the dilutive mark after cancellation would, presumably, be actionable under section 43(c). This would appear to require the dilution plaintiff to bring two actions — one seeking cancellation, and then a second one seeking an injunction (and damages if the dilution was willful). Had Congress intended this result, it seems likely that it would have expressed this intent in the legislative record.[652]

---

[649] 15 U.S.C. § 1125(c)(3) (prior to 2006 amendments).

[650] 15 U.S.C. § 1125(c)(6) (as amended).

[651] 15 U.S.C. §§ 1052(f), 1064, 1092.

[652] This two-step process was already possible under the original FTDA, as a way to avoid the federal registration defense to state dilution claims. In the Ninth Circuit's view, both steps could be

The legislative history of the TDRA offers no explanation for this change, nor any indication that it was even intentional. It may simply be a drafting error. The language of the 2005 House bill was written ambiguously, and could be read to preclude only state dilution claims (as in the original FTDA) or to preclude *both* state and federal dilution claims:

> (5) Ownership of valid registration a complete bar to action. The ownership by a person of a valid registration under the Act of March 3, 1881, or the Act of February 20, 1905, or on the principal register under this Act shall be a complete bar to an action against that person, with respect to that mark, that is brought by another person under the common law or a statute of a State and that seeks to prevent dilution by blurring or dilution by tarnishment, or that asserts any claim of actual or likely damage or harm to the distinctiveness or reputation of a mark, label, or form of advertisement.[653]

When the House bill was reported in the Senate several months later, the Senate replaced all of the original House language with its own language (for example, introducing subsection (c)(4) pertaining to dilution of trade dress). The Senate's version of the registration defense was ultimately enacted in the TDRA.[654] Although the language of the Senate version is almost identical to that of the original House version, the Senate's hierarchical structuring of this language — splitting it into clauses (A) and (B), where clause (B) is apparently not limited to state law dilution claims — appears to explicitly preclude section 43(c) claims against marks that are registered on the Principal Register.[655]

Because the legislative history gives no indication that Congress intended to bar federal dilution claims against registered marks, it seems more likely that the purpose of inserting the reference to claims asserting "harm to the distinctiveness or reputation" of a mark was simply to broaden the original defense to preclude the possibility of state law claims that are the *equivalent* of dilution claims but that do not employ the specific "blurring" or "tarnishment" terminology of the federal statute.

---

accomplished in a single legal proceeding. *See* Jada Toys, Inc. v. Mattel, Inc., 496 F.3d 974, 981 & n.4 (9th Cir. 2007) (rejecting federal registration defense to state dilution claim because defendant counterclaimed for cancellation).

[653] H.R. 683, 109th Cong., 1st Sess. (as introduced February 9, 2005).

[654] The Senate version read as follows:

(6) Ownership of valid registration a complete bar to action. The ownership by a person of a valid registration under the Act of March 3, 1881, or the Act of February 20, 1905, or on the principal register under this Act shall be a complete bar to an action against that person, with respect to that mark, that —

(A)(i) is brought by another person under the common law or a statute of a State; and

(ii) seeks to prevent dilution by blurring or dilution by tarnishment; or

(B) asserts any claim of actual or likely damage or harm to the distinctiveness or reputation of a mark, label, or form of advertisement.

[655] H.R. 683, 109th Cong., 2d Sess. (as reported Feb. 27, 2006). The only difference between the Senate version of subsection(c)(6) and the language ultimately enacted is the change from "under this Act" to "under this chapter."

Unless Congress enacts a technical correction, the courts will have to decide whether a literal interpretation of subsection (c)(6) reflects the true intent of Congress.

PART V:
CYBERSQUATTING

§ 3.08   ANTICYBERSQUATTING CONSUMER PROTECTION ACT (ACPA)

The popularity of the Internet as a channel for commercial activities soon led to the phenomenon of "cybersquatting," which occurs, in the words of one court, "when a person other than the trademark holder registers the domain name of a well-known trademark and then attempts to profit from this by either ransoming the domain name back to the trademark holder or by using the domain name to divert business from the trademark holder to the domain name holder."[656]

In 1999, Congress enacted section 43(d) of the Lanham Act, the Anticybersquatting Consumer Protection Act (ACPA), to clarify and strengthen the remedies available against users of domain names that incorporate registered marks or marks that are protected under section 43(a) or (c).

Congress was concerned that cybersquatters were committing fraud and causing consumer confusion in ways that would "impair electronic commerce, deprive trademark owners of substantial revenues and consumer goodwill, and place overwhelming burdens on trademark owners in protecting their valuable intellectual property."[657] Three types of conduct were of particular concern: (1) registering domain names that are similar to famous marks in order to profit by selling those domain names to the owners of the marks; (2) attaching offensive (e.g., pornographic) matter to an infringing domain name in order to tarnish the mark; and (3) attempting to divert a trademark owner's customers to a competitor's website.[658]

The legislative history of the ACPA defines cybersquatters as those who: (1) "register well-known brand names as Internet domain names in order to extract payment from the rightful owners of the marks;" (2) "register well-known marks as domain names and warehouse those marks with the hope of selling them to the highest bidder;" (3) "register well-known marks to prey on consumer confusion by misusing the domain name to divert customers from the mark owner's site to the cybersquatter's own site;" or (4) "target distinctive marks to defraud

---

[656] DaimlerChrysler v. The Net, Inc., 388 F.3d 201, 204 (6th Cir. 2004); *see also* Virtual Works, Inc. v. Volkswagen of America, Inc. 238 F.3d 264 (4th Cir. 2001).

[657] Coca-Cola Co. v. Purdy, 382 F.3d 774, 778 (8th Cir. 2004).

[658] *Id.*; *see also* Lucent Techs., Inc. v. Lucentsucks.com, 95 F. Supp. 2d 528, 530 n. 1 (E.D. Va. 2000); H.R. Rep. No. 106-412, 106th Cong., 1st Sess. 6 (1999).

consumers, including to engage in counterfeiting activities."[659]

[A]   Elements of a Cybersquatting Claim

Section 43(d) gives the trademark owner a cause of action against anyone who, with a bad faith intent to profit from the mark, registers, traffics in, or uses a domain name that (1) is identical or confusingly similar to a mark that was distinctive at the time the defendant's domain name was registered; or (2) is identical or confusingly similar to, or dilutive of, a mark that was famous at the time the defendant's domain name was registered.[660] A trademark owner asserting a claim under the ACPA must therefore establish the following: (1) it has a valid trademark entitled to protection; (2) its mark is distinctive or famous; (3) the defendant's domain name is identical or confusingly similar to, or in the case of famous marks, dilutive of, the owner's mark; and (4) the defendant used, registered, or trafficked in the domain name; (5) with a bad faith intent to profit.[661] Liability under section 43(d) may be imposed only on the domain name registrant or an authorized licensee of the registrant.[662]

The question whether a domain name is "confusingly similar" to a famous mark is not analyzed under the traditional likelihood-of-confusion analysis for trademark infringement. The latter considers a wide variety of factors that may affect a consumer's perception of the junior user's mark, including the similarity of the goods or services.[663] In contrast, the question of confusing similarity under the ACPA has a narrower focus, looking only at the senior user's mark and the junior user's domain name.[664] The fact that a consumer's confusion could be alleviated by actually visiting the junior user's website is therefore irrelevant.[665] Courts generally hold that a domain name is confusingly similar to a senior user's trademark if "consumers might think that [the domain name] is used, approved, or permitted" by the senior user.[666] In making this assessment, courts consider only the second-level domain name (for example, "pepsi" in pepsi.com), and disregard the top-level domain name (for example, .com, .org, .net).[667] They also disregard "slight differences" between the domain name and

---

[659] S. Rep. No. 106-140, at 5-6 (1999), quoted in *Lucas Nursery and Landscaping, Inc. v. Grosse*, 359 F.3d 806, 809 (6th Cir. 2004).

[660] 15 U.S.C. § 1125(d)(1)(A). This provision also applies to registration, trafficking, or use of a mark, word, or name protected under 18 U.S.C. § 706 (the Red Cross) or 36 U.S.C. § 220506 (the Olympics).

[661] *DaimlerChrysler*, 388 F.3d at 204.

[662] 15 U.S.C. § 1125(d)(1)(D).

[663] *See* § 3.02 [B] *supra*.

[664] *Coca-Cola*, 382 F.3d at 783; *Northern Light Tech., Inc. v. Northern Lights Club*, 236 F.3d 57, 66 (1st Cir. 2001).

[665] *Coca-Cola*, 382 F.3d at 783; *People for Ethical Treatment of Animals v. Doughney*, 263 F.3d 359 (4th Cir. 2001); *Virtual Works, Inc. v. Volkswagen of Am., Inc.*, 238 F.3d 264, 266 (4th Cir. 2001); *Sporty's Farm L.L.C. v. Sportsman's Market, Inc.*, 202 F.3d 489, 497-98 (2d Cir. 2000).

[666] *DaimlerChrysler*, 388 F.3d at 205-06 (citing *Ford Motor Co. v. Greatdomains.com, Inc.*, 177 F. Supp. 2d 635, 641 (E.D. Mich. 2001); *Harrods Ltd. v. Sixty Internet Domain Names*, 157 F. Supp. 2d 658, 677 (E.D. Va. 2001)).

[667] *Coca-Cola*, 382 F.3d at 783-84.

the senior user's mark, "such as the addition of minor or generic words,"[668] or common misspellings or similar errors.[669]

Domain names may also violate the ACPA if they are "dilutive" of a senior user's mark. Pornographic websites, for example, are routinely held to be dilutive when they incorporate well-known trademarks in their domain names.[670]

The statutory phrase "traffics in" includes, without limitation, sales, purchases, loans, pledges, licenses, exchanges of currency, and "any other transfer for consideration or receipt in exchange for consideration."[671]

Congress imposed the threshold requirement of "bad faith intent to profit" in order to target cybersquatters who act with an "intent to trade on the goodwill of another's mark."[672] In determining whether a defendant acted with such bad faith intent, courts may consider the following non-exhaustive[673] list of factors: (1) the defendant's intellectual property rights, if any, in the domain name; (2) the extent to which the domain name constitutes the defendant's legal name or a name commonly used to identify the defendant; (3) the defendant's prior use of the domain name in connection with the bona fide offering of goods or services; (4) the defendant's bona fide noncommercial use or fair use of the mark in a site accessible under the domain name; (5) the defendant's intent to divert customers from the mark owner's online location to a site accessible under the domain name that could harm the goodwill represented by the mark, either for commercial gain or with the intent to tarnish or disparage the mark, by creating a likelihood of confusion as to the source, sponsorship, affiliation, or endorsement of the defendant's site; (6) the defendant's offer to assign the

---

[668] *See, e.g., DaimlerChrysler*, 188 F.3d at 205-06 ("foradodge.com" domain name was confusingly similar to DODGE mark); *Ford Motor Co.*, 177 F. Supp. 2d at 641 (domain names "4fordparts.com," "jaguarcenter.com," and "volvoguy.com" were confusingly similar to the marks FORD, JAGUAR, and VOLVO); Spear, Leeds, & Kellogg v. Rosado, 122 F. Supp. 2d 403, 406 (S.D.N.Y. 2000) (domain names redi-ecn.com and redixt.com, which combined "redi" with generic or descriptive financial industry terms, were confusingly similar to plaintiff's REDI and REDIBOOK marks).

[669] *See, e.g.*, Shields v. Zuccarini, 254 F.3d 476, 483-84 (3d Cir. 2001) (defendant's domain names were confusingly similar where they differed from the senior user's mark only by slight misspellings or typographical differences).

[670] *See, e.g.*, Lucent Techs., Inc. v. Johnson, 56 U.S.P.Q.2d (BNA) 1637 (C.D. Cal 2000) (allegation that defendant used plaintiff's mark as domain name for pornographic web site stated a claim for dilution); Mattel, Inc. v. Internet Dimensions, Inc., 2000 U.S. Dist. LEXIS 9747 (S.D.N.Y. July 13, 2000) (finding defendant's registration of barbiesplaypen.com to divert users to a site displaying pornographic content tarnished the goodwill of plaintiff's BARBIE mark); Hasbro Inc. v. Internet Entertainment Group, Ltd., 40 U.S.P.Q.2d (BNA) 1479, 1480, 1996 U.S. Dist. LEXIS 11626 (W.D. Wash. 1996) (finding defendants had diluted plaintiff's mark for its board game "Candy Land," by registering the domain name candyland.com and displaying pornography there).

[671] 15 U.S.C. § 1125(d)(1)(E).

[672] S. Rep. No. 106-140, 106th Cong., 1st Sess. 9 (1999); *see* Ford Motor Co. v. Catalanotte, 342 F.3d 543, 549 (6th Cir. 2003) ("Registering a famous trademark as a domain name and then offering it for sale to the trademark owner is exactly the wrong Congress intended to remedy when it passed the ACPA.").

[673] As permitted by the ACPA, courts have considered factors other than the nine listed. *See, e.g.*, Virtual Works, Inc. v. Volkswagen of America, Inc., 238 F.3d 264, 57 U.S.P.Q.2d (BNA) 1547 (4th Cir. 2001).

domain name to the mark owner or any other person for financial gain without having used, or having an intent to use, the domain name in the bona fide offering of goods or services, or the defendant's prior conduct indicating a pattern of such conduct; (7) the defendant's provision of material and misleading false contact information when applying for the domain name's registration, intentional failure to maintain accurate contact information, or prior conduct indicating a pattern of such conduct; (8) the defendant's registration or acquisition of multiple domain names with the knowledge that those names were identical or confusingly similar to distinctive marks of others, or dilutive of famous marks of others, without regard to the goods or services of the parties; and (9) the extent to which the mark incorporated in the defendant's domain name is or is not distinctive and famous within the meaning of section 43(c) (the federal dilution statute).[674] The first four factors represent reasons why a defendant, acting in good faith, might register a domain name that incorporates another's mark, while the last five factors are considered indicia of bad faith.[675] In applying these factors, courts consider the totality of the circumstances, including "the purely circumstantial indicia of bad faith, as well as the direct evidence of the statements made at the time of registration and the direct evidence regarding terms of the sale" of the domain name.[676] Under the ACPA's "safe harbor" provision, bad faith intent to profit will not be found where a court determines that the defendant reasonably believed that the use of the domain name was a fair use or otherwise lawful.[677]

In *Coca-Cola Co. v. Purdy*, for example, the court found a violation of the ACPA where the defendant registered domain names that were confusingly similar to the plaintiff's trademarks for the purpose of diverting the plaintiff's customers to noncommercial websites carrying an anti-abortion message.[678] In *People for the Ethical Treatment of Animals v. Doughney*, an ACPA violation was found where the defendant registered the plaintiff organization's acronym (PETA) as a domain name, which he publicly offered to sell to the plaintiff.[679] In *Sporty's Farm L.L.C. v. Sportsman's Market, Inc.*, a finding of bad faith was based, *inter alia*, on the fact the defendant registered its domain name for the primary purpose of depriving a competitor of the use of that domain name.[680] And in *Harrods, Ltd. v. Sixty Internet Domain Names*,[681] the Fourth Circuit found bad faith where the registrant of multiple domain names using the "Harrods" mark was the lawful user of this mark in South America but intended to use the domain names to confuse customers outside of South America into

---

[674] 15 U.S.C. § 1125(d)(1)(B)(i); *See, e.g.*, *Shields*, 254 F.3d at 485 (applying these factors); People for the Ethical Treatment of Animals v. Doughney, 263 F.3d 359, 369 (4th Cir. 2001) (similar).

[675] *Coca-Cola*, 382 F.3d at 785 (citing Lucas Nursery & Landscaping, Inc. v. Grosse, 359 F.3d 806, 809-10 (6th Cir. 2004)).

[676] *Virtual Works*, 238 F.3d at 270.

[677] 15 U.S.C. § 1125(d)(1)(B)(ii).

[678] *Coca-Cola*, 382 F.3d at 785.

[679] 263 F.3d 359 (4th Cir. 2001); *see also* BroadBridge Media, L.L.C. v. Hypercd.com. 106 F. Supp. 2d 505 (S.D.N.Y. 2000) (bad faith found where defendant offered to sell domain name to plaintiff).

[680] 202 F.3d 489, 499 (2d Cir. 2000).

[681] 302 F.3d 214, 233-34 (4th Cir. 2002).

believing that they were doing business with the Harrods company that was based in the United Kingdom. In addition to these examples, bad faith is commonly found when a defendant uses a plaintiff's mark in the domain name of a pornographic website.[682]

In contrast, courts have *not* found bad faith intent to profit where the defendant has incorporated a trademark into its domain name for the purpose of criticizing the owner of that mark.[683] The question of whether a domain name is being used for a legitimate "gripe site" is not always clear-cut; an ACPA violation may be established where the criticisms on a website are merely camouflage for a bad faith intent to profit. As one court has noted:

> [E]xcluding cyber-gripers from the scope of the ACPA has the potential of "eviscerat[ing]" the protections of the bill by suggesting a blueprint for cybersquatters who would simply create criticism sites in order to immunize themselves from liability despite their bad-faith intentions." For that reason, it is important to carefully examine the entire record, to ascertain the context surrounding the formation and use of the disputed domain name, and to scrutinize the defendant's actions for any evidence that the griping may in fact be a pretext disguising an underlying profit motive.[684]

The presence or absence of various bad faith factors is helpful in distinguishing true gripe sites from cybersquatting. In *Coca-Cola Co. v. Purdy*, for example, the Eighth Circuit noted the absence of bad faith indicia in two cases where consumer gripe sites were held *not* to violate the ACPA despite their incorporation of a senior user's trademarks: "Neither customer in those cases had registered multiple infringing domain names or offered to transfer the names in exchange for valuable consideration. Neither had linked the names to websites about issues other than the company's business or to websites that solicited donations or sold merchandise."[685] In contrast, the putative "gripe sites" in *Toronto-Dominion Bank v. Karpachev*[686] violated the ACPA because numerous bad faith indicia were present:

> The defendant, a disgruntled customer, registered sixteen domain names composed of various misspellings of the name tdwaterhouse.com. On the web sites associated with these names, the defendant attacked Toronto-Dominion for "webfascism" and involvement with white collar crime, among other things. The court concluded that the defendant had acted in bad faith, citing four factors: (1) his intention to divert customers from the "tdwaterhouse" web site by creating confusion as to its source or sponsorship; (2) the fact that he had registered sixteen

---

[682]   *See, e.g.*, Lucent Techs., Inc. v. Johnson, 56 U.S.P.Q.2d (BNA) 1637 (C.D. Cal 2000).

[683]   *See, e.g., Coca-Cola*, 382 F.3d at 786-87; *Lucas Nursery*, 359 F.3d at 811; TMI, Inc. v. Maxwell, 368 F.3d 433 (5th Cir. 2004); Mayflower Transit, L.L.C. v. Prince, 314 F. Supp. 2d 362, 369-70 (D.N.J. 2004) (collecting "gripe site" cases).

[684]   *Mayflower Transit*, 314 F. Supp. 2d at 372 (quoting S. Rep. 106-140, at 9).

[685]   *Coca-Cola*, 382 F.3d at 786-87; *see also Mayflower Transit*, 314 F. Supp. 2d at 369-71 (collecting cases).

[686]   188 F. Supp. 2d 110 (D. Mass. 2002).

domain names; (3) the fact that he offered no goods or services on the site; and (4) the fact that he had no intellectual property rights in the site.[687]

Where at least some elements of bad faith are present, defendants are unlikely to succeed in invoking the safe harbor provision of section 43(d)(1)(B)(ii), which provides that bad faith may not be found where a defendant "believed and had reasonable grounds to believe that the use of the domain name was fair use or otherwise lawful."[688] Thus, for example, a mere offer to sell a domain name, without more, does not necessarily establish bad faith intent.[689] However, courts have held that a defendant "who acts even partially in bad faith in registering a domain name is not, as a matter of law, entitled to benefit from [the ACPA's] safe harbor provision."[690] In *Virtual Works, Inc. v. Volkswagen of America*, for example, the Fourth Circuit rejected a defendant's invocation of the safe harbor provision, because the evidence clearly established the defendant's intent to create and profit from the confusion caused by its domain name registration. The court observed:

> Just as we are reluctant to interpret the ACPA's liability provisions in an overly aggressive manner, we decline to construe the safe harbor so broadly as to undermine the rest of the statute. All but the most blatant cybersquatters will be able to put forth at least some lawful motives for their behavior. To hold that all such individuals may qualify for the safe harbor would frustrate Congress' purpose by artificially limiting the statute's reach. We do not think Congress intended the safe harbor to protect defendants operating, at least in part, with unlawful intent.[691]

[B]   *In Rem* Jurisdiction

Perhaps the ACPA's greatest enhancement to existing Lanham Act protections was the authorization of *in rem* jurisdiction over domain names when *in personam* jurisdiction over the user of the domain name cannot be obtained. Unfortunately, the *in rem* provisions have also given rise to significant interpretive problems.

When a defendant is beyond the reach of a court's *in personam* jurisdiction, the ACPA permits the exercise of *in rem* jurisdiction over the domain name itself.[692] Where the conditions for *in rem* jurisdiction are satisfied, the plaintiff may file the *in rem* action in the judicial district in which the domain name registrar, domain name registry, or other domain name authority that

---

[687] *Lucas Nursery*, 359 F.3d at 810-11 (citing *Toronto-Dominion Bank*, 188 F. Supp. 2d at 111-14); *see also* Shields v. Zuccarini, 254 F.3d 476, 485 (3d Cir. 2001) (rejecting as "spurious" defendant's characterization of his websites as "protest pages"). *Cf. People for the Ethical Treatment of Animals*, 263 F.3d at 369 (rejecting defendant's characterization of his website as parody).

[688] 15 U.S.C. § 1125(d)(1)(B)(ii).

[689] *Virtual Works*, 238 F.3d at 270 (citing H.R. Conf. Rep. No. 106-464, at 111 (1999)).

[690] *Virtual Works*, 238 F.3d at 270; *accord, People for the Ethical Treatment of Animals*, 263 F.3d at 369.

[691] *Virtual Works*, 238 F.3d at 270.

[692] *E.g.*, Porsche Cars N.A., Inc. v. Porsche.net, 302 F.3d 248 (4th Cir. 2002).

registered or assigned the domain name is located (which, for ".com" top-level domains, is the Northern District of California or the Eastern District of Virginia).[693] *In rem* jurisdiction is authorized only if the court finds that the plaintiff (1) cannot obtain *in personam* jurisdiction over the party that is acting in violation of section 43(d); or (2) through due diligence was unable to find that person by (a) sending notice to the domain name registrant at the postal and e-mail addresses that the latter provided to the registrar and (b) by publishing notice of the action, as directed by the court, promptly after filing.[694] Although several district courts have held that the publication requirement is mandatory even when the registrant receives actual notice,[695] others have held that, upon a motion by the plaintiff, the court can waive the publication requirement if actual notice is established.[696]

Subsection (d)(2)(C) further provides that the "situs" of a domain name is the judicial district where either (i) the domain name authority that registered or assigned the domain name is located, or (ii) documents sufficient to establish control and authority regarding disposition of the registration and use of the domain name are deposited with the court.[697] The relationship between subsections (d)(2)(A) (the jurisdictional provision) and (d)(2)(C) (the situs provision) is ambiguous, but courts have generally concluded that subsection (d)(2)(C) does not provide an alternative basis for *in rem* jurisdiction.[698] To conclude otherwise, courts have noted, would render subsection (d)(2)(C)(i) superfluous,[699] and treating (d)(2)(C)(ii) as an independent basis for *in rem* jurisdiction would violate the "minimum contacts" requirement of due process, at least if the domain name registrar is statutorily *required* to deposit the documents necessary to trigger this provision upon service of the complaint, as appears to be the case under subsection (d)(2)(D)(i)(I).[700] It appears that a proper reading of the statute treats the question of the domain name's legal "situs" as separate from the question of jurisdiction. The registrar's act of

---

[693] 15 U.S.C. § 1125(d)(2)(A). A domain name registrar "is one of several entities, for a given TLD, that is authorized by ICANN [Internet Corporation for Assigned Names and Numbers] to grant registration of domain names to registrants." FleetBoston Financial Corp. v. FleetBostonFinancial-.com, 138 F. Supp. 2d 121, 123 n. 2 (D. Mass. 2001). In contrast, a domain name registry "is the single official entity that maintains all official records regarding registrations in the TLD (top level domain)." *Id.* (internal citations and quotation marks omitted). There is one registry for each TLD, such as ".com," ".org," and ".edu." *See generally* Cable News Network, LP, LLLP v. CNNews.com, 162 F. Supp. 2d 484, 486 n. 4 (E.D. Va. 2001), *aff'd in relevant part*, 56 Fed. Appx. 599 (4th Cir. 2003).

[694] 15 U.S.C. § 1125(d)(2)(A). *See* Lucent Techs, Inc. v. Lucentsucks.com, 95 F. Supp. 2d 528, 534 (E.D. Va. 2000) (purpose of ACPA's in rem provisions is "to provide a last resort where in personam jurisdiction is impossible, because the domain name resident is foreign or anonymous").

[695] *See, e.g.*, Investools, Inc. v. Investtools.com, 81 U.S.P.Q.2d (BNA) 2019 (E.D. Va. 2006).

[696] *See, e.g.*, Yahoo!, Inc. v. Yahooahtos.com, 82 U.S.P.Q.2d (BNA) 1361 (E.D. Va. 2006).

[697] 15 U.S.C. § 1125(d)(2)(C).

[698] *See, e.g.*, Mattel, Inc. v. Barbie-Club.com, 310 F.3d 293, 299-301 (2d Cir. 2002); Ford Motor Co. v. Greatdomains.com, 177 F. Supp. 2d 656, 658-60 (E.D. Mich. 2001): *FleetBoston Financial Corp.*, 138 F. Supp. 2d at 124-29; *Cable News Network*, 162 F. Supp. 2d at 489 n. 15.

[699] *See, e.g.*, *Cable News Network*, 162 F. Supp. 2d at 489 n. 15; *Ford Motor Co.*, 177 F. Supp. 2d at 659 n.4; *Mattel*, 310 F.3d at 301.

[700] *Ford Motor Co.*, 177 F. Supp. 2d at 658-60.; *FleetBoston Financial Corp.*, 138 F. Supp. 2d at 125.

depositing the appropriate documents with a court that *already* has jurisdiction establishes that the domain name's situs is in the judicial district that has jurisdiction, and this gives the court authority to exercise control over the domain name throughout the litigation, even if the location of the registrar or registry changes after the litigation commences.[701]

Unfortunately, the ACPA is also ambiguous with respect to the substantive scope of the *in rem* cause of action. Initially, district courts disagreed on whether the *in rem* cause of action was available *only* in cases involving "bad faith intent to profit" under section 43(d)(1), or whether it could also be invoked against domain names that violated section 32, 43(a), or 43(c) even without a showing of bad faith.[702] In 2002, the Fourth Circuit adopted the latter interpretation in its thoughtful opinion in *Harrods, Ltd. v. Sixty Internet Domain Names*,[703] and treatise author Thomas McCarthy agrees with that analysis.[704] Because most *in rem* actions are brought in the Fourth Circuit (where the ".com" registry is located), this probably settles the matter. Thus, where personal jurisdiction cannot be obtained over a defendant, plaintiffs may invoke the *in rem* cause of action in order to remedy trademark infringement, dilution, and unfair competition claims under the Lanham Act, as well as "bad faith intent to profit" claims.

Conversely, there is some uncertainty as to whether an *in rem* action can be predicated *solely* on the act of registering a domain name, regardless of whether the registrant has a bad intent to profit. While the ACPA's *in personam* provision (subsection (d)(1)) provides a cause of action against a person who registers, traffics in, or uses a domain name that resembles another's mark only when there is a bad faith intent to profit, the *in rem* provision (subsection (d)(2)) is worded differently, providing a cause of action against a domain name if and only if "the domain name violates any right of the owner of a mark registered in the Patent and Trademark Office or protected under subsection (a) or (c)" of section 43. Based on this difference in wording, one district court held that an *in rem* cause of action could be based on the act of registration alone, even in the absence of bad faith as defined in section 43(d).[705] In that court's view, the *in rem* cause of action applied because the mere act of registering another person's mark as a domain name was a "use in commerce" that was likely to cause confusion, mistake, or deception within the meaning of section 32(1) or section 43(a):

> The act of registration was in connection with the sale of the right to use the domain name, arguably either a good or service. This sale (from the

---

[701]   *Mattel*, 310 F.3d at 303-06.

[702]   *Compare* V'soske, Inc. v. Vsoske.com, 2001 U.S. Dist. LEXIS 6675, *20 (S.D.N.Y. 2001) (bad faith required); Hartog & Co. v. swix.com, 136 F. Supp. 2d 531, 539 (E.D. Va. 2001) (similar); *and* Broadbridge Media, LLC v. Hypercd.com, 106 F. Supp. 2d 505, 511 (S.D.N.Y. 2000) (similar) *with* Jack in the Box, Inc. v. Jackinthebox.org, 143 F. Supp. 2d 590, 591 (E.D. Va. 2001) (*in rem* provision not limited to section 43(d) claims).

[703]   302 F.3d 214, 228, 232 (4th Cir. 2002); *accord* Cable News Network, L.P. v. CNNews.com, 56 Fed. Appx. 599, 603 (4th Cir. 2003) (unpub.).

[704]   *See* McCarthy on Trademarks, *supra* note 223, at § 25:79 (2001).

[705]   Jack in the Box, Inc. v. Jackinthebox.org, 143 F. Supp. 2d 590, 591-92 (E.D. Va. 2001).

domain name registrar to the unknown registrants) constituted "use in commerce." A domain name registrant need not actually develop a working website for the illegal use of the mark to constitute commercial use. The act of registering a domain name is a commercial act because it involves a sale between the registrant and the registrar. The infringing domain name is used in this commercial act because it itself becomes the good or service that is sold. It thus meets the definition of "use in commerce" under 15 U.S.C. § 1127, 15 U.S.C. § 1114(1)(a), and 15 U.S.C. § 1125.[706]

Accordingly, the court held that a bad faith intent to profit was not a necessary element of an *in rem* cause of action predicated solely on the act of domain name registration.[707] However, another district court disagreed:

> I first address plaintiff's concern regarding the necessity of showing bad faith at all in an *in rem* proceeding, but conclude that bad faith intent to profit is a necessary element to plaintiff's case for two reasons. First, Congress clearly intended to use the bad faith element of the statute as a way to narrow the breadth of the statute. "The bill is carefully and narrowly tailored, however, to extend only to cases where the plaintiff can demonstrate the defendant . . . *used* the offending domain name with bad-faith intent to profit from the goodwill of a mark belonging to someone else. Thus, the bill does not extend to innocent domain name registrations by . . . someone who is aware of the trademark status of the name but registers a domain name containing the mark for any reason other than with bad faith intent to profit from the goodwill associated with that mark." Reflecting this intent, Congress limited the in rem action against a domain name to those situations where the court finds the owner is unable "to obtain *in personam* jurisdiction over a person *who would have been a defendant under paragraph (1)*." To be brought in as a defendant under paragraph (1) requires, in addition to other elements, a bad faith intent to profit.[708]

The court noted, however, that there was also a second reason to require bad faith in that case — because the plaintiff had specifically pleaded a violation of subsection (d)(1) as the basis for his *in rem* proceeding.[709]

In *Harrods, Ltd. v. Sixty Internet Domain Names*,[710] the Fourth Circuit did not resolve this conflict, and indeed was not squarely presented with the issue. The holding in that case — that section 43(d) authorizes *in rem* actions "against domain names based on claims of infringement and dilution as well as bad faith registration"[711] — does not answer the question whether domain name regis-

---

[706] 143 F. Supp. 2d at 592; *see* §§ 3.02 [E], *supra* (discussing the "use in commerce" requirement for violations of sections 32, 43(a), and 43(c)).

[707] *Id.* at 592.

[708] Broadbridge Media, LLC v. Hypercd.com, 106 F. Supp. 2d 505, 511 (S.D.N.Y. 2000) (quoting H.R. Conf. Rep. 106-412 (emphasis added)).

[709] *Id.*

[710] Harrods, Ltd. v. Sixty Internet Domain Names, 302 F.3d 214, 222-23, 228, 247 (4th Cir. 2002).

[711] *Id.* at 247.

tration, without more, constitutes an infringing or dilutive use in commerce. However, implicit in the court's holding is an acknowledgment that the plaintiff in an *in rem* proceeding must show that the domain name registration does *one* of the following: (1) creates a likelihood of confusion, (2) creates a likelihood of dilution, or (3) involves a bad faith intent to profit.

[C]   Personal Names

With respect to unauthorized domain name registrations of personal names, both the civil action under section 43(d)(1)(A) and the *in rem* action under section 43(d)(2) apply to "a personal name which is protected as a mark" under section 43.[712] With respect to personal names that lack sufficient secondary meaning to qualify as trademarks, however, the ACPA affords a narrower range of protection. Section 47 of the Lanham Act provides:

> Any person who registers a domain name that consists of the name of another living person, or a name substantially and confusingly similar thereto, without that person's consent, with the specific intent to profit from such name by selling the domain name for financial gain to that person or any third party, shall be liable in a civil action by such person.[713]

Thus, in contrast to section 43(d)(1), which provides a cause of action whenever a trademark-protected personal name is used in a domain name with a "bad faith intent to profit," section 47 provides a cause of action for unauthorized use of a personal name in a domain name *only* against a party that (1) registers that domain name, (2) "with the specific intent to profit from such name by selling the domain name for financial gain to that person or any third party."[714]

In addition to these restrictions, one court has held that no liability arises under section 43(d) where a political figure's name is used as the domain name for a noncommercial website devoted to criticism of that person, because, *inter alia*, such use is protected by the First Amendment.[715]

Because of the limited scope of anticybersquatting protection which sections 43(d) and 47 provide for personal names, section 3006 of the ACPA directed the Secretary of Commerce to recommend to Congress guidelines and procedures for protecting personal names against the following unauthorized uses:

(1)   registration by another person as a domain name for the purposes of profiting from the sale or transfer of the domain name;

(2)   bad faith uses of personal names as domain names by others with malicious intent to harm the reputation of the individual or the goodwill associated with the individual's name; or,

---

[712]   15 U.S.C. § 1125(d)(1)(A).

[713]   *Id.* § 1129(1)(A).

[714]   *Id.*; *See, e.g.*, Schmidheiny v. Weber, 285 F. Supp. 2d 613 (E.D. Pa. 2003) (granting summary judgment to plaintiff based on domain name registrant's intent to profit from the sale of domain name consisting of plaintiff's personal name).

[715]   Ficker v. Tuohy, 305 F. Supp. 2d 569, 572 (D. Md. 2004).

(3)   use that is intended or likely to confuse or deceive the consumer as to the affiliation, connection, or association of the domain name registrant, or the domain name site with the individual.[716]

The Secretary was also asked to recommend guidelines and procedures for protecting the public against registration and use of domain names that include the personal names of government officials and candidates for office.[717] In a 2001 report submitted to Congress pursuant to this directive, however, the Commerce Department concluded that current federal and state laws, together with the ICANN dispute resolution mechanism, already provided sufficient remedies against such unauthorized uses, so that no further legislation was needed.[718]

[D]   ACPA Remedies

Where a violation of section 43(d) is established, the court may order the forfeiture or cancellation of the domain name, or may order that it be transferred to the owner of the mark.[719] In an action under section 43(d)(2), these remedies are exclusive.[720] In an action under section 43(d)(1), however, the full array of Lanham Act remedies are available.[721] In addition, section 35(d) of the Lanham Act permits a plaintiff bringing a claim under section 43(d)(1) to elect statutory damages in place of actual damages and profits; a court may award an amount of statutory damages between $1,000 and $100,000 per domain name, as the court considers just.[722]

§ 3.09   ALTERNATIVE FORUMS FOR DOMAIN NAME DISPUTES

The ACPA does not preclude states from providing their own remedies for cybersquatting laws. California, for example, has enacted its own legislation prohibiting the bad faith domain registration of the name of a "living person or deceased celebrity."[723]

However, the main mechanism for resolving domain name disputes outside of the Lanham Act is the Uniform Domain Name Dispute Resolution Policy (UDRP) of the Internet Corporation for the Assigned Names and Numbers (ICANN), a non-profit, non-governmental organization that administers the domain name registration system under a Memorandum of Understanding with

---

[716] Sec. 3006, ACPA, Pub. L. No. 106-113, 113 Stat. 1501 (1999).

[717] *Id.*

[718] Report to Congress: The Anticybersquatting Consumer Protection Act of 1999, section 3006 concerning the abusive registration of domain names, available at http://www.uspto.gov/web/offices/dcom/olia/tmcybpiracy/repcongress.pdf.

[719] 15 U.S.C. § 1125(d)(1)(C).

[720] *Id.* § 1125(d)(2)(D); *see* Harrods Ltd. v. Sixty Internet Domain Names, 302 F.3d 214, 232 (4th Cir. 2002).

[721] For a detailed discussion of Lanham Act remedies, *see* §§ 3.13–3.15 *infra.*

[722] 15 U.S.C. § 1117(d).

[723] Calif. Bus. & Prof. Code, Art. 1.6, sec. 17525(a) (signed into law Aug.21, 2000).

the United States Department of Commerce.[724] Since 1999 the UDRP provisions have been incorporated into all domain name registration agreements, and acceptance of these provisions is a condition of the domain name registration. The purpose of the UDRP is to afford a non-judicial option to trademark owners that will allow them to resolve domain name disputes quickly and inexpensively through a form of non-binding arbitration utilizing approved dispute resolution providers. Remedies are limited to cancellation of the offending domain name registration or transfer of that registration to the successful complainant. Complaining parties are not required to utilize the UDRP, and may opt instead to pursue their legal claims in court. Initiating a UDRP proceeding does not foreclose a complainant from pursuing legal remedies.[725]

Paragraph 4 of the UDRP sets forth the procedures for arbitration. To prevail in a UDRP proceeding, the complainant must generally establish (1) that the domain name is identical or confusingly similar to a trademark or service mark in which the complainant has rights (either through trademark registration or under common law), (2) that the domain name holder does not have legitimate interests in the domain name, and (3) that the domain name was registered and being used in bad faith.[726] The policy sets forth a non-exhaustive list of bad faith indicia.[727] The domain name holder must respond by demonstrating a legitimate interest in the domain name. Proof of such a legitimate interest should include (1) whether the name used in the domain name is connected to the bona fide offering of goods or services; (2) whether the domain name holder is commonly known by the name used as a domain name; or (3) whether the domain name holder is making a legitimate noncommercial or a fair use of the domain name without intent to divert consumers or tarnish the trademark in question.[728]

A party that is dissatisfied with the outcome of a UDRP proceeding may pursue a separate legal action in a court of competent jurisdiction. If the UDRP panel orders cancellation or transfer of the domain name registration, the domain name registrar will implement that decision within ten business days unless it receives official documentation (such as a copy of the complaint) indicating that the registrant has commenced legal action.

UDRP arbitration decisions are reported at http://www.icann.org/udrp/proceedings-list-name.htm.

---

[724] *See* Sallen v. Corinthians Licenciamentos LTDA, 273 F.3d 14, 20 (1st Cir. 2001).

[725] BroadBridge Media, L.L.C. v. Hypercd.com, 106 F. Supp. 2d 505, 509 (S.D.N.Y. 2000).

[726] UDRP, ¶ 4(a), available at http://www.icann.org/en/dndr/udrp/policy.htm.

[727] *Id.* ¶ 4(b).

[728] *Id.* ¶ 4(c).

PART VI:
SECONDARY LIABILITY

§ 3.10   CONTRIBUTORY AND VICARIOUS LIABILITY

Although the Lanham Act contains no statutory provisions for imposing liability on parties other than direct infringers, the courts have turned to the common law of torts in order to develop doctrines of contributory and vicarious liability that apply to claims involving registered trademarks as well as violations of section 43(a). More recently, courts have begun to explore the concept of secondary liability (contributory or vicarious) for violations of section 43(c). Applying secondary liability concepts derived from tort law to the Lanham Act is particularly appropriate because the law of trademarks and unfair competition is itself a species of tort law.[729]

[A]   Contributory Liability

Even prior to the Lanham Act, the common law recognized contributory liability in the context of unfair competition when a party supplied goods to another knowing or intending that the latter would pass off the goods as those of a competitor.[730] In a leading case imposing such liability, *William R. Warner & Co. v. Eli Lilly & Co.*, the Supreme Court in 1924 held a drug manufacturer liable for actively encouraging pharmacists to pass off the defendant's medicine as a competitor's more expensive medicine that was similar in taste and color: "The wrong was in designedly enabling the dealers to palm off the preparation as that of the respondent. One who induces another to commit a fraud and furnishes the means of consummating it is equally guilty and liable for the injury."[731]

As discussed below, it is now well settled that contributory liability under section 32 or 43(a) of the Lanham Act arises when a defendant either: (1) actively induces another to infringe, or (2) continues to supply a product to a party that it knows or has reason to know is using the product in an infringing activity. More recently, the latter test has been extended to the provision of services.

---

[729] *See* AT&T v. Winback & Conserve Program, 42 F.3d 1421, 1433 (3d Cir. 1994) (collecting cases).

[730] *See* Smith, Kline & French Labs. v. Clark & Clark, 157 F.2d 725, 731 (3d Cir.), *cert. denied*, 329 U.S. 796 (1946); F.W. Fitch Co. v. Camille, Inc., 106 F.2d 635, 640 (8th Cir. 1939); Coca-Cola Co. v. Gay-Ola Co., 200 F. 720, 722-23 (6th Cir. 1912); N.K. Fairbank Co. v. R.W. Bell Manuf'g. Co., 77 F. 869, 875, 877-78 (2d Cir. 1896); Hiram Walker & Sons v. Grubman, 224 F. 725, 733-34 (S.D.N.Y. 1915); Enoch Morgan's Sons Co. v. Whittier-Coburn Co., 118 F. 657, 661-62 (N.D. Cal. 1902); Hostetter Co. v. Brueggeman-Reinert Distilling Co., 46 F. 188, 189 (E.D. Mo. 1891); Robert Reis & Co. v. Herman B. Reiss, Inc., 63 N.Y.S.2d 786, 798-803 (N.Y. Sup. Ct. 1946) (collecting cases).

[731] 265 U.S. 526, 530-31 (1924) (citations omitted).

The leading case on contributory liability for trademark infringement is the Supreme Court's decision in *Inwood Laboratories v. Ives Laboratories*.[732] The defendant in *Inwood Labs* was a drug manufacturer/supplier who continued to supply generic drugs to a pharmacist who was mislabeling them with another maker's trademark. In determining whether the manufacturer/supplier could be held liable under section 32 for the infringing actions of the pharmacists, the Court held that:

> Liability for trademark infringement can extend beyond those who actually mislabel goods with the mark of another. Even if a manufacturer does not directly control others in the chain of distribution, it can be held responsible for their infringing activities under certain circumstances. Thus, if a manufacturer or distributor intentionally induces another to infringe a trademark, or if it continues to supply its product to one whom it knows or has reason to know is engaging in trademark infringement, the manufacturer or distributor is contributorily responsible for any harm done as a result of the deceit.[733]

Both prongs of the *Inwood Labs* test have been extended beyond the manufacturer/supplier context.[734] In *Mini Maid Services Co. v. Maid Brigade Systems, Inc.*, the Eleventh Circuit applied *Inwood Labs* to the relationship between a franchisor and its franchisees:

> Although *Inwood Laboratories* involved the relationship between manufacturers and retailers, the analysis employed in that case governs the relationship between a franchisor and its franchisees. Following the lead of *Inwood Laboratories*, we conclude that liability for trademark infringement can extend beyond those entities that actually perform the acts of infringement, but only under certain circumstances. With respect to a franchisor's liability for the independent infringing acts of its franchisees, we hold that the franchisor may be held accountable only if it intentionally induced its franchisees to infringe another's trademark or if it knowingly participated in a scheme of trademark infringement carried out by its franchisees.
>
> As in *Inwood Laboratories*, any liability for contributory infringement will necessarily depend upon whether or not the contributing party intended to participate in the infringement or actually knew about the

---

[732] 456 U.S. 844 (1982).

[733] *Id.* at 854-55 (emphasis added). Procter & Gamble Co. v. Haugen, 317 F.3d 1121, 1129-30 (10th Cir. 2003) ("An action for contributory liability is not limited to a manufacturer, but may also extend to licensors, franchisers, or to similarly situated third parties.").

[734] *See* Procter & Gamble Co. v. Haugen, 317 F.3d 1121, 1129-30 (10th Cir. 2003) ("An action for contributory liability is not limited to a manufacturer, but may also extend to licensors, franchisers, or to similarly situated third parties."); AT&T v. Winback & Conserve Program, 42 F.3d 1421, 1432 (3d Cir. 1994) (noting that contributory liability is not limited to manufacturers, but finding no contributory liability where provider of telecommunications services "took appropriate steps to reprimand and discipline" its sales representatives for their infringing conduct), *cert. denied*, 514 U.S. 1103 (1995); Mini Maid Servs Co. v. Maid Brigade Sys., Inc., 967 F.2d 1516, 1522 (11th Cir. 1992) (imposing liability on franchisor that "explicitly or implicitly encouraged" trademark infringements by its franchisees).

infringing activities. In making these determinations of intent and knowledge, a district court should consider the nature and extent of the communication between a franchisor and its franchisees regarding the infringing acts; specifically, the court should decide whether or not the franchisor explicitly or implicitly encouraged the trademark violations. In addition, the court may wish to consider the extent and nature of the violations being committed. If the infringement is serious and widespread, it is more likely that the franchisor knows about and condones the acts of its franchisees. Finally, under appropriate facts, contributory trademark infringement might be grounded upon a franchisor's bad faith refusal to exercise a clear contractual power to halt the infringing activities of its franchisees.[735]

Mini Maid refused to impose on franchisors a "duty to supervise with reasonable diligence," noting that "the law imposes no duty upon a franchisor to diligently prevent the independent acts of trademark infringement that may be committed by a single franchisee."[736]

Similarly, in *Hard Rock Café Licensing Corp. v. Concession Services, Inc.,*[737] the Seventh Circuit held that the operator of a flea market could be contributorily liable for violations of sections 32 and 43(a) by one of its vendors. The court relied on the common law of torts, and specifically the rule of the *Restatement (Second) of Torts* that a company "is responsible for the torts of those it permits on its premises 'knowing or having reason to know that the other is acting or will act tortiously,' "[738] and concluded that "[t]he common law . . . imposes the same duty on landlords and licensors that the Supreme Court has imposed on manufacturers and distributors."[739]

However, even as it used common law principles to broaden the *Inwood Labs* doctrine beyond the manufacturer/supplier context, the *Hard Rock* court expressed uncertainty as to the full scope of contributory liability:

[I]t is not clear how the doctrine applies to people who do not actually manufacture or distribute the good that is ultimately palmed off as made by someone else. A temporary help service, for example, might not be liable if it furnished [the infringing flea market vendor] Parvez the workers he employed to erect his stand, even if the help service knew that Parvez would sell counterfeit goods. Thus we must ask whether the operator of a flea market is more like the manufacturer of a mislabeled good or more like a temporary help service supplying the purveyor of goods.[740]

---

[735] *Mini Maid Servs,* 967 F.2d at 1521-22 (11th Cir. 1992) (citations omitted).

[736] *Id.* at 1519-21.

[737] 955 F.2d 1143, 1149 (7th Cir. 1992). The Ninth Circuit adopted the *Hard Rock Café* approach in Fonovisa, Inc. v. Cherry Auction, Inc., 76 F.3d 259, 265 (9th Cir. 1996), holding that a flea market operator could be contributorily liable for "blatant" trademark infringements by its vendors.

[738] 955 F.2d at 1149 (quoting Restatement (Second) of Torts § 877(c) & cmt. d (1979)).

[739] *Id.*

[740] *Hard Rock Café,* 955 F.2d at 1148.

In the absence of proof that the flea market operator had actual knowledge of the infringements, *Hard Rock* held that contributory liability could be imposed if the operator was "willfully blind" to the infringing activities, because "willful blindness is equivalent to actual knowledge for purposes of the Lanham Act."[741] To be willfully blind, the court held, "a person must suspect wrongdoing and deliberately fail to investigate."[742] Contributory liability could not, therefore, be premised on mere failure to take reasonable precautions to prevent infringement:

> [Flea market operator] CSI has no affirmative duty to take precautions against the sale of counterfeits. Although the "reason to know" part of the standard for contributory liability requires CSI (or its agents) to understand what a reasonably prudent person would understand, it does not impose any duty to seek out and prevent violations. We decline to extend the protection that Hard Rock finds in the common law to require CSI, and other landlords, to be more dutiful guardians of Hard Rock's commercial interests.[743]

The Seventh Circuit's expansion of the *Inwood Labs* doctrine was later adopted by the Ninth Circuit in *Fonovisa, Inc. v. Cherry Auction, Inc.*, where it held that a flea market operator could be contributorily liable for its vendors' sales of infringing goods because it was "supplying the necessary marketplace for their sale."[744]

Courts have yet to establish a clear standard for imposing contributory liability based on the provision of services that facilitate infringing activity. However, they have begun to explore this question in the specific context of Internet-related services.

For example, in *Lockheed Martin Corp. v. Network Solutions, Inc.*,[745] the Ninth Circuit held that a domain name registrar could not be liable for contributory infringement simply because it registered, and refused to cancel, certain domain names that contained or resembled the plaintiff's registered service mark. The "supplying a product" aspect of the *Inwood* test, in the court's view, would be satisfied only if the registrar controlled and monitored the infringing activities:

> *Hard Rock* and *Fonovisa* teach us that when measuring and weighing a fact pattern in the contributory infringement context without the convenient "product" mold dealt with in *Inwood Lab.*, we consider the extent of control exercised by the defendant over the third party's means of infringement. Direct control and monitoring of the instrumentality used by a third party to infringe the plaintiff's mark permits the expansion of *Inwood Lab*'s "supplies a product" requirement for contributory infringement.

---

[741] *Hard Rock Café*, 955 F.2d at 1149.

[742] *Id.* at 1149.

[743] *Id.* (citing Restatement (Second) of Torts § 12(1) & cmt. a (1965)).

[744] 76 F.3d 259, 265 (9th Cir. 1996).

[745] 194 F.3d 980 (9th Cir. 1999).

. . .

The "direct control and monitoring" rule established by *Hard Rock* and *Fonovisa* likewise fails to reach the instant situation. The district court correctly recognized that NSI's rote translation service does not entail the kind of direct control and monitoring required to justify an extension of the "supplies a product" requirement. Such a stretch would reach well beyond the contemplation of *Inwood Lab.* and its progeny.

In an attempt to fit under *Fonovisa*'s umbrella, Lockheed characterizes NSI's service as a licensing arrangement with alleged third-party infringers. Although we accept Lockheed's argument that NSI licenses its routing service to domain-name registrants, the routing service is just that — a service. In *Fonovisa* and *Hard Rock*, by contrast, the defendants licensed real estate, with the consequent direct control over the activity that the third-party alleged infringers engaged in on the premises.[746]

In an earlier proceeding in *Lockheed Martin*, the district court distinguished the role of a domain name registrar from that of "an Internet service provider whose computers provide the actual storage and communications for infringing material, and who therefore might be more accurately compared to the flea market vendors in *Fonovisa* and *Hard Rock*."[747] It noted, however, that even an Internet service provider might avoid contributory liability for the infringing conduct of its customers, because "[e]ven though Internet service providers directly provide the storage and communications facilities for Internet communication, they cannot be held liable merely for failing to monitor the information posted on their computers for tortious content."[748]

In *Playboy Enterprises v. Netscape Communications Corp.*,[749] the Ninth Circuit allowed Playboy Enterprises to proceed against service provider Netscape for trademark infringement and dilution, because the latter caused banner ads from Playboy's competitors to "pop up" whenever users conducted key word searches on a Netscape search engine using either of Playboy's trademarked terms "playboy" and "playmate." The banner ads were not labeled to indicate that they had a source other than Playboy. Clicking on one of these banner ads would take the user to the advertiser's Web site, and high "click-through" rates encouraged advertisers to continue to purchase banner ads on Netscape. The Ninth Circuit reversed a summary judgment for Netscape, holding that triable issues of fact existed with respect to Netscape's liability for infringement and dilution of Playboy's marks, either as a direct infringer or as a contributory infringer. However, the court declined to decide which theory of liability applied, and therefore did not explore the standard for contributory infringement.

---

[746] *Id.* at 984-85 (citations omitted).

[747] Lockheed Martin Corp. v. Network Solutions, Inc., 985 F. Supp. 949, 962 (C.D. Cal. 1997).

[748] *Id.* at 962 n. 7.

[749] 354 F.3d 1020 (9th Cir. 2004).

Two district courts applied a similar analysis to conclude that that the operator of a search engine could be liable for infringements by its advertisers. In *Government Employees Insurance Co. v. Google, Inc.* ("*GEICO*"),[750] the Eastern District of Virginia held that the operator of the Google search engine could be held liable under a theory of contributory or vicarious liability — the court did not specify which — for the actions of banner advertisers that used plaintiff's trademarks by incorporating them into their ads in a way that was likely to confuse consumers as to the affiliation of those advertisers. The court based its conclusion on the fact that Google "exercise[d] significant control over the content of advertisements that appear on their search results pages." It rejected the defendant's argument that, under *Inwood Labs*, there could be no contributory liability unless the defendant intentionally induced the infringement or continued to supply a product to the infringer with actual or constructive knowledge of infringing activity. In the court's view, it would be sufficient for the plaintiff to show that the defendant monitored and controlled the third-party advertisements.[751]

In *Google, Inc. v. American Blind & Wallpaper Factory, Inc.*,[752] an unpublished opinion, the Northern District of California applied *Netscape* and *GEICO* to hold that Google could be contributorily liable for infringement arising from its keyword-triggered advertising program. Google allowed, and even encouraged, its advertisers to "purchase" trademarked keywords that, when entered into a search engine, would generate "sponsored links" to the advertisers' Web sites, which appeared at the top and in the margins of the search results page. Google received a payment from the advertiser each time a user clicked on its sponsored link. The court noted that while Google had the technological capacity to block the purchase of keywords, it chose not to do so, nor did it disable sponsored links that had purchased trademarked terms.

In *Perfect 10, Inc. v. Visa Int'l Serv. Ass'n*,[753] the Ninth Circuit considered a contributory infringement claim against credit card companies that processed payments for customers purchasing infringing images over the Internet from websites that infringed the plaintiff's mark. The plaintiff argued that the credit card companies were contributorily liable because they "provid[ed] critical support" to the infringing websites.[754] Because there was no indication that the defendants intentionally induced the websites' infringing activities, and because the defendants supplied services rather than goods, the court applied the *Lockheed Martin* version of *Inwood Labs*: "When the alleged direct infringer supplies a service rather than a product, under the second prong of this test, the court must 'consider the extent of control exercised by the defendant over the third party's means of infringement.' For liability to attach, there must be '[d]irect control and monitoring of the instrumentality used by a third party to

---

[750] 330 F. Supp. 2d 700, 704 (E.D. Va. 2004).

[751] *Id.* at 705 (citing Size v. Network Solutions. Inc., 255 F. Supp. 2d 568, 573 (E.D. Va. 2003); Lockheed Martin Corp. v. Network Solutions, Inc., 194 F.3d 980 (9th Cir. 1999)).

[752] 74 U.S.P.Q.2d (BNA) 1385 (N.D. Cal. 2005) (unpub.).

[753] 494 F.3d 788 (9th Cir. 2007), *cert. denied*, 128 S. Ct. 2871 (2008).

[754] *Id.* at 807.

infringe the plaintiff's mark.' "[755] Here, the plaintiff argued that the "instrumentality" was the defendants' credit card payment network. However, in the court's view, the payment network was not the instrument that was used to infringe the plaintiff's mark; the infringement "occur[ed] without any involvement of Defendants and their payment systems."[756] Furthermore, the plaintiffs did not allege that the defendants had the power to remove the infringing materials from the websites, or to stop the distribution of those materials over the Internet. Although the defendants might have the power to stop processing payments to the websites, which could then have the practical effect of stopping or reducing the infringing activity, the court held that "[t]his, without more, does not constitute 'direct control.' "[757] The court noted its own observation in *Lockheed Martin* that "[w]hile the landlord of a flea market might reasonably be expected to monitor the merchandise sold on his premises, [defendant] NSI cannot reasonably be expected to monitor the Internet."[758] Dissenting, Judge Kozinski argued that the credit card companies satisfied the *Lockheed Martin* control test because "not only do they process the payment for virtually every sale of pirated images by the Stolen Content Websites, they control whether such transactions will go forward."[759]

In *Tiffany, Inc. v. eBay, Inc.*,[760] a district court in the Second Circuit considered whether Internet auction site eBay was contributorily liable for sales of counterfeit Tiffany goods by merchants using its website. Tiffany did not allege inducement; thus, the contributory liability question turned on whether eBay continued to supply its services to vendors that it knew or had reason to know were infringing. Although eBay promptly removed, without question, any listings that Tiffany identified as infringing, Tiffany argued that eBay was required to monitor its website and to preemptively remove any listings that *might* be infringing based on its generalized knowledge that infringing activities were taking place. Tiffany had notified eBay that there were no authorized third-party vendors for Tiffany merchandise and, therefore, that any vendor offering five or more Tiffany items was almost certainly selling counterfeit goods;[761] in Tiffany's view, this imposed on eBay an affirmative duty to monitor its website and remove listings from merchants offering multiple Tiffany items, even without having specific knowledge that the items were counterfeit. The district court rejected this argument, noting that, under *Inwood Labs*, "the standard is not whether eBay could reasonably anticipate possible infringement, but rather whether eBay continued to supply its services to sellers when it knew or had reason to know of infringement by those sellers."[762] The court continued:

---

[755] *Id.* at 807 (quoting *Lockheed Martin*, 194 F.3d at 984).

[756] *Id.*

[757] *Id.*

[758] *Id.* (quoting *Lockheed Martin*, 194 F.3d at 985).

[759] *Id.* at 822 (Kozinski, J., dissenting).

[760] 576 F. Supp. 2d 463 (S.D.N.Y. 2008).

[761] *Id.* at 481.

[762] *Id.* at 469.

The law does not impose liability for contributory trademark infringement on eBay for its refusal to take such preemptive steps in light of eBay's "reasonable anticipation" or generalized knowledge that counterfeit goods might be sold on its website. Quite simply, the law demands more specific knowledge as to which items are infringing and which seller is listing those items before requiring eBay to take action.[763]

Because eBay ceased to provide its services to specific sellers whom it knew or had reason to know were selling infringing goods, it satisfied its obligations under *Inwood Labs*.

In applying the *Inwood Labs* standard, the *Tiffany* court and many others have expressly rejected the "reasonable anticipation" standard derived from section 27 of the Restatement (Third) of Unfair Competition, which would impose contributory liability for trademark infringement when "the actor fails to take reasonable precautions against the occurrence of the third person's infringing conduct in circumstances in which the infringing conduct can be reasonably anticipated."[764] These courts have concluded that the reasonable anticipation standard is specifically foreclosed by the Supreme Court's decision in *Inwood Labs*.[765]

Courts and commentators have only recently begun to explore the concept of contributory liability for dilution.[766] Although several cases have discussed contributory dilution,[767] only one district court (in the Northern District of Illinois) has actually recognized this cause of action, holding that encouraging others to dilute a trademark can constitute contributory dilution.[768] That court did not address the applicability of the second *Inwood Labs* test (supplying a

---

[763] *Id.* at 470.

[764] *Id.* at 502.

[765] *Id.* at 502-503. *Accord*, GMC v. Keystone Auto. Indus., No. 02-74587, 2005 U.S. Dist. LEXIS 23168, at *35 n. 21 (E.D. Mich. May 10, 2005), *rev'd on other grounds*, 453 F.3d 351 (6th Cir. 2006); P&G v. Haugen, 158 F. Supp. 2d 1286, 1294 (D. Utah 2001); Medic Alert Found. United States, Inc. v. Corel Corp., 43 F. Supp. 2d 933, 940 (N.D. Ill. 1999); Lockheed Martin Corp. v. Network Solutions, 175 F.R.D. 640, 646 (C.D. Cal. 1997); David Berg & Co. v. Gatto Int'l Trading Co., 9 U.S.P.Q.2d (BNA) 1070, *11 (N.D. Ill. 1988); *but see* Ciba-Geigy Corp. v. Bolar Pharm. Co., 547 F. Supp. 1095, 1116 (D.N.J. 1982), *aff'd*, 719 F.2d 56 (3d Cir. 1983).

[766] *See, e.g.*, John T. Cross, *Contributory and Vicarious Liability for Trademark Dilution*, 80 Or. L. Rev. 625 (2001).

[767] Tiffany, Inc. v. eBay, Inc., 576 F. Supp. 2d 463, 526 (S.D.N.Y. 2008) (finding it unnecessary to determine whether contributory dilution should be recognized, because the facts failed to show that defendant eBay either (1) knowingly encouraged its sellers to dilute, or (2) knew or had reason to know of specific instances of dilution by its sellers, and failed to take action against those sellers); Medline Indus., Inc. v. Strategic Commercial Solutions, Inc., 553 F. Supp. 2d 979, 992 (N.D. Ill. 2008) (finding it unnecessary to decide whether to recognize contributory dilution because plaintiff failed to state such a claim); Google, Inc. v. American Blind & Wallpaper Factory, Inc., 74 U.S.P.Q.2d (BNA) 1385, 1394 (N.D. Cal. 2005) (unpub.) (declining to decide whether such cause of action exists); Steinway, Inc. v. Ashley, 2002 U.S. Dist. LEXIS 1372, *7 (S.D.N.Y. 2002) (declining to dismiss contributory dilution claim, and describing the cause of action as "entirely plausible"); *Lockheed Martin*, 194 F.3d at 986; Academy of Motion Picture Arts & Sciences v. Network Solutions, Inc., 989 F. Supp. 1276, 1278-81 (C.D. Cal. 1997) (finding no precedent or statutory basis for contributory dilution).

[768] Kegan v. Apple Computer Inc., 42 U.S.P.Q.2d (BNA) 1053, 1062 (N.D. Ill. 1996).

product to the diluting party with actual or constructive knowledge of the dilution) or the expanded version of that test (monitoring and controlling the dilutive activity).

In *Lockheed Martin*, the Ninth Circuit rebuffed the plaintiff's belated attempt to add a contributory dilution claim based on NSI's refusal to cancel dilutive domain name registrations. Although the court saw this claim as unlikely to succeed on the facts presented, it acknowledged that the plaintiff's argument was consistent with the second *Inwood Labs* test:

> . . . Lockheed's proposed amended complaint alleged that NSI contin-
> ued to supply its routing service to registrants, knowing that these
> parties were diluting Lockheed's "Skunk Works" service mark. As we
> have already concluded, however, NSI does not supply a product or
> engage in the kind of direct control and monitoring required to extend
> the *Inwood Lab.* rule.[769]

Despite the dearth of authority, there should be little doubt that a cause of action for contributory dilution will ultimately be recognized under the Lanham Act. Although the specific legal standards remain to be established, they are likely to develop along the same lines as the contributory infringement standards that have evolved from *Inwood Labs*.

[B]   Vicarious Liability

Courts generally apply common law principles of agency in determining whether, and under what circumstances, to impose vicarious liability under state trademark law and under the Lanham Act.[770] Accordingly, the concept of vicarious liability in trademark law is narrower than the concept of vicarious liability in federal copyright law, which is a form of strict liability that does not comport with the common law standards.[771]

Where an infringement action concerns common law trademarks under section 43(a), some courts have expressed uncertainty on the question of whether the pertinent agency principles are those of federal common law or, where different, the common law of the state where the infringing conduct took place.[772] Where the action involves federally registered marks under section 32, however, state law principles would not appear to be relevant.

The seminal case on vicarious liability under the Lanham Act is *Hard Rock Café Licensing Corp. v. Concession Services, Inc.*, where the Seventh Circuit

---

[769] *Lockheed Martin*, 194 F.3d at 986.

[770] *See AT&T*, 42 F.3d at 1433-34; W.T. Rogers Co., Inc. v. Keene, 778 F.2d 334 (7th Cir. 1985).

[771] *Hard Rock Café*, 955 F.2d at 1150. Under copyright law, a defendant is vicariously liable for copyright infringement if it has "the right and ability to supervise the infringing activity and also has a direct financial interest in such activities." *Id.* (quoting Gershwin Publishing Corp. v. Columbia Artists Mgt., Inc., 443 F.2d 1159, 1162 (2d Cir. 1971)).

[772] *See AT&T*, 42 F.3d at 1435 n. 16; W.T. Rogers Co., Inc. v. Keene, 778 F.2d 334 (7th Cir. 1985); Fare Deals, Ltd. v. World Choice Travel.com, Inc., 180 F. Supp. 2d 678, 684 n. 2 (D. Md. 2001). In many cases, of course, the law will be the same. *See, e.g., AT&T*, 42 F.3d at 1435 n. 16; *Fare Deals*, 180 F. Supp. 2d at 684 n. 2; Procter & Gamble Co. v. Haugen, 317 F.3d 1121, 1127-28 (10th Cir. 2003).

considered whether to hold a flea market operator liable, under theories of contributory[773] and vicarious liability, for violations of section 32 and 43(a) by a vendor who operated a booth at the market. Relying on common law standards, the court applied a "joint tortfeasor" analysis to determine whether vicarious liability should be imposed:

> We have recognized that a joint tortfeasor may bear vicarious liability for trademark infringement by another. This theory of liability requires a finding that the defendant and the infringer have an apparent or actual partnership, have authority to bind one another in transactions with third parties or exercise joint ownership or control over the infringing product.[774]

Because the relationship between the flea market operator and its vendor did not fit this description, there was no basis for imposing vicarious liability. Applying the same test, the Third Circuit reached a similar conclusion in *AT&T v. Winback & Conserve Program*, on the ground that the defendant entity and its sales representatives (the direct infringers) did not "act in concert to commit a tort, pursuant to a common purpose."[775]

In *SB Designs v. Reebok Int'l, Ltd.*,[776] the district court applied *Hard Rock*'s joint tortfeasor concept of vicarious liability in concluding that apparel maker Reebok was not vicariously liable for violations of sections 32 and 43(a) by third-party websites:

> Plaintiffs attach various screen shots and print-outs of several allegedly infringing Web sites, but these exhibits show no indication that the Web sites are owned by, endorsed by, or otherwise affiliated with Reebok. In general, the Web sites contain what appear to be comments and postings by basketball fans about Iverson and other players, and some of the Web sites offer Reebok shoes and apparel for sale. There is no evidence that Reebok supplied the products for sale on the Web sites, or permitted the sales or the use of Reebok's tradename or logos. Lynch stated in his affidavit that at no time has Reebok authorized, licensed, permitted, or encouraged the use of Reebok's trademarks, trade name, service marks, or trade dress on any of the Web sites cited by plaintiffs. Plaintiffs do not refute this claim, and thus create no triable issue as to whether there is a relationship between Reebok and these Web sites that would subject Reebok to vicarious liability.[777]

The court also declined to impose vicarious liability on Reebok for infringements by a basketball player's promotional company; although Reebok had occasional

---

[773] *Hard Rock Café*'s analysis of contributory liability is discussed at § 3.10 [A] *supra*.

[774] 955 F.2d at 1150 (citation omitted). The court relied on its previous decision in David Berg & Co. v. Gatto Internat'l Trading Co., 884 F.2d 306, 311 (7th Cir. 1989), in which it applied the joint tortfeasors doctrine to a section 32 action, holding that "[e]very person actively partaking in, lending aid to, or ratifying and adopting such acts is liable equally with the party itself performing these acts."

[775] *AT&T*, 42 F.3d at 1441 n. 22.

[776] 338 F. Supp. 2d 904 (2004).

[777] *Id.* at 911.

business dealings with that company and an endorsement deal with the player, there was no evidence that Reebok's relationship with either the company or the player amounted to a partnership, a joint venture, or an employment relationship.[778]

Although the stringency of the common law standard makes vicarious liability for trademark infringement difficult to establish, it is not impossible. In *Government Employees Insurance Co. v. Google*,[779] for example, the district court refused to dismiss the plaintiff's vicarious liability claim against two Internet search engines where the latter sold advertising opportunities triggered by trademarked "keywords" (including the plaintiff's "GEICO" mark) to competitors of the trademark owner, so that the competitors' Web sites would appear as "sponsored links" on the search results page whenever a user entered the trademarked terms into the search engine. The court rejected the argument that vicarious liability applied only when the defendant and the direct infringer have a principal-agent relationship,[780] interpreting *Hard Rock* as establishing "that a principal-agent relationship is only one example of a relationship that can give rise to vicarious liability, and that vicarious liability can also occur if the defendant and the infringer 'exercise joint ownership and control over the infringing product.'"[781] In the court's view, this standard was satisfied by GEICO's allegation that both the search engine and the advertisers controlled the appearance of the advertisements on the search results page and the use of GEICO's trademarks in those advertisements.[782]

In *Perfect 10, Inc. v. Visa Int'l Serv. Ass'n*,[783] the Ninth Circuit rejected a vicarious liability claim against the credit card companies that processed customers' payments for purchases made on websites that allegedly infringed the plaintiff's mark. In the court's view, the defendants' payment processing services did not amount to a "symbiotic" relationship or a "joint ownership and control" relationship with the infringing websites. The court rejected the plaintiff's argument that the credit card companies' acceptance of a payment created a contract that bound the customer to purchase from the website; rather, the contract arose between the customer and the website, and the credit card companies merely provided a means to settle the customer's debt.[784] In his dissent, Judge Kozinski argued that the plaintiffs had alleged sufficient facts to support vicarious liability: "[T]he Stolen Content Websites cannot operate without the use of credit cards, while defendants make huge profits by

---

[778] *Id.* at 910.

[779] 330 F. Supp. 2d 700 (E.D. Va. 2004).

[780] In support of this approach, the defendant relied on Fare Deals, Ltd. v. World Choice Travel.com, Inc., 180 F. Supp. 2d 678, 686 (D. Md. 2001), which appears to hold that a principal-agent relationship is a necessary prerequisite to vicarious liability under the Lanham Act. However, the opinion in that case did not even discuss *Hard Rock*. The *Fare Deals* approach has not been endorsed by other courts.

[781] 330 F. Supp. 2d at 705 (*quoting Hard Rock Café*, 955 F.2d at 1150).

[782] *Id.*

[783] 494 F.3d 788 (9th Cir. 2007), *cert. denied*, 128 S. Ct. 2871 (2008).

[784] *Id.* at 808.

processing these illegal transactions. If this is not symbiosis, what is?"[785] He agreed with the plaintiff's argument that it was the actions of the credit card companies that bound the websites to deliver the infringing content to purchasers.[786]

In cases where a claim of vicarious liability is premised on a principal-agent relationship, courts look to the common law of agency to determine whether the direct infringer was acting as an agent for the defendant when it engaged in the infringing activities.[787] Common law agency principles are complex and multifaceted, extending to situations involving both actual and apparent authority.[788] As a result, determinations as to agency are highly fact-specific.

Although no court has yet imposed vicarious liability for trademark dilution, and only one court has considered such a claim,[789] on an appropriate set of facts there would appear to be no legal barrier to imposing such liability under the Lanham Act where the common law standard is satisfied.

PART VII:
DEFENSES

§ 3.11   FIRST AMENDMENT CONSIDERATIONS

Because trademark and unfair competition laws regulate speech, these laws are sometimes in tension with the First Amendment. As discussed in this section, courts have adopted a number of different approaches to resolving these conflicts. Their approaches, however, are not always consistent.

Although it is convenient to discuss First Amendment concerns in connection with defenses to trademark and unfair competition claims, in many cases courts have treated First Amendment considerations as distinct from true affirmative defenses to infringement. For example, as discussed below,[790] where a defendant has used another's trademark in the context of literary and artistic expression, some courts have held that trademark and unfair competition laws either do not apply, or must be narrowly construed, because the defendant is not using the mark to indicate the origin of goods or services. Other courts have engaged in a balancing analysis, weighing the rights of the trademark owner (and the public interest in avoiding consumer confusion) against the public interest in free expression. In contrast, where the defendant uses another's trademark in a parodic fashion either in commercial advertising or on ordinary merchandise, courts will generally treat this as a commercial use that falls within the scope of

---

[785] *Id.* at 822-23.

[786] *Id.* at 823.

[787] *See, e.g., AT&T*, 42 F.3d at 1434-40 (collecting authorities).

[788] *See, e.g., id.*

[789] *See* Fare Deals, Ltd. v. World Choice Travel.com, Inc., 180 F. Supp. 2d 678, 685-86 (D. Md. 2001) (finding no vicarious liability for false designation of origin or trademark dilution in the absence of facts establishing a principal-agent relationship).

[790] See § 3.11 [B] below.

trademark and unfair competition laws;[791] however, courts disagree on the extent to which the parodic context of this commercial use warrants special consideration in light of First Amendment concerns. Another context in which courts have not reached a consensus is that of expressive merchandise (such as posters and T-shirts), which are commercial goods but often have a strong expressive component.[792] And while political speech normally receives a high degree of First Amendment protection, courts generally have not treated it as outside the scope of trademark laws.[793]

Unfortunately, many court opinions, especially those involving parodies, do not clearly indicate whether the court considers the defendant's work to be one of artistic expression or one that is purely commercial (such as commercial advertising or ordinary merchandise), thus making it difficult to assess whether those courts would apply the same analysis in both contexts. Indeed, some decisions fail to draw any distinction between purely commercial uses and protected expression. In addressing the scope of First Amendment protection against infringement and dilution claims, courts frequently rely indiscriminately on precedents involving artistic expression, ordinary commercial goods, and/or expressive merchandise, apparently without recognizing that these different categories may not be interchangeable in terms of their degree of First Amendment protection.

In the context of infringement and unfair competition claims, courts also disagree on whether the analysis of First Amendment issues should be integrated with the analysis of the likelihood of confusion,[794] or whether consideration of these issues should be undertaken only if a likelihood of confusion is found to exist.[795] The Eighth Circuit, for example, has held that failure to separate the parody analysis from the standard likelihood-of-confusion analysis is reversible error.[796]

---

[791] See § 3.11 [A] below.

[792] See § 3.11 [D] below.

[793] See § 3.11 [C] below.

[794] *E.g.*, Dr. Seuss Enters., L.P. v. Penguin Books USA, Inc., 109 F.3d 1394, 1407 (9th Cir. 1997); Nike, Inc. v. "Just Did It" Enters., 6 F.3d 1225, 1231 (7th Cir. 1993); Jordache Enters. v. Hogg Wyld, Ltd., 828 F.2d 1482, 1486 (10th Cir. 1987).

[795] *E.g.*, Anheuser-Busch, Inc. v. Balducci Pubs., 28 F.3d 769, 775 (8th Cir. 1994). In Elvis Presley Enters. v. Capece, 141 F.3d 188, 200 n. 5 (5th Cir. 1998), the Fifth Circuit noted: "We have considered parody separately from the other digits of confusion and recommend this approach, but in no way do we suggest at this time that the district court's approach of considering parody within its analysis of the standard digits of confusion in itself constitutes reversible error."

[796] *Balducci*, 28 F.3d at 775. The court noted that:

> Rather than first considering whether Balducci's ad parody was likely to confuse the public and then considering the scope of First Amendment protection, the district court conflated the two. The court essentially skewed its likelihood of confusion analysis in an attempt to give "special sensitivity" to the First Amendment, holding Anheuser Busch to a higher standard than required in a "classic trademark infringement case."

Id. at 773 (citation omitted).

[A]   Commercial Parodies

Allegations of trademark infringement or unfair competition sometimes arise in the context of commercial advertising or the offering of goods or services that involves the parody of a protected mark. Such cases require courts to determine whether and to what extent the parodic aspect of the defendant's actions should affect the likelihood-of-confusion analysis. A similar problem arises when the parodic use of a plaintiff's mark gives rise to a dilution claim, based on blurring or, more often, tarnishment of the parodied mark, although the analysis in those cases does not involve a likelihood of confusion.

[1]   Infringement and Unfair Competition

In the context of trademark infringement or unfair competition claims, parody is generally not treated as an affirmative defense. Rather, it serves as an additional consideration in the likelihood-of-confusion analysis,[797] one that tends to weigh against a finding that consumers are likely to be confused as to the source, sponsorship, or approval of the defendant's goods or services.[798]

For example, in *Hormel Foods Corp. v. Jim Henson Productions*,[799] the defendant parodied the plaintiff's SPAM trademark for canned meat products by introducing a wild boar "Muppet" character named "Spa'am" in a children's movie and related merchandise. Although the district court had rejected the plaintiff's claims of trademark infringement and dilution arising from the movie itself (which it analyzed as a work of artistic expression), additional issues involved the movie company's use of this character in merchandise related to the film, including food, candy, and cereal boxes. Hormel contended that this imitation of its SPAM trademark for canned meat created a likelihood of confusion, especially because Hormel sometimes used a character named "SPAM-man" (described as "a giant can of SPAM with arms and legs") to market its product, and had also begun its own merchandising efforts under the SPAM mark, including clothing, watches, golf balls, and toy cars — some of the same items that Henson's licensees were planning to issue. On appeal, the Second Circuit applied the traditional likelihood-of-confusion factors to the

---

[797] *See, e.g.*, Utah Lighthouse Ministry v. Found. For Apologetic Info. & Resch., 527 F.3d 1045, 1057 (10th Cir. 2008); Louis Vuitton Malletier S.A. v. Haute Diggity Dog, LLC, 507 F.3d 252, 263 (4th Cir. 2007); Elvis Presley Enters. v. Capece, 141 F.3d 188, 194 (5th Cir. 1998); Dr. Seuss Enters. v. Penguin Books USA, Inc., 109 F.3d 1394, 1407 (9th Cir. 1997); Nike, Inc. v. "Just Did It" Enters., 6 F.3d 1225, 1231 (7th Cir. 1993); Anheuser-Busch, Inc. v. L & L Wings, Inc., 962 F.2d 316, 321 (4th Cir. 1992); Jordache Enters. v. Hogg Wyld, Ltd., 828 F.2d 1482, 1486 (10th Cir. 1987); Anheuser-Busch, Inc. v. VIP Prods., LLC, 2008 U.S. Dist. LEXIS 82258, *22-23 (E.D. Mo. 2008); Tommy Hilfiger Licensing, Inc. v. Nature Labs, LLC, 221 F. Supp. 2d 410 (S.D.N.Y. 2002); Hard Rock Licensing Corp. v. Pacific Graphics, Inc., 776 F. Supp. 1454, 1462 (W.D. Wash. 1991); Schieffelin & Co. v. Jack Co. of Boca, 725 F. Supp. 1314, 1323 (S.D.N.Y. 1989); Mutual of Omaha Ins. Co. v. Novak, 648 F. Supp. 905, 910 (D. Neb. 1986), *aff'd*, 836 F.2d 397 (8th Cir. 1987); Tetley, Inc. v. Topps Chewing Gum, Inc., 556 F. Supp. 785 (E.D.N.Y. 1983).

[798] *E.g., Utah Lighthouse Ministry*, 527 F.3d at 1057; *Elvis Presley Enters.*, 141 F.3d at 198-99 ("while not a defense, parody is relevant to a determination of a likelihood of confusion and can even weigh heavily enough to overcome a majority of the digits of confusion weighing in favor of a likelihood of confusion"); *Dr. Seuss Enters.*, 109 F.3d at 1405; *Mutual of Omaha*, 648 F. Supp. at 910.

[799] 73 F.3d 497, 503 (2d Cir. 1996).

movie merchandise; however, in evaluating each factor it gave significant weight to the parodic context. The court emphasized that, well before the release of the Muppets movie and merchandise, the SPAM mark was already a frequent target of ridicule. Because the defendant's parody was not subtle, the court found that consumers would clearly understand that the character was a parody, and they would not be confused as to the origin or sponsorship of the movie-related merchandise:[800]

> Henson's use of the name "Spa'am" is simply another in a long line of Muppet lampoons. Moreover, this Muppet brand of humor is widely recognized and enjoyed. Thus, consumers of Henson's merchandise, all of which will display the words "Muppet Treasure Island," are likely to see the name "Spa'am" as the joke it was intended to be.[801]

The court treated the parodic aspect of the "Spa'am" character as particularly important to its analysis of the following factors:

Strength of the plaintiff's mark: Although the SPAM mark was "undeniably strong," a fact that would ordinarily weigh in the plaintiff's favor, the court concluded that in the context of an obvious parody the strength of the plaintiff's mark could actually favor the defendant, especially where, as here, consumers were already very familiar with the defendant's distinctive style of humor:

> "[W]here the plaintiff's mark is being used as part of a jest or commentary. . . . [and] both plaintiff['s] and defendant's marks are strong, well recognized, and clearly associated in the consumers' mind with a particular distinct ethic . . . confusion is avoided . . ." Indeed, a parody depends on a lack of confusion to make its point. "A parody must convey two simultaneous — and contradictory — messages: that it is the original, but also that it is *not* the original and is instead a parody."[802]

Similarity of the marks: Although the marks were superficially similar, the court concluded that the obvious parodic context would sufficiently distinguish them.[803]

Bad faith: The parody's lack of subtlety indicated that the defendant had no intent to create confusion.[804]

Some decisions analyzing commercial parodies have drawn guidance from the Supreme Court's decision in *Campbell v. Acuff-Rose Music*,[805] which analyzed a copyright infringement claim in the context of a parody. There, the Supreme Court noted that:

---

[800] *Id.* For a discussion of the plaintiff's dilution claim, *see* § 3.11 [A][2] *infra*.

[801] *Id.*

[802] *Id.* at 503 (quoting Yankee Publishing Inc. v. News America Publishing Inc., 809 F. Supp. 267, 273 (S.D.N.Y. 1992)).

[803] *Id.* at 503-04

[804] *Id.* at 505.

[805] 510 U.S. 569 (1994).

[T]he heart of any parodist's claim to quote from existing material, is the use of some elements of a prior author's composition to create a new one that, at least in part, comments on that author's works. If, on the contrary, the commentary has no critical bearing on the substance or style of the original composition, which the alleged infringer merely uses to get attention or to avoid the drudgery in working up something fresh, the claim to fairness in borrowing from another's work diminishes accordingly (if it does not vanish), and other factors, like the extent of its commerciality, loom larger. Parody needs to mimic an original to make its point, and so has some claim to use the creation of its victim's (or collective victims') imagination, whereas satire can stand on its own two feet and so requires justification for the very act of borrowing.[806]

Applying these principles to trademark parody in *Elvis Presley Enterprises v. Capece*, the Fifth Circuit observed:

From the Supreme Court's statements, it is clear that a parody derives its need and justification to mimic the original from its targeting of the original for comment or ridicule. ("When parody takes aim at a particular original work, the parody must be able to 'conjure up' at least enough of that original to make the object of its critical wit recognizable."). If the original is not a target of the parody, the need to "conjure up" the original decreases as the parody's aim moves away from the original.

This same need to conjure up the original exists when a parody targets a trademark or service mark. In the case of the standard likelihood-of-confusion analysis, a successful parody of the original mark weighs against a likelihood of confusion because, even though it portrays the original, it also sends the message that it is not the original and is a parody, thereby lessening any potential confusion. Therefore, a parody of a mark needs to mimic the original mark and from this necessity arises the justification for the mimicry, but this necessity wanes when the original mark is not the target of the parody.[807]

In the *Elvis Presley* case, the defendant had used a number of the plaintiff's trademarks to create an Elvis-themed bar called "The Velvet Elvis." The Fifth Circuit rejected the defendant's characterization of this use as a parody, because the plaintiff's marks were not the true object of the defendant's humorous message:

The Defendants' parody of the faddish bars of the sixties does not require the use of EPE's marks because it does not target Elvis Presley; therefore, the necessity to use the marks significantly decreases and does not justify the use. Capece himself conceded that the Defendants

---

[806] *Id.* at 580-81 (citations and footnotes omitted) (considering parody in relation to the fair-use defense to copyright infringement).

[807] 141 F.3d 188, 199-200 (5th Cir. 1998) (citing Cliffs Notes, Inc. v. Bantam Doubleday Dell Publ'g Group, Inc., 886 F.2d 490, 494 (2d Cir. 1989) ("A parody must convey two simultaneous — and contradictory — messages: that it is the original, but also that it is not the original and is instead a parody."); *see also* Anheuser-Busch, Inc. v. L & L Wings, Inc., 962 F.2d 316, 321 (4th Cir. 1992).

could have performed their parody without using Elvis's name. Without the necessity to use Elvis's name, parody does not weigh against a likelihood of confusion in relation to EPE's marks. It is simply irrelevant.[808]

The *Campbell* decision also influenced the Second Circuit's analysis in *Harley-Davidson, Inc. v. Grottanelli*,[809] where the defendant parodied the plaintiff's marks in promoting his motorcycle parts and repair business. Because the defendant did not use the marks primarily to comment on Harley-Davidson, the Second Circuit held that, under *Campbell*, this was "not a permitted trademark parody use."[810]

Courts routinely hold that, the more obvious the parody, the less likely it is that consumers will be confused about its source;[811] a true parody is "so obvious and heavy-handed that a clear distinction [is] preserved in the viewer's mind between the source of the actual product and the source of the parody."[812] Conversely, a parody that is too subtle is more likely to give rise to liability,[813] and a defendant's parody argument will be disregarded completely if the court does not perceive the mark as a true parody in the first place.[814]

As the Second Circuit has noted: "[A] parody depends on a lack of confusion to make its point. A parody must convey two simultaneous — and contradictory — messages: that it is the original, but also that it is *not* the original and is instead a parody."[815] Under this approach, in jurisdictions that consider the defendant's good or bad faith as one of the likelihood-of-confusion factors, an intent to parody is not equated with an intent to confuse or mislead.[816]

On occasion, courts or the PTO have completely disregarded the parodic nature of the defendant's mark,[817] or have expressly held it irrelevant.[818] In such cases, a finding of likelihood of confusion is almost inevitable, due to the similarity between the defendant's mark and the parodied mark, and the

---

[808] 141 F.3d at 200.

[809] 164 F.3d 806 (2d Cir. 1999).

[810] *Id.* at 813.

[811] New York Stock Exch., Inc. v. New York, New York Hotel, LLC, 69 F. Supp. 2d 479, 487 (S.D.N.Y. 1999), aff'd in relevant part, 293 F.3d 550 (2d Cir. 2002); see, e.g., Cardtoons, L.C. v. Major League Baseball Players Ass'n, 95 F.3d 959, 967 (10th Cir. 1996); Tommy Hilfiger, 221 F. Supp. 2d at 416.

[812] *Mutual of Omaha*, 648 F. Supp. at 910, *aff'd*, 836 F.2d 397 (8th Cir. 1987); *accord, Hard Rock Licensing*, 776 F. Supp. at 1462.

[813] *E.g.*, Schieffelin & Co. v. Jack Co., 850 F. Supp. 232, 250 (S.D.N.Y. 1994).

[814] *E.g., Hard Rock Licensing*, 776 F. Supp. at 1462.

[815] Hormel Foods Corp. v. Jim Henson Prods., 73 F.3d 497, 503 (2d Cir. 1996) (quoting Cliff Notes, Inc. v. Bantam Doubleday Dell Publishing Group, Inc., 886 F.2d 490, 494 (2d Cir. 1989)) (internal quotation marks omitted).

[816] *E.g., Tommy Hilfiger*, 221 F. Supp. 2d at 418-20; *Jordache*, 828 F.2d at 1486.

[817] *E.g.*, Grey v. Campbell Soup Co., 650 F. Supp. 1166, 1173 (C.D. Cal. 1986), *aff'd without op.*, 830 F.2d 197 (9th Cir. 1987); Recot, Inc. v. Becton, 56 U.S.P.Q.2d 1859 (TTAB 2000) (refusing to register FIDO LAY for dog treats, due to likelihood of confusion with FRITO LAY).

[818] Gucci Shops, Inc. v. R.H. Macy & Co., 446 F. Supp. 838, 840 (S.D.N.Y. 1977).

defendant's intentional copying. However, this approach appears to be a minority view.[819]

[2]   Dilution

Because dilution claims do not require a likelihood of consumer confusion, it can be more difficult to define the scope of First Amendment protection for commercial activities involving allegedly dilutive uses of trademarks. Because, unlike the federal statute, most state dilution statutes do not contain explicit exemptions for expressive or noncommercial works, the vulnerability of such works to state dilution claims is directly dependent on courts' sensitivity to First Amendment considerations.

Where the allegedly dilutive use takes place in the context of ordinary commercial advertising or the sale of goods (as opposed to artistic expression), courts generally will give little weight to a defendant's First Amendment arguments. However, they will consider whether, in the context in which the allegedly diluting use takes place, it is truly likely that the defendant's use of the mark will undermine the selling power of that mark. Nonetheless, the results in the dilution cases are inconsistent, and reflect courts' widely disparate levels of tolerance for commercial parody.

Several cases from the Second Circuit provide useful, and contrasting, illustrations. In *Deere & Co. v. MTD Products*,[820] the plaintiff charged that a competing lawnmower manufacturer had violated New York's antidilution statute in a television commercial that poked fun at the proud, majestic deer in plaintiff's well-known trademark by depicting it as cowardly and afraid. Although no blurring was involved, and the court rejected a tarnishment claim (based on its narrow view of tarnishment as requiring "a context of sexual activity, obscenity, or illegal activity"[821]), the court held that the defendant had nonetheless diluted the plaintiff's mark, because "alterations of that sort, accomplished for the sole purpose of promoting a competing product . . . risk the possibility that consumers will come to attribute unfavorable characteristics to a mark and ultimately associate the mark with inferior goods and services."[822] The fact that the parties were competitors was critical: "Dilution of this sort is more likely to be found when the alterations are made by a competitor with both an incentive to diminish the favorable attributes of the mark and an ample opportunity to promote its products in ways that make no significant alteration."[823]

In another suit brought under the New York dilution statute, the same court held in *Hormel Foods Corp. v. Jim Henson Productions*,[824] that the plaintiff's "SPAM" trademark for canned meat products was not diluted when a children's

---

[819] *See Tommy Hilfiger*, 221 F. Supp. 2d at 420 (disagreeing with these precedents).

[820] 41 F.3d 39 (2d Cir. 1994).

[821] 41 F.3d at 44.

[822] *Id.* at 45.

[823] *Id.*

[824] 73 F.3d 497, 503 (2d Cir. 1996).

entertainment company known for its famous "Muppet" characters produced a movie featuring a character named "Spa'am." At the appellate level, the plaintiff's dilution claim was based not on the movie itself, but on the defendant's sale of movie-related merchandise referencing the Spa'am character. The court concluded that blurring would not occur, for three reasons: First, the defendant's parody was so obvious that it would not weaken the association of the mark with the plaintiff's products — indeed, the court held, the humorous reference would strengthen that association.[825] Second, the marks were dissimilar, because the name "Spa'am" would always appear in conjunction with the character's image and other source identifiers. Finally, the defendant was not using "Spa'am" as a product brand name: "Rather, Spa'am is a character in products branded with Henson's own trademark."[826] The court concluded that: "Viewed against the backdrop of Henson's transparent parodic intent and the contextual dissimilarity between the two marks, it is clear that use of the name 'Spa'am' does not blur Hormel's mark."[827]

On the tarnishment claim, the *Hormel* court drew three distinctions between the defendant's use of the "Spa'am" character and the depiction of the cowardly deer in *Deere*. First, the "Spa'am" character was depicted in a positive, likeable way, which would not cause consumers to develop negative associations with SPAM-branded meat products. Second, the defendant's products — children's entertainment and related merchandise — did not directly compete with the plaintiff's products. Thus, the defendant was not ridiculing the plaintiff's mark in order to sell more of its own competing goods. Finally, the court noted that this was a case in which the defendant's parody was part of the product itself: "Without Spa'am, the joke is lost."[828]

A third parody case from the Second Circuit reached opposite conclusions on the blurring and tarnishment aspects of a dilution claim. In *New York Stock Exchange v. New York, New York Hotel, LLC,*[829] the plaintiff brought a state law dilution claim against a New York-themed casino for using the terms "NY$E" and "New York $lot Exchange" in connection with its gambling services and related merchandise. In the court's view, the "humor or parody" in the casino's modification of the plaintiff's marks prevented any diminution in the capacity of those marks to serve as unique identifiers of the plaintiff's stock trading services; thus, no blurring occurred. However, the court held that this same "humorous analogy" could injure the plaintiff's reputation; accordingly, the plaintiff could proceed to trial on the question of tarnishment.

The close relationship between dilution theory and parodic purpose created analytical problems for the Tenth Circuit in *Jordache Enters. v. Hogg Wyld, Ltd.,*[830] where a blue jeans maker brought a state law dilution claim against a competitor that marketed blue jeans for larger women with the word

---

[825] *Id.* at 506.

[826] *Id.* at 508.

[827] *Id.*

[828] *Id.*.

[829] 293 F.3d 550 (2d Cir. 2002).

[830] 828 F.2d 1482 (10th Cir. 1987).

"Lardashe" on the seat of the pants, accompanied by an image of a smiling pig. The appellate court upheld the district court's holding that no blurring occurred, because "parody tends to increase public identification of a plaintiff's mark with the plaintiff."[831] The court also rejected the tarnishment claim, but in doing so the court applied a narrow concept of tarnishment that is almost indistinguishable from a likelihood of confusion:

> To be actionable, . . . the association of the two marks must tarnish or appropriate the good will and reputation of the owner of the mark. If the public associates the two marks for parody purposes only and does not associate the two sources of the products, appellant suffers no actionable injury. Indeed, a manufacturer of a high quality product will typically benefit if its competitors are marketing a poor quality product at similar prices — *unless* the public associates the manufacturer of the poor quality product with the manufacturer of the high quality product. Thus, the actionable association of marks is limited to an association of the source of the marks. Association of marks for parody purposes without corresponding association of manufacturers does not tarnish or appropriate the good will of the manufacturer of the high quality similar product.[832]

In contrast to *Jordache*, some courts have not hesitated to treat commercial parody as actionable dilution. For example, in *Gucci Shops, Inc. v. R.H. Macy & Co.*,[833] a district court granted a preliminary injunction against the distribution of "Gucchi Goo" diaper bags. After ruling in the plaintiff's favor on the infringement claims, the court limited its dilution discussion to a footnote, where it held, without distinguishing between blurring and tarnishment, that the defendant's ridicule "would debilitate the potency of plaintiff's mark."[834] As in the *Deere* case, this court assigned no positive value to the defendant's parodic intent.

In contrast to the state dilution laws at issue in these cases, when claims against commercial uses are brought under the federal dilution statute, First Amendment considerations tend to be subsumed under the statutory exceptions. As discussed in § 3.07[H] above, the original version of section 43(c) included an exception for "noncommercial use" of a famous mark,[835] which courts interpreted as applying to expressive works protected by the First Amendment; however, courts did not apply that exception to commercial advertising. As revised in 2006, the federal dilution statute now exempts not only "any noncommercial use" of a famous mark (section 43(c)(3)(C),[836] but also "any fair use . . . other than as a designation of source for the person's own goods or services . . . including use in connection with . . . identifying and parodying, criticizing, or commenting upon the famous mark owner or the goods or services of the famous mark owner"

---

[831] *Id.* at 1490.

[832] *Id.* at 1490-91.

[833] 446 F. Supp. 838 (S.D.N.Y. 1977).

[834] *Id.* at 840 n. 6.

[835] 15 U.S.C. § 1125(c)(4)(B) (prior to 2006 amendments).

[836] *Id.* § 43 (c)(3)(C).

(section 43(c)(3)(A)(ii)).[837] While this new parody exception may ultimately be applied to some commercial parodies of famous marks, it does not apply to a commercial parody that uses the famous mark as an origin indicator for the defendant's products. Thus, in *Louis Vuitton Malletier S.A. v. Haute Diggity Dog LLC*,[838] the Fourth Circuit held that that the federal parody exception did not apply to a defendant's use of "Chewy Vuiton" as a trademark for dog toys. In contrast, this exception would permit a merchant to poke fun at its competitor's famous mark in comparative advertising. Thus, on the facts of the *Deere* case discussed above, the federal parody exception would probably allow the defendant to prevail against a federal dilution claim, even without resort to First Amendment arguments.

[B]   Noncommercial Expression

Where a defendant uses a plaintiff's trademark in a work of literary or artistic expression in order to convey an idea or a point of view, rather than for a purely commercial purpose, First Amendment considerations tend to weigh heavily in the defendant's favor. Therefore, in contrast to cases involving parodic uses of trademarks in connection with the advertising or sale of merchandise, courts have generally applied a different analysis where a trademark is used in a traditional expressive work — typically, a work of artistic, musical, or literary expression.

[1]   Infringement and Unfair Competition

Where a plaintiff alleges that the use of its mark in a work of artistic expression gives rise to a likelihood of confusion about the origin or sponsorship of that work, most courts have employed a balancing test that weighs the public interest in free expression against the public interest in avoiding consumer confusion.[839] In carrying out this balancing test, courts are generally willing to tolerate some degree of consumer confusion in order to avoid chilling protected speech.[840]

A leading case in this area, *Rogers v. Grimaldi*,[841] involved the application of the Lanham Act to the title of an expressive work. In that case, the defendant had made a film about fictional ballroom dancers who became known in Italy as "Ginger and Fred," which was also the title of the movie. Ginger Rogers brought suit, arguing that the film's title violated her rights under section 43(a) and the common law right of publicity. The district court granted summary judgment to the defendant on the ground that the film and its title were works of artistic expression rather than commercial speech. The Second Circuit affirmed. Although it noted that the First Amendment did not completely insulate artistic

---

[837] *Id.* § 43(c)(3)(A)(ii).

[838] 507 F.3d 252 (4th Cir. 2007).

[839] *Cliffs Notes*, 886 F.2d at 494.

[840] *Id.* at 495.

[841] 875 F.2d 994 (2d Cir. 1989). The Second Circuit applied the same approach four years later, in another case involving a title. *See* Twin Peaks Productions v. Publications Intern., 996 F.2d 1366, 1379 (2d Cir. 1993).

speech from Lanham Act claims, the expressive element of the film's title warranted "more protection than the labeling of ordinary commercial products."[842] The court concluded that the Lanham Act "should be construed to apply to artistic works only where the public interest in avoiding consumer confusion outweighs the public interest in free expression."[843] In the context of titles, the court held, "that balance will normally not support application of the Act unless the title has no artistic relevance to the underlying work whatsoever, or, if it has some artistic relevance, unless the title explicitly misleads as to the source or the content of the work."[844] The court rejected the narrower test proferred by the plaintiff, under which First Amendment considerations would be "implicated only where a title is so intimately related to the subject matter of a work that the author has no alternative means of expressing what the work is about,"[845] holding that this approach would not "sufficiently accommodate the public's interest in free expression."[846]

The Sixth Circuit applied the *Rogers* approach to the title of a musical work in *Parks v. LaFace Records*,[847] where famed civil rights figure Rosa Parks brought a section 43(a) claim against a record company, arguing that the use of her name in the title of a song, and on the album cover, falsely suggested that she had sponsored or approved of the song. The appellate court questioned the artistic relevance of the title (because the song lyrics were not about Rosa Parks), but held that it was not explicitly misleading. The court remanded the case so that a jury could determine whether the title was artistically relevant. If the jury found no artistic relevance, the court held, then Rosa Parks should prevail, but if the title was artistically relevant, then the defendant should prevail.[848]

The Second Circuit expanded the *Rogers* balancing approach beyond titles in *Cliffs Notes, Inc. v. Bantam Doubleday Dell Publishing Group, Inc.*,[849] where the defendant had published a series of literary parodies that spoofed the plaintiff's study aids summarizing major literary works by presenting summaries and pseudo-scholarly critiques of lesser contemporary works that were popular among college-age readers. The defendant's works used a cover design that was very similar to the plaintiff's. However, the Second Circuit noted that the defendant must be permitted to "conjure up" the original in order to parody it successfully. Although it would be fairly obvious to most consumers that the work was a parody, there remained, in the court's view, some slight risk of confusion. The court held, however, that this small risk of confusion was outweighed by First Amendment considerations. In so holding, the court expanded the *Rogers* balancing test beyond the context of titles to include all

---

[842] *Id.* at 998.

[843] *Id.* at 999.

[844] *Id.*

[845] *Id.* at 998.

[846] *Id.* at 999.

[847] 329 F.3d 437 (6th Cir. 2003).

[848] *Id.* at 458.

[849] 886 F.2d 490 (2d Cir. 1989).

works of artistic expression, including but not limited to parodies:[850]

> We believe that the overall balancing approach of *Rogers* and its emphasis on construing the Lanham Act "narrowly" when First Amendment values are involved are both relevant in this case. That is to say, in deciding the reach of the Lanham Act in any case where an expressive work is alleged to infringe a trademark, it is appropriate to weigh the public interest in free expression against the public interest in avoiding consumer confusion.[851]

The court concluded that "the *Rogers* balancing approach is generally applicable to Lanham Act claims against works of artistic expression, a category that includes parody."[852] Accordingly, "somewhat more risk of confusion is to be tolerated when a trademark holder seeks to enjoin artistic expression such as a parody."[853] Although the court did not abandon the likelihood-of-confusion test, it held that "a balancing approach allows greater latitude for works such as parodies, in which expression, and not commercial exploitation of another's trademark, is the primary intent, and in which there is a need to evoke the original work being parodied."[854] Thus, in the case of parody, the *Polaroid* factors must be applied "with proper weight given to First Amendment considerations."[855] Even if some consumers might be confused, the court found it sufficient that "most consumers will realize it is a parody."[856] Here, the label "A Satire" appeared five times on the cover of the defendant's work, and four times on the back. This reduced the likelihood that a consumer would purchase the defendant's book by mistake, and discover the error only after the purchase. Although the court conceded that there was a "slight risk of consumer confusion," this risk was "outweighed by the public interest in free expression, especially in a form of expression that must to some extent resemble the original."[857]

A similar analysis favored the defendant in *Hormel Foods Corp. v. Jim Henson Productions, Inc.*,[858] where the plaintiff argued that the presence of a Muppet character named "Spa'am" in the defendant's film infringed its SPAM trademark for canned meat. Adhering closely to the Second Circuit's guidance in *Cliffs Notes*, the Southern District of New York found that the character was an obvious parody, and treated this parodic context as relevant to each of the traditional *Polaroid* factors. The court concluded that the analysis of these factors overwhelmingly favored the defendant, and that the plaintiff could not

---

[850] *Id.* at 495.

[851] *Id.* at 494.

[852] *Id.* at 495.

[853] *Id.* at 495.

[854] *Id.*.

[855] *Id.* at 495 n. 3.

[856] *Id.* at 496.

[857] *Id.* at 497.

[858] 36 U.S.P.Q.2d (BNA) 1812, 1995 U.S. Dist. LEXIS 13886 (S.D.N.Y. 1995), *aff'd*, 73 F.3d 497 (2d Cir. 1996).

"use federal trademark laws to enjoin what is obviously a joke at its expense."[859] Likewise, in *Yankee Publishing, Inc. v. News Am. Publishing, Inc.*,[860] the same court applied the *Rogers/Cliffs Notes* balancing approach to the cover of a magazine issue (containing an article about Christmas gifts ranging from thrifty to frivolous) that imitated the cover of a popular almanac known for its emphasis on thrift. Although the court found that the cover image was not a true parody, the court held that it was "artistic editorial expression" that warranted the same degree of First Amendment protection as a parody.[861] Even if some readers did not comprehend the joke — thus giving rise to some potential for confusion — this was "far outweighed by First Amendment considerations protecting the right of commentary and artistic expression."[862] In addition, however, upon applying the *Polaroid* factors the court found that there was little likelihood of confusion because it would be obvious to most readers that the reference to the almanac was intended as a joke.

The Ninth Circuit applied the *Rogers* balancing approach to the lyrics of a musical work in *Mattel, Inc. v. MCA Records, Inc.*[863] In that case, toy manufacturer Mattel brought trademark infringement as well as dilution claims against the record companies that produced and distributed "Barbie Girl," a song that poked fun at Mattel's famous "Barbie" doll. The Ninth Circuit noted that the parodic use of the plaintiff's iconic trademark in this case was distinctly different from the garden-variety infringements that are the central concern of both trademark and dilution doctrine, both because the defendant's work was a work of artistic expression, and because the "Barbie" mark had achieved independent cultural significance apart from its origin-identifying function:

> The problem arises when trademarks transcend their identifying purpose. Some trademarks enter our public discourse and become an integral part of our vocabulary. How else do you say that something's "the Rolls Royce of its class?" What else is a quick fix, but a Band-Aid? Does the average consumer know to ask for aspirin as "acetyl salicylic acid?" Trademarks often fill in gaps in our vocabulary and add a contemporary flavor to our expressions. Once imbued with such expressive value, the trademark becomes a word in our language and assumes a role outside the bounds of trademark law.

> Our likelihood-of-confusion test generally strikes a comfortable balance between the trademark owner's property rights and the public's expressive interests. But when a trademark owner asserts a right to control how we express ourselves — when we'd find it difficult to describe the product any other way (as in the case of aspirin), or when the mark (like Rolls Royce) has taken on an expressive meaning apart from its source-identifying function — applying the traditional test fails to account for the full weight of the public's interest in free expression.

---

[859] *Id.* at *27.

[860] 809 F. Supp. 267 (S.D.N.Y. 1992).

[861] *Id.* at 278-80.

[862] *Id.* at 272.

[863] 296 F.3d 894 (9th Cir. 2002), *cert. denied*, 537 U.S. 1171 (2003).

The First Amendment may offer little protection for a competitor who labels its commercial good with a confusingly similar mark, but "trademark rights do not entitle the owner to quash an unauthorized use of the mark by another who is communicating ideas or expressing points of view." Were we to ignore the expressive value that some marks assume, trademark rights would grow to encroach upon the zone protected by the First Amendment. Simply put, the trademark owner does not have the right to control public discourse whenever the public imbues his mark with a meaning beyond its source-identifying function.[864]

In this case, the defendant was squarely targeting the Barbie mark itself as the object of parody, rather than merely using the mark as a convenient vehicle for a broader social commentary, such as satire.

Following the leads of the Second and Ninth Circuits, the Sixth Circuit expanded the *Rogers* balancing test beyond titles, applying it to works of artistic expression in *ETW Corp. v. Jireh Publishing, Inc.*,[865] which held that, with respect to a limited edition print of a painting that depicted champion golfer Tiger Woods, the slight risk that some members of the public would believe that Woods endorsed the painting was outweighed by the public interest in artistic expression.

Several courts have extended the *Rogers* approach to video games, treating them as works of artistic expression.[866]

A few courts have been less solicitous of First Amendment considerations, even where purely expressive works are involved. For example, in *Anheuser-Busch, Inc. v. Balducci Publications*,[867] the Eighth Circuit held that a humor magazine infringed the plaintiff's marks when it published a fictitious print advertisement for a beer called "Michelob Oily." The court held that the defendant's fictitious print ad in a magazine created a likelihood of confusion because the defendant "carefully designed the fictitious ad to appear as authentic as possible" and "sought to do far more than 'conjure up' [the original]."[868]

In applying the likelihood-of-confusion factors, the *Balducci* court noted that the absence of direct competition between the parties did not negate the possibility of confusion. The fact that the parodied trademarks were strong marks, which appeared "virtually unaltered" in the parody, favored the plaintiff. Furthermore, the fact that the defendant published its parody "on the back cover of a magazine — a location frequently devoted to real ads" enhanced the possibility of confusion.[869]

---

[864] *Id.* at 900 (citations omitted).

[865] 332 F.3d 915 (6th Cir. 2003).

[866] E.S.S. Entertainment 2000, Inc. v. Rock Star Videos, Inc., 547 F.3d 1095, 1099–1101 (9th Cir. 2008); Romantics v. Activision Pub., Inc., 574 F. Supp. 2d 758, 768–69 (E.D. Mich. 2008).

[867] 28 F.3d 769 (8th Cir. 1994), *cert. denied*, 513 U.S. 1112 (1995).

[868] *Id.* at 774.

[869] *Id.*

The defendant's intent was also problematic: Although the defendant intended to create a parody, the apparent authenticity of the fictitious ad suggested that the defendant was indifferent to the possibility that consumers would be misled or confused, a factor that weighed against the defendant's claim of good faith:

> For example, no significant steps were taken to remind readers that they were viewing a parody and not an advertisement sponsored or approved by Anheuser-Busch. Balducci carefully designed the fictitious ad to appear as authentic as possible. Several of Anheuser-Busch's marks were used with little or no alteration. The disclaimer is virtually undetectable. Balducci even included a (R) symbol after the words Michelob Oily. These facts suggest that Balducci sought to do far more than just "conjure up" an image of Anheuser-Busch in the minds of its readers. These factors limit the degree to which Balducci's intent to parody weighs in favor of a finding of no likelihood of confusion.[870]

Survey evidence, moreover, indicated a substantial degree of actual confusion. On balance, the court concluded, there was a strong likelihood of confusion.[871]

Under the second step of its analysis, the *Balducci* court considered whether the First Amendment insulated the defendant from liability for infringement, noting that while there is no absolute First Amendment right to parody another's trademarks, "[p]arody does implicate the First Amendment's protection of artistic expression."[872] The court adopted a balancing approach:

> There is no simple, mechanical rule by which courts can determine when a potentially confusing parody falls within the First Amendment's protective reach. Thus, "in deciding the reach of the Lanham Act in any case where an expressive work is alleged to infringe a trademark, it is appropriate to weigh the public interest in free expression against the public interest in avoiding consumer confusion." "This approach takes into account the ultimate test in trademark law, namely, the likelihood of confusion as to the source of the goods in question."[873]

In this case, the court concluded, the First Amendment did not preclude liability for infringement, because the confusion generated by the parody was simply not necessary for the defendant to achieve its parodic purpose of social commentary: "By using an obvious disclaimer, positioning the parody in a less-confusing location, altering the protected marks in a meaningful way, or doing some collection of the above, Balducci could have conveyed its message with substantially less risk of consumer confusion."[874] The appellate court recognized that the fictitious ad was a type of editorial parody, providing social commentary on environmental concerns and "brand proliferation," but held, in effect, that the parody was too subtle to satisfy the *Cliffs Notes*[875] balancing test:

---

[870] *Id.* (citation omitted).

[871] *Id.* at 775.

[872] *Id.*

[873] *Id.* at 776 (citations omitted).

[874] *Id.*

[875] *Cliffs Notes*, 886 F.2d at 494.

A parody must convey two simultaneous — and contradictory — messages: that it is the original, but also that it is not the original and is instead a parody. To the extent that it does only the former but not the latter, it is not only a poor parody but also vulnerable under trademark law, since the customer will be confused.[876]

Although the parody in *Cliffs Notes* may indeed have been more obvious, and thus less likely to confuse, nonetheless, had *Balducci* arisen in a different circuit, the same balancing test might have been resolved in the defendant's favor, because the defendant was engaging in pure expressive speech. Indeed, the district court in *Balducci* had struck the balance in the defendant's favor before it was reversed by the Eighth Circuit.

Sometimes an expressive work is so obviously a parody that it eliminates any likelihood of confusion as to source or sponsorship, in which case some courts will rule in the defendant's favor without even applying a First Amendment analysis. The parody in the *Cliffs Notes* case, discussed above, was arguably obvious enough to meet this standard. In a case involving a T-shirt that parodied the Budweiser beer label, the Fourth Circuit found that the parody was so obvious that there was no likelihood of confusion, and thus no need to address the defendant's First Amendment arguments.[877] More recently, a district court in the Ninth Circuit dismissed comedian Carol Burnett's section 43(a) claim against a television show that parodied her famous "charwoman" character, depicting her as mopping the floor in a porn shop.[878] The court held that the depiction was an obvious parody, giving rise to no likelihood of confusion; accordingly, the court did not address the First Amendment issues.

Another example of obvious parody is *Pillsbury Co. v. Milky Way Productions, Inc.*,[879] where a pornographic magazine published a fictional advertisement featuring an unsavory depiction of Pillsbury's distinctive characters "Poppin' Fresh" and "Poppie Fresh," together with additional Pillsbury trademarks. Applying the Fifth Circuit's traditional likelihood-of-confusion factors, the district court found no likelihood of confusion, even though the plaintiff's marks were strong, and the defendant's depiction of them was intentional and nearly identical. The court pointed out that (1) the defendant's "product" was the expressive work itself, (2) the fictional "ad" was not offering any real goods or services, (3) the defendant did not intend to deceive consumers, (4) the defendant's magazine was offered in different retail outlets, (5) there was little evidence of actual confusion, and (6) most of Pillsbury's customers would never even see the defendant's magazine. Accordingly, the court found it unnecessary even to consider a First Amendment defense.[880] Comparing the facts of

---

[876] *Balducci*, 28 F.3d at 776.

[877] Anheuser-Busch, Inc. v. L&L Wings, Inc., 962 F.2d 316, 321 n. 2 (4th Cir. 1992).

[878] Burnett v. Twentieth Century Fox Film, 491 F. Supp. 2d 962 (C.D. Cal. 2007).

[879] 215 U.S.P.Q. (BNA) 124 (N.D. Ga. 1981).

[880] The Ninth Circuit applied a similar analysis in Walt Disney Productions v. Air Pirates, 581 F.2d 751 (9th Cir. 1978), holding that the analysis of the likelihood of confusion must consider the context in which the defendant's imitation of Disney's trademarked characters occurred, which, in that case, was in the middle of a comic book sold in adult, counter-culture stores; here, too, the court

Pillsbury with those of *Balducci,* discussed above, which also involved a fictitious ad that was (arguably) a fairly obvious parody, raises further doubt as to the correctness of the *Balducci* decision, but also demonstrates that determinations of likelihood of confusion are highly fact-specific and can be especially difficult to predict in the context of expressive works.

In contrast, where an expressive work uses a trademark in a manner that does *not* qualify as a parody of the trademark itself, or the business associated with that trademark, a First Amendment defense is less likely to succeed. For example, in the *Mattel* parody case discussed above, the court distinguished its earlier decision in *Dr. Seuss Ents., L.P. v. Penguin Books USA,*[881] in which the defendant had used the distinctive Dr. Seuss marks in writing a satirical commentary about the O.J. Simpson trial. In the *Mattel* court's view, the defendant in *Dr. Seuss* was less justified in imitating the plaintiff's expressive works and distinctive characters, because these were not the target of the defendant's commentary.[882]

The defendant's claim of parody was even weaker in *Dallas Cowboys Cheerleaders, Inc. v. Pussycat Cinema, Ltd.,*[883] where the defendant's adult film featured a promiscuous cheerleader character wearing a costume that resembled the distinctive uniform of the Dallas Cowboys Cheerleaders. The film also alluded to her as a "Texas Cowgirl," another trademark used by the plaintiff's organization, and advertisements for the film falsely described the lead actress as a former Dallas Cowboys Cheerleader. The Second Circuit upheld a preliminary injunction under section 43(a), finding that confusion was likely because the public would believe that the plaintiff sponsored or was somehow connected with the film. The court discerned no element of parody in the film, and found no other basis for a First Amendment defense. Notably, the court applied a particularly rigorous test for giving First Amendment protection to the use of trademarks in expressive works:

> That defendants' movie may convey a barely discernible message does not entitle them to appropriate plaintiff's trademark in the process of conveying that message. Plaintiff's trademark is in the nature of a property right, and as such it need not "yield to the exercise of First Amendment rights under circumstances where adequate alternative avenues of communication exist." Because there are numerous ways in which defendants may comment on "sexuality in athletics" without infringing plaintiff's trademark, the district court did not encroach upon their first amendment rights in granting a preliminary injunction.[884]

Few courts have applied this "alternative avenues" test to expressive works. One district court applied it to a movie title,[885] and the Eighth Circuit applied it

---

did not consider a separate First Amendment defense.

[881]   109 F.3d 1394, 1400 (9th Cir. 1997).

[882]   *Mattel,* 296 F.3d at 901.

[883]   604 F.2d 200 (2d Cir. 1979).

[884]   *Id.* at 206 (quoting Lloyd Corp. v. Tanner, 407 U.S. 551, 567 (1972)).

[885]   American Dairy Queen Corp. v. New Line Prods., Inc., 35 F. Supp. 2d 727, 734 (D. Minn. 1998).

to satirical T-shirts.[886] In *Reddy Communications, Inc. v. Environmental Action Found., Inc.*,[887] a district court applied this test to books and periodicals that were critical of the plaintiff's industry and that included caricatures of the plaintiff's "Reddy Kilowatt" character. The test was also applied by the district court in the *Dr. Seuss* case,[888] although that aspect of the case was not addressed on appeal, and may no longer be good law in the Ninth Circuit since the latter's adoption of the *Rogers* balancing test in *Mattel*. Most courts that have considered the "alternative avenues" test have rejected it as insufficiently sensitive to First Amendment values in the context of expressive works.[889] Indeed, the Second Circuit itself arguably retreated from this standard some years later, when it articulated the balancing test in *Rogers v. Grimaldi* and stated: "We do not read *Dallas Cowboys Cheerleaders* as generally precluding all consideration of First Amendment concerns whenever an allegedly infringing author has 'alternative avenues of communication.' "[890] The outcome in the *Cheerleaders* case was almost certainly influenced by the exploitative nature of the film, which predisposed the court to treat it more as a commercial product than a work of artistic or literary expression.

[2]   Dilution

The application of dilution laws to traditional expression has an even greater potential to chill protected speech than their application to trademark infringement or unfair competition claims, because dilution (or the likelihood thereof) can be established without any likelihood of consumer confusion or deception. As the Ninth Circuit has observed:

> [A] trademark injunction, even a very broad one, is premised on the need to prevent consumer confusion. This consumer protection rationale — averting what is essentially a fraud on the consuming public — is wholly consistent with the theory of the First Amendment, which does not protect commercial fraud. Moreover, avoiding harm to consumers is an important interest that is independent of the senior user's interest in protecting its business.

> Dilution, by contrast, does not require a showing of consumer confusion, and dilution injunctions therefore lack the built-in First Amendment compass of trademark injunctions. In addition, dilution law protects only the distinctiveness of the mark, which is inherently less weighty than the

---

[886] Mutual of Omaha Ins. Co. v. Novak, 836 F.2d 397, 402 (8th Cir. 1987).

[887] 199 U.S.P.Q. (BNA) 630, 634 (D.D.C. 1977). The test was not outcome-determinative in this case, because the court found no likelihood of confusion.

[888] Dr. Seuss Enters., L.P. v. Penguin Book USA, Inc., 924 F. Supp. 1559, 1573 (S.D. Cal. 1996), *aff'd*, 109 F.3d 1394 (9th Cir. 1997).

[889] *See, e.g.*, Parks v. LaFace Records, 329 F.3d 437, 448-50 (6th Cir. 2003); Westchester Media v. PRL USA Holdings, Inc., 214 F.3d 658, 672 (5th Cir. 2000); L.L. Bean, Inc. v. Drake Publishers, Inc., 811 F.2d 26, 29 (1st Cir. 1987).

[890] *Rogers*, 875 F.2d at 999 n. 4.

dual interest of protecting trademark owners and avoiding harm to consumers that is at the heart of every trademark claim.[891]

Furthermore, when traditional expression or expressive merchandise parodies or otherwise criticizes a plaintiff's trademark, this can damage the prestige of the mark, thus establishing one important element of a tarnishment claim. Thus, there is inherent tension between dilution law's goal of protecting the reputation of a mark and the First Amendment's goal of fostering criticism and commentary. The *Restatement (Third) of Unfair Competition* advises that this tension should be resolved against the trademark owner, on the ground that such uses simply do not use the mark *as a trademark*:

> There is no indication that the first amendment limits application of the antidilution statutes in the context of a subsequent use of a mark as a trademark by another. Use of another's trademark, not as a means of identifying the user's own goods or services, but as an incident of speech directed at the trademark owner, however, raises serious free speech concerns that cannot be easily accommodated under traditional trademark doctrine. The expression of an idea by means of the use of another's trademark in a parody, for example, will often lie within the substantial constitutional protection accorded noncommercial speech and may thus be the subject of liability only in the most narrow circumstances. Although such nontrademark uses of another's mark may undermine the reputation and value of the mark, they should not be actionable under the law of trademarks.[892]

As discussed in § 3.07[H] above, the federal dilution statute contains specific exemptions for news reporting and other noncommercial speech, as well as many instances of comparative advertising and criticism, including parody. Even in a case where none of these exceptions applied, because the defendant was using its parody as an origin indicator for its goods, the Fourth Circuit in *Louis Vuitton Malletier S.A. v. Haute Diggity Dog, LLC* gave significant weight to the parodic context in evaluating the likelihood of dilution by blurring.[893] And in its 2007 dismissal of Carol Burnett's federal dilution claim against a television show that depicted her famous charwoman character mopping the floor of a porn shop, a district court did not rely on the statutory exemptions at all, squarely holding that "[a] dilution action only applies to purely commercial speech."[894]

Most state dilution laws, however, contain no specific exemptions distinguishing expressive uses from purely commercial uses, and courts applying these laws have shown varying degrees of solicitude for First Amendment considerations.

An early and influential case involving an allegedly dilutive parody is *L.L. Bean, Inc. v. Drake Publishers, Inc.*,[895] in which the plaintiff brought a tarnishment claim under Maine's antidilution statute against a magazine that

---

[891]   Mattel, Inc. v. MCA Records, 296 F.3d 894, 905 (9th Cir. 2002).

[892]   Rest. (3d) Unfair Competition, § 25 comment (i) (1995).

[893]   507 F.3d 252 (4th Cir. 2007); *see supra* § 3.07 [G][3][a].

[894]   Burnett v. Twentieth Century Fox Film, 491 F. Supp. 2d 962, 974 (C.D. Cal. 2007).

[895]   811 F.2d 26 (1st Cir. 1987).

used its trademarks in "a prurient parody of Bean's famous catalog."[896] Because the products listed in the fictitious catalog were not actually offered for sale, it was clear that the purpose of the defendant's parody was to spoof the plaintiff's catalog rather than to sell merchandise. This was an expressive use that warranted a substantial degree of First Amendment protection. Because the plaintiff's claim involved state dilution law, and indeed predated enactment of the federal dilution statute, the defendant could not invoke any express statutory exception for works of artistic expression; thus, its defense was based on general First Amendment principles. The *L.L. Bean* court took note of the concern (expressed by Professor Robert C. Denicola) that too-liberal application of the tarnishment doctrine raises serious First Amendment concerns:

> Famous trademarks offer a particularly powerful means of conjuring up the image of their owners, and thus become an important, perhaps at times indispensable, part of the public vocabulary. Rules restricting the use of well-known trademarks may therefore restrict the communication of ideas. . . . If the defendant's speech is particularly unflattering, it is also possible to argue that the trademark has been tarnished by the defendant's use. The constitutional implications of extending the misappropriation or tarnishment rationales to such cases, however, may often be intolerable. Since a trademark may frequently be the most effective means of focusing attention on the trademark owner or its product, the recognition of exclusive rights encompassing such use would permit the stifling of unwelcome discussion.[897]

Based on these concerns, the appellate court reversed a grant of summary judgment for the plaintiff:

> The district court's opinion suggests that tarnishment may be found when a trademark is used without authorization in a context which diminishes the positive associations with the mark. Neither the strictures of the First Amendment nor the history and theory of anti-dilution law permit a finding of tarnishment based solely on the presence of an unwholesome or negative context in which a trademark is used without authorization. Such a reading of the anti-dilution statute unhinges it from its origins in the marketplace. A trademark is tarnished when consumer capacity to associate it with the appropriate products or services has been diminished. The threat of tarnishment arises when the goodwill and reputation of a plaintiff's trademark is linked to products which are of shoddy quality or which conjure associations that clash with the associations generated by the owner's lawful use of the mark.[898]

In this case, the court held, the defendant's disparaging use of the plaintiff's trademarks was strictly noncommercial:

---

[896] *Id.* at 27.

[897] *Id.* at 30-31 (quoting Robert C. Denicola, *Trademarks as Speech*, 1982 Wis. L. Rev. 158, 195-96).

[898] *Id.* at 31.

Appellant's parody constitutes an editorial or artistic, rather than a commercial, use of plaintiff's mark. The article was labeled as "humor" and "parody" in the magazine's table of contents section; it took up two pages in a one-hundred-page issue; neither the article nor appellant's trademark was featured on the front or back cover of the magazine. Drake did not use Bean's mark to identify or promote goods or services to consumers; it never intended to market the "products" displayed in the parody.[899]

The court noted, however, that its analysis did not extend to traditional infringement claims premised on a likelihood of confusion, because "[a] parody which causes confusion in the marketplace implicates the legitimate commercial and consumer protection objectives of trademark law."[900]

The First Circuit specifically rejected the argument that the First Amendment could not shield the defendant's parody because "alternative avenues of communication" were available for the defendant to convey its message. Because the plaintiff and its trademark were the specific targets of the parody, the defendant's message necessitated the use of the identifying trademark:

> [W]e reject Bean's argument that enjoining the publication of appellant's parody does not violate the First Amendment because "there are innumerable alternative ways that Drake could have made a satiric statement concerning 'sex in the outdoors' or 'sex and camping gear' without using plaintiff's name and mark." This argument fails to recognize that appellant is parodying L.L. Bean's catalog, not "sex in the outdoors." The central role which trademarks occupy in public discourse (a role eagerly encouraged by trademark owners), makes them a natural target of parodists. Trademark parodies, even when offensive, do convey a message. The message may be simply that business and product images need not always be taken too seriously; a trademark parody reminds us that we are free to laugh at the images and associations linked with the mark. The message also may be a simple form of entertainment conveyed by juxtaposing the irreverent representation of the trademark with the idealized image created by the mark's owner. While such a message lacks explicit political content, that is no reason to afford it less protection under the First Amendment. Denying parodists the opportunity to poke fun at symbols and names which have become woven into the fabric of our daily life, would constitute a serious curtailment of a protected form of expression.[901]

The *L.L. Bean* case arguably represents the high water mark in First Amendment defenses against dilution claims. Several other courts have held trademark parodies to be actionable simply because they potentially have a negative effect on consumer perceptions of a trademark, even when the parody takes the form of traditionally protected expression.

---

[899] *Id.* at 32.

[900] *Id.* at 32 n. 3.

[901] 811 F.2d at 34.

In the *Balducci* case,[902] for example, the defendant's fictitious ad (appearing in a humor magazine) parodied various trademarks associated with Michelob beer, and implied that the beer was made from water polluted by an oil spill. There was no evidence that the parody led consumers to believe that the plaintiff's beer was actually tainted. Nonetheless, the Eighth Circuit held that plaintiff's claim under Missouri's dilution law should not have been dismissed, because the mere suggestion that a product is tainted, regardless of its believability, "obviously tarnishes the marks' well-developed images."[903] The court completely rejected the defendant's First Amendment arguments, and distinguished the *L.L. Bean* case:

> [T]he facts in *Bean* differ significantly from the facts in this appeal. First, the catalog parody made no derogatory comment about Bean's products' quality. Balducci's parody, as demonstrated by the survey, suggested that Anheuser-Busch products were contaminated with oil. This unsupported attack was not even remotely necessary to Balducci's goals of commenting on the Gasconade oil spill and water pollution generally. Nor does Balducci's asserted purpose of commenting on Anheuser-Busch's brand proliferation give it carte blanche to attack Anheuser-Busch's products. Second, and more importantly, the catalog parody was located inside a 100-page magazine. Readers presumably discovered it only after perusing the magazine or reviewing the table of contents, which labeled the article as "humor" and "parody." In contrast, Balducci placed its parody on the back cover with only a tiny disclosure. Thus, the casual viewer might fail to appreciate its editorial purpose. Even the *Bean* court felt it significant that "neither the [catalog parody] nor appellant's trademark was featured on the front or back cover of the magazine."[904]

The First Amendment also provided no defense to dilution claims in the *Pillsbury* case,[905] where a sexually explicit cartoon in a humor magazine targeted Pillsbury's "Poppin' Fresh" Dough Boy character. Here, the district court granted a preliminary injunction under the Georgia dilution statute, limiting its analysis to a conclusory statement that the cartoon "could injure the business reputation of the plaintiff or dilute the distinctive quality of its trademarks."[906] The court made no mention of First Amendment considerations.

In contrast, in the *Yankee Publishing* case,[907] the district court applied the *Rogers/Cliffs Notes* balancing approach in rejecting a dilution claim where the cover of a magazine issue imitated the cover of the plaintiff's well-known almanac. The almanac was known for its emphasis on thrift, and the magazine contained an article on Christmas gift ideas ranging from thrifty to frivolous. The court described the defendant's cover illustration as "artistic editorial commen-

---

[902] Anheuser-Busch, Inc. v. Balducci Pubs., 28 F.3d 769 (8th Cir. 2001).

[903] *Id.* at 777.

[904] *Id.* at 778 (citations omitted).

[905] Pillsbury Co. v. Milky Way Prods., Inc., 215 U.S.P.Q. (BNA) 124 (N.D. Ga. 1981).

[906] *Id.* at 135.

[907] 809 F. Supp. 267 (S.D.N.Y. 1992).

tary"; although the court did not perceive it to be parody, the court found that it was a "joking reference" that was "part of a socio-economic commentary." In the court's view, this kind of "expressive message" merited the same degree of First Amendment protection as parody, even if some consumers did not comprehend the joke.

In evaluating state law dilution claims against motion pictures, courts have been less receptive to First Amendment arguments when the film is sexually exploitative, reflecting perhaps the low social utility of the subject matter, or simply a recognition that such works are not primarily designed as vehicles for humor and parody. For example, in the *Dallas Cowboys Cheerleaders* case, where the defendants' adult film purported to portray a promiscuous Dallas Cowboys Cheerleader (wearing the plaintiff's distinctive costume), in addition to finding a likelihood of confusion as to sponsorship, the Second Circuit upheld a preliminary injunction under the New York dilution statute, offering no analysis separate from its likelihood-of-confusion analysis, other than noting that no likelihood of confusion was required. The court had already rejected the defendants' First Amendment arguments in analyzing the traditional infringement claim, holding that the film was not a parody, and that, to the extent it was a commentary on "sexuality in athletics," it could not satisfy the "adequate alternative avenues" standard.[908] The court implicitly applied the same standard to the dilution claim. In a case marked by even less analysis, a district court in California held that the "Tarzan" mark was diluted by the use of "Tarz" as the name of a character in an X-rated film (and also as an element of the film's title).[909] In contrast, where a *federal* dilution claim was brought against a pornographic film, a district court in California held that the film was clearly protected by the federal statute's exemption for "noncommercial" uses.[910]

Where a motion picture targets a famous trademark in a humorous but disparaging way, but does not involve sexual exploitation, one might expect courts evaluating state dilution claims to be more receptive to First Amendment considerations. However, such a trend has not yet emerged. In *American Dairy Queen Corp. v. New Line Prods.*,[911] a district court applied the rigorous "alternative avenues" test in granting a preliminary injunction against the use of the phrase "Dairy Queens" in the title of a movie about beauty pageant contestants in the Midwest. Despite the obvious play on words, the court held that the defendant could easily have chosen a title that did not reference the plaintiff's trademark. The court also relied on "the somewhat lesser protection afforded commercial speech,"[912] thus implicitly refusing to recognize films (or, at least, film titles) as noncommercial speech. Even the *Hormel* case,[913] where a district court rejected a dilution claim arising from the good-natured spoofing of

---

[908] *See supra* § 3.11 [B][1].

[909] Edgar Rice Burroughs, Inc. v. Manns Theaters, 195 U.S.P.Q. (BNA) 159 (C.D. Cal. 1976).

[910] Lucasfilm Ltd. v. Media Market Group, Ltd., 182 F. Supp. 2d 897 (N.D. Cal. 2002).

[911] 35 F. Supp. 2d 727 (D. Minn. 1998).

[912] *Id.* at 735.

[913] Hormel Foods Corp. v. Jim Henson Prods., Inc., 36 U.S.P.Q.2d (BNA) 1812 (S.D.N.Y. 1995), *aff'd*, 73 F.3d 497 (2d Cir. 1996).

SPAM in the context of a Muppet movie featuring a character named "Spa'am," was not decided on First Amendment considerations. Rather, the court simply found that, based on the parodic and wholesome nature of the film, blurring and tarnishment of the mark were unlikely to occur.

[C]   Political Speech

Political speech is the one arena in which courts have consistently subordinated the rights of trademark owners in the interest of free expression, regardless of whether the claim is based on infringement/unfair competition or dilution. The outcomes in these cases are more consistent than in cases involving artistic and literary expression, because courts generally view political speech as entirely noncommercial, while artistic and literary expression often have a commercial aspect. Even in the context of political speech, however, some of these decisions rest solely on the plaintiff's failure to make out the elements of its claim, without any express mention of the First Amendment.

For example, one district court held that the use of the term "Star Wars" by public interest groups in "political propaganda, newspapers or noncommercial, [or] non-trade references" to the Strategic Defense Initiative[914] neither infringed nor diluted the plaintiff's trademark in the title of its motion picture. The court did not expressly rely on the First Amendment, relying instead on the conclusory statement that political speech of this nature would "not affect the distinct, and still strong secondary meaning of STAR WARS in trade and entertainment;" however, the court also noted that "[i]t would be wholly unrealistic and unfair to allow the owner of a mark to interfere in the give-and-take of normal political discourse."[915]

A district court also permitted the use of Mastercard's "Priceless" slogan and distinctive advertising format in a series of television ads for a presidential candidate,[916] in an analysis that turned entirely on the plaintiff's failure to satisfy the elements of its infringement and dilution claims; the court's opinion does not even mention the First Amendment, although it does invoke the noncommercial use exception of the federal dilution statute. In rejecting the state law dilution claim, the court simply held that there was no evidence of either dilution or tarnishment.

Another district court permitted the imitation of AFLAC's famous "quacking duck" character in ads for a gubernatorial candidate.[917] Although it rejected the plaintiff's infringement claim based on the absence of any likelihood of confusion, without expressly considering First Amendment values, those values were clearly central to its conclusion that political speech falls squarely within the noncommercial use exception in the federal dilution statute.

---

[914] Lucasfilm, Ltd. v. High Frontier, 622 F. Supp. 931 (D.D.C. 1985)

[915] *Id.* at 935.

[916] Mastercard Int'l, Inc. v. Nader 2000 Primary Comm., Inc., 70 U.S.P.Q.2d (BNA) 1046, 2004 U.S. Dist. LEXIS 3644 (S.D.N.Y. 2004).

[917] American Family Life Insurance Company v. Hagan, 266 F. Supp. 2d 682 (N.D. Ohio 2002).

In contrast, political and public service *organizations* have been held liable for infringement and dilution when they adopt names that are likely to cause confusion as to source or affiliation. The courts in these cases have reasoned that the use of another party's mark as the organization's name constitutes its use as a source identifier, rather than as a means of expressing an idea, and thus is not protected by the First Amendment.[918]

[D]   Expressive Merchandise

Between the two extremes of purely commercial speech and traditional forms of artistic, political, or literary expression lies the realm of what might be "expressive merchandise" — a wide variety of items such as posters, T-shirts, and coffee mugs, which may carry parodic or satirical messages incorporating well-known trademarks. The analyses of infringement and dilution claims in these cases have been inconsistent. To a large extent, this is due to the difficulty of determining the level of First Amendment protection that such merchandise should receive — in other words, how to weigh the commerciality of the merchandise against its expressive content. In contrast to "purer" forms of expression, the use of another's mark on expressive merchandise is more likely to be perceived by consumers as an indication of source or sponsorship. Another factor that appears to influence courts in expressive merchandise cases is the extent to which the parodic message targets the trademark itself (or the associated goods and services) as opposed to commenting on a largely unrelated topic.

Notably, infringement and unfair competition claims are more prevalent than dilution claims with respect to this class of merchandise. The crucial factor in many of the infringement and unfair competition cases has been the presence or absence of actual confusion as to source or sponsorship; in the context of expressive merchandise, courts seem unwilling to tolerate consumer confusion in the name of free expression.

The inconsistent treatment of expressive merchandise is illustrated by two decisions involving parodic posters, decided just three years apart, by district courts in the Second Circuit. In *Girl Scouts of United States of America v. Personality Posters Mfg. Co.*,[919] the court found no likelihood of confusion as to source or sponsorship where a poster depicted a pregnant Girl Scout along with the message "Be Prepared." Although members of the public had called the Girl Scouts to express indignation over the poster, the court held that, far from demonstrating confusion, this evidence showed that the public fully understood that the Girl Scouts were not the source of the "lampooning" poster. The court also rejected the plaintiff's dilution claim because, at that time, courts interpreted New York's dilution law as requiring a likelihood of confusion. Two remaining causes of action, however, more closely resembled modern dilution claims — a defamation claim, and a state statutory claim alleging unauthorized

---

[918] *See, e.g.*, United We Stand America, Inc. v. United We Stand, America New York, Inc., 128 F.3d 86, 93 (2d Cir. 1997); MGM-Pathe Communications v. Pink Panther Patrol, 774 F. Supp. 869 (S.D.N.Y. 1991); Tomei v. Finley, 512 F. Supp. 695, 698 (N.D. Ill. 1981).

[919] 304 F. Supp. 1228 (S.D.N.Y. 1969).

commercial exploitation of a nonprofit organization's name, device, symbol, or other identification. With respect to both of these claims, the court held that injunctive relief would constitute an unlawful prior restraint of protected expression in violation of the First Amendment; the poster was "satirical expression 'deserving of substantial freedom — both as entertainment and as a form of social . . . criticism.' "[920] The court relied specifically on New York case law holding that posters were "a form of expression which may be constitutionally protected."[921] In addition, the court found no evidence that the poster would injure the Girl Scouts' reputation. The court's conclusion hints that the iconic status of the Girls Scouts made their trademarks a legitimate target for parody:

> Those who may be amused at the poster presumably never viewed the reputation of the plaintiff as being inviolable. Those who are indignant obviously continue to respect it. Perhaps it is because the reputation of the plaintiff is so secure against the wry assault of the defendant that no such damage has been demonstrated.[922]

In contrast, three years later, in *Coca-Cola Co. v. Gemini Rising, Inc.*,[923] another district court in the same circuit granted a preliminary injunction against distribution of a poster that closely mimicked Coca-Cola's marks as well as its distinctive typeface and trade dress, except that in place of the plaintiff's "Enjoy Coca-Cola" slogan it displayed the message "Enjoy Cocaine." The plaintiff asserted both a likelihood of confusion and dilution. When the defendant asserted that it intended the poster to be "satirical," the court described this as a type of "predatory intent."[924] The defendant argued that it was not selling competing merchandise, and it was unlikely that anyone would be confused about the origin or sponsorship of the poster. However, the plaintiff had received numerous communications about the poster from members of the public, at least some of whom appeared to attribute the poster to the plaintiff. Although the court concluded that there was "a high probability of confusion,"[925] it also appeared to concern itself with tarnishment: "To associate such a noxious substance as cocaine with plaintiff's wholesome beverage as symbolized by its 'Coca-Cola' trademark and format would clearly have a tendency to impugn that product and injure plaintiff's business reputation, as plaintiff contends."[926] Addressing the defendant's First Amendment arguments, the court rejected the argument that injunctive relief would be an unconstitutional prior restraint. It distinguished the *Girl Scouts* decision on the erroneous ground that the Girls Scouts' name, insignia, uniform, and slogan were not trademarks; in fact, the *Girls Scouts* opinion itself expressly noted that the Girl Scouts held a registered

---

[920] *Id.* at 1235.

[921] *Id.*

[922] *Id.* at 1235-36.

[923] 346 F. Supp. 1183, 1192 (E.D.N.Y. 1972).

[924] *Id.* at 1187.

[925] *Id.* at 1190.

[926] *Id.* at 1189.

trademark in their name and insignia.[927] The court concluded that Coca-Cola was entitled to injunctive relief because of "special circumstances" that were absent in the *Girl Scouts* case — an "imitative use of [a] trademark in a manner injurious to the mark and to plaintiff's business reputation and good will."[928]

A more recent pair of decisions, illustrating sharply different approaches to trademark claims involving expressive merchandise, involves parodic T-Shirts. The 1989 decision by the Eighth Circuit in *Mutual of Omaha Ins. Co. v Novak*[929] applied the "adequate alternative avenues" test to parodic T-shirts, without regard to the obviousness of the parody. (As noted earlier,[930] the "alternative avenues" test has been widely criticized in the context of more traditional expressive works.) The appellate court permanently enjoined a defendant from distributing T-shirts, caps, buttons, and coffee mugs displaying the words "Mutant of Omaha" and "Nuclear Holocaust Insurance," and depicting an emaciated, feather-bonneted human head that imitated Mutual of Omaha's distinctive "Indian head" logo. The court applied the traditional likelihood-of-confusion factors, giving significant weight to survey evidence indicating the existence of actual confusion. (The plaintiff did not allege dilution.) Although it was clear that the defendant's intent was to convey a satirical message opposing nuclear war, the court rejected his First Amendment defense. Holding that the rights of the trademark owner "need not 'yield to the exercise of First Amendment rights under circumstances where adequate alternative avenues of communication exist,' " the court noted that the injunction applied only to the defendant's sale of "services and products," and that the defendant was free to express his views through "an editorial parody in a book, magazine, or film."[931] The court distinguished cases such as *L.L. Bean* as involving "editorial or artistic" use of a mark "solely for noncommercial purposes."[932]

In contrast, the Fourth Circuit's 1992 decision in *Anheuser-Busch, Inc. v. L&L Wings, Inc.*[933] purports to treat T-shirts like any other form of merchandise, but questions the appropriateness of the traditional likelihood-of-confusion factors in a way that suggests the influence of case law involving traditional expression. The plaintiff in *L&L Wings* brought a trademark infringement claim (but no dilution claim) against a defendant that sold souvenir T-shirts with a design that imitated Budweiser's beer label while promoting Myrtle Beach as the "King of Beaches." Reinstating a jury verdict for the defendant, the majority applied the traditional likelihood-of-confusion factors, and concluded that a reasonable jury could find that the differences between the designs were sufficient to dispel confusion. However, the opinion also comments that the traditional confusion factors are "at best awkward in the context of parody," and that while successful parodies necessarily imitate the original trademarks, they

---

[927] 304 F. Supp. at 1233.

[928] 346 F. Supp. at 1193.

[929] 836 F.2d 397 (8th Cir. 1987).

[930] *See supra* § 3.11 [B][1].

[931] *Id.* at 402.

[932] *Id.* at 403 n. 9.

[933] 962 F.2d 316 (4th Cir. 1992).

also "dispel consumer confusion by conveying just enough of the original design to allow the consumer to appreciate the point of the parody."[934] Although the majority expressly declined to consider whether the First Amendment provided a defense for trademark parodies, in concluding that a reasonable jury could find that the T-shirts were obvious parody, the opinion cited a mix of precedents involving both traditional expression and conventional merchandise.

In a notable dissent from the majority's opinion in *L&L Wings*, Associate Justice Powell of the United States Supreme Court (retired and sitting by designation) argued that trademark parody deserves special treatment only when it is parody in the "editorial or artistic" sense (as in *L.L. Bean*), because only then does it implicate sufficiently strong First Amendment concerns:

> Such would be the case, for instance, if Mothers Against Drunk Driving [MADD] marketed T-shirts bearing a caricature of the Budweiser trademark. (In that context, incidentally, consumers would purchase the T-shirts precisely because they were not affiliated with Anheuser-Busch. That is not true here.) I would conclude that the defendants' commercial speech, whose avowed aim was to convey "how great Myrtle Beach is," is not protected by the First Amendment from enforcement of the Lanham Act.[935]

Unfortunately, Justice Powell did not make clear exactly why MADD's T-shirts should be treated differently from the Myrtle Beach T-shirts. Thus, it is unclear whether Justice Powell's approach requires a close relationship between the nature of the targeted mark (a beer mark) and the parodist's message (anti-drunk-driving), whether it requires an examination of the parodist's motives (profit versus social benefit), or whether it depends on the social importance of the parodist's message (anti-drunk-driving versus extolling the virtues of a beach resort).

In *World Wrestling Fedn. Ent't, Inc. v. Big Dog Holdings, Inc.*,[936] the plaintiff brought infringement and dilution claims against a defendant that sold T-shirts, mugs, sports bottles, and beanie dolls using dog caricatures and a variety of puns to parody the plaintiff's wrestler characters. In this case, the designs on the merchandise were accompanied by the words "This is a parody." The court's analysis closely tracked that of the *Hormel* decision involving movie merchandise featuring the "Spa'am" character.[937] The court treated the parodic context as relevant to the likelihood of confusion analysis, noting that "where the unauthorized use of a trademark is part of an expressive work, such as a parody, the Lanham Act must be construed narrowly,"[938] but it also held that the ultimate question was still the likelihood of confusion. Unlike the *Mutual of Omaha* and *Gemini Rising* cases, here there was no evidence of actual confusion. Citing both *Hormel* and the *Yankee Publishing* decision involving editorial parody, the court

---

[934] *Id.* at 321.

[935] 962 F.2d at 327 n. 8.

[936] 280 F. Supp. 2d 413 (W.D. Pa. 2003).

[937] *See* § 3.11 [A][1] *supra*.

[938] 280 F. Supp. 2d at 431 n. 10.

held that, because of the clarity of the defendant's parodic intent, the strength of the WWF marks weighed *against* a likelihood of confusion. The court's ultimate conclusion indicated that it had taken account of First Amendment considerations, without indicating how much weight it had given them:

> Big Dog's graphics spoofing the WWE wrestling characters and phrases are parodies that entitle its WBDF merchandise to First Amendment protection when analyzing the *Lapp* [likelihood of confusion] factors. Evaluating the *Lapp* factors, while applying First Amendment principles to Big Dog's parodies of WWE, the Court finds that the factors favor Big Dog and that there is no likelihood of confusion.[939]

In rejecting the plaintiff's state and federal dilution claims, the court again relied on a mix of authorities involving traditional expression and conventional merchandise, citing *Hormel*'s interpretation of tarnishment as limited to "inferior or offensive" products while also stating that "tarnishment caused merely by an editorial or artistic parody which satirizes plaintiff's product or its image carries the free speech protections of the First Amendment."[940]

§ 3.12   AFFIRMATIVE DEFENSES

The infringement defenses listed in section 33(b) with respect to incontestable marks[941] are available for contestable marks as well.[942] Thus, for example, the "limited area" defense described by section 33(b)(5) with respect to incontestable registered marks also applies to contestable registered marks, as well as to unregistered marks that are protected by section 43(a).[943]

Unless otherwise indicated, the defenses discussed below apply to an action for infringement of any trademark or service mark, without regard to whether the mark is registered or, if registered, has become incontestable.

[A]   Abandonment

Abandonment is both a defense to infringement of a mark and a ground for cancellation of a federal registration.[944] Common law has long recognized abandonment as a defense to trademark infringement. This rule derives from the basic principle that:

> [T]he right to a particular mark grows out of its use, not its mere adoption; its function is simply to designate the goods as the product of a particular trader and to protect his good will against the sale of

---

[939] 280 F. Supp. 2d at 440.

[940] *Id.* at 443 (citing McCarthy on Trademarks, *supra* note 223, at § 24.105).

[941] 15 U.S.C. § 1115(b); *see* § 2.13 *supra* (discussing the effect of incontestability).

[942] Matador Motor Inns, Inc. v. Matador Motel, Inc., 376 F. Supp. 385, 388 (D.N.J. 1974).

[943] *Id.*

[944] 15 U.S.C. §§ 1115(b)(2), 1064(3).

another's product as his; and it is not the subject of property except in connection with an existing business.[945]

However, non-use does not, by itself, constitute abandonment; common law abandonment requires that the cessation of use be coupled with an intent to abandon.[946] Thus, for example, in *Beech-Nut Co. v. Lorillard Co.*, the Supreme Court held that non-use for four years did not constitute abandonment in light of the trademark owner's intent to resume use.[947]

Abandonment may be raised as an affirmative defense to infringement, or as a ground for cancelling a mark's registration, even after the party that abandoned the mark has resumed use of the mark in commerce.[948] This is because the mark, once abandoned, loses its trademark status and enters the public domain. At this point it becomes equally available for the use of any party, including, but not limited to, its previous owner.[949] A right of priority in a previously abandoned mark will therefore belong to whichever party, if any, first establishes trademark rights through use of the mark on goods or services after the abandonment takes place.[950] Thus, where a trademark owner abandons a mark and then wishes to resume use of the mark at a later date, an intervening use by another party may give the latter a right of priority in the mark, enabling it to enjoin the original owner's resumption of use or cancel the original owner's registration.[951] If the abandonment leads to cancellation of the mark's registration, then even if the original owner resumes use before another party establishes priority in the mark, the original owner's rights will be limited to those arising from use of an unregistered mark; once registration has been cancelled due to abandonment, the mark must be registered anew in order to enjoy the rights appurtenant to registration.[952]

Courts disagree, however, on the standard of proof that applies to the abandonment defense; some courts require "clear and convincing evidence" of abandonment,[953] while others require only a "preponderance of the evidence."[954] Still others have been less precise, asserting that the proponent of an abandonment defense bears a "stringent," "heavy," or "strict" burden of proof.[955]

---

[945] United Drug Co. v. Theodore Rectanus Co., 248 U.S. 90, 97 (1918).

[946] Baglin v. Cusenier Co., 221 U.S. 580, 598 (1910).

[947] 273 U.S. 629, 633 (1926).

[948] *See, e.g.*, Ambrit, Inc. v. Kraft, Inc., 812 F.2d 1531, 1551 (11th Cir. 1986) (collecting cases).

[949] Major League Baseball Properties, Inc. v. Sed Non Olet Denarius, Ltd., 817 F. Supp. 1103, 1132-33 (S.D.N.Y. 1993), *vacated pursuant to settlement*, 859 F. Supp. 80 (S.D.N.Y. 1994).

[950] *Id.*

[951] *Id.*; Conwood Corp. v. Loew's Theatres, Inc., 173 U.S.P.Q. (BNA) 829, 830 (T.T.A.B. 1972).

[952] *Ambrit*, 812 F.2d at 1551 n. 114.

[953] The Second Circuit requires clear and convincing evidence. *See, e.g.*, Saratoga Vichy Spring Co., Inc. v. Lehman, 625 F.2d 1037, 1044 (2d Cir. 1980).

[954] The Federal Circuit requires only a preponderance of the evidence. *See, e.g.*, West Florida Seafood, Inc. v. Jet Restaurants, Inc., 31 F.3d 1122, 1124 (Fed. Cir. 1994).

[955] *See, e.g.*, Grocery Outlet, Inc. v. Albertson's, Inc., 497 F.3d 949 (9th Cir. 2007) (separate opinions disagreeing on meaning of "high" or "strict" standard of proof); Cumulus Media, Inc. v. Clear Channel Communs., Inc., 304 F.3d 1167, 1175 & n. 12 (11th Cir. 2002) (acknowledging the

The concept of abandonment under federal trademark law is derived from the common law rule. Under section 45 of the Lanham Act, a mark is deemed abandoned under either of two circumstances: (1) when its bona fide use in the ordinary course of trade has been discontinued with intent not to resume such use, or (2) when the conduct of the mark's owner, including acts of commission or omission, causes the mark to become generic.[956] These rules, discussed below, apply to both registered and unregistered marks.[957]

[1]   Cessation of Use

Abandonment under subsection (1) of the Lanham Act definition may occur either through express abandonment, such as the owner's cancellation of the mark, or through cessation of use with intent not to resume use.[958]

Intent not to resume use of a mark may be inferred from circumstances; in addition, nonuse for three (formerly two) consecutive years constitutes prima facie evidence that the mark has been abandoned.[959] Where a mark is used legitimately and in a nondeceptive manner by a related company, such use will inure to the benefit of the trademark owner under section 5 of the Lanham Act,[960] and will defeat a claim of abandonment due to nonuse.[961]

Where the prima facie case of abandonment based on three years of nonuse cannot be established, the party challenging a trademark must show that the trademark owner is not using the mark and has no intention to resume its use in the reasonably foreseeable future.[962]

The federal courts appear to have reached a general consensus on the effect that a showing of prima facie abandonment under the three-year rule has on the burden of proof on the ultimate question of abandonment. The emerging consensus indicates that the prima facie showing does not shift the ultimate

---

ambiguity); Conagra, Inc. v. Singleton, 743 F.2d 1508, 1516 (11th Cir. 1984) ("strict"); Citibank, N.A. v. Citibanc Group, Inc., 724 F.2d 1540, 1545 (11th Cir. 1984) ("strict"); Moore Business Forms, Inc. v. Ryu, 960 F.2d 486 (5th Cir. 1992) ("stringent"); Lipton Indus., Inc. v. Ralston Purina Co., 670 F.2d 1024, 1031, 213 U.S.P.Q. 185, 191 (C.C.P.A. 1982) ("heavy"); Seidelmann Yachts, Inc. v. Pace Yacht Corp., 1989 U.S. Dist. LEXIS 17486 (D. Md. 1989), *aff'd*, 898 F.2d 147 (4th Cir. 1990) ("Because abandonment constitutes a forfeiture of a property interest, both non-use and intent not to resume use must be strictly proved.").

[956] 15 U.S.C. § 1127 (defining "abandonment").

[957] Sweetheart Plastics, Inc. v. Detroit Forming, Inc., 743 F.2d 1039, 1047 n. 4 (4th Cir. 1984).

[958] Defiance Button Mach. Co. v. C&C Metal Prods. Corp., 759 F.2d 1053, 1059 (2d Cir.), *cert. denied*, 474 U.S. 844 (1985); Sands, Taylor & Wood Co. v. Quaker Oats Co., 978 F.2d 947 (7th Cir. 1992), *cert. denied*, 507 U.S. 1042 (1993); *see, e.g.*, Major League Baseball Properties, Inc. v. Sed Non Olet Denarius, Ltd., 817 F. Supp. 1103 (S.D.N.Y. 1993), *vacated pursuant to settlement*, 859 F. Supp. 80 (S.D.N.Y. 1994) ("Brooklyn Dodgers" mark for baseball team was abandoned when registrant moved the team, changed its name to the "Los Angeles Dodgers," and subsequently used the name only in conjunction with items of historical interest between 1958 and 1981).

[959] 15 U.S.C. § 1127.

[960] 15 U.S.C. § 1055.

[961] Turner v. HMH Pub. Co., 380 F.2d 224 (5th Cir. 1967), *cert. denied*, 389 U.S. 1006 (1967); Alligator Co. v. Robert Bruce, Inc., 176 F. Supp. 377 (E.D. Pa. 1953).

[962] Stetson v. Howard D. Wolf & Assocs., 955 F.2d 847, 850 (2d Cir. 1992).

burden of persuasion to the trademark owner, but merely the burden of production.[963] Thus, the trademark owner need only produce some evidence to rebut the prima facie case of abandonment — such as evidence of intent to resume use — and the challenger still bears the burden of proving that abandonment occurred.[964]

To rebut a prima facie case of abandonment based on cessation of use, the trademark owner must demonstrate that there were reasonable grounds for suspending use of the mark,[965] and must produce evidence of an intent to resume use of the mark "within the reasonably foreseeable future."[966] A bare assertion of possible future use is insufficient, and the trademark owner must produce more than conclusory testimony or affidavits of intent.[967]

In establishing a sufficient intent to resume use, there is no hard-and-fast rule as to what constitutes "the reasonably foreseeable future," and courts have held that this determination "will vary depending on the industry and the particular circumstances of the case."[968] Thus, for example, a longer period of nonuse may be tolerated when the mark is used on goods that are extremely durable (such as fire trucks), because the persistence of previously sold goods will keep the mark in the public eye even during a hiatus in its use on newly produced goods. In contrast, if a trademark for potato chips is discontinued, it will lose its visibility in the marketplace as soon as the existing merchandise is consumed, and failure to resume use in the near future could cause the mark to lose its origin-identifying function.[969]

The Second Circuit has expressly held that the intent to resume use must exist during the three-year period of non-use. In other words, "[a]n intent to resume use of the mark formulated after more than three years of non-use cannot be invoked to dislodge the rights of another party who has commenced use of a mark" at the end of that three-year period.[970]

---

[963] *See* Cumulus Media, Inc. v. Clear Channel Communs., Inc., 304 F.3d 1167, 1177 (11th Cir. 2002); Emergency One, Inc. v. American FireEagle, Ltd., 228 F.3d 531, 536 (4th Cir. 2000); Cerveceria Centroamericana, S.A. v. Cerveceria India, Inc., 892 F.2d 1021, 1025 (Fed Cir. 1989); Silverman v. CBS Inc., 870 F.2d 40, 47 (2d Cir.), *cert. denied*, 492 U.S. 907 (1989); Roulo v. Russ Berrie & Co., 886 F.2d 931, 938 (7th Cir. 1989); Star-Kist Foods, Inc. v. P.J. Rhodes & Co., 769 F.2d 1393, 1396 (9th Cir. 1985); Exxon Corp. v. Humble Exploration Co., 695 F.2d 96, 99 (5th Cir. 1983); Saratoga Vichy Spring Co. v. Lehman, 625 F.2d 1037, 1043-44 (2d Cir. 1980); Sterling Brewers, Inc. v. Schenley Industries, Inc., 441 F.2d 675, 679 (C.C.P.A. 1971); Societe de Developments et D'Innovations des Marches Agricoles et Alimentaires-SODIMA-Union de Cooperatives Agricoles v. International Yogurt Co., 662 F. Supp. 839, 844-45 (D. Or. 1987) (collecting cases).

[964] *Societe de Developments et D'Innovations*, 662 F. Supp. at 845.

[965] Silverman v. CBS, 870 F.2d 40, 47 (2d Cir. 1989).

[966] *Emergency One*, 228 F.3d at 537; *Silverman*, 870 F.2d at 46-47.

[967] *Silverman*, 870 F.2d at 47; Imperial Tobacco Ltd. v. Phillip Morris, Inc., 899 F.2d 1575, 1581 (Fed. Cir. 1990); Rivard v. Linville, 133 F.3d 1446, 1449 (Fed. Cir. 1998); Hughes v. Design Look, Inc., 693 F. Supp. 1500, 1506 (S.D.N.Y. 1988) (citation omitted).

[968] *Emergency One*, 228 F.3d at 537; *accord*, Defiance Button Mach. Co. v. C & C Metal Prods. Corp., 759 F.2d 1053, 1060-62 (2d Cir. 1985).

[969] *Emergency One*, 228 F.3d at 537.

[970] ITC Ltd. v. Punchgini, Inc., 482 F.3d 135, 149 n. 9 (2d Cir. 2007) (noting, however, that evidence arising after three years of non-use may be used to demonstrate the existence of intent

In determining whether the use of the mark has been resumed, mere token or sporadic use is insufficient to overcome a showing of abandonment due to nonuse.[971] Moreover, once a mark has been abandoned, subsequent commercial use cannot retroactively cure the abandonment.[972]

In appropriate cases, the concept of trademark tacking[973] may be invoked to overcome a defense of abandonment.[974] Thus, if the trademark owner makes only minor changes to a mark that do not change its overall commercial impression, the altered version of the mark will be treated as a continuing use of the earlier mark, because the marks are considered legal equivalents: "As long as the key elements of the mark remain, it has not been abandoned."[975]

[2]   Other Causes of Abandonment

Abandonment under subsection (2) of the federal definition arises from acts of commission or omission by the trademark owner that cause the mark to become generic or otherwise to lose its significance as a mark.[976] In contrast to voluntary abandonment under subsection (1), these acts or omissions constitute involuntary abandonment. Mere failure to pursue infringers does not, by itself, constitute abandonment of a mark. Such unauthorized uses can lead to a weakening of the strength of the mark, however, and this weakening can, in turn, cause the mark to become generic; genericism, whatever its cause, will lead to a finding of abandonment under subsection (2), because the mark will have lost its significance as an origin indicator.[977]

As discussed below, abandonment will also be found under section (2) when a mark loses its significance as an indicator of goods or services, through (a) unrestricted ("naked") licensing, (b) assignment of the mark without an accompanying assignment of the goodwill that is associated with it ("assignment in gross"), or (c) any circumstance that causes the mark to become generic.[978]

---

during that three-year period) (citing Imperial Tobacco, Ltd. v. Philip Morris, Inc., 899 F.2d 1575, 1580-81 (Fed. Cir. 1990) (intent must be formulated during non-use period); Emergency One, Inc. v. American FireEagle, Ltd., 228 F.3d 531, 537 (4th Cir. 2000) (similar)).

[971] *See, e.g.*, Pilates, Inc. v. Current Concepts, Inc., 120 F. Supp. 2d 286, 307-10 (S.D.N.Y. 2000) (finding that two to three sales, a single brochure and limited advertising over a three-year period were insufficient to overcome prima facie evidence of abandonment); *accord*, Kusek v. Family Circle, Inc., 894 F. Supp. 522 (D. Mass. 1995); Hughes v. Design Look Inc., 693 F. Supp. 1500, 1506 (S.D.N.Y. 1988).

[972] *Societe de Developments et D'Innovations*, 662 F. Supp. at 851.

[973] For a general discussion of tacking, see § 3.02 [A] *supra.*

[974] Sands, Taylor & Wood Co. v. Quaker Oats Co., 978 F.2d 947, 955 (7th Cir. 1992); Children's Legal Services PLLC v. Kresch, 87 U.S.P.Q.2d (BNA) 1765 (E.D. Mich. 2008); MB Financial Bank, N.A. v. MB Real Estate Servs., L.L.C., 2003 U.S. Dist. LEXIS 10578, *31-32 (N.D. Ill. 2003); Paris Glove of Canada Ltd. v. SBC/Sporto Corp., 84 U.S.P.Q.2d (BNA) 1856 (T.T.A.B. 2007).

[975] Miyano Mach. USA, Inc. v. Miyanohitec Mach., Inc., 576 F. Supp. 2d 868, 882 (N.D. Ill. 2008).

[976] 15 U.S.C. § 1127.

[977] *See* Sweetheart Plastics, Inc. v. Detroit Forming, Inc., 743 F.2d 1039, 1047-48 (4th Cir. 1984) (collecting authorities); Exxon Corp. v. Oxxford Clothes, Inc., 109 F.3d 1070, 1080 (5th Cir.), *cert. denied*, 522 U.S. 915 (1997); *see generally* § 2.07 [A][4] *supra* (discussing genericism).

[978] *Defiance Button Mach.*, 759 F.2d at 1059.

[a]   Naked Licensing

Naked licensing occurs "when a trademark owner fails to exercise reasonable control over the use of a mark by a licensee," such that "the presence of the mark on the licensee's goods or services misrepresents their connection with the trademark owner since the mark no longer identifies goods or services that are under the control of the owner of the mark" and the mark can no longer provide "a meaningful assurance of quality."[979] Thus, the policy consideration underlying the naked licensing defense is the concern that "if a trademark owner allows licensees to depart from his quality standards, the public will be misled, and the trademark will cease to have utility as an informational device."[980] As the Second Circuit explained in *Dawn Donut Co. v. Hart's Food Stores, Inc*:[981]

> Without the requirement of control, the right of a trademark owner to license his mark separately from the business in connection with which it has been used would create the danger that products bearing the same trademark might be of diverse qualities. If the licensor is not compelled to take some reasonable steps to prevent misuses of his trademark in the hands of others the public will be deprived of its most effective protection against misleading uses of a trademark. The public is hardly in a position to uncover deceptive uses of a trademark before they occur and will be at best slow to detect them after they happen. Thus, unless the licensor exercises supervision and control over the operations of its licensees the risk that the public will be unwittingly deceived will be increased and this is precisely what the Act is in part designed to prevent. Clearly the only effective way to protect the public where a trademark is used by licensees is to place on the licensor the affirmative duty of policing in a reasonable manner the activities of his licensees.[982]

Some courts have held that, to defeat a naked licensing defense, the licensor must have contractually reserved the right to control the licensee's use of the mark.[983] However, this a minority view. The majority of courts have held that the crucial question is whether the licensor in fact exercised such control; under this

---

[979] Tumblebus, Inc. v. Cranmer, 2005 Fed. App. 0021P, 2005 U.S. App. LEXIS 603 (6th Cir. 2005) (quoting Restatement (Third) of Unfair Competition § 33 cmt. b (1995)). Some courts cite section 5 of the Lanham Act, 15 U.S.C. § 1055, often together with the statutory definition of abandonment, as the statutory basis for the naked licensing defense under the Lanham Act. *See Exxon*, 109 F.3d at 1079 n. 12 (collecting cases). In the case of certification marks, the general principle that naked licensing is grounds for canceling a federal registration is expressly incorporated in section 14(5)(A) of the Lanham Act, which states that a certification mark may be cancelled when the registrant "does not control, or is not able legitimately to exercise control over, the use of such mark." 15 U.S.C. § 1064(5)(A).

[980] *Exxon*, 109 F.3d at 1079 (quoting Kentucky Fried Chicken Corp. v. Diversified Packaging Corp., 549 F.2d 368, 387 (5th Cir. 1977).

[981] 267 F.2d 358 (2d Cir. 1959).

[982] *Id.* at 367 (citing Sen. Report No. 1333, 79th Cong., 2d Sess. (1946)).

[983] *E.g.*, E. I. Du Pont de Nemours & Co. v. Celanese Corp. of America, 167 F.2d 484 (C.C.P.A. 1948) (treating abandonment as a question of intent, and holding that presence of quality requirements, inspection rights, and cancellation provision in license defeated naked licensing claim, without inquiring into whether those license terms were actually enforced); Robinson Co. v. Plastics

approach, the contractual reservation of a right to control is neither necessary nor sufficient to avoid naked licensing.[984] While there are no clear-cut rules for determining whether the licensor has exercised sufficient quality control, courts have considered the actual quality of the goods produced, the existence or absence of consumer complaints about quality, and the extent to which the licensor actually inspected the goods or the facilities where they were produced.[985] In appropriate circumstances, such as where there is a close working relationship between the parties, or where the licensor is familiar with the quality control practices of the licensee, it may be reasonable for the licensor to rely on the quality control measures of the licensee.[986]

A naked license must be distinguished from a consent-to-use agreement, which "is not an attempt to transfer or license the use of a trademark . . . but fixes and defines the existing trademark of each [party] . . . [so] that confusion and infringement may be prevented."[987] To avoid being recharacterized as a naked license, a consent-to-use agreement must be "structured in such a way as to avoid misleading or confusing consumers as to the origin and/or nature of the respective parties' goods."[988] In contrast, the permitted use under a licensing agreement is one that would be an infringing use but for the existence of the license; that is, it could mislead customers as to the origin or quality of the goods if the licensor did not exercise sufficient control over the licensee's use of the mark.[989]

Courts have construed a wide variety of agreements and relationships entered into for a range of reasons, including the cessation or forbearance of litigation, as trademark licenses that are subject to the naked licensing defense.[990] Whether

---

Research & Development Corp., 264 F. Supp. 852 (W.D. Ark. 1967) (right to control, rather than actual control, is determinative).

[984] *See, e.g.,* Dawn Donut Co. v. Hart's Food Stores, Inc., 267 F.2d 358 (2d Cir. 1959); Barcamerica Int'l USA Trust v. Tyfield Imps., Inc., 289 F.3d 589, 596-97 (9th Cir. 2002); Carl Zeiss Stiftung v. V.E.B. Carl Zeiss, Jena, 293 F. Supp. 892 (S.D.N.Y. 1968), *supp. op. at* 298 F. Supp. 1309 (S.D.N.Y. 1969), *mod.,* 433 F.2d 686 (2d Cir. 1970), *cert. denied,* 403 U.S. 905 (1971).

[985] *See, e.g., Exxon,* 109 F.3d at 1077; *Carl Zeiss Stiftung,* 293 F. Supp. at 918.

[986] *See, e.g.,* Barcamerica Int'l USA Trust v. Tyfield Imps., Inc., 289 F.3d 589, 596-97 (9th Cir. 2002); Transgo, Inc. v. Ajac Transmission Parts Corp., 768 F.2d 1001, 1017-18 (9th Cir. 1985); Taco Cabana Int'l, Inc. v. Two Pesos, Inc., 932 F.2d 1113, 1121 (5th Cir. 1991), *aff'd,* 505 U.S. 763 (1992); Taffy Original Designs, Inc. v. Taffy's Inc., 161 U.S.P.Q. (BNA) 707, 713 (N.D. Ill. 1966).

[987] *Exxon,* 109 F.3d at 1076 (quoting Waukesha Hygeia Mineral Springs Co. v. Hygeia Sparkling Distilled Water Co., 63 F. 438, 441 (7th Cir. 1894)).

[988] *Exxon,* 109 F.3d at 1076.

[989] *Id.*

[990] *Id.* at 1078 n. 9; *see, e.g,* E. & J. Gallo Winery v. Gallo Cattle Co., 967 F.2d 1280, 1289-1290 (9th Cir. 1992) (settlement agreement); Stock Pot Restaurant, Inc. v. Stockpot, Inc., 737 F.2d 1576, 1579-1580 (Fed. Cir. 1984) (lease); United States Jaycees v. Philadelphia Jaycees, 639 F.2d 134, 139 n. 7 (3d Cir. 1980) (affiliated organizations); Professional Golfers Ass'n v. Bankers L. & C. Co., 514 F.2d 665, 668-669 (5th Cir. 1975) (settlement and lease); Sheila's Shine Products, Inc. v. Sheila Shine, Inc., 486 F.2d 114, 123 (5th Cir. 1973) (purchase agreement); Express, Inc. v. Sears, Roebuck & Co., 840 F. Supp. 502, 509-510 (S.D. Ohio 1993) (settlement agreements); Engineered Mechanical Services, Inc., 584 F. Supp. at 1158-1159; Universal City Studios, Inc. v. Nintendo Co., 578 F. Supp. 911, 929 (S.D.N.Y. 1983) (covenant not to sue), *aff'd,* 746 F.2d 112 (2d Cir. 1984); Hodge Chile Co. v. KNA Food Distributors, Inc., 575 F. Supp. 210, 213 (E.D. Mo. 1983) (settlement agreement), *aff'd,*

a particular agreement constitutes a license is a question of fact that depends on the particular facts and circumstances of the case.[991]

Just as rights in a mark may be established in one geographic market but not in others, a number of courts have recognized that a mark may be partially abandoned — that is, abandoned in fewer than all of the markets where it has been used.[992] Thus, naked licensing in one territory may lead to a finding of abandonment in that territory but not in other regions.[993]

[b] Assignment in Gross

Under both common law and the Lanham Act, a mark is deemed to be abandoned when it is transferred separately from the goodwill that it represents — in other words, when it is the subject of an "assignment in gross."[994] Because a trademark has no independent significance apart from its function as a symbol of the goodwill associated with the goods or services to which it is attached, the mark cannot be sold or otherwise assigned apart from the business with which it is associated.[995] Thus, a mark is assigned "in gross" when it is assigned "separately from the essential assets used to make the product or service that the trademark identifies," because in such a case "[t]he consumer would have no assurance that he was getting the same thing (more or less) in buying the product or service from its new maker."[996] The rationale for the prohibition against assignments in gross has been explained as follows:

---

741 F.2d 1086 (8th Cir. 1984); Acme Valve & Fittings Co. v. Wayne, 386 F. Supp. 1162, 1165-1166 (S.D. Tex. 1974) (purchase order form); Naclox, Inc. v. Lee, 231 U.S.P.Q. 395, 399 (T.T.A.B.1986) (release on promissory note).

[991] *Exxon*, 109 F.3d at 1076-78.

[992] *See, e.g., Tumblebus*, 2005 U.S. App. LEXIS 603, at *24-28; Sheila's Shine Prods., Inc. v. Sheila Shine, Inc., 486 F.2d 114, 124-25 (5th Cir. 1973); E. F. Prichard Co. v. Consumers Brewing Co., 136 F.2d 512, 522 (6th Cir. 1943), *cert. denied*, 321 U.S. 763 (1944) ("While a trade-mark extends to every market where the trader's goods have become known and identified by his use of the mark, the mark itself cannot travel to markets where the trader does not offer, or has not offered, the articles for sale. Such permission for use north of the Ohio river, would be a naked license and void, resulting in an abandonment by Prichard of any rights to the mark in that area.") (citations omitted); Restatement (Third) of Unfair Competition § 30 cmt. a ("Priority at common law . . . extends only to the geographic areas in which the trademark owner uses the designation or in which the designation is associated with the trademark owner. Common law priority in a particular geographic area is thus lost if the designation has been abandoned by the owner in that geographic area.") (citation omitted); Restatement (Third) of Unfair Competition § 33 cmt. b ("If substantial uncontrolled use is confined to a particular geographic or product market, a court may conclude that the mark has been abandoned only in that geographic area or in connection with use on that product. The trademark owner then retains its priority in the use of the mark in other areas or on other products.").

[993] *See, e.g., Sheila's Shine Prods.*, 486 F.2d at 123-24.

[994] Sands, Taylor & Wood Co. v. Quaker Oats Co., 978 F.2d 947, 956 (7th Cir. 1992), *cert. denied*, 507 U.S. 1042 (1993); Money Store v. Harriscorp Finance, Inc., 689 F.2d 666, 676 (7th Cir. 1982).

[995] Dial-A-Mattress Operating Corp. v. Mattress Madness, Inc., 841 F. Supp. 1339, 1350 (E.D.N.Y. 1994); *see also* 15 U.S.C. § 1060(a); United Drug Co. v. Theodore Rectanus Co., 248 U.S. 90, 97, 39 S. Ct. 48, 50-51, 63 L. Ed. 141 (1918). Goodwill has been defined as "the value attributable to a going concern apart from its physical asserts — the intangible worth of buyer momentum emanating from the reputation and integrity earned by the company." *Dial-A-Mattress*, 841 F. Supp. at 1350.

[996] Green River Bottling Co. v. Green River Corp., 997 F.2d 359, 362 (7th Cir. 1993).

If one obtains a trademark through an assignment in gross, divorced from the good will of the assignor, the assignee obtains the symbol, but not the reality. Any subsequent use of the mark by the assignee will necessarily be in connection with a different business, a different good will and a different type of product. The continuity of the things symbolized by the mark is broken. Use of the mark by the assignee in connection with a different good will and different product would result in a fraud on the purchasing public, who reasonably assume that the mark signified the same things, whether used by one person or another . . .[997]

An assignment of physical assets is not essential to a valid trademark assignment, as long as the assignment includes the goodwill of the business in connection with which the mark is used.[998] However, where no physical assets are transferred, it can be difficult to determine whether, in fact, the assignment of a mark includes the goodwill of the business in which the mark has been used.[999] Although a trademark assignment agreement typically recites that the trademark is being assigned together with its associated goodwill, such a recitation does not, by itself, prevent a finding of an assignment in gross; instead, courts will look at the reality of the transaction as a whole.[1000]

Goodwill has been defined as "the advantage obtained from use of a trademark."[1001] Although that definition is somewhat circular, the "advantage" is said to consist of "public confidence in the quality of the product and in the warranties made on behalf of the product, and the 'name recognition' of the product that differentiates that product from others."[1002] Somewhat more helpfully, Professor McCarthy defines goodwill as "the favorable consideration shown by the purchasing public to goods known to emanate from a particular source," and describes it as "a business value that reflects the basic human propensity to continue doing business with a seller who has offered goods and services that the customer likes and has found adequate to fulfill his needs."[1003] However, determining when this value has effectively been transferred to a trademark assignee can be difficult.

An assignment of a mark will typically *not* be an assignment in gross if: (1) it is accompanied by an assignment of the physical assets used in the associated

---

[997] Money Store v. Harriscorp Finance, Inc., 689 F.2d 666, 676 (7th Cir. 1982) (quoting McCarthy on Trademarks § 18.1, at 607). *See also Green River*, 997 F.2d at 362 ("The point is not that the product to which a trademark is affixed can never change. Many trademarked products, ranging from Chevrolets to Coca-Cola, have changed enormously over the years. But in these cases the consumer always knew whose product it was that he was getting. The prohibition of sales in gross protects his expectations.").

[998] *See, e.g.*, Sands, Taylor & Wood Co. v. Quaker Oats Co., 978 F.2d 947, *cert. denied*, 507 U.S. 1042 (1993).

[999] Money Store v. Harriscorp Finance, Inc., 689 F.2d 666, 676 (7th Cir. 1982).

[1000] *Money Store*, 689 F.2d at 676; Haymaker Sports, Inc. v. Turian, 581 F.2d 257 (C.C.P.A. 1978); Colonial Elec. & Plumbing Supply v. Colonial Elec., 2007 U.S. Dist. LEXIS 94417, *17 (D.N.J. 2007).

[1001] Premier Dental Prods. Co. v. Darby Dental Supply Co., 794 F.2d 850, 853 n. 3 (3d Cir. 1986).

[1002] *Id.*

[1003] McCarthy on Trademarks, *supra* note 223, at § 2.17.

line of business, *or* (2) the assignee "is producing a product or providing a service which is substantially similar to that of the assignor and where consumers will not be deceived or harmed."[1004] However, if the physical assets are not transferred, *and* there is no continuity in the line of business in which the mark is used (as, for example, where the assignee uses the mark on a substantially different product or service), then the assignment is deemed not to include the goodwill associated with the mark, and is treated as an assignment in gross.[1005]

[B]   First Sale Doctrine

Under common law as well as the Lanham Act, the first sale doctrine permits a purchaser of lawfully trademarked goods to display, offer, and sell those goods under their original trademark.[1006] The rationale is that "when a retailer merely resells a genuine, unaltered good under the trademark of the producer, the use of the producer's trademark by the reseller will not deceive or confuse the public as to the nature, qualities, and origin of the good."[1007]

The courts have recognized several exceptions to the first sale doctrine. First, the doctrine does not apply where a reseller uses the mark in a manner that is likely to cause the public to believe that the reseller was part of the producer's authorized sales force or one of its franchisees.[1008] Second, the doctrine does not apply when the goods sold are materially different from those that the trademark owner has authorized for sale.[1009] Third, several courts have held that the doctrine does not apply to goods that have been repackaged if there is inadequate notice of the repackaging.[1010]

[1004] *Colonial Elec.*, 2007 U.S. Dist. LEXIS 94417 at *16-17; Pilates, Inc. v. Current Concepts, Inc., 120 F. Supp. 2d 286, 311 (S.D.N.Y. 2000); *accord* Defiance Button Machine Co. v. C & C Metal Prods. Corp., 759 F.2d 1053, 1059 (2d Cir. 1985); *see also* InterState Net Bank v. NetB@nk, Inc., 348 F. Supp. 2d 340 (D.N.J. 2004) (holding that a domain name is not a tangible asset whose transfer in conjunction with a trademark can avoid a finding of assignment in gross).

[1005] *See, e.g.,* Pepsico, Inc. v. Grapette Co., 416 F.2d 285, 289-90 (8th Cir. 1969) (assignment in gross found where assignor had used "Peppy" mark on a cola drink, assignment included neither tangible assets nor formula for producing the cola beverage, and assignee used the mark on a pepper-type drink).

[1006] Tumblebus, Inc. v. Cranmer, 399 F.3d 754, 766-67 (6th Cir. 2005); Sebastian Int'l, Inc. v. Longs Drug Stores Corp., 53 F.3d 1073, 1076 (9th Cir.), *cert. denied*, 516 U.S. 914 (1995); NEC Electronics v. CAL Circuit Abco, 810 F.2d 1506, 1509 (9th Cir. 1987); *see also* PACCAR Inc. v. TeleScan Techs., L.L.C., 319 F.3d 243, 257 (6th Cir. 2003); Restatement (Third) of Unfair Competition § 24 cmt. b (1995) ("Trademark owner cannot ordinarily prevent or control the sale of goods bearing the mark once the owner has permitted those goods to enter commerce.").

[1007] *Tumblebus*, 399 F.3d at 766; *see also NEC Electronics*, 810 F.2d at 1509; Restatement (Third) of Unfair Competition § 24 cmt. b.

[1008] *PACCAR*, 319 F.3d at 257. *Cf.* H.L. Hayden Co. of New York, Inc. v. Siemens Med. Sys., Inc., 879 F.2d 1005, 1023-24 (2d Cir. 1989) (allowing first-sale defense in trademark infringement suit on the basis that customers knew that purchases from the defendant included the product only and not its installation, which plaintiff's authorized distributors provided).

[1009] *Brilliance Audio*, 474 F.3d at 369.

[1010] Prestonettes, Inc. v. Coty, 264 U.S. 359, 368-69 (1924); Brilliance Audio Inc. v. Haights Cross Commun., Inc., 474 F.3d 365, 369 (6th Cir. 2007); Enesco Corp. v. Price/Costco Inc., 146 F.3d 1083, 1085-86 (9th Cir. 1998).

Each of these exceptions is discussed below.

[1]   Misrepresentation by Non-Authorized Resellers

Under the first sale rule, the mere sale of a lawfully trademarked product by an unauthorized reseller does not, by itself, constitute trademark infringement or unfair competition.[1011] Therefore, a person who purchases an authentic designer handbag (or receives one as a gift) is free to offer it for sale on eBay. Likewise, any person or entity that purchases a large inventory of authentic designer handbags is, in general, free to offer those bags for sale to others. Even if purchasers mistakenly believe that the reseller is authorized by or affiliated with the trademark owner, this does not give rise to actionable misrepresentation if the reseller has done no more than stock, display, and resell the goods.[1012]

However, conduct that goes beyond the mere stocking, display, and sale of merchandise may violate the Lanham Act. If a reseller falsely represents to purchasers that the reseller is an authorized agent of the trademark holder, this false representation is not permitted by the first sale defense. For example, courts have imposed liability where a reseller's print advertising displayed a trademark in a way that suggested that the reseller was a franchisee of the trademark owner,[1013] and where a reseller used the maker's trademark at a trade show and in a trade journal ad, and stamped the reseller's name on the maker's promotional literature, which it then used to advertise the reseller's wares.[1014]

[2]   Materially Different Goods

Because the first sale defense applies only when the reseller's goods are lawfully trademarked, a question may arise as to whether the goods offered by a particular reseller are "genuine" trademarked goods. As discussed below, this question may arise when the goods have been altered after their initial manufacture, or when, at some point in the chain of manufacturing and distribution, they have not been subjected to the quality control standards imposed by the trademark owner on its licensees.

[a]   Used, Altered, or Refurbished Goods

In the case of used, altered, or refurbished goods, the courts generally examine the extent to which the goods differ from their new, unaltered, counterparts in order to determine whether the use of the original manufacturer's mark is infringing.[1015] Two unsettled issues, however, are: (1)

[1011] NEC Electronics v. CAL Circuit Abco, 810 F.2d 1506, 1508-09 (9th Cir. 1987); Matrix Essentials v. Emporium Drug Mart, 988 F.2d 587, 593 (5th Cir. 1993); H.L. Hayden Co. v. Siemens Medical Sys., 879 F.2d 1005, 1023 (2d Cir. 1989).

[1012] Sebastian Int'l v. Longs Drug Stores Corp., 53 F.3d 1073, 1076 (9th Cir. 1995).

[1013] Bandag, Inc. v. Al Bolser's Tire Stores, 750 F.2d 903, 911, 916 (Fed. Cir. 1984).

[1014] Stormor, a Div. of Fuqua Indus. v. Johnson, 587 F. Supp. 275, 279 (W.D. Mich. 1984).

[1015] Champion Spark Plug Co. v. Sanders, 331 U.S. 125 (1947); Nitro Leisure Prods., L.L.C. v.

the question of the type and degree of differences or alterations that can give rise to infringement, and (2) the question of whether the same legal standards should apply to both used and new goods.

Champion Spark Plug Co. v. Sanders,[1016] the leading case on the sale of refurbished goods, involved the repair, reconditioning, and resale of used spark plugs under the original manufacturer's trademark. Although the plugs and their packaging were marked "renewed," that legend was not always legible, and the packaging did not indicate any source other than the original manufacturer. The district court found infringement of the plaintiff's mark, and issued an injunction requiring, *inter alia*, that the defendant remove the manufacturer's trademark and other identifying marks from the spark plugs, repaint them, stamp them prominently as "repaired," and print a legend on the package identifying them as "Used spark plug(s) originally made by Champion Spark Plug Company repaired and made fit for use up to 10,000 miles by Perfect Recondition Spark Plug Co., 1133 Bedford Avenue, Brooklyn, N.Y."[1017] On appeal, the Second Circuit modified the injunction in several respects, most notably by eliminating the requirement that the original manufacturer's trademark and other identifying marks be removed, and by replacing the district court's precise legend with a more general one that nonetheless indicated clearly that the plugs: (1) were used, and (2) had been reconditioned by the defendants.[1018] In its decision upholding these modifications, the Supreme Court made clear that selling used or refurbished goods under their original trademark is not an infringement, even if the secondhand goods are inferior to their newly manufactured counterparts, provided that the seller does not misrepresent the goods as new, and has not made material alterations to the goods:

> Cases may be imagined where the reconditioning or repair would be so extensive or so basic that it would be a misnomer to call the article by its original name, even though the words "used" or "repaired" were added. But no such practice is involved here. The repair or reconditioning of the plugs does not give them a new design. It is no more than a restoration, so far as possible, of their original condition. The type marks attached by the manufacturer are determined by the use to which the plug is to be put. But the thread size and size of the cylinder hole into which the plug is fitted are not affected by the reconditioning. The heat range also has relevance to the type marks. And there is evidence that the reconditioned plugs are inferior so far as heat range and other qualities are concerned. But inferiority is expected in most second-hand articles. Indeed, they generally cost the customer less. That is the case here. Inferiority is immaterial so long as the article is clearly and distinctly sold as repaired or reconditioned rather than as new. The result is, of course, that the second-hand dealer gets some advantage from the trade

---

Acushnet Co., 341 F.3d 1356 (Fed. Cir. 2003). Davidoff & Cie, S.A. v. PLD Int'l Corp., 263 F.3d 1297 (11th Cir. 2001).

[1016] 331 U.S. 125 (1947).

[1017] *Id.* at 126-27.

[1018] *Id.* at 127-28.

mark. But . . . that is wholly permissible so long as the manufacturer is not identified with the inferior qualities of the product resulting from wear and tear or the reconditioning by the dealer. Full disclosure gives the manufacturer all the protection to which he is entitled.[1019]

Several appellate courts have had occasion to apply *Champion*'s observation that "[c]ases may be imagined where the reconditioning or repair would be so extensive or so basic that it would be a misnomer to call the article by its original name, even though the words 'used' or 'repaired' were added." In a series of cases involving reconditioned Rolex and Bulova watches, for example, the Fifth, Seventh, and Ninth Circuits held that the sale of such watches under their original trademarks creates a likelihood of confusion that cannot be negated by a disclosure that the original watches have been altered or that they contain some non-original components.[1020] The defendant's alterations resulted in the creation of a "new product" that could not be sold under the original manufacturer's trademark.[1021]

In contrast to *Champion* and other cases addressing the sale of used or refurbished goods, the Eleventh Circuit applied the "material differences" test to the resale of *new* trademarked goods in *Davidoff & Cie, S.A. v. PLD Int'l Corp.*[1022] In that case, the appellate court upheld a district court's finding that etching the glass on a fragrance bottle in order to remove the original batch code degraded the appearance of the product, creating a "material difference," and therefore gave rise to a likelihood of confusion: "[T]he resale of a trademarked product that is materially different can constitute a trademark infringement . . . because materially different products that have the same trademark may confuse consumers and erode consumer goodwill toward the mark."[1023] A finding of material differences, it noted, may be based on differences in quality control or in the goods themselves.[1024] The court then attempted to define material differences:

> Not just any difference will cause consumer confusion. A material difference is one that consumers consider relevant to a decision about whether to purchase a product. Because a myriad of considerations may influence consumer preferences, the threshold of materiality must be kept low to include even subtle differences between products.

[1019] 331 U.S. at 129-30 (citations and footnotes omitted). The Court in *Champion* relied in part on its prior decision in Prestonettes, Inc. v. Coty, 264 U.S. 359 (1924), in which the purchaser of trademarked perfume and face powder had rebottled the perfumes and combined the face powder with other ingredients for resale. The Court held that the original manufacturer, Coty, could not prevent the reseller from using the manufacturer's trademark to identify the original source of the goods, provided that the product packaging bore an inscription that accurately indicated the reseller's role in repackaging and/or combining Coty's goods with other ingredients.

[1020] Rolex Watch, U.S.A., Inc. v. Michel Co., 179 F.3d 704 (9th Cir. 1999); Rolex Watch USA, Inc., v. Meece, 158 F.3d 816 (5th Cir. 1998), *cert. denied*, 526 U.S. 1133 (1999); Bulova Watch Co. v. Allerton Co., 328 F.2d 20 (7th Cir. 1964).

[1021] *Michel,* 179 F.3d at 710.

[1022] 263 F.3d 1297 (11th Cir. 2001).

[1023] *Id.* at 1301-02.

[1024] *Id.* at 1302.

The case law supports the proposition that the resale of a trademarked product that has been altered, resulting in physical differences in the product, can create a likelihood of consumer confusion. Such alteration satisfies the material difference exception and gives rise to a trademark infringement claim.[1025]

The appropriateness of applying the material differences standard to used or refurbished goods, however, was questioned by the Federal Circuit in *Nitro Leisure Products, L.L.C. v. Acushnet Co.*,[1026] in which the defendant reconditioned golf balls by removing and replacing the outer layers of paint, and reapplying the manufacturer's trademark. Prior to sale, the defendant marked the balls and their packaging with legends clearly indicating that the balls had been refurbished. The Federal Circuit upheld the district court's determination that, under *Champion*, the alterations to the balls were not so substantial as to create a likelihood of consumer confusion: "[S]o long as the customer is getting a product with the expected characteristics, and so long as the goodwill built up by the trademark owner is not eroded by being identified with inferior quality, the Lanham Act does not prevent the truthful use of trademarks, even if such use results in the enrichment of others."[1027] Furthermore, the court held, because the case involved used goods rather than new, it was not strictly necessary for the court to apply *Davidoff*'s "material differences" standard:

> The fundamental question examined in *Davidoff* was the same question considered in *Champion* — likelihood of confusion — but presented in the context of re-sales of new goods. The context is important because consumers of new goods have different expectations than consumers of used goods. For new goods, any variation of the product from a new condition — even as relatively modest as the obliteration of a name or

---

[1025] *Id.* (citations omitted). The court's definition of a material difference as "one that consumers consider relevant to a decision about whether to purchase a product" is consistent with the standard that has been adopted in five other circuits; many, though not all, of those cases involved "gray goods" imported without the consent of the trademark owner. Societe des Produits Nestle, S.A. v. Casa Helvetia, Inc., 982 F.2d 633, 644 (1st Cir. 1992) (finding material differences based on quality control, composition, configuration, packaging, and price); Original Appalachian Artworks, Inc. v. Granada Elecs., Inc., 816 F.2d 68, 73 (2d Cir. 1987) (finding material differences where an imported doll came with foreign language "adoption papers" and was not permitted to be "adopted" domestically); Iberia Foods Corp. v. Romeo, 150 F.3d 298, 302 (3d Cir. 1998) (finding material differences where quality control measures differed); Martin's Herend Imports Inc. v. Diamond & Gem Trading USA, Co., 112 F.3d 1296, 1302 (5th Cir. 1997) (finding material differences when the trademark holder had chosen to sell only selected pieces in the United States and the accused infringer was selling other, genuine pieces in the United States); Enesco Corp. v. Price/Costco Inc., 146 F.3d 1083, 1087 (9th Cir. 1998) (finding material differences where quality control measures differed). *Compare* Graham Webb International Ltd. Partnership v. Emporium Drug Mart, Inc., 916 F. Supp. 909 (E.D. Ark. 1995) (removal of batch codes from hair care products was not a material difference where it did not significantly affect overall appearance of product, and thus would not materially affect consumer decision to purchase), *and* John Paul Mitchell Systems v. Randall's Food Markets, Inc., 17 S.W.3d 721 (Tex. Ct. App. 2000) (similar), *with* John Paul Mitchell Systems v. Pete-N-Larry's Inc., 862 F. Supp. 1020, 1027 (W.D.N.Y. 1994) (removal of batch codes from hair care products was a material difference, giving rise to infringement, where it left noticeable scars on bottles and erased some of the information printed).

[1026] 341 F.3d 1356 (Fed. Cir. 2003).

[1027] *Id.* at 1362.

batch number from the bottom of a container — may signal imitation, counterfeiting, falsity or some other irregularity affecting a customer's decision whether to purchase the product. . . . For new goods, consumers are likely to be confused by the presence of such "material differences."

For used or refurbished goods, customers have a different expectation. They do not expect the product to be in the same condition as a new product. There is an understanding on the part of consumers of used or refurbished products that such products will be degraded or will show signs of wear and tear and will not measure up to or perform at the same level as if new. For used or refurbished products, consumers are not likely to be confused by — and indeed expect — differences in the goods compared to new, unused goods. Thus, the tests applied to assess likelihood of confusion by courts will not necessarily be the same when determining trademark infringement in the resale of altered new goods and when considering trademark infringement in the resale of used and refurbished goods.

. . .

The *Davidoff* test looks to the effect on a consumer's decision to purchase of differences in an altered or modified new product from the original. It is a reasonable and workable test of the likelihood of confusion and the loss of goodwill represented by the trademark applied to the product, given consumer expectations as to the nature and quality of new products as offered for sale . . .

. . .

The *Champion* Court recognizes that consumers do not expect used or refurbished goods to be the same as new goods and that for such goods, "material differences" do not necessarily measure consumer confusion. According to *Champion*, what is more telling on the question of likelihood of confusion in the context of used goods is whether the used or refurbished goods are so different from the original that it would be a misnomer for them to be designated by the original trademark.[1028]

Therefore, the court concluded, the district court was not required to apply the "material differences" test to the refurbished golf balls, and the district court had properly concluded that the plaintiff had not established a likelihood of confusion because "the differences in the goods were nothing more than what would be expected for used golf balls," and it was therefore not a "misnomer" to apply the original manufacturer's mark to the refurbished balls.[1029]

The Ninth Circuit formulated a test for determining whether a product has been so altered that the use of the original trademark would infringe in *Karl Storz Endoscopy-America, Inc. v. Surgical Technologies, Inc.*,[1030] which in-

---

[1028] *Id.* at 1362-63 (citations omitted).

[1029] *Id.* at 1364.

[1030] 285 F.3d 848, 856-57 (9th Cir. 2002).

volved the activities of a contractor that provided repair services for endoscopes. The court distinguished between normal repairs in which a product is repaired, and returned to its owner, and the defendant's endoscope repairs, which involved replacing every essential component of a customer's endoscope and reattaching this to the original base bearing the plaintiff's trademark, and that therefore constituted the functional equivalent of a sale:

> A mere repair for an owner's personal use must be contrasted with a complete rebuild where the rebuilt product will be used by a third party. If the reconstructed product still bearing the original manufacturer's trademark is so altered as to be a different product from that of the original manufacturer, the repair transaction involves a "use in commerce." The repair company in that situation is trading on the goodwill of, or association with, the trademark holder.[1031]

Even though the customer requesting the repair (a hospital, for example) might not be confused about the origin of the reconstructed endoscope, an actual user of the endoscope (such as a surgeon working at the hospital) who was unaware of the full extent of the repair might experience post-sale confusion, and might therefore blame the original manufacturer for any defects in the product.[1032] The court distinguished the right of property owners to repair or alter trademarked goods without incurring liability for trademark infringement, noting that when the repairs or alterations are done by an outside contractor, "the question is whether the trademarked product is so altered that the substance of the transaction is a sale, and it would be misleading to sell the product without noting the alterations," thus raising the same question that the Supreme Court had addressed in *Champion*.[1033] Merely cleaning, sterilizing, and resharpening medical instruments, for example, would not constitute trademark infringement.[1034] Eschewing any bright-line test for determining whether a contractor's repair or reconstruction of goods that retain their original trademark constitutes a use in commerce, the court of appeals suggested that a number of factors should be considered in determining whether the contractor "has made a different product":

> Those factors include the nature and extent of the alterations, the nature of the device and how it is designed (whether some components have a shorter useful life than the whole), whether a market has developed for service and spare parts, and, most importantly, whether end users of the product are likely to be misled as to the party responsible for the composition of the product.[1035]

The court relied in part on the factors that are used by the Federal Circuit to distinguish a permissible repair from an infringing reconstruction for purposes

---

[1031] *Id.* at 856.

[1032] *Id.* at 855-56.

[1033] *Id.* at 856.

[1034] *Id.* (citing U.S. Surgical Corp. v. Orris, Inc., 5 F. Supp. 2d 1201, 1209 (D. Kan. 1998)).

[1035] *Id.* at 856-57 (citations omitted).

of federal patent law.[1036]

[b]   Other Non-Genuine Goods

In some cases, an unauthorized reseller may be ineligible for the first sale defense because its merchandise has not been subjected to the quality control standards that the trademark owner imposes on its licensees, even if there is no evidence that the goods have in fact been altered since their initial manufacture. The failure of quality control may occur at any point in the manufacturing and distribution process. In these cases, courts have held that the first sale defense does not apply, because the goods are not "genuine." The rationale underlying these decisions is that the sale of such goods under the original trademark falsely implies to consumers that the goods have been subjected to the trademark owner's quality control standards from the point of manufacture to the point of sale.

In some cases, the failure of quality control occurs in the manufacturing process. For example, a retailer was held liable for infringing the Candie's trademark for shoes because the shoes it had purchased and then resold to customers were part of a cancelled order that had never been subjected to a final quality control inspection at the factory as required under the terms of the manufacturing license from the trademark owner. Without this final inspection, there could be no certainty that the shoes met the trademark owner's quality standards; accordingly, the goods were not "genuine."[1037]

On other occasions, the failure of quality control may take place after the initial manufacture. In one such case, a company that purchased Shell motor oil from authorized distributors and then resold it in bulk under Shell's trademark was liable for trademark infringement because its handling of the oil did not meet Shell's quality control standards — for example, the reseller transported the bulk oil in tankers that had not been cleaned after hauling diesel fuel, creating the potential for contamination.[1038] A likelihood of confusion arose because the use of Shell's trademark falsely implied to purchasers that the oil offered for sale had been subjected to Shell's quality control procedures throughout the entire manufacturing and distribution process.[1039] Applying similar reasoning, another court held that the Coors beer sold by a distributor was not genuine; although the beer had been manufactured and labeled by Coors, the distributor did not abide by Coors' standards for transporting and storing the product. Because the beer contained no preservatives, inadequate refrigeration could cause it to deteriorate.[1040]

In contrast, it appears that some restrictions imposed by trademark owners on their licensed distributors may be ignored without affecting the

---

[1036] *Id.* at 857 (citing Bottom Line Mgmt., Inc. v. Pan Man, Inc., 228 F.3d 1352, 1355-56 (Fed. Cir. 2000)).

[1037] El Greco Leather Prods. Co. v. Shoe World, Inc., 806 F.2d 392, 395-96 (2d Cir. 1986).

[1038] Shell Oil Co. v. Commercial Petroleum, Inc., 928 F.2d 104, 106 n. 2 (4th Cir. 1991).

[1039] *Id.* at 108.

[1040] Adolph Coors Co. v. A. Genderson & Sons, Inc., 486 F. Supp. 131 (D. Colo. 1980).

"genuineness" of the merchandise. For example, where a retailer sold but did not install the plaintiff's trademarked dental equipment, the Second Circuit held that the equipment was still genuine, even though the plaintiff required its authorized distributors to install the equipment they sold. In the court's view, customers were not deceived if they understood that the product they purchased under the plaintiff's trademark included only the equipment and not the installation.[1041]

[3] Undisclosed Repackaging

Several courts have recognized a "repackaging" exception to the first sale rule. Under this exception, a reseller is permitted to repackage lawfully trademarked goods provided that the reseller adequately discloses to consumers that the goods have been repackaged by someone other than the trademark owner. This rule appears to be grounded in the concern that a reseller's repackaging may be inadequate or inappropriate for the product. For example, the new packaging may provide inadequate damage protection, or may permit the product to deteriorate more quickly after purchase, leading consumers to blame their dissatisfaction on the trademark owner unless they are made aware that the reseller is responsible for the packaging. This rationale is similar to that which underlies the exception for goods that have been materially altered or that have not been subjected to the trademark owner's quality control standards.

The repackaging exception is derived from the Supreme Court's decision in *Prestonettes, Inc. v. Coty,*[1042] in which the defendant repackaged Coty's powders and perfumes for resale. The plaintiff did not allege that the defendant had materially altered the products, although it implied that the new packaging might hasten their deterioration. The Court held that the defendant was permitted to identify the repackaged goods as Coty products provided that consumers were aware that the defendant was responsible for the repackaging:

> If a man bought a barrel of a certain flour, or a demijohn of Old Crow whiskey, he certainly could sell the flour in smaller packages or in former days could have sold the whiskey in bottles, and tell what it was, if he stated that he did the dividing up or the bottling. And this would not be because of a license implied from the special facts but on the general ground that we have stated. It seems to us that no new right can be evoked from the fact that the perfume or powder is delicate and likely to be spoiled, or from the omnipresent possibility of fraud. If the defendant's rebottling the plaintiff's perfume deteriorates it and the public is adequately informed who does the rebottling, the public, with or without the plaintiff's assistance, is likely to find it out. And so of the powder in its new form.[1043]

[1041] H.L. Hayden Co. v. Siemens Med. Sys., Inc., 879 F.2d 1005, 1023 (2d Cir. 1989).

[1042] 264 U.S. 359 (1924).

[1043] *Coty,* 264 U.S. at 369.

In *Enesco Corp. v. Price/Costco, Inc.*,[1044] the defendant removed the plaintiff's collectible porcelain figurines from the plaintiff's packaging and substituted its own prior to resale. The plaintiff argued that the figurines as sold by the defendant were no longer "genuine," because the defendant's inferior packaging was inadequate to protect the fragile figurines. Although the Ninth Circuit agreed that the defendant had exceeded the bounds of the first sale defense, the court did *not* hold that the goods themselves were no longer genuine. Instead, relying on *Coty*, the court held that the defendant was required to disclose to customers that it had repackaged the figurines.

The repackaging exception was also addressed in *Brilliance Audio, Inc. v. Haight Cross Communications, Inc.*[1045] The plaintiff packaged its audiobooks in two versions — library and retail editions. The defendant purchased the plaintiff's retail editions and repackaged them as library editions, which it then resold under the plaintiff's trademark. The plaintiff argued that this repackaging vitiated the first sale defense, because "the notice of repackaging is inadequate because it creates the misrepresentation that '[d]efendants have a long-standing relationship with Plaintiff and that the activities of Defendants are authorized and sponsored by Plaintiff' [and] . . . the inadequate packaging is likely to result in consumer confusion that will dilute the value of the trademark."[1046] Applying *Coty*, the Sixth Circuit held that, even though it was unclear whether the products themselves were materially different, the allegation of differences in "packaging and marketing" was sufficient to withstand a motion to dismiss.[1047]

[4]   Gray Market Goods

The problem of "gray market goods" represents a special application of the first sale rule. Gray market goods, also known as "parallel imports," are goods that bear a legitimate trademark, but that are manufactured outside the United States under a restricted trademark license that prohibits their importation into the United States. Because the use of the trademark on the licensed goods is an authorized use, the mark is not counterfeit. However, the restricted license limits the geographic markets in which the goods bearing this mark can be sold. When goods are manufactured abroad under a license that prohibits their importation into the United States, the question arises whether the subsequent importation of those goods infringes the rights of the domestic trademark owner.

When such goods are purchased overseas and then imported into the United States for domestic distribution, the United States trademark owner may have a cause of action for trademark infringement, or may be able to invoke Customs laws to prevent the goods from entering the United States.

Several statutes offer avenues of relief for a domestic trademark owner seeking a remedy against importation of gray market goods. These include

---

[1044] 146 F.3d 1083, 1085-86 (9th Cir. 1998).

[1045] 474 F.3d 365 (6th Cir. 2007).

[1046] *Id.* at 371.

[1047] *Id.* at 370-71.

sections 32, 42, 43(a) and 43(b) of the Lanham Act,[1048] as well as section 526 of the 1930 Tariff Act.[1049]

Under sections 32, 43(a), and 43(b),[1050] the plaintiff must establish that the importation of the gray market goods creates a likelihood of confusion. However, courts generally will not find a likelihood of confusion unless the imported goods are "materially different" from the authorized goods.[1051]

The rationale for the material differences test has been expressed as follows:

> Under the Lanham Act, only those appropriations of a mark that are likely to cause confusion are prohibited. Ergo, when a product identical to a domestic product is imported into the United States under the same mark, no violation of the Lanham Act occurs. In such a situation, consumers get exactly the bundle of characteristics that they associate with the mark and the domestic distributor can be said to enjoy in large measure his investment in goodwill. By the same token, using the same mark on two blatantly different products normally does not offend the

---

[1048] *See, e.g.,* R.J. Reynolds Tobacco Co. v. Premium Tobacco Stores, Inc., 52 U.S.P.Q.2d (BNA) 1052 (N.D. Ill. 1999), *dismissed in part on other grounds,* 1999 U.S. Dist. LEXIS 19641 (N.D. Ill. 1999); Societe Des Produits Nestle, S.A. v. Casa Helvetia, Inc., 982 F.2d 633 (1st Cir. 1992).

[1049] 19 U.S.C. § 1526. Under section 526(a) of the Tariff Act, it is "unlawful to import into the United States any merchandise of foreign manufacture if such merchandise . . . bears a trademark owned by a citizen of, or by a corporation or association created or organized within, the United States," if the trademark is properly registered, unless the owner of the registration provides written consent. 19 U.S.C. § 1526(a). Section 526(b) subjects such merchandise to seizure and forfeiture. Section 526(c) provides that any person dealing in such merchandise may be enjoined from doing so or may be required to export or destroy the merchandise or remove the trademark; and subjects the vendor to liability for the same damages and profits as in an action for trademark infringement.

[1050] Section 43(b) prohibits importation of goods that are marked in contravention of section 43 and provides that such goods shall not be admitted into the country by U.S. Customs. 15 U.S.C. § 1125(b). This prohibition is enforced through U.S. Customs regulations providing that "[a]rticles which bear, or the containers of which bear, false designations of origin, or false descriptions or representations, including words or other symbols tending falsely to describe or represent the articles, are prohibited importation and shall be detained." 19 C.F. R. § 11.13(a). The United States Court of International Trade has held that, in exercising its authority under these provisions, Customs is permitted to make an independent determination as to whether section 43(a) has been violated, and thus may deny entry to goods without a court order finding a violation of section 43(a), subject to the rights of the importer, owner, or consignee of the goods to appeal this decision under section 43(b). United States v. Nippon Miniature Bearing Corp., 155 F. Supp. 2d 707 (C.I.T. 2001).

[1051] *E.g., Societe des Produits Nestle,* 982 F.2d at 638; NEC Elecs., Inc. v. Cal Circuit Abco, 810 F.2d 1506 (9th Cir.), *cert. denied,* 484 U.S. 851 (1987); Weil Ceramics & Glass, Inc. v. Dash, 878 F.2d 659, 668 (3d Cir. 1989); Lever Bros. Co. v. United States, 877 F.2d 101, 105-07 (D.C. Cir. 1989); Olympus Corp. v. United States, 792 F.2d 315, 321 (2d Cir. 1986), *cert. denied,* 486 U.S. 1042 (1988). The rationale for the "material differences" approach has been expressed as follows:

> [A]lthough it has been said that "trademark law generally does not reach the sale of genuine goods bearing a true mark even though such sale is without the mark owner's consent," the maxim does not apply when genuine, but unauthorized, imports differ materially from authentic goods authorized for sale in the domestic market. . . . [A]n unauthorized importation may well turn an otherwise "genuine" product into a "counterfeit" one. In other words, the unauthorized importation and sale of materially different merchandise violates Lanham Act section 32 because a difference in products bearing the same name confuses consumers and impinges on the local trademark holder's goodwill.

Societe des Produits Nestle, 982 F.2d at 638 (quoting *NEC Elecs.,* 810 F.2d at 1509); *see also* Shell Oil Co. v. Commercial Petroleum, Inc., 928 F.2d 104, 107 (4th Cir. 1991).

Lanham Act, for such use is unlikely to cause confusion and is, therefore, unlikely to imperil the goodwill of either product.

The probability of confusion is great, however, when the same mark is displayed on goods that are not identical but that nonetheless bear strong similarities in appearance or function. Gray goods often fall within this category. Thus, when dealing with the importation of gray goods, a reviewing court must necessarily be concerned with subtle differences, for it is by subtle differences that consumers are most easily confused. For that reason, the threshold of materiality must be kept low enough to take account of potentially confusing differences — differences that are not blatant enough to make it obvious to the average consumer that the origin of the product differs from his or her expectations.[1052]

Where courts have required a showing of "material differences" between the domestic goods and the imported goods, they have not required the plaintiff to establish that the gray market goods are inferior in quality; it is sufficient that the goods are different.[1053] Furthermore, courts have not limited their analysis to physical differences. In determining whether products are "materially different," it has been said that "differences in . . . warranty protection or service commitments . . . may well render products non-identical in the relevant Lanham Act sense."[1054] For example, in *Original Appalachian Artworks, Inc. v. Granada Electronics, Inc.*, the Second Circuit upheld a finding of infringement under section 32 against a defendant that imported "Cabbage Patch" dolls that bore a lawful trademark (licensed from the plaintiff) but that were manufactured abroad under a license prohibiting the sale of the dolls outside of Spain and several other overseas markets. The court found that the defendant's dolls differed materially from the plaintiff's dolls because their "birth certificates," "adoption papers," and instructions were in Spanish. This created consumer confusion over the source of the product, which had the potential to injure the plaintiff's domestic goodwill:

> Jesmar's dolls were not intended to be sold in the United States and, most importantly, were materially different from the Coleco Cabbage Patch Kids dolls sold in the United States. There is a very real difference in the product itself — the foreign language adoption papers and birth certificate, coupled with the United States fulfillment houses' inability or unwillingness to process Jesmar's adoption papers or mail adoption certificates and birthday cards to Jesmar doll owners, and the concomitant inability of consumers to "adopt" the dolls. It is this difference that creates the confusion over the source of the product and results in a loss of OAA's and Coleco's good will. Thus, even though the goods do bear

---

[1052] *Societe des Produits Nestle*, 982 F.2d at 641 (citations omitted).

[1053] *Id.* at 640. For examples of material differences, see Martin's Herend Imports, Inc. v. Diamond and Gem Trading USA, Co., 112 F.3d 1296 (5th Cir. 1997); Lever Brothers Co. v. United States, 981 F.2d 1330 (D.C. Cir. 1993); *Societe Des Produits Nestle*, 982 F.2d at 641–44; Lever Brothers Co. v. United States, 877 F.2d 101 (D.C. Cir. 1989); and Philip Morris Inc. v. Allen Distributors, Inc., 48 F. Supp. 2d 844 (S.D. Ind. 1999).

[1054] *Id.* at 639 n. 7.

OAA's trademark and were manufactured under license with OAA, they are not "genuine" goods because they differ from the Coleco dolls and were not authorized for sale in the United States.[1055]

Even where the packaging of gray market goods clearly identifies their geographic origin, courts have held that actionable confusion regarding the source of materially different goods can still arise from the use of the similar trademarks or trade dress.[1056]

The standard of materiality which the courts apply is low:

There is no mechanical way to determine the point at which a difference becomes "material." Separating wheat from chaff must be done on a case-by-case basis. Bearing in mind the policies and provisions of the Lanham Act as they apply to gray goods, we can confidently say that the threshold of materiality is always quite low in such cases. We conclude that the existence of any difference between the registrant's product and the allegedly infringing gray good that consumers would likely consider to be relevant when purchasing a product creates a presumption of consumer confusion sufficient to support a Lanham Act claim. Any higher threshold would endanger a manufacturer's investment in product goodwill and unduly subject consumers to potential confusion by severing the tie between a manufacturer's protected mark and its associated bundle of traits.[1057]

[1055] Original Appalachian Artworks, Inc. v. Granada Electronics, Inc., 816 F.2d 68, 73 (2d Cir. 1987); see also Societe des Produits Nestle, 982 F.2d at 639 n. 7 (noting that material differences may include differences in "warranty protection or service commitments").

[1056] See, e.g., Societe des Produits Nestle, 982 F.2d at 639 (noting that actionable confusion under section 43(a)(1) was possible "in light of the overall appearance of the package, despite the existence of fine print identifying the true origin; that is, such a package may falsely convey the impression that the domestic mark holder intended the importation of the good into the local market"); see also Ferrero U.S.A., Inc. v. Ozak Trading, Inc., 753 F. Supp. 1240, 1243, 1247 (D.N.J.), aff'd, 935 F.2d 1281 (3d Cir. 1991) (enjoining parallel importation of TIC TAC mints under section 43(a), despite the fact that the infringing product was identified as originating with the "sole importer for the U.K.," because material differences in caloric content and size, in conjunction with a virtually identical outward appearance, created the distinct potential for consumer confusion).

[1057] Societe des Produits Nestle, 982 F.2d at 641 (citations omitted) (finding differences between chocolates to be "material in the aggregate," based on differences in quality control, ingredients, shape, packaging, and price); accord, Gamut Trading Co. v. ITC, 200 F.3d 775, 779 (Fed. Cir. 1999) (applying "low threshold of materiality, requiring no more than showing that consumers would be likely to consider the differences between the foreign and domestic products to be significant when purchasing the product, for such differences would suffice to erode the goodwill of the domestic source"); see also El Greco Leather Products Co. v. Shoe World Inc., 806 F.2d 392 (2d Cir. 1986) (holding that differences in quality control were material); Lever Bros., 877 F.2d at 103, 108 (finding minor differences in ingredients and packaging between versions of deodorant soap to be material); Ferrero U.S.A., Inc. v. Ozak Trading, Inc., 753 F. Supp. 1240, 1247 (D.N.J. 1991) (finding a one-half calorie difference in chemical composition of breath mints, coupled with slight differences in packaging and labeling, to be material); PepsiCo, Inc. v. Nostalgia Prods. Corp., 18 U.S.P.Q.2d (BNA) 1404, 1405 (N.D. Ill. 1991) (finding "differences in labeling, packaging and marketing methods" to be material); PepsiCo v. Giraud, 7 U.S.P.Q.2d (BNA) 1371, 1373 (D.P.R. 1988) (finding differences not readily apparent to the consumer — container volume, packaging, quality control, and advertising participation — to be material); Dial Corp. v. Encina Corp., 643 F. Supp. 951, 952 (S.D. Fla. 1986) (finding differences in formulation and packaging of soap products to be material).

However, if the goods fail to meet the trademark owner's quality standards, that can be sufficient to establish material differences, even if these differences are not blatant enough to frustrate the expectations of the average consumer.[1058]

In the case of registered marks, the trademark owner also has the option of blocking their importation under section 42, which bars importation of goods that "copy or simulate" a registered trademark.[1059] Courts have held that even when imported goods bear non-counterfeit marks, they may be found to "copy or simulate" registered marks in violation of section 42. Although section 42 does not expressly articulate a "likelihood of confusion" standard, courts appear to have reached a consensus that section 42 is violated only when there are "material differences" between the imported goods and the goods authorized for domestic distribution:[1060]

> [T]he potential for consumer confusion is extremely high when a product catering to the indigenous conditions of a foreign country competes domestically against a physically different product that bears the same name. In such a case, the foreign product can legitimately be said to "copy or simulate" the domestic mark because use of the identical nomenclature "is simply not truthful."

> Accordingly, the importation of a gray good identical to a good authorized for sale in the domestic market does not violate section 42. But, the existence of physical differences changes the result.[1061]

In contrast, under section 526 of the Tariff Act,[1062] if a United States person owns a trademark that is registered with the PTO, the parallel importation of foreign-made goods bearing that trademark is prohibited absent the written consent of the U.S. trademark owner, even if the goods are *identical* to the domestically authorized goods, and without regard to the presence or absence of a likelihood of confusion.[1063]

[1058] Abercrombie & Fitch Trading Co. v. Fashion Shops, Inc., 363 F. Supp. 2d 952, 966 (S.D. Ohio Feb. 16, 2005).

[1059] 15 U.S.C. § 1124. The prohibition also applies to imported goods that "copy or simulate the name of any domestic manufacture, or manufacturer, or trader," even if it is not registered as a trademark. *Id.*

[1060] Lever Bros. Co. v. United States, 877 F.2d 101, 111 (D.C. Cir. 1989) ("the natural, virtually inevitable reading of § 42 is that it bars foreign goods [that] bear a trademark identical to a valid U.S. trademark but [that] physically differ, regardless of the trademarks' [sic] genuine character abroad"); *accord Societe des Produits Nestle*, 982 F.2d at 639; Weil Ceramics & Glass, Inc. v. Dash, 878 F.2d 659, 668 (3d Cir.), *cert. denied*, 493 U.S. 853 (1989); Olympus Corp. v. United States, 792 F.2d 315, 321 (2d Cir. 1986), *cert. denied*, 486 U.S. 1042 (1988); Lever Bros. Co. v. United States, 981 F.2d 1330 (D.C. Cir. 1993).

[1061] *Societe des Produits Nestle*, 982 F.2d at 639 (quoting *Lever Bros.*, 877 F.2d at 108).

[1062] 19 U.S.C. § 1526 (2009).

[1063] Premier Dental Prods. Co. v. Darby Dental Supply Co., 794 F.2d 850, 857 (3d Cir. 1986) (noting that the legislative history of § 526 "amply demonstrates Congress's intent to bar imports even of 'genuine' goods, where the importation is not authorized by the domestic trademark owner"), *cert. denied*, 479 U.S. 950 (1986); *see also id.* at 859 (noting that "an American distributor's goodwill can be harmed even by the sale of gray market goods that are identical to those sold by the distributor"); United States v. Eighty-Nine (89) Bottles of "Eau de Joy," 797 F.2d 767, 771 (9th Cir.

The crucial difference between section 526 and the Lanham Act provisions pertaining to gray market goods (which apply only when there are material differences between the domestic and imported goods) is that section 526 applies only to goods that are *manufactured outside the United States*.[1064] Thus, section 526 does not apply where goods are manufactured in the United States for sale in foreign territories, and then are imported without the consent of the United States trademark owner. Also, there is one additional restriction on the application of section 526. In construing the Customs regulations issued under section 526,[1065] the Supreme Court has held that the "extraordinary protection" provided by these regulations applies only when the domestic trademark owner has no corporate affiliation with the foreign manufacturer,[1066] and subsequent decisions from some of the lower federal courts have treated this restriction as implicit in the statute itself.[1067]

[C] Laches

Laches, or "estoppel by laches," is an equitable doctrine that can be invoked as a defense when a plaintiff has failed to act diligently in asserting its rights. The defense of laches derives from the maxim that "those who sleep on their rights, lose them."[1068]

Laches is a valid defense to trademark, false advertising, and unfair competition claims under both state law and the Lanham Act.[1069] To establish laches, a defendant must show that: (a) the claimant unreasonably delayed in filing suit, and (b) as a result of the delay, the defendant suffered prejudice.[1070] The defense of laches is available even when the mark alleged to have been infringed is incontestable.[1071]

In determining whether a plaintiff has unreasonably delayed in filing suit, it must be determined when the plaintiff first had knowledge of the defendant's infringing activity.[1072] That knowledge may be actual or constructive.[1073] In determining whether and when a trademark plaintiff had constructive

---

1986). *Cf.* K-Mart Corp. v. Cartier, Inc., 486 U.S. 281 (1988) (addressing validity of Customs regulations under § 526).

[1064] *Id.* (referring to "merchandise of foreign manufacture"); *see* Bourdeau Bros. v. ITC, 444 F.3d 1317, 1322 (Fed. Cir. 2006).

[1065] 19 C.F.R. § 133.23 (2009).

[1066] K Mart Corp. v. Cartier, Inc., 486 U.S. 281, 291 (1988).

[1067] *See, e.g.*, Weil Ceramics & Glass, Inc. v. Dash, 878 F.2d 659, 665 n. 6 (3d Cir. 1989).

[1068] Hot Wax, Inc. v. Turtle Wax, Inc., 191 F.3d 813, 820 (7th Cir. 1999).

[1069] *See, e.g.*, Danjaq LLC v. Sony Corp., 263 F.3d 942, 955 (9th Cir. 2001); Conopco, Inc. v. Campbell Soup Co., 95 F.3d 187 (2d Cir. 1996); Tillamook Country Smoker, Inc. v. Tillamook County Creamery Ass'n, 311 F. Supp. 2d 1023, 1030 (D. Or. 2004).

[1070] *Tillamook*, 311 F. Supp. 2d at 1030; *see* Carl Zeiss Stiftung v. VEB Carl Zeiss, Jena, 433 F.2d 686, 704 (2d Cir. 1970) (court "may find laches if the passing of time can be shown to have lulled the defendant into a false sense of security, and the defendant acts in reliance thereon").

[1071] 15 U.S.C. § 1115(b)(9).

[1072] Chattanooga Mfg., Inc. v. Nike, Inc., 301 F.3d 789, 793 (7th Cir. 2002).

[1073] *Id.*

knowledge, "the plaintiff is chargeable with such knowledge as he may have obtained upon inquiry, provided the facts already known by him were such as to put upon a man of ordinary intelligence the duty of inquiry."[1074] Thus, for example, where a defendant's infringing activity was evident from its prominent national advertising campaign, the court held that the plaintiff had constructive notice of the infringement beginning with the first year of the defendant's campaign.[1075]

In evaluating a laches defense to a trademark claim, courts may consider all relevant circumstances. However, some courts have enumerated a list of factors that should be considered. For example, courts in the Ninth Circuit have directed district courts to consider six factors in determining whether laches bars a claim for either damages or injunctive relief based on a claim of trademark infringement: (1) the strength and value of the trademark rights asserted; (2) the plaintiff's diligence in enforcing its mark; (3) the harm to the senior user if relief is denied; (4) good faith ignorance by the junior user; (5) the degree of competition between the senior and junior users; and (6) the extent of harm that was suffered by the junior user because of the senior user's delay.[1076] Ultimately, the doctrine of laches requires "a consideration of the circumstances of each particular case and a balancing of the interests and equities of the parties."[1077]

Even though laches is an equitable defense, it is a defense to claims for damages under the Lanham Act.[1078] In fact, most courts permit laches as a defense *only* to a damages claim, and not as a defense to a claim for injunctive relief, because a damages claim is based on past infringement, while injunctive relief protects against the harm to the public that will be caused by future infringement.[1079] This view is endorsed by the *Restatement (Third) of Unfair*

[1074] *Id.* (quoting Johnston v. Standard Mining Co., 148 U.S. 360, 370 (1893)).

[1075] *Id.*

[1076] Grupo Gigante SA de CV v. Dallo & Co., 391 F.3d 1088, 1102 (9th Cir. 2004); E-Systems, Inc. v. Monitek, Inc., 720 F.2d 604, 607 (9th Cir. 1983); *Tillamook*, 311 F. Supp. 2d at 1030.

[1077] *Tillamook*, 311 F. Supp. 2d at 1030-31 (internal quotation marks omitted).

[1078] *Hot Wax*, 191 F.3d at 822.

[1079] *See, e.g.*, Kellogg Co. v. Exxon Corp., 209 F.3d 562, 568 (6th Cir.), *cert. denied*, 531 U.S. 944 (2000); TWM Mfg. Co., Inc. v. Dura Corp., 592 F.2d 346, 349-50 (6th Cir. 1979); Sara Lee Corp., v. Kayser-Roth Corp., 81 F.3d 455 (4th Cir. 1996); *see also* Kason Indus. v. Component Hardware Grp., 120 F.3d 1199, 1207 (11th Cir. 1997) (noting that laches is not a bar to injunctive relief in cases of intentional infringement, and that there may also be other instances in which such relief is appropriate: "if the likelihood of confusion is inevitable, or so strong as to outweigh the effect of the plaintiff's delay in bringing a suit, a court may in its discretion grant injunctive relief, even in cases where a suit for damages is appropriately barred"); SunAmerica Corp. v. Sun Life Assurance Co. of Can., 77 F.3d 1325, 1334 (11th Cir. 1996) (recognizing that "inevitable confusion" revives a plaintiff's claim for injunctive relief from estoppel). *But see* University of Pittsburgh v. Champion Products, Inc., 686 F.2d 1040, 1044-45 (3d Cir. 1982) (describing the "common situation" in which a plaintiff's delay "will bar its claim for an accounting for past infringement but not for prospective injunctive relief," but noting that "there is that narrow class of cases where the plaintiff's delay has been so outrageous, unreasonable and inexcusable as to constitute a virtual abandonment of its right"); Anheuser-Busch, Inc. v. DuBois Brewing Co., 175 F.2d 370, 374 (3d Cir. 1949) ("Mere delay by the injured party in bringing suit would not bar injunctive relief. This doctrine, however, has its limits; for example, had there been a lapse of a hundred years or more, we think it highly dubious that any

Competition: "Because of the public interest in preventing the deception of consumers, delay by the trademark owner will not ordinarily disable it from obtaining an injunction if there is strong evidence of likely or actual confusion."[1080]

Courts that treat laches as a bar only to damages typically require the stronger showing of acquiescence in order to bar injunctive relief.[1081] Other courts, however, will deny injunctive relief on the basis of laches alone, at least where the defendant would be prejudiced by an injunction.[1082] In the Ninth Circuit, laches will bar injunctive relief unless the suit alleges "that the product is harmful or otherwise a threat to public safety and well being."[1083]

In determining whether a defendant has been prejudiced by a plaintiff's delay, courts consider whether "a defendant has changed his position in a way that would not have occurred if the plaintiff had not delayed."[1084] Typically, prejudice is established where the plaintiff's unexcused delay "caused the defendant to rely to its detriment and build up a valuable business around its trademark."[1085] Because laches is "a question of degree," courts often apply a sliding scale to determine whether the defense should apply: "[I]f only a short period of time has elapsed since the accrual of the claim, the magnitude of prejudice required before the suit should be barred is great, whereas if the delay is lengthy, prejudice is more likely to have occurred and less proof of prejudice is required."[1086]

Because the Lanham Act does not contain a statute of limitations, federal courts have looked to analogous state limitations statutes to determine whether a presumption of laches should apply.[1087] However, a laches defense is not per se unavailable for claims brought within the limitations period; rather, courts use the state limitations period as a "baseline" for determining whether a presumption of laches is appropriate:

> In the context of the Lanham Act, this framework makes particularly good sense. The notion of a "continuing wrong," which is so prevalent in Lanham Act cases, provides a strong justification for the application of the doctrine of laches in appropriate circumstances regardless of whether the plaintiff has brought suit within the analogous statute of limitations. Under the notion of a continuing wrong, "only the last infringing act need be within the statutory period." Without the

---

court of equity would grant injunctive relief against even a fraudulent infringer.").

[1080] Restatement (Third) of Unfair Competition § 31, cmt. e (1995); *accord*, Profitness Physical Therapy Ctr. v. Pro-Fit Orthopedic & Sports Physical Therapy P.C., 314 F.3d 62, 68 (2d Cir. 2002).

[1081] *See* § 3.12 [D] *infra*.

[1082] *See, e.g.*, Jarrow Formulas, Inc. v. Nutrition Now, Inc., 304 F.3d 829, 840 (9th Cir.), *cert. denied*, 537 U.S. 1047 (2002).

[1083] Tillamook Country Smoker, Inc. v. Tillamook County Creamery Ass'n, 465 F.3d 1102, 1111 (9th Cir. 2006); Jarrow Formulas, Inc. v. Nutrition Now, Inc., 304 F.3d 829, 841 (9th Cir. 2002).

[1084] Chattanooga Mfg. Co. v. Nike, Inc., 301 F.3d 789, 795 (7th Cir. 2002).

[1085] *Id.* at 795.

[1086] *Hot Wax*, 191 F.3d at 824.

[1087] *Id.* at 820-21.

availability of the application of laches to a claim arising from a continuing wrong, a party could, theoretically, delay filing suit indefinitely. It would certainly be inequitable to reward this type of dilatory conduct and such conduct would necessarily warrant application of laches in appropriate circumstances. Thus, . . . whether a Lanham Act claim has been brought within the analogous state statute of limitations is not the sole indicator of whether laches may be applied in a particular case.[1088]

Accordingly, federal courts will typically "presume that an action is barred if not brought within the period of the statute of limitations and is alive if brought within the period."[1089] That presumption is rebuttable.[1090]

In the context of trademark and unfair competition claims, another factor relevant to determining whether the defense of laches should apply is whether "its application is equitable in light of the public's interest in being free from confusion and deception."[1091] Indeed, the importance of this factor has been described as "paramount."[1092] Thus, the availability of a laches defense in a particular case "must be considered in light of the consuming public's right to be free from confusion with respect to product marketing and advertisements."[1093] However, concerns about the public interest must be well-founded. Thus, for example, where a plaintiff failed to demonstrate that the defendant's conduct had had a negative impact on the public interest, a federal court of appeals held that the application of laches was not barred.[1094]

The laches defense may be negated if the plaintiff establishes "progressive encroachment" by the defendant. Progressive encroachment applies:

> where the defendant has engaged in some infringing use of its trademark — at least enough of an infringing use so that it may attempt to avail itself of a laches or acquiescence defense — but the plaintiff does not bring suit right away because the nature of defendant's infringement is such that the plaintiff's claim has yet to ripen into one sufficiently colorable to justify litigation.[1095]

For example, progressive encroachment may occur when the defendant alters its mark so that it more closely resembles the plaintiff's mark, or where the

---

[1088] *Id.* at 821-22 (citations omitted).

[1089] *Id.* at 821 (quoting Tandy Corp. v. Malone & Hyde, Inc., 769 F.2d 362, 365 (6th Cir. 1985) (internal quotation marks omitted).

[1090] *Chattanooga Mfg.*, 301 F.3d at 793-94.

[1091] Conopco, Inc. v. Campbell Soup Co., 95 F.3d 187, 193 (2d Cir. 1996).

[1092] *Id.*

[1093] *Hot Wax*, 191 F.3d at 826.

[1094] *Id.* at 826-27.

[1095] Kellogg Co. v. Exxon Corp., 209 F.3d 562, 570 (6th Cir. 2003); *see also* Kason Indus., Inc. v. Component Hardware Grp., 120 F.3d 1199, 1205 (11th Cir. 1997) ("where a defendant begins use of a trademark or trade dress in the market, and then directs its marketing or manufacturing efforts such that it is placed more squarely in competition with the plaintiff, the plaintiff's delay is excused").

defendant expands its market to compete more directly with the plaintiff.[1096] Market expansion that constitutes progressive encroachment occurs when the junior user expands into a different region or a different market; mere growth in the junior user's existing business does not qualify.[1097] For example, Ralph Lauren demonstrated progressive encroachment against its POLO mark for clothing and accessories when POLO magazine, after 20 years as an insider's publication about the sport of polo, began featuring mainstream fashion news.[1098] In contrast, progressive encroachment did not occur where a food distributor that initially sold its products to small grocery stores begin increasing its direct sales to larger chains.[1099] Similarly, a progressive encroachment argument was rejected where the senior user did not file its infringement suit until it decided to expand into the junior user's geographic area.[1100]

Courts developed the doctrine of progressive encroachment in response to the concern that infringement plaintiffs sometimes face a difficult choice in determining how to time an infringement suit in order to present the strongest possible case:

> If [the trademark owner] waits for substantial injury and evidence of actual confusion, it may be faced with a laches defense. If it rushes immediately into litigation, it may have little or no evidence of actual confusion and real commercial damage, may appear at a psychological disadvantage as "shooting from the hip" and may even face a counterclaim for overly aggressive use of litigation.[1101]

In evaluating the merits of a progressive encroachment argument, courts often find it necessary to engage in a likelihood-of-confusion analysis to determine whether the plaintiff would have had a valid infringement claim at the earlier time when the plaintiff opted not to pursue litigation.[1102]

[D] Acquiescence

In contrast to laches, the defense of acquiescence arises only if the plaintiff gave the defendant an express or implied assurance that the plaintiff would not assert its trademark rights against the defendant.[1103] Thus, acquiescence

---

[1096] *Kellogg Co.*, 209 F.3d at 570-73 (collecting cases).

[1097] *Tillamook*, 465 F.3d at 1110; Grupo Gigante S.A. de C.V. v. Dallo & Co., 391 F.3d 1088, 1103 (9th Cir. 2004); ProFitness Phys. Therapy Ctr. v. Pro-Fit Orthopedic & Sports Phys. Therapy P.C., 314 F.3d 62, 65 (2d Cir. 2002) (encroachment involves "using the mark in a different manner or in new geographic area").

[1098] Westchester Media v. PRL USA Holdings, Inc., 214 F.3d 658 (5th Cir. 2000).

[1099] *Tillamook*, 465 F.3d at 1109.

[1100] *Grupo Gigante*, 391 F.3d at 1103.

[1101] Sara Lee Corp. v. Kayser-Roth Corp., 81 F.3d 455, 462 (4th Cir. 1996) (internal quotation marks and citation omitted).

[1102] *See, e.g., Chattanooga Mfg.*, 301 F.3d at 794-95; *Kellogg Co.*, 209 F.3d at 571-73 (collecting cases).

[1103] Creative Gifts, Inc. v. UFO, 235 F.3d 540 (10th Cir. 2000); Sweetheart Plastics, Inc. v. Detroit Forming, Inc., 743 F.2d 1039, 1046 (4th Cir. 1984) (citing Carl Zeiss Stiftung v. Veb Carl Zeiss Jena, 433 F.2d 686, 704 (2d Cir. 1970), *cert. denied*, 403 U.S. 905 (1971); Exxon Corp. v. Humble Exploration

involves active consent, while laches involves passive consent.[1104] However, acquiescence need not be explicit, and can be inferred from the trademark owner's affirmative conduct toward the defendant.[1105] Several federal courts of appeals have set forth strict criteria for acquiescence, requiring three elements: (1) the senior user actively represented that it would not assert a right or a claim; (2) the delay between the active representation and assertion of the right or claim was not excusable; and (3) the delay caused the defendant undue prejudice.[1106] However, some courts are less precise, and occasionally use the term acquiescence as a synonym for laches.[1107]

Acquiescence may bar injunctive relief as well as monetary damages:

> To defeat a suit for injunctive relief, a defendant must also prove elements of estoppel which requires more than a showing of mere silence on the part of the plaintiff; defendant must show that it had been misled by plaintiff through actual misrepresentations, affirmative acts of misconduct, intentional misleading silence, or conduct amounting to virtual abandonment of the trademark.[1108]

However, even where a finding of acquiescence is otherwise warranted, a strong showing of likelihood of confusion may persuade a court that injunctive relief is nonetheless appropriate in order to protect the public.[1109] Furthermore, as in the case of a laches defense, a showing of progressive encroachment may negate a defense of acquiescence.[1110]

[E]   Unclean Hands

The equitable defense of unclean hands is available as a defense against trademark or unfair competition claims under state or federal law. Although the scope of conduct by a plaintiff that warrants invocation of this doctrine is not well defined, it is not limited to illegal conduct. Rather, the Supreme Court has described it as "any willful act concerning the cause of action which rightfully

---

Co., Inc., 524 F. Supp. 450, 467 (N.D. Tex. 1981), *aff'd in part, rev'd and remanded in part*, 695 F.2d 96 (5th Cir. 1983)).

[1104] Profitness Physical Therapy Ctr. v. Pro-Fit Orthopedic & Sports Physical Therapy P.C., 314 F.3d 62, 67-68 (2d Cir. 2002); Kellogg Co. v. Exxon Corp., 209 F.3d 562, 569 n. 2 (6th Cir. 2000); Sara Lee Corp. v. Kayser-Roth Corp., 81 F.3d 455, 460, 462 (4th Cir. 1996); Kellogg Co. v. Exxon Corp., 209 F.3d 562, 569 n. 2 (6th Cir. 2000).

[1105] *Sweetheart Plastics*, 433 F.2d at 1046; *see, e.g.*, Ambrosia Chocolate Co. v. Ambrosia Cake Bakery, 165 F.2d 693 (4th Cir. 1947), *cert. denied*, 333 U.S. 882 (1948); *Tillamook*, 311 F. Supp. 2d at 1031 and n. 2.

[1106] *See, e.g.*, Times Mirror Magazines, Inc. v. Field & Stream Licenses Co., 294 F.3d 383, 395 (2d Cir. 2002); SunAmerica Corp. v. Sun Life Assurance Co. of Can., 77 F.3d 1325 (11th Cir. 1996).

[1107] *See, e.g.*, University of Pittsburgh v. Champion Prods., Inc., 686 F.2d 1040, 1045 (3d Cir.), *cert. denied*, 459 U.S. 1087 (1982).

[1108] Kellogg Co. v. Exxon Corp., 209 F.3d 562, 574 (6th Cir. 2000).

[1109] *See, e.g.*, *Profitness*, 314 F.3d at 68; Sara Lee Corp. v. Kayser-Roth Corp., 81 F.3d 455 (4th Cir. 1996); Coach House Rest., Inc. v. Coach & Six Rests., Inc., 934 F.2d 1551 (11th Cir. 1991).

[1110] *Profitness*, 314 F.3d at 68; *Kellogg*, 209 F.3d at 570.

can be said to transgress equitable standards of conduct."[1111] Intentional misrepresentations regarding a product have been held to constitute unclean hands, provided they pertain to the subject matter of the plaintiff's cause of action.[1112] Thus, for example, plaintiffs may be denied relief on the grounds that their marks are deceptive.[1113] The defense may also apply where marks have been used in violation of antitrust laws.[1114] Fraud in obtaining federal trademark registration can also provide an unclean hands defense to infringement of the registered mark; however, this will not bar an action based on common law rights in that mark.[1115]

[F]   "Classic" Fair Use

Section 33(b)(4) of the Lanham Act provides an affirmative "fair use" defense to trademark infringement in the case of an incontestable mark, under which "the use of the name, term, or device charged to be an infringement is a use, otherwise than as a mark, . . . of a term or device which is descriptive of and used fairly and in good faith only to describe the goods or services of such party, or their geographic origin."[1116] Like the other section 33(b) defenses, fair use applies even if the plaintiff's mark has become incontestable.[1117]

The fair use defense of section 33(b)(4) applies when the defendant has used the plaintiff's trademark only to describe the defendant's own goods or services, and not to describe or identify the plaintiff's goods or services.[1118] This defense exists both at common law and under the Lanham Act.[1119] It protects a junior user's right "to use a descriptive term in good faith in its primary, descriptive sense other than as a trademark."[1120] As one court has noted, "[t]he 'fair-use' defense, in essence, forbids a trademark registrant to appropriate a descriptive term for his exclusive use and so prevent others from accurately describing a

---

[1111] Precision Instr. Mfg. Co. v. Automotive Maint. Mach. Co., 324 U.S. 806, 815 (1945).

[1112] Havana Club Holding S.A. v. Galleon S.A., 49 U.S.P.Q.2d 1296, 1998 U.S. Dist. LEXIS 4065, *18-20 (S.D.N.Y. 1998) (plaintiff's use of "HAVANA CLUB" mark for Panamanian rum supported unclean hands defense).

[1113] See, e.g., id. Compare Worden v. California Fig Syrup Co., 187 U.S. 516 (1903) (recovery for infringement was barred because plaintiff's "SYRUP OF FIGS" trademark, used for a product that contained no figs, was misleading), with Holeproof Hosiery Co. v. Wallach Bros., 172 F. 859 (2d Cir. 1909) (relief against infringer of plaintiff's "Holeproof" mark for socks was not inequitable, because no one would be misled into believing that the socks would never wear out).

[1114] Phi Delta Theta Fraternity v. J. A. Bochroeder & Co., 251 F. Supp 968 (W.D. Mo. 1966); Sanitized, Inc. v. S.C. Johnson & Sons, Inc., 23 F.R.D. 230, 231 (S.D.N.Y. 1959); Phi Delta Theta Fraternity v. J. A. Bochroeder & Co., 251 F. Supp. 968 (W.D. Mo. 1966).

[1115] Orient Express Trading Co. v. Federated Dept. Stores, Inc., 842 F.2d 650 (2d Cir. 1988). Fraud as grounds for cancelling a federal registration and as a defense to infringement of an incontestable mark is discussed at §§ 2.12 [A] and 2.13[A] supra.

[1116] 15 U.S.C. § 1115(b)(4).

[1117] Abercrombie & Fitch Co. v. Hunting World, Inc., 537 F.2d 4, 12 (2d Cir. 1976).

[1118] Cairns v. Franklin Mint Co., 292 F.3d 1139, 1150 (9th Cir. 2002).

[1119] Id. at 1150; Ideal Indus., Inc. v. Gardner Bender, Inc., 612 F.2d 1018, 1027 (7th Cir. 1979), cert. denied, 447 U.S. 924 (1980).

[1120] Cairns, 292 F.3d at 1150.

characteristic of their goods."[1121] This defense is sometimes referred to as "classic" fair use, to distinguish it from "nominative" fair use, which is discussed in the next section.[1122]

To establish classic fair use, a defendant must prove that: (1) its use of the plaintiff's mark was not as a trademark or service mark, (2) it is using the mark "fairly and in good faith," and (3) it is using the mark only to describe its goods or services.[1123]

A strong example of classic fair use is *In re Dual-Deck Video Cassette Recorder Antitrust Litigation.*[1124] In this case, the plaintiff adopted the trademark "VCR-2" for its dual-deck videocassette recorder. The defendant sold various audiovisual devices to which two videocassette recorders could be connected simultaneously, and accordingly labeled the connection terminals "VCR-1" and "VCR-2." The Ninth Circuit held that the defendant's use of the term "VCR-2" was descriptive, and that there was no evidence from which bad faith could be inferred.[1125] Similarly, fair use was established in *Zatarain's, Inc. v. Oak Grove Smokehouse, Inc.,*[1126] in which each of the defendants used the term "fish fry" (which was similar to the plaintiff's trademarked term "Fish-Fri") to describe their batter mixes for coating fish, and in *Abercrombie & Fitch Co. v. Hunting World, Inc.,* in which the defendant used the plaintiff's incontestable "Safari" mark, in combination with other words, on hunting boots imported from Africa. In the latter case, the court noted that the defendant's use was "a purely descriptive use to apprise the public of the type of product by referring to its origin and use," and that the fair use analysis should focus on the "use of the words, not on their nature or meaning in the abstract," adding: "When a plaintiff has chosen a mark with some descriptive qualities, he cannot altogether exclude some kinds of competing uses even when the mark is properly on the register."[1127] In assessing whether the defendant was using "Safari" in its descriptive sense or its trademark sense, the court found it "significant that [the defendant] did not use 'Safari' alone on its shoes, as it would doubtless have done if confusion had been intended."[1128]

In other cases, a fair use defense has failed because the defendant did not use the plaintiff's mark primarily to describe the defendant's goods or services, but instead used it primarily as a trademark — that is, as an indication of source. Such a conclusion typically follows where the defendant has used the mark in a way that "attracts public attention, is the most prominent element on the

---

[1121] Soweco, Inc. v. Shell Oil Co., 617 F.2d 1178, 1185 (5th Cir. 1980), *cert. denied*, 450 U.S. 981 (1981).

[1122] *See* § 3.12 [G] *infra.*

[1123] *Cairns*, 292 F.3d at 1151; *see, e.g.*, Victoria's Secret Stores v. Artco Equip. Co., 194 F. Supp. 2d 704 (S.D. Ohio 2002).

[1124] 11 F.3d 1460 (9th Cir. 1993).

[1125] *Id.* at 1467.

[1126] 698 F.2d 786 (5th Cir. 1983).

[1127] *Abercrombie & Fitch*, 537 F.2d at 12.

[1128] *Id.* at 13.

package, and dominates the package as a whole."[1129] For example, in *Beer Nuts, Inc. v. Clover Club Foods Co.*,[1130] the defendant's fair use argument failed where the term "Brew Nuts" (which was similar to the plaintiff's mark "Beer Nuts") had special prominence on its packaging:

> In this case, the words "Brew Nuts" are much larger than the other lettering on the package and in a different type style. The words are set off in a distinctive red-brown oval, outlined in dark brown and topped by a conspicuous white circle containing a picture of an overflowing beer stein. Below or above the oval, depending on the particular package, is the phrase actually used to describe the product: "sweetened salted peanuts." Furthermore, the president of [defendant] Clover Club, Robert Sanders, testified repeatedly that Clover Club uses secondary trademarks on some of its products in addition to the company name, and that "Brew Nuts" is such a trademark.[1131]

Ideal Industries, Inc. v. Gardner Bender, Inc.[1132] represents a somewhat closer case. There, the plaintiff originally used the designation "71B" as a model number referring to the smallest electrical connectors that it produced (and used 72B, etc. as model numbers for progressively larger connectors), but over time "71B" and the like came to serve both as descriptions of the size of each connector and as common law trademarks. Several of the plaintiff's competitors sold comparably-sized connectors in packages bearing their own trademarks and model numbers, but also displaying "71B," etc., next to the word "size." In contrast, the defendant adopted "71B," etc., as the model numbers for its comparable connectors, and its packaging displayed "71B," etc., next to the word "style." Although the appellate court left the full scope of the fair use defense to be developed at trial, it upheld the portion of the district court's preliminary injunction, which barred the defendant from using the plaintiff's model numbers as model designations on the connectors themselves, but modified the portion of the injunction that had barred the defendant from using the plaintiff's model numbers in any manner on its packaging; instead, the appellate court held that the defendant should be permitted to use "71B" and the other model numbers adjacent to the word "size," in a manner comparable to that employed by the other competitors.[1133]

Fair use has also been held to apply where a defendant uses another's mark in an index or catalog to indicate the source of its items, or to describe the defendant's relationship to the trademark owner.[1134] For example, courts have

---

[1129] Beer Nuts, Inc. v. Clover Club Foods Co., 711 F.2d 934, 938 (10th Cir. 1983); *see also* Sands, Taylor & Wood Co. v. Quaker Oats Co., 978 F.2d 947, 953-54 (7th Cir. 1992); Venetianaire Corp. v. A & P Import Co., 429 F.2d 1079, 1082 (2d Cir. 1970); Feathercombs, Inc. v. Solo Prods. Corp., 306 F.2d 251, 256 (2d Cir. 1962), *cert. denied*, 371 U.S. 910 (1962).

[1130] 711 F.2d 934 (10th Cir. 1983).

[1131] *Id.* at 938.

[1132] 612 F.2d 1018 (7th Cir. 1979), *cert. denied*, 447 U.S. 924 (1980).

[1133] *Id.* at 1027-28.

[1134] Bihari v. Gross, 119 F. Supp. 2d 309 (S.D.N.Y. 2000).

applied fair use to a news clipping service that used the plaintiff's mark in accurately identifying the source of the abstracted articles that it offered for sale.[1135]

Although there is limited authority on the question, it appears that the classic fair use defense is not limited to word marks, but may be applied to trade dress as well.[1136]

There is some disagreement in the courts as to whether the fair use defense applies only to descriptive, or perhaps suggestive, trademarks, or whether it extends also to arbitrary and fanciful marks, which have no descriptive aspect.[1137] Although the language of *Abercrombie & Fitch*, above, indirectly lends support to the narrower view, the text of section 33(b)(4) implies no such limitation, and the better answer appears to be that the defense applies without regard to the nature of the plaintiff's mark, so long as the defendant is using it descriptively. It is likely, however, that the defense will be successful most often in cases involving descriptive marks, because marks that are already inherently descriptive will be the ones most often needed by competitors to describe their own goods and services. On the other hand, an arbitrary mark, such as APPLE for computers, should be freely available for use by apple merchants to describe their goods.

In 2004, the Supreme Court resolved a longstanding circuit split regarding the classic fair use defense, holding in *KP Permanent Make-Up, Inc. v. Lasting Impression I*[1138] that a defendant may prevail on a fair use defense without being required to prove the absence of a likelihood of confusion. Thus, a defendant's unauthorized use of another's trademark can be a permissible fair use even if it creates a likelihood of confusion. Although the Court rested its decision largely on an analysis of the statutory language of sections 32 and 33(b)(4), it also noted that the plaintiff has the burden of demonstrating a likelihood of confusion, because the latter is essential to establishing a prima facie case of infringement, and an affirmative defense such as fair use should have legal significance that is independent of any challenge to the strength of the plaintiff's prima facie case:

> Finally, a look at the typical course of litigation in an infringement action points up the incoherence of placing a burden to show nonconfusion on a defendant. If a plaintiff succeeds in making out a prima facie case of

---

[1135] Nihon Keizai Shimbun, Inc. v. Comline Bus. Data, Inc., 166 F.3d 65, 73-74 (2d Cir. 1999).

[1136] *See* Car-Freshner Corp. v. S.C. Johnson & Son, Inc., 70 F.3d 267 (2d Cir. 1995) (holding that defendant's sale of a pine-tree-shaped plug-in air freshener during Christmas season was fair use of, and thus did not infringe, plaintiff's own pine-tree-shaped air freshener design, because shape of defendant's product was intended to call to mind both product's scent and time of year); *accord*, Mattel Inc. v. Walking Mt. Prods., 353 F.3d 792, 810 (9th Cir. 2003) (approving Car-Freshner's extension of fair use defense to trade dress).

[1137] *See Car-Freshner Corp.*, 70 F.3d at 269 (collecting cases); DowBrands, L.P. v. Helene Curtis, Inc., 863 F. Supp. 963, 967-69 (D. Minn. 1994) (collecting cases); National Football League Properties v. Playoff Corp., 808 F. Supp. 1288, 1293 (N.D. Tex. 1992) (holding that classic fair use defense is unavailable in Fifth Circuit when plaintiff's marks are arbitrary or fanciful, even if defendant has used them descriptively, but finding this conclusion "troubling").

[1138] 543 U.S. 111, 547 (2004) (discussing circuit split).

trademark infringement, including the element of likelihood of consumer confusion, the defendant may offer rebutting evidence to undercut the force of the plaintiff's evidence on this (or any) element, or raise an affirmative defense to bar relief even if the prima facie case is sound, or do both. But it would make no sense to give the defendant a defense of showing affirmatively that the plaintiff cannot succeed in proving some element (like confusion); all the defendant needs to do is to leave the factfinder unpersuaded that the plaintiff has carried its own burden on that point. A defendant has no need of a court's true belief when agnosticism will do. Put another way, it is only when a plaintiff has shown likely confusion by a preponderance of the evidence that a defendant could have any need of an affirmative defense . . .[1139]

The Supreme Court acknowledged that its decision in *KP Permanent Make-Up* authorizes certain uses of a trademark that will lead to a likelihood of confusion, but it concluded that, in light of the purposes of the fair use defense, some confusion must be tolerated in order to preserve the rights of competitors to describe their goods and services accurately:

> Since the burden of proving likelihood of confusion rests with the plaintiff, and the fair use defendant has no free-standing need to show confusion unlikely, it follows . . . that some possibility of consumer confusion must be compatible with fair use, and so it is. The common law's tolerance of a certain degree of confusion on the part of consumers followed from the very fact that in cases like this one an originally descriptive term was selected to be used as a mark, not to mention the undesirability of allowing anyone to obtain a complete monopoly on use of a descriptive term simply by grabbing it first. The Lanham Act adopts a similar leniency, there being no indication that the statute was meant to deprive commercial speakers of the ordinary utility of descriptive words. "If any confusion results, that is a risk the plaintiff accepted when it decided to identify its product with a mark that uses a well known descriptive phrase." This right to describe is the reason that descriptive terms qualify for registration as trademarks only after taking on secondary meaning as "distinctive of the applicant's goods," with the registrant getting an exclusive right not in the original, descriptive sense, but only in the secondary one associated with the markholder's goods. . . .[1140]

However, the Court noted that the degree of likely confusion was not necessarily irrelevant to the determination of whether the defendant's use was fair within the meaning of section 33(b):

> [O]ur holding that fair use can occur along with some degree of confusion does not foreclose the relevance of the extent of any likely consumer confusion in assessing whether a defendant's use is objectively fair. Two Courts of Appeals have found it relevant to consider such scope, and

---

[1139] *KP Permanent Make-Up*, 543 U.S. at 549.

[1140] *Id.* at 550 (quoting Cosmetically Sealed Industries, Inc. v. Chesebrough-Pond's USA Co., 125 F.3d 28, 30 (2d Cir. 1997)) (citations omitted).

commentators and amici here have urged us to say that the degree of likely consumer confusion bears not only on the fairness of using a term, but even on the further question whether an originally descriptive term has become so identified as a mark that a defendant's use of it cannot realistically be called descriptive.[1141]

The Court declined an invitation to rule on the exact meaning of the term "used fairly" in section 33(b), which the United States (as amicus) had argued "demands only that the descriptive term describe the goods accurately." While acknowledging that accuracy "has to be a consideration in assessing fair use," the Court noted that "the door is not closed" to the possibility of other considerations, including, but not limited to, "commercial justification and the strength of the plaintiff's mark."[1142]

The fair use defense has also been recognized under common law and under section 43(a) of the Lanham Act; thus, it applies to both registered and unregistered marks.[1143] It performs the same function as the early common law rule that barred trademark protection for descriptive marks — ensuring that competitors are not precluded from describing their goods or services accurately to the public.

The concept of fair use is also incorporated into one of the statutory exemptions to the federal dilution statute, as discussed in § 3.07 [H] above.

[G]   Nominative Fair Use

Some courts have recognized a second type of fair use defense, known as "nominative fair use." Nominative fair use, which is not grounded specifically in section 33(b)(4), applies when the defendant has used the plaintiff's trademark to describe or identify the *plaintiff's* goods or services, even though the defendant's ultimate goal is to describe the defendant's own goods or services.[1144] Typically, this use occurs because the plaintiff's mark is the only practical way to refer to a particular subject matter.[1145] In contrast to "classic" fair use under common law and section 33(b)(4), where the defendant uses the plaintiff's mark in its primary, descriptive sense, in nominative fair use the defendant uses the plaintiff's mark in its trademark sense (which, in the case of suggestive or descriptive marks, means its "secondary" sense).[1146]

[1141] *Id.* at 550-51.

[1142] *Id.* at 551.

[1143] *Car-Freshner Corp.*, 70 F.3d at 269; Soweco, Inc. v. Shell Oil Co., 617 F.2d 1178, 1190 (5th Cir. 1980); Robert B. Vance & Assocs., Inc. v. Baronet Corp., 487 F. Supp. 790, 797 (N.D. Ga. 1979); Restatement (Third) Unfair Competition § 28 comment (a) (1995).

[1144] *E.g.*, Cairns v. Franklin Mint Co., 292 F.3d 1139, 1151 (9th Cir. 2002).

[1145] *E.g.*, New Kids on the Block v. News Am. Publ'g, Inc., 971 F.2d 302, 308 (9th Cir. 1992) (noting that nominative fair use may occur where plaintiff's trademark is the "only word reasonably available to describe a particular thing").

[1146] Brother Records, Inc. v. Jardine, 318 F.3d 900, 908 (9th Cir. 2003), *cert. denied*, 540 U.S. 824 (2003).

The leading case on nominative fair use is the Ninth Circuit's decision in *New Kids on the Block v. News America Publishing, Inc.*,[1147] where defendant newspapers used the trademarked name of a popular musical group to promote their telephone polls regarding the relative popularity of the individual band members. The Ninth Circuit held that the newspapers were using the trademarked name to describe the plaintiff's goods or services (that is, the musical group itself) for the ultimate purpose of describing the defendants' own goods or services — the telephone polls. The court explained:

> With many well-known trademarks, such as Jell-O, Scotch tape and Kleenex, there are equally informative non-trademark words describing the products (gelatin, cellophane tape and facial tissue). But sometimes there is no descriptive substitute, and a problem closely related to genericity and descriptiveness is presented when many goods and services are effectively identifiable only by their trademarks. For example, one might refer to "the two-time world champions" or "the professional basketball team from Chicago," but it's far simpler (and more likely to be understood) to refer to the Chicago Bulls. In such cases, use of the trademark does not imply sponsorship or endorsement of the product because the mark is used only to describe the thing, rather than to identify its source.
>
> . . .
>
> Indeed, it is often virtually impossible to refer to a particular product for purposes of comparison, criticism, point of reference or any other such purpose without using the mark. For example, reference to a large automobile manufacturer based in Michigan would not differentiate among the Big Three; reference to a large Japanese manufacturer of home electronics would narrow the field to a dozen or more companies. Much useful social and commercial discourse would be all but impossible if speakers were under threat of an infringement lawsuit every time they made reference to a person, company or product by using its trademark.[1148]

To establish nominative fair use, the Ninth Circuit held that a defendant must establish: (1) that the plaintiff's goods or services at issue are not readily identifiable without use of the plaintiff's trademark; (2) that the defendant used only as much of the mark as was reasonably necessary to identify the plaintiff's goods or services; and (3) that the defendant did nothing that would, in conjunction with the mark, suggest sponsorship or endorsement by the trademark owner.[1149]

Rather than attempt to ground the nominative fair use defense in the specific language of the Lanham Act, the Ninth Circuit noted that "[c]ases like these are

---

[1147] 971 F.2d 302 (9th Cir. 1992).

[1148] *New Kids*, 971 F.2d at 306-07.

[1149] *Cairns*, 292 F.3d at 1151; *New Kids*, 971 F.2d at 308.

best understood as involving a non-trademark use of a mark — a use to which the infringement laws simply do not apply," because it "lies outside the strictures of trademark law."[1150]

For example, the Ninth Circuit applied the nominative fair use defense to reject a claim of trade dress infringement where a photographer used images of Mattel's "Barbie" doll in a series of satirical photos:

> All three elements weigh in favor of [defendant] Forsythe. Barbie would not be readily identifiable in a photographic work without use of the Barbie likeness and figure. Forsythe used only so much as was necessary to make his parodic use of Barbie readily identifiable, and it is highly unlikely that any reasonable consumer would have believed that Mattel sponsored or was affiliated with his work.[1151]

Nominative fair use was also found where an automobile maker referred to basketball star Kareem Abdul-Jabbar, who won an award three years in a row, in a commercial for a car that won an award three years in a row;[1152] where a maker of memorabilia used the name and likeness of Diana, Princess of Wales, on merchandise commemorating the late princess;[1153] and where a former Playboy "Playmate" used the terms "Playboy" and "Playmate" to describe herself on her website.[1154]

A nominative fair use defense failed, however, where a defendant's ads for car wax prominently featured the trade dress and trademarks of the Porsche 911; the district court held that the defendant's use failed all three prongs of the *New Kids* test.[1155] The defense also failed where the website used by a defendant to promote its pharmaceutical products repeatedly used the name of a competitor's product in metatags that were used by search engines to identify the website's contents; even if the defendant's use of the plaintiff's trademark could pass muster under the first two prongs of the *New Kids* test, the court held, it clearly failed the third prong, because it "spawn[ed] confusion as to sponsorship and attempt[ed] to appropriate the cachet of the trademark."[1156]

In the Ninth Circuit, when a defendant raises a nominative fair use defense, the three-part *New Kids* test for nominative fair use *replaces* the likelihood-of-confusion analysis. Thus, instead of assessing the likelihood of confusion under

---

[1150] *New Kids*, 971 F.2d at 307-08.

[1151] Mattel, Inc. v. Walking Mountain Prods., 353 F.3d 792, 812 (9th Cir. 2003).

[1152] Abdul-Jabbar v. Gen. Motors Corp., 85 F.3d 407 (9th Cir. 1996).

[1153] Cairns v. Franklin Mint Co., 292 F.3d 1139, 1153 (9th Cir. 2002).

[1154] Playboy Enters., Inc. v. Welles, 279 F.3d 796, 803-04 (9th Cir. 2002). An earlier opinion in the same case had applied the classic fair use analysis. Playboy Enters., Inc. v. Welles, 7 F. Supp. 2d 1098 (S.D. Cal. 1998), *aff'd without op.*, 162 F.3d 1169 (9th Cir. 1998); *accord Bihari*, 119 F. Supp. at 322-23. However, the earlier opinion predated the Ninth Circuit's recognition of nominative fair use in the *New Kids* case.

[1155] Liquid Glass Enters., Inc. v. Dr. Ing. h.c. F. Porsche AG, 8 F. Supp. 2d 398, 402-03 (D.N.J. 1998).

[1156] Horphag Research, Ltd. v. Pellegrini, 337 F.3d 1036, 1041 (9th Cir. 2003).

the usual multifactor tests (discussed in § 3.02 [B][2] above), under *New Kids* the burden is on the defendant to establish the elements of nominative fair use.[1157]

In contrast, the Third Circuit adopted a different approach to nominative fair use in *Century 21 Real Estate Corp. v. Lending Tree, Inc.*[1158] The court disagreed with the Ninth Circuit's decision to apply the nominative fair use test in place of the likelihood of confusion analysis, for several reasons. First, "even an accurate nominative use could potentially confuse consumers about the plaintiff's endorsement or sponsorship of the defendant's products or services."[1159] Second, the court suggested that the Supreme Court's decision in *KP Permanent Make-Up* (discussed in § 3.12 [F] above), holding that a classic fair use defense under section 33(b)(4) does not require a defendant to prove the absence of a likelihood of confusion, should also apply to nominative fair use.[1160] Finally, the court believed that the Ninth Circuit's three-part test suffered from a lack of clarity. Accordingly, the Third Circuit adopted a two-step approach to analyzing claims of nominative fair use. The first step is a modified likelihood-of-confusion test, applicable only in nominative fair use cases, which considers only those likelihood-of-confusion factors that the court considers most relevant to the nominative use in question. On the specific facts of *Century 21*, the appellate court deemed those factors to be: (1) the price of the goods and other factors indicative of the care and attention expected of consumers when making a purchase; (2) the length of time the defendant has used the mark without evidence of actual confusion; (3) the intent of the defendant in adopting the mark; and (4) the evidence of actual confusion.[1161] However, the court noted that different factors might be relevant in other cases, and that this determination would have to be made on a case-by-case basis by the district court in the first instance. Under the second step of the Third Circuit's analysis, if the plaintiff succeeds in establishing a likelihood of confusion under the modified test, then the burden shifts to the defendant to show that: (1) the use of the plaintiff's mark is necessary to describe both the plaintiff's product or service and the defendant's product or service; (2) the defendant uses only so much of the plaintiff's mark as is necessary to describe the plaintiff's product; and (3) the defendant's conduct or language reflects the true and accurate relationship between the plaintiff and the defendant's products or services.[1162]

The nominative fair use defense has won increasing acceptance outside the Third and Ninth Circuits. The Ninth Circuit's approach has been adopted by

---

[1157] *Cairns*, 292 F.3d at 1151; *New Kids*, 971 F.2d at 308; Playboy Enters., Inc. v. Welles, 279 F.3d 796, 801 (9th Cir. 2002).

[1158] 425 F.3d 211 (3d Cir. 2005).

[1159] 425 F.3d at 221 & n. 1.

[1160] *Id.* at 222 & n. 3. In *KP Permanent Make-Up*, the Supreme Court specifically declined to address nominative fair use. 125 S. Ct. at 546 n. 3. A district court in the Seventh Circuit has expressly held that *KP Permanent Make-Up* applies with equal force to nominative fair use, thus permitting this defense to succeed even where the defendant's use gives rise to some likelihood of confusion. Ty, Inc. v. Pubs. Int'l, Ltd., 2005 U.S. Dist. LEXIS 23420 (N.D. Ill. Feb. 25, 2005).

[1161] *Id.* at 225-26.

[1162] *Id.* at 222.

district courts in the Second,[1163] Sixth,[1164] and Seventh[1165] Circuits, although it was rejected by a district court in the Fourth Circuit.[1166] In the context of comparative advertising, the Fifth Circuit applied only the second and third prongs of the *New Kids* test in *Pebble Beach Co. v. Tour 18 I, Ltd.*,[1167] and also declined to dispense with the traditional likelihood-of-confusion factors.[1168] The Third Circuit's approach has been applied by a district court in the Eighth Circuit.[1169]

The underlying principle on which the defense is based — that a merchant may use another's trademark to identify the latter's goods or services in the course of truthfully advertising its own goods or services, provided the use does not mislead or confuse consumers — has been widely recognized both before and after the *New Kids* decision, although not formally denominated in those cases as "fair use." Examples include *Smith v. Chanel*, Inc., in which the defendant described its knock-off perfume as identical to the trademarked brand "Chanel #5,"[1170] *Volkswagenwerk Aktiengesellschaft v. Church*, where the defendant advertised its auto repair service by posting a sign that read "Modern Volkswagen Porsche Service,"[1171] *WCVB-TV v. Boston Athletic Association*, in which the defendant television station used the trademarked term "Boston Marathon" to promote its broadcast of that event,[1172] and *Scott Fetzer Co. v. House of Vacuums, Inc.*,[1173] in which the Fifth Circuit held that an independent retailer or second-hand dealer may truthfully advertise the brand names of the merchandise it sells, provided the use does not suggest affiliation or endorsement.

In the 2006 amendments to the federal dilution statute (discussed in § 3.07 [H] above), Congress modified the statutory exemptions in section 43(c) to expressly

---

[1163] Audi AG v. Shokan Coachworks, Inc., 2008 U.S. Dist. LEXIS 92021 (N.D.N.Y. 2008); Yurman Studio, Inc. v. Castaneda, 2008 U.S. Dist. LEXIS 63158 (S.D.N.Y. 2008); Tiffany (NJ) Inc. v. eBay, Inc., 576 F. Supp. 2d 460 (S.D.N.Y. 2008); S&L Vitamins, Inc. v. Australian Gold, Inc., 521 F. Supp. 2d 188, 207 (E.D.N.Y. 2007); Merck & Co., Inc. v. Mediplan Health Consulting, Inc., 425 F. Supp. 2d 402, 413 (S.D.N.Y. 2006); Nasdaq Stock Mkt., Inc. v. Archipelago Holdings, LLC, 336 F. Supp. 2d 294, 304 (S.D.N.Y. 2004).

[1164] Romantics v. Activision Publishing, 532 F. Supp. 2d 884, 890 (E.D. Mich. 2008). Five years earlier, the Sixth Circuit had declined to recognize nominative fair use, in PACCAR, Inc. v. TeleScan Techs., 319 F.3d 243, 256 (6th Cir. 2003), *overruled on other grounds*, KP Permanent Make-Up, Inc. v. Lasting Impression I, Inc., 543 U.S. 111 (2004), but the appellate court went on to apply the Ninth Circuit's test to the facts of that case, concluding that the test was not satisfied.

[1165] DeVry Inc. v. Univ. of Med. & Health Sci., 2009 U.S. Dist. LEXIS 7876 (N.D. Ill. Feb. 2009); Ty, Inc. v. Pubs. Int'l, Ltd., 2005 U.S. Dist. LEXIS 23420 (N.D. Ill. Feb. 25, 2005); World Impressions Corp. v. McDonald's Corp., 235 F. Supp. 2d 831, 844 (N.D. Ill. 2002).

[1166] Nat'l Fed. of the Blind, Inc. v. Loompanics Enters., Inc., 936 F. Supp. 1232, 1241 (D. Md. 1996).

[1167] 155 F.3d 526, 545 (5th Cir. 1998).

[1168] *Id.* at 546–47.

[1169] Edina Realty v. TheMLSOnline.com, 80 U.S.P.Q.2d (BNA) 1039 (D. Minn. 2006).

[1170] 402 F.2d 562 (9th Cir. 1968).

[1171] 411 F.2d 350, *as amended*, 413 F.2d 1126 (9th Cir. 1969).

[1172] 926 F.2d 42 (1st Cir. 1991); *see* Universal Commun. Sys. v. Lycos, Inc., 478 F.3d 413, 424 (1st Cir. 2007) (acknowledging that this is the principle underlying nominative fair use).

[1173] 381 F.3d 477, 484–85 (5th Cir. 2004).

include nominative fair use. Although this congressional endorsement of the nominative fair use concept occurred only within the context of dilution, it is likely to lead more courts to recognize the concept with respect to other Lanham Act claims as well.

[H]   Comparative Advertising

Although the Ninth Circuit's precise formulation of nominative fair use in *New Kids* has not received universal acceptance, the underlying principle from which it is derived has been widely employed to permit the use of trademarks in order to draw truthful comparisons between one merchant's goods and those of a competitor, provided that the use is not likely to create consumer confusion as to source. This is the principle of comparative advertising:

> An imitator may use in a truthful way an originator's trademark when advertising that the imitator's product is a copy so long as that use is not likely to create confusion in the consumer's mind as to the source of the product being sold . . . The underlying rationale is that an imitator is entitled to truthfully inform the public that it believes that it has produced a product equivalent to the original and that the public may benefit through lower prices by buying the imitation.[1174]

For example, courts have held that it is permissible for a maker of a "knock-off" perfume to identify the brand-name perfume that it imitates,[1175] for a party that sells imitations of designer clothing to identify the famous couturier whose designs are being copied,[1176] for a seller of "artificial" water to identify the brand of natural spring water that its product resembles,[1177] and for a seller of a pharmaceutical product to identify the brand-name medicine for which it can be substituted.[1178]

In contrast, the bounds of truthful comparative advertising were exceeded where a maker of knock-off perfumes used the name-brand perfume's exact

---

[1174] Calvin Klein Cosmetics Corp. v. Lenox Labs., Inc., 815 F.2d 500, 503 (8th Cir. 1987) (citations omitted); *see, e.g.*, Pebble Beach Co. v. Tour 18 I, 155 F.3d 526, 545-46 (5th Cir. 1998) (collecting cases); Lindy Pen Co. v. Bic Pen Corp., 725 F.2d 1240 (9th Cir. 1984), *cert. denied*, 469 U.S. 1188 (1985); Mattel, Inc. v. Azrak-Hamway Int'l, Inc., 724 F.2d 357, 361 (2d Cir. 1983); SSP Agricultural Equipment, Inc. v. Orchard-Rite Ltd., 592 F.2d 1096, 1103 (9th Cir. 1979); Anti-Monopoly, Inc. v. General Mills Fun Group, 611 F.2d 296, 301 n. 2 (9th Cir. 1979); Saxony Products, Inc. v. Guerlain, Inc., 513 F.2d 716, 722 (9th Cir. 1975); Smith v. Chanel, 402 F.2d 562, 563 (9th Cir. 1968); Nautilus Group, Inc. v. Icon Health & Fitness, Inc., 308 F. Supp. 2d 1208, 1212 (W.D. Wash. 2003), *aff'd*, 372 F.3d 1330 (Fed. Cir. 2004); Shepard's Co. v. Thomson Corp., 1999 U.S. Dist. LEXIS 21051, *21-23 (S.D. Ohio 1999); Cumberland Packing Corp. v. Monsanto Co., 32 F. Supp. 2d 561 (E.D.N.Y. 1999); American Angus Ass'n v. Sysco Corp., 829 F. Supp. 807, 817-18 (W.D. N.C. 1992); Weight Watchers Int'l., Inc. v. Stouffer Corp., 744 F. Supp. 1259, 1269 (S.D.N.Y. 1990); Sykes Laboratory, Inc. v. Kalvin, 610 F. Supp. 849, 855 (C.D. Cal. 1985); Invicta Plastics (USA) Ltd. v. Mego Corp., 523 F. Supp. 619, 623 (S.D.N.Y. 1981); McDonald's Corp. v. Gunvill, 441 F. Supp. 71, 74 (N.D. Ill. 1977), *aff'd without op.*, 622 F.2d 592 (7th Cir. 1980).

[1175] R.G. Smith v. Chanel, Inc., 402 F.2d 562 (9th Cir. 1968).

[1176] Societe Comptoir de l'Industrie Cotonniere Etablissements Boussac v. Alexander's Dept. Stores, Inc., 299 F.2d 33, 36 (2d Cir. 1962).

[1177] Saxlehner v. Wagner, 216 U.S. 375, 380-81 (1910).

[1178] Viavi Co. v. Vimedia Co., 245 F. 289, 292 (8th Cir. 1917).

mark on its packaging and used a disclaimer that failed to obviate consumer confusion because it was in small type and was not prominently positioned,[1179] and where a golf course that replicated the designs of golf holes at famous courses displayed the marks of those courses so prominently in its materials that consumers perceived them as indications of endorsement or approval.[1180]

As discussed in § 3.07 [H] above, the express exemptions in the federal dilution statute include any "fair use" in the context of comparative advertising.

[I]   Federal Preemption

In certain circumstances, state trademark or unfair competition laws may be unenforceable because they are preempted by federal patent or copyright law. For example, the functionality bar to trademark protection, discussed in § 2.03 above, illustrates the preemptive effect of federal patent law.

The seminal cases on federal preemption of state unfair competitions laws are the Supreme Court's decisions in *Sears, Roebuck & Co. v. Stiffel Co.*,[1181] and *Compco Corp. v. Day-Brite Lighting, Inc.*[1182] In *Sears*, the Court considered an Illinois unfair competition law under which a finding of likelihood of confusion was based solely on the fact that the defendant's lamp was a virtually identical copy of the plaintiff's unpatented lamp, both in appearance and in functional details. Although it acknowledged that the similarity between the lamps might cause some consumers to be confused about the source of each lamp, the Court held that this similarity alone, without more, could not lead to an award of injunctive relief or monetary damages against the copier, because this would allow the state to give the plaintiff the equivalent of a patent monopoly, thus invading the exclusive province of federal law:

> An unpatentable article, like an article on which the patent has expired, is in the public domain and may be made and sold by whoever chooses to do so. What Sears did was to copy Stiffel's design and to sell lamps almost identical to those sold by Stiffel. This it had every right to do under the federal patent laws. That Stiffel originated the pole lamp and made it popular is immaterial. "Sharing in the goodwill of an article unprotected by patent or trade-mark is the exercise of a right possessed by all — and in the free exercise of which the consuming public is deeply interested." To allow a State by use of its law of unfair competition to prevent the copying of an article which represents too slight an advance to be patented would be to permit the State to block off from the public something which federal law has said belongs to the public. The result would be that while federal law grants only 14 or 17 years' protection to genuine inventions, States could allow perpetual protection to articles too lacking in novelty to merit any patent at all under federal constitu-

---

[1179] Charles of the Ritz Group, Ltd. v. Quality King Distrs., Inc., 832 F.2d 1317, 1324 (2d Cir. 1987).

[1180] Pebble Beach Co. v. Tour 18 I, 942 F. Supp. 1513, 1553 (S.D. Tex. 1996).

[1181] 376 U.S. 225 (1964).

[1182] 376 U.S. 234 (1964).

tional standards. This would be too great an encroachment on the federal patent system to be tolerated. . . .

Doubtless a State may, in appropriate circumstances, require that goods, whether patented or unpatented, be labeled or that other precautionary steps be taken to prevent customers from being misled as to the source, just as it may protect businesses in the use of their trademarks, labels, or distinctive dress in the packaging of goods so as to prevent others, by imitating such markings, from misleading purchasers as to the source of the goods. But because of the federal patent laws a State may not, when the article is unpatented and uncopyrighted, prohibit the copying of the article itself or award damages for such copying.[1183]

In *Compco*, the same Illinois law had been applied against a defendant that had copied the plaintiff's unpatented design for a lamp reflector. The trial court had awarded damages and an injunction, based on the finding that the reflector design had the capacity to identify the plaintiff, so that the defendant's use of the same design was likely to cause confusion as to the source of the defendant's lamps. The Supreme Court reversed, holding that even if the reflector design had developed secondary meaning, state law could not forbid the defendant from copying it. The Court noted, however, that state law could require the defendant to take steps to mitigate the potential for confusion:

As we have said in *Sears*, while the federal patent laws prevent a State from prohibiting the copying and selling of unpatented articles, they do not stand in the way of state law, statutory or decisional, which requires those who make and sell copies to take precautions to identify their products as their own. A State of course has power to impose liability upon those who, knowing that the public is relying upon an original manufacturer's reputation for quality and integrity, deceive the public by palming off their copies as the original. That an article copied from an unpatented article could be made in some other way, that the design is "nonfunctional" and not essential to the use of either article, that the configuration of the article copied may have a "secondary meaning" which identifies the maker to the trade, or that there may be "confusion" among purchasers as to which article is which or as to who is the maker, may be relevant evidence in applying a State's law requiring such precautions as labeling; however, and regardless of the copier's motives, neither these facts nor any others can furnish a basis for imposing liability for or prohibiting the actual acts of copying and selling. And of course a State cannot hold a copier accountable in damages for failure to label or otherwise to identify his goods unless his failure is in violation of valid state statutory or decisional law requiring the copier to label or take other precautions to prevent confusion of customers as to the source of the goods.[1184]

[1183] *Sears*, 376 U.S. at 232-33 (citations and footnote omitted).

[1184] *Compco*, 376 U.S. at 238-39.

The broad language of *Sears* and *Compco* led to some confusion over the scope of the Court's federal preemption doctrine, with resulting uncertainty as to the power of a state to protect distinctive trade dress. In *Bonito Boats, Inc. v. Thunder Craft Boats, Inc.*,[1185] the Court acknowledged this confusion, and sought to clarify the scope of federal preemption. Preemption of the state law in *Sears* and *Compco* was warranted because "[a] state law that substantially interferes with the enjoyment of an unpatented utilitarian or design conception which has been freely disclosed by its author to the public at large impermissibly contravenes the ultimate goal of public disclosure and use which is the centerpiece of federal patent policy."[1186] The Court characterized the Illinois law in *Sears* as violating this principle, because it afforded "the equivalent of a patent monopoly" to "functional aspects" of the plaintiff's lamp.[1187] Nonetheless,

> The *Sears* Court made it plain that the States "may protect businesses in the use of their trademarks, labels, or distinctive dress in the packaging of goods so as to prevent others, by imitating such markings, from misleading purchasers as to the source of the goods." Trade dress is, of course, potentially the subject matter of design patents. Yet our decision in *Sears* clearly indicates that the States may place limited regulations on the circumstances in which such designs are used in order to prevent consumer confusion as to source. Thus, while *Sears* speaks in absolutist terms, its conclusion that the States may place some conditions on the use of trade dress indicates an implicit recognition that all state regulation of potentially patentable but unpatented subject matter is not ipso facto pre-empted by the federal patent laws.[1188]

The Court distinguished the Illinois law in *Sears* and *Compco* from more typical unfair competition laws, which are "limited to protection against copying of nonfunctional aspects of consumer products which have acquired secondary meaning,"[1189] thus implying that the case for federal preemption is strongest where a state law protects functional features of a product.

In *Bonito Boats*, the Court held that a Florida statute that prohibited the use of a particular molding process for copying the design of boat hulls, as well as the sale of such unlawfully duplicated hulls, was preempted because it conflicted with the "strong federal policy favoring free competition in ideas which do not merit patent protection."[1190] While holding that the Florida statute impermissibly invaded the province of federal patent and copyright laws, the Court emphasized that the states may still impose restrictions on the copying of designs if those restrictions are "limited to those necessary to promote goals outside the contemplation of the federal patent scheme."[1191]

[1185] 489 U.S. 141 (1989).

[1186] *Id.* at 156-57.

[1187] *Id.*

[1188] *Id.* at 154.

[1189] *Id.* at 157-58.

[1190] *Id.* at 168.

[1191] *Id.* at 166.

Bonito Boats noted that the long-term "peaceful coexistence" of state unfair competition laws and federal patent law signals that "Congress has indicated its awareness of the operation of state law in a field of federal interest, and has nonetheless decided to 'stand by both concepts and to tolerate whatever tension there [is] between them.' "[1192] The Florida statute, like the Illinois unfair competition law, exceeded the scope of traditional unfair competition laws, and "rais[ed] the spectre of state-created monopolies in a host of useful shapes and processes for which patent protection has been denied or is otherwise unobtainable."[1193] The Court also suggested that section 43(a) of the Lanham Act indicates Congress's recognition of the same type of concerns that underlie traditional unfair competition law.[1194]

Some courts have suggested that the scope of federal preemption and the functionality bar are coextensive.[1195] It is true that the Court's analysis in *Bonito Boats* emphasizes that states should not interfere with the free circulation of designs that are "useful" or "functional." Moreover, the Court specifically noted that states may impose "limited regulations" on the use of designs in order to prevent consumer confusion, even though the designs might be the subject of design patent protection.[1196] However, federal preemption is not necessarily limited to state laws protecting the functional aspects of an article. In both *Sears* and *Compco*, the lamp designs that were held to be unworthy of utility patents had received design patents that were later held to be invalid. In a case decided before *Bonito Boats*, the Federal Circuit held in *Litton Systems, Inc. v. Whirlpool Corp.*[1197] that federal law preempted the application of a state law prohibiting the copying of product configuration trade dress, noting that "[t]he key to determining whether the *Sears* and *Compco* cases prohibit a state action is whether a design is of the type on which a patent may issue."[1198] In decisions issued after *Bonito Boats*, several courts have suggested that state trade dress protection of product configuration (as opposed to product packaging) is preempted.[1199] Attempts to protect product configuration under state antidilution laws may be particularly vulnerable to preemption, because dilution laws do not require a likelihood of consumer confusion; one federal district court has already held that, under *Bonito Boats*, federal patent law preempts the

---

[1192] *Id.*

[1193] *Id.* at 167.

[1194] *Id.* at 166.

[1195] *See, e.g.*, I.P. Lund Trading ApS v. Kohler Co., 163 F.3d 27, 36 (1st Cir. 1998) (stating that "the functionality doctrine marks the boundaries of trade dress protection").

[1196] 489 U.S. at 154.

[1197] 728 F.2d 1423 (Fed. Cir. 1984).

[1198] *Id.* at 1448.

[1199] Landscape Forms, Inc. v. Columbia Cascade Corp., 113 F.3d 373, 383 (2d Cir. 1997) (suggesting in dicta that federal design patent law would preempt state law protection for furniture design); PAF S.r.l. v. Lisa Lighting Co., 712 F. Supp. 394, 412 n. 19 (S.D.N.Y. 1989) (state protection for product configuration trade dress may be preempted by federal patent law if state law does not require proof of secondary meaning).

application of New York's antidilution statute to protect the decorative shape of a fragrance bottle.[1200]

Ironically, it is well settled that *non*functional aspects of product configuration can be protected under section 43(a) of the Lanham Act;[1201] thus, a plaintiff that seeks to protect the goodwill associated with its product configuration may have more success bringing its claims under section 43(a) than under the corresponding provisions of state law. A number of courts have also held that section 43(c), the federal dilution statute, applies to nonfunctional product configurations.[1202] The conflict between a potentially unlimited term of federal dilution protection for product configurations and the limited 14-year term[1203] of federal design patent protection is obvious, yet the language of section 43(c) does not suggest that Congress intended to exclude otherwise-eligible product configurations from its scope.[1204]

Federal copyright law can also preempt the enforcement of some state trademark and unfair competition laws, because some trademarks are also copyrightable works of authorship, and some unfair competition claims may involve false representations about copyrightable works of authorship. Preemption arguments based on copyright law may involve either express preemption or conflict preemption.

The express preemption provisions of the copyright statutes prohibit enforcement of any state law claim that: (1) is the equivalent of any of the exclusive rights of a copyright owner and (2) involves a work that falls within the general scope of copyrightable subject matter[1205] (which encompasses original works of authorship fixed in any tangible medium of expression[1206]). The purpose of the

---

[1200] *See* Escada AG v. Limited, Inc., 810 F. Supp. 571 (S.D.N.Y. 1993).

[1201] *See* TrafFix Devices, Inc. v. Marketing Displays, Inc., 532 U.S. 23 (2001) (holding that, in determining whether product design features are protectible under section 43(a), a particularly strong presumption of functionality applies to features that were claimed in an expired utility patent); Wal-Mart Stores, Inc. v. Samara Bros., Inc., 529 U.S. 205 (2000) (holding that product configuration may be protected by section 43(a) only if it has secondary meaning). For a more detailed discussion of the Lanham Act's application to trade dress, see § 2.07 [C] *supra.*

[1202] I.P. Lund Trading ApS v. Kohler Co., 163 F.3d 27, 45 (1st Cir. 1998); Sunbeam Prods., Inc. v. West Bend Co., 39 U.S.P.Q.2d (BNA) 1545, 1555 (S.D. Miss. 1996), *aff'd on other grounds*, 123 F.3d 246 (5th Cir. 1997), *cert. denied*, 523 U.S. 1118 (1998), *overruled in part on other grounds*, *TrafFix*, 523 U.S. at 28; *see also* GMC v. Urban Gorilla, LLC, 500 F.3d 1222, 1228-29 (10th Cir. 2007) (addressing section 43(c) claim involving product configuration, but upholding denial of preliminary injunction due to failure to demonstrate actual dilution under pre-2006 statute); Hammerton, Inc. v. Heisterman, 2008 U.S. Dist. LEXIS 38036 (D. Utah 2008) (product configuration must be nonfunctional and have secondary meaning to be protected under 43(c)).

[1203] 35 U.S.C. § 173.

[1204] *See I.P. Lund Trading ApS*, 163 F.3d at 50 ("It is possible that Congress did not really envision protection for product design from dilution by a competing product under the FTDA, but the language it used does not permit us to exclude such protection categorically and rare cases can be imagined."); *see also* Gary Myers, *Statutory Interpretation, Property Rights, and Boundaries: The Nature and Limits of Protection in Trademark Dilution, Trade Dress, and Product Configuration Cases*, 23 Colum.-VLA J.L. & Arts 241, 291-305 (2000) (examining conflict between federal patent policy and protection of product configuration under section 43(c)).

[1205] 17 U.S.C. § 301 (2009).

[1206] 17 U.S.C. § 102(a) (2009).

express preemption provisions is to prevent states from duplicating or expanding the scope of federal copyright protection. Thus, a state law claim is not preempted if it involves an "extra element" that makes it qualitatively different from a copyright claim.[1207] Most trademark infringement and false designation of origin claims avoid express preemption because they require proof of a likelihood of confusion; because this extra element is not a requirement for copyright infringement, such claims neither duplicate nor enlarge the scope of federal copyright protection.[1208] In contrast, courts have held that copyright law preempts state law "reverse passing off" claims arising from the unauthorized (and uncredited) copying of copyrightable expression.[1209] The scope of copyright preemption of state law dilution claims is less clear, however, because those claims do not require a plaintiff to demonstrate a likelihood of confusion. However, because a dilution plaintiff must still establish that its mark is a distinctive (and famous, under some statutes) indication of the origin of goods or services, and that the mark's ability to function in this capacity is likely to be undermined (that is, diluted or tarnished) by the defendant's unauthorized use, several courts have held that a dilution claim is not the equivalent of any of the exclusive rights of the copyright owner, and that, accordingly, the dilution claim is not subject to express preemption.[1210]

Even where a claim is not expressly preempted by federal copyright law, the principle of conflict preemption will prevent enforcement of state trademark and unfair competition claims that would unduly interfere with the purposes underlying the overall federal scheme of copyright protection — for example, by preventing the public from freely reproducing works that have entered the public domain, or by allowing someone other than the copyright owner to control the exploitation of a copyrighted work.

Although, in general, Lanham Act claims are not subject to preemption by other federal laws, the federal courts have applied a principle analogous to conflict preemption in order to reject Lanham Act claims that interfere with the general scheme of copyright protection. In *Dastar Corp. v. Twentieth Century Fox Film Corp.*,[1211] discussed in § 3.03 above, the Supreme Court rejected a claim of reverse passing off under section 43(a) of the Lanham Act, where the defendant had reproduced the plaintiff's videos (which had entered the public domain due to failure to renew the copyright registration) and represented itself as the author of those videos; the Court held that a false designation of origin claim under the Lanham Act could not be used to create a "mutant" form of copyright protection for public domain works. *Dastar* specifically held that the "origin" of goods for purposes of section 43(a) refers to the origin of *tangible* goods, and not to the ideas or intangible intellectual property content of those goods; thus, it does not permit authors to bring reverse passing off claims based

---

[1207] Computer Assocs. Int'l v. Altai, Inc., 982 F.2d 693, 716 (2d Cir. 1992).

[1208] *See, e.g.*, Warner Bros. v. American Broadcasting Co., 720 F.2d 231, 247 (2d Cir. 1983).

[1209] *See* Waldman Pub. Corp. v. Landoll, Inc., 848 F. Supp. 498, 505 (S.D.N.Y. 1994) (collecting cases), *vacated and remanded on other grounds*, 43 F.3d 775 (2d Cir. 1994).

[1210] *See, e.g.*, Eliya, Inc. v. Kohl's Dep't Stores, 82 U.S.P.Q.2d (BNA) 1088 (S.D.N.Y. 2006); Gateway 2000 v. Cyrix Corp., 942 F. Supp. 985, 995 (D.N.J. 1996).

[1211] 539 U.S. 23 (2003).

on misattribution of authorship.[1212] In accordance with this holding, federal courts have broadened the *Dastar* analysis to encompass Lanham Act claims involving copyrighted works regardless of whether those works have entered the public domain.[1213] For example, the Ninth Circuit recently applied *Dastar's* analysis in *Sybersound Records, Inc. v. UAV Corp.*,[1214] to reject a karaoke record producer's false advertising claim under section 43(a) against a competitor for falsely representing to customers that it had obtained the proper copyright licenses for its products.

Although *Dastar* was not, strictly speaking, a preemption case, because it did not involve a conflict between state and federal laws, its holding brings consistency to the treatment of reverse passing off claims brought under state and federal law. Prior to *Dastar*, a common law reverse passing off claim based on unauthorized copying of copyrightable expression would be preempted, while the identical claim under section 43(a) would be allowed.[1215] After *Dastar*, this is no longer the case.[1216]

[J]   Eleventh Amendment

The Lanham Act provides that the rights of a trademark owner to sue an infringer under sections 32 and 43 extend to suits against "any State, any instrumentality of a State, and any officer or employee of a State or instrumentality of a State acting in his or her official capacity," and "[a]ny State, and any such instrumentality, officer, or employee, shall be subject to the provisions of this Act in the same manner and to the same extent as any nongovernmental entity."[1217]

Furthermore, section 40 of the Lanham Act expressly abrogates the sovereign immunity of states and state actors with respect to violations of the Act:

> Any State, instrumentality of a State or any officer or employee of a State or instrumentality of a State acting in his or her official capacity, shall not be immune, under the Eleventh Amendment of the Constitution of the United States or under any other doctrine of sovereign immunity, from suit in Federal court by any person, including any governmental or non-governmental entity for any violation under this Act.[1218]

Despite these clear indications of congressional intent to abrogate the sovereign immunity of state actors for purposes of federal trademark and unfair

---

[1212] 539 U.S. at 37.

[1213] *See* Richard Feiner & Co. v. New York Times Co., 88 U.S.P.Q.2d (BNA) 1951 (S.D.N.Y. 2008) (collecting cases).

[1214] 517 F.3d 1137, 1143-44 (9th Cir. 2008).

[1215] *See, e.g., Waldman Pub. Corp.*, 848 F. Supp. at 500-05.

[1216] *See, e.g.*, Atrium Group de Ediciones y Publicaciones, S.L. v. Harry N. Abrams, Inc., 565 F. Supp. 2d 505, 511-13 (S.D.N.Y. 2008).

[1217] 15 U.S.C. §§ 1114(1), 1127 (definition of "person").

[1218] 15 U.S.C. § 1122(b).

competition law, the Supreme Court held in *College Savings Bank v. Florida Prepaid Postsecondary Education Expense Board* that this abrogation exceeded Congress's powers and was invalid under the Eleventh Amendment to the United States Constitution, which provides that "[t]he Judicial power of the United States shall not be construed to extend to any suit in law or equity, commenced or prosecuted against one of the United States by Citizens of another State, or by Citizens or Subjects of any Foreign State."

The Supreme Court has interpreted the Eleventh Amendment as precluding federal court jurisdiction over any suit brought against a state, and has recognized only two exceptions to this rule:

> First, Congress may authorize such a suit in the exercise of its power to enforce the Fourteenth Amendment — an Amendment enacted after the Eleventh Amendment and specifically designed to alter the federal-state balance. Second, a State may waive its sovereign immunity by consenting to suit.[1219]

In *Florida Prepaid*, the Court held that Congress's attempt to abrogate sovereign immunity in the context of a false advertising claim under section 43(a) of the Lanham Act was an exercise of its power under the Commerce Clause, rather than the Fourteenth Amendment. Because the state of Florida had not waived its sovereign immunity for purposes of the Lanham Act, a complaint against the state for false advertising under section 43(a) did not fall within either of the Court's two recognized exceptions to the Eleventh Amendment. Accordingly, the federal courts had no jurisdiction to adjudicate the claim. This jurisdictional bar is equally applicable whether the plaintiff's claim is for monetary damages or for injunctive relief.[1220]

After *Florida Prepaid* invalidated Congress's attempt to abrogate Eleventh Amendment immunity for purposes of false advertising claims under section 43(a), a federal district court held that this same conclusion applied to trademark infringement claims under section 32 and false designation of origin claims under section 43(a).[1221] No court has held to the contrary.

It remains unclear, however, whether and under what circumstances federal courts may consider a claim for injunctive relief under the Lanham Act that is brought against a state officer, as distinguished from the state or an agency thereof. The Supreme Court has recognized that the Eleventh Amendment does not always bar suits for injunctive relief under state officers, even where it would bar a similar suit against the state itself.[1222] In *Sofamor Danek Group v. Brown*,[1223] for example, the Ninth Circuit held that the Eleventh Amendment

---

[1219] College Savings Bank v. Florida Prepaid Postsecondary Educ. Expense Bd., 527 U.S. 666, 670 (1999) (citation omitted).

[1220] Federal Maritime Comm'n v. South Carolina State Ports Auth., 535 U.S. 743, 766 (2002); Seminole Tribe of Florida v. Florida, 517 U.S. 44, 58 (1996).

[1221] Regents of Univ. Wisc. Sys. v. Phoenix Software Int'l Inc., 565 F. Supp. 2d 1007, 1013 (W.D. Wisc. 2008).

[1222] *Seminole Tribe*, 517 U.S. at 71 n. 14; Ex Parte Young, 209 U.S. 123 (1908).

[1223] 124 F.3d 1179 (9th Cir. 1997).

did not preclude federal court adjudication of a claim for injunctive relief against a state official for making false statements in an official state document in violation of section 43(a), even though it would have barred an action against the state itself; however, because this decision predates *Florida Prepaid*, it should be viewed with caution.

Also unclear are the circumstances under which a state may be deemed to have voluntarily waived its Eleventh Amendment immunity to suit. In *Florida Prepaid*, the Supreme Court stated that the test for waiver "is a stringent one," and will generally be found only if the state voluntarily invokes the jurisdiction of the federal courts, or makes a "clear declaration" that it intends to submit itself to federal jurisdiction.[1224] Since then, a federal district court has held that a state does not waive its immunity by participating in the federal trademark system or by filing a suit to review the cancellation of its mark.[1225] However, in contexts not involving trademark law, courts have held that a state waives its immunity when it voluntarily invokes the jurisdiction of the federal courts, although the waiver reaches only as far as necessary to adjudicate the state's claims,[1226] and this analysis should apply equally to trademark law.

However, the Eleventh Amendment does not preclude *state* courts from exercising jurisdiction over Lanham Act claims against a state or its agencies. Because state and federal courts have concurrent jurisdiction over Lanham claims,[1227] it is possible to adjudicate such a claim in state court, regardless of whether the plaintiff seeks monetary damages, injunctive relief, or both.

The Eleventh Amendment also does not bar a state court from adjudicating claims against states or their agencies under state trademark and unfair competition laws. In this case, the question of sovereign immunity would be determined by state law.

Since the Supreme Court's decision in *Florida Prepaid*, Congress has considered a number of bills that would require states to waive their Eleventh Amendment immunity as a condition to securing federal protection for their own intellectual property. However, no such legislation has been enacted.

[K]   Statute of Limitations

The Lanham Act does not have its own statute of limitations, and federal courts have developed two different approaches to filling this void. Some circuits follow the Supreme Court's instruction in *Wilson v. Garcia*, applicable generally to federal statutes that fail to specify limitations periods, to "adopt a local time limitation as federal law if it is not inconsistent with federal law or policy to do so."[1228] Accordingly, courts in these circuits follow the statute of limitations that

---

[1224] 527 U.S. at 675-76.

[1225] Regents of Univ. Wisc. Sys., 565 F. Supp. 2d at 1014-15.

[1226] *Id.* at 1014.

[1227] *See* § 3.17 *infra*.

[1228] Wilson v. Garcia, 471 U.S. 261, 266-67 (1985); *accord* Reed v. United Transp. Union, 488 U.S. 319, 334 (1989).

applies to the most closely analogous action under state law.[1229] Other courts, however, do not interpret *Wilson v. Garcia* as requiring the application of state limitations statutes to Lanham Act claims; these courts rely on the equitable doctrine of laches in place of a formal limitations period.[1230] However, the courts that have adopted this approach typically treat the analogous state limitations statute as relevant to determining whether a "presumption of laches" should apply.[1231]

PART VIII:
REMEDIES

§ 3.13   NON-MONETARY REMEDIES

[A]   Injunctions

Under both state and federal law, injunctions are the predominant and most traditional remedy for violations of trademark and unfair competition law. Injunctive relief, unlike monetary damages, protects the consuming public from the danger of continuing confusion and deception. It also protects the trademark owner from the irreparable injury that could be caused by another party's appropriation or tarnishment of the goodwill embodied in the mark.[1232]

Under section 34(a) of the Lanham Act, both permanent and temporary injunctive relief are available for infringements of registered trademarks under section 32, as well as for violations of sections 43(a), (c), or (d) with respect to both registered and unregistered marks. Section 34 grants state and federal courts broad powers to fashion injunctions "according to the principles of equity and upon such terms as the court may deem reasonable." Where the injunction is issued by a federal district court, section 34(a) provides that the relief is nationwide in effect, and may be enforced by proceedings for contempt.[1233]

[1229] *See, e.g.*, Santana Prods. v. Bobrick Washroom Equip., Inc., 401 F.3d 123, 135 (3d Cir. 2005); Jarrow Formulas, Inc. v. Nutrition Now, Inc., 304 F.3d 829, 836 (9th Cir.), *cert. denied*, 537 U.S. 1047 (2002); Island Insteel Sys., Inc. v. Waters, 296 F.3d 200, 203 (3d Cir. 2002); Beauty Time v. VU Skin Sys., 118 F.3d 140, 143 (3d Cir. 1997) (applying state tolling principles as well); Lamparello v. Falwell, 360 F. Supp. 2d 768, 775 (E.D. Va. 2004); Unlimited Screw Products, Inc. v. Malm, 781 F. Supp. 1121, 1125 (E.D. Va. 1991); Fox Chemical Co. v. Amsoil, Inc., 445 F. Supp. 1355, 1357 (D. Minn. 1978).

[1230] Ford Motor Co. v. Catalanotte, 342 F.3d 543, 550 (6th Cir. 2003); Hot Wax, Inc. v. Turtle Wax, Inc., 191 F.3d 813, 820-21 (7th Cir. 1999); Conopco, Inc. v. Campbell Soup Co., 95 F.3d 187, 191 (2d Cir. 1996); AmBrit, Inc. v. Kraft, Inc., 812 F.2d 1531, 1546 (11th Cir. 1986); Tandy Corp. v. Malone & Hyde, Inc., 769 F.2d 362, 365 (6th Cir. 1985). For a discussion of laches, see § 3.12 [C] *supra*.

[1231] *Hot Wax*, 191 F.3d at 820-21; *AmBrit*, 812 F.2d at 1545; *Tandy*, 769 F.2d at 365.

[1232] *See, e.g.*, Lone Star Steakhouse & Saloon v. Alpha of Virginia, 43 F.3d 922 (4th Cir. 1995); Opticians Ass'n v. Independent Opticians, 920 F.2d 187, 195 (3d Cir. 1990); Century 21 Real Estate Corp. v. Sandlin, 846 F.2d 1175 (9th Cir. 1988); Times Mirror Magazines, Inc. v. Las Vegas Sports News, 212 F.3d 157, 169 (3d Cir. 2000).

[1233] 15 U.S.C. § 1116(a).

Injunctive relief — both permanent and temporary — is typically available under state law as well, both for unfair competition and for infringement of marks that are registered under state law. It has been held that state courts exercising personal jurisdiction over a defendant have the authority to issue nationwide injunctions.[1234]

Section 34(a) of the Lanham Act affords courts a great degree of latitude in fashioning injunctive relief, and in exercising their broad discretion courts will consider all of the equities of a case, including but not limited to the extent of the injury that the plaintiff and the public would suffer from continuing concurrent use of the mark under limitations or conditions (such as concurrent uses in distinct geographic territories), and the good or bad faith of the defendant in adopting the mark. In *King-Seeley Thermos Co. v. Aladdin Industries*, for example, where the court recognized that the term "thermos" had become largely generic, but still retained some small degree of its origin-identifying function, the defendant was permitted to use the term "thermos" on its insulated vacuum bottle, but was enjoined from capitalizing the "t" or from referring to its product as an "original" or "genuine" thermos.[1235]

While a permanent injunction will be issued only after a plaintiff has prevailed on the merits, the court may exercise its discretion to grant a preliminary injunction prior to the resolution of the case in order to prevent irreparable harm to the plaintiff during the pendency of the litigation. In determining whether a preliminary injunction is warranted, a court will ordinarily consider the following criteria: (1) the likelihood that the plaintiff will ultimately succeed on the merits; (2) whether the plaintiff is likely to suffer irreparable harm if the defendant is permitted to continue the allegedly infringing activities during the litigation; (3) whether the hardship to the plaintiff in the absence of a preliminary injunction is likely to be greater than the hardship to the defendant that will result from preliminary injunction; and (4) whether a preliminary injunction would serve the public interest (e.g., by preventing consumer confusion during pendency of the litigation).[1236]

[1234] *See, e.g.*, Allied Artists Pictures Corp. v. Friedman, 68 Cal. App. 3d 127, 136-37 (1977).

[1235] King-Seeley Thermos Co. v. Aladdin Industries, Inc., 321 F.2d 577 (2d Cir. 1963). The flexibility afforded to courts fashioning injunctions under the Lanham Act reflects the traditionally broad discretion afforded by the common law of unfair competition. *See, e.g.*, David B. Findlay, Inc. v. Findlay, 18 N.Y.S.2d 12 (N.Y. App. 1966) (upholding injunction providing that junior user of surname who was sibling of senior user could not use the same surname as a mark for a similar business located on the same street as the senior user, but could use that surname as a mark for a similar business located elsewhere).

[1236] These four criteria represent the most common formulation. *See, e.g.*, Abbott Laboratories v. Mead Johnson & Co., 971 F.2d 6 (7th Cir. 1992). However, the federal circuits (and some state courts) have each developed their own version of these factors. The Ninth Circuit, in particular, has adopted a somewhat less demanding standard, under which "the moving party must demonstrate either a combination of probable success on the merits and the possibility of irreparable injury, or that serious questions are raised and the balance of hardships tips sharply in the moving party's favor." Beltran v. Myers, 677 F.2d 1317, 1320 (9th Cir. 1982). The Ninth Circuit uses a "sliding scale" approach, under which "the greater the relative hardship to the moving party, the less strong need be the showing of probable success that is required." *Id.*

In trademark infringement, false designation of origin, and false advertising cases, most federal and state courts have routinely granted permanent injunctions to prevailing plaintiffs, on the ground that irreparable harm to the plaintiff can be presumed once a likelihood of confusion is established.[1237] Some courts have applied this presumption to dilution and cybersquatting claims as well, once the plaintiff has prevailed on the merits.[1238] Preliminary injunctions, too, have routinely been granted once a plaintiff establishes a likelihood of success on the merits; here, too, irreparable harm has generally been presumed.[1239] However, the Supreme Court's 2006 decision in *eBay, Inc. v. MercExchange, L.L.C.*,[1240] has cast doubt on the appropriateness of such presumptions. In *eBay*, a patent infringement case, the Court disapproved the Federal Circuit's policy of routinely granting permanent injunctions against infringers absent "exceptional circumstances," and instead ordered the Federal Circuit to apply the traditional principles of equity in determining whether injunctive relief is warranted. Those principles require a plaintiff to demonstrate: "(1) that it has suffered an irreparable injury; (2) that remedies available at law, such as monetary damages, are inadequate to compensate for that injury; (3) that, considering the balance of hardships between the plaintiff and defendant, a remedy in equity is warranted; and (4) that the public interest would not be disserved by a permanent injunction."[1241] If a district court applies these principles, then its decision to grant or deny injunctive relief is reviewable only for an abuse of discretion.[1242]

While the Supreme Court did not indicate whether the *eBay* analysis should apply to claims involving trademark infringement, unfair competition, and false advertising, most courts that have considered the question have so held,[1243] although several district courts in New York have continued to presume

---

[1237] *E.g.*, Brennan's, Inc. v. Brennan's Rest., L.L.C., 360 F.3d 125, 129 (2d Cir. 2004); Ty, Inc. v. Jones Group, Inc., 237 F.3d 891, 902 (7th Cir. 2001); GoTo.com, Inc. v. Walt Disney Co., 202 F.3d 1199, 1209 (9th Cir. 2000); Circuit City Stores, Inc. v. CarMax, Inc., 165 F.3d 1047, 1056 (6th Cir. 1999); McDonald's Corp. v. Robertson, 147 F.3d 1301, 1310 (11th Cir. 1998); Pappan Enters., Inc. v. Hardee's Food Sys., Inc., 143 F.3d 800, 805 (3d Cir. 1998); Societe Des Produits Nestle, S.A. v. Casa Helvetia, Inc., 982 F.2d 633, 640 (1st Cir. 1992); Black Hills Jewelry Mfg. Co. v. Gold Rush, Inc., 633 F.2d 746, 753 n. 7 (8th Cir. 1980). The Fifth Circuit, in contrast, has never adopted this presumption. Paulsson Geophysical Servs., Inc. v. Sigmar, 529 F.3d 303 (5th Cir. 2008). In false advertising cases, some courts have limited the presumption to claims of false *comparative* advertising. *See* Scotts Co. v. United Indus. Corp., 315 F.3d 264, 273-74 (4th Cir. 2002) (collecting cases).

[1238] *E.g.*, Verizon Calif., Inc. v. Navigation Catalyst Sys., Inc., 568 F. Supp. 2d 1088 (C.D. Cal. 2008) (cybersquatting); AM Gen. Corp. v. Daimlerchrysler Corp., 311 F.3d 796, 832 (7th Cir. 2002) (dilution); Asia Apparel, LLC v. RIPSwear, Inc., 2004 U.S. Dist. LEXIS 29208 (W.D.N.C. 2004) (cybersquatting), *aff'd sub nom.* Asia Apparel, LLC v. Cunneen, 118 Fed. Appx. 782 (4th Cir. 2005); Nabisco, Inc. v. PF Brands, Inc., 50 F. Supp. 2d 188, 210 (S.D.N.Y.) (dilution), *aff'd*, 191 F.3d 208 (2d Cir. 1999); Deere & Co. v. MTD Prods., Inc., 860 F. Supp. 113, 122 (S.D.N.Y.) (dilution), *aff'd*, 41 F.3d 39 (2d Cir. 1994).

[1239] *See, e.g.*, Tally-Ho, Inc. v. Coast Cmty. Coll. Dist., 889 F.2d 1018, 1029 (11th Cir. 1989).

[1240] 547 U.S. 388 (2006).

[1241] *eBay*, 547 U.S. at 391.

[1242] *Id.*

[1243] *See, e.g.*, Reno Air Racing Ass'n, Inc. v. McCord, 452 F.3d 1126 (9th Cir. 2006); Audi AG v. D'Amato, 469 F.3d 534, 550 (6th Cir. 2006); Funai Elec Co, LTD v. Daewoo Elecs. Corp., 2009 U.S. Dist. LEXIS 1618 (N.D. Cal. 2009); Avid Identification Sys. v. Phillips Elecs. N. Am., 2008 U.S. Dist.

irreparable harm whenever a likelihood of confusion is established.[1244] At least one court has applied *eBay* to a federal dilution claim.[1245]

The *eBay* decision is unlikely to lead courts to refuse permanent injunctions against activities that constitute trademark infringement, unfair competition, or false advertising, at least where the plaintiff makes a reasonable showing under the four equitable factors,[1246] because denial of an injunction in such situations is likely to harm the public interest by allowing consumers to be confused or misled. In contrast, denial of an injunction in a patent or copyright case is likely to harm only the patentee or copyright owner, respectively. Courts are unlikely to impose a compulsory license in trademark cases because: (1) permitting an infringer to continue making false representations regarding goods or services would cause harm to the public, and because (2) as a remedy for trademark infringement, a compulsory license would lack the quality controls that are necessary to prevent a finding that the trademark has been abandoned due to "naked licensing." It is also unlikely that *eBay* will lead courts to deny permanent injunctions in dilution cases; while there is typically less of a public interest at stake in these cases, injunctive relief is typically the only remedy available.

It is unsettled whether *eBay* also alters the current standard for granting preliminary injunctions. In the past, courts considering motions for preliminary injunctions in trademark, unfair competition, false advertising, cybersquatting, and dilution cases have typically presumed irreparable injury once a plaintiff demonstrates a likelihood of success on the merits. While some courts have continued this practice post-*eBay*,[1247] a larger number of courts have concluded that *eBay* makes this presumption impermissible.[1248]

LEXIS 23648 (E.D. Tex. 2008); Mannatech, Inc. v. Glycoproducts Int'l, Inc., 2008-2 U.S. Trade Cas. (CCH) P76, 236 (N.D. Tex. 2008); Microsoft Corp. v. AGA Solutions, Inc., 2008 U.S. Dist. LEXIS 95181 (E.D.N.Y. 2008); American Taxi Dispatch, Inc. v. American Metro Taxi & Limo Co., 582 F. Supp. 2d 999 (N.D. Ill. 2008); Baden Sports, Inc. v. Kabushiki Kaisha Molten, 2007 U.S. Dist. LEXIS 70776 (W.D. Wash. 2007); Propet USA, Inc. v. Shugart, 2007 U.S. Dist. LEXIS 94979 (W.D. Wash. 2007); Panda Invs., Inc. v. Jabez Enters., 2007 U.S. Dist. LEXIS 93542 (N.D. Iowa 2007); Western Union Holdings, Inc. v. Eastern Union, Inc., 2007 U.S. Dist. LEXIS 66281 (N.D. Ga. 2007).

[1244] Microsoft Corp. v. Atek 3000 Computer, Inc., 2008 U.S. Dist. LEXIS 56689 (E.D.N.Y. 2008); JA Apparel Corp. v. Abboud, 2008 U.S. Dist. LEXIS 44599 (S.D.N.Y. 2008); Cartier v. Aaron Faber, Inc., 512 F. Supp. 2d 165 (S.D.N.Y. 2007).

[1245] *See* Nike, Inc. v. Nikepal Intern., Inc., 84 U.S.P.Q.2d (BNA) 1521 (E.D. Cal. 2007).

[1246] *See* Microsoft Corp. v. AGA Solutions, Inc., 2008 U.S. Dist. LEXIS 95181 (E.D.N.Y. 2008) (denying permanent injunction where the plaintiff made no attempt to satisfy the four equitable factors, and where the last act of infringement took place three years earlier).

[1247] *See, e.g.,* Lorillard Tobacco Co. v. Amouri's Grand Foods, Inc., 453 F.3d 377 (6th Cir. 2006); Canfield v. Health Communs., Inc. 2008 U.S. Dist. LEXIS 28662, *6 (C.D. Cal. 2008); Verizon Calif., Inc. v. Navigation Catalyst Sys., Inc., 568 F. Supp. 2d 1088 (C.D. Cal. 2008).

[1248] *See, e.g.,* North American Medical Corp. v. Axiom Worldwide, Inc., 522 F.3d 1211, 1228 (11th Cir. 2008); Lorillard Tobacco Co. v. Engida, 213 Fed. Appx. 654 (10th Cir.) (unpub.), *cert. denied*, 127 S. Ct. 3016 (2007); Auburn Univ. v. Moody, 2008 U.S. Dist. LEXIS 89578, *28-29 (M.D. Ala. 2008); MyGym, LLC v. Engle, 2006 U.S. Dist. LEXIS 88375 (D. Utah 2006); Harris Research, Inc. v. Lydon, 505 F. Supp. 2d 1161 (D. Utah 2007).

[B]   Seizure of Counterfeit Goods and Related Materials

In the case of marks registered on the Principal Register, upon ex parte application section 34(d) authorizes seizure of any goods bearing counterfeit marks, as well as the counterfeit marks themselves, the means for making the counterfeit marks, and records relating to the counterfeiting. An ex parte seizure order may be granted only if the court determines that the following conditions have been met:

(i)   an order other than an ex parte seizure order is not adequate to achieve the purposes of section 32;

(ii)   the applicant has not publicized the requested seizure;

(iii) the applicant is likely to succeed in showing that the person against whom seizure would be ordered used a counterfeit mark in connection with the sale, offering for sale, or distribution of goods or services;

(iv)   an immediate and irreparable injury will occur if such seizure is not ordered;

(v)   the matter to be seized will be located at the place identified in the application;

(vi)   the harm to the applicant of denying the application outweighs the harm to the legitimate interests of the person against whom seizure would be ordered of granting the application; and

(vii) the person against whom seizure would be ordered, or persons acting in concert with such person, would destroy, move, hide, or otherwise make such matter inaccessible to the court, if the applicant were to proceed on notice to such person.[1249]

For purposes of section 34(a), a "counterfeit" mark is a spurious mark that is identical to, or substantially indistinguishable from, a mark that is: (1) in use, and (2) registered in the Principal Register for the same goods or services, regardless of whether the counterfeiter knew that the mark was registered, except that a mark is *not* counterfeit if, at the time the goods or services in question were manufactured or produced, the holder of the right to use the genuine mark had authorized the maker or producer of the goods or services in question to use that mark.[1250]

The party requesting an order for seizure must provide security adequate to pay any damages arising from wrongful seizure,[1251] and the court must issue any protective orders necessary to prevent disclosure of any trade secrets or other confidential information as a result of the seizure.[1252] The defendant is entitled to a post-seizure hearing to determine whether the findings of fact and

---

[1249] 15 U.S.C. § 1116(d)(4)(B).

[1250] 15 U.S.C. §§ 1116(d)(1)(B), 1127.

[1251] 15 U.S.C. § 1116(d)(4)(A).

[1252] 15 U.S.C. §§ 1116(d)(7), (9).

conclusions of law on which the order was based are still in effect.[1253] Any person who suffers damage as the result of a wrongful seizure may bring an action against the party that requested seizure, and may recover such relief as the court finds appropriate, including lost profits, cost of materials, loss of good will, punitive damages if the seizure was sought in bad faith, and, in the absence of extenuating circumstances, a reasonable attorney's fee. The court also has discretion to award prejudgment interest.[1254]

The seizure provisions of section 34(a) also apply to counterfeiting of various names and symbols pertaining to the Olympics.[1255]

[C]   Destruction of Infringing Articles

In the case of infringement of a registered mark under section 32, a violation of section 43(a), or a willful violation of section 43(c), a court may order the surrender and destruction of all infringing materials in the defendant's possession, together with all means of making the infringing marks.[1256]

[D]   Cancellation of Federal Registration

Section 37 of the Lanham Act authorizes a court to determine whether a federally registered mark is entitled to continued registration or whether the registration of the mark should be cancelled.[1257] The court's cancellation authority is concurrent with that of the PTO, and may be exercised on the same grounds. Grounds for cancellation are discussed in § 2.12 [A] above.

[E]   Disclaimers

Because courts enjoy a wide range of discretion and flexibility in framing relief for trademark infringement, in some cases a court may appropriately determine that a disclaimer will be sufficient to alleviate the likelihood of confusion arising from the defendant's use of the disputed trademark.[1258] A court is particularly likely to find that a disclaimer is an appropriate remedy

---

[1253] 15 U.S.C. § 1116(d)(10).

[1254] 15 U.S.C. § 1116(d)(11).

[1255] 15 U.S.C. § 1116(d).

[1256] 15 U.S.C. § 1118.

[1257] 15 U.S.C. § 1119. *See, e.g.*, Brittingham v. Jenkins, 914 F.2d 447, 453, 16 U.S.P.Q.2d 1121 (4th Cir. 1990); Loctite Corp. v. National Starch & Chemical Corp., 516 F. Supp. 190, 211 U.S.P.Q. 237 (S.D.N.Y. 1981); Polaroid Corp. v. Berkey Photo, Inc., 425 F. Supp. 605, 193 U.S.P.Q. 183 (D. Del. 1976).

[1258] *See, e.g.*, Champion Spark Plug Co. v. Sanders, 331 U.S. 125 (1947) (finding disclaimer adequate to prevent likelihood of confusion arising from sale of refurbished spark plugs bearing original manufacturer's trademark); Nitro Leisure Prods., L.L.C. v. Acushnet Co., 341 F.3d 1356 (Fed. Cir. 2003) (denying preliminary injunction against sale of refurbished golf balls that bore original manufacturer's mark as well as disclaimer indicating they were refurbished); Soltex Polymer Corp. v. Fortex Indus., Inc., 832 F.2d 1325, 1329 (2d Cir. 1987); Springs Mills, Inc. v. Ultracashmere House, Ltd., 724 F.2d 352, 355 (2d Cir. 1983); Berlitz Schools of Languages v. Everest House, 619 F.2d 211, 215 (2d Cir. 1980); Mushroom Makers, Inc. v. R. G. Barry Corp., 441 F. Supp. 1220 (S.D.N.Y. 1977), *aff'd*, 580 F.2d 44 (2d Cir. 1978), *cert. denied*, 439 U.S. 1116 (1979) (requiring junior

where the likelihood of confusion is modest,[1259] or where other equitable considerations weigh in favor of allowing the junior user to continue its use of the mark — for example, where the mark in question is the legitimate surname of the junior user.[1260]

In many cases, however, courts have held that a disclaimer is inadequate to eliminate the likelihood of confusion. Depending on the circumstances, courts have expressed concern that a disclaimer may not be used consistently,[1261] that it might not be noticed by consumers,[1262] that it will not be incorporated in every channel of communication between consumers and the junior user,[1263] and that, where the likelihood of confusion is particularly strong, a disclaimer might simply be insufficient to completely eliminate the confusion.[1264] Recently, courts have taken notice of academic literature questioning the effectiveness of disclaimers, especially those "which employ brief negator words such as 'no' or 'not,' ";[1265] as a result, some courts have held that the infringer has an affirmative duty to come forward with "evidence sufficient to demonstrate that any proposed material would significantly reduce the likelihood of consumer confusion,"[1266] and some have required the use of more prominent and affirmative disclaimers rather than mere "negator"-type disclaimers.[1267]

---

user of MUSHROOM mark on women's sportswear to disclaim association with MUSHROOM brand of women's footwear).

[1259] *See, e.g.*, Soltex Polymer Corporation v. Fortex Industries, Inc., 832 F.2d 1325 (2d Cir. 1987) (minimal to moderate amount of consumer confusion could be cured effectively by disclaimer).

[1260] *See, e.g.*, Coty, Inc. v. Parfums De Grande Luxe, Inc., 298 F. 865 (2d Cir.), *cert. denied*, 266 U.S. 609 (1924) (allowing defendant to use "Ernest Coty" mark if accompanied by "Not connected with the original Coty"); Taylor Wine Co. v. Bully Hill Vineyards, Inc., 590 F.2d 701 (2d Cir. 1978) (allowing grandson sharing Taylor surname to place his signature on labels of his competing wines); Joseph Scott Co. v Scott Swimming Pools, Inc., 764 F.2d 62 (2d Cir. 1985) (where principals of competing companies were brothers, and junior user split off from family's pool company); G. & C. Merriam Co. v. Saalfield, 198 F. 369 (6th Cir. 1912) (allowing use of "Webster's" on dictionary not affiliated with original publisher); G. & C. Merriam Co. v. Ogilvie, 170 F. 167 (1st Cir. 1909) (similar).

[1261] *See, e.g.*, International Kennel Club, Inc. v. Mighty Star, Inc., 846 F.2d 1079, 1093 (7th Cir. 1988).

[1262] *See, e.g.*, *International Kennel Club*, 846 F.2d at 1093; Gilliam v. American Broadcasting Cos., 538 F.2d 14, 25 n. 13 (2d Cir. 1976); Home Box Office, Inc. v. Showtime/Movie Channel, Inc., 832 F.2d 1311, 1315 (2d Cir. 1987).

[1263] *See, e.g.*, Volkswagenwerk Aktiengesellschaft v. Karadizian, 170 U.S.P.Q. (BNA) 565, 567 (C.D. Cal. 1971).

[1264] *See, e.g.*, *Gilliam*, 538 F.2d at 25 n. 13; Boston Pro Hockey Association v. Dallas Cap & E. Manufacturing, Inc., 510 F.2d 1004, 1013 (5th Cir.), *cert. denied*, 423 U.S. 868 (1975) (holding a proposed disclaimer "insufficient to remedy the illegal confusion"); Marquis Who's Who v. North American Ad Associates, 426 F. Supp. 139, 143 n. 5 (D.D.C. 1976), *aff'd*, 574 F.2d 637, 187 U.S. App. D.C. 426 (D.C. Cir. 1978); United States Jaycees v. Philadelphia Jaycees, 639 F.2d 134, 142 (3d Cir. 1981); Miss Universe, Inc. v. Flesher, 605 F.2d 1130, 1134-35 (9th Cir. 1979).

[1265] Charles of the Ritz Group, Ltd. v. Quality King Distribs., Inc., 832 F.2d 1317, 1324 (2d Cir. 1987) (collecting authorities); *accord* Profitness Phys. Therapy Ctr. v. Pro-Fit Orthopedic & Sports Phys. Therapy P.C., 314 F.3d 62, 70 (2d Cir. 2002); *Home Box Office*, 832 F.2d at 1315-16.

[1266] *See, e.g.*, *Home Box Office*, 832 F.2d at 1316; *accord, Profitness*, 314 F.3d at 71.

[1267] *See, e.g.*, *Charles of the Ritz*, 832 F.2d at 1324 (requiring disclaimer to be prominent and to indicate that parties were competitors, rather than allowing ambiguous "not related to" wording).

§ 3.14   MONETARY AWARDS

[A]   Actual Damages, Defendants' Profits, and Costs

In the case of infringement of a registered mark under section 32(1)(a), a violation of section 43(a) or 43(d), or a willful violation of section 43(c), section 35 of the Lanham Act permits a plaintiff to recover the defendant's profits, the plaintiff's damages, and costs.[1268] However, duplicative recoveries (for example, defendant's profits plus damages representing plaintiff's lost profits) are not permitted.[1269] In an infringement action under section 32(1), a plaintiff can be awarded damages or profits only for infringing activities that took place after the plaintiff became the owner of the federal registration.[1270]

In assessing damages, courts will consider a plaintiff's lost sales, as well as other damage to the plaintiff's goodwill, provided that these were a proximate result of the infringing activity.[1271] The damages award may include the costs of corrective advertising to restore the value that the plaintiff's trademark has lost due to the defendant's infringement; such an award may cover the costs a plaintiff has already incurred, and/or the costs of prospective corrective advertising.[1272]

For example, in a false advertising case under section 43(a), the plaintiff's damages may include (1) lost profits from sales diverted to the defendant, (2) lost profits resulting from sales made at prices reduced as a demonstrated result of the false advertising, (3) the costs of any completed advertising that actually and reasonably responds to the defendant's offending ads, and (4) quantifiable harm to the plaintiff's goodwill, to the extent that completed corrective advertising has not repaired that harm.[1273] Where a plaintiff seeks recovery for lost sales, lost profits, or loss of goodwill, many courts require the plaintiff to demonstrate that the defendant's false statements caused actual confusion in the marketplace.[1274] In contrast, where a false advertising plaintiff seeks recovery for the costs of corrective advertising or other "damage control"

[1268]   15 U.S.C. § 1117(a).

[1269]   *See, e.g.*, United Phosphorus, Ltd. v. Midland Fumigant, Inc., 205 F.3d 1219 (10th Cir. 2000).

[1270]   *See, e.g.*, Reliable Tire Distributors, Inc. v. Kelly Springfield Tire Co., 592 F. Supp. 127 (E.D. Pa. 1984).

[1271]   Ramada Inns, Inc. v. Gadsden Motel Co., 804 F.2d 1562 (11th Cir. 1986); Heaton Distrib. Co. v. Union Tank Car Co., 387 F.2d 477 (8th Cir. 1967); Aladdin Mfg. Co. v. Mantle Lamp Co., 116 F.2d 708 (7th Cir. 1941); Lawrence-Williams Co. v. Societe Enfants Gombault et Cie, 52 F.2d 774 (6th Cir. 1931), *cert. denied*, 285 U.S. 549 (1932): Tillman & Bendel, Inc. v. California Packing Co., 63 F.2d 498 (9th Cir.), *cert. denied*, 290 U.S. 638 (1933).

[1272]   Adray v. Adry-Mart, Inc., 68 F.3d 362 (9th Cir. 1995), *as amended*, 76 F.3d 984, 988-89 (9th Cir. 1996); Zazu Designs v. L'Oreal, S.A., 979 F.2d 499, 506 (7th Cir. 1992); U-Haul Int'l, Inc. v. Jartran, Inc., 793 F.2d 1034, 1041 (9th Cir. 1986); Cher v. Forum Int'l., Ltd., 213 U.S.P.Q. 96, 103 (C.D. Cal.), *aff'd in pertinent part*, 692 F.2d 634, 640 (9th Cir. 1982); Big O Tire Dealers, Inc. v. Goodyear Tire & Rubber Co., 561 F.2d 1365, 1374-76 (10th Cir. 1977); Bellagio v. Denhammer, 2001 U.S. Dist. LEXIS 24764, *11-12 (D. Nev. 2001).

[1273]   ALPO Petfoods, Inc. v. Ralston Purina Co., 913 F.2d 958, 969 (D.C. Cir. 1990).

[1274]   Balance Dynamics Corp. v. Schmitt Indus., Inc., 204 F.3d 683, 690-91 (6th Cir.), *cert. denied*, 531 U.S. 927 (2000).

measures, rather than recovery for "marketplace damage," some courts dispense with the requirement of actual confusion.[1275] One such court explained its reasoning as follows:

> Actual confusion is a prerequisite to an award of such "marketplace damages" because actual confusion tends to show that these hard-to-prove damages probably exist. Yet there is no need to use such proxies with regard to damage control expenses, for the proof of such expenses is in the possession of the plaintiff and is therefore easily produced. Hence, there seems little reason to require "actual confusion" before awarding compensation for damage control expenses, even though such an award is "monetary."[1276]

Prior to 1999, courts interpreted section 35(a) as authorizing an accounting of the infringer's profits in an action for infringement of a registered mark under section 32, or for a violation of section 43(a), only if the defendant acted willfully or in bad faith,[1277] even though section 35(a) did not expressly impose such a requirement. In 1999, however, Congress amended the language of section 35(a) to authorize an award of profits for infringement of a registered mark or for "a violation under section 43(a), or a willful violation under section 43(c)."[1278] As a result of this change, the Third and Fifth Circuits have concluded, by reverse implication, that willfulness is no longer a prerequisite to an award of the defendant's profits for infringement of a registered mark under section 32(1)(a), or for a violation under section 43(a).[1279] A district court in the Ninth Circuit has also adopted this view.[1280] Within the Second Circuit, there is an intra-circuit (indeed, intra-district) split of authority. In the Southern District of New York, one district judge has agreed with the Third and Fifth Circuits,[1281] but four others have reached the opposite conclusion,[1282] and, accordingly, have continued to treat willfulness as a prerequisite to profits recovery for trademark infringement or false designation of origin claims under the Lanham Act. Leading commentator J. Thomas McCarthy suggests that the latter courts have reached

---

[1275] *See, e.g., id.*

[1276] *Id.*

[1277] ALPO Petfoods, Inc. v. Ralston Purina Co., 913 F.2d 958, 968 (D.C. Cir. 1990); George Basch Co. v. Blue Coral, Inc., 968 F.2d 1532 (2d Cir. 1992), *cert. denied,* 506 U.S. 991 (1992); International Star Class Yacht Racing Ass'n v. Tommy Hilfiger U.S.A., 146 F.3d 66 (2d Cir. 1998); Banff, Ltd. v. Colberts, Inc., 996 F.2d 33 (2d Cir. 1993).

[1278] Pub. L. No. 106-43, § 3(b), 113 Stat. 219 (Aug. 5, 1999).

[1279] *See, e.g.,* Banjo Buddies, Inc. v. Renosky, 399 F.3d 168, 174-75 (3d Cir. 2005); Quick Technologies, Inc. v. Sage Group PLC, 313 F.3d 338, 347-48 (5th Cir. 2002).

[1280] R&R Partners, Inc. v. Tovar, 2007 U.S. Dist. LEXIS 29819, *4-5 (D. Nev. 2007).

[1281] Nike, Inc. v. Top Brand Co., 2005 U.S. Dist. LEXIS 42374 (S.D.N.Y. 2005).

[1282] Aedes de Venustas v. Venustas Int'l, LLC, 2008 U.S. Dist. LEXIS 86581 (S.D.N.Y. 2008); Life Services Supps., Inc. v. Natural Organics, Inc., 86 U.S.P.Q.2d (BNA) 1639 (S.D.N.Y. 2007); Louis Vuitton Malletier v. Dooney & Bourke, Inc., 500 F. Supp. 2d 276 (S.D.N.Y. 2007); MasterCard Int'l, Inc. v. First Nat'l Bank of Omaha, Inc., 2004 U.S. Dist. LEXIS 2485 (S.D.N.Y. 2004). A fifth decision from this district acknowledges that willfulness is not a statutory requirement for a profits award under § 43(a), but suggests that in some cases principles of equity will dictate a willfulness prerequisite. Gucci America, Inc. v. Exclusive Imports Int'l, 2007 U.S. Dist. LEXIS 19532, *26 (S.D.N.Y. 2007).

the correct conclusion; he expressly disagrees with the Third and Fifth Circuits, and argues that the only purpose of the 1999 amendment was to clarify that willfulness is a prerequisite to a damages award for dilution under section 43(c).[1283] Other circuits have not squarely addressed this question; as recently as 2004, the Tenth Circuit continued to require either willfulness or actual damage as a prerequisite to a profits award, without considering the effect of the 1999 amendments.[1284]

Subsection (e), which was added to section 35 by the Intellectual Property Protection and Courts Amendments Act of 2004,[1285] provides that:

> In the case of a violation referred to in this section, it shall be a rebuttable presumption that the violation is willful for purposes of determining relief if the violator, or a person acting in concert with the violator, knowingly provided or knowingly caused to be provided materially false contact information to a domain name registrar, domain name registry, or other domain name registration authority in registering, maintaining, or renewing a domain name used in connection with the violation.[1286]

The purpose of this amendment is not entirely clear. Section 35 refers to "willful" violations in two contexts: (1) in limiting damages awards for dilution claims under section 43(c) to cases involving willful dilution,[1287] and (2) in setting a maximum statutory damages award of $1,000,000 for the willful use of a counterfeit mark.[1288] Thus, it would appear that the rebuttable presumption of willfulness arising under subsection (e) applies to dilution claims as well as counterfeiting claims.

In a series of amendments to section 35(a) in 1999[1289] and in 2002,[1290] Congress authorized an award of profits for cybersquatting violations under section 43(d). Because it implemented this amendment by replacing the phrase "a violation under section 1125(a)" with the phrase "a violation under section 1125(a) or (d)," the question arises whether willfulness is a prerequisite to an award of profits under section 43(d), just as that question has arisen with respect to sections 32 and 43(a). No court has addressed this question in the section 43(d) context; however, it seems likely that individual courts will reach the same conclusion in this context that they have reached in the section 43(a) context. On

---

[1283] McCarthy on Trademarks, *supra* note 223, at § 30:62.

[1284] Western Diversified Servs., Inc. v. Hyundai Motor America, Inc., 427 F.3d 1269, 1272-73 (10th Cir. 2004). A district court in the First Circuit reached the same conclusion after full consideration of the 1999 amendments, Hipsaver Co., Inc. v. J.T. Posey Co., 497 F. Supp. 2d 96, 107 (D. Mass. 2007), although the First Circuit itself has declined to decide the question. Venture Tape Corp. v. McGills Glass Warehouse, 540 F.3d 56, 63 (1st Cir. 2008).

[1285] Pub. L. No. 108-482, 108th Cong., 2d Sess. (2004).

[1286] 15 U.S.C. § 1117(e).

[1287] 15 U.S.C. § 1117(a).

[1288] *Id.* § 1117(c)(2).

[1289] Pub. L. No. 106-113, Div. B, § 1000(a)(9), 113 Stat. 1536, 1501A-54 (Nov. 29, 1999).

[1290] Pub. L. No. 107-273, Div. C, Tit. III, § 13207(a), 116 Stat. 1906 (Nov. 2, 2002).

the other hand, because a violation under section 43(d) by definition requires a "bad faith intent to profit," willfulness will probably be found in most cases.

Even if willfulness is no longer required for an award of profits in actions under sections 32(1)(a), 43(a), and 43(d), section 35(a) nonetheless provides that any award of profits, damages, or costs is "subject to the principles of equity." In making this equitable determination, the factors that courts may consider "include, but are not limited to (1) whether the defendant had the intent to confuse or deceive, (2) whether sales have been diverted, (3) the adequacy of other remedies, (4) any unreasonable delay by the plaintiff in asserting his rights, (5) the public interest in making the misconduct unprofitable, and (6) whether it is a case of palming off."[1291] Courts considering such a monetary award may therefore consider a defendant's willfulness or bad faith as one factor in weighing the equities.[1292] Courts typically justify awarding a defendant's profits based on theories of unjust enrichment or deterrence of willful infringement.[1293]

With respect to most Lanham Act claims, courts generally apply a rebuttable presumption that all of the infringer's profits resulted from the infringing activity,[1294] and the burden falls on the infringer to establish the portion of its profits that were not attributable to the infringement.[1295] However, in false advertising cases under section 43(a)(1)(B), some courts have required the plaintiff to prove that the defendant's profits, or the plaintiff's lost sales, were actually caused by the defendant's false statements.[1296]

In establishing the amount of an infringer's profits under the Lanham Act, the plaintiff need only establish the amount of the defendant's sales; the defendant must prove any elements of cost or deduction claimed.[1297]

[1291] Banjo Buddies, Inc. v. Renosky, 399 F.3d 168, 175, 2005 U.S. App. LEXIS 3014, *14 (3d Cir. 2005) (quoting Quick Technologies, Inc. v. Sage Group PLC, 313 F.3d 338, 349 (5th Cir. 2002)) (internal quotation marks and citations omitted); Gucci America, Inc. v. Daffy's Inc., 354 F.3d 228, 241-43 (3d Cir. 2003).

[1292] *See, e.g., Banjo Buddies*, 399 F.3d at 175-76; *Quick Technologies*, 313 F.3d at 349.

[1293] *See, e.g.*, Estate of Bishop v Equinox Int'l Corp., 256 F.3d 1050 10th Cir. 2001), *cert. denied*, 534 U.S. 1130 (2002).

[1294] Mishawaka Rubber & Woolen Mfg. Co. v. S. S. Kresge Co., 316 U.S. 203, 206-07 (1942); Obear-Nester Glass Co. v. United Drug Co., 149 F.2d 671 (8th Cir. 1945), *cert. denied*, 326 U.S. 761 (1945); Century Distilling Co. v. Continental Distilling Corp., 205 F.2d 140, 146 (3d Cir. 1953), *cert. denied*, 346 U.S. 900 (1953).

[1295] *Mishawaka Rubber*, 316 U.S. at 206-07; *see, e.g.*, WMS Gaming, Inc. v. WPC Productions Ltd., 542 F.3d 601 (7th Cir. 2008); Maier Brewing Co. v. Fleischmann Distilling Corp., 390 F.2d 117 (9th Cir. 1968).

[1296] Logan v. Burgers Ozark Country Cured Hams, Inc., 263 F.3d 447, 464-65 (5th Cir. 2001); Balance Dynamics Corp. v. Schmitt Indus., 204 F.3d 683, 695 (6th Cir. 2000).

[1297] 15 U.S.C. § 1117(a); *see, e.g.*, Wynn Oil Co. v. American Way Service Corp., 943 F.2d 595 (6th Cir. 1991).

[B]   Enhanced Damages and Prejudgment Interest

With respect to damages, section 35(a) of the Lanham Act permits a court, "according to the circumstances of the case," to award more than the amount found as actual damages, but not in excess of three times that amount.[1298] Thus, for example, damages representing lost sales and corrective advertising costs are subject to trebling.[1299] However, trebling of damages is normally reserved for cases of willful infringement.[1300]

A different rule applies to an award of defendant's profits: if the court finds that the amount of profits is inadequate or excessive to compensate the plaintiff, the court may award any amount that is just, based on the circumstances of the case.[1301] In either event, the award must be compensatory rather than punitive.[1302]

Under section 35(b), the court must, in the absence of extenuating circumstances, award the plaintiff treble damages or profits (whichever is greater), as well as a reasonable attorney's fee, against a defendant that (1) violates section 32(1)(a) by intentionally using a mark, knowing it to be a counterfeit mark within the meaning of section 34(d), or (2) provides goods or services necessary to the commission of such a violation, with the intent that those goods or services would be used in that violation.[1303] A counterfeit mark is a spurious mark that is "identical with, or substantially indistinguishable from," a mark registered on the Principal Register.[1304]

Although section 35(b) requires a showing that the defendant used a counterfeit mark "knowing such mark . . . is counterfeit," the knowledge requirement will be satisfied if the defendant was willfully blind — that is, if the defendant "failed to inquire further because he was afraid of what the inquiry would yield."[1305] At the court's discretion in such cases, the court may also award prejudgment interest for the period from the date the pleadings were

---

[1298] 15 U.S.C. § 1117(a).

[1299] Thompson v. Haynes, 305 F.3d 1369, 1380 (Fed. Cir. 2002).

[1300] *See, e.g.*, Scovill Mfg. Co. v. United States Electric Mfg. Corp., 47 F. Supp. 619 (C.D.N.Y. 1942).

[1301] 15 U.S.C. § 1117(a); *see* Thompson v. Haynes, 305 F.3d 1369 (Fed. Cir. 2002) (distinguishing enhancement rules for damages and profits under section 1117(a)).

[1302] 15 U.S.C. § 1117(a); *see* ALPO Petfoods, Inc. v. Ralston Purina Co., 997 F.2d 949, 955 (D.C. Cir. 1993) (applying damages enhancement provisions in false advertising context); *see also* ALPO Petfoods, Inc. v. Ralston Purina Co., 913 F.2d 958, 970 & n. 13 (D.C. Cir. 1990) (noting uncertainty as to whether the antipenalty language of section 1117(a) applies only to enhanced awards, or to unenhanced awards as well).

[1303] 15 U.S.C. § 1117(b). Clause (2) was added by the Prioritizing Resources and Organization for Intellectual Property ("Pro IP") Act of 2008, Pub. L. 110-403,122 Stat. 4259 (Oct. 13, 2008).

[1304] 15 U.S.C. §§ 1116(d), 1127. These provisions also apply to counterfeiting of various names and symbols pertaining to the Olympics. *Id.* § 1116(d).

[1305] Louis Vuitton S.A. v. Lee, 875 F.2d 584, 590 (7th Cir. 1989) (*citing* Joint Statement on Trademark Counterfeiting Legislation, 130 Cong. Rec. at H12076-77 (daily ed. Oct. 10, 1984) ("Of course, if the prosecution proves that the defendant was 'willfully blind' to the counterfeit nature of the mark, it will have met its burden of showing 'knowledge' ")).

filed to the date judgment was entered, or for such shorter period as the court deems appropriate.[1306]

In contrast to the Lanham Act, which does not provide for punitive damages, some states allow for recovery of punitive damages for trademark infringement or unfair competition.[1307]

[C]   Attorney's Fees

Section 35(a) provides that, in exceptional cases, a court may award reasonable attorney's fees to the prevailing party, who may be either the plaintiff or the defendant.[1308] Typically, a plaintiff will recover attorney's fees when the infringing conduct was malicious, fraudulent, deliberate, or willful.[1309] In addition, attorney's fees may be awarded to the prevailing party (plaintiff or defendant) when the opponent engaged in bad faith or vexatious litigation,[1310] or litigation misconduct.[1311] However, courts disagree on the standard of proof for establishing that a case is "exceptional." Several courts have required "clear and convincing evidence" of exceptional circumstances,[1312] another has rejected this heightened standard of proof,[1313] and most decisions are simply silent on the question. Courts also disagree on the standard of review applicable to these determinations.[1314]

In contrast to the general rule of section 35(a) requiring exceptional circumstances for an award of attorney's fees, section 35(b) provides that, in the absence of extenuating circumstances, an award of attorney's fees is mandatory for violations of section 32(1)(a) in which the defendant intentionally uses a mark registered on the Principal Register, knowing it to be a counterfeit mark.[1315]

[1306] 15 U.S.C. § 1117(b).

[1307] *See* JCW Invs., Inc. v. Novelty, Inc., 482 F.3d 910 (7th Cir. 2007) (holding that Lanham Act does not preempt punitive damages award under state unfair competition law); Gai Audio of New York, Inc. v. Columbia Broadcasting Sys., Inc., 27 Md. App. 172, 201-03 (1975) (collecting cases).

[1308] 15 U.S.C. § 1117(a).

[1309] Nike, Inc. v. Variety Wholesalers, Inc., 274 F. Supp. 2d 1352 (S.D. Ga. 2003), *aff'd*, 107 Fed. Appx. 183 (11th Cir. 2004); Reader's Digest Assoc. v. Conservative Digest, 821 F.2d 800, 808 (D.C. Cir. 1987); Hard Rock Café, International, Inc. v. Texas Pig Stands, Inc., 951 F.2d 684, 697 (5th Cir. 1992); S. Rep. No. 1400, 93d Cong., 2d Sess., *reprinted in* 1974 U.S.C.C.A.N. 7132, 7136.

[1310] *See, e.g.*, SecuraComm Consulting, Inc. v. Securacom, Inc., 224 F.3d 273 (3d Cir. 2000) (award to plaintiff); Universal City Studios, Inc. v. Nintendo, Inc., 797 F.2d 70, 77 (2d Cir.) (award to defendant), *cert. denied*, 479 U.S. 987 (2d Cir. 1986); Mattel, Inc. v. Walking Mountain Prods., 353 F.3d 792, 816 (9th Cir. 2003).

[1311] TE-TA-MA Truth Foundation-Family of URI, Inc. v. World Church of the Creator, 392 F.3d 248, 261-63 (7th Cir. 2004); *SecuraComm Consulting*, 224 F.3d at 281-82; Patsy's Brand, Inc. v. I.O.B. Realty, Inc., 317 F.3d 209 (2d Cir. 2003).

[1312] *See, e.g.*, Finance Investment Co. v. Geberit AG, 165 F.3d 526, 533 (7th Cir. 1998); Proctor & Gamble Co. v. Amway Corp., 280 F.3d 519, 526 (5th Cir. 2002).

[1313] Eagles, Ltd. v. Am. Eagle Found., 356 F.3d 724, 729 (6th Cir. 2004).

[1314] *Compare* Earthquake Sound Corp. v. Bumper Indus., 352 F.3d 1210, 1216-1219 (9th Cir. 2003) (applying abuse of discretion standard), *with* Tamko Roofing Prods., Inc. v. Ideal Roofing Co., Ltd., 282 F.3d 23, 29 (1st Cir. 2002) (applying de novo review).

[1315] 15 U.S.C. § 1117(b).

For this purpose, a counterfeit mark is "a spurious mark that is identical with, or substantially indistinguishable from" a mark that is registered on the Principal Register.[1316]

A recent Ninth Circuit decision holds that attorney's fees cannot be awarded to a plaintiff that elects statutory damages under section 35(c) in place of actual damages or profits under section 35(a), reasoning that subsection (c) makes no provision for attorney's fees, and subsection (b) authorizes attorney's fees only for awards under subsection (a).[1317] It can also be argued, however, that nothing in section 35 expressly *precludes* an award of attorney's fees together with statutory damages. No other circuit has squarely addressed this issue. District courts that have considered the question have reached varying conclusions, and others have awarded both statutory damages and attorney's fees without even considering whether this is permitted under the statute. The Third Circuit has held that attorney's fees may be awarded to a cybersquatting plaintiff that elects statutory damages under section 35(d) in a section 43(d) action[1318] (a conclusion with which the Ninth Circuit would probably disagree), but it reached this conclusion without analyzing the statutory language that the Ninth Circuit found to be problematic.

[D]   Statutory Damages

In two situations, a prevailing plaintiff may elect, any time before the trial court renders final judgment, to recover statutory damages in place of actual damages and profits.

In a case involving the use of a counterfeit mark as defined in section 34(d),[1319] the amount of statutory damages may be such amount as the court considers just, but it may not be less than $1,000 or more than $200,000[1320] per counterfeit mark per type of goods or services sold, offered for sale, or distributed. However, if the use of the counterfeit mark was willful, the maximum award increases to $2,000,000 per counterfeit mark per type of goods or services sold, offered for sale, or distributed.[1321]

In a cybersquatting case under section 43(d)(1), the amount of statutory damages must be not less than $1,000 and not more than $100,000 per domain name, as the court considers just.[1322]

[1316] 15 U.S.C. §§ 1116(d), 1127. These provisions also apply to counterfeiting of various names and symbols pertaining to the Olympics. *Id.* § 1116(d).

[1317] K & N Eng'g, Inc. v. Bulat, 510 F.3d 1079, 1082 (9th Cir. 2007).

[1318] Shields v. Zuccarini, 254 F.3d 476, 481-82 (3d Cir. 2001).

[1319] 15 U.S.C. § 1116(d).

[1320] Before October 13, 2008, the effective date of the Pro IP Act, these amounts were $500 and $100,000, respectively.

[1321] 15 U.S.C. § 1117(c); *see, e.g.,* Taylor Made Golf Co. v. MJT Consulting Group, 265 F. Supp. 2d 732 (N.D. Tex. 2003) (denying statutory damages absent evidence that counterfeiting was knowing and willful). The $2,000,000 maximum replaces the $1,000,000 maximum that preceded the enactment of the Pro IP Act, which took effect on October 13, 2008.

[1322] 15 U.S.C. § 1117(d); *see, e.g.,* Bellagio v. Denhammer, 2001 U.S. Dist. LEXIS 24764, *12 (D. Nev. 2001).

As noted in § 3.14 [C] above, the Ninth Circuit has held that if a plaintiff elects statutory damages, an award of attorney's fees is precluded,[1323] but the correctness of this conclusion is debatable.

Although it is well settled that the Seventh Amendment right to a jury trial applies to awards of actual damages in trademark cases, only recently have courts begun to apply this rule to statutory damages. However, based on the Supreme Court's ruling in a 1998 copyright infringement case, it now appears that the Seventh Amendment right to a jury trial applies to an award of statutory damages under the Lanham Act. In *Feltner v. Columbia Pictures Television, Inc.*,[1324] the Court held that if a defendant elects statutory damages in a copyright infringement suit, the defendant is entitled to have a jury determine the amount of the award, because damages are a legal remedy rather than an equitable one. Although there is surprisingly little authority on the question, the two courts that have addressed this issue in the Lanham Act context agree that *Feltner* applies.[1325]

[E]   Enhanced Monetary Awards in Counterfeiting Cases

As is evident from the preceding materials, monetary awards arising from the use of counterfeit marks are more generous than those arising from other infringements of registered marks, in several respects:

(1)   Attorney's fees are mandatory (absent extenuating circumstances) in counterfeiting cases,[1326] but are available for other infringements only in exceptional cases;[1327]

(2)   Treble damages or profits are mandatory (absent extenuating circumstances) in counterfeiting cases,[1328] but enhancements of damages are left to the court's discretion in other infringement cases;[1329]

(3)   Prejudgment interest is available only in counterfeiting cases;[1330] and

(4)   Statutory damages are available for counterfeiting claims[1331] (as well as cybersquatting claims, under section 43(d)[1332]), but not for other infringements.

[1323]   *K & N Eng'g*, 510 F.3d at 1082.

[1324]   523 U.S. 340, 353-54 (1998).

[1325]   Bar-Meir v. North Am. Die Casting Ass'n, 55 Fed. Appx. 389, 390-91 (8th Cir. 2003) (per curiam); Microsoft Corp. v. Ion Technologies Corp., 2003 U.S. Dist. LEXIS 9946, *20 (D. Minn. 2003).

[1326]   15 U.S.C. § 1117(b).

[1327]   *Id.* § 1117(a).

[1328]   *Id.* § 1117(b).

[1329]   *Id.* § 1117(a).

[1330]   *Id.* § 1117(b).

[1331]   *Id.* § 1117(c).

[1332]   *Id.* § 1117(d).

In order to benefit from these enhancements, owners of registered marks that have been infringed have an incentive to characterize their section 32(1) claims as counterfeiting claims rather than as mere infringements. As defined in the Lanham Act, however, a defendant's mark is a "counterfeit" mark only if it is "identical with, or substantially indistinguishable from," the plaintiff's registered mark.[1333] A defendant's mark may be similar enough to lead to a likelihood of confusion (under the traditional multi-factor analysis), and yet may not be so similar as to be "substantially indistinguishable" from the plaintiff's mark. Accordingly, courts have rejected plaintiffs' efforts to characterize infringing marks as counterfeits when the marks, while similar, are nonetheless distinguishable.[1334]

[F]   The Requirement of Marking or Actual Notice

In an action for infringement of a federally registered mark under section 32 of the Lanham Act, section 29 provides that profits or damages may be recovered only if the defendant had notice of the registration.[1335] The notice requirement may be satisfied by either statutory notice or actual notice. The requirement of statutory notice is satisfied when the mark is accompanied by the words "Registered in U.S. Patent and Trademark Office," or "Reg. U.S. Pat. & Tm. Off.," or the (r) symbol.[1336] In the absence of statutory notice, damages or profits for infringement may be recovered for infringing acts that took place after the defendant received actual notice of the registration.[1337]

Because the notice requirement of section 29 applies only to infringement actions involving registered marks, it does not apply to a section 43(a) claim involving an unregistered mark.

One court has held that the marking requirement also does not apply to recovery of statutory damages for counterfeiting under section 35(c),[1338] because the definition of a counterfeit mark in section 34(d)(1)(B)(i)[1339] does not require that the defendant have notice that the mark is registered.[1340]

[1333] *Id.* § 1116(d), 1127.

[1334] *See, e.g.,* Louis Vuitton Malletier v. Haute Diggity Dog, LLC, 507 F.3d 252 (4th Cir. 2007) ("CV" versus "LV," and "Chewy Vuiton" versus "Louis Vuitton" — not substantially indistinguishable); Colgate-Palmolive Co. v. J.M.D. All-Star Import & Export, Inc., 486 F. Supp. 2d 286 (S.D.N.Y. 2007) ("Colddate" versus "Colgate," "Cavity Fighter" versus "Cavity Protection" — not substantially indistinguishable).

[1335] 15 U.S.C. § 1111.

[1336] *Id.*

[1337] *Id.*; Stark Bros. Nurseries & Orchards Co. v. Stark, 255 U.S. 50 (1921); Treasure Imports, Inc. v. Henry Amdur & Sons, Inc., 127 F.2d 3 (2d Cir. 1942); G. Heileman Brewing Co. v. Independent Brewing Co., 191 F. 489 (9th Cir. 1911); Bambu Sales, Inc. v. Sultana Crackers, Inc., 683 F. Supp. 899 (E.D.N.Y. 1988); Scovill Mfg. Co. v. United States Elec. Mfg. Corp., 47 F. Supp. 619 (S.D.N.Y. 1942).

[1338] 15 U.S.C. § 1117(c).

[1339] *Id.* § 1116(d)(1)(B)(i).

[1340] Playboy Enterprises, Inc. v. Universal Tel-A-Talk, Inc., 1999 U.S. Dist. LEXIS 6124 (E.D. Pa. Apr. 26, 1999).

Failure to provide notice of registration does not preclude recovery of attorney's fees.[1341]

Although the "TM" and "SM" symbols have no legal significance, merchants sometimes use them to assert trademark status for their unregistered trademarks and service marks, respectively, and to foster the development of secondary meaning if their marks are not inherently distinctive.

[G] Limited Availability of Damages Under Federal Dilution Law

Ordinarily, injunctive relief under section 34[1342] of the Lanham Act is the sole remedy available for dilution of a famous mark under section 43(c)(1).[1343] However, if the owner of the mark also establishes that the defendant's use of a dilutive mark was willful, then, subject to the principles of equity and the discretion of the court, the full array of remedies under section 35(a)[1344] (damages, profits, costs, and, in exceptional cases, attorneys fees) and section 36[1345] (destruction of infringing articles) are available.[1346] In this context, the meaning of willfulness was revised in the 2006 TDRA; thus, the rules governing remedies for willful dilution depend on whether the willful conduct commenced before and after the effect date of this amendment (October 6, 2006). These standards are discussed in §§ 3.07[I] - [J] above.

[H] False or Fraudulent Registration

Section 38 of the Lanham Act permits any person injured by another party's procurement of a false or fraudulent federal trademark registration to bring a civil action for damages.[1347] As interpreted by the Tenth Circuit, section 38 requires a plaintiff to prove that: (1) the registrant made a representation to the PTO during the registration process that was false and material, (2) the registrant knew or believed that its representation was false, (3) the registrant intended to induce action or forbearance in reliance on the false representation, (4) the PTO reasonably relied on the false representation, and (5) the plaintiff's damages resulted from this reliance.[1348]

[1341] Schroeder v. Lotito, 747 F.2d 801 (1st Cir. 1984).

[1342] 15 U.S.C. § 1116.

[1343] *Id.* § 1125(c)(1).

[1344] *Id.* § 1117(a).

[1345] *Id.* § 1118.

[1346] *Id.* § 1125(c)(2); *see, e.g.,* Sporty's Farm, L.L.C. v. Sportsman's Market, Inc., 202 F.3d 489, 500 (2d Cir.) (upholding, under clear error standard of review, district court's finding that dilution was not willful), *cert. denied,* 530 U.S. 1262 (2000).

[1347] 15 U.S.C. § 1120.

[1348] San Juan Prods., Inc. v. San Juan Pools, Inc., 849 F.2d 468, 473 (10th Cir. 1988) (citing McCarthy on Trademarks, *supra* note 223, at § 31:21).

§ 3.15 LIMITATIONS ON REMEDIES AGAINST CERTAIN DEFENDANTS

[A] Makers of Labels, Signs, Packaging, or Advertisements

Section 32(1)(b) of the Lanham Act imposes infringement liability on parties that do no more than "reproduce, counterfeit, copy, or colorably imitate a registered mark" and apply that mark to labels, signs, packaging, or advertisements intended to be used in connection with goods or services offered to the public, if such use is likely to cause confusion, mistake, or deception.[1349] However, it also imposes a limitation on the remedies to which such parties are subject. Specifically, a party found to have infringed a registered mark under section 32(1)(b) is not liable for damages or profits unless that party committed the infringing acts "with knowledge that such imitation is intended to be used to cause confusion, or to cause mistake, or to deceive."[1350] Thus, those who violate section 32(1)(b) may be enjoined from continuing the infringing activity regardless of their state of mind,[1351] but will not be subject to damages or an accounting of profits unless they know that their work product will be used in an infringing activity.

[B] Printers and Publishers

Section 32(2) limits the remedies available to a plaintiff bringing a Lanham Act claim (under section 32(1), 43(a), or 43(d)) against a party that is engaged solely in the printing or publishing of infringing materials. Section 32(2) does not create an independent cause of action against printers and publishers; it only limits their liability.[1352]

Two of these provisions, subsections (A) and (B), apply only to defendants that qualify as "innocent infringers" or "innocent violators." In this context, the term "violator" refers specifically to a party that is liable for violating section 43(a),[1353] as distinguished from an "infringer" of a registered mark under section 32(1).

Under section 32(2)(A), if a defendant is engaged solely in the business of printing the mark or violating matter for others, and qualifies as an innocent infringer or an innocent violator, the plaintiff's remedies are limited to an injunction against future printing.[1354]

[1349] 15 U.S.C. § 1114(1)(b).

[1350] *Id.*

[1351] *See, e.g.*, Union Tank Car Co. v. Lindsay Soft Water Corp. of Omaha, Inc., 257 F. Supp. 510, 517 (D.C. Neb. 1966) (enjoining telephone company from accepting yellow pages advertising that contained infringing mark), *aff'd*, 387 F.2d 477 (8th Cir. 1967).

[1352] Lockheed Martin Corp. v. Network Solutions, Inc., 194 F.3d 980, 985 (9th Cir. 1999); Lockheed Martin Corp. v. Network Solutions, Inc., 141 F. Supp. 2d 648 (N.D. Tex. 2001); Barrios v. American Thermal Instruments, Inc., 712 F. Supp. 611, 620 (S.D. Ohio 1988).

[1353] 15 U.S.C. § 1114(2)(E).

[1354] *Id.* § 1114(2)(A).

If the infringement is contained in paid advertising material in a newspaper, magazine, or similar periodical, or in an electronic communication defined in 18 U.S.C. § 2510(12), and the defendant is an innocent infringer or innocent violator, limitations on remedies are imposed by sections 32(2)(B) and (C). Section 32(2)(B) limits the plaintiff's remedies to an injunction against the presentation of this advertising matter in future issues of the periodical(s) or future transmissions of such electronic communications. Section 32(2)(C) imposes an additional limitation, providing that injunctive relief in these situations will not be available where it would delay the delivery of the periodical or electronic transmission. This denial of injunctive relief applies only if the delay would arise from the customary method of delivery or transmission "in accordance with sound business practice," and not from any method or device adopted to evade the injunction.

The Lanham Act does not define what it means to be an "innocent" infringer or violator. Some courts have held that innocence is established by the absence of "actual malice" in the defamation sense; under this standard, a defendant qualifies as innocent unless he or she acted with knowledge of the infringement or with reckless disregard as to whether the material was infringing.[1355] Other courts take an objective approach that disregards the defendant's state of mind, treating the defendant as innocent if his or her conduct is "reasonable."[1356]

[C]   Domain Name Registration Authorities

Section 32(2)(D) limits the liability of domain name registration authorities arising from certain actions they may take in response to infringement or dilution claims brought against domain names. The purpose of subsections (D)(i)-(ii) is "to encourage domain name registrars . . . to work with trademark owners to prevent cybersquatting through a limited exemption from liability for domain name registrars . . . that suspend, cancel, or transfer domain names pursuant to a court order or in the implementation of a reasonable policy prohibiting cybersquatting."[1357]

Subsection (D)(ii) provides that, in general, registration authorities are immune from both monetary and injunctive relief if they refuse to register a domain name, remove it from registration, or transfer, temporarily disable, or cancel a domain name either: (1) in compliance with a court order under section 43(d) (the cybersquatting provisions of the Lanham Act), or (2) pursuant to a "reasonable policy" under which they prohibit registration of domain names that are identical or confusingly similar to, or dilutive of, another's mark.[1358] If a domain name is suspended, disabled, or transferred under a policy of the latter

---

[1355] *E.g.*, Gucci Am., Inc. v. Hall & Assocs., 135 F. Supp. 2d 409, 420 (S.D.N.Y. 2001); World Wrestling Fed. Inc. v. Posters Inc., 58 U.S.P.Q.2d (BNA) 1783, 1785 (N.D. Ill. 2000); NBA Props. v. Untertainment Records LLC, 1999 U.S. Dist. LEXIS 7780 (S.D.N.Y. 1999).

[1356] *E.g.*, Dial One of the Mid-South, Inc. v. Bellsouth Telecomm'ns, Inc., 269 F.3d 523, 525 (5th Cir. 2001).

[1357] Sallen v. Corinthians Licenciamentos LTDA, 273 F.3d 14, 28 (1st Cir. 2001) (quoting H.R. Conf. Rep. No. 106-464, at 116 (1999)); *see also* H.R. Rep. No. 106-412, at 15.

[1358] 15 U.S.C. § 1114(2)(D)(ii).

sort, subsection (D)(v) provides that the domain name registrant may, upon notice to the trademark owner, bring a civil action to establish that its use or registration of the domain name is not unlawful,[1359] and if the action succeeds, the court may issue an injunction reactivating the domain name or transferring it back to the domain name registrant.[1360] Section (D)(v) is designed to prevent overreaching by trademark owners who seek to use ICANN's UDRP process to compel domain name registrants to transfer their rights to lawfully-held domain names, a process sometimes referred to as "reverse domain name hijacking,"[1361] and "to preserve the rights of Internet users to engage in protected expression online and to make lawful uses of others' trademarks in cyberspace."[1362]

Furthermore, if the domain name registration authority has undertaken either of the actions authorized by subsection (D)(ii) based on a "knowing and material representation" by another person regarding the infringing or dilutive nature of the domain name, subsection (D)(iv) provides that the party making the misrepresentation is liable for any damages, including costs and attorneys' fees, incurred by the domain name registrant as a result of such action, and permits the court to issue an injunction reactivating the domain name or transferring it back to the domain name registrant.[1363] Subsection D(iv) was designed to "protect[] the rights of domain name registrants against overreaching trademark owners."[1364] Whereas subsections (D)(i) and (ii) facilitate enforcement of anti-cybersquatting policies by encouraging cooperation between registrars and trademark owners, subsection (D)(iv) "provides a counterweight to ensure that this cooperation does not result in reverse domain name hijacking, whereby trademark holders abuse anticybersquatting provisions to take domain names from rightful, noninfringing registrants."[1365]

Notwithstanding the general bar on injunctive relief against domain name registration authorities under subsection (D)(ii), injunctive relief may be imposed on a registration authority that has: (1) failed to comply with the requirement of section 43(d)(2)(D) that it expeditiously deposit with the court those documents that enable the court to establish its control or authority over the domain name; (2) transferred, suspended, or modified the domain name

---

[1359] The statutory language authorizing this civil action is ambiguous, stating that the domain name registrant may file a civil action to establish that the domain name "is not unlawful under this Act," without specifying whether the "Act" refers to the entire Lanham Act or only the Anticybersquatting Consumer Protection Act of 1999, which consists primarily of 15 U.S.C. § 1125(d) (section 43(d) of the Lanham Act). *See* Storey v. Cello Holdings, L.L.C., 347 F.3d 370, 382 n.9 (2d Cir. 2003) (noting conflicting authorities).

[1360] 15 U.S.C. § 1114(2)(D)(v); *See, e.g.*, Sallen v. Corinthians Licenciamentos LTDA, 273 F.3d 14 (1st Cir. 2001).

[1361] *Sallen*, 273 F.3d at 29; *accord* 145 Cong. Rec. S10,516 (1999) (statement of Sen. Hatch).

[1362] 145 Cong. Rec. S10,515 (1999) (statement of Sen. Hatch).

[1363] 15 U.S.C. § 1114(2)(D)(iv).

[1364] *Sallen*, 273 F.3d at 29 (quoting H.R. Conf. Rep. No. 106-464, at 117).

[1365] *Id.*

during the pendency of the legal action, except upon court order; or (3) willfully failed to comply with any such court order.[1366]

Under subsection (D)(iii), registration authorities are not liable for damages under section 32 for registering or maintaining a domain name for another party absent a showing of bad faith intent to profit from the registration or maintenance of that domain name.[1367]

[D] The Family Movie Act of 2005

The Family Movie Act of 2005 (FMA)[1368] added another limited-liability provision to the Lanham Act, section 32(3),[1369] which provides that parties engaged in certain types of unauthorized film editing are immune from liability for infringement of any right under the Lanham Act.

Section 32(3) is a companion provision to section 110(11) of the Copyright Act (Title 17), also added by the FMA, which permits:

> the making imperceptible, by or at the direction of a member of a private household, of limited portions of audio or video content of a motion picture, during a performance in or transmitted to that household for private home viewing, from an authorized copy of the motion picture, or the creation or provision of a computer program or other technology that enables such making imperceptible and that is designed and marketed to be used, at the direction of a member of a private household, for such making imperceptible, if no fixed copy of the altered version of the motion picture is created by such computer program or other technology.[1370]

This provision was designed to preclude copyright infringement claims against parties that make and distribute software that enables home viewers of a DVD to "skip" or "mute" specific portions of a motion picture that might be considered offensive.[1371]

Section 32(3) provides that the activities that are permitted by section 110(11) of the Copyright Act will not give rise to liability for violation of any right under the Lanham Act.[1372] However, it also imposes certain conditions on this immunity. Specifically, a manufacturer, licensee, or licensor of the technology permitted by the FMA is immune from suit under the Lanham Act only if it "ensures that the technology provides a clear and conspicuous notice at the

---

[1366] 15 U.S.C. § 1114(2)(D)(i)(II).

[1367] *Id.* § 1114(2)(D)(iii).

[1368] Pub. L. No. 109-9, Title II, § 202(b), 119 Stat. 223 (April 27, 2005).

[1369] 15 U.S.C. § 1114(3).

[1370] 17 U.S.C. § 110(11), added by P.L. 109-9, Title II, § 202(a), 119 Stat. 223 (April 27, 2005).

[1371] *See* Gail H. Cline, *On a ClearPlay, You Can See Whatever: Copyright and Trademark Issues Arising from Unauthorized Film Editing*, 27 Hastings Comm. & Ent. L. J. (Comm/Ent) 567, 611-14 (2005) (discussing legislative history of FMA).

[1372] 15 U.S.C. § 1114(3)(A).

beginning of each performance that the performance of the motion picture is altered from the performance intended by the director or copyright holder of the motion picture."[1373]

[E]   Remedies against Federal and State Governments

Under section 40 of the Lanham Act, the federal government and persons acting on its behalf are subject to the full array of remedies for Lanham Act violations.

Although section 40 contains a similar provision for state governments, the Eleventh Amendment makes this provision largely ineffective unless the Lanham Act claims are adjudicated in a state court. Eleventh Amendment immunity does not, however, extend to state and county governments, except where they act as an arm of the state.[1374] For a more detailed discussion of Eleventh Amendment immunity, see § 3.12 [J] above.

§ 3.16   CRIMINAL PENALTIES

[A]   Counterfeit Marks

Increased concerns regarding infringement of registered marks led Congress in 1984 to enact criminal penalties for counterfeiting in the Trademark Counterfeiting Act,[1375] which is codified in 18 U.S.C. § 2320. Section 2320 imposes criminal penalties on "[w]hoever intentionally traffics or attempts to traffic in goods or services and knowingly uses a counterfeit mark on or in connection with such goods or services."[1376]

Penalties for individuals include a fine of up to $2 million and/or up to 10 years in prison; for corporate violators, the penalty is a fine of up to $5 million. In the case of a subsequent violation following a conviction, an individual may be fined up to $5 million and/or imprisoned for up to 20 years, and a corporation may be fined up to $15 million.[1377] The government may also obtain an order for destruction of the infringing articles.[1378] All of the defenses otherwise available under the Lanham Act are equally available to a criminal defendant under section 2320.[1379]

For purposes of section 2320, a "counterfeit mark" is defined as a mark: (1) that is used in connection with trafficking in goods or services; (2) that is identical with, or substantially indistinguishable from, a mark registered for

---

[1373] *Id.* § 1114(3)(B). This requirement applies only to technology manufactured more than 180 days after the FMA's effective date of April 27, 2005. *Id.* § 1114(3)(C).

[1374] Monell v. Dep't of Soc. Servs., 436 U.S. 658, 690 n. 54 (1978); Mt. Healthy City Sch. Dist. Bd. of Educ. v. Doyle, 429 U.S. 274, 280 (1977).

[1375] Pub. L. No. 98-473, 98 Stat. 1837 (1984).

[1376] 18 U.S.C. § 2320(a); *see* United States v. Sultan, 115 F.3d 321, 325 (5th Cir. 1997).

[1377] 18 U.S.C. § 2320(a).

[1378] *Id.* § 2320(b).

[1379] *Id.* § 2320(c).

those goods or services on the Principal Register, and in use, whether or not the defendant knew the mark was so registered; and (3) the use of which is likely to cause confusion, to cause mistake, or to deceive.[1380] It has been held that the government must establish that the defendant had knowledge or intent with respect to every element of this definition.[1381]

Counterfeit marks do not include "any mark or designation used in connection with goods or services of which the manufacturer or producer was, at the time of the manufacture or production in question authorized to use the mark or designation for the type of goods or services so manufactured or produced, by the holder of the right to use such mark or designation."[1382] However, counterfeit marks do include genuine trademarks that are attached to the packaging of products that were not made by or under license from the trademark owner.[1383]

Courts generally apply the same likelihood-of-confusion analysis in analyzing section 2320 violations that they apply to infringement actions under the Lanham Act, and have considered both point-of-sale and post-sale confusion.[1384]

Because section 2320(a) requires that the defendant both traffic in goods or services and use a counterfeit mark in connection with those goods or services, it has been held that a defendant who merely traffics in counterfeit labels or tags, unattached to any goods, does not violate section 2320, both because labels or tags are not "goods," and because a spurious mark is not counterfeit unless the defendant used it in connection with the goods or services for which the genuine mark is registered.[1385]

The penalties of forfeiture, destruction and restitution also apply to proceedings under section 2320.[1386]

All defenses, affirmative defenses, and limitations on remedies under the Lanham Act apply to prosecutions under section 2320, and the defendant must prove them by a preponderance of the evidence.[1387]

[1380] *Id.* § 2320(e)(1)(A). Section 2320(e)(1)(B) extends coverage also to counterfeiting of Olympics trademarks, under 36 U.S.C. § 220506.

[1381] United States v. Infurnari, 647 F. Supp. 57 (W.D.N.Y. 1986).

[1382] 18 U.S.C. § 2320(e)(1).

[1383] United States v. Petrosian, 126 F.3d 1232 (9th Cir. 1997), *cert. denied*, 522 U.S. 1138 (1998).

[1384] *See, e.g.*, United States v. Foote, 413 F.3d 1240, 1246 (10th Cir. 2005); United States v Hon, 904 F.2d 803 (2d Cir. 1990), *cert. denied*, 498 U.S. 1069 (1991); United States v. Torkington, 812 F.2d 1347 (11th Cir. 1987); United States v. Infurnari, 647 F. Supp. 57 (W.D.N.Y. 1986).

[1385] United States v. Giles, 213 F.3d 1247, 1251-53 (10th Cir. 2000) (noting, however, that such a defendant might be charged with "aiding and abetting" a party that used the labels in violation of § 2320). *But see* United States v. Nunez, 127 F. Supp. 2d 53 (D.P.R. 2000) (treating counterfeit tax stamps as "goods for purposes of § 2320); *cf.* Boston Professional Hockey Ass'n v. Dallas Cap & Emblem Mfg., Inc., 510 F.2d 1004 (5th Cir. 1975) (treating "patches" bearing sports team logos, which purchasers could sew onto jackets or caps, as "goods" for purposes of civil liability for infringement of registered marks under section 32 of Lanham Act).

[1386] 18 U.S.C. §§ 2320(b), 2323.

[1387] 18 U.S.C. § 2320(c).

[B]   Counterfeit Labels

In the Anti-Counterfeiting Amendments Act of 2004,[1388] Congress amended section 2318 of title 18 of the United States Code to provide both criminal and civil penalties for trafficking in counterfeit labels, documentation, or packaging designed to accompany copyrighted works; such counterfeit labels and packaging facilitate the distribution of pirated copies of such works. Specifically, section 2318 applies to knowingly trafficking in counterfeit physical documentation or packaging, or counterfeit or illicit labels, that are designed to accompany any of the following: a phonorecord, a copy of a computer program, a copy of a motion picture or other audiovisual work, a copy of a literary work, a copy of a pictorial, graphic, or sculptural work, a work of visual art, or documentation or packaging.[1389] "Illicit" labels, for this purpose, are certificates, licensing documents, registration cards, or similar labeling components that are genuine rather than counterfeit, and that are ordinarily used by copyright owners to identify authorized copies of their works, but that are being distributed separately from the authorized copies of these works, without the authority of the copyright owner, or that have been knowingly falsified to designate a larger number of licensed users or copies than the copyright owner has authorized.[1390]

While section 2318 is not limited to counterfeit labels that display registered marks, it applies only to labels, documentation, and packaging that are associated with the specified categories of copyrightable works; its purpose is to enhance the remedies available for unauthorized duplication and distribution of such works. It provides both criminal penalties and civil remedies.[1391]

PART IX:
ADJUDICATION

§ 3.17   SUBJECT MATTER JURISDICTION

Plaintiffs alleging violations of trademark or unfair competition laws may generally combine their federal and state claims and bring those claims either in federal or state court.

Federal and state courts have concurrent subject matter jurisdiction to adjudicate claims arising under sections 32, 43(a), 43(c), and 43(d) of the Lanham Act.[1392] Note, however, that an *in rem* action under section 43(d) should be

---

[1388] Intellectual Property Protection and Courts Amendments Act of 2004, Title I, Pub. L. 108-482, 108th Cong., 2d Sess. (Dec. 23, 2004), 118 Stat. 3915.

[1389] 18 U.S.C. § 2318(a).

[1390] *Id.* § 2318(b)(4).

[1391] *Id.* § 2318(a), (f). Criminal penalties include fines and/or imprisonment for up to 5 years. *Id.* § 2318(a).

[1392] 15 U.S.C. § 1121(a) (granting original and appellate jurisdiction to federal courts, but not exclusively); *see, e.g.,* Aquatherm Indus. v. Florida Power & Light Co., 84 F.3d 1388, 1394 (11th Cir. 1996); Scientific Tech., Inc. v. Stanford Telecomm., Inc. (N.D. Cal. 1988); La Chemise Lacoste v.

brought only in a federal district court, because only the latter is empowered to award the statutory remedy under section 43(d)(2)(D). Decisions of the federal district courts in trademark and unfair competition matters are appealable to the regional circuit courts of appeal.

Claims arising under state statutes or common law can be adjudicated in federal courts only under two circumstances: (1) where there is diversity of citizenship between the parties and the amount in controversy exceeds $75,000;[1393] or (2) where the complaint also includes federal claims, in which case the federal court will hear the state claims pursuant to its pendent jurisdiction.[1394] Because federal trademark and unfair competition laws closely parallel their state counterparts, trademark and unfair competition plaintiffs ordinarily have no difficulty pleading a Lanham Act violation that enables them to invoke federal court jurisdiction.

In contrast, federal courts have exclusive jurisdiction over claims arising from PTO decisions involving trademark registrations. Decisions of the Trademark Trial and Appeals Board (TTAB), which conducts opposition and cancellation proceedings and hears appeals from registration denials, can be appealed by either of two routes: (1) by direct appeal, on a closed record, to the United States Court of Appeal for the Federal Circuit,[1395] or (2) by filing a civil action in a federal district court,[1396] in which case the review is de novo.[1397]

§ 3.18 STANDING

[A] Standing to Cancel or Oppose Federal Registration

The standing rules for cancelling a registered mark are the same as those for opposing a registration.[1398] In general, a party has standing only if it has "a real commercial interest in its own marks and a reasonable basis for its belief that it would be damaged" by the registration.[1399] For example, courts have held that this standard is satisfied where: (1) the trademark for which cancellation is

---

Alligator Co., 506 F.2d 339 (3d Cir. 1974), *cert. denied*, 421 U.S. 937 (1975); Pennsylvania State University v. University Orthopedics, Ltd., 706 A.2d 863, n. 2 (Pa. Super. 1998); Mastro Plastics Corp. v. Emenee Indus., Inc., 19 App. Div. 2d 600, 240 N.Y.S.2d 624 (1st Dept. 1963), *aff'd*, (1964) 14 N.Y.2d 498 (1964); Dell Pub. Co. v. Stanley Pubs., Inc., 9 N.Y.2d 126 (1961); Brown & Bigelow v Remembrance Advertising Products, Inc., 279 App. Div. 410, 110 N.Y.S.2d 441 (1952), *aff'd*, 304 N.Y. 909 (1953); Thomas J. Valentino, Inc. v. Majar Discs, Inc., 138 N.Y.S.2d 494 (Sup. 1955).

[1393] 28 U.S.C. § 1332(a); *see, e.g.*, Cohn v. Petsmart, Inc., 281 F.3d 837 (9th Cir. 2002).

[1394] *See, e.g.*, Lone Star Steakhouse & Saloon, Inc. v. Longhorn Steaks, Inc., 106 F.3d 355 (11th Cir. 1997). The decision to exercise pendent jurisdiction, however, is discretionary. *See, e.g.*, Travelers Ins. Co. v. Keeling, 996 F.2d 1485, 1490 (2d Cir. 1993) (addressing the discretion to exercise jurisdiction over state law claims); United Mine Workers of Am. v. Gibbs, 383 U.S. 715, 726 (1966); Christopher D. Smithers Found., Inc. v. St. Lukes-Roosevelt Hosp. Ctr., 2001 U.S. Dist. LEXIS 9293, *16 (S.D.N.Y. 2001).

[1395] 15 U.S.C. § 1071(a).

[1396] *Id.* § 1071(b).

[1397] *See, e.g.*, Gillette Co. v. "42" Prods., Ltd., 435 F.2d 1114 (9th Cir. 1970).

[1398] Ritchie v. Simpson, 170 F.3d 1092, n. 2 (Fed. Cir. 1999).

[1399] Citigroup, Inc. v. City Holding Co., 2003 U.S. Dist. LEXIS 1845, *37 (S.D.N.Y. 2003) (quoting

sought has been cited against the registration applications of the plaintiff's own trademarks,[1400] or (2) the party seeking cancellation is using the same or a similar mark for the same or similar goods.[1401] In a pair of TTAB decisions, standing was denied where a party sought to cancel a registration on the ground that the mark had been abandoned and that its registration might in future be a bar to the petitioner's own not-yet-filed applications,[1402] but a party that had already filed an intent-to-use application was found to have standing to cancel another party's potentially conflicting registration on abandonment grounds.[1403]

The prevailing defendant in an infringement proceeding was held to have standing to seek cancellation of the unsuccessful plaintiff's registration because the outcome of the infringement suit established that both parties had equal rights to use the mark.[1404]

The TTAB has been especially liberal where the defendant in an opposition proceeding seeks to cancel the opposer's mark on the basis of genericness or descriptiveness; in these situations, the Board has held, the defendant need not have any interest in using the mark for which cancellation is sought.[1405]

Although in most cases the opposer or party seeking cancellation will have a commercial interest in the outcome of the proceeding, this is not necessarily true in the case of oppositions or petitions to cancel under section 2(a) that allege that a mark is disparaging or scandalous, or falsely suggests an affiliation with a person or institution. In such cases, courts have held that a party need not have a "commercial" interest in order to have standing; it is sufficient to have a "real interest" and a "reasonable basis" for believing it will be damaged by the registration.[1406] A party has a "real interest" if it has a "direct and personal stake in the outcome" of the proceeding.[1407] In the case of marks alleged to be disparaging under section 2(a), for example, an opposer (or party seeking cancellation) will have standing simply by being a member of the

---

Aerogroup Int'l Inc. v. Marlboro Footworks, Ltd., 977 F. Supp. 264, 266-67 (S.D.N.Y. 1997)); *accord* Lipton Industries, Inc. v. Ralston Purina Co., 670 F.2d 1024, 213 U.S.P.Q. (BNA) 185 (C.C.P.A. 1982).

[1400] *E.g.*, Cerveceria Modelo, S.A. de C.V. v. R.B. Marco & Sons, Inc., 55 U.S.P.Q.2d (BNA) 1298, 1299-1300 (T.T.A.B. 2000); Jewelers Vigilance Comm., Inc. v. Ullenberg Corp. 823 F.2d 490, 493 (Fed. Cir. 1987); *see also* BankAmerica Corp. v. Invest America, 5 U.S.P.Q.2d (BNA) 1076 (T.T.A.B. 1987) (allowing defendant in opposition proceeding to bring counterclaim for cancellation of opposer's mark); Syntex (U.S.A.), Inc. v. E.R. Squibb & Sons, Inc., 14 U.S.P.Q.2d (BNA) 1879 (T.T.A.B. 1990) (applying similar rule even though opposer failed to prosecute its opposition and lost).

[1401] *E.g.*, Selva & Sons, Inc. v. Nina Footwear, Inc., 705 F.2d 1316, 1326 (Fed. Cir. 1983).

[1402] International Tel. & Tel. Corp. v. International Mobile Machines Corp., 218 U.S.P.Q. (BNA) 1024 (T.T.A.B. 1983).

[1403] Hartwell Co. v. Shane, 17 U.S.P.Q.2d (BNA) 1569 (T.T.A.B. 1990).

[1404] International Order of Job's Daughters v. Lindeburg & Co., 727 F.2d 1087 (Fed. Cir. 1984).

[1405] BankAmerica Corp. v. Invest America, 5 U.S.P.Q.2d (BNA) 1076 (T.T.A.B. 1987); *see also* Aruba v. Excelsior Inc., 5 U.S.P.Q.2d (BNA) 1685, 1686, 1987 TTAB LEXIS 4 (recognizing standing of Commonwealth of Aruba to oppose registration of its name on grounds of geographic descriptiveness under section 2(e)(2)).

[1406] Ritchie v. Simpson, 170 F.3d 1092, 1095 (Fed Cir. 1999).

[1407] *Id.*

disparaged group. Thus, in *Bromberg v. Carmel Self-Service, Inc.*,[1408] the Board granted standing to two women to oppose registration of the mark, ONLY A BREAST IN THE MOUTH IS BETTER THAN A LEG IN THE HAND, for restaurant services.[1409] The women alleged that they would be damaged by the registration because it disparaged women as a class, and they filed affidavits from women's groups in support in support of that belief.[1410] The TTAB granted them standing because they had a "real interest" in the registration, even though that interest was no different from that of other women, who comprised more than one-half of the general population.[1411] Likewise, where a mark is alleged to falsely suggest an affiliation with the opposer or party seeking cancellation, standing under section 2(a) exists if the mark refers "uniquely and unmistakably to the identity or persona" of that party.[1412]

In *Ritchie v. Simpson*, the Federal Circuit granted standing to oppose registration of three marks — O.J. SIMPSON, O.J., and THE JUICE — to an individual who alleged that these marks were "synonymous with wife-beater and wife-murderer" and, accordingly, that their registration would damage him "because the marks disparage[d] his values."[1413] He also alleged that the marks were disparaging because they "would attempt to justify physical violence against women."[1414] The TTAB had denied standing on the ground that the opposer had not established that he had any special interest in the outcome of the proceeding that was greater than that of the general public.[1415] The Federal Circuit, however, reversed:

> It would be inconsistent to deny standing to persons in a situation similar to that in Bromberg who happen to be members of a different general group, on the grounds that their concerns are widely shared. The Board erred by requiring the opposer in this case to somehow show that his interest is not shared by any substantial part of the general population. On the contrary, the purpose of the opposition proceeding is to establish what a substantial composite of the general public believes. The limitation placed upon standing in this case by the Board undermines this very purpose.[1416]

The Court held that the opposer had a "real interest" in the outcome of the opposition proceeding, because he would suffer a "real injury" if the marks were registered — "the disparagement of his alleged belief in a loving and nurturing

---

[1408]　198 U.S.P.Q. (BNA) 176, 179 (T.T.A.B. 1978).

[1409]　*Id.* at 177.

[1410]　*Id.*

[1411]　*Id.* at 179; *see also* Harjo v. Pro Football Inc., 30 U.S.P.Q.2d (BNA) 1828, 1830 (T.T.A.B. 1994).

[1412]　*See* Internet, Inc. v. Corporation for Nat'l Research Initiatives, 38 U.S.P.Q.2d (BNA) 1435 (T.T.A.B. 1996); Estate of Biro v. Bic Corp., 18 U.S.P.Q.2d 1382 (T.T.A.B. 1991).

[1413]　*Ritchie*, 170 F.3d at 1097.

[1414]　*Id.*

[1415]　*Id.* at 1095.

[1416]　*Id.* at 1097.

relationship between husband and wife."[1417] The opposer also established that his belief that he would be damaged was a reasonable one, by submitting proof that other people shared that belief.[1418]

[B]   Standing under Section 32

According to section 32(1), "the registrant" of a trademark may bring an infringement action against unauthorized users.[1419] Accordingly, as a general rule, only the owner of the federal registration has standing to sue for infringement under section 32. The owner may be the actual registrant, or the registrant's "legal representatives, successors, and assigns."[1420] Thus, assignees have standing to sue.[1421]

As a general rule, mere licensees lack standing to sue under section 32(1).[1422] However, some courts have recognized a limited exception to this rule in the case of exclusive licensees. According to these courts, under certain circumstances an exclusive licensee's interest in a registered trademark will be sufficient to confer standing.[1423] Specifically, a licensee has standing "only where the licensing agreement grants the licensee either a property interest in the trademark or rights tantamount to an assignment."[1424] By analogy to federal patent law, these courts have reasoned that, where a license is truly exclusive, the licensee has the right to exclude even the owner of the mark from using it in the same marketplace,[1425] and thus stands in much the same position as an assignee.[1426] This approach would, for example, confer standing on the exclusive retailer or distributor of trademarked goods or services.[1427] Non-exclusive licensees, in contrast, would have no standing.[1428]

Because licensee standing applies only when the licensee's rights are sufficiently exclusive that they are tantamount to an assignment, courts recognizing this approach have developed some general principles to assist in determining which licenses are sufficiently exclusive to qualify.[1429] Under these guidelines, a licensee will have standing where the agreement transfers to the

---

[1417] *Id.*

[1418] *Id.* at 1098.

[1419] 15 U.S.C. § 1114(1).

[1420] *Id.* § 1127; Berni v. International Gourmet Restaurants, Inc., 838 F.2d 642 (2d Cir. 1988).

[1421] Quabaug Rubber Co. v. Fabiano Shoe Co., Inc., 567 F.2d 154, 159-60 (1st Cir. 1977).

[1422] *Id.*; Finance Investment Co. (Bermuda) Ltd. v. Geberit AG, 165 F.3d 526 (7th Cir. 1998); Gruen Marketing Corp. v. Benrus Watch Co., 955 F. Supp. 979, 982 (N.D. Ill. 1997).

[1423] Bliss Clearing Niagara, Inc. v. Midwest Brake Bond Co., 339 F. Supp. 2d 944, 958-60 (W.D. Mich. 2004).

[1424] *Id.* at 959 (citing Calvin Klein Jeanswear Co. v. Tunnel Trading, 2001 U.S. Dist. LEXIS 18738 (S.D.N.Y. Nov. 16, 2001).

[1425] *Quabaug Rubber,* 567 F.2d at 159.

[1426] Fin. Inv. Co. (Bermuda) Ltd. v. Geberit AG, 165 F.3d 526, 531-32 (7th Cir. 1998).

[1427] *Quabaug Rubber,* 567 F.2d at 159.

[1428] *Id.*; Icee Distribs., Inc. v. J & J Snack Foods Corp., 325 F.3d 586, 598-99 (5th Cir. 2003).

[1429] *Bliss Clearing Niagara,* 339 F. Supp. 2d at 958-60.

licensee all of the licensor's rights in the use of the trademark,[1430] or where the agreement grants the licensee exclusive use of the mark without imposing any restrictions on the licensee's ability to enforce the mark.[1431] In contrast, the following factors, although non-exhaustive, tend to indicate that a license is not sufficiently exclusive to confer standing:[1432] (1) the licensee lacks the power to exclude the licensor from using the mark in the licensee's territory,[1433] (2) the license provides that the licensor retains exclusive ownership of the mark,[1434] (3) the license imposes geographical restrictions on the licensee's use of the mark,[1435] (4) the licensing agreement requires the licensee to maintain the quality of the mark or reserves to the licensor the right to monitor the quality of the licensee's products,[1436] (5) the license contains duties and rights between the parties that are inconsistent with an assignment,[1437] and (6) the license limits the licensee's ability to enforce the mark against infringers.[1438]

A party that does not have standing to sue under section 32(1) because it is not the owner of the federal registration may nonetheless have standing to sue under section 43(a) if it is likely to be injured as a result of the defendant's actions.[1439]

[C] Standing under Section 43(c)

Standing to bring a federal dilution claim under section 43(c) is limited to "the owner of a famous mark." Thus, in general, an exclusive licensee does not have standing under section 43(c).[1440]

However, courts that recognize the standing of certain exclusive licensees under section 32 (as discussed above) have applied a similar rule to dilution claims under section 43(c), requiring that the exclusive license be tantamount to an assignment before standing will be recognized.[1441]

[1430] *Id.* (citing Etri, Inc. v. Nippon Miniature Bearing Corp., 1989 U.S. Dist. LEXIS 10129 (N.D. Ill. Aug. 18, 1989)).

[1431] *Id.* at 960 (citing Ultrapure Sys., Inc. v. Ham-Let Group, 921 F. Supp. 659, 665-66 (N.D. Cal. 1996)).

[1432] *See generally Bliss Clearing Niagara*, 339 F. Supp. 2d at 959-60 (collecting cases).

[1433] *Quabaug Rubber*, 567 F.2d at 159; *Icee Distribs., Inc.*, 325 F.3d at 598-99.

[1434] Ultrapure Sys., Inc. v. Ham-Let Group, 921 F. Supp. 659, 665 (N.D. Cal. 1996) (*citing* DEP Corp. v. Interstate Cigar Co., 622 F.2d 621, 623 (2d Cir. 1980)).

[1435] *Calvin Klein Jeanswear*, 2001 U.S. Dist. LEXIS 18738 (S.D.N.Y. 2001).

[1436] *Id.* at *5; Gruen Mktg. Corp. v. Benrus Watch Co., 955 F. Supp. 979, 983 (N.D. Ill. 1997).

[1437] *Fin. Inv. Co. (Bermuda) Ltd.*, 165 F.3d at 532.

[1438] STX, Inc. v. Bauer USA, Inc., 1997 U.S. Dist. LEXIS 16250 (N.D. Cal. June 5, 1997).

[1439] *See* § 3.18 [D] *infra.*

[1440] *See, e.g.*, STX, Inc. v. Bauer USA, Inc., 1997 U.S. Dist. LEXIS 16250 (N.D. Cal. June 5, 1997).

[1441] *See Icee Distribs.*, 325 F.3d at 597-98 (holding, however, that the plaintiff was merely an exclusive licensee and therefore lacked standing); *Bliss Clearing Niagara*, 339 F. Supp. 2d at 958-60 n. 4; World Championship Wrestling v. Titan Sports, Inc., 46 F. Supp. 2d 118, 122 (D. Conn. 1999); BMW of N. Am., Inc. v. Au-Tomotive Gold, Inc., 1996 U.S. Dist. LEXIS 22828 (M.D. Fla. June 19, 1996).

[D]   Standing under Section 43(a) and the Common Law of Unfair Competition

Under both section 43(a) and the common law of unfair competition, standing is not limited to trademark owners. Under section 43(a), the plaintiff may be "any person who believes that he or she is or is likely to be damaged" by the defendant's actions.[1442] However, notwithstanding the breadth of the statutory language, courts have consistently held that consumers do not have standing to sue under section 43(a).[1443] Instead, standing under section 43(a) is limited to parties alleging a competitive or commercial injury (or likelihood thereof).[1444] This can include licensees of a mark, whether exclusive[1445] or non-exclusive.[1446] Courts have held that even a non-competitor of the defendant — such as a trade association[1447] — may have standing to sue based on commercial injury.[1448] At least three circuits have adopted a five-factor test, proposed by commentator J. Thomas McCarthy,[1449] to determine when a non-competitor has standing under section 43(a). This test considers: (1) whether the plaintiff's injury is of a type that Congress intended section 43(a) to redress; (2) the directness or indirectness of the injury; (3) the proximity or remoteness of the party to the injurious conduct; (4) the speculativeness of the damages claimed; and (5) the risk of duplicative damages or complexity in apportioning damages.[1450] In applying this test, no single factor is determinative.[1451]

[1442] 15 U.S.C. § 1125(a).

[1443] *See, e.g.*, Colligan v. Activities Club of New York, Ltd., 442 F.2d 686 (2d Cir.), *cert. denied*, 404 U.S. 1004 (1971).

[1444] *See, e.g.*, Dovenmuehle v. Gilldorn Mortg. Midwest Corp., 871 F.2d 697 (7th Cir. 1989). A non-profit entity may have standing even though it is not a commercial enterprise, provided that it can assert a competitive injury. *See, e.g.*, United We Stand America, Inc. v. United We Stand, America New York, Inc., 128 F.3d 86 (2d Cir. 1997); Shiraz Univ. Sch. of Med. Alumni Ass'n USA, Inc. v. Sheik, 1999 U.S. Dist. LEXIS 11566 (S.D.N.Y. July 29, 1999); Gideons Int'l, Inc. v. Gideon 300 Ministries, Inc., 94 F. Supp. 2d 566 (E.D. Pa. 1999); Healing the Children, Inc. v. Heal the Children, Inc., 786 F. Supp. 1209 (W.D. Pa. 1992); Christopher D. Smithers Found., Inc. v. St. Lukes-Roosevelt Hosp. Ctr., 2001 U.S. Dist. LEXIS 9293, *12-13 (S.D.N.Y. 2001).

[1445] *See, e.g.*, Frisch's Restaurants v. Elby's Big Boy, 670 F.2d 642 (6th Cir.), *cert. denied*, 459 U.S. 916 (1982); Business Trends Analysts v. Freedonia Group, Inc., 650 F. Supp. 1452 (S.D.N.Y. 1987).

[1446] Quabaug Rubber Co. v. Fabiano Shoe Co., 567 F.2d 154 (1st Cir. 1977); Murphy v. Provident Mut. Life Ins. Co., 756 F. Supp. 83, 86 (D. Conn. 1990), *aff'd*, 923 F.3d 923 (2d Cir. 1990).

[1447] National Ass'n of Pharm. Mfrs., Inc. v. Ayerst Labs., 850 F.2d 904 (2d Cir. 1988); Camel Hair & Cashmere Inst., Inc. v. Associated Dry Goods Corp., 799 F.2d 6 (1st Cir. 1986).

[1448] *See, e.g.*, Berni v. International Gourmet Rests., Inc., 838 F.2d 642, 648 (2d Cir. 1988). In *Waits v. Frito-Lay, Inc.*, 978 F.2d 1093 (9th Cir. 1992), the Ninth Circuit held that singer Tom Waits had standing to sue the defendant for running a commercial in which his voice was imitated. The court noted that plaintiffs in Waits's position "will rarely if ever be a competitor, and yet [are] the parties best situated to enforce the Lanham Act's prohibition on such conduct." *Id.* at 1107.

[1449] McCarthy on Trademarks, *supra* note 223, § 27:32.

[1450] Phoenix of Broward, Inc. v. McDonald's Corp., 489 F.3d 1156 (11th Cir. 2007); Procter & Gamble Co. v. Amway Corp., 242 F.3d 539 (5th Cir.), *cert. denied*, 534 U.S. 945 (2001); Joint Stock Society v. UDV North America, Inc., 266 F.3d 164, 179-80 (3d Cir. 2001); Conte Bros. Automotive, Inc. v. Quaker State-Slick 50, Inc., 165 F.3d 221 (3d Cir. 1998).

[1451] *Joint Stock Society*, 266 F.3d at 180.

Several circuits require a plaintiff to assert a competitive injury in order to bring a false advertising claim under section 43(a), but require only a commercial injury in order to bring a false designation/false endorsement claim. In the Ninth Circuit, for example, a party has standing to bring a false designation of origin claim if it has a "commercial interest in the product wrongfully identified,"[1452] but a "discernibly competitive injury" is required to bring a false advertising claim.[1453] The requirement of a competitive injury for a false advertising claim has also been adopted by the Seventh[1454] and Tenth[1455] Circuits.

Even where a false advertising claim is raised by a competitor of the defendant, it can be difficult for the plaintiff to establish a commercial injury. In a market where there are sellers other than the plaintiff and the defendant, the plaintiff is likely to be denied standing because it cannot establish that, but for the defendant's false statements, customers would have dealt with the plaintiff rather than the defendant.[1456] In contrast, a plaintiff will typically have standing to sue where it is the only source of the goods or services to which a competitor's false advertising pertains, or where the plaintiff and the false advertiser are the only sellers of those goods or services.[1457]

§ 3.19   DECLARATORY JUDGMENTS

A recent decision by the Supreme Court in the context of patent litigation may broaden the availability of declaratory judgment actions in federal courts for controversies arising under trademark and unfair competition laws.

The authority of federal courts to issue declaratory judgments is governed by the Declaratory Judgment Act, which provides that "[i]n a case of actual controversy within its jurisdiction," a federal court "may declare the rights and other legal relations of any interested party seeking such declaration, whether or not further relief is or could be sought."[1458] Until 2007, courts held that no justiciable "controversy" existed unless the party seeking the declaratory judgment had a "reasonable apprehension" that litigation was "imminent." This requirement was typically not satisfied unless the party reasonably believed that it was about to be sued (e.g., for infringement or dilution) by the declaratory judgment defendant. However, in its 2007 decision in *MedImmune, Inc. v.*

[1452] Waits v. Frito-Lay, Inc., 978 F.2d 1093, 1109 (9th Cir. 1992), *cert. denied*, 506 U.S. 1080 (1993); Smith v. Montoro, 648 F.2d 602 (9th Cir. 1981).

[1453] *Waits*, 978 F.2d at 1109; *accord* Halicki v. United Artists Communications, Inc., 812 F.2d 1213 (9th Cir. 1987).

[1454] L.S. Heath & Son, Inc. v. AT & T Info. Sys., Inc., 9 F.3d 561, 575 (7th Cir. 1993).

[1455] Hutchinson v. Pfeil, 211 F.3d 515 (10th Cir.), *cert. denied*, 531 U.S. 959 (2000); Stanfield v. Osborne Indus., Inc., 52 F.3d 867, 872 (10th Cir.), *cert. denied*, 516 U.S. 920 (1995).

[1456] *See, e.g.*, Burndy Corp. v. Teledyne Industries, Inc., 584 F. Supp. 656 (D. Conn. 1984), *aff'd*, 748 F.2d 767 (2d Cir. 1984); Construction Technology v. Lockformer Co., 704 F. Supp. 1212 (S.D.N.Y. 1989).

[1457] Mosler Safe Co. v. Ely-Norris Safe Co., 273 U.S. 132 (1927); Electronics Corp. of America v. Honeywell, Inc., 428 F.2d 191 (1st Cir. 1970).

[1458] 28 U.S.C. § 2201(a).

Genentech, Inc.,[1459] the Supreme Court rejected the "reasonable apprehension" test in the context of patent infringement. Instead, the Court held, the dispute must be "definite and concrete, touching the legal relations of parties having adverse legal interests," must be "real and substantial," and must "admit of specific relief through a decree of a conclusive character, as distinguished from an opinion advising what the law would be upon a hypothetical state of facts;" in other words, "the question in each case is whether the facts alleged, under all the circumstances, show that there is a substantial controversy, between parties having adverse legal interests, of sufficient immediacy and reality to warrant the issuance of a declaratory judgment."[1460] On the facts of *MedImmune*, this meant that a patent licensee in good standing could seek a declaratory judgment of patent invalidity or non-infringement; the licensee did not have to cease paying royalties so as to be in breach of its license and facing imminent infringement litigation. Because nothing in the *MedImmune* decision appears to limit its scope to the patent context, the new standard should be equally applicable to trademark and unfair competition claims.

In its 2008 decision in *Surefoot LC v. Sure Foot Corp.*,[1461] the Tenth Circuit became the first federal appellate court to apply *MedImmune* to a trademark case. In that case, Sure Foot (the declaratory judgment defendant) had repeatedly accused Surefoot (the declaratory judgment plaintiff) of infringing Sure Foot's registered trademarks, had threatened litigation if Surefoot did not change its name, and had initiated four oppositions and one cancellation proceeding against Surefoot's trademark registrations. Three of these oppositions took place in a one-year period from 2005 to 2006. However, when Surefoot sought a declaratory judgment of non-infringement in 2006, the district court dismissed the suit, finding no "reasonable apprehension" of imminent litigation, because Sure Foot had not threatened infringement litigation in the past seven years. Shortly after this decision, the Supreme Court issued its *MedImmune* decision. When Surefoot appealed, the Tenth Circuit held that the "reasonable apprehension" standard no longer applied. Applying the *MedImmune* formulation, the court held that the mere passage of time since Sure Foot's litigation threat had not dissipated the controversy between the parties, and that Sure Foot's recent opposition and cancellation proceedings, as well as its repeated accusations, signaled its continued belief that Surefoot was infringing its marks. Accordingly, the district court had jurisdiction to hear Surefoot's declaratory judgment suit. This did not, however, resolve the question whether, as a prudential matter, the court *should* hear the suit, because the Declaratory Judgment Act does not *require* a district court to hear a request for a declaratory judgment. The Tenth Circuit therefore instructed the district court on remand to consider the following factors:

> [1] whether a declaratory action would settle the controversy; [2] whether it would serve a useful purpose in clarifying the legal relations at issue; [3] whether the declaratory remedy is being used merely for the purpose of "procedural fencing" or "to provide an arena for a race to *res*

[1459] 549 U.S. 118 (2007).

[1460] *Id.* at 127.

[1461] 531 F.3d 1236 (10th Cir. 2008).

judicata"; [4] whether use of a declaratory action would increase friction between our federal and state courts and improperly encroach upon state jurisdiction; and [5] whether there is an alternative remedy which is better or more effective.[1462]

[1462] *Id.* at 1248.

TABLE OF CASES

[References are to pages]

A

A&H Sportswear Co. v. Victoria's Secret Stores, Inc.. . . . . 139, 140; 142; 149

A.W. Cox Dep't Store Co. v. Cox's, Inc.. 63

Abbott Laboratories v. Mead Johnson & Co.. . .338

Abdul-Jabbar v. Gen. Motors Corp.. 324

Abercrombie & Fitch Co. v. Hunting World, Inc.. . .47; 49; 51–53; 55; 58; 61; 112, 113; 152; 317, 318

Abercrombie & Fitch Stores, Inc. v. Am. Eagle Outfitters, Inc.. 31

Abercrombie & Fitch Trading Co. v. Fashion Shops, Inc.. 310

Academy of Motion Picture Arts & Sciences v. Creative House Promotions, Inc.. 210

Academy of Motion Picture Arts & Sciences v. Network Solutions, Inc.. 256

Accurate Leather & Novelty Co. Inc. v. LTD Commodities Inc.. 203

Acme Valve & Fittings Co. v. Wayne. . . .37; 294

Acxiom Corp. v. Axiom, Inc.. 173

Addison-Wesley Pub. Co. v. Brown. 4, 5

Adidas Am., Inc. v. Payless Shoesource, Inc.. 216; 220

Admark, Inc., In re Application of 103

Admiral Corp. v. Penco, Inc.. 186

Adolph Coors Co. v. A. Genderson & Sons, Inc.. 304

Adray v. Adry-Mart, Inc.. 344

Advantage Rent-A-Car, Inc. v. Enter. Rent-A-Car Co.. .209

Advertising & Marketing Dev., Inc., In re . . . 103

Aedes de Venustas v. Venustas Int'l, LLC . . . 345

Aerogroup Int'l v. Marlboro Footworks. . 190; 361

Aktieselskabet. 85

Aladdin Mfg. Co. v. Mantle Lamp Co.. 344

Alderman v. Iditarod Props.. 139

Alfacell Corp. v. Anticancer, Inc.. 38

Alfred Dunhill of London, Inc. v. Dunhill Tailored Clothes, Inc.. 88

The All England Lawn Tennis Club (Wimbledon) Ltd. v. Creations Aromatiques, Inc.. 43

Allen v. National Video, Inc.. 72

Allied Artists Pictures Corp. v. Friedman. . . .338

Alligator Co. v. Robert Bruce, Inc.. 290

Alpha Indus., Inc. v. Alpha Steel Tube & Shapes, Inc.. . . . . .143; 155

Alpo Petfoods, Inc. v. Ralston Purina Co.. . . .193; 344, 345; 348

Alum-A-Fold Shutter Corporation v. Folding Shutter Corporation. 193

AM General Corp. v. DaimlerChrysler Corp. . 143; 339

Am. Safety Razor Co., In re 74, 75

Am. Throwing Co. v. Famous Bathrobe Co.. . . 145

AmBrit, Inc. v. Kraft, Inc.. . . . . . 155; 289; 337

Ambrosia Chocolate Co. v. Ambrosia Cake Bakery. 316

American Angus Ass'n v. Sysco Corp.. 327

American Chicle Co. v. Topps Chewing Gum, Inc.. 139

American Council of Certified Podiatric Physicians & Surgeons v. American Bd. of Podiatric Surgery, Inc.. 201

American Dairy Queen Corp. v. New Line Prods., Inc.. . . . . .276; 282

American Diabetes Ass'n, Inc. v. Nat'l Diabetes Ass'n. 38

American Express Co. v. Goetz 69; 86

American Family Life Ins. Co. v. Hagan . 213; 231, 232; 283

American Foods, Inc. v. Golden Flake, Inc.. . . 128

American Greetings Corp. v. Dan-Dee Imports, Inc.. 27

American Home Prods. Corp. v. Johnson Chem. Co.. 54

American Hosp. Ass'n v. Bankers Commercial Life Ins. Co.. 186

American Mensa, Ltd. v. Inpharmatica, Ltd.. . . 220

American Paging, Inc. v. American Mobilphone, Inc.. 137

American Precast Corp. v. Maurice Concrete Products. 193

American Soc'y of Plumbing Eng'rs v. TMB Publ'g, Inc.. 116

American Speech-Language-Hearing Ass'n v. National Hearing Aid Soc'y 81

American Stock Exch., Inc. v. American Express Co.. 86

American Sugar Refining Co. v. Andreassen . . 148

American Taxi Dispatch, Inc. v. American Metro Taxi & Limo Co.. 339

American White Cross Labs., Inc. v. H.M. Cote, Inc.. 190

Ameritech, Inc. v. American Information Technologies Corp.. . . . . 162, 163; 165

AMF, Inc. v. American Leisure Prods., Inc.. . . .146

AMF Inc. v. Sleekcraft Boats . 141; 154, 155; 158; 160, 161; 168

TC-1

Amstar Corp. v. Domino's Pizza, Inc..52; 153, 154

Anheuser-Busch, Inc. v. Balducci Pubs. . 156; 261; 273; 275; 281

Anheuser-Busch, Inc. v. DuBois Brewing Co. . 312

Anheuser-Busch, Inc. v. L & L Wings, Inc. . . 262; 264; 275; 286

Anheuser-Busch, Inc. v. Stroh Brewery Co. . . . 76

Anheuser-Busch, Inc. v. VIP Prods., LLC. . . .262

Anti-Cori-Zine Chem. Co., In re 52; 55

Anti-Monopoly, Inc. v. General Mills Fun Group .327

Antidote Int'l Films, Inc. v. Bloomsbury Pub'g, PLC 196; 204

Antioch Co. v. West Trimming Corp 21

Anvil Brand, Inc. v. Consolidated Foods Corp. . 36

Application of (see name of party) . . . .

Aquatherm Indus. v. Florida Power & Light Co.. 360

Armstrong Paint & Varnish Works v. Nu-Enamel Corp.. .55

Arrow Distilleries, Inc. v. Globe Brewing Co.. .51

Arrow Fastener Co. v. Stanley Works 74

Arrow United Indus., Inc. v. Hugh Richards, Inc.. .193

Artic Electronics Co., In re 175

Aruba v. Excelsior Inc.. 362

Ashe v. Pepsico, Inc.. 153

Asia Apparel, LLC v. Cunneen 339

Asia Apparel, LLC v. RIPSwear, Inc.. 339

Astra Pharmaceutical Prods., Inc. v. Beckman Instruments, Inc.. 209

AT&T v. Winback & Conserve Program . 198; 249; 250; 257; 258; 260

Atrium Group de Ediciones y Publicaciones, S.L. v. Harry N. Abrams, Inc.. 334

Au-Tomotive Gold, Inc. v. Volkswagen of America, Inc.. 32

Auburn Farms, Inc. v. McKee Foods Corp.. . .114

Auburn Univ. v. Moody 340

Audi AG v. D'Amato 339

Audi AG v. Shokan Coachworks, Inc.. . . .220; 326

Aunt Jemima Mills Co. v. Rigney & Co.. . . .149

Auscape Int'l v. National Geographic Soc'y . .196, 197

Australian Gold v. Hatfield. . .167; 170; 178; 180; 182

AutoZone, Inc. v. Tandy Corp.. . . .143; 221, 222

Avakoff v. Southern Pacific Co.. 36

Avery Dennison Corp. v. Acco Brands, Inc. . . 231

Avery Dennison Corp. v. Sumpton . 215, 216; 218; 219

Avid Identification Sys. v. Phillips Elecs. N. Am.. .339

Avon Shoe Co. v. David Crystal, Inc.. 88

Azteca Rest. Enters., Inc., In re. 88

B

Babbit Elecs., Inc. v. Dynascan Corp.. 189

Babson Bros. Co. v. Surge Power Corp.. 98

Baden Sports, Inc. v. Kabushiki Kaisha Molten. 204; 339

Baglin v. Cusenier Co.. 289

Balance Dynamics Corp. v. Schmitt Indus., Inc.. . . . . .175; 344; 347

Bally Total Fitness Holding Corp. v. Faber . . 232, 233

Bambu Sales, Inc. v. Sultana Crackers, Inc.. . . 352

Bandag, Inc. v. Al Bolser's Tire Stores 298

Banff, Ltd. v. Colberts, Inc.. 345

Banff Ltd. v. Express, Inc. 31

Banff, Ltd. v. Federated Dept. Stores, Inc.. . . .152; 161; 162; 163; 164; 165

Bangor Punta Operations, Inc. v. Universal Marine Co.. .194

Banjo Buddies, Inc. v. Renosky 345; 347

BankAmerica Corp. v. Invest America 362

Bar-Meir v. North Am. Die Casting Ass'n . . . 351

Barcamerica Int'l USA Trust v. Tyfield Imps., Inc.. 294

Barrios v. American Thermal Instruments, Inc..354

BASF Corp. v. Old World Trading Co. . . . 200, 201

Basile, S.p.A. v. Basile 62

Bath & Body Works, Inc. v. Luzier Personalized Cosmetics, Inc.. 61

Baughman Tile Co. v. Plastic Tubing, Inc.. . . . 116

Bayer Co. v. United Drug Co. 60

Beacon Mut. Ins. Co. v. OneBeacon Ins. Group 175, 176

Beatrice Foods, In re 14; 88; 91

Beauty Time v. VU Skin Sys.. 337

Beaverton Foods, Inc., In re 94

Beckwith Builders, Inc. v. Depietri 196

Becoming, Inc. v. Avon Products, Inc.. . . .162, 163

Beech-Nut, Inc. v. Warner-Lambert Co.. 139

Beech-Nut Packing Co. v. P. Lorillard Co.. . . . 289

Beer Nuts, Inc. v. Clover Club Foods Co.. . . . 139; 161; 319

Bellagio v. Denhammer 344; 350

BellSouth Adv'g & Pub'g Corp. v. The Real Color Pages. .54

Beltran v. Myers. 338

[References are to pages]

Benthin Mgt. GmbH, In re 96

Berlitz Schools of Languages v. Everest House 342

Berni v. International Gourmet Restaurants, Inc. .364; 366

Best Software, Inc., In re 80; 117

BIC Corp. v. Far Eastern Source Corp. 54

BidZirk, LLC v. Smith. 233

Big O Tire Dealers, Inc. v. Goodyear Tire & Rubber Co. 162; 165; 344

Bihari v. Gross. 182, 183; 319; 324

Bijur Lubricating Corp. v. Devco Corp. . . .183; 231

Bird v. Parsons. 215

Biro, Estate of v. Bic Corp. 363

Bishop, Estate of v. Equinox Int'l Corp. 347

Bit, Inc. v. Poly-Tech Indus. 175

Black Hills Jewelry Mfg. Co. v. Gold Rush, Inc. 339

Blinded Veterans Ass'n v. Blinded American Veterans Found. 52; 53; 55; 57; 59

Bliss Clearing Niagara 364, 365

Blue & White Food Prods. Corp. v. Shamir Food Indus., Ltd. 74

Blue Bell, Inc. v. Farah Mfg. Co. 33, 34; 37

Blue Bell, Inc. v. Jaymar-Ruby, Inc. 46

Blue Nile, Inc. v. Ice.com, Inc. 64

BMW of N. Am., Inc. v. Au-Tomotive Gold, Inc. 365

Board of Supervisors for Louisiana State Univ. v. Smack Apparel Co. 29

Bongrain Int'l Corp. v. Delice de France, Inc. . .78

Bonito Boats v. Thunder Craft Boats 14; 330

Bose Corp. v. Linear Design Labs, Inc. 143

Bose Corp., In re 26

Bosley Med. Inst. 177, 178; 183

Boston Duck Tours, LP v. Super Duck Tours, LLC 178, 179

Boston Pro Hockey Association v. Dallas Cap & E. Manufacturing, Inc. 343; 359

Boswell v. Mavety Media Group, Ltd. 83

Bottom Line Mgmt., Inc. v. Pan Man, Inc. 304

Boule v. Hutton 202

Boulevard Entertainment, Inc., In re 82; 83

Bourdeau Bros. v. ITC. 311

Branch v. Federal Trade Commission 188

Brennan's, Inc. v. Brennan's Rest., L.L.C. 339

Bretford Mfg. v. Smith Sys. Mfg. Co. 194

Brilliance Audio, Inc. v. Haights Cross Communs., Inc. .297; 306

Bristol-Myers Squibb. Co. v. McNeil-P.P.C., Inc. 49; 141

Brittingham v. Jenkins. 342

BroadBridge Media, L.L.C. v. Hypercd.com. . 240; 244, 245; 248

Brockmeyer v. Hearst Corp. 163

Brody's, Inc. v. Brody Bros., Inc. 62, 63

Bromberg v. Carmel Self Service, Inc. 363

Brookfield Comms., Inc. v. West Coast Entert. Corp. 38, 39; 137; 142; 145; 154; 165–169; 182, 183

Brother Records, Inc. v. Jardine 322

Brown & Bigelow v. Remembrance Advertising Products, Inc. 360

Browne-Vintners Co. v. National Distillers & Chem. Corp. 39

Brunswick Corp. v. British Seagull. 25; 65

Budge Mfg. Co., In re 83

Buffett v. Chi-Chi's, Inc. 84

Bulova Watch Co. v. Allerton Co. 300

Bulova Watch Co. v. Steele 185

Burger King of Florida, Inc. v. Hoots . 14; 116; 127

Burger King of Florida, Inc., In re 102

Burndy Corp. v. Teledyne Industries, Inc. 367

Burnett v. Twentieth Century Fox Film . . 275; 278

Business Trends Analysts v. Freedonia Group, Inc. 366

Buti v. Impressa Perosa S.R.L. 40

Buying for the Home, LLC v. Humble Abode, LLC 179

C

Cable News Network L.P. v. CNNews.com . . 186; 243; 244

CAE, Inc. v. Clean Air Eng'g, Inc. 112

Cahn, Belt, & Co., In re. 84

Cairns v. Franklin Mint Co. 230; 317, 318; 322–325

California Cooler, Inc. v. Loretto Winery, Ltd.. .50

California Innovations, Inc., In re 81; 93

Calvin Klein Cosmetics Corp. v. Lenox Labs., Inc. 327

Calvin Klein Indus., Inc. v. BFK Hong Kong, Ltd. 189

Calvin Klein Jeanswear Co. v. Tunnel Trading.364, 365

Camel Hair & Cashmere Inst., Inc. v. Associated Dry Goods Corp. 366

Campbell v. Acuff-Rose Music 263

Canfield v. Health Communs., Inc. 340

Canovas v. Venezia 84

Capital Films Corp. v. Charles Fries Productions 165

Car-Freshner Corp. v. S.C. Johnson & Son, Inc.. . . . . .320; 322

Cardtoons, L.C. v. Major League Baseball Players Ass'n 265

Carefirst of Md., Inc. v. First Care, P.C. 223

Carl Zeiss Stiftung v. VEB Carl Zeiss, Jena. .294; 311; 315

Cartier v. Aaron Faber, Inc. 340

Cashmere & Camel Hair Mfrs. Inst. v. Saks Fifth Ave. 201

Castrol, Inc. v. Quaker State Corp.. .198; 200, 201

CBS, Inc. v. Liederman . . 138; 148; 154; 156, 157

CCS Communications Control, Inc. v. Law Enforcement Assoc., Inc.. 193

Century 21 Real Estate Corp. v. Lendingtree, Inc. 325

Century 21 Real Estate Corp. v. Sandlin 337

Century Distilling Co. v. Continental Distilling Corp.. .347

Cerveceria Modelo, S.A. de C.V. v. R.B. Marco & Sons, Inc.. 362

Champion Spark Plug Co. v. Sanders. . .298, 299; 342

Champions Golf Club, Inc. v. The Champions Golf Club, Inc.. 55

Charles Atlas, Ltd. v. D.C. Comics, Inc. 232

Charles of the Ritz Group, Ltd. v. Quality King Distrs., Inc. 328; 343

Charles R. DeBevoise Co. v. H. & W. Co. 60

Chattanooga Mfg., Inc. v. Nike, Inc. . . . 311; 313; 314; 315

Checkpoint Sys. v. Check Point Software Techs., Inc. 165

Cher v. Forum Int'l., Ltd. 344

Chicago Rawhide Mfg. Co., In re 36

Children's Legal Services PLLC v. Kresch. . .292

China Healthways Inst., Inc. v. Wang. 142

Christopher D. Smithers Found., Inc. v. St. Lukes-Roosevelt Hosp. Ctr. 361; 366

Chrysler Corp. v. Silva. 173

Ciba-Geigy Corp. v. Bolar Pharm. Co. 256

Cincinnati, City of v. Discovery Network, Inc..202

Circuit City Stores, Inc. v. CarMax, Inc. . 129; 339

Citibank, N.A. v. Citibanc Group, Inc. . . . 128; 289

Citigroup Inc. v. City Holding Co. . 145; 147; 148; 154; 361

City of (see name of city). . . . .

Clairol, Inc. v. Roux Distr. Co., Inc. 118

Clark Tile Co. v. Red Devil, Inc.. 20

Clarke, In re 68

Cleary v. News Corp.. . . . . .192; 195

Clicks Billiards, Inc. v. Sixshooters, Inc.. . . 31, 32; 143

Cliffs Notes, Inc. v. Bantam Doubleday Dell Publ'g Group, Inc.. . . . . . .264; 265; 269, 270; 274

Clorox v. Procter & Gamble. 198, 199

Clorox Chem. Co. Chlorit Mfg. Corp.. 51

Clorox Co. v. Chemical Bank. 130

CMM Cable Rep., Inc. v. Ocean Coast Props. . 176

Coach House Rest., Inc. v. Coach & Six Rests., Inc. 316

Coach, Inc. v. We Care Trading Co. 32

Coalgate Abstract Co. v. Coal County Abstract Co. 52

Coastal Abstract Serv., Inc. v. First Am. Tit. Ins. Co.. . . . . .201; 203

Coca-Cola Co. v. Gay-Ola Co. 249

Coca-Cola Co. v. Gemini Rising, Inc.. . .206; 285

Coca-Cola Co. v. Purdy. 237, 238; 240, 241

Coca-Cola Co. v. Snow Crest Beverages, Inc. . 138

Coca-Cola Co. v. Tropicana Prods., Inc.. .155; 198

The Coca-Cola Co. v. Overland, Inc.. 76

Coffee Dan's, Inc. v. Coffee Don's Charcoal Broiler. 206

Cohn v. Petsmart, Inc.. 361

Colgate-Palmolive Co. v. J.M.D. All-Star Import & Export, Inc. 352

Coll-Monge, Estate of v. Inner Peace Movement 39

College Savings Bank v. Florida Prepaid Postsecondary Educ. Expense Bd.. 335

Colligan v. Activities Club of New York, Ltd. . 366

Colonial Elec. & Plumbing Supply v. Colonial Elec.. . . . . .296, 297

Colston Inv. Co. v. Home Supply Co. 56

Comedy III Prods., Inc. v. New Line Cinema . . 73

Comidas Exquisitos, Inc. v. O'Malley & McGee's, Inc.. 128

Commerce Bancorp, Inc. v. BankAtlantic. . . .128

Commodore Import Co. v. Hiraoka. 193

Community of Roquefort v. William Faehndrich, Inc.. 101

Compco Corp. v. Day-Brite Lighting, Inc..14; 328; 329

Componentone, L.L.C. v. Componentart, Inc. . 220

Compuclean Mktg. & Design v. Berkshire Prods., Inc.. 107

Computer Assocs. Int'l v. Altai, Inc. 333

Computer Food Stores Inc. v. Corner Store Franchises, Inc.. 86

ConAgra, Inc. v. Geo. A. Hormel & Co. . 142; 156

[References are to pages]

Conagra, Inc. v. Singleton 140; 289

Conopco, Inc. v. Campbell Soup Co.. . . .311; 314; 337

Conopco, Inc. v. Cosmair, Inc. 156

Construction Technology v. Lockformer Co.. . . 367

Conte Bros. Automotive, Inc. v. Quaker State-Slick 50, Inc. 366

Continental Connector Corp. v. Continental Specialties Corp. 150

Conwood Corp. v. Loew's Theatres, Inc. 289

Cook, Perkiss & Liehe, Inc. v. Northern California Collection Serv., Inc. 198

Cooper, In re. 73

Cork 'N Cleaver of Colorado, Inc. v. Keg 'N Cleaver of Utica, Inc. 157

Corporate Document Services, Inc. v. I.C.E.D. Mgt., Inc. 85, 86

Corporate Fitness Programs v. Weider Health and Fitness. .138

Cosmetically Sealed Industries, Inc. v. Chesebrough-Pond's USA Co. 321

Coty, Inc. v. Parfums De Grande Luxe, Inc.. . . 343

Courtenay Comms. Corp. v. Hall 152

CPP Ins. Agency, Inc. v. General Motors Corp. . 76

CreAgri, Inc. v. USANA Health Scis., Inc.. . . .38

Creative Gifts, Inc. v. UFO 114; 315

Cridlebaugh v. Rudolph. 52

Crocker Nat'l Bank v. Canadian Imperial Bank of Commerce. 121

Crossbow, Inc. v. Dan-Dee Imports Inc. 193

Crowell Pub. Co. v. Italian Monthly Co. 3

Cuisinart, Inc. v. Robot-Coupe Int'l Corp. . . . 199

Cumberland Packing Corp. v. Monsanto Co.. .231; 327

Cumulus Media, Inc. v. Clear Channel Communs., Inc.. . . . . .289; 291

Custom Mfg. & Eng'g, Inc. v. Midway Servs..135; 141; 176

Custom Vehicles, Inc. v. Forest River, Inc.. . . 136

D

D'Innovations 33; 35; 291; 292

Daddy's Junky Music Stores, Inc. v. Big Daddy's Family Music Center 52; 142–144; 149

DaimlerChrysler v. The Net, Inc.. . . .237; 238; 239

Dallas Cowboys Cheerleaders, Inc. v. Pussycat Cinema, Ltd.. . . . . .184; 206; 276

Danjaq LLC v. Sony Corp. 311

Dastar Corp. v. Twentieth Century Fox Film Corp. 71; 135; 194; 195; 197; 203; 333

David Berg & Co. v. Gatto Int'l Trading Co.. . 16; 256; 258

Davidoff & Cie, S.A. v. PLD Int'l Corp. . 298; 300

Dawn Donut Co. v. Day. . 77; 128; 131; 139; 150; 186; 293, 294

Days-Ease Home Products Corp., In re. 65

Dayton Progress Corp. v. Lane Punch Corp.. . . .57

De Costa v. Columbia Broadcasting System, Inc. 155

Deborah Heart & Lung Ctr. v. Children of the World Found., Ltd.. 214

Deere & Co. v. Farmhand, Inc.. 25

Deere & Co. v. MTD Holdings, Inc. . . . 154; 160

Deere & Co. v. MTD Prods.. . . . . . . .266; 339

Defiance Button Mach. Co. v. C&C Metal Prods. Corp. 290–292; 297

DeGidio v. West Group Corp. 53, 54

Deister Concentrator Co., In re 98

Delaware & Hudson Canal Co. v. Clark 55

Dell Pub. Co. v. Stanley Pubs., Inc.. 360

DEP Corp. v. Interstate Cigar Co.. 365

Department of Justice v. Calspan Corp.. 186

DeVry Inc. v. Univ. of Med. & Health Sci.. . .326

Diagnostics Technology, Inc. v. Miles Labs., Inc. 146

Dial-A-Mattress 295

Dial Corp. v. Encina Corp. 309

Dial One of the Mid-South, Inc. v. Bellsouth Telecomm'ns, Inc. 355

Dickinson v. Zurko. 111

Dieter v. B&H Indus. of Southwest Fla., Inc. . 116; 140

Dippin' Dots, Inc. v. Frosty Bites Dist., L.L.C.. 30; 32; 64, 65; 142; 150

Dixie Rests., In re. 88

Dodd v. Fort Smith Special School Dist.. . . . 195

Dolphin Homes Corp. v. Tocomc Dev. Corp.. . .209

Dorr-Oliver, Inc. v. Fluid-Quip, Inc.. 168

Dovenmuehle v. Gilldorn Mortg. Midwest Corp.. .366

DowBrands, L.P. v. Helene Curtis, Inc.. 320

Dr. Pepper Co., In re. 103

Dr. Seuss Enters. v. Penguin Books. 165; 184; 221; 232; 261, 262; 276; 277

Dreamwerks Prod. Grp. v. SKG Studio. .161; 163, 164

Dresser Indus., Inc. v. Heraeus Engelhard Vacuum, Inc. 60

Drexel Enters., Inc. v. Hermitage Cabinet Shop, Inc.. . . . . .138; 158

Drop Dead Co. v. S.C. Johnson & Son, Inc.. . . 186

Dual-Deck Video Cassette Recorder Antitrust Litig., In re. 318

DuPont Cellophane Co. v. Waxed Prods. Co. . 2, 3; 60

Dyneer Corp. v. Automotive Prods. PLC. . .86, 87

E

E. & J. Gallo Winery v. Consorzio Del Gallo Nero 211

E. & J. Gallo Winery v. Gallo Cattle Co. . .61; 63; 149; 294

E. F. Prichard Co. v. Consumers Brewing Co. . 295

E. I. Du Pont de Nemours & Co. v. Celanese Corp. of America 293

E.I. DuPont de Nemours & Co. v. Yoshida Int'l, Inc. 150

E.I. DuPont de Nemours & Co., In re.88; 111; 141

E-Systems, Inc. v. Monitek, Inc.. 312

E.T. Browne Drug Co. v. Cococare Prods. . . . 136

Eagles, Ltd. v. Am. Eagle Found. 349

Earthquake Sound Corp. v. Bumper Indus. . . . 349

Eastman Kodak Co. v. Bell & Howell Document Mgt. Prods. Co. 74

Eastman Kodak Co. v. Rakow 158; 206

eBay Inc. v. MercExchange, L.L.C.. 339

Eclipse Assocs. Ltd. v. Data Gen. Corp. 154

Eco Mfg. LLC v. Honeywell Int'l, Inc. . . . 29; 65

Edgar Rice Burroughs, Inc. v. Manns Theaters . 72; 282

Edina Realty, Inc. v. TheMLSonline.com . 179; 326

Edison Bros. Stores, Inc. v. Cosmair, Inc.. . . .157

Educational Dev't Corp. v. Economy Co. 91

Eighty-Nine (89) Bottles of "Eau de Joy"; United States v. 310

800 Contacts, Inc. v. WhenU.com, Inc.. .178; 180; 182

El Greco Leather Prods. Co. v. Shoe World, Inc.. . . . . .304; 309

Electronic Design & Sales, Inc. v. Electronic Data Sys. Corp.. 165

Electronics Corp. of America v. Honeywell, Inc. 367

Eli Lilly & Co. v. Natural Answers, Inc.. 170; 182; 222

Eliya, Inc. v. Kohl's Dep't Stores 333

Elvis Presley Enters. v. Capece . . . 139; 142; 166; 167; 261; 262; 264

Empresa Cubana Del Tabaco v. Culbro Corp.. .42; 39; 135; 159

Enesco Corp. v. Price/Costco Inc. . . 297; 301; 306

Engineered Mechanical Services, Inc.. 294

Ennco Display Sys., Inc., In re 96

Enoch Morgan's Sons Co. v. Whittier-Coburn Co.. 249

Enterprise Rent-A-Car Co. v. Advantage Rent-A Car, Inc.. 98–100

Eppendorf-Netheler-Hinz   GMBH   v.   Ritter GMBH 21

Era Corp. v. Electronic Realty Associates, Inc. . 86

Ernst Hardware Co. v. Ernst Home Ctr.. .164, 165

Escada AG v. Limited, Inc. 332

Esercizio v. Roberts 173

ESPN, Inc. v. Quiksilver, Inc. 209

Essence Communications, Inc. v. Singh Indus.. 159

Estate LLC v. Century Ins. Group. 222

Estate of (see name of party) . . . .

Estee Lauder v. Gap, Inc. 139

Etri, Inc. v. Nippon Miniature Bearing Corp.. .365

ETW Corp. v. Jireh Pub., Inc.. . . . . . .72; 273

Eurostar, Inc. v. Euro-Star" Reitmoden GMBH & Co.. .114

Evans v. Paramount Pictures Corp.. 73

Evans Chemetics, Inc. v. Chemetics International Ltd.. 86

Everest Capital, Ltd. v. Everest Funds Mgt., L.L.C.. . . . . 142; 219

Ex parte (see name of relator). . . . .

Express, Inc. v. Sears, Roebuck & Co. 294

Exxon Corp. v. Humble Exploration Co., Inc.. 291; 315

Exxon Corp. v. Oxxford Clothes, Inc.. . . .292–295

Exxon Corp. v. Texas Motor Exch., Inc. 155

F

F.E.L. Publications, Ltd. v. Catholic Bishop of Chicago .195

F.R. Lepage Bakery, Inc. v. Roush Bakery Prods. Co.. 102

F.W. Fitch Co. v. Camille, Inc. 249

Facenda v. N.F.L. Films, Inc. 142

Fair Indigo LLC v. Style Conscience. 85, 86

Family Inns of America, Inc., In re 108

Family of U.R.I., Inc. v. World Church of the Creator. 116

Feathercombs, Inc. v. Solo Prods. Corp. 319

Federal Elec. Co. v. Flexlume Corp. 194

Federal Express Corp. v. Federal Espresso, Inc. 206

Federal Maritime Comm'n v. South Carolina State Ports Auth. 335

Felix the Cat Prods., Inc. v. New Line Cinema Corp. 177–179; 184

Feltner v. Columbia Pictures TV 351

Ferrero U.S.A., Inc. v. Ozak Trading, Inc. . . . 309

Ficker v. Tuohy. 246

[References are to pages]

Field Enters. Educ. Corp. v. Cove Industries, Inc. 160

Field Enters. Educ. Corp. v. Grosset & Dunlap, Inc. 160

Filipino Yellow Pages, Inc. v. Asian Journal Publ'n, Inc. 57

Fils S.A. v. J. Young Enters., Inc. 31

Finance Investment Co. v. Geberit AG . . 349; 364, 365

Fioravanti v. Fioravanti Corrado S.R.L.. 107

First Franklin Fin. Corp. v. Franklin First Fin., LTD. 161

First Nat'l Bank v. First Wyo. S&L Ass'n . . . 127

First National Bank, in Sioux Falls v. First National Bank, South Dakota. 161

First Niagara Ins. Brokers, Inc. v. First Niagara Fin. Group, Inc.. . . . . .43; 85

Fisher Stoves, Inc. v. All Nighter Stove Works, Inc. 143

FleetBoston Financial Corp. v. FleetBostonFinancial.com 243

Fleischmann Distilling Corp. v. Maier Brewing Co.. . . . . .52; 139; 149

Fleischmann Distilling Corp. v. Maier Brewing Co.. 186

Florida Citrus Comm'n, In re 101

Folmer Graflex Corp. v. Graphic Photo Serv. . . 52

Fonovisa, Inc. v. Cherry Auction, Inc.. . . .251, 252

Foote; United States v.. 359

Ford Motor Co. v. Catalanotte. 239; 337

Ford Motor Co. v. Greatdomains.com, Inc. . . 238, 239; 243

Ford Motor Co. v. 2600 Enters. . . . 178; 183; 232

The Forschner Group, Inc. v. Arrow Trading Co., Inc. 143

Forum Corp. of N. Am. v. Forum, Ltd.. 167

Fox Chemical Co. v. Amsoil, Inc.. 337

Foxtrap, Inc. v. Foxtrap, Inc. 128

Foxworthy v. Custom Tees. 69; 155; 177

FragranceNet.com, Inc. v. FragranceX.com, Inc.. . . . . .178, 179; 182

Franchised Stores of New York, Inc. v. Winter. 186

Frederick Warne & Co. v. Book Sales, Inc.. . . . 71

Frisch's Restaurants v. Elby's Big Boy . .141; 160; 366

Fruit of the Loom, Inc. v. Girouard. 206

Fuddruckers, Inc. v. Doc's B.R. Others, Inc.. . . .32

Fuente Cigar, Ltd. v. Opus One 202, 203

Fuji Photo Film Co., Inc. v. Shinohara Shoji Kabushiki Kaisha. 39; 161

Funai Elec Co, LTD v. Daewoo Elecs. Corp.. . .339

G

G & C Merriam Co. v. Saalfield 56; 343

G. & C. Merriam Co. v. Ogilvie 343

G.D. Searle & Co. v. Nutrapharm, Inc.. 38

G. Heileman Brewing Co. v. Anheuser-Busch, Inc.. . . . . .57; 76

G. Heileman Brewing Co. v. Independent Brewing Co.. 352

G. Wentworth, S.S.C. Ltd. P'ship v. Settlement Funding LLC 170; 179; 182

Gai Audio of New York, Inc. v. Columbia Broadcasting Sys., Inc.. 349

Galerie Furstenberg v. Coffaro 71

Galerie Gmurzynska v. Hutton 202

Gamut Trading Co. v. ITC. 309

Garcia, In re. 98

Gartside, In re 111

Gateway 2000 v. Cyrix Corp.. 333

Gay Toys, Inc. v. McDonalds Corp. 36

GEICO v. Google, Inc.. 178

General Healthcare, Ltd. v. Qashat. 35; 37

General Motors Corp. v. Urban Gorilla, LLC . 142; 173; 221; 223; 332

General Shoe Corp. v. Rosen. 53

General Univ. Sys. v. Lee 193

Geoffrey, Inc. v. Stratton. 146

George Basch Co. v. Blue Coral, Inc.. 345

Gershwin Publishing Corp. v. Columbia Artists Mgt., Inc.. 257

Gibson Guitar Corp. v. Paul Reed Smith Guitars, LP 167, 168; 173

Gideons Int'l, Inc. v. Gideon 300 Ministries, Inc.. 366

Giles; United States v.. 359

Gilliam v. American Broadcasting Cos. . . 197; 343

Girl Scouts of United States v. Personality Posters Mfg. Co.. 284

Glen Raven Mills, Inc. v. Ramada Int'l, Inc.. . 211

GMA Accessories, Inc. v. Croscill, Inc.. 220

GMC v. Keystone Auto. Indus.. 256

Gnesys, Inc. v. Greene.. 135

Gold Seal Co. v. Weeks. 92

Google Inc. v. Am. Blind & Wallpaper Factory, Inc.. . . . . .179; 254; 256

Gordon & Breach Sci. Pubs., S.A. v. American Inst. of Physics. 201, 202

Gorham Mfg. Co., In re. 84

[References are to pages]

Gort Girls Frocks, Inc. v. Princess Pat Lingerie, Inc. 160
GoTo.com v. Walt Disney Co. . 150; 152; 168; 339
Gov't Employees Ins. Co. v. Google, Inc. . . . 180; 254; 259
Goya Foods, Inc. v. Condal Distribs., Inc. . . . 155
Gracie v. Gracie 113
Graham Webb International Ltd. Partnership v. Emporium Drug Mart, Inc. 301
Great S. Bank v. First S. Bank. 129; 210
Green River Bottling Co. v. Green River Corp.. . . . . .295, 296
Grey v. Campbell Soup Co. 211; 265
Greyhound Corp. v. Armour Life Ins. Co. 37
Greyhound Corp. v. Both Worlds, Inc. 83
Griffith v. Fenrick 232
Grocery Outlet, Inc. v. Albertson's, Inc.. 289
Groden v. Random House, Inc. 202
Grotrian, Helfferich, Schulz, Th. Steinweg Nachf. v. Steinway & Sons 155; 166
Grove Labs. v. Brewer & Co.. 76
Gruen Marketing Corp. v. Benrus Watch Co. . 364, 365
Grupo Gigante S.A. de C.V. v. Dallo & Co.. . .33; 39; 43; 57; 218; 312; 315
GTE Corp. v. Williams. 152
Gucci Am., Inc. v. Hall & Assocs. 355
Gucci America, Inc. v. Daffy's Inc. 347
Gucci America, Inc. v. Exclusive Imports Int'l.345
Gucci Shops, Inc. v. R.H. Macy & Co. . . 265; 268

H

H&R Indus. v. Kirshner 202, 203
H-D Michigan, Inc. v. Top Quality Serv., Inc.. . .59
H.L. Hayden Co. of New York, Inc. v. Siemens Med. Sys., Inc.. . . . . .297, 298; 305
Haig & Haig, Ltd., Ex parte 65
Halicki v. United Artists Communications, Inc..367
Haltom v. Haltom's Jewelers, Inc. 63
Hammerton, Inc. v. Heisterman 332
Hamzik v. Zale Corp./Delaware 182
Hanover Star Milling Co. v. Metcalf. 33; 34
Hard Rock Café International, Inc. v. Texas Pig Stands, Inc.. 349
Hard Rock Café Licensing Corp. v. Concession Services, Inc.. 251
Hard Rock Licensing Corp. v. Pacific Graphics, Inc.. . . . . .262; 265
Harjo v. Pro Football Inc. 363
Harley-Davidson, Inc. v. Grottanelli. 265
Harris Research, Inc. v. Lydon 340

Harrods Ltd. v. Sixty Internet Domain Names.238; 240; 244, 245; 247
Hartford House, Ltd. v. Hallmark Cards, Inc. . . 70
Hartog & Co. v. swix.com. 244
Hartwell Co. v. Shane 362
Hasbro, Inc. v. Clue Computing, Inc. 171
Hasbro Inc. v. Internet Entertainment Group, Ltd.. . . . . .207; 214; 239
Haughton Elev. Co. v. Seeberger 60
Havana Club Holding S.A. v. Galleon S.A. . . 121; 317
Haymaker Sports, Inc. v. Turian. 296
Healing the Children, Inc. v. Heal the Children, Inc. 366
Heaton Distrib. Co. v. Union Tank Car Co. . . 344; 354
Heavenly Creations, Inc., In re 103
Helena Rubenstein, Inc., In re. 118
Henri's Food Prods. Co., Inc. v. Kraft, Inc.. . .143
Herbko Int'l, Inc. v. Kappa Books, Inc. . . . 73; 85
Hermes, Int'l v. Lederer de Paris Fifth Ave., Inc. 177
Hershey Co. v. Art Van Furn., Inc. 220
Hesmer Foods, Inc. v. Campbell Soup Co.. . . .50
Hess's of Allentown, Inc. v. National Bellas Hess, Inc. 137
HI Limited Partnership v. Winghouse of Florida, Inc. 221
Hipsaver Co., Inc. v. J.T. Posey Co.. 346
Hiram Walker & Sons v. Grubman 249
HMH Pub. Co. v. Lambert. 138
Hodge Chile Co. v. KNA Food Distributors, Inc. 294
Holeproof Hosiery Co. v. Wallach Bros. 317
Holiday Inns of America, Inc. v. B & B Corp..128
Home Box Office, Inc. v. Showtime/Movie Channel, Inc. 343
Hon, United States v. 359
Hormel Foods Corp. v. Jim Henson Prods.. . . .150; 159; 184; 207; 226; 262; 265, 266
Horn's, Inc. v. Sanofi Beaute, Inc. 75
Horphag Research, Ltd. v. Garcia . 215; 223, 224
Horphag Research, Ltd. v. Pellegrini 324
Hostetter Co. v. Brueggeman-Reinert Distilling Co.. 249
Hot Wax, Inc. v. Turtle Wax, Inc. . . 311–314; 337
House of Westmore v. Denney. 3
House of Windsor, Inc., In re. 93
HQM, Ltd. v. Hatfield 129
Huang v. Tzu Wei Chen Food Co. 106
Hughes v. Design Look Inc.. . . . . .71; 291, 292

Hunt Foods & Indus., Inc. v. Gerson Stewart Corp............................148

Hunt Masters, Inc. v. Landry's Seafood Rest., Inc............................58

Hurricane Fence Co. v. A-1 Hurricane Fence Co............................39

Hutchinson v. Essence Communications, Inc.. .156

Hutchinson v. Pfeil..............367

Hutchinson Tech., Inc., In re..........62

Hydro-Dynamics, Inc. v. George Putnam & Co., Inc........................33; 36

Hylo Co. v. Jean Patou, Inc............39

Hyundai Constr. Equip. U.S.A., Inc. v. Chris Johnson Equip., Inc..............215

I

I.P. Lund Trading ApS v. Kohler Co.. . . .205; 218, 219; 222, 223; 331; 332

Iberia Foods Corp. v. Romeo..........301

Icee Distribs., Inc. v. J & J Snack Foods Corp........................364, 365

Ideal Indus., Inc. v. Gardner Bender, Inc. . 74; 317; 319

Ideal Toy Corp. v. Cameo Exclusive Prods., Inc............................37

Iding v. Anaston..................185

IMAF, S.P.A. v. J.C. Penney Co..........95

Imperial Service Systems, Inc. v. ISS Int'l Service System, Inc..................155

Imperial Tobacco Ltd. v. Phillip Morris, Inc.. .291

In re Application of (see name of party)......

In re (see name of party)..............

Indianapolis Colts, Inc. v. Metropolitan Baltimore Football Club L.P..........139; 141; 156

Induct-O-Matic Corp. v. Inductotherm Corp.. . . 53; 55; 57; 144

Industrie Cotonniere Etablissements Boussac v. Alexander's Dept. Stores, Inc..........327

Information Clearing House, Inc. v. Find Magazine................154; 158

Infurnari; United States v............359

Int'l Ass'n of Lions Clubs v. Mars, Inc.....102

Int'l Bancorp, LLC v. Societe Des Bains De Mer Et Du Cercle Des Etrangers a Monaco . 41; 42; 44

Int'l Taste, Inc., In re..............92

Intermatic v. Toeppen............184; 187

Intermed Communications, Inc. v. Chaney. . . .40

International Flavors & Fragrances Inc., In re. .81, 82

International Kennel Club, Inc. v. Mighty Star, Inc..............144; 154; 175; 343

International News Service v. Associated Press . . 5

International Order of Job's Daughters v. Lindeburg & Co............................362

International Profit Assocs., Inc. v. Paisola. . . 179

International Star Class Yacht Racing Ass'n v. Tommy Hilfiger U.S.A...........345

International Tel. & Tel. Corp. v. International Mobile Machines Corp...........362

Internet, Inc. v. Corporation for Nat'l Research Initiatives..................363

Interpace Corp. v. Lapp, Inc............149

Interstellar Starship Servs. v. Epix, Inc.. .145; 168; 171

Investacorp, Inc. v. Arabian Inv. Banking Corp.. .57

Investools, Inc. v. Investtools.com.......243

Invicta Plastics (USA) Ltd. v. Mego Corp.. . . .327

Inwood Laboratories, Inc. v. Ives Laboratories, Inc..................18, 19; 47; 250

Island Insteel Sys., Inc. v. Waters........337

IT&T Corp. v. General Instr. Corp..........86

ITC Ltd. v. Punchgini, Inc.........44, 45; 291

J

J & J Snack Foods Corp. v. McDonald's Corp........................145; 146

J.L. Prescott Co. v. Blue Cross Laboratories (Inc.)........................107

J.R. Wood & Sons, Inc. v. Reese Jewelry Corp........................138

JA Apparel Corp. v. Abboud..........340

Jack in the Box, Inc. v. Jackinthebox.org. . . .244

Jada Toys, Inc. v. Mattel, Inc.....223; 234; 235

Jahr USA Pub'g v. Meredith Corp.......159

James Burrough, Ltd. v. Sign of Beefeater, Inc............................155

Japan Telecom, Inc. v. Japan Telecom Am., Inc..56

Jarritos, Inc. v. Los Jarritos..........220

Jarrow Formulas, Inc. v. Nutrition Now, Inc. . 313; 337

JCW Invs., Inc. v. Novelty, Inc..........349

Jeffrey Milstein, Inc. v. Greger, Lawlor, Roth, Inc........................32; 68

Jellibeans, Inc. v. Skating Clubs of Georgia, Inc..................141, 142; 185

Jenkins, Estate of v. Paramount Pictures Corp. . 73

Jet, Inc. v. Sewage Aeration Sys........221

Jewelers Vigilance Comm., Inc. v. Ullenberg Corp........................107

Jewelers Vigilance Comm., Inc. v. Ullenberg Corp........................362

Jews for Jesus v. Brodsky......177; 183; 232

Jim Dandy Co. v. Martha White Foods......86

Jimlar Corp. v. Army & Air Force Exchange Serv. 85

John H. Harland Co. v. Clarke Checks, Inc. . . . 64

John Paul Mitchell Systems v. Pete-N-Larry's Inc. 301

John Paul Mitchell Systems v. Randall's Food Markets, Inc. 301

John R. Thompson Co. v. Holloway 63; 77

John Walker & Sons, Ltd. v. Bethea 148

Johnston v. Standard Mining Co. 312

Joint Stock Society v. UDV North America, Inc. 366

Jones Day v. Blockshopper, LLC 233

Jordache Enters. v. Hogg Wyld, Ltd. . . . 261, 262; 265; 267

Joseph Scott Co. v. Scott Swimming Pools, Inc. 343

JR Cigar, Inc. v. GoTo.com, Inc. 179

K

K & N Eng'g, Inc. v. Bulat 350, 351

K Mart Corp. v. Cartier, Inc. 310; 311

Kappa Sigma Fraternity v. Kappa Sigma Gamma Fraternity 38

Karl Storz Endoscopy-Am., Inc. v. Surgical Techs., Inc. 175; 302

Kasco Corp. v. General Services, Inc. 192

Kason Indus. v. Component Hardware Grp. . . . 312; 314

Keebler Co. v. Rovira Biscuit Corp. 143

Keebler Co., Application of. 55

Keene Corp. v. Paraflex Indus., Inc. 24; 27

Kegan v. Apple Computer Inc. 256

Keller Prods., Inc. v. Rubber Linings Corp. . . . 50

Kellogg Co. v. Exxon Corp. 312; 314–316

Kellogg Co. v. Nat'l Biscuit Co. 56; 60

Kendall-Jackson Winery, Ltd. v. E. & J. Gallo Winery 59

Kentucky Fried Chicken Corp. v. Diversified Packaging Corp. 293

KeyCorp. v. Key Bank & Trust 128

Kinetic Concepts, Inc. v. Bluesky Med. Group .215

King v. Innovation Books 197

King-Seeley Thermos Co. v. Aladdin Indus., Inc. 59, 60; 338

Knitwaves, Inc. v. Lollytogs Ltd. 31

Koffler Stores, Ltd. v. Shoppers Drug Mart, Inc. 37; 43

Kohler v. Moen 14; 65

KP Permanent Make-Up, Inc. v. Lasting Impression I, Inc. 321; 326

Kraft Foods Holdings, Inc. v. Helm. 214

Kraft Gen. Foods, Inc. v. Allied Old English, Inc. 150

Krueger Int'l v. Nightingale Inc. 31

L

L. & J.G. Stickley, Inc. v. Cosser. 86

L.L. Bean Inc. v. Drake Publishers, Inc. . . 184; 213; 277, 278

L.S. Heath & Son, Inc. v. AT & T Info. Sys., Inc. 367

A La Carte v. Culinary Enters. 54; 155

La Chemise Lacoste v. Alligator Co. 360

La Peregrina Ltd., In re 75

Lamothe v. Atlantic Recording Co. 192–195

Lamparello v. Falwell. 135; 173; 337

Lands' End, Inc. v. Manback 37

Landscape Forms, Inc. v. Columbia Cascade Co. .175; 331

Lane Capital Mgt., Inc. v. Lane Capital Mgt., Inc. 62

Lang v. Retirement Living Pub. Co. 157

Larry Harmon Pictures Corp. v. Williams Rest. Corp. 36

Larsen v. Terk Technologies 57

Laura Scudder's v. Pacific Gamble Robinson Co. 137

Leatherman Tool Group, Inc. v. Cooper Indus., Inc. 96

Leelanau Wine Cellars v. Black & Red 142

Leigh v. Warner Bros., Inc. 70; 71

Les Ballets Trockadero De Monte Carlo, Inc. v. Trevino 190

Les Halles de Paris, J.V., In re 93, 94

Lever Bros. Co. v. American Bakeries Co. . . .158; 159

Lever Bros. Co. v. United States. 307–310

Levi Strauss & Co. v. Blue Bell, Inc. 57; 153

Levi Strauss & Co. v. Sunrise Int'l Trading Inc. 189

Lewis v. Marriott Int'l, Inc. 61

Liberty Mutual Ins. Co. v. Liberty Ins. Co. . . . 84

Libman Co. v. Vining Indus., Inc. 154

Life Savers Corp. v. Curtiss Candy Co. 139

Life Services Supps., Inc. v. Natural Organics, Inc. 345

Lindy Pen Co. v. Bic Pen Corp. 327

Linville v. Rivard 40

Lipscher v. LRP Pubs., Inc. 192

Lipton v. Nature Co. 198

[References are to pages]

Lipton Industries, Inc. v. Ralston Purina Co.. .107; 289; 361

Liqwacon Corp. v. Browning-Ferris Industries, Inc. 86

Little Caesar Enters., Inc. v. Pizza Caesar, Inc.. 143

Little Tavern Shops v. Davis 63

Litton Systems, Inc. v. Whirlpool Corp.. 331

Lloyd Corp. v. Tanner 276

Lockheed Martin Corp. v. Network Solutions, Inc. 252; 253; 254–257; 354

Loctite Corp. v. National Starch & Chemical Corp.. 342

Logan v. Burgers Ozark Country Cured Hams, Inc. 347

Lois Sportswear, U.S.A., Inc. v. Levi Strauss & Co.. . . . . 156; 160; 173; 177

London Regional Transport v. The William A. Berden & Edward C. Goetz, III Partnership . 43

Lone Star Steakhouse & Saloon, Inc. v. Longhorn Steaks, Inc. 361

Lone Star Steakhouse & Saloon v. Alpha of Virginia 337

Lopez; United States v. 36

Lorillard Tobacco Co. v. Amouri's Grand Foods, Inc. 340

Lorillard Tobacco Co. v. Engida. 340

Louis Vuitton Malletier v. Dooney & Bourke, Inc.. . . . . 135; 140; 345

Louis Vuitton Malletier S.A. v. Haute Diggity Dog, LLC . .214; 220; 225; 228; 231; 262; 269; 278; 352

Louis Vuitton S.A. v. Lee 348

Lucas Nursery and Landscaping, Inc. v. Grosse 238; 240–242

Lucasfilm, Ltd. v. High Frontier, et al. . . 178; 184; 283

Lucasfilm Ltd. v. Media Market Group, Ltd.. . .282

Lucent Techs., Inc. v. Johnson 207; 239; 241

Lucent Techs., Inc. v. Lucentsucks.com . .237; 243

Lucky Brand Dungarees, Inc. v. Ally Apparel Resources LLC 116

Luigino's, Inc. v. Stouffer Corp.. 222

Lycee Francais de New York v. Reynaud. . . . 144

M

M&G Elecs. Sales Corp. v. Sony Kabushiki Kaisha. 159; 164

Macia v. Microsoft Corp. 50; 152; 157

Madison Reprographics v. Cook's Reprographics 57

Maharishi Hardy Blechman Ltd. v. Abercrombie & Fitch Co. 68

Maier Brewing Co. v. Fleischmann Distilling Corp.. .347

Maison Prunier v. Prunier's Restaurant & Cafe, Inc. 42, 43

Major League Baseball Properties, Inc. v. Sed Non Olet Denarius, Ltd. 289, 290

Maple Grove Farms v. Euro-Can Prods. 65

Marcon Ltd. v. Avon Prods., Inc. 106

Marker Int'l v. DeBruler 61

Market America v. Optihealth Prods. . . . 180; 182

Marling v. Ellison 195

Marque le Fouquet's 122

Marquis Who's Who v. North American Ad Associates. 343

Marriott Corp., In re. 37

Martin's Herend Imports Inc. v. Diamond & Gem Trading USA, Co.. . . . . .301; 308

Mashantucket Pequot Tribe v. Redican 223

MasterCard Int'l, Inc. v. First Nat'l Bank of Omaha, Inc. 345

Mastercard Int'l, Inc. v. Nader 2000 Primary Comm., Inc. 206; 232; 283

Mastercrafters Clock & Radio Co. v. Vacheron & Constantin-Le Coutre Watches, Inc. 177

Mastro Plastics Corp. v. Emenee Indus., Inc.. .360

Matador Motor Inns, Inc. v. Matador Motel, Inc. 288

Matrix Essentials v. Emporium Drug Mart . . . 298

Matrix Motor Co. v. Toyota Jidosha Kabushiki Kaisha 135, 136; 164

Matsushita Elec. Corp. of Am. v. Solar Sound Sys., Inc. 193

Mattel, Inc. v. Azrak-Hamway Int'l, Inc. 327

Mattel, Inc. v. Internet Dimensions, Inc. . 207; 239

Mattel, Inc. v. MCA Records. .184; 213; 231; 232; 272; 276; 278

Mattel Inc. v. Walking Mt. Prods. . . 320; 324; 349

Mavety Media Group Ltd., In re 112

Mayflower Transit 241

MB Financial Bank, N.A. v. MB Real Estate Services, L.L.C. 143, 144; 292

McBee v. Delica Co.. 192

McDonald's Corp. v. Gunvill 327

McDonald's Corp. v. McKinley 145, 146

McDonald's Corp. v. Robertson 339

McFly, Inc. v. Universal City Studios. 155

McGinley, In re 83

McGregor-Doniger Inc. v. Drizzle Inc. . . 150–153; 156; 160

McLean v. Fleming. 7

McNeil Nutritionals, LLC v. Heartland Sweeteners, LLC. 167

McNeil-P.C.C., Inc. v. Bristol-Myers Squibb Co.. .198

McNeilab, Inc. v. American Home Prods. Corp.. .198

Mead Data Cent., Inc. v. Toyota Motor Sales, U.S.A., Inc.. . . . . .206; 210–212

Medic Alert Found. United States, Inc. v. Corel Corp.. .256

Medical Modalities Association, Inc. v. ARA Corporation 145

MedImmune, Inc. v. Genentech, Inc. 368

Medinol Ltd. v. Neuro Vasx, Inc. 115

Medline Indus., Inc. v. Strategic Commercial Solutions, Inc.. 256

Members First Fed. Credit Union v. Members 1st Fed. Credit Union. 128; 149

Merchants' Syndicate Catalog Co. v. Retailers' Factory Catalog Co.. 4

Merck & Co. v. Mediplan Health Consulting . 178, 179; 326

Merck & Co. v. Mediplan Health Consulting, Inc.. 179

Meridian Mut. Ins. Co. v. Meridian Ins. Group, Inc.. . . . . .144; 175

Merriam-Webster, Inc. v. Random House, Inc.. . 153

Metromedia, Inc. v. American Broadcasting Co's., Inc.. 55

MGM-Pathe Communications v. Pink Panther Patrol 284

Microsoft Corp. v. AGA Solutions, Inc.. . .339, 340

Microsoft Corp. v. Atek 3000 Computer, Inc.. .340

Microsoft Corp. v. Ion Technologies Corp.. . . .351

Midwest Plastic Fabricators 101; 113

Miller Brewing Co. v. G. Heileman Brewing Co.. 50

Mini Maid Servs Co. v. Maid Brigade Sys., Inc.. .250, 251

Minnesota Mining & Mfg. Co. v. Taylor. . . . 145

Minnesota Mining and Mfg. Co., In re. 65

Mishawaka Rubber & Woolen Mfg. Co. v. S.S. Kresge. 16; 347

Miss Universe, Inc. v. Flesher. 343

Miss World (UK), Ltd. v. Mrs. America Pageants, Inc. 150

Mister Donut of America, Inc. v. Mr. Donut, Inc. 128

Miyano Mach. USA, Inc. v. Miyanohitec Mach., Inc. 292

Mobil Oil Corp. v. Pegasus Petroleum Corp. . 158; 166, 167

Mobile Office Solutions, Inc. 172

Modern Optics v. Univis Lens Co.. 76

Mogen David Wine Corp., In re 24; 65

Monell v. Dep't of Soc. Servs. 358

Money Store v. Harriscorp Fin., Inc..152; 295, 296

Monsanto Chem. Co. v. Perfect Fit Prods. Mfg. Co.. 186

Monsanto Co. v. Syngenta Seeds, Inc.. 204

Montgomery v. Noga. 195

Moore Business Forms, Inc. v. Ryu. 289

Moose Creek, Inc. v. Abercrombie & Fitch Co..51; 151

Morningside Group, Ltd. v. Morningside Capital Group, L.L.C.. 40

Morton-Norwich Products, Inc., In re. .22; 26; 65; 96

Moseley v. V Secret Catalogue, Inc.. .1; 212; 214; 223

Mosler Safe Co. v. Ely-Norris Safe Co.. 367

Mother's Restaurants, Inc. v. Mother's Other Kitchen, Inc.. . . . . .40; 43

Motorola, Inc. v. Griffiths Elecs., Inc.. 146

Mt. Healthy City Sch. Dist. Bd. of Educ. v. Doyle 358

Murphy v. Provident Mut. Life Ins. Co. 366

Murphy Door Bed Co. v. Interior Sleep Sys., Inc.. .3; 60

Mushroom Makers, Inc. v. R. G. Barry Corp.. . 138; 342

Mustang Motels, Inc. v. Patel. 52

Mutual of Omaha Ins. Co. v. Novak . . . 155; 262; 265; 277; 286

MyGym, LLC v. Engle 340

N

N.K. Fairbank Co. v. R.W. Bell Manuf'g. Co.. . 249

Nabisco, Inc. v. PF Brands, Inc. 215; 218; 221–223; 339

Naclox, Inc. v. Lee. 294

Nasdaq Stock Mkt., Inc. v. Archipelago Holdings, LLC. 326

Nat'l Fed. of the Blind, Inc. v. Loompanics Enters., Inc.. 326

Nat'l Football League Props., Inc. v. New Jersey Giants, Inc.. 155

National Artists Mgt. Co. v. Weaving . . . 202, 203

National Ass'n of Pharm. Mfrs., Inc. v. Ayerst Labs.. .366

National Auto. Club v. National Auto Club, Inc. . 3

National Cable Television Ass'n, Inc. v. American Cinema Editors, Inc.. 86

[References are to pages]

National Conf. of Bar Examiners v. Multistate Legal Studies, Inc. 51; 58

National Football League Properties v. Playoff Corp.. 320

Natural Footwear Ltd. v. Hart, Schaffner & Marx 78

NBA Props. v. Untertainment Records LLC . . 355

NBBJ East L.P. v. NBBJ Training Acad., Inc. . 216

NEC Electronics v. CAL Circuit Abco . . 297, 298; 307

Nelson Souto Major Piquet, In re. 62

New Colt Holding Corp. v. RJG Holdings of Fla., Inc. 159

New Kayak Pool v. R & P Pools, Inc. 141

New Kids on the Block v. News Am. Publ'g, Inc. 213; 230; 322–325

New York Stock Exch., Inc. v. New York, New York Hotel, LLC 206; 207; 211; 265; 267

Nihon Keizai Shimbun, Inc. v. Comline Bus. Data, Inc. 320

Nike, Inc. v. "Just Did It"' Enters.. . . . .261, 262

Nike, Inc. v. Nikepal Int'l, Inc. . 99; 220; 227; 228; 340

Nike, Inc. v. Top Brand Co.. 345

Nike, Inc. v. Variety Wholesalers, Inc.. 349

Nikon, Inc. v. Ikon Corp. 159

Nintendo of Am., Inc. v. Aeropower Co.. . . . 189

Nippon Miniature Bearing Corp.; United States v.. 307

Nissan Motor Co. v. Nissan Computer Corp. . 171; 177; 220; 221

Nissen Trampoline Co. v. American Trampoline Co.. 60

Niton Corp. v. Radiation Monitoring Devices, Inc. 182

Nitro Leisure Prods., L.L.C. v. Acushnet Co. . 298; 301; 342

No Nonsense Fashions, Inc. v. Consolidated Foods Corp.. .107

Nor-Am Chemical Co. v. O.M. Scott & Sons Co.. 27

Nora Beverages, Inc. v. Perrier Group of Am., Inc.. . . . . .21; 64

North Am. Med. Corp. v. Axiom Worldwide, Inc.. . . . . .170; 182; 340

Northern Light Tech., Inc. v. Northern Lights Club. .238

Northland Ins. Cos. v. Blaylock 183; 232

Novartis Consumer Health, Inc. v. Johnson & Johnson-Merck Consumer Pharms. Co.. . . .155; 198–201

Novo Nordisk of N. Am. v. Eli Lilly & Co. . . 156

Nunez; United States v.. 359

Nupla Corp. v. IXL Mfg. Co.. 50

NutraSweet Co. v. Stadt Corp.. 68

O

Obear-Nester Glass Co. v. United Drug Co. . . 347

OBH, Inc. v. Spotlight Magazine, Inc.. . . 172; 177; 183

Odol-Werke Wien Gesellschaft M.B.H., Ex parte. 75

Oklahoma Beverage Co. v. Dr. Pepper Love Bottling Co. (of Muskogee) 129

Old Dutch Foods, Inc. v. Dan Dee Pretzel & Potato Chip Co.. . . . . .77; 88; 91

Old Glory Condom Corp., In re 83

Oliveira v. Frito-Lay, Inc.. 69

Olympus Corp. v. United States 307; 310

Omega S.A. v. Omega Eng'g, Inc.. 223

Opticians Ass'n v. Independent Opticians. . . .337

Oreck Corp. v. U.S. Floor Sys., Inc. 116

Orient Express Trading Co. v. Federated Dept. Stores, Inc.. 317

Oriental Foods, Inc. v. Chun King Sales, Inc. . 139

Original Appalachian Artworks, Inc. v. Granada Elecs., Inc.. . . . . .301; 309

Orion Pictures Co. v. Dell Pub. Co. 73

Orion Research, Inc., In re. 103

Otokoyama Co. v. Wine of Japan Import, Inc. . 74, 75

Ott v. Target Corp.. 219

Owens-Corning Fiberglas Corp., In re 65; 68

Oxford Indus., Inc. v. JBJ Fabrics, Inc.. 151

P

P&G v. Haugen 256

P.J. Valckenbeg, GmbH, In re. 83

PACCAR, Inc. v. TeleScan Techs., L.L.C.. . . .167; 168; 297; 326

Packman v. Chicago Tribune Co.. 143

Paco Sport, Ltd. v. Paco Rabanne Parfums . . .158

PacTel Teletrac v. T.A.B. Systems 87

Paddington Corp. v. Attiki Imp. & Distrib., Inc.. .46; 67

PAF S.r.l. v. Lisa Lighting Co. 331

Palm Bay Imps. 74, 75; 141; 218

Panavision Int'l, L.P. v. Toeppen 232

Panavision International, L.P. v. Toeppen.184; 210; 215

Panda Invs., Inc. v. Jabez Enters.. 339

Pappan Enters., Inc. v. Hardee's Food Sys., Inc.. 339

Paramount Pictures Corp. v. White. 36

[References are to pages]

Paris Glove of Canada Ltd. v. SBC/Sporto Corp.. .292

Park N' Fly v. Dollar Park and Fly, Inc.. . .59; 114; 116

Parks v. LaFace Records. 270; 277

Patsy's Brand, Inc. v. I.O.B. Realty, Inc. . 150; 349

Paulsson Geophysical Servs., Inc. v. Sigmar . . 339

Payless Shoesource, Inc. v. Reebok Int'l, Ltd.. 173, 174

Peaceable Planet, Inc. v. Ty, Inc.. . . . . . .61, 62

Pebble Beach Co. v. Tour 18 I. . . .326, 327; 328

Pennsylvania State University v. University Orthopedics, Ltd.. 360

Penthouse Int'l Ltd., In re.. 65

Pepcom Indus., Inc., In re.. 38

PepsiCo, Inc. v. #1 Wholesale, LLC. . . .213; 220

PepsiCo v. Giraud 309

Pepsico, Inc. v. Grapette Co.. 297

PepsiCo, Inc. v. Nostalgia Prods. Corp.. 309

Perfect 10, Inc. v. Visa Int'l Serv. Ass'n . 254; 259

Perini Corp. v. Perini Construction, Inc.. . .47; 57; 175

Person's Co. v. Christman.. 39

PETA v. Doughney . 177, 178; 183; 226; 238; 240; 242

Petrosian; United States v.. 359

Phat Fashions, L.L.C. v. Phat Game Ath. Apparel, Inc.. 146

PHC, Inc. v. Pioneer Healthcare, Inc.. 112

Philip Morris Inc. v. Allen Distributors, Inc. . .308

Phillips Beverage Co., In re. 106

Phoenix of Broward, Inc. v. McDonald's Corp.. 366

PIC Design Corp. v. Sterling Precision Corp.. .193

Pignons S.A. de Mecanique de Precision v. Polaroid Corp.. .143

Pilates, Inc. v. Current Concepts, Inc.. . . .292; 297

Pilates, Inc. v. Georgetown Bodyworks Deep Muscle Massage Ctrs., Inc.. 81

Pillsbury Co. v. Milky Way Prods., Inc.. 281

Pillsbury Flour Mills Co., Ex Parte. 81

Pinaud, Inc. v. Huebschman. 52

Pioneer Hi-Bred Int'l v. Holden Found. Seeds . 194

Pirone v. MacMillan, Inc.. 72

Pizza Hut, Inc. v. Papa John's Int'l, Inc.. 201

Pizzeria Uno Corp. v. Temple 128; 152

Planetary Motion, Inc. v. Techsplosion, Inc. . .134

Planned Parenthood Fed'n of America v. Bucci.36; 145; 172; 183; 187; 232

Playboy Enters. v. Netscape Communs. Corp.. 166; 169; 179, 180; 253

Playboy Enters., Inc. v. Asiafocus Int'l, Inc.. . .182

Playboy Enters., Inc. v. Welles.183; 205; 210; 221, 222; 230; 324, 325

Plus Prods. v. Plus Discount Foods, Inc. . 159; 163

Polaroid Corp. v. Berkey Photo, Inc.. 342

Polaroid Corp. v. Polarad Elecs. Corp. . . 140; 168

Polaroid Corp. v. Polaraid, Inc.. . . . . . .51; 211

Polo Fashions v. Craftex, Inc.. 173

Polo Fashions, Inc. v. Extra Special Products, Inc.. 138

Poloskey v. Pantano.. 63

Porsche Cars N.A., Inc. v. Porsche.net 242

Precision Instr. Mfg. Co. v. Automotive Maint. Mach. Co.. 317

Premier Dental Prods. Co. v. Darby Dental Supply Co.. . . . . .296; 310

Presley, Estate of v. Russen. 72

Prestonettes, Inc. v. Coty. 297; 300; 305

Pro-Cuts v. Schilz-Price Enters 137

Pro-Football, Inc. v. Harjo. 83; 112; 114

Procter & Gamble Co. v. Amway Corp.. . . . 366

Procter & Gamble Co. v. Chesebrough-Pond's, Inc.. . . . . .200, 201

Procter & Gamble Co. v. Haugen. .201; 203; 250; 257

Procter & Gamble Co. v. Johnson & Johnson, Inc.. 158

Proctor & Gamble Co. v. Amway Corp.. . . . 349

Prof'l Photographers of Ohio, Inc., In re 101

Professional Economics Inc. v. Professional Economic Servs., Inc.. 119

Professional Golfers Ass'n of America v. Bankers Life & Cas. Co.. . . . . .102; 294

Profitness Physical Therapy Ctr. v. Pro-Fit Orthopedic & Sports Physical Therapy P.C.. . . . . .313; 315; 316; 343

Promatek Indus., Ltd. v. Equitrac Corp. . 168; 170; 182, 183

Propet USA, Inc. v. Shugart. 339

Public Serv. Co. v. Nexus Energy Software, Inc.. 145

Publications Int'l, Ltd. v. Landoll, Inc.. . . . .29; 64

Pure Foods, Inc. v. Minute Maid Corp.. 186

Q

Q-Tips, Inc. v. Johnson & Johnson. 53, 54

Quabaug Rubber 364–366

Qualitex Co. v. Jacobson Prods. Co. Inc..1; 16, 17; 19; 27; 67, 68

Quality Inns Int'l, Inc. v. McDonald's Corp.. . . 148

[References are to pages]

Quantum Fitness Corp. v. Quantum Lifestyle Ctrs., L.L.C. 145
Quick Technologies, Inc. v. Sage Group PLC . 345; 347
Quiksilver, Inc. v. Kymsta Corp. 138

R

R&R Partners, Inc. v. Tovar. 345
R.G. Barry Corp. v. A. Sandler Co.. 143
R.J. Reynolds Tobacco Co. v. Premium Tobacco Stores, Inc. 307
R.M. Smith, Inc., In re 26; 96
Racine Indus., Inc. v. Bane-Clene Corp. . . 76; 102
Radolf v. University of Connecticut. 204
Ralston Purina Co. v. Saniwax Paper Co.. . . . 138
Ramada Inns, Inc. v. Gadsden Motel Co.. . . . 344
Ramex Records, Inc. v. Guerrero 107
Reader's Digest Assoc. v. Conservative Digest . 349
Recot, Inc. v. M.C. Becton 111; 148; 265
Reddy Comms., Inc. v. Environmental Action Foundation 153
Reebok Int'l, Ltd. v. Marnatech Enters., Inc.. . 190, 191
Reed v. United Transp. Union. 336
Regents of Univ. Wisc. Sys. v. Phoenix Software Int'l Inc.. . . . . 335; 336
Reliable Tire Distributors, Inc. v. Kelly Springfield Tire Co.. 344
Reno Air Racing Ass'n, Inc. v. McCord 339
Rescue.com Corp. v. Google, Inc.. 179
Resorts Int'l, Inc. v. Greate Bay Hotel & Casino, Inc.. 43
Resource Developers Inc. v. Statue of Liberty-Ellis Island Foundation, Inc.. 155
Retail Servs. v. Freebies Pub'g 151
Richard Feiner & Co. v. New York Times Co.. 196; 334
Ringling Bros.-Barnum & Bailey Combined Shows, Inc. v. B.E. Windows Corp. 213
Ringling Bros.-Barnum & Bailey Combined Shows, Inc. v. Celozzi-Ettelson Chevrolet, Inc. . . . 211
Ringling Bros.-Barnum & Bailey Combined Shows, Inc. v. Utah Div. of Travel Dev. . 216; 218; 222
Ritchie v. Simpson 361–363
Rivard v. Linville. 291
Riverbank Canning Co., In re 83
RJR Foods, Inc. v. White Rock Corp.. 155
Robert B. Vance & Assocs., Inc. v. Baronet Corp.. 322
Robert Reis & Co. v. Herman B. Reiss, Inc.. . 249
Roberts, In re 38

Robinson Co. v. Plastics Research & Development Corp.. 293
Rock & Roll Hall of Fame & Museum, Inc. v. Gentile Prods.. . . . . 69; 71
Rogers v. Grimaldi. 269
Rogers, In re. 97
Roho, Inc. v. Marquis 193
Rolex Watch USA, Inc. v. Meece 300
Roller Derby Skate Corp. v. Bauer Nike Hockey, Inc.. . . . . 22; 99
Rolls-Royce Motors, Ltd. v. A & A Fiberglass, Inc.. 135
Romantics v. Activision Publishing 326
Romm Art Creations, Ltd. v. Simcha Int'l, Inc.. . 70
Rose Art Indus., Inc. v. Swanson. 64
Roulo v. Russ Berrie & Co.. 291
Roux Labs., Inc. v. Clairol, Inc.. . . . . 91, 92
Rudolph Int'l, Inc. v. Realys, Inc.. 59
Runsdorf, In re. 83

S

S&L Vitamins, Inc. v. Australian Gold, Inc.. . . 179; 182; 326
S.C. Johnson & Son, Inc. v. Gold Seal Co.. . . . 92
S.S. Kresge Co. v. Winget Kickernick Co.. . . . 138
Safeway Stores, Inc. v. Safeway Properties, Inc.. . 3
Saks & Co. v. Hill 211
Sallen v. Corinthians Licenciamentos LTDA. . 248; 355, 356
Sally Beauty Co. v. Beautyco., Inc.. 161
Salton, Inc. v. Cornwall Corp.. 116
San Juan Prods., Inc. v. San Juan Pools, Inc.. . 353
Sands, Taylor & Wood Co. v. Quaker Oats Co.. . . . . . 163, 164; 290; 292; 295, 296; 319
Sanitized, Inc. v. S.C. Johnson & Sons, Inc.. . . 317
Santana Prods. v. Bobrick Washroom Equip., Inc.. 337
Sara Lee Corp. v. Kayser-Roth Corp.. . 51, 52; 54, 55; 58; 148; 155; 312; 315, 316
Saratoga Vichy Spring Co., Inc. v. Lehman . . 289; 291
Sardi's Rest. Corp. v. Sardie 63
Sarkli, Ltd., In re 74, 75
Savannah College of Art & Design, Inc. v. Houeix 177; 183; 233
Savin Corp. v. Savin Group . . . 95; 159; 217–219; 223, 224
Saxlehner v. Wagner. 327
Saxony Products, Inc. v. Guerlain, Inc.. 327
SB Designs v. Reebok Int'l, Ltd. 258

[References are to pages]

Scandia Down Corp. v. Euroquilt, Inc. 142

Scanvec Amiable, Ltd. v. Chang. 189

Scarves by Vera, Inc. v. Todo Imports, Ltd.. . . 153; 156; 159

Schieffelin & Co. v. Jack Co. . 149; 155; 156; 262; 265

Schlotzky's Ltd. v. Sterling 135

Schmidheiny v. Weber. 246

Scholastic, Inc. v. Stouffer. 209

Scholastic, Inc. v. Time Warner Ent. Co., L.P. . 209

Schroeder v. Lotito. 353

Schwartz v. Slenderella Systems of California, Inc. 155

SCM Corp. v. Langis Foods, Ltd. 121

Scott Fetzer Co. v. House of Vacuums, Inc. . . 326

Scotts Co. v. United Indus. Corp. 339

Scovill Mfg. Co. v. United States Electric Mfg. Corp. 348; 352

Seabrook Foods, Inc. v. Bar-Well Foods, Ltd.. . 52

Sealol, Inc., In re. 118

Sears, Roebuck & Co. v. Stiffel Co. 14; 328

Sebastian Int'l, Inc. v. Longs Drug Stores Corp. 297, 298

Secular Orgs. for Sobriety, Inc. v. Ullrich 39

SecuraComm Consulting, Inc. v. SecuraCom Inc. 167; 349

Seidelmann Yachts, Inc. v. Pace Yacht Corp.. . 289

Self-Realization Fellowship Church v. Ananda Church of Self-Realization. 59

Selva & Sons, Inc. v. Nina Footwear, Inc. . . . 362

Semco, Inc. v. Amcast, Inc. 202

Seven-Up Co. v. Coca-Cola Co. 201

Shatel Corp. v. Mao Ta Lumber & Yacht Corp.. .185

Shaw v. Lindheim 195

Sheila's Shine Products, Inc. v. Sheila Shine, Inc. 294, 295

Shell Oil Co. v. Commercial Petroleum, Inc. . 304; 307

Shepard's Co. v. Thomson Corp. 327

Shields v. Zuccarini 239, 240; 242; 350

Shiraz Univ. Sch. of Med. Alumni Ass'n USA, Inc. v. Sheik. 366

Shire US, Inc. v. Barr Labs., Inc. 21

Silverman v. CBS Inc. 291

Simmons Co., In re 117

Simon & Schuster v. Dove Audio 73

Singer Mfg. Co. v. June Mfg. Co. 60

Site Pro-1, Inc. v. Better Metal, LLC . . . 179; 182

Size v. Network Solutions. Inc. 254

Sleeper Lounge Co. v. Bell Mfg. Co. 144

Slokevage, In re 67

Smith v. Chanel, Inc.. . . . . .73; 326, 327

Smith v. Montoro 192–194; 367

Smith v. New Line Cinema 196

Smith, Kline & French Labs. v. Clark & Clark.249

Sociedade Agricola, In re v. Commercial Dos Vinhos Messias, S.A.R.L. 83

Societe des Produits Nestle, S.A. v. Casa Helvetia, Inc. 301; 307–310; 339

Sofamor Danek Group v. Brown 335

Soltex Polymer Corp. v. Fortex Indus., Inc. . . 342, 343

Soweco, Inc. v. Shell Oil Co. 50; 318; 322

Spangler Candy Co. v. Crystal Pure Candy Co.. 56

Spartan Food Sys., Inc. v. HFS Corp. . 34, 35; 127

Spear, Leeds, & Kellogg v. Rosado. 239

The Sports Authority, Inc. v. Prime Hospitality Corp.. . . . . .175; 206

Sporty's Farm L.L.C. v. Sportsman's Market, Inc. 219; 238; 240; 353

Springs Mills, Inc. v. Ultracashmere House, Ltd. 342

SquirtCo v. Seven-Up Co. 141

SSP Agricultural Equipment, Inc. v. Orchard-Rite Ltd. 327

Standard Process, Inc. v. Banks 183

Stanfield v. Osborne Indus., Inc.. 367

Star-Kist Foods, Inc. v. P.J. Rhodes & Co.. . . 291

Starbucks Corp. v. Wolfe's Borough Coffee, Inc.. . . . . .227, 228

Stark Bros. Nurseries & Orchards Co. v. Stark.352

Steele v. Bulova Watch Co. 188

Steinway, Inc. v. Ashley 256

Sterling Brewers, Inc. v. Schenley Industries, Inc. 291

Sterling Drug, Inc. v. Bayer AG . . . 161, 162; 189

Sterling Drug, Inc. v. Knoll A.-G. Chemische Fabriken 41

Stern's Miracle-Gro Prods., Inc. v. Shark Prods., Inc.. . . . . .157, 158

Stetson v. Howard D. Wolf & Assocs. 290

Stix Prods., Inc. v. United Merchants & Mfrs., Inc.. 53

Stock Pot Restaurant, Inc. v. Stockpot, Inc.. . .294

Storey v. Cello Holdings, L.L.C. 356

Stork Restaurant v. Sahati 35; 138, 139

Stormor, a Div. of Fuqua Indus. v. Johnson. . .298

STX, Inc. v. Bauer USA, Inc.. 365

Sullivan v. CBS Corp. 141; 144; 160, 161

Sultan; United States v. 358

[References are to pages]

Summit Mach. Tool Mfg. Corp. v. Victor CNC Sys., Inc.. 193

Sun Banks of Florida, Inc. v. Sun Federal Sav. & Loan Ass'n 153; 157

SunAmerica Corp. v. Sun Life Assurance Co. of Canada. 135; 312; 316

Sunbeam Prods., Inc. v. West Bend Co.. 141

Sunenblick v. Harrell. 161–164

Sunmark Inc. v. Ocean Spray Cranberries, Inc..164

Surefoot LC v. Sure Foot Corp.. 368

Sweetarts v. Sunline, Inc.. 34

Sweetheart Plastics, Inc. v. Detroit Forming, Inc.. . . . . .290; 292; 315; 316

Sweetwater Brewing Co. LLC v. Great American Restaurants, Inc.. . . . . .143, 144

Swift & Co., In re.. 69

Sybersound Records, Inc. v. UAV Corp. . 204; 334

Sykes Laboratory, Inc. v. Kalvin 327

Syntex (U.S.A.), Inc. v. E.R. Squibb & Sons, Inc.. 362

T

T.A.B. Sys. v. Pactel Teletrac. 86

Taco Cabana Int'l, Inc. v. Two Pesos, Inc.. . . .294

Tactica Int'l, Inc. v. Atlantic Horizon, Int'l, Inc..39

Taffy Original Designs, Inc. v. Taffy's Inc.. . . .294

Talking Rain Bev. Co. v. South Beach Bev. Co.. . . . . .23; 96, 97

Tally-Ho, Inc. v. Coast Community College Dist.. . . . . .34, 35; 339

Tamko Roofing Prods., Inc. v. Ideal Roofing Co., Ltd.. 349

Tandy Corp. v. Malone & Hyde, Inc.. . . .314; 337

Taubman Co. v. Webfeats 177; 183

Taylor Made Golf Co. v. MJT Consulting Group 350

Taylor Wine Co. v. Bully Hill Vineyards, Inc.. .63; 343

TCPIP Holding Co. v. Haar Communications, Inc.. . . . . 153; 213; 217–219

Tdata Inc. v. Aircraft Technical Publishers . . . 170

TE-TA-MA Truth Foundation-Family of URI, Inc. v. World Church of the Creator. 349

Techex, Ltd. v. Dvorkovitz 40

Tetley, Inc. v. Topps Chewing Gum, Inc.. . . . 262

Therma-Scan, Inc. v. Thermoscan. 152

Thomas J. Valentino, Inc. v. Majar Discs, Inc.. 360

Thomas Pub'g Co., LLC v. Technology Evaluation Ctrs., Inc.. . . . . 196; 204

Thompson v. Haynes. 348

Thrifty Rent-A-Car Sys.. 34

Tia Maria, Inc., In re 74

Tie Tech, Inc. v. Kinedyne Corp.. 96

Tiffany & Co. v. Boston Club, Inc.. . . . 186; 211

Tiffany & Co. v. Tiffany Prods., Inc.. 211

Tiffany Inc. v. eBay, Inc.. 255

Tillamook Country Smoker, Inc. v. Tillamook County Creamery Ass'n. . .311; 312; 313; 315; 316

Tillery v. Leonard & Sciolla, LLP 61

Time, Inc. v. Life Television Corp.. 149

Time, Inc. v. T.I.M.E., Inc.. 149

Times Mirror Magazines, Inc. v. Field & Stream Licenses Co.. 316

Times Mirror Magazines, Inc. v. Las Vegas Sports News, L.L.C.. . . . . .219; 222, 223; 337

Tinseltown, Inc., In re. 83

Tisch Hotels, Inc. v. Americana Inn, Inc.. . . . 157

TMI, Inc. v. Maxwell 241

Tomei v. Finley. 284

Tommy Hilfiger Licensing, Inc. v. Nature Labs, LLC. 160, 161; 262; 265, 266

Top Tobacco, LP v. North Atlantic Operating Co.. . . . . .219, 220

Torkington; United States v.. . . . . . . 175; 359

Toronto-Dominion Bank v. Karpachev . . 241; 242

Torres v. Cantine Torresella S.r.l.. 115

Toys "R" Us v. Abir 145; 172

Toys "R" Us, Inc. v. Akkaoui 146

Toys "R" Us, Inc. v. Canarsie Kiddie Shop, Inc.. . . . . 138; 146; 156; 158

TrafFix Devices, Inc. v. Mktg. Displays, Inc.. . 19; 21; 28; 97; 332

Trans Union L.L.C. v. Credit Research, Inc.. . . 183

Transgo, Inc. v. Ajac Transmission Parts Corp..294

Travelers Ins. Co. v. Keeling 361

Treasure Imports, Inc. v. Henry Amdur & Sons, Inc.. 352

Tri-Star Pictures, Inc. v. Leisure Time Prods., B.V.. 73

Trouble v. Wet Seal. 161; 163

Truck Equipment Service Co. v. Fruehauf Co..192; 203

Trustees of Columbia University v. Columbia/HCA Healthcare Corp.. . . . . .161; 163, 164

Tumblebus, Inc. v. Cranmer . . 142; 293; 295; 297

Turner v. H M H Pub. Co. 39; 290

Twin Peaks Productions v. Publications Intern..269

TWM Mfg. Co., Inc. v. Dura Corp.. 312

Two Pesos, Inc. v. Taco Cabana, Inc. 64, 65

Ty, Inc. v. Jones Group, Inc.. 339

Ty, Inc. v. Perryman 208; 216; 218

[References are to pages]

Ty, Inc. v. Pubs. Int'l, Ltd 325, 326

Ty, Inc. v. Softbelly's, Inc 60

U

U-Haul Int'l, Inc. v. Jartran, Inc 344

U-Haul Int'l, Inc. v. WhenU.com, Inc . . . 178; 180

U.S. Conference of Catholic Bishops v. Media Research Center 76

U.S. Surgical Corp. v. Orris, Inc 303

UDOR U.S.A., Inc., In re 22

Ultrapure Sys., Inc. v. Ham-Let Group 365

Union Carbide Corp. v. Ever-Ready, Inc . . . 50; 53; 56; 91; 97; 143; 152

Union des Cooperatives Agricoles v. International Yogurt 33; 291

Union Nat'l Bank of Texas v. Union Nat'l Bank of Texas 54; 59

Union Tank Car Co. v. Lindsay Soft Water Corp. of Omaha, Inc 354

United Drug Co. v. Theodore Rectanus Co 1; 32–35; 289; 295

United Indus. Corp. v. Clorox Co . . . 198; 200, 201

United Mine Workers of Am. v. Gibbs 361

United Phosphorus, Ltd. v. Midland Fumigant, Inc 38; 344

United States v. (see name of defendant) . . . . . .

United States Jaycees v. Philadelphia Jaycees . .38; 294; 343

United States Jaycees v. San Francisco Junior Chamber of Commerce 38

United States Steel Corp. v. Vasco Metals Corp 80, 81

United We Stand 38; 178; 186; 284; 366

Universal City Studios, Inc. v. Nintendo, Inc . . 294; 349

Universal Commun. Sys. v. Lycos, Inc 326

Universal Nutrition Corp. v. Carbolite Foods, Inc 78

Universal Oil Products Co., In re 37

University of Florida v. KPB, Inc 186

University of Kansas v. Sinks 234

University of Notre Dame du Lac v. J.C. Gourmet Food Imports Co., Inc 84

University of Pittsburgh v. Champion Products, Inc 312; 316

Unlimited Screw Products, Inc. v. Malm 337

Utah Lighthouse Ministry v. Found. For Apologetic Info. & Resch 262

V

V Secret Catalogue, Inc. v. Moseley .220; 227, 228

V'soske, Inc. v. Vsoske.com 244

Valu Eng'g, Inc. v. Rexnord Corp 22; 96, 97

Value House v. Phillips Mercantile Co 77; 128

Vanity Fair Mills, Inc. v. T. Eaton Co 189–191

Vaudable v. Montmartre, Inc 42

Venetianaire Corp. v. A & P Import Co 319

Venture Tape Corp. v. McGills Glass Warehouse 346

Verizon Calif., Inc. v. Navigation Catalyst Sys., Inc .339, 340

Vertex Group LLC, In re 22

Viacom, Inc. v. Ingram Enters., Inc 210

Viavi Co. v. Vimedia Co 327

Victoria's Secret Stores v. Artco Equip. Co . . . 318

Vidal Sassoon, Inc. v. Bristol-Myers Co 198

Virgin Enters., Ltd. v. Nawab . .150, 151; 153; 160

Virtual Works, Inc. v. Volkswagen of America, Inc 237–240; 242

Visa Int'l Serv. Ass'n v. JSL Corp . . .220; 227, 228

Visa, USA, Inc. v. Birmingham Trust Nat'l Bank 130

Vitarroz Corp. v. Borden, Inc 150

Viviane Woodard Corp. v. Roberts 138

Volkswagenwerk Aktiengesellschaft v. Church .326

Volkswagenwerk Aktiengesellschaft v. Karadizian 343

Volkswagenwerk Aktiengesellschaft v. Tatum . .138

W

W.F. & John Barnes Co. v. Vandyck-Churchill Co 160

W.T. Rogers Co., Inc. v. Keene 257

W.W.W. Pharm. Co. v. Gillette Co . . .50; 150; 152; 157–159; 162, 163

Wada, In re 81; 93

Waits v. Frito-Lay, Inc 367

Wal-Mart v. Samara Bros 47; 65, 66; 332

Waldman Pub. Corp. v. Landoll, Inc 195; 333, 334

Walgreen Drug Stores v. Obear-Nester Glass Co 138

Wall v. Rolls-Royce of America, Inc 211

Wallace Int'l Silversmiths, Inc. v. Godinger Silver Art Co 31

Walt Disney Co. v. Goodtimes Home Video Corp 68

Walt Disney Productions v. Air Pirates 275

Warner Bros. v. American Broadcasting Co . . . 333

Warner-Lambert Co. v. BreathAsure, Inc . .198, 199

Warner Lambert Co. v. McCrory's Corp 27

[References are to pages]

Waukesha Hygeia Mineral Springs Co. v. Hygeia Sparkling Distilled Water Co. 294

WCVB-TV v. Boston Athletic Ass'n 326

Web Printing Controls Co. v. Oxy-Dry Corp.. .194

Wedgwood Homes, Inc. v. Lund 209

Weight Watchers Intern. v. Stouffer Corp..156; 327

Weil Ceramics & Glass, Inc. v. Dash. . .307; 310, 311

Weiss Assocs., Inc. v. HRL Assocs. Inc. 112

Weiss Noodle Co. v. Golden Cracknel & Specialty Co. 75

Welding Services, Inc. v. Forman. 76

Wells Fargo & Co. v. WhenU.com, Inc. . 178, 179; 190; 191

Wendt v. Host Int'l, Inc.. 72

West Fla. Seafood v. Jet Rests.. . . . . . .114; 289

Westchester Media v. PRL USA Holdings, Inc.. .277; 315

Western Diversified Servs., Inc. v. Hyundai Motor America, Inc.. 346

Western Union Holdings, Inc. v. Eastern Union, Inc. 339

Westward Coach Mfg. Co. v. Ford Motor Co..156; 165

White v. Samsung Elecs. America, Inc.. . . . .4; 72

Wilchcombe v. Teevee Toons, Inc. 204

Wilcher Corp., In re. 82

Wilhelm Pudenz, GmbH v. Littlefuse, Inc. . 16; 17; 65

Willhelm Pudenz 17

William & Scott Co. v. Earl's Restaurants Ltd..107

William Connors Paint Mfg. Co., In re. 84

William R. Warner & Co. v. Eli Lilly & Co..3; 17; 52; 55; 249

Williams v. Curtiss-Wright Corp. 194

Williams v. UMG Recordings. 196

Williamson-Dickie Mfg. Co. v. Davis Mfg. Co..95

Wilson v. Garcia. 336

WMS Gaming, Inc. v. WPC Productions Ltd. . 347

Woodstock's Enters., Inc. v. Woodstock's Enters., Inc.. 114

Worden v. California Fig Syrup Co.. 317

World Championship Wrestling v. Titan Sports, Inc.. . . . . .232; 365

World Impressions Corp. v. McDonald's Corp..326

World's Finest Chocolate, Inc., In re. 10

World Wrestling Fedn. Entm't, Inc. v. Big Dog Holdings, Inc.. 287

Wynn Oil Co. v. American Way Service Corp..347

Y

Yahoo!, Inc. v. Yahooahtos.com. 243

Yale Elec. Corp. v. Robertson 148, 149

Yankee Publ'g Inc. v. News Am. Publ'g Inc. . 226; 263; 272; 281

Yeley, In re. 96

Yocono's Restaurant v. Yocono. 56

Young, Ex Parte 335

Yurman Design, Inc. v. Golden Treasure Imps., Inc.. 31

Yurman Design, Inc. v. PAJ, Inc.. 31

Yurman Studio, Inc. v. Castaneda. 326

Z

Zapata Corp. v. Zapata Trading Int'l, Inc.. . . . 56

Zatarains, Inc. v. Oak Grove Smokehouse, Inc..59; 318

Zazu Designs v. L'Oreal, S.A.. 344

Zimmerman v. National Ass'n of Realtors . . . 102

Zyla v. Wadsworth 135; 151; 196; 204

TABLE OF STATUTES

[References are to pages]

CALIFORNIA
CALIFORNIA STATUTES

Business and Professions Code

Sec.	Page
14210	126
14220	126

MAINE

Maine Revised Statutes

Tit.:Sec.	Page
10:1530	212

NEVADA
NEVADA STATUTES

Nevada Revised Statutes Annotated

Sec.	Page
600.435(1)	212

NEW YORK

New York General Business Law

Sec.	Page
360-a	126
360-l	211

OHIO

Ohio Revised Code

Sec.	Page
4165.02	134

OREGON

Oregon Revised Statutes

Sec.	Page
647.107	209

WASHINGTON

Washington Revised Code

Sec.	Page
19.77.010(6)	209

FEDERAL STATUTES, RULES, AND REGULATIONS

United States Constitution

Amend.	Page
amend.:1	184; 202; 213; 231– 233; 246; 260, 261; 266; 268–288
amend.:7	351
amend.:11	334–336; 358
amend.:14	335
art.:1:8:3	6; 13; 41; 184, 185; 335
art.:1:8:8	13
art.:4:3:2	13
art.:6:2	17
art.:I:8:3	6; 36

United States Code

Title:Sec.	Page
5:706	111
9:1526(a)	307
15:43(a)(1)(B)	4
15:43(a)(3)	65
15:43(c)(3)(A)(ii)	269
15:43(c)(3)(C)	268
15:1051(a)(1)	106
15:1051(b)	46
15:1051(b)(1) to (3)	104
15:1051(c)	105
15:1051(d)(1)	105, 106
15:1051(d)(2)	106
15:1051(d)(4)	106
15:1052	79; 106; 126
15:1052(a)	82
15:1052(b)	84
15:1052(c)	84
15:1052(d)	85; 108; 143
15:1052(e)	91
15:1052(e)(2)	93
15:1052(e)(5)	65
15:1052(f)	217; 235
15:1053	102
15:1054	93; 100
15:1055	39; 131; 290; 293
15:1056(a)	80
15:1056(b)	81
15:1057(b)	76; 112; 136; 151

United States Code—Cont.

Title:Sec.	Page
15:1057(c)	77
15:1058	109
15:1058(b)	109
15:1059	110
15:1059(b)	110
15:1060(a)	295
15:1060(a)(1) to (2)	130
15:1062	104
15:1062(b)	119
15:1062(c)	109
15:1063	99
15:1063(a)	107
15:1063(b)	105
15:1064	99; 101; 113; 235
15:1064(3)	65; 116; 288
15:1064(5)	101; 113
15:1064(5)(A)	293
15:1065	77; 113, 114; 117
15:1065(4)	116
15:1067	107, 108
15:1071	111; 119
15:1071(a)	361
15:1071(b)	361
15:1072	77
15:1091	118
15:1091(a)	118, 119
15:1091(b)	119
15:1092	99; 113; 119; 235
15:1094	118, 119; 136
15:1111	352
15:1114	134
15:1114(1)	334; 364
15:1114(1)(a)	134; 173; 245
15:1114(1)(b)	354
15:1114(2)(D)(i)(II)	357
15:1114(2)(D)(ii)	355
15:1114(2)(D)(iii)	357
15:1114(2)(D)(iv)	356
15:1114(2)(D)(v)	356
15:1114(2)(E)	354
15:1114(3)	357
15:1114(3)(A)	357
15:1115(6)	116
15:1115(a)	76
15:1115(b)	114; 136; 288
15:1115(b)(2)	288
15:1115(b)(4)	317
15:1115(b)(5)	116; 127
15:1115(b)(5)(A) to (C)	116

United States Code—Cont.

Title:Sec.	Page
15:1115(b)(8)	65
15:1115(b)(9)	311
15:1116	233; 353
15:1116(9)	341
15:1116(a)	337
15:1116(d)	78; 342; 348; 350
15:1116(d)(1)(B)	341
15:1116(d)(1)(B)(i)	352
15:1116(d)(4)(A)	341
15:1116(d)(4)(B)	341
15:1116(d)(7)	341
15:1116(d)(10)	342
15:1116(d)(11)	342
15:1117(a)	234; 344; 346–349; 353
15:1117(b)	78; 348, 349; 351
15:1117(c)	78; 350; 352
15:1117(d)	247; 350
15:1117(e)	346
15:1118	234; 342; 353
15:1119	342
15:1120	353
15:1121(a)	360
15:1122(b)	334
15:1124	77; 310
15:1125	245
15:1125(a)	129; 134; 366
15:1125(a)(1)(A)	135; 173; 215
15:1125(a)(1)(B)	134; 197; 215
15:1125(a)(3)	138
15:1125(b)	307
15:1125(c)	8; 129; 134
15:1125(c)(1)	213; 217; 233; 353
15:1125(c)(1)(F)	219
15:1125(c)(2)	353
15:1125(c)(2)(A)	220
15:1125(c)(2)(B)	214; 224
15:1125(c)(3)	212; 235
15:1125(c)(4)	221
15:1125(c)(4)(B)	268
15:1125(c)(5)	233
15:1125(c)(5)(B)(i)	234
15:1125(c)(6)	212; 235
15:1125(d)	9; 129; 134; 184; 356
15:1125(d)(1)(A)	238; 246
15:1125(d)(1)(B)(i)	240
15:1125(d)(1)(B)(ii)	240; 242
15:1125(d)(1)(C)	247
15:1125(d)(1)(D)	238
15:1125(d)(1)(E)	239

[References are to pages]

United States Code—Cont.

Title:Sec.	Page
15:1125(d)(2)(A)	243
15:1125(d)(2)(C)	243
15:1126	118; 121
15:1126(c)	122
15:1126(d)	77; 121
15:1126(d)(3)	122
15:1127	6; 36–39; 46; 48; 100; 102; 131; 187; 215; 245; 290; 292; 334; 341; 348; 350; 364
15:1141a(a)	124
15:1141a(b)	123
15:1141f	118
15:1141h(4)	124
15:1141h(c)(1)	124
15:1141l	131
15:1441g	120
17:102(a)	332
17:110(11)	357
17:301	332
17:302 to 304	12
18:706	238
18:2318	360
18:2318(a)	360
18:2320	358
18:2320(a)	358
18:2320(b)	359
18:2320(c)	359
18:2320(e)(1)	359
18:2323	359
18:2510(12)	355
19:1526	77; 307; 310
28:1332(a)	361
28:2201(a)	367
35:154(a)(2)	12
35:156	12
35:173	12; 332

United States Code—Cont.

Title:Sec.	Page
36:220506	238; 359
43:651	56

Code of Federal Regulations

Title:Sec.	Page
19:11.13(a)	307
19:133.23	311
27:2.47(a)	118
37:2.33(b)(2)	104
37:2.34	103
37:2.47(b) to (c)	118
37:2.47(d)	118
37:2.56(a)	104
37:2.66	106
37:2.71(d)	106
37:2.76	105
37:2.76(c)	109
37:2.87(a)	109
37:2.88	105
37:2.88(c)	109
37:2.89(c)	105
37:2.89(d)	105
37:2.91	108
37:2.91(a)	108
37:2.92 to 93	108
37:2.99	109
37:2.133(c)	100
37:2.141	104; 106
37:2.182	110
37:2.183	110
37:2.183(a)	110
37:3.71	130
37:7.3	126
87:2.89(f)	106

INDEX

[References are to page numbers.]

A

ABANDONMENT
Generally . . . 288, 292
Assignment in gross . . . 295
Cessation of use . . . 290
Naked licensing . . . 293

C

COMMON LAW
Early common law . . . 2
Modern common law, evolution of . . . 3

CONSTITUTIONAL LAW
Eleventh Amendment . . . 334
First Amendment considerations
Generally . . . 260
Commercial parodies
Generally . . . 262
Dilution . . . 266
Infringement and unfair competition
. . . 262
Expressive merchandise . . . 284
Noncommercial expression
Dilution . . . 277
Infringement and unfair competition
. . . 269
Political speech . . . 283

COPYRIGHT LAW
Comparison of trademark, copyright, and patent
law
Congressional authority, source of . . . 13
Duration of protection . . . 11
Geographic scope of protection . . . 13
Rights, scope of . . . 11
State and Federal law, relationship between
. . . 14
Subject matter . . . 9

CRIMINAL PENALTIES
Labels, counterfeit . . . 360
Marks, counterfeit . . . 358

D

DAMAGES (See MONETARY AWARDS)

DECLARATORY JUDGMENTS
Adjudication . . . 367

DEFENSES
Generally . . . 260
Affirmative defenses
Generally . . . 288
Abandonment
Generally . . . 288, 292
Assignment in gross . . . 295
Cessation of use . . . 290

DEFENSES—Cont.
Affirmative defenses—Cont.
Abandonment—Cont.
Naked licensing . . . 293
Acquiescence . . . 315
Comparative advertising . . . 327
Eleventh Amendment . . . 334
Fair use
"Classic" fair use . . . 317
Nominative fair use . . . 322
Federal preemption . . . 328
First sale doctrine
Generally . . . 287
Gray market goods . . . 306
Materially different goods . . . 298
Misrepresentations by non-authorized
resellers . . . 298
Non-genuine goods . . . 304
Undisclosed repackaging . . . 305
Used, altered, or refurbished goods
. . . 298
Laches . . . 311
Statute of limitations . . . 336
Unclean hands . . . 316
First Amendment considerations
Generally . . . 260
Commercial parodies
Generally . . . 262
Dilution . . . 266
Infringement and unfair competition
. . . 262
Expressive merchandise . . . 284
Noncommercial expression
Dilution . . . 277
Infringement and unfair competition
. . . 269
Political speech . . . 283

DILUTION
Generally . . . 204
Federal Trademark Dilution Act
Generally . . . 213
Actual dilution versus likelihood of dilution
Generally . . . 222
Judicial interpretations . . . 225
Likely dilution under the FTDA
. . . 224
Moseley and the FTDA . . . 222
Defense, Federal registration as . . . 235
Distinctiveness . . . 216
Effective date of . . . 234
Elements of claim under . . . 213
Exceptions
Generally . . . 229
Fair use . . . 230
News reporting and commentary
. . . 233
Noncommercial use . . . 231
Fair use . . . 230
Famous marks . . . 216

[References are to page numbers.]

DILUTION—Cont.
Federal Trademark Dilution Act—Cont.
   History of . . . 213
   News reporting and commentary . . . 233
   Noncommercial use . . . 231
   Nontraditional marks . . . 221
   Registration as defense, Federal . . . 235
   Remedies . . . 233
   Similarity . . . 221
   Trade dress . . . 221
   Trademark use . . . 215
Lanham act, treatment under . . . 8
State dilution laws . . . 208

DISTINCTIVENESS
Generally . . . 46, 49
Arbitrary marks . . . 51
Descriptive marks
   Common law proscription . . . 55
   Secondary meaning . . . 56
Fanciful marks . . . 51
Federal Trademark Dilution Act . . . 216
Generic terms . . . 57
Suggestive marks . . . 52

E

ESTABLISHING TRADEMARK RIGHTS
Lanham Act
   Commerce, use in . . . 35
   Constructive use . . . 46
   Famous marks doctrine . . . 42
   Foreign use . . . 39
   Intent to Use (ITU) applications . . . 45
Use in trade
   Generally . . . 32
   Lanham Act (See subhead: Lanham Act)
   Priority of use, establishing . . . 33

EXPRESSIVE WORKS
Generally . . . 69
Titles of . . . 73

F

FAIR USE
"Classic" fair use . . . 317
Federal Trademark Dilution Act, fair use under
   . . . 230
Nominative fair use . . . 322

FALSE ADVERTISING
Federal law of . . . 197

FEDERAL LAW
Constitutional issues
   Eleventh Amendment . . . 334
   First Amendment considerations (See sub-
     head: First Amendment considerations)
Dilution
   Federal Trademark Dilution Act (See FED-
     ERAL TRADEMARK DILUTION ACT)
   Lanham Act . . . 8
Early federal law, overview of . . . 6

FEDERAL LAW—Cont.
First Amendment considerations
   Generally . . . 260
   Commercial parodies
     Generally . . . 262
     Dilution . . . 266
     Infringement and unfair competition
       . . . 262
   Expressive merchandise . . . 284
   Noncommercial expression
     Dilution . . . 277
     Infringement and unfair competition
       . . . 269
   Political speech . . . 283
Lanham Act
   Generally . . . 6
   Anticybersquatting provisions . . . 9
   Dilution doctrine . . . 8
   Establishing trademark rights
     Commerce, use in . . . 35
     Constructive use . . . 46
     Famous marks doctrine . . . 42
     Foreign use . . . 39
     Intent to Use (ITU) applications
       . . . 45
   Recent amendments . . . 8
Preemption
   Affirmative defense of . . . 328
   State registration statutes, preemption of
     . . . 127
Registration of trademarks under (See FEDERAL
   TRADEMARK REGISTRATION)

FEDERAL TRADEMARK DILUTION ACT
Generally . . . 213
Actual dilution versus likelihood of dilution
   Generally . . . 222
   Judicial interpretations . . . 225
   Likely dilution under the FTDA . . . 224
   Moseley and the FTDA . . . 222
Defense, Federal registration as . . . 235
Distinctiveness . . . 216
Effective date of . . . 234
Elements of claim under . . . 213
Exceptions
   Generally . . . 229
   Fair use . . . 230
   News reporting and commentary . . . 233
   Noncommercial use . . . 231
Fair use . . . 230
Famous marks . . . 216
History of . . . 213
News reporting and commentary . . . 233
Noncommercial use . . . 231
Nontraditional marks . . . 221
Registration as defense, Federal . . . 235
Remedies . . . 233
Similarity . . . 221
Trade dress . . . 221
Trademark use . . . 215

FEDERAL TRADEMARK REGISTRATION
Benefits of . . . 76

[References are to page numbers.]

FEDERAL TRADEMARK REGISTRATION—Cont.
Cancellation
    Grounds for cancellation . . . 112
    Procedure . . . 113
Collective marks . . . 101
Eligibility for
    Generally . . . 78
    Ineligible marks (See subhead: Ineligible marks)
Foreign registrations, domestic priority based on
    Generally . . . 121
    International agreements . . . 120
    Madrid Agreement and Madrid Protocol . . . 123
    National treatment . . . 121
Incontestability
    Effect of status . . . 114
    Establishing . . . 117
Ineligible marks
    Generally . . . 80
    Confusion with existing marks, marks likely to cause . . . 84
    Deceptive marks . . . 82
    Descriptive marks . . . 91
    Dilutive marks . . . 98
    Disparaging marks . . . 82
    False geographic indications for wines and spirits . . . 82
    Functional marks . . . 91
    Immoral marks . . . 82
    Insignia, national, state, or municipal . . . 84
    Misdescriptive marks . . . 91
    Names, portraits, or signatures . . . 84
    National, state, or municipal insignia, . . . 84
    Overcoming bars to registration . . . 97
    Scandalous marks . . . 82
    Wines and spirits, false geographic indications for . . . 82
Judicial review . . . 111
Process of registration
    Generally . . . 103
    Concurrent use . . . 108
    Dividing applications . . . 109
    Intent to use . . . 104
    Interferences . . . 108
    Maintaining and renewing registrations . . . 109
    Opposition to registration . . . 107
    Renewing and maintaining registrations . . . 109
    Use . . . 103
    Who may register mark . . . 106
Service marks . . . 102
Supplemental register
    Generally . . . 117
    Cancellation . . . 120
    Effect of supplemental registration . . . 119
    Eligibility . . . 118
    Procedure for registration . . . 119

FIRST AMENDMENT CONSIDERATIONS
Generally . . . 260
Commercial parodies
    Generally . . . 262
    Dilution . . . 266
    Infringement and unfair competition . . . 262
Expressive merchandise . . . 284
Noncommercial expression
    Dilution . . . 277
    Infringement and unfair competition . . . 269
Political speech . . . 283

FIRST SALE DOCTRINE
Generally . . . 287
Gray market goods . . . 306
Materially different goods . . . 298
Misrepresentations by non-authorized resellers . . . 298
Non-genuine goods . . . 304
Undisclosed repackaging . . . 305
Used, altered, or refurbished goods . . . 298

FOREIGN TRADEMARKS AND USE
Domestic priority based on foreign registrations
    Generally . . . 121
    International agreements . . . 120
    Madrid Agreement and Madrid Protocol . . . 123
    National treatment . . . 121
Foreign words as trademark . . . 74
Lanham Act, Foreign use of trademarks under . . . 39

I

INFRINGEMENT
Generally . . . 133
Elements of infringement
    Generally . . . 134
    Initial interest confusion . . . 163
    Jurisdictional predicate . . . 184
    Likelihood of confusion
        Generally . . . 138
        Actual confusion . . . 154
        Bridging the gap . . . 156
        Competitive proximity . . . 148
        Consumer sophistication . . . 153
        Factors . . . 140
        Good faith, defendant's . . . 157
        Jurisdictional variations on the *Polaroid* test . . . 160
        Polaroid test, jurisdictional variations on the . . . 160
        Relative quality of defendant's goods or services . . . 158
        Reverse confusion . . . 161
        Similarity . . . 142
        Strength of plaintiff's mark . . . 150
    Ownership of valid mark . . . 136
    Post-sale confusion . . . 173

[References are to page numbers.]

INFRINGEMENT—Cont.
Elements of infringement—Cont.
    Purchasing decision, confusion before or after the
        Generally . . . 163
        Initial interest confusion . . . 163
        Post-sale confusion . . . 173
    Reverse confusion . . . 161
    Territorial limitations . . . 187
    Use of trademark
        Generally . . . 177
        Domain names . . . 183
        Expressive works . . . 184
        Keyword-triggered advertising . . . 179
        Metatags . . . 182
Reverse passing off . . . 192

INTERNET LAW
Cybersquatting
    Generally . . . 237
    Alternative forums for domain name disputes . . . 247
    Anticybersquatting Consumer Protection Act (ACPA)
        Generally . . . 237
        Elements of claim . . . 238
        In rem jurisdiction . . . 242
        Personal names . . . 246
        Remedies . . . 247
    Lanham Act, anticybersquatting provisions of . . . 9
Lanham Act, anticybersquatting provisions of . . . 9

J

JURISDICTION
Anticybersquatting Consumer Protection Act (ACPA), *In rem* jurisdiction IN . . . 242
Elements of infringement, Jurisdictional predicate to . . . 184
Polaroid test, Jurisdictional variations on the . . . 160
Subject matter jurisdiction . . . 360

L

LANHAM ACT
Generally . . . 6
Anticybersquatting provisions . . . 9
Dilution doctrine . . . 8
Establishing trademark rights
    Commerce, use in . . . 35
    Constructive use . . . 46
    Famous marks doctrine . . . 42
    Foreign use . . . 39
    Intent to Use (ITU) applications . . . 45
Recent amendments . . . 8

M

MONETARY AWARDS
Generally . . . 344
Actual damages . . . 344
Actual notice requirement . . . 352
Attorneys' fees . . . 349
Costs . . . 344
Counterfeiting cases, enhanced monetary awards in . . . 351
Defendants' profits . . . 344
Dilution law, limited availability of damages under Federal . . . 353
Enhanced damages . . . 348
False or fraudulent registration . . . 353
Marking requirement . . . 352
Prejudgment interest . . . 348
Statutory damages . . . 350

N

NATURE OF TRADEMARKS
Nonfunctionality, requirement of
    Aesthetic functionality . . . 24
    Definition of functionality, evolving . . . 18
    Public policy . . . 16
Origin identifiers, trademarks as . . . 15

P

PATENT LAW
Comparison of trademark, copyright, and patent law
    Congressional authority, source of . . . 13
    Duration of protection . . . 11
    Geographic scope of protection . . . 13
    Rights, scope of . . . 11
    State and Federal law, relationship between . . . 14
    Subject matter . . . 9

PREEMPTION
Affirmative defense of . . . 328
State registration statutes, preemption of . . . 127

R

REGISTRATION OF TRADEMARKS
Assignments . . . 129
Federal trademark registration
    Benefits of . . . 76
    Cancellation
        Grounds for cancellation . . . 112
        Procedure . . . 113
    Collective marks . . . 101
    Eligibility for
        Generally . . . 78
        Ineligible marks (See within this,subhead: Ineligible marks)
    Foreign registrations, domestic priority based on
        Generally . . . 121
        International agreements . . . 120

[References are to page numbers.]

REGISTRATION OF TRADEMARKS—Cont.
Federal trademark registration—Cont.
  Foreign registrations, domestic priority based
    on—Cont.
    Madrid Agreement and Madrid Protocol
      . . . 123
    National treatment . . . 121
  Incontestability
    Effect of status . . . 114
    Establishing . . . 117
  Ineligible marks
    Generally . . . 80
    Confusion with existing marks, marks
      likely to cause . . . 84
    Deceptive marks . . . 82
    Descriptive marks . . . 91
    Dilutive marks . . . 98
    Disparaging marks . . . 82
    False geographic indications for wines
      and spirits . . . 82
    Functional marks . . . 91
    Immoral marks . . . 82
    Insignia, national, state, or municipal
      . . . 84
    Misdescriptive marks . . . 91
    Names, portraits, or signatures . . . 84
    National, state, or municipal insignia,
      . . . 84
    Overcoming bars to registration
      . . . 97
    Scandalous marks . . . 82
    Wines and spirits, false geographic in-
      dications for . . . 82
  Judicial review . . . 111
  Process of registration
    Generally . . . 103
    Concurrent use . . . 108
    Dividing applications . . . 109
    Intent to use . . . 104
    Interferences . . . 108
    Maintaining and renewing registrations
      . . . 109
    Opposition to registration . . . 107
    Renewing and maintaining registrations
      . . . 109
    Use . . . 103
    Who may register mark . . . 106
  Service marks . . . 102
  Supplemental register
    Generally . . . 117
    Cancellation . . . 120
    Effect of supplemental registration
      . . . 119
    Eligibility . . . 118
    Procedure for registration . . . 119
Licensing . . . 131
State registration statutes
  Generally . . . 126
  Preemption . . . 127
Unregistered marks, protection of
  Generally . . . 129
  Federal law . . . 129
  State law . . . 129

REMEDIES
Generally . . . 337
Cancellation of Federal registration . . . 342
Criminal penalties
  Labels, counterfeit . . . 360
  Marks, counterfeit . . . 358
Destruction of infringing articles . . . 342
Disclaimers . . . 342
Injunctions . . . 337
Limitations on remedies against certain defendants
  Generally . . . 354
  Domain name registration authorities
    . . . 355
  Family Movie Act of 2005 . . . 357
  Governments, Federal and state . . . 358
  Makers of labels, signs, packaging, or adver-
    tisements . . . 354
  Printers and publishers . . . 354
Monetary awards
  Generally . . . 344
  Actual damages . . . 344
  Actual notice requirement . . . 352
  Attorneys' fees . . . 349
  Costs . . . 344
  Counterfeiting cases, enhanced monetary
    awards in . . . 351
  Defendants' profits . . . 344
  Dilution law, limited availability of damages
    under Federal . . . 353
  Enhanced damages . . . 348
  False or fraudulent registration . . . 353
  Marking requirement . . . 352
  Prejudgment interest . . . 348
  Statutory damages . . . 350
Non-monetary remedies . . . 337
Seizure of counterfeit goods and related materials
  . . . 341

REVERSE PASSING OFF
Unfair competition . . . 192

S

SECONDARY LIABILITY
Contributory liability . . . 249
Vicarious liability . . . 249, 257

STANDING
Cancel or oppose Federal registration, standing to
  . . . 361
Section 32 standing . . . 364
Section 43(a) standing and the common law of
  unfair competition . . . 366
Section 43(c) standing . . . 365

STATE TRADEMARK LAW
Dilution laws, state . . . 208
Evolution of . . . 3
Federal law, relationship between state and
  . . . 14
Preemption of state registration statutes . . . 127
Registration of trademarks under state registration
  statutes
    Generally . . . 126
    Preemption . . . 127

STATE TRADEMARK LAW—Cont.
Registration of trademarks under state registration statutes—Cont.
    Preemption of state registration statutes
      . . . 127
Unregistered marks, protection of . . . 129

STATUTE OF LIMITATIONS
Affirmative defenses . . . 336

SUBJECT MATTER JURISDICTION
Adjudication . . . 360

T

TYPES OF TRADEMARKS
Abbreviations of generic or descriptive terms
    . . . 76
Alphanumeric combinations . . . 74
Artistic works . . . 69
Celebrity likenesses . . . 72
Color, sound, and scent . . . 68
Descriptive terms, abbreviations of generic or
    . . . 76
Distinctiveness
    Generally . . . 46, 49
    Arbitrary marks . . . 51
    Descriptive marks
        Common law proscription . . . 55
        Secondary meaning . . . 56
    Fanciful marks . . . 51

TYPES OF TRADEMARKS—Cont.
Distinctiveness—Cont.
    Generic terms . . . 57
    Suggestive marks . . . 52
Expressive works
    Generally . . . 69
    Titles of . . . 73
Fictional characters . . . 72
Foreign words . . . 74
Generic or descriptive terms, abbreviations of
    . . . 76
Maintaining trademark rights . . . 47
Musical works . . . 69
Numbers . . . 74
Personal names . . . 61
Protectible marks . . . 48
Trade dress . . . 64

U

UNFAIR COMPETITION
False advertising, Federal law of . . . 197
Infringement (See INFRINGEMENT)
Reverse passing off . . . 192

UNREGISTERED MARKS
Protection of
    Generally . . . 129
    Federal law . . . 129
    State law . . . 129